A Handbook of

HUMAN RESOURCE MANAGEMENT PRACTICE

A Handbook of

HUMAN RESOURCE MANAGEMENT PRACTICE

10TH EDITION

Michael Armstrong

KOGAN
PAGE

London and Philadelphia

First published by Kogan Page Limited as *A Handbook of Personnel Management Practice* in 1977
Second edition 1984
Third edition 1988
Fourth edition 1991
Fifth edition 1995
Sixth edition 1996
Seventh edition published by Kogan Page Limited as *A Handbook of Human Resource Management Practice* in 1999
Eighth edition 2001
Ninth edition 2003
Tenth edition 2006

120 Pentonville Road
London N1 9JN
United Kingdom
www.kogan-page.co.uk

525 South 4th Street, #241
Philadelphia, PA 19147
USA

British Library Cataloguing in Publication Data

A CIP record for this book is available from the British Library.

ISBN 0 7494 4631 5

Library of Congress Cataloging-in-Publication Data

Armstrong, Michael, 1928-
   A handbook of human resource management practice/Michael Armstrong.–10th ed.
      p.cm.
   Includes bibliographical references and index.
   ISBN 0-7494-4631-5
  1. Personnel management–Handbooks, manuals, etc. I. Title.
HF5549.17.A76 2006
658.3–dc22

                              2005032487

Typeset by Jean Cussons Typesetting, Diss, Norfolk
Printed and bound in Great Britain by Cambridge University Press

Contents

PART I   MANAGING PEOPLE

PART IV   ORGANIZATIONAL BEHAVIOUR

List of figures

List of tables

About the author

Michael Armstrong is an honours graduate in economics from the London School of Economics, a Companion of the Chartered Institute of Personnel and Development and a Fellow of the Institute of Management Consultancy.

This book is largely based on Michael Armstrong's hands-on experience as a personnel practitioner, initially in the engineering industry, specializing in industrial relations, and then in the engineering and food industries as an employee development specialist.

For 12 years he was an executive director with responsibility for HR in a large publishing firm and for three years of that period also acted as general manager for an operating division. For a further 10 years he headed up the HR consultancy division of Coopers & Lybrand. He is Managing Partner of e-reward.uk and also practises as an independent consultant. This experience has been supplemented recently by a number of research projects carried out on behalf of the Chartered Institute of Personnel and Development. These covered the personnel function's contribution to the bottom line, strategic HRM, incentive pay, job evaluation, team rewards, broad-banded pay structures, and performance management. He was Chief Examiner Employee Reward for the CIPD from 1997–2001.

His publications for Kogan Page include *Reward Management, Performance Management, How to Be an Even Better Manager, A Handbook of Management Techniques* and *A Handbook of Employee Reward, Management and Leadership.*

Preface

This tenth edition of *A Handbook of Human Resource Management Practice* contains many additions and revisions. It refers to major developments in HR practice in the last two to three years such as the development of the theory and practice of human capital management, talent management and approaches to learning and development, all covered in new or substantially revised chapters. Reference is also made to a number of significant research projects including those conducted by the CIPD, IES and e-reward. Chapters on the following subjects have been either wholly replaced or extensively revised in the light of new concepts of good practice, the experience of the author as a practitioner and the outcomes of research:

- human resource management;
- role of the HR function;
- role of the HR practitioner;
- strategic human resource management;
- competency-based HRM;
- the delivery of learning and training;
- performance management;
- reward management fundamentals;
- grade and pay structures.

The plan of the handbook is illustrated in the 'route map' shown in Figure 0.1.

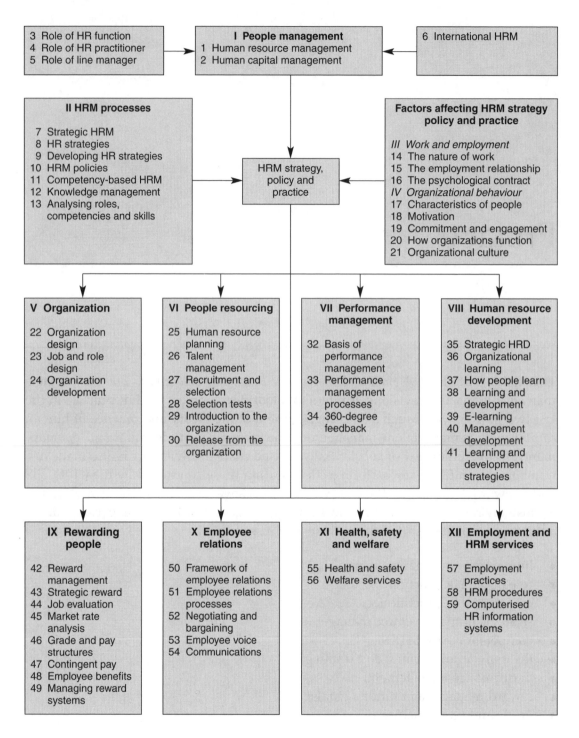

Figure 0.1 Route map

Part I

Managing people

This part underpins the rest of the Handbook. It deals with the approaches and philosophies that affect how people are managed in organizations, the roles of the HR function and its members, and the special considerations that affect international people management. The term 'people management' embraces the two related concepts of human resource management (HRM) and human capital management (HCM), which are defined and explained in the first two chapters. These have virtually replaced the term 'personnel management', although the philosophies and practices of personnel management still provide the foundations for the philosophy and practices of HRM and HCM. The relationships between these aspects of people management are modelled in Figure 0.2.

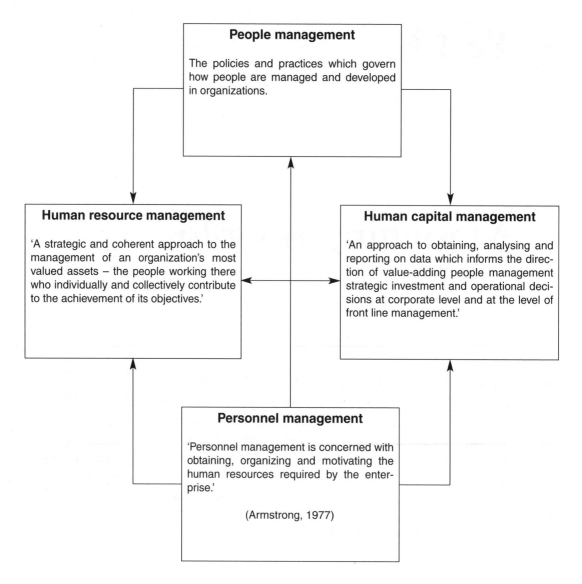

Figure 0.2 Relationship between aspects of people management

1

Human resource management

The terms 'human resource management' (HRM) and 'human resources' (HR) have largely replaced the term 'personnel management' as a description of the processes involved in managing people in organizations. The concept of HRM underpins all the activities described in this book, and the aim of this chapter is to provide a framework for what follows by defining the concepts of HRM and an HR system, describing the various models of HRM and discussing its aims and characteristics. The chapter continues with a review of reservations about HRM and the relationship between HRM and personnel management and concludes with a discussion of the impact HRM can make on organizational performance.

HUMAN RESOURCE MANAGEMENT DEFINED

Human resource management is defined as a strategic and coherent approach to the management of an organization's most valued assets – the people working there who individually and collectively contribute to the achievement of its objectives.

Storey (1989) believes that HRM can be regarded as a 'set of interrelated policies with an ideological and philosophical underpinning'. He suggests four aspects that constitute the *meaningful* version of HRM:

1. a particular constellation of beliefs and assumptions;
2. a strategic thrust informing decisions about people management;
3. the central involvement of line managers; and
4. reliance upon a set of 'levers' to shape the employment relationship.

HUMAN RESOURCE SYSTEM

Human resource management operates through human resource systems that bring together in a coherent way:

- *HR philosophies* describing the overarching values and guiding principles adopted in managing people.
- *HR strategies* defining the direction in which HRM intends to go.
- *HR policies*, which are the guidelines defining how these values, principles and the strategies should be applied and implemented in specific areas of HRM.
- *HR processes* consisting of the formal procedures and methods used to put HR strategic plans and policies into effect.
- *HR practices* comprising the informal approaches used in managing people.
- *HR programmes*, which enable HR strategies, policies and practices to be implemented according to plan.

Becker and Gerhart (1996) have classified these components into three levels: the system architecture (guiding principles), policy alternatives and processes and practices.

See Figure 1.1.

MODELS OF HRM

The matching model of HRM

One of the first explicit statements of the HRM concept was made by the Michigan School (Fombrun *et al*, 1984). They held that HR systems and the organization structure should be managed in a way that is congruent with organizational strategy (hence the name 'matching model'). They further explained that there is a human resource cycle (an adaptation of which is illustrated in Figure 1.2), which consists of four generic processes or functions that are performed in all organizations. These are:

1. *selection* – matching available human resources to jobs;

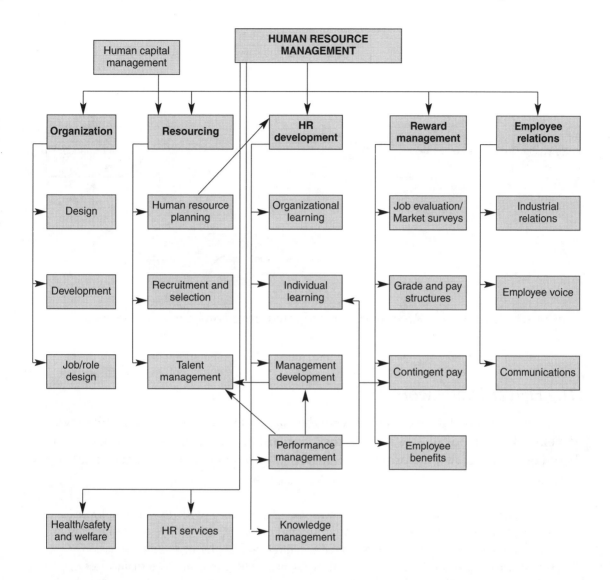

Figure 1.1 HRM activities

2. *appraisal* – performance management;
3. *rewards* – 'the reward system is one of the most under-utilized and mishandled managerial tools for driving organizational performance'; it must reward short as well as long-term achievements, bearing in mind that 'business must perform in the present to succeed in the future';
4. *development* – developing high quality employees.

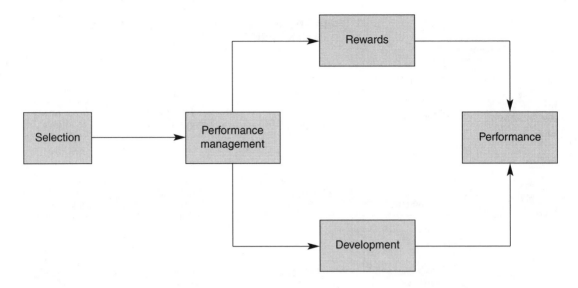

Figure 1.2   The Human Resource Cycle (adapted from Fombrun *et al*, 1984)

The Harvard framework

The other founding fathers of HRM were the Harvard School of Beer *et al* (1984) who developed what Boxall (1992) calls the 'Harvard framework'. This framework is based on the belief that the problems of historical personnel management can only be solved:

> when general managers develop a viewpoint of how they wish to see employees involved in and developed by the enterprise, and of what HRM policies and practices may achieve those goals. Without either a central philosophy or a strategic vision – which can be provided *only* by general managers – HRM is likely to remain a set of independent activities, each guided by its own practice tradition.

Beer and his colleagues believed that 'Today, many pressures are demanding a broader, more comprehensive and more strategic perspective with regard to the organization's human resources.' These pressures have created a need for: 'A longer-term perspective in managing people and consideration of people as potential assets rather than merely a variable cost.' They were the first to underline the HRM tenet that it belongs to line managers. They also stated that: 'Human resource management involves all management decisions and action that affect the nature of the relationship between the organization and its employees – its human resources.'

The Harvard school suggested that HRM had two characteristic features: 1) line managers accept more responsibility for ensuring the alignment of competitive strategy and personnel policies; 2) personnel has the mission of setting policies that govern how personnel activities are developed and implemented in ways that make them more mutually reinforcing. The Harvard framework as modelled by Beer *et al* is shown in Figure 1.3.

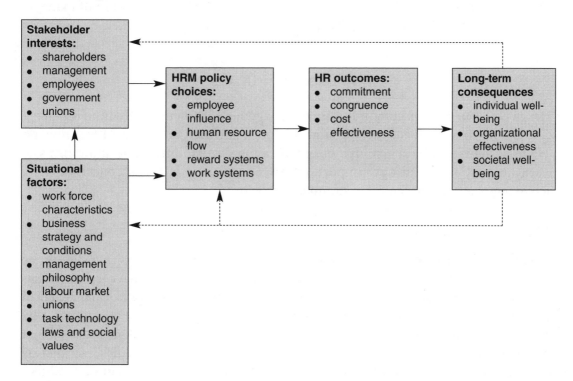

Figure 1.3 The Harvard Framework for Human Resource Management (*Source*: Beer *et al*, 1984)

According to Boxall (1992) the advantages of this model are that it:

- incorporates recognition of a range of stakeholder interests;
- recognizes the importance of 'trade-offs', either explicitly or implicitly, between the interests of owners and those of employees as well as between various interest groups;
- widens the context of HRM to include 'employee influence', the organization of work and the associated question of supervisory style;

- acknowledges a broad range of contextual influences on management's choice of strategy, suggesting a meshing of both product-market and socio-cultural logics;
- emphasizes strategic choice – it is not driven by situational or environmental determinism.

The Harvard model has exerted considerable influence over the theory and practice of HRM, particularly in its emphasis on the fact that HRM is the concern of management in general rather than the personnel function in particular.

AIMS OF HRM

The overall purpose of human resource management is to ensure that the organization is able to achieve success through people. As Ulrich and Lake (1990) remark: 'HRM systems can be the source of organizational capabilities that allow firms to learn and capitalize on new opportunities.' Specifically, HRM is concerned with achieving objectives in the areas summarized below.

Organizational effectiveness

'Distinctive human resource practices shape the core competencies that determine how firms compete' (Cappelli and Crocker-Hefter, 1996). Extensive research has shown that such practices can make a significant impact on firm performance. HRM strategies aim to support programmes for improving organizational effectiveness by developing policies in such areas as knowledge management, talent management and generally creating 'a great place to work'. This is the 'big idea' as described by Purcell *et al* (2003), which consists of a 'clear vision and a set of integrated values'. More specifically, HR strategies can be concerned with the development of continuous improvement and customer relations policies.

Human capital management

The human capital of an organization consists of the people who work there and on whom the success of the business depends. Human capital has been defined by Bontis *et al* (1999) as follows:

> Human capital represents the human factor in the organization; the combined intelligence, skills and expertise that give the organization its distinctive character. The human elements of the organization are those that are capable of learning, changing, innovating and providing the creative thrust which if properly motivated can ensure the long-term survival of the organization.

Human capital can be regarded as the prime asset of an organization and businesses need to invest in that asset to ensure their survival and growth. HRM aims to ensure that the organization obtains and retains the skilled, committed and well-motivated workforce it needs. This means taking steps to assess and satisfy future people needs and to enhance and develop the inherent capacities of people – their contributions, potential and employability – by providing learning and continuous development opportunities. It involves the operation of 'rigorous recruitment and selection procedures, performance-contingent incentive compensation systems, and management development and training activities linked to the needs of the business' (Becker *et al*, 1997). It also means engaging in talent management – the process of acquiring and nurturing talent, wherever it is and wherever it is needed, by using a number of interdependent HRM policies and practices in the fields of resourcing, learning and development, performance management and succession planning.

The process of human capital management (HCM) as described in the next chapter is closely associated with human resource management. However, the focus of HCM is more on the use of metrics (measurements of HR and people performance) as a means of providing guidance on people management strategy and practice.

Knowledge management

Knowledge management is 'any process or practice of creating, acquiring, capturing, sharing and using knowledge, wherever it resides, to enhance learning and performance in organizations' (Scarborough *et al*, 1999). HRM aims to support the development of firm-specific knowledge and skills that are the result of organizational learning processes.

Reward management

HRM aims to enhance motivation, job engagement and commitment by introducing policies and processes that ensure that people are valued and rewarded for what they do and achieve and for the levels of skill and competence they reach.

Employee relations

The aim is to create a climate in which productive and harmonious relationships can be maintained through partnerships between management and employees and their trade unions.

Meeting diverse needs

HRM aims to develop and implement policies that balance and adapt to the needs of its stakeholders and provide for the management of a diverse workforce, taking into account individual and group differences in employment, personal needs, work style and aspirations and the provision of equal opportunities for all.

Bridging the gap between rhetoric and reality

The research conducted by Gratton *et al* (1999) found that there was generally a wide gap between the sort of rhetoric expressed above and reality. Managements may start with good intentions to do some or all of these things but the realization of them – 'theory in use' – is often very difficult. This arises because of contextual and process problems: other business priorities, short-termism, limited support from line managers, an inadequate infrastructure of supporting processes, lack of resources, resistance to change and lack of trust. An overarching aim of HRM is to bridge this gap by making every attempt to ensure that aspirations are translated into sustained and effective action. To do this, members of the HR function have to remember that it is relatively easy to come up with new and innovatory policies and practice. The challenge is to get them to work. They must appreciate, in the phrase used by Purcell *et al* (2003) that it is the front line managers who bring HR policies to life, and act accordingly.

POLICY GOALS OF HRM

The models of HRM, the aims set out above and other definitions of HRM have been distilled by Caldwell (2004) into 12 policy goals:

1. Managing people as assets that are fundamental to the competitive advantage of the organization.
2. Aligning HRM policies with business policies and corporate strategy.
3. Developing a close fit of HR policies, procedures and systems with one another.
4. Creating a flatter and more flexible organization capable of responding more quickly to change.
5. Encouraging team working and co-operation across internal organizational boundaries.
6. Creating a strong customer-first philosophy throughout the organization.
7. Empowering employees to manage their own self-development and learning.

8. Developing reward strategies designed to support a performance-driven culture.
9. Improving employee involvement through better internal communication.
10. Building greater employee commitment to the organization.
11. Increasing line management responsibility for HR policies.
12. Developing the facilitating role of managers as enablers.

CHARACTERISTICS OF HRM

The characteristics of the HRM concept as they emerged from the writings of the pioneers and later commentators are that it is:

- diverse;
- strategic with an emphasis on integration;
- commitment-oriented;
- based on the belief that people should be treated as assets (human capital);
- unitarist rather than pluralist, individualistic rather than collective in its approach to employee relations;
- a management-driven activity – the delivery of HRM is a line management responsibility;
- focused on business values.

The diversity of HRM

But these characteristics of HRM are by no means universal. There are many models, and practices within different organizations are diverse, often only corresponding to the conceptual version of HRM in a few respects.

Hendry and Pettigrew (1990) play down the prescriptive element of the HRM model and extend the analytical elements. As pointed out by Boxall (1992), such an approach rightly avoids labelling HRM as a single form and advances more slowly by proceeding more analytically. It is argued by Hendry and Pettigrew that 'better descriptions of structures and strategy-making in complex organizations, and of frameworks for understanding them, are an essential underpinning for HRM'.

A distinction was made by Storey (1989) between the 'hard' and 'soft' versions of HRM. The hard version of HRM emphasizes that people are important resources through which organizations achieve competitive advantage. These resources have therefore to be acquired, developed and deployed in ways that will benefit the organization. The focus is on the quantitative, calculative and business-strategic aspects of managing human resources in as 'rational' a way as for any other economic factor. As Guest (1999a) comments:

> The drive to adopt HRM is... based on the business case of a need to respond to an external threat from increasing competition. It is a philosophy that appeals to managements who are striving to increase competitive advantage and appreciate that to do this they must invest in human resources as well as new technology.

He also commented that HRM 'reflects a long-standing capitalist tradition in which the worker is regarded as a commodity'. The emphasis is therefore on the interests of management, integration with business strategy, obtaining added value from people by the processes of human resource development and performance management and the need for a strong corporate culture expressed in mission and value statements and reinforced by communications, training and performance management processes.

The soft version of HRM traces its roots to the human-relations school; it emphasizes communication, motivation and leadership. As described by Storey (1989) it involves 'treating employees as valued assets, a source of competitive advantage through their commitment, adaptability and high quality (of skills, performance and so on)'. It therefore views employees, in the words of Guest (1999a), as means rather than objects, but it does not go as far as following Kant's advice: 'Treat people as ends unto themselves rather than as means to an end.' The soft approach to HRM stresses the need to gain the commitment – the 'hearts and minds' – of employees through involvement, communications and other methods of developing a high-commitment, high-trust organization. Attention is also drawn to the key role of organizational culture.

In 1998, Legge defined the 'hard' model of HRM as a process emphasizing 'the close integration of human resource policies with business strategy which regards employees as a resource to be managed in the same rational way as any other resource being exploited for maximum return'. In contrast, the soft version of HRM sees employees as 'valued assets and as a source of competitive advantage through their commitment, adaptability and high level of skills and performance'.

It has, however, been observed by Truss (1999) that 'even if the rhetoric of HRM is soft, the reality is often hard, with the interests of the organization prevailing over those of the individual'. And research carried out by Gratton *et al* (1999) found that in the eight organizations they studied, a mixture of hard and soft HRM approaches was identified. This suggested to the researchers that the distinction between hard and soft HRM was not as precise as some commentators have implied.

The strategic nature of HRM

Perhaps the most significant feature of HRM is the importance attached to strategic integration, which flows from top management's vision and leadership, and which requires the full commitment of people to it. Guest (1987, 1989a, 1989b, 1991) believes that this is a key policy goal for HRM, which is concerned with the ability of the organization to integrate HRM issues into its strategic plans, to ensure that the various aspects of HRM cohere, and to encourage line managers to incorporate an HRM perspective into their decision-making.

Legge (1989) considers that one of the common themes of the typical definitions of HRM is that human resource policies should be integrated with strategic business planning. Sisson (1990) suggests that a feature increasingly associated with HRM is a stress on the integration of HR policies both with one another and with business planning more generally.

Storey (1989) suggests that: 'The concept locates HRM policy formulation firmly at the strategic level and insists that a characteristic of HRM is its internally coherent approach.'

The commitment-oriented nature of HRM

The importance of commitment and mutuality was emphasized by Walton (1985a) as follows:

> The new HRM model is composed of policies that promote mutuality – mutual goals, mutual influence, mutual respect, mutual rewards, and mutual responsibility. The theory is that policies of mutuality will elicit commitment, which in turn will yield both better economic performance and greater human development.

Guest (1987) wrote that one of the HRM policy goals was the achievement of high commitment – 'behavioural commitment to pursue agreed goals, and attitudinal commitment reflected in a strong identification with the enterprise'.

It was noted by Legge (1995) that human resources 'may be tapped most effectively by mutually consistent policies that promote commitment and which, as a consequence, foster a willingness in employees to act flexibly in the interests of the "adaptive organization's" pursuit of excellence'.

But this emphasis on commitment has been criticized from the earliest days of HRM. Guest (1987) asked: 'commitment to what?' and Fowler (1987) has stated:

> At the heart of the concept is the complete identification of employees with the aims and values of the business – employee involvement but on the company's terms. Power in

the HRM system remains very firmly in the hands of the employer. Is it really possible to claim full mutuality when at the end of the day the employer can decide unilaterally to close the company or sell it to someone else?

People as 'human capital'

The notion that people should be regarded as assets rather than variable costs, in other words, treated as human capital, was originally advanced by Beer *et al* (1984). HRM philosophy, as mentioned by Karen Legge (1995), holds that 'human resources are valuable and a source of competitive advantage'. Armstrong and Baron (2002) stated that:

> People and their collective skills, abilities and experience, coupled with their ability to deploy these in the interests of the employing organization, are now recognized as making a significant contribution to organizational success and as constituting a significant source of competitive advantage.

Unitary philosophy

The HRM approach to employee relations is basically unitary – it is believed that employees share the same interests as employers. This contrasts with what could be regarded as the more realistic pluralist view, which says that all organizations contain a number of interest groups and that the interests of employers and employees do not necessarily coincide.

Individualistic

HRM is individualistic in that it emphasizes the importance of maintaining links between the organization and individual employees in preference to operating through group and representative systems.

HRM as a management-driven activity

HRM can be described as a central, senior management-driven strategic activity that is developed, owned and delivered by management as a whole to promote the interests of the organization that they serve. Purcell (1993) thinks that 'the adoption of HRM is both a product of and a cause of a significant concentration of power in the hands of management', while the widespread use 'of the language of HRM, if not its practice, is a combination of its intuitive appeal to managers and, more importantly, a response to the turbulence of product and financial markets'. He asserts that HRM is about the rediscovery of management prerogative. He considers that HRM policies and practices, when applied within a firm as a break from the past, are often associated with words such as commitment, competence, empowerment, flexibility, culture, performance, assessment, reward, teamwork, involvement, cooperation, harmonization, quality and learning. But 'the danger of descriptions of HRM as modern best-management practice is that they stereotype the past and idealize the future'.

Sisson (1990) suggested that: 'The locus of responsibility for personnel management no longer resides with (or is "relegated to") specialist managers.' More recently, Purcell *et al* (2003) underlined the importance of line management commitment and capability as the means by which HR policies are brought to life.

Focus on business values

The concept of HRM is largely based on a management and business-oriented philosophy. It is concerned with the total interests of the organization – the interests of the members of the organization are recognized but subordinated to those of the enterprise. Hence the importance attached to strategic integration and strong cultures, which flow from top management's vision and leadership, and which require people who will be committed to the strategy, who will be adaptable to change, and who will fit the culture. By implication, as Guest (1991) says: 'HRM is too important to be left to personnel managers.'

In 1995 Legge noted that HRM policies are adapted to drive business values and are modified in the light of changing business objectives and conditions. She describes this process as 'thinking pragmatism' and suggests that evidence indicates more support for the hard versions of HRM than the soft version.

RESERVATIONS ABOUT HRM

For some time HRM was a controversial topic, especially in academic circles. The main reservations have been that HRM promises more than it delivers and that its morality is suspect.

HRM promises more than it can deliver

Noon (1992) has commented that HRM has serious deficiencies as a theory:

> It is built with concepts and propositions, but the associated variables and hypotheses are not made explicit. It is too comprehensive... If HRM is labelled a 'theory' it raises expectations about its ability to describe and predict.

Guest (1991) believes that HRM is an 'optimistic but ambiguous concept'; it is all hype and hope.

Mabey *et al* (1998) follow this up by asserting that 'the heralded outcomes (of HRM) are almost without exception unrealistically high'. To put the concept of HRM into practice involves strategic integration, developing a coherent and consistent set of employment policies, and gaining commitment. This requires high levels of determination and competence at all levels of management and a strong and effective HR function staffed by business-oriented people. It may be difficult to meet these criteria, especially when the proposed HRM culture conflicts with the established corporate culture and traditional managerial attitudes and behaviour.

Gratton *et al* (1999) are convinced on the basis of their research that there is:

> a disjunction between rhetoric and reality in the area of human resource management between HRM theory and HRM practice, between what the HR function says it is doing and that practice as perceived by employers, and between what senior management believes to be the role of the HR function, and the role it actually plays.

In their conclusions they refer to the 'hyperbole and rhetoric of human resource management'.

Caldwell (2004) believes that HRM 'is an unfinished project informed by a self-fulfilling vision of what it *should* be'.

In response to the above comments it is agreed that many organizations that think they are practising HRM are doing nothing of the kind. It is difficult, and it is best not to expect too much. Most of the managements who hurriedly adopted performance-related pay as an HRM device that would act as a lever for change have been sorely disappointed.

But the research conducted by Guest and Conway (1997) covering a stratified random sample of 1,000 workers established that a notably high level of HRM was found to be in place. This contradicts the view that management has tended to 'talk up' the adoption of HRM practices. The HRM characteristics covered by the survey included the opportunity to express grievances and raise personal concerns on such matters as opportunities for training and development, communications about business issues, single status, effective systems for dealing with bullying and harassment at work, making jobs interesting and varied, promotion from within, involvement programmes, no compulsory redundancies, performance-related pay, profit sharing and the use of attitude surveys.

The morality of HRM

HRM is accused by many academics of being manipulative if not positively immoral.

Willmott (1993) remarks that HRM operates as a form of insidious 'control by compliance' when it emphasizes the need for employees to be committed to do what the organization wants them to do. It preaches mutuality but the reality is that behind the rhetoric it exploits workers. It is, they say, a wolf in sheep's clothing (Keenoy, 1990a). As Legge (1998) pointed out:

> Sadly, in a world of intensified competition and scarce resources, it seems inevitable that, as employees are used as means to an end, there will be some who will lose out. They may even be in the majority. For these people, the soft version of HRM may be an irrelevancy, while the hard version is likely to be an uncomfortable experience.

The accusation that HRM treats employees as means to an end is often made. However, it could be argued that if organizations exist to achieve ends, which they obviously do, and if those ends can only be achieved through people, which is clearly the case, the concern of managements for commitment and performance from those people is not unnatural and is not attributable to the concept of HRM – it existed in the good old days of personnel management before HRM was invented. What matters is how managements treat people as ends and what managements provide in return.

Much of the hostility to HRM expressed by a number of academics is based on the belief that it is hostile to the interests of workers, ie that it is managerialist. However, the Guest and Conway (1997) research established that the reports of workers on outcomes showed that a higher number of HR practices were associated with higher ratings of fairness, trust and management's delivery of their promises. Those experiencing more HR activities also felt more secure in and more satisfied with their jobs. Motivation was significantly higher for those working in organizations where more HR practices were in place. In summary, as commented by Guest (1999b), it appears that workers like their experience of HRM. These findings appear to contradict the 'radical critique' view produced by academics such as Mabey *et al* (1998) that HRM has been ineffectual, pernicious (ie managerialist) or both. Some of those who adopt this stance tend to dismiss favourable reports from workers about HRM on the grounds that they have been brainwashed by management. But there is no evidence to support this view. Moreover, as Armstrong (2000a) pointed out:

> HRM cannot be blamed or given credit for changes that were taking place anyway. For example, it is often alleged to have inspired a move from pluralism to unitarism in industrial relations. But newspaper production was moved from Fleet Street to Wapping by Murdoch, not because he had read a book about HRM but as a means of breaking the print unions' control.

Contradictions in the reservations about HRM

Guest (1999a) has suggested that there are two contradictory concerns about HRM. The first as formulated by Legge (1995, 1998) is that while management rhetoric may express concern for workers, the reality is harsher. Keenoy (1997) complains that: 'The real puzzle about HRMism is how, in the face of such apparently overwhelming critical "refutation", it has secured such influence and institutional presence.'

Other writers, however, simply claim that HRM does not work. Scott (1994) for example, finds that both management and workers are captives of their history and find it very difficult to let go of their traditional adversarial orientations. But these contentions are contradictory. Guest (1999b) remarks that, 'It is difficult to treat HRM as a major threat (though what it is a threat to is not always made explicit) deserving of serious critical analysis while at the same time claiming that it is not practiced or is ineffective.'

HRM AND PERSONNEL MANAGEMENT

A debate about the differences, if any, between HRM and personnel management went on for some time. It has died down recently, especially as the terms HRM and HR are now in general use both in their own right and as synonyms for personnel management. But understanding of the concept of HRM is enhanced by analysing what the differences are and how traditional approaches to personnel management have evolved to become the present day practices of HRM.

Some commentators (Hope-Hailey *et al*, 1998; Keenoy, 1990b; Legge, 1989, 1995; Sisson, 1990; Storey, 1993) have highlighted the revolutionary nature of HRM. Others have denied that there is any significant difference in the concepts of personnel management and HRM. Torrington (1989) suggested that: 'Personnel management has grown through assimilating a number of additional emphases to produce an even richer combination of experience... HRM is no revolution but a further dimension to a multi-faceted role.'

The conclusion based on interviews with HR and personnel directors reached by Gennard and Kelly (1994) on this issue was that 'it is six of one and half a dozen of the other and it is a sterile debate'. An earlier answer to this question was made by Armstrong (1987):

> HRM is regarded by some personnel managers as just a set of initials or old wine in new bottles. It could indeed be no more and no less than another name for personnel management, but as usually perceived, at least it has the virtue of emphasizing the virtue of treating people as a key resource, the management of which is the direct concern of

top management as part of the strategic planning processes of the enterprise. Although there is nothing new in the idea, insufficient attention has been paid to it in many organizations.

The similarities and differences between HRM and personnel management are summarized in Table 1.1.

Table 1.1   Similarities and differences between HRM and personnel management

Similarities	Differences
1. Personnel management strategies, like HRM strategies, flow from the business strategy. 2. Personnel management, like HRM, recognizes that line managers are responsible for managing people. The personnel function provides the necessary advice and support services to enable managers to carry out their responsibilities. 3. The values of personnel management and at least the 'soft' version of HRM are identical with regard to 'respect for the individual', balancing organizational and individual needs, and developing people to achieve their maximum level of competence both for their own satisfaction and to facilitate the achievement of organizational objectives. 4. Both personnel management and HRM recognize that one of their most essential functions is that of matching people to ever-changing organizational requirements – placing and developing the right people in and for the right jobs. 5. The same range of selection, competence analysis, performance management, training, management development and reward management techniques are used both in HRM and personnel management. 6. Personnel management, like the 'soft' version of HRM, attaches importance to the processes of communication and participation within an employee relations system.	1. HRM places more emphasis on strategic fit and integration. 2. HRM is based on a management and business orientated philosophy. 3. HRM attaches more importance to the management of culture and the achievement of commitment (mutuality). 4. HRM places greater emphasis on the role of line managers as the implementers of HR policies. 5. HRM is a holistic approach concerned with the total interests of the business – the interests of the members of the organization are recognized but subordinated to those of the enterprise. 6. HR specialists are expected to be business partners rather than personnel administrators. 7. HRM treats employees as assets not costs.

The differences between personnel management and human resource management appear to be substantial but they can be seen as a matter of emphasis and approach rather than one of substance. Or, as Hendry and Pettigrew (1990) put it, HRM can be perceived as a 'perspective on personnel management and not personnel management itself'.

HOW HR IMPACTS ON ORGANIZATIONAL PERFORMANCE

The assumption underpinning the practice of HRM is that people are the organization's key resource and organizational performance largely depends on them. If, therefore, an appropriate range of HR policies and processes are developed and implemented effectively, then HR will make a substantial impact on firm performance.

The Holy Grail sought by many commentators on human resource management is to establish that a clear positive link between HRM practices and organizational performance exists. There has been much research, as summarized in Table 1.2, over the last decade or so that has attempted to answer two basic questions: 'Do HR practices make a positive impact on organizational performance?' 'If so, how is the impact achieved?' The second question is the most important one. It is not enough to justify HRM by proving that it is a good thing. What counts is what can be done to ensure that it is a good thing. This is the 'black box' mentioned by Purcell *et al* (2003) that lies between intentions and outcomes.

Ulrich (1997a) has pointed out that: 'HR practices seem to matter; logic says it is so; survey findings confirm it. Direct relationships between investment and attention to HR practices are often fuzzy, however, and vary according to the population sampled and the measures used'.

Purcell *et al* (2003) have cast doubts on the validity of some of the attempts through research to make the connection:

> Our study has demonstrated convincingly that research which only asks about the number and extent of HR practices can never be sufficient to understand the link between HR practices and business performance. As we have discussed it is misleading to assume that simply because HR policies are present that they will be implemented as intended.

Further comments about attempts to trace the link have been made by Truss (2001) who, following research in Hewlett-Packard, remarked that:

Our findings did lend strong support to the argument put forward by Mueller (1996) that the informal organization has a key role to play in the HRM process such that informal practice and norms of behaviour interact with formal HR policies... We cannot consider how HRM and performance are linked without analysing, in some detail, how policy is turned into practice through the lens of the informal organization.

Research outcomes

A considerable amount of research has been carried out to establish the link between HRM and firm performance. The outcomes of some of the main projects are summarized in Table 1.2.

Table 1.2 Outcomes of research on the link between HR and organizational performance

Researcher(s)	Methodology	Outcomes
Arthur (1990, 1992, 1994)	Data from 30 US strip mills used to assess impact on labour efficiency and scrap rate by reference to the existence of either a high commitment strategy* or a control strategy*.	Firms with a high commitment strategy had significantly higher levels of both productivity and quality than those with a control strategy.
Huselid (1995)	Analysis of the responses of 968 US firms to a questionnaire exploring the use of high performance work practices*, the development of synergies between them and the alignment of these practices with the competitive strategy.	Productivity is influenced by employee motivation; financial performance is influenced by employee skills, motivation and organizational structures.
Huselid and Becker (1996)	An index of HR systems in 740 firms was created to indicate the degree to which each firm adopted a high performance work system.	Firms with high values on the index had economically and statistically higher levels of performance.
Becker *et al* (1997)	Outcomes of a number of research projects were analysed to assess the strategic impact on shareholder value of high performance work systems.	High performance systems make an impact as long as they are embedded in the management infrastructure.

Table 1.2 *continued*

Patterson *et al* (1997)	The research examined the link between business performance and organization culture and the use of a number of HR practices.	HR practices explained significant variations in profitability and productivity (19% and 18% respectively). Two HR practices were particularly significant: (1) the acquisition and development of employee skills and (2) job design including flexibility, responsibility, variety and the use of formal teams.
Thompson (1998)	A study of the impact of high performance work practices such as teamworking, appraisal, job rotation, broad-banded grade structures and sharing of business information in 623 UK aerospace establishments.	The number of HR practices and the proportion of the workforce covered appeared to be the key differentiating factor between more and less successful firms.
The 1998 Workplace Employee Relations Survey (as analysed by Guest *et al* 2000a)	An analysis of the survey which sampled some 2,000 workplaces and obtained the views of about 28,000 employees.	A strong assocation exists between HRM and both employee attitudes and workplace performance.
The Future of Work Survey, Guest *et al* (2000b)	835 private sector organizations were surveyed and interviews were carried out with 610 HR professionals and 462 chief executives.	A greater use of HR practices is associated with higher levels of employee commitment and contribution and is in turn linked to higher levels of productivity and quality of services.
Purcell *et al* (2003)	A University of Bath longitudinal study of 12 companies to establish how people management impacts on organizational performance.	The most successful companies had what the researchers called 'the big idea'. The companies had a clear vision and a set of integrated values which were embedded, enduring, collective, measured and managed. They were concerned with sustaining performance and flexibility. Clear evidence existed between positive attitudes towards HR policies and practices, levels of satisfaction, motivation and

continued

Table 1.2   *continued*

			commitment, and operational performance. Policy and practice implementation (not the number of HR practices adopted) is the vital ingredient in linking people management to business performance and this is primarily the task of line managers.

* In the US research projects set out in Table 1.2 reference is made to the impact made by the following strategies: *A commitment strategy* – a strategy, as described by Walton (1985b) which promotes mutuality between employers and employees. *A control strategy* – as described by Walton (1985b), one in which the aim is to establish order, exercise control and achieve efficiency in the application of the workforce but where employees did not have a voice except through their unions. *High performance work systems* – these aim to impact on performance through its people by the use of such practices as rigorous recruitment and selection procedures, extensive and relevant training and management development activities, incentive pay systems and performance management processes.

How HR makes an impact

In Guest *et al* (2000b) the relationship between HRM and performance was modelled as shown in Figure 1.4.

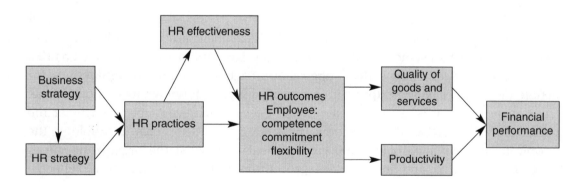

Figure 1.4   Model of the link between HRM and performance (*Source*: Guest *et al*, 2000b)

The messages from research, especially that carried out by Purcell *et al* (2003), are that HR can make an impact by leading or contributing to:

- the development and successful implementation of high performance work practices, particularly those concerned with job and work design, flexible working, resourcing (recruitment and selection and talent management), employee development (increasing skills and extending the skills base), reward, and giving employees a voice;
- the formulation and embedding of a clear vision and set of values (the big idea);
- the development of a positive psychological contract and means of increasing the motivation and commitment of employees;
- the formulation *and* implementation of policies which, in the words of Purcell *et al* (2003) meet the needs of individuals and 'create a great place to work';
- the provision of support and advice to line managers on their role in implementing HR policies and practices;
- the effective management of change.

HRM IN CONTEXT

HRM processes take place within the context of the internal and external environment of the organization. They will be largely contingent on the environmental factors that affect them.

Contingency theory

Contingency theory tells us that definitions of aims, policies and strategies, lists of activities, and analyses of the role of the HR department are valid only if they are related to the circumstances of the organization. Descriptions in books such as this can only be generalizations that suggest approaches and provide guidelines for action; they cannot be prescriptive in the sense of laying down what should be done. Contingency theory is essentially about the need to achieve *fit* between what the organization is and wants to become (its strategy, culture, goals, technology, the people it employs and its external environment) and what the organization does (how it is structured, and the processes, procedures and practices it puts into effect).

Contextual factors

There are three main contextual factors that influence HR policies and practices.

1. Technology

The technology of the business exerts a major influence on the internal environment – how work is organized, managed and carried out. The introduction of new technology may result in considerable changes to systems and processes. Different skills are required and new methods of working are developed. The result may be an extension of the skills base of the organization and its employees, including multiskilling (ensuring that people have a range of skills that enable them to work flexibly on a variety of tasks, often within a teamworking environment). But it could result in de-skilling and a reduction in the number of jobs (downsizing).

New technology can therefore present a considerable threat to employees. The world of work has changed in many ways. Knowledge workers are employed in largely computerized offices and laboratories, and technicians work in computer integrated manufacturing systems. They may have to be managed differently from the clerks or machine operators they displace. The service industries have become predominant and manufacturing is in decline. New work environments such as call centres have become common and tele-working (working from home with a networked computer) is increasing.

2. Competitive pressures

Global competition in mature production and service sectors is increasing. This is assisted by easily transferable technology and reductions in international trade barriers. Customers are demanding more as new standards are reached through international competition. Organizations are reacting to this competition by becoming 'customer-focused', speeding up response times, emphasizing quality and continuous improvement, accelerating the introduction of new technology, operating more flexibly and 'losing cost'.

The pressure has been for businesses to become 'lean organizations', downsizing and cutting out layers of management and supervision. They are reducing permanent staff to a core of essential workers, increasing the use of peripheral workers (subcontractors, temporary staff) and 'outsourcing' work to external service providers. The aim is to reduce employment costs and enable the enterprise easily to increase or reduce the numbers available for work in response to fluctuations in the level of business activity. They become the so-called 'flexible firms'. The ultimate development of this process is the 'virtual' firm or corporation, where through the extensive use of information technology a high proportion of marketing and professional staff mainly work from home, only coming into the office on special occasions to occupy their 'hot desks', and spending more time with their customers or clients.

Another response to competitive pressures is business process re-engineering (BPR), which examines the process that contains and links those functions together from initiation to completion. It looks at processes in organizations horizontally to establish how they can be integrated more effectively as well as streamlined. It can therefore form the basis for an organizational redesign exercise. From an HR point of view, the outcome of a BPR exercise may well be the need to attract or develop people with new skills as well as pressure for the improvement of team working. It also emphasizes the importance of an integrated – a coherent – approach to the development and implementation of HR policies and employment practices. Re-engineering often promises more than it achieves and is not regarded as highly as it once was, not least because it often neglected the human aspects, giving insufficient attention to the management of change and retraining staff.

3. Responses affecting people

The responses to the increased use of technology and to economic and competitive pressures have changed the nature of people management in a number of ways. These include slimmer and flatter organization structures in which cross-functional operations and teamworking have become more important, more flexible working patterns, total quality and lean production initiatives, and the decentralization and devolvement of decision-making.

The challenge to HRM

Ulrich (1998) suggests that environmental and contextual changes present a number of competitive challenges to organizations that mean that HR has to be involved in helping to build new capabilities. These comprise:

- *Globalization*, which requires organizations to move people, ideas, products and information around the world to meet local needs. New and important ingredients must be added to the mix when making strategy: volatile political situations, contentious global trade issues, fluctuating exchange rates and unfamiliar cultures.
- *Profitability through growth* – the drive for revenue growth means that companies must be creative and innovative and this means encouraging the free flow of information and shared learning among employees.
- *Technology* – the challenge is to make technology a viable, productive part of the work setting.
- *Intellectual capital* – this is the source of competitive advantage for organizations. The challenge is to ensure that firms have the capability to find, assimilate,

compensate and retain human capital in the shape of the talented individuals they need who can drive a global organization that is both responsive to its customers and 'the burgeoning opportunities of technology'. They have also to consider how the social capital of the organization – the ways in which people interact – can be developed. Importantly, organizations have to focus on organizational capital – the knowledge they own and how it should be managed.

- *Change, change and more change* – the greatest challenge companies face is adjusting to – indeed, embracing – non-stop change. They must be able to 'learn rapidly and continuously, and take on new strategic imperatives faster and more comfortably'.

2

Human capital management

Human capital management (HCM) has been described as 'a paradigm shift' from the traditional approach to human resource management (Kearns, 2005b) – a large claim. It is considered in this chapter initially by defining the concept of human capital management and its relationship to the concept of human resource management. To understand HCM it is necessary to know about the concept of human capital, which is the next section heading. The chapter is completed with an analysis of the processes involved in HCM including a discussion of human capital measurement and reporting.

HUMAN CAPITAL MANAGEMENT DEFINED

Human capital management (HCM) is concerned with obtaining, analysing and reporting on data that informs the direction of value-adding people management, strategic investment and operational decisions at corporate level and at the level of front line management. The defining characteristic of HCM is this use of metrics to guide an approach to managing people that regards them as assets and emphasizes that competitive advantage is achieved by strategic investments in those assets through employee engagement and retention, talent management and learning and development programmes.

The Accounting for People Task Force Report (2003) stated that HCM involves the systematic analysis, measurement and evaluation of how people policies and practices create value. The report defined HCM as 'an approach to people management that treats it as a high level strategic issue rather than an operational matter "to be left to the HR people" '. The Task Force expressed the view that HCM 'has been under-exploited as a way of gaining competitive edge'. As John Sunderland, Task Force member and Executive Chairman of Cadbury Schweppes plc commented: 'An organization's success is the product of its people's competence. That link between people and performance should be made visible and available to all stakeholders.'

Nalbantian *et al* (2004) emphasize the measurement aspect of HCM. They define human capital as, 'The stock of accumulated knowledge, skills, experience, creativity and other relevant workforce attributes' and suggest that human capital management involves 'putting into place the metrics to measure the value of these attributes and using that knowledge to effectively manage the organization'. HCM is defined by Kearns (2005b) as 'The total development of human potential expressed as organizational value.' He believes that 'HCM is about creating value through people' and that it is 'a people development philosophy, but the only development that means anything is that which is translated into value'.

HUMAN CAPITAL MANAGEMENT AND HUMAN RESOURCE MANAGEMENT

In the opinion of Mayo (2001) the essential difference between HCM and HRM is that the former treats people as assets while the latter treats them as costs. Kearns (2005b) believes that in HCM 'people are value adders, not overheads' while in HRM 'people are (treated as) a significant cost and should be managed accordingly'. According to Kearns, in HRM 'the HR team is seen as a support service to the line' – HR is based around the function and the HR team performs 'a distinct and separate role from other functions'. Conversely, 'HCM is clearly seen and respected as an equal business partner at senior levels' and is 'holistic, organization-wide and systems-based' as well as being strategic and concerned with adding value.

The claim that in HRM employees are treated as costs is not supported by the descriptions of the *concept* of HRM produced by American writers such as Beer *et al* (1984). In one of the seminal texts on human resource management, they emphasized the need for: 'a longer-term perspective in managing people and consideration of people as potential assets rather than merely a variable cost'. Fombrun *et al* (1984), in the other seminal text, quite explicitly presented workers as a key resource that managers use to achieve competitive advantage for their companies. Grant (1991) lists the main characteristics of human resources in his general classification of a firm's potential resources as follows:

- The training and expertise of employees determines the skills available to the firm.
- The adaptability of employees determines the strategic flexibility of the firm.
- The commitment and loyalty of employees determine the firm's ability to maintain competitive advantage.

Cappelli and Singh (1992) propose that competitive advantage arises from firm-specific, valuable resources that are difficult to imitate, and stress 'the role of human resource policies in the creation of valuable, firm-specific skills'.

Other writers confirmed this view. For example:

> HRM is an 'approach to labour management which treats labour as a valued *asset* rather than a variable cost and which consequently counsels investment in the labour resource through training and development and through measures designed to attract and retain a committed workforce'. (Storey, 1989)

> Human resource management is a distinctive approach to employment management that seeks to obtain competitive advantage through the strategic deployment of a highly committed and capable workforce, using an integrated array of cultural, structural and personnel techniques. (Storey, 1995)

The HRM argument is that people... are not to be seen as a cost, but as an *asset* in which to invest, so adding to their inherent value. (Torrington, 1989, emphasis in the original)

Of course, all these commentators are writing about HRM as a belief system, not about how it works in practice. The almost universal replacement of the term 'personnel management' with HR or HRM does not mean that everyone with the job title of HR director or manager is basing their approach on the HRM philosophy. Guest commented in 1991 that HRM was 'all hype and hope'.

A survey conducted by Caldwell (2004) provided some support to this view by establishing that the five most important HR policy areas identified by respondents were also the five in which the least progress had been made. For example, while 89 per cent of respondents said the most important HR policy was 'managing people as assets which are fundamental to the competitive advantage of the organization', only 37 per cent stated that they had made any progress in implementing it.

However, research conducted by Hoque and Moon (2001) found that there were significant differences between the activities of those described as HR specialists and those described as personnel specialists. For example, workplace-level strategic plans are more likely to emphasize employee development in workplaces with an HR specialist rather than a personnel specialist, and HR specialists are more likely to be involved in the development of strategic plans than are personnel specialists.

Both HRM in its proper sense and HCM as defined above treat people as assets. Although, as William Scott-Jackson, Director of the Centre for Applied HR Research at Oxford Brookes University argues (Oracle, 2005), 'You can't simply treat people as assets, because that depersonalizes them and leads to the danger that they are viewed in purely financial terms, which does little for all-important engagement.'

However, there is more to both HRM and HCM than simply treating people as assets. Each of them also focuses on the importance of adopting an integrated and strategic approach to managing people, which is the concern of all the stakeholders in an organization, not just the people management function. So how does the concept of HCM reinforce or add to the concept of HRM? The answers to that question are that HCM:

- draws attention to the importance of what Kearns (2005b) calls 'management through measurement', the aim being to establish a clear line of sight between HR interventions and organizational success;
- strengthens the HRM belief that people are assets rather than costs;
- focuses attention on the need to base HRM strategies and processes on the requirement to create value through people and thus further the achievement of organizational goals;
- reinforces the need to be strategic;
- emphasizes the role of HR specialists as business partners;
- provides guidance on what to measure and how to measure;
- underlines the importance of using the measurements to prove that superior people management is delivering superior results and to indicate the direction in which HR strategy needs to go.

The concept of HCM complements and strengthens the concept of HRM. It does not replace it. Both HCM and HRM can be regarded as vital components in the process of people management.

THE CONCEPT OF HUMAN CAPITAL

Individuals generate, retain and use knowledge and skill (human capital) and create intellectual capital. Their knowledge is enhanced by the interactions between them (social capital) and generates the institutionalized knowledge possessed by an organization (organizational capital). These concepts of human, intellectual, social and organizational capital are explained below.

Human capital

The term 'human capital' was originated by Schultz (1961) who elaborated his concept in 1981 as follows: 'Consider all human abilities to be either innate or acquired. Attributes... which are valuable and can be augmented by appropriate investment will be human capital.'

A more detailed definition was put forward by Bontis *et al* (1999) as follows:

> Human capital represents the human factor in the organization; the combined intelligence, skills and expertise that gives the organization its distinctive character. The human elements of the organization are those that are capable of learning, changing, innovating and providing the creative thrust which if properly motivated can ensure the long-term survival of the organization.

Scarborough and Elias (2002) believe that: 'The concept of human capital is most usefully viewed as a bridging concept – that is, it defines the link between HR practices and business performance in terms of assets rather than business processes.' They point out that human capital is to a large extent 'non-standardized, tacit, dynamic, context dependent and embodied in people'. These characteristics make it difficult to evaluate human capital bearing in mind that the 'features of human capital that are so crucial to firm performance are the flexibility and creativity of individuals, their ability to develop skills over time and to respond in a motivated way to different contexts'.

It is indeed the knowledge, skills and abilities of individuals that create value, which is why the focus has to be on means of attracting, retaining, developing and maintaining the human capital they represent. Davenport (1999) comments that:

> People possess innate abilities, behaviours and personal energy and these elements make up the human capital they bring to their work. And it is they, not their employers, who own this capital and decide when, how and where they will contribute it. In other words, they can make choices. Work is a two-way exchange of value, not a one-way exploitation of an asset by its owner.

The choices they make include how much discretionary behaviour they are prepared to exercise in carrying out their role (discretionary behaviour refers to the discretion people at work can exercise about the way they do their job and the amount of effort, care, innovation and productive behaviour they display). They can also choose whether or not to remain with the organization.

Intellectual capital

The concept of human capital is associated with the overarching concept of intellectual capital, which is defined as the stocks and flows of knowledge available to an organization. These can be regarded as the intangible resources associated with people who, together with tangible resources (money and physical assets), comprise the market or total value of a business. Bontis (1996, 1998) defines intangible resources as the factors other than financial and physical assets that contribute to the value-generating processes of a firm and are under its control.

Social capital

Social capital is another element of intellectual capital. It consists of the knowledge derived from networks of relationships within and outside the organization. The concept of social capital has been defined by Putnam (1996) as 'the features of social life – networks, norms and trust – that enable participants to act together more effectively to pursue shared objectives'. The World Bank (2000) offers the following definition:

> Social capital refers to the institutions, relationships and norms that shape the quality and quantity of a society's social interactions... Social capital is not just the sum of the institutions that underpin a society – it is the glue that holds them together.

It is necessary to capture individual knowledge through knowledge management processes, as described in Chapter 12, but it is equally important to take into account social capital considerations, that is, the ways in which knowledge is developed through interaction between people. Bontis *et al* (1999) point out that it is flows as well as stocks that matter. Intellectual capital develops and changes over time and a significant part is played in these processes by people acting together.

Organizational capital

Organizational capital is the institutionalized knowledge possessed by an organization, which is stored in databases, manuals, etc (Youndt, 2000). It is often called *structural capital* (Edvinson and Malone, 1997), but the term 'organizational capital' is preferred by Youndt because, he argues, it conveys more clearly that this is the knowledge that the organization actually *owns*.

The significance of human capital theory

The added value that people can contribute to an organization is emphasized by human capital theory. It regards people as assets and stresses that investment by organizations in people will generate worthwhile returns. The theory therefore underpins the philosophies of human resource management and human capital management.

Human capital theory is associated with the resource-based view of the firm as developed by Barney (1991). This proposes that sustainable competitive advantage is attained when the firm has a human resource pool that cannot be imitated or substituted by its rivals. Boxall (1996) refers to this situation as one that confers 'human capital advantage'. But he also notes (1996 and 1999), that a distinction should be made between 'human capital advantage' and 'human process advantage'. The former results from employing people with competitively valuable knowledge and skills, much of it tacit. The latter, however, follows from the establishment of:

> difficult to imitate, highly evolved processes within the firm, such as cross-departmental co-operation and executive development. Accordingly, 'human resource advantage', the superiority of one firm's labour management over another's, can be thought of as the product of its human capital and human process advantages.

For the employer, investments in training and developing people is a means of attracting and retaining human capital as well as getting better returns from those investments. These returns are expected to be improvements in performance, productivity, flexibility and the capacity to innovate that should result from enlarging the skill base and increasing levels of knowledge and competence. Schuller (2000) suggests that: 'The general message is persuasive: skills, knowledge and competences are key factors in determining whether organizations and nations will prosper.' This point is also made powerfully by Reich (1991).

But Davenport (1999) has some cautionary words about the asset-based content of human capital theory. He argues that workers should not be treated as passive assets to be bought, sold and replaced at the whim of their owners – increasingly, they actively control their own working lives. Workers, especially knowledge workers, may regard themselves as free agents who can choose how and where they invest their talents, time and energy. He suggests that the notion that companies own human assets as they own machines is unacceptable in principle and inapplicable in practice; it short-changes people by placing them in the same category as plant and equipment.

Important though human capital theory may be, interest in it should not divert attention from the other aspects of intellectual capital – social and organizational capital – which are concerned with developing and embedding the knowledge possessed by the human capital of an organization. Schuller (2000) contends that:

> The focus on human capital as an individual attribute may lead – arguably has already led – to a very unbalanced emphasis on the acquisition by individuals of skills and competences which ignores the way in which such knowledge is embedded in a complex web of social relationships.

HUMAN CAPITAL MANAGEMENT: PRACTICE AND STRATEGY

Practice

Human capital management is concerned with measurement, reporting measurements and drawing conclusions about the significance of the outcomes of measurement as a guide to future action. This is the process of human capital measurement and reporting that is considered separately in the next two sections of this chapter. But it is not the sole purpose. There is more to HCM than measurement. Human capital management focuses the attention of an organization's leadership team on the strategies it should adopt as outlined below to increase the added value they obtain from people. It identifies those aspects of people management that demonstrably have the greatest bearing on business performance. It clarifies the returns that can be obtained in terms of increased profitability, productivity and overall effectiveness arising from the deployment, development and engagement of the people the organization needs to achieve its goals. HCM points the way to achieving human capital advantage by highlighting where and how investments in people generate the highest returns. It ensures that HRM policies and practices are developed to attain this end. These policies include knowledge management, resourcing, talent management, performance management, learning and development programmes, and reward and recognition processes.

From an organizational perspective, an HCM approach generates the following practical questions:

- What are the key performance drivers that create value?
- What skills have we got?

- What skills do we need now and in the future to meet our strategic aims?
- How are we going to attract, develop and retain these skills?
- How can we develop a culture and environment in which organizational and individual learning takes place that meets both our needs and the needs of our employees?
- How can we provide for both the explicit and tacit knowledge created in our organization to be captured, recorded and used effectively?

Strategy

To provide guidelines for action a human capital strategy can be developed making use of the data provided by human capital measurement and reporting. The Mercer HR consulting organizational performance model (CIPD, 2004a) describes a firm's human capital strategy as consisting of six interconnected factors:

1. *People* – who is in the organization, their skills and competencies on hiring; what skills competences they develop through training and experience; their level of qualification; and the extent to which they apply firm-specific or generalized human capital.
2. *Work processes* – how work gets done; the degree of teamwork and interdependence amongst organizational units; and the role of technology.
3. *Managerial structure* – the degree of employee discretion, management direction and control; spans of control; performance management and work procedures.
4. *Information and knowledge* – how information is shared and interchanged between employees and with suppliers and customers through formal or informal means.
5. *Decision-making* – how important decisions are made and who makes them; the degree of decentralization, participation and timeliness of decisions.
6. *Rewards* – how monetary and non-monetary incentives are used; how much pay is at risk; individual versus group rewards; current versus longer-term 'career rewards'.

The human capital strategy of an organization can be regarded as complementary to its human resource strategy, as discussed in Chapters 7 and 8.

HUMAN CAPITAL MEASUREMENT

As Becker *et al* (2001) emphasize: 'The most potent action HR managers can take to ensure their strategic contribution is to develop a measurement system that convincingly showcases HR's impact on business performance.' They must 'understand how the firm creates value and how to measure the value creation process'. This means getting involved in human capital measurement as defined and described below.

Human capital measurement defined

Human capital measurement has been defined by IDS (2004) as being 'about finding links, correlations and, ideally, causation, between different sets of (HR) data, using statistical techniques'. The CIPD (2004a) emphasizes that it deals with the analysis of 'the actual experience of employees, rather than stated HR programmes and policies'.

The need for human capital measurement

There is an overwhelming case for evolving methods of valuing human capital as an aid to decision-making. This may mean identifying the key people management drivers and modelling the effect of varying them. The issue is to develop a framework within which reliable information can be collected and analysed such as added value per employee, productivity and measures of employee behaviour (attrition and absenteeism rates, the frequency/severity rate of accidents, and cost savings resulting from suggestion schemes).

Becker *et al* (2001) refer to the need to develop a 'high-performance perspective' in which HR and other executives view HR as a system embedded within the larger system of the firm's strategy implementation. They state that: 'The firm manages and measures the relationship between these two systems and firm performance.' A high-performance work system is a crucial part of this approach in that it:

● links the firm's selection and promotion decisions to validated competency models;
● develops strategies that provide timely and effective support for the skills demanded by the firm's strategy implementation;
● enacts compensation and performance management policies that attract, retain and motivate high-performance employees.

Reasons for the interest in measurement

The recognized importance of achieving human capital advantage has led to an interest in the development of methods of measuring the value of that capital for the following reasons:

● Human capital constitutes a key element of the market worth of a company. A research study conducted in 2003 (CFO Research Studies) estimated that the value of human capital represented over 36 per cent of total revenue in a typical organization.

- People in organizations add value and there is a case for assessing this value to provide a basis for HR planning and for monitoring the effectiveness and impact of HR policies and practices.
- The process of identifying measures and collecting and analysing information relating to them will focus the attention of the organization on what needs to be done to find, keep, develop and make the best use of its human capital.
- Measurements can be used to monitor progress in achieving strategic HR goals and generally to evaluate the effectiveness of HR practices.
- You cannot manage unless you measure.

However, three voices have advised caution about measurement. Leadbeater (2000) observed that measuring can 'result in cumbersome inventories which allow managers to manipulate perceptions of intangible values to the detriment of investors. The fact is that too few of these measures are focused on the way companies create value and make money'. The Institute of Employment Studies (Hartley, 2005) emphasized that reporting on human capital is not simply about measurement. Measures on their own such as those resulting from benchmarking are not enough; they must be clearly linked to business performance. And Scarborough and Elias (2002) concluded from their investigations that the specific set of measures or metrics organizations reported were less important than the process of measuring and the uses for the information gathered.

Approaches to measurement

Six of the main approaches to measurement are described below.

The human capital index – Watson Wyatt

On the basis of a survey of companies that have linked together HR management practices and market value, Watson Wyatt (2001) identified four major categories of HR practice that could be linked to a 30 per cent increase in shareholder value creation. These are:

Practice	Impact on market value (per cent)
total rewards and accountability	16.5
collegial, flexible workforce	9.0
recruiting and retention excellence	7.9
communication integrity	7.1

The organizational performance model – Mercer HR Consulting

As described by Nalbantian *et al* (2004) the Organizational Performance Model developed by Mercer HR Consulting is based on the following elements: people, work processes, management structure, information and knowledge, decision-making and rewards, each of which plays out differently within the context of the organization, creating a unique DNA. If these elements have been developed piecemeal, as often happens, the potential for misalignment is strong and it is likely that human capital is not being optimised, creating opportunities for substantial improvement in returns. Identifying these opportunities requires disciplined measurement of the organization's human capital assets and the management practices that affect their performance. The statistical tool, 'Internal Labour Market Analysis' used by Mercer draws on the running record of employee and labour market data to analyse the actual experience of employees rather than stated HR programmes and policies. Thus gaps can be identified between what is required in the workforce to support business goals and what is actually being delivered.

The human capital monitor – Andrew Mayo

Mayo (2001) has developed the 'human capital monitor' to identify the human value of the enterprise or 'human asset worth', which is equal to 'employment cost × individual asset multiplier'. The latter is a weighted average assessment of capability, potential to grow, personal performance (contribution) and alignment to the organization's values set in the context of the workforce environment (ie how leadership, culture, motivation and learning are driving success). The absolute figure is not important. What does matter is that the process of measurement leads you to consider whether human capital is sufficient, increasing, or decreasing, and highlights issues to address. Mayo advises against using too many measures and instead to concentrate on a few organization-wide measures that are critical in creating shareholder value or achieving current and future organizational goals.

A number of other areas for measurement and methods of doing so have been identified by Mayo (1999, 2001). He believes that value added per person is a good measure of the effectiveness of human capital, especially for making inter-firm comparisons. But he considers that the most critical indicator for the value of human capital is the level of expertise possessed by an organization. He suggests that this could be analysed under the headings of identified organizational core competencies. The other criteria he mentions are measures of satisfaction derived from employee opinion surveys and levels of attrition and absenteeism.

The Sears Roebuck model

The Sears Roebuck model (Rucci *et al*, 1998) defines the employee-customer-profit chain. It is sometimes called the 'engagement model'. It explains that if you keep employees satisfied in terms of their attitude to the company and their job you will create a *'compelling place to work'*, which will encourage retention and lead to service helpfulness and merchandize value, which leads to customer satisfaction, retention and recommendations, thus creating *'a compelling place to shop'*. This in turn creates *'a compelling place to invest'*, because of its impact on return on assets, operating margins and revenue growth (Figure 2.1).

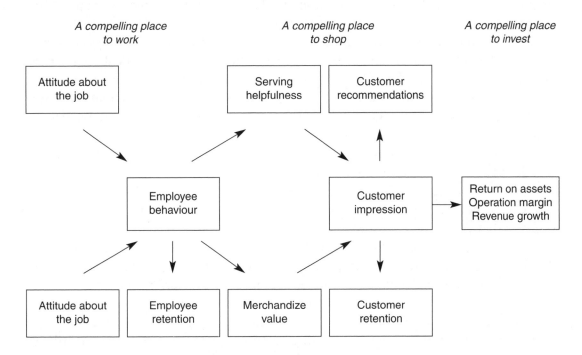

Figure 2.1   The Sears Roebuck Model: Employee-Customer-Profit chain

This model encourages the use of attitude surveys to measure job satisfaction and engagement and has been used in a number of organizations in the UK.

Nationwide has developed its 'Genome' human capital investment model to quantify the impact that employee commitment has on customer satisfaction and business performance. The model uses data from existing sources such as employee opinion surveys, customer satisfaction indices, business performance statistics and employee metrics covering turnover, length of service and absence. Use of the model enabled

Nationwide to prove statistically that the more committed the employee the happier the customer. It is possible to use data modelling to predict the impact that a change in one factor affecting employee commitment would have on customer satisfaction and ultimately on business performance. For example, increasing employee satisfaction with basic pay by 5 per cent would produce an overall rise in customer satisfaction of 0.5 per cent and an increase in personal loan sales of 2.3 per cent.

The balanced scorecard

The balanced scorecard as originally developed by Kaplan and Norton (1992, 1996) is frequently used as the basis for measurement. Their aim was to counter the tendency of companies to concentrate on short-term financial reporting. They take the view that 'what you measure is what you get', and they emphasize that 'no single measure can provide a clear performance target or focus attention on the critical areas of the business. Managers want a balanced presentation of both financial and operational measures'. Their original concept of the scorecard required managers to answer four basic questions, which means looking at the business from four related perspectives, as shown in Figure 2.2.

Some organizations have replaced the innovation and learning perspective with a broader people or human capital element.

Kaplan and Norton emphasize that the balanced scorecard approach 'puts strategy and vision, not control at the centre'. They suggest that while it defines goals, it assumes that people will adopt whatever behaviours and take whatever actions are required to achieve those goals: 'Senior managers may know what the end result should be, but they cannot tell employees exactly how to achieve that result, if only because the conditions in which employees operate are constantly changing.'

They suggest that the balanced scorecard can help to align employees' individual performance with the overall strategy: 'Scorecard users generally engage in three activities: communicating and educating, setting goals, and linking rewards to performance measures'. They comment that:

> Many people think of measurement as a tool to control behaviour and to evaluate past performance. The measures on a Balanced Scorecard, however, should be used as the cornerstone of a management system that communicates strategy, aligns individuals and teams to the strategy, establishes long-term strategic targets, aligns initiatives, allocates long- and short-term resources and, finally, provides feedback and learning about the strategy.

Research by Deloitte & Touche and *Personnel Today* (2002) found that 32 per cent of large UK companies are using the balanced scorecard methodology, although the

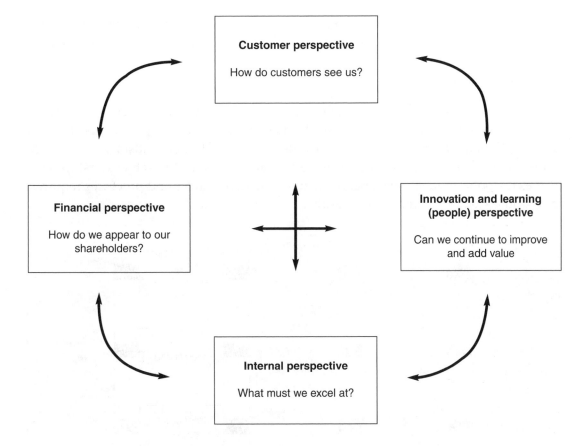

Figure 2.2 The balanced scorecard

methods adopted vary. At Lloyds TSB the balanced scorecard blends a mix of financial metrics and non-financial indicators to provide a single integrated measure of performance that focuses on key indicators, from which a true reflection of organization performance can be accomplished. The scorecard thus enables the organization to focus on a small number of critical measures that create value for the organization.

Norwich Union Insurance describes its balanced scorecard as a 'mechanism for implementing our strategy and measuring performance against our objectives and critical success factors to achieve the strategy'. The scorecard is cascaded throughout the organization to measure the operational activities that are contributing to the overall company strategy. The balanced scorecard changes from year to year. Most recently, it set out to achieve three goals: positive benefit, staff impacts and financial performance – in short, service, morale and profits. Previously, the emphasis was predominantly on profit, in order to deliver the promises made to the City and share-holders, but the company feels that more focus is now needed on service and morale.

The EFQM model of quality

The European Foundation for Quality Management (EFQM) model of quality as shown in Figure 2.3 provides another framework for measuring and reporting on human capital management. It indicates that customer satisfaction, people (employee) satisfaction and impact on society are achieved through leadership. This drives the policy and strategy, people management, resources and processes required to produce excellence in business results.

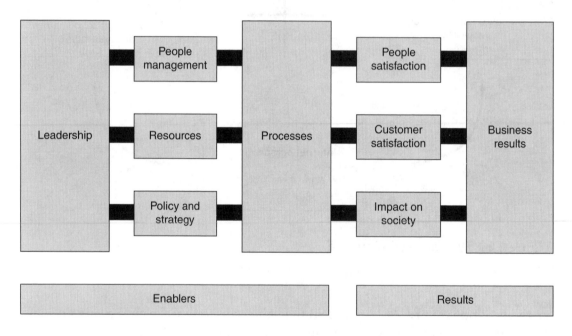

Figure 2.3 The EFQM model

The nine elements in the model are defined as follows:

1. *Leadership* – how the behaviour and actions of the executive team and all other leaders inspire, support and promote a high performance culture.
2. *Policy and strategy* – how the organization formulates, deploys and reviews its policy and strategy and turns them into plans and actions.
3. *People management* – how the organization realizes the full potential of its people.

4. *Resources* – how the organization manages resources effectively and efficiently.
5. *Processes* – how the organization identifies, manages, reviews and improves its processes.
6. *Customer satisfaction* – what the organization is achieving in relation to the satisfaction of its external customers.
7. *People satisfaction* – what the organization is achieving in relation to the satisfaction of its people.
8. *Impact on society* – what the organization is achieving in satisfying the needs and expectations of the local, national and international community at large.
9. *Business results* – what the organization is achieving in relation to its planned business objectives and in satisfying the needs and expectations of everyone with a financial interest or stake in the organization.

Organizations that adopt the EFQM model accept the importance of performance measurement and work all the time to improve the usefulness of their measures, but they also recognize that simply measuring a problem does not improve it. There is a risk that managers will exert their best energies to the analysis, leaving little left for the remedy.

Measurement elements

The main data elements used for measurement are as follows:

- *Basic workforce data* – demographic data (numbers by job category, sex, race, age, disability, working arrangements, absence and sickness, turnover and pay).
- *People development and performance data* – learning and development programmes, performance management/potential assessments, skills and qualifications.
- *Perceptual data* – attitude/opinion surveys, focus groups, exit interviews.
- *Performance data* – financial, operational and customer.
- *Non-financial variables* – the top 10 as listed by Low and Siesfield (1998) are:
  - quality of corporate strategy;
  - execution of corporate strategy;
  - management credibility;
  - innovation;
  - research leadership;
  - ability to attract and retain talented people;
  - market share;
  - management expertise;
  - alignment of compensation with shareholders' interests;
  - quality of major business processes.

In more detail the Council for Excellence in Management and Leadership (2002) report listed the following measures:

A. *Morale*

1. Absenteeism.
2. Accidents.
3. Employee turnover.
4. Director and manager turnover.
5. Employee satisfaction (staff survey measure).
6. Sickness.

B. *Motivation*

1. Appraisal – completion rates.
2. Per cent of employees for whom documented annual appraisal has been agreed.
3. Per cent of jobs for which objectives have been documented.
4. Per cent of jobs for which job descriptions exist.
5. Employee understanding of strategy (staff survey measure).
6. Employee understanding of vision (staff survey measure).
7. Employee retention.
8. Director and manager retention.
9. Working hours.

C. *Investment*

1. Benchmarked remuneration levels.
2. Directors and managers' salaries as a percentage of total salaries.
3. Human resource spend per employee.
4. Training investment.

D. *Long-term development*

1. Current management and leadership capability.
2. Potential management and leadership capability.
3. Management and leadership skill gaps.
4. Per cent of job holders for whom a development plan has been agreed.
5. Per cent of jobs for which competencies have been audited.
6. Training days.

E. *External perception*

1. Job applications: vacancies.
2. Job offers: job acceptances.

Measuring human capital

The points that should be borne in mind when measuring human capital are:

- Identify sources of value including the competencies and abilities that drive business performance.
- Analyse the relationships between people management practices and outcomes and organizational effectiveness.
- Remember that human capital measurement is concerned with the impact of people management practices on performance so that steps can be taken to do better. It is not just about measuring the efficiency of the HR department in terms of activity levels. It needs to be value-focused rather than activity-based. For example, it is not enough just to record the number of training days or the expenditure on training; it is necessary to assess the return on investment generated by that training.
- Keep measurements simple – concentrate on key areas of outcomes and behaviour.
- Only measure activities if it is clear that such measurements will inform decision-making.
- Analyse and evaluate trends rather than simply record actuals – compare the present position with baseline data.
- Focus on readily available and reliable quantified information; however, although quantification is desirable it should not be based on huge, loose assumptions.
- Remember that measurement is a means to an end, not an end in itself. Do not get so mesmerized by the process of collecting data as to forget that the data is there to be used to support decision-making and generate action.

HUMAN CAPITAL REPORTING

Human capital reporting is concerned with providing information on how well the human capital of an organization is managed. There are two aspects: first, external reporting to stakeholders through, in the UK, the compulsory Operating and Financial Review (OFR). The second aspect is internal reporting, which also informs the leadership team and stakeholders generally about how human capital is being managed, but extends this with statements of how the information will be used to guide future action. The purpose is to inform decision-making about human capital management, not just to record the figures.

External reporting

The Accounting for People Task Force Report (2003) recommended that operating and financial review reports (OFRs) should be made by companies which have a strategic focus, are balanced and objective and based on sound data'. The Task Force specified that:

> The report should clearly represent the Board's understanding of the links between HCM policies and practices and its business strategy and performance. This means that it should normally include details on the size and composition of the workforce, employee retention and motivation, skills, competencies and training, remuneration and fair employment practice, and leadership and succession planning. The report should follow a process that is susceptible to review by auditors, provide information in a form that enables comparison over time, and use commonly accepted terms and definitions.

The CIPD (2003b) has recommended that the OFR should provide information on:

- the profile of the workforce and its diversity;
- senior executive remuneration;
- the quality of leadership and management strength;
- how well labour costs have been managed over time;
- evidence of a coherent, robust people strategy that is mapped to the stated business strategy for the next three years;
- evidence that current people management practice (especially regarding acquisition, motivation and retention) are affecting organizational and business performance;
- current and forecasted returns on people investment in the next three to five years;
- the value of human capital assets and future investments, especially in major corporate decisions such as mergers and acquisitions;
- comparator listings in financial league tables – such as industry FTSE or analyst ratings.

The CIPD (2003b) also proposed the external reporting framework illustrated in Figure 2.4.

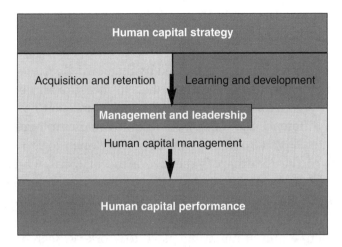

Figure 2.4   Human capital external reporting framework (CIPD, 2003b)

Internal reporting

Internal reporting should be linked to the external reporting framework but will focus more on the practical implications of the data that has been assembled and analysed. The information and the headings of the internal report have to be tailored to the context and needs of the organization, but it could:

- set out the quantitative and qualitative information – this could include data on the size and composition of the workforce, attraction and retention, absence, motivation, skills and competencies, learning and development activities, remuneration and fair employment practices, leadership and succession planning, and the outcomes of opinion or job satisfaction surveys;
- analyse measures of employee satisfaction and engagement, compare them with data on business performance and demonstrate the links between them;
- analyse the outcomes of external benchmarking;
- identify the key performance drivers in the organization and indicate how human capital management is contributing to adding value in each of these areas;
- review the extent to which people management strategy, policies and practices are contributing to the achievement of business goals;

- set out the returns on investments in people management and development projects and evaluate the effectiveness of the investments;
- draw conclusions on the implications of the data for future people management strategy, policy and practice.

An example of internal reporting is provided by Standard Chartered Bank. A range of processes and benchmarks has been established to measure and enhance the contribution of its employees. Work on human capital measurement has enabled the bank to understand the difference that talented and motivated employees can make to the business. A 'Human Capital Roadmap' has been developed to provide a clear people agenda. The core of the roadmap is the five areas of focus which drive business performance that are supported by key people processes and interventions. The latter form the framework for metrics and evaluations. These include an engagement survey (G12) developed by the Gallop Organization covering 12 factors that underpin a productive and stimulating place to work. Research has established a powerful link between engagement scores and business performance.

At Nationwide regular reports are made to area managers on key drivers. These are presented graphically on dashboards, as illustrated in Figure 2.5, enabling the manager to identify problem areas, investigate the circumstances and initiate action.

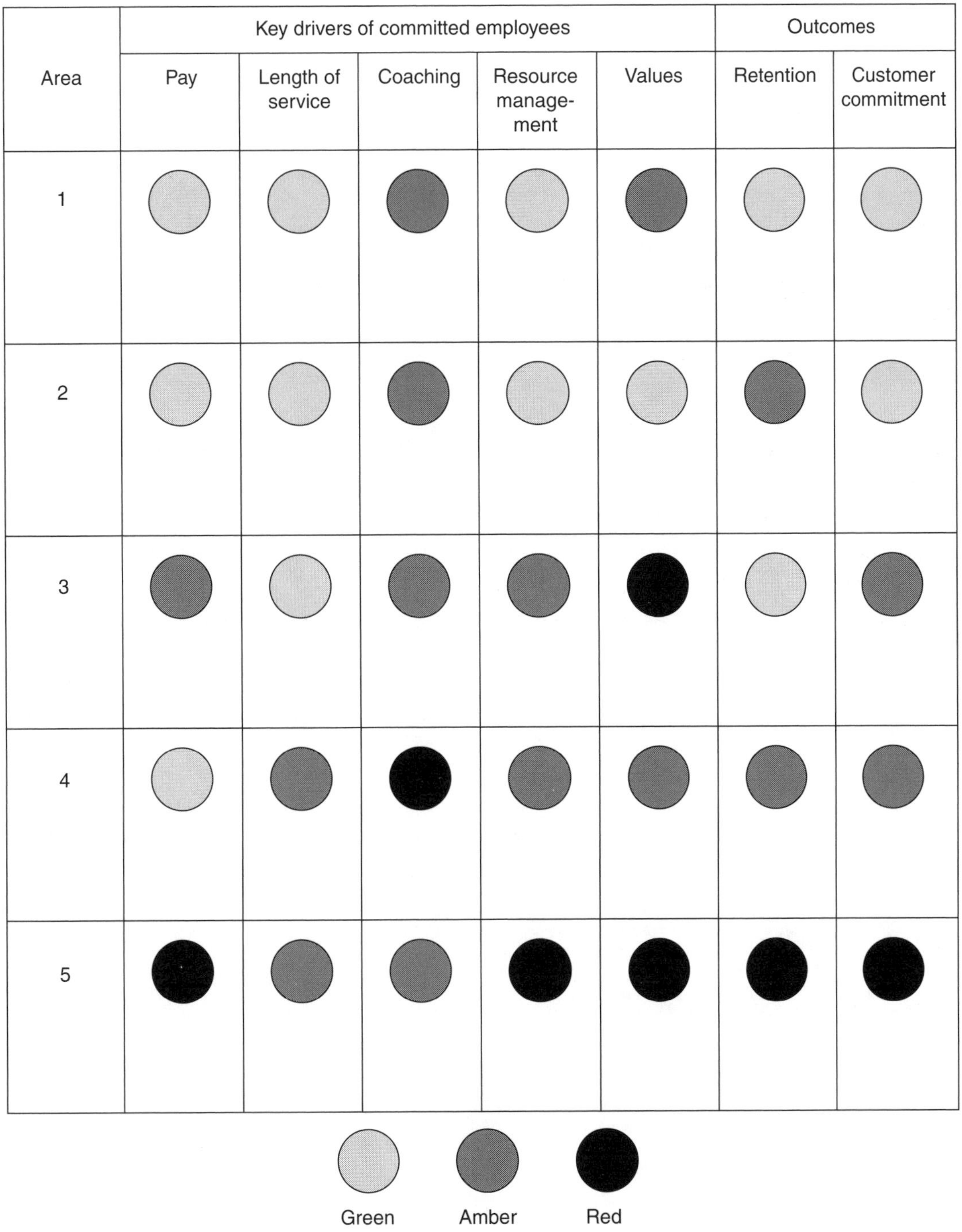

Area	Key drivers of committed employees					Outcomes	
	Pay	Length of service	Coaching	Resource manage-ment	Values	Retention	Customer commitment
1	🟢	🟢	🟡	🟢	🟡	🟢	🟢
2	🟢	🟢	🟡	🟢	🟢	🟡	🟢
3	🟡	🟢	🟡	🟡	🔴	🟢	🟡
4	🟢	🟡	🔴	🟡	🟡	🟡	🟡
5	🔴	🟡	🟡	🔴	🔴	🔴	🔴

🟢 Green 🟡 Amber 🔴 Red

Figure 2.5 Human capital reporting dashboard for area managers: Nationwide

3

Role of the HR function

HR functions are concerned with the management and development of people in organizations. They are involved in the development and implementation of HR strategies and policies and some or all of the following people management activities: organization development, human resource planning, talent management, knowledge management, recruitment and selection, learning and development, reward management, employee relations, health and safety, welfare, HR administration, fulfilment of statutory requirements, equal opportunity and diversity issues, and any other matters related to the employment relationship.

The IRS survey of HR roles and responsibilities (IRS, 2004b) found that HR functions were spending 20 per cent of their time on strategic activities, 40 per cent on administration, 30 per cent on providing a consultancy service, and 10 per cent on other activities.

The 'clients' or 'customers' of the HR function are not just management. They also comprise the front-line managers who actually implement HR policies and on whom the function relies to get things done, employees, and potential recruits.

This chapter deals with:

- the overall role of the function;
- the role of HR in facilitating and managing change;
- variations in practice;
- organization of the function;

- marketing the function;
- preparing, justifying and protecting the HR budget;
- outsourcing;
- the provision of shared services;
- the use of external consultants;
- evaluating the HR function.

THE OVERALL ROLE OF THE HR FUNCTION

The role of the HR function is to enable the organization to achieve its objectives by taking initiatives and providing guidance and support on all matters relating to its employees. The basic aim is to ensure that the organization develops HR strategies, policies and practices that cater effectively for everything concerning the employment and development of people and the relationships that exist between management and the workforce. The HR function can play a major part in the creation of an environment that enables people to make the best use of their capacities and to realize their potential to the benefit of both the organization and themselves.

Essentially, the HR function provides the advice and services that enable organizations to get things done through people. It is in the delivery business. Ulrich (1998) points out that: 'The activities of HR appear to be and often are disconnected from the real work of the organization.' He believes that HR 'should not be defined by what it does but by what it delivers'.

The more sophisticated HR functions aim to achieve strategic integration and coherence in the development and operation of HRM policies and employment practices. Strategic integration could be described as vertical integration – the process of ensuring that HR strategies are integrated with or 'fit' business strategies. The concept of coherence could be defined as horizontal integration – the development of a mutually reinforcing and interrelated set of HR employment and development policies and practices. These strategic aspects of the work of the function are dealt with in Chapters 7, 8 and 9 of this book.

THE ROLE OF HR IN FACILITATING AND MANAGING CHANGE

If HR is concerned – as it should be – with playing a major role in the achievement of continuous improvement in organizational and individual performance and in the HR processes that support that improvement, then it will be concerned with facilitating change. Ulrich (1997a) believes that one of the key roles of HR professionals is to act as change agents, delivering organizational transformation and culture change.

Strategic HRM is as much if not more about managing change during the process of implementation as it is about producing long-term plans; a point emphasized by Purcell (1999) who believes that: 'We should be much more sensitive to processes of organizational change and avoid being trapped in the logic of rational choice.' In 2001 Purcell suggested that change is specially important in HRM strategies, 'since their concern is with the future, the unknown, thinking of and learning how to do things differently, undoing the ways things have been done in the past, and managing its implementation'. He believes that the focus of strategy is on implementation, where HR can play a major part.

The importance of the human resource element in achieving change has been emphasized by Johnson and Scholes (1997):

> Organizations which successfully manage change are those which have integrated their human resource management policies with their strategies and the strategic change process... training, employee relations, compensation packages and so on are not merely operational issues for the personnel department; they are crucially concerned with the way in which employees relate to the nature and direction of the firm and as such they can both block strategic change and be significant facilitators of strategic change.

The contribution of HR to change management

The HR function may be involved in initiating change but it can also act as a stabilizing force in situations where change would be damaging. Mohrman and Lawler (1998) believe that:

> The human resources function can help the organization develop the capability to weather the changes that will continue to be part of the organizational landscape. It can help with the ongoing learning processes required to assess the impact of change and enable the organization to make corrections and enhancements to the changes. It can help the organization develop a new psychological contract and ways to give employees a stake in the changes that are occurring and in the performance of the organization.

How HR can facilitate change

Ulrich (1998) argues that HR professionals are 'not fully comfortable or compatible in the role of change agent', and that their task is therefore not to carry out change but to get change done. But HR practitioners are in a good position to understand possible points of resistance to change and they can help to facilitate the information flow and understanding that will help to overcome that resistance.

Change guidelines for HR

To facilitate change, HR has to be fully aware of the reasons why people resist change and the approaches that can be adopted to overcome that resistance, indeed to gain agreement that change is desirable. These approaches are described in Chapter 24.

Useful guidelines (quoted by Ulrich, 1998) on how HR can facilitate change have been produced by the HR department in General Electric. These are to ensure that:

- employees see the reason for change;
- employees understand why change is important and see how it will help them and the business in the long and short term;
- the people who need to be committed to the change to make it happen are recognized;
- a coalition of support is built for the change;
- the support of key individuals in the organization is enlisted;
- the link between the change and other HR systems such as staffing, training, appraisal, rewards, structure and communication is understood;
- the systems implications of the change are recognized;
- a means of measuring the success of the change is identified;
- plans are made to monitor progress in the implementation of change;
- the first steps in getting change started are recognized;
- plans are made to keep attention focused on the change;
- the likely need to adapt the change over time is recognized and plans can readily be made and implemented for such adaptations.

VARIATIONS IN THE PRACTICE OF HR

The role of the HR function and the practice of human resource management vary immensely in different organizations. As Sisson (1995) has commented, HR management is not a single homogeneous occupation – it involves a variety of roles and activities that differ from one organization to another and from one level to another in the same organization. Tyson (1987) has claimed that the HR function is often 'balkanized' – not only is there a variety of roles and activities but these tend to be relatively self-centred, with little passage between them. Hope-Hailey *et al* (1998) believe that HR could be regarded as a 'chameleon function' in the sense that the diversity of practice established by their research suggests that 'contextual variables dictate different roles for the function and different practices of people management'.

Adams (1991) has identified four approaches to the role of the function, each of which can be seen as representing a 'kind of scale of increasing degrees of external-ization, understood as the application of market forces to the delivery of HR activi-ties':

1. The *in-house agency*, in which the HR department is seen as a cost centre and the activities are cross-charged to other departments or divisions.
2. The *internal consultancy*, in which the HR department sells its services to internal customers (line managers), the implication being that managers have some freedom to go elsewhere if they are not happy with the service that is being provided.
3. The *business within a business*, in which some of the activities of the function are formed into a quasi-independent organization that may trade not only with orga-nizational units but also externally.
4. *External consultancy*, in which the organizational units go outside to completely independent businesses for help and advice.

The common feature of all these approaches is that the services delivered are charged for in some form of contract, which may incorporate a service level agreement.

The approach to the provision of services and their externalization will vary between different organizations because of contextual factors such as the way in which the business is organized and the type of people employed, the values and beliefs of top management about the need for HR and the extent to which it will make a contribution to the 'bottom line', and the reputation and credibility of the HR func-tion.

Another area for variation is the extent to which the traditional methods of managing HR functions have changed in the direction of setting up shared services and outsourcing, as described later in this chapter.

ORGANIZING THE HR FUNCTION

The organization and staffing of the HR function clearly depends on the size of the business, the extent to which operations are decentralized, the type of work carried out, the kind of people employed and the role assigned to the HR function.

There is no standard ratio for the number of HR specialists to the number of employees. It can vary from 1 to 80, to 1 to 1,000 or more. In the 128 organizations covered by the IRS 2004b survey, there was on average one HR practitioner for every 109 employees.

The ratio is affected by all the factors mentioned above and can only be decided empirically by analysing what HR services are required and then deciding on the extent to which they are provided by full-time professional staff or can be purchased from external agencies or consultants. The degree to which the organization believes that the management of human resources is the prime responsibility of line managers and team leaders affects not only the numbers of HR staff but also the nature of the guidance and support services they provide.

There are, therefore, no absolute rules for organizing the HR function, but current practice suggests that the following guidelines should be taken into account:

- The head of the function should report directly to the chief executive and should be on the board, or at least be a member of the senior management or leadership team, in order to contribute to the formulation of corporate strategies and play a full part in the formulation and integration of HR strategies and policies. In practice, however, this does not happen as frequently as one would wish. Only four out of 10 of the organizations surveyed by IRS in 2004 had a director with sole responsibility for HR.

- In a decentralized organization, subsidiary companies, divisions, or operational units should be responsible for their own HR management affairs within the framework of broad strategic and policy guidelines from the centre.

- The central HR function in a decentralized organization should be slimmed down to the minimum required to develop group human resource strategies and policies. It will probably be concerned with resourcing throughout the group at senior management level and advising on both recruitment and career development. It may also control remuneration and benefits policies for senior management. The centre may co-ordinate industrial-relations negotiating if bargaining has been decentralized, especially where bargaining is related to terms and conditions such as hours of work, holidays and employee benefits. Although rates of pay may vary among subsidiaries, it is generally desirable to develop a consistent approach to benefit provision. A recent development is to operate as a 'service centre', providing shared HR services to other parts of the organization, as described later in this chapter.

- The HR function has to be capable of delivering the level of advice and services required by the organization. Delivery may be achieved by the direct provision of services but may be outsourced.

- The function will be organized in accordance with the level of support and services it is required to give and the range of activities that need to be catered for, which could include resourcing, management development, training, reward management, employee relations, knowledge management and HR services in such areas as health and safety, welfare, HR information systems and employment matters generally. In a large department, each of these areas may be provided for separately, but they can be combined in various ways.

The organization and staffing of the HR function needs to take account of its role in formulating HR strategies and policies and intervening and innovating as required. But the function also has to provide efficient and cost-effective services. These cannot be neglected; the credibility and reputation of the function so far as line managers are concerned will be largely a function of the quality of those services to the HR department's internal customers. It is, in fact, important for members of the function to remember that line managers are their customers and deserve high levels of personal service that meet their needs.

The most important principle to bear in mind about the organization of the HR function is that it should fit the needs of the business. Against that background, there will always be choice about the best structure to adopt, but this choice should be made on the basis of an analysis of what the organization wants in the way of HR management guidance and services. This is why there are considerable variations in HR practice.

MARKETING THE HR FUNCTION

Top management and line managers are the internal customers whose wants and needs the HR function must identify and meet. How can this be done?

First, it is necessary to understand the needs of the business and its critical success factors – where the business is going, how it intends to get there and what are the things that are going to make the difference between success and failure.

Market research data needs to be converted into marketing plans for the development of products and services to meet ascertained needs – of the business and its managers and employees. The marketing plan should establish the costs of introducing and maintaining these initiatives and the benefits that will be obtained from them. Every effort must be made to quantify these benefits in financial terms.

The next step in the marketing process is to persuade management that this is a product or service the business needs. This means spelling out its costs and benefits, covering the financial and human resources required to develop, introduce and maintain it, and the impact it will make on the performance of the business. Identifying the business need and convincing management that a product or service is worthwhile will be easier if the initial customer research and product development activities have been carried out thoroughly. Credibility is vital. This will be achieved if the proposal for expenditure is credible in itself, but the track record of the HR function in delivering its promises is equally important.

This approach is akin to 'branding' in product planning. This identifies the product or service, spells out the benefits it provides and differentiates it from other services, thus bringing it to the attention of customers. Presentation is important through logos and distinctive brochures. Some HR departments brand products with an immediately identifiable name such as 'Genome' or 'Gemini'.

PREPARING, JUSTIFYING AND PROTECTING THE HR BUDGET

Preparation

HR budgets are prepared like any other functional department budget in the following stages:

1. Define functional objectives and plans.
2. Forecast the activity levels required to achieve objectives and plans in the light of company budget guidelines and assumptions on future business activity levels and any targets for reducing overheads or for maintaining them at the same level.
3. Assess the resources (people and finance) required to enable the activity levels to be achieved.
4. Cost each activity area – the sum of these costs will be the total budget.

Justification

Justifying budgets means ensuring in advance that objectives and plans are generally agreed – there should be no surprises in a budget submitted to top management. A cast-iron case should then be prepared to support the forecast levels of activity in each area and, on a cost/benefit basis, to justify any special expenditure. Ideally, the benefit should be defined as a return on investment expressed in financial terms.

Protection

The best way to protect a budget is to provide in advance a rationale for each area of expenditure that proves that it is necessary and will justify the costs involved. The worst thing that can happen is to be forced on to the defensive. If service delivery standards (service level agreements) are agreed and achieved these will provide a further basis for protecting the budget.

OUTSOURCING HR WORK

Increasingly, HR services, which would previously have been regarded as a business's own responsibility to manage, are now routinely being purchased from external suppliers. Managements are facing Tom Peters' (1988) challenge: 'Prove it can't be subcontracted.' The formal policy of a major global corporation reads: 'Manufacture only those items – and internally source only those support services – that directly contribute to, or help to maintain, our competitive advantage.' The IPD (1998a) states that 'the biggest single cause in the increase of outsourcing has been the concept of the core organization which focuses its in-house expertise on its primary function and purchases any necessary support from a range of sources in its periphery'.

The HR function is well positioned to outsource some of its activities to management consultancies and other agencies or firms that act as service providers in such fields as training, recruitment, executive search, occupational health and safety services, employee welfare and counselling activities, childcare, payroll administration and legal advisory services. HR functions, which have been given responsibility for other miscellaneous activities such as catering, car, fleet management, facilities management and security (because there is nowhere else to put them), may gladly outsource them to specialist firms.

The case for outsourcing

There are three reasons for outsourcing:

1. *Cost saving* – HR costs are reduced because the services are cheaper and the size of the function can be cut back.
2. *Concentration of HR effort* – members of the function are not diverted from the key tasks that add value.
3. *Obtaining expertise* – know-how and experience that are unavailable in the organization can be purchased.

Problems with outsourcing

The advantages of outsourcing seem to be high, but there are problems. Some firms have unthinkingly outsourced core activities on an *ad hoc* basis to gain short-term advantage, while others found that they were being leveraged by their suppliers to pay higher rates. Firms may focus on a definition of the core activities and those that can be outsourced that may be justified at the time but do not take account of the future. Additionally, a seemingly random policy of outsourcing can lead to lower employee morale and to a 'who next' atmosphere.

Deciding to outsource

The decision to outsource should be based on rigorous analysis and benchmarking to establish how other organizations manage their HR activities. This will define the level of service required. The cost of providing the existing service internally should also be measured. This will be easier if an activity-based costing system is used in the organization.

To minimize problems, careful consideration should be given to the case for out-sourcing. It is necessary to assess each potential area with great care in order to determine whether it can and should be outsourced and exactly what such outsourcing is intended to achieve. The questions to be answered include: Is the activity a core one or peripheral? How efficiently is it run at present? What contribution does it make to the qualitative and financial well-being of the organization? This is an opportunity to re-engineer the HR function, subjecting each activity to critical examination to establish whether the services can be provided from within or outside the organization, if at all. Outsourcing may well be worthwhile if it is certain that it can deliver a better service at a lower cost.

Selecting service providers

Potential service providers should be required to present tenders in response to a brief. Three or four providers should be approached so that a choice can be made. The tender should set out how the brief will be met and how much it will cost. Selection should take into account the degree to which the tender meets the specification, the quality and reputation of the firm and the cost (this is an important consideration but not the only one – the level of service that will be provided is critical). References should be obtained before a contract is drawn up and agreed. The contract should be very clear about services, costs and the basis upon which it can be terminated.

Managerial and legal implications of outsourcing

Service providers need to be managed just as carefully – if not more so – than internal services. Service standards and budgets should be reviewed and agreed regularly and management information systems should be set up so that performance can be monitored. Swift corrective action should be taken if things go wrong, and the contract terminated if there is a serious shortcoming.

The legal implications of outsourcing are that it will be based on a service contract and the purchaser of the services has the right to insist that the terms of the contract are fulfilled. Purchasers also have a duty to fulfil their side of the contract, for example, providing agreed facilities, meeting the leasing terms set out in a car fleet management contract, and paying for the services as required by the contract.

SHARED HR SERVICES

The term 'shared services' refers to the central provision of HR services that are available to a number of parties and are therefore the same for all those who take them up. The nature of the services is determined by both the provider and the user. The customer or user defines the level of the service and decides which services to take up. Thus, 'the user is the chooser' (Ulrich, 1995). As described by Reilly (2000), administrative tasks tend to be those most commonly covered by shared services, for example:

- payroll changes;
- relocation services;
- recruitment administration;
- benefits administration (including flexible benefits and share schemes);
- company car provision;
- pensions administration;
- employee welfare support;
- training support;
- absence monitoring;
- management information.

Services can be provided through the internet, a telephone customer help line, a consultancy pool of advisers, or 'centres of excellence' with expertise in such areas as resourcing, employee relations, reward or training. The increasing interest in shared services has been prompted by the more extensive and strategic use of HR information systems.

The organizations covered by the research conducted by Reilly (2000) on behalf of the Institute of Employment Studies identified one or more of the following reasons for providing shared services:

- HR will be consumer-driven, more accessible, and more professional;
- the quality of HR services will be improved in terms of using better processes, delivery to specification, time and budget, incorporation of good practice, the achievement of greater consistency and accuracy;
- the process can help to achieve organizational flexibility – a common service will support customers during business change;
- it can support the repositioning of HR, moving it from a purely operational to a more strategic role so that HR is carrying out the role of 'acting as a catalyst for change… anticipating problems and making things happen' (Hutchinson and Wood, 1995).

The advantages of providing shared services include lower costs, better quality, more efficient resourcing and better customer service. But there are disadvantages, which include loss of face-to-face contact, de-skilling administrative jobs and, potentially, remoteness from the users.

The steps required to introduce shared services in what is often described as an 'HR service centre' are as follows (all should involve users as well as providers):

1. Identify present arrangements.
2. Obtain views from customers on the quality of existing services and what could be done to improve them (including the scope for sharing services).
3. Define the areas for shared services.
4. Define how shared services would be supplied, including who provides the service, where it is provided, how it is provided (this will include consideration of outsourcing as discussed later in this chapter).
5. Decide on priorities.
6. Plan programme (this could be phased and might involve pilot testing).

USING MANAGEMENT CONSULTANTS

Management consultants act as service providers in such fields as recruitment, executive search and training. They also provide outside help and guidance to their clients by advising on the introduction of new systems or procedures or by going through processes of analysis and diagnosis in order to produce recommendations or to assist generally in the improvement of organizational performance. Their role is to provide expertise and resources to assist in development and change.

The steps required to select and use consultants effectively are:

1. Define the business need – what added value consultants will provide.
2. Justify their use in terms of their expertise, objectivity and ability to bring resources to bear that might otherwise be unavailable. If the need has been established in cost/benefit terms, the use of external consultants rather than internal resources has to be justified.
3. Define clearly the objectives of the exercise in terms of the end-results and deliverables.
4. Invite three or four firms or independent consultants to submit proposals.
5. Select the preferred consultants on the basis of their proposal and an interview (a 'beauty contest') – the criteria should be the degree to which the consultants understand the need, the relevance and acceptability of their proposed deliverables and programme of work, the capacity of the firm and the particular consultants to deliver, whether the consultants will be able to adopt to the culture and management style of the organization, the extent to which they are likely to be acceptable to the people with whom they will work, and the cost (a consideration but, as for service providers, not the ultimate consideration).
6. Take up references before confirming the appointment.
7. Agree and sign a contract – this should always be in writing and should set out deliverables, timing and costs, methods of payment and arrangements for termination.
8. Agree detailed project programme.
9. Monitor the progress of the assignment carefully without unduly interfering in the day-to-day work of the consultants, and evaluate the outcomes.

Legal implications

If there is a serious problem, a consultancy assignment can be cancelled if either party has clearly failed to meet the terms of the contract (whether this is a formal contract or simply an exchange of letters). Clients can also sue consultants for professional negligence if they believe that their advice or actions have caused financial or some other form of measurable loss. Professional negligence is, however, not always easy to prove, especially in HR assignments. Consultants can always claim that their advice was perfectly good but that it has been used incorrectly by the client (this may also be difficult to prove). Suing consultants can be a messy business and should only be undertaken when it is felt that they (or their insurers) should pay for their mistakes and thus help to recoup the client's losses. It should also be remembered that independent consultants and even some small firms might not have taken out professional liability insurance. If that is the case, all the aggrieved client who sues would do is to bankrupt them, which may give the client some satisfaction but could be a somewhat pointless exercise. The latter problem can be overcome if the client selects only consultants who are insured.

EVALUATING THE HR FUNCTION

It is necessary to evaluate the contribution of the HR function to ensure that it is effective at both the strategic level and in terms of service delivery and support. In evaluation it is useful to remember the distinction made by Tsui and Gomez-Mejia (1988) between *process criteria* – how well things are done, and *output criteria* – the effectiveness of the end-result. A 'utility analysis' approach as described by Boudreau (1988) can be used. This focuses on the impact of HR activities measured wherever possible in financial terms (*quantity*), improvements in the *quality* of those activities, and *cost/benefit* (the minimization of the cost of the activities in relation to the benefits they provide).

Huselid *et al* (1997) believe that HR effectiveness has two dimensions: 1) *strategic HRM* – the delivery of services in a way that supports the implementation of the firm's strategy; and 2) *technical HRM* – the delivery of HR basics such as recruitment, compensation and benefits. The methods that can be used to evaluate these dimensions are described below.

Quantitative criteria

- *Organizational:* added value per employee, profit per employee, sales value per employee, costs per employee and added value per £ of employment costs.
- *Employee behaviour:* retention and turnover rates, absenteeism, sickness, accident rates, grievances, disputes, references to employment tribunals, successful suggestion scheme outcomes.
- *HR service levels and outcomes:* time to fill vacancies, time to respond to applicants, ratio of acceptances to offers made, cost of replies to advertisements, training days per employee, time to respond to and settle grievances, measurable improvements in organizational performance as a result of HR practices, ratio of HR costs to total costs, ratio of HR staff to employees, the achievement of specified goals.

User reactions

The internal customers of HR (the users of HR services) can provide important feedback on HR effectiveness. Users can be asked formally to assess the extent to which the members of the HR function demonstrate that they:

- understand the business strategy;
- anticipate business needs and produce realistic proposals on how HR can help to meet them;
- are capable of meeting performance standards and deadlines for the delivery of HR initiatives and projects;
- provide relevant, clear, convincing and practical advice;
- provide efficient and effective services with regard to response and delivery times and quality;
- generally demonstrate their understanding and expertise.

Service level agreements

A service level agreement (SLA) is an agreement between the provider of a service and the customers who use the service on the level of service that should be provided. It sets out the nature of the service provided, the volume and quality to be achieved by the service, and the response times the provider must attain after receiving requests for help. The headings of the agreement can be drawn from the list of HR service level areas set out above. The agreement provides the basis for monitoring and evaluating the level of service.

Employee satisfaction measures

The degree to which employees are satisfied with HR policies and practices can be measured by attitude surveys. These can obtain opinions on such matters as their work, their pay, how they are treated, their views about the company and their managers, how well they are kept informed, the opportunities for learning and career development, and their working environment and facilities.

Benchmarking

In addition to internal data it is desirable to benchmark HR services. This means comparing what the HR function is doing with what is happening in similar organizations. This may involve making direct comparisons using quantified performance data or exchanging information on 'good practice' that can be used to indicate where changes are required to existing HR practices or to provide guidance on HR innovations. Organizations such as Saratoga provide benchmarking data under standardized and therefore comparable headings for their clients.

Measuring performance

The following key points about measuring HR performance have been made by Likierrnan (2005):

- agree objectives against budget assumptions: this will ensure HR's role reflects changes in strategy implementation;
- use more sophisticated measures – get underneath the data and look not only at the figures but also at the reasons behind them;
- use comparisons imaginatively, including internal and external benchmarking;
- improve feedback through face-to-face discussion rather than relying on questionnaires;
- be realistic about what performance measures can deliver – many measurement problems can be mitigated, not solved.

The HR scorecard

The HR scorecard developed by Beatty *et al* (2003) follows the same principle as the balanced scorecard described in Chapter 2, ie it emphasizes the need for a balanced presentation and analysis of data. The four headings of the HR scorecard are:

1. *HR competencies* – administrative expertise, employee advocacy, strategy execution and change agency.
2. *HR practices* – communication, work design, selection, development, measurement and rewards.
3. *HR systems* – alignment, integration and differentiation.
4. *HR deliverables* – workforce mindset, technical knowledge, and workforce behaviour.

These are all influenced by the factors that determine the strategic success of the organization, ie operational excellence, product leadership and customer intimacy.

Preferred approach to evaluation

There is much to be said for the systematic HR scorecard approach, although every organization would have to develop its own headings as a basis for evaluation. There are plenty of typical measures but no standard set exists. Perhaps, as Guest and Peccei (1994) suggest:

The most sensible and important indicator of HRM effectiveness will be the judgements of key stakeholders... The political, stakeholder, perspective on organizations acknowledges that it is the interpretation placed on effectiveness in organizations and the attributions of credit and blame that are derived from them that matter most in judging effectiveness. In other words, at the end of the day, it is always the qualitative interpretation by those in positions of power that matters most.

However, they recognized 'the desirability of also developing clearly specified goals and quantitative indicators, together with financial criteria'.

4

The role of the HR practitioner

This chapter is concerned with what HR professionals do and how they do it, bearing in mind the comment of Boxall and Purcell (2003) that 'HRM does not belong to HR specialists'. HRM belongs to line managers and the people they manage – the stakeholders in people management.

This chapter starts with an analysis of the basic roles and activities of HR professionals and of the various models of these roles. A number of issues that affect the role of HR people are then explored; these comprise gaining support and commitment, role ambiguity, role conflict, ethics, and professionalism. The chapter concludes with a discussion of the competencies required by HR practitioners.

THE BASIC ROLES

The roles of HR practitioners vary widely according to the extent to which they are generalist (eg, HR director or HR manager), or specialist (eg, head of learning and development, head of talent management, or head of reward), the level at which they work (strategic, executive or administrative) the needs of the organization, the context within which they work and their own capabilities.

The role can be proactive, reactive or a mixture of both. At a strategic level, HR people take on a proactive role. Research conducted by Hoque and Moon (2001) established that: 'The growing number of specialists using the HR title are well qualified, are more likely to be involved in strategic decision-making processes and are most likely to be found in workplaces within which sophisticated methods and techniques have been adopted.' As such, they act as business partners, develop integrated HR strategies, intervene, innovate, operate as internal consultants and volunteer guidance on matters concerning upholding core values, ethical principles and the achievement of consistency. They focus on business issues and working with line managers to deliver performance targets.

In some situations they play a mainly reactive role. They spend much of their time doing what they are told or asked to do. They provide the administrative systems required by management. This is what Storey (1992a) refers to as the non-interventionary role, in which HR people merely provide a service to meet the demands of management and front-line managers. The various roles are described in more detail below.

Service provision

The basic role of HR specialists is that of providing services to internal customers. These include management, line managers, team leaders and employees. The services may be general, covering all aspects of HRM: human resource planning, recruitment and selection, employee development, employee reward, employee relations, health and safety management and welfare. Alternatively, services may only be provided in one or two of these areas by specialists. The focus may be on the requirements of management (eg, resourcing), or it may extend to all employees (eg, health and safety).

The aims are to provide effective services that meet the needs of the business, its management and its employees and to administer them efficiently.

Guidance and advice

To varying degrees, HR practitioners provide guidance and advice to management. At the highest level, this will include recommendations on HR strategies that have been developed by processes of analysis and diagnosis to address strategic issues arising from business needs and human, organizational or environmental factors. They will also provide advice on issues concerning culture change and approaches to the improvement of process capability – the ability of the organization to get things done through people.

Guidance will be given to managers to ensure that consistent decisions are made on such matters as performance ratings, pay increases and disciplinary actions. At all levels, guidance may be provided on HR policies and procedures and the implications of employment legislation. In the latter area, HR practitioners are concerned with compliance – ensuring that legal requirements are met.

The business partner role

HR practitioners as business partners share responsibility with their line management colleagues for the success of the enterprise and get involved with them in running the business. They must have the capacity to identify business opportunities, to see the broad picture and to understand how their HR role can help to achieve the company's business objectives.

As defined by Tyson (1985), HR professionals integrate their activities closely with management and ensure that they serve a long-term strategic purpose. This is one of the key roles assigned to HR by Ulrich (1998), who stated that HR should become a partner with senior and line managers in strategy execution and that 'HR executives should impel and guide serious discussion of how the company should be organized to carry out its strategy'. He suggested that HR should join forces with operating managers in systematically assessing the importance of any new initiatives they propose by asking: 'Which ones are really aligned with strategy implementation? Which ones should receive immediate attention and which can wait? Which ones, in short, are truly linked to business results?' But there is a danger of over-emphasizing the glamorous albeit necessary role of business or strategic partner at the expense of the service delivery aspect of the HR specialist's role. As an HR specialist commented to Caldwell (2004): 'My credibility depends on running an extremely efficient and cost-effective administrative machine… If I don't get that right, and consistently, then you can forget about any big ideas.' Another person interviewed during Caldwell's research referred to personnel people as 'reactive pragmatists', a view that is in accord with reality in many organizations.

The strategist role

As strategists, HR professionals address major long-term organizational issues concerning the management and development of people and the employment relationship. They are guided by the business plans of the organization but they also contribute to the formulation of those business plans. This is achieved by ensuring that top managers focus on the human resource implications of the plans. HR strategists persuade top managers that they must develop business strategies that make the best use of the core competences of the organization's human resources. They emphasize, in the words of Hendry and Pettigrew (1986), that people are a strategic resource for the achievement of competitive advantage.

The innovation and change agent role

In their proactive role, HR practitioners are well placed to observe and analyse what is happening in and to their organizations as it affects the employment of people, and intervene accordingly. Following this analysis, they produce diagnoses that identify opportunities and threats and the causes of problems. They propose innovations in the light of these diagnoses that may be concerned with organizational processes such as interaction between departments and people, teamwork, structural change and the impact of new technology and methods of working, or HR processes such as resourcing, employee development or reward. As innovators they have to be experts in change management.

Impression management

The danger, according to Marchington (1995a), is that HR people may go in for 'impression management' – aiming to make an impact on senior managers and colleagues through publicizing high-profile innovations. HR specialists who aim to draw attention to themselves simply by promoting the latest flavour of the month, irrespective of its relevance or practicality, are falling into the trap that Drucker (1955), anticipating Marchington by 40 years, described as follows:

> The constant worry of all personnel administrators is their inability to prove that they are making a contribution to the enterprise. Their preoccupation is with the search for a 'gimmick' that will impress their management colleagues.

The HR specialist as change agent

Caldwell (2001) categorizes HR change agents in four dimensions:

1. *Transformational change* – a major change that has a dramatic effect on HR policy and practice across the whole organization.
2. *Incremental change* – gradual adjustments of HR policy and practices that affect single activities or multiple functions.
3. *HR vision* – a set of values and beliefs that affirm the legitimacy of the HR function as strategic business partner.
4. *HR expertise* – the knowledge and skills that define the unique contribution the HR professional can make to effective people management.

Across these dimensions, the change agent roles that Caldwell suggests can be carried out by HR professionals are those of change champions, change adapters, change consultants and change synergists.

Gratton (2000) stresses the need for HR practitioners to: 'Understand the state of the company, the extent of the embedding of processes and structures throughout the organization, and the behaviour and attitudes of individual employees'. She believes that 'The challenge is to implement the ideas' and the solution is to 'build a guiding coalition by involving line managers', which means 'creating issue-based cross-functional action teams that will initially make recommendations and later move into action'. This approach 'builds the capacity to change'.

Guidelines for innovation and change

The following are 10 guidelines for HR innovators and change agents:

1. Be clear on what has to be achieved and why.
2. Ensure that what you do fits the strategy, culture and circumstances of the organization.
3. Don't follow fashion – do your own thing.
4. Keep it simple – over-complexity is a common reason for failure.
5. Don't rush – it will take longer than you think.
6. Don't try to do too much at once – an incremental approach is generally best.
7. Assess resource requirements and costs.
8. Pay close attention to project planning and management.
9. Remember that the success of the innovation rests as much on the effectiveness of the process of implementation (line manager buy-in and skills are crucial) as it does on the quality of the concept, if not more so.
10. Pay close attention to change management – communicate, involve and train.

The internal consultancy role

As internal consultants, HR practitioners function like external management consultants, working alongside their colleagues – their clients – in analysing problems, diagnosing issues and proposing solutions. They will be involved in the development of HR processes or systems and in 'process consulting'. The latter deals with process areas such as organization, team building and objective setting.

The monitoring role

As monitors of the application of HR policies and procedures and the extent to which the organization's values relating to people management are upheld, HR practitioners have a delicate, indeed a difficult, role to play. They are not there to 'police' what line managers do but it is still necessary to ensure that the policies and procedures are implemented with a reasonable degree of consistency. This role as described by Storey (1992a) can mean that HR specialists can act as 'regulators' who are 'managers of discontent' involved in formulating and monitoring employment rules. The monitoring role is particularly important with regard to employment legislation. HR practitioners have to ensure that policies and procedures comply with the legislation and that they are implemented correctly by line managers.

Although the tendency is to devolve more responsibility for HR matters to line managers, the latter cannot be given total freedom to flout company policy or to contravene the provisions of employment, equal opportunity and health and safety legislation. A balance has to be struck between freedom, consistency and legal obligations.

The guardian of values role

HR practitioners may act as the guardians of the organization's values concerning people. They point out when behaviour conflicts with those values or where proposed actions would be inconsistent with them. In a sense, their roles require them to act as the 'conscience' of management – a necessary role but not an easy one to play.

MODELS OF THE PRACTITIONERS OF HR

A number of models classifying types of roles have been produced, as summarized below. These simplify the complex roles that HR professionals often have to play which, in different contexts or times, may change considerably or may mean adopting varied approaches to meet altering circumstances. They are therefore not universal but they do provide some insight into the different ways in which HR specialists operate.

Karen Legge (1978)

Two types of HR managers are described in this model: 1) *Conformist innovators* who go along with their organization's ends and adjust their means to achieve them. Their expertise is used as a source of professional power to improve the position of their departments. 2) *Deviant innovators* who attempt to change this means/ends relationship by gaining acceptance for a different set of criteria for the evaluation of organizational success and their contribution to it.

The Tyson and Fell (1986) model

This is the classic model, which describes three types of practitioner:

1. *The clerk of works* – all authority for action is vested in line managers. HR policies are formed or created after the actions that led to the need. Policies are not integral to the business and are short term and *ad hoc*. Authority is vested in line managers and HR activities are largely routine – employment and day-to-day administration.
2. *The contracts manager* – policies are well established, often implicit, with a heavy industrial relations emphasis, possibly derived from an employers association. The HR department will use fairly sophisticated systems, especially in the field of employee relations. The HR manager is likely to be a professional or very experienced in industrial relations. He or she will not be on the board and, although having some authority to 'police' the implementation of policies, acts mainly in an interpretative, not a creative or innovative, role.
3. *The architect* – explicit HR policies exist as part of the corporate strategy. Human resource planning and development are important concepts and a long-term view is taken. Systems tend to be sophisticated. The head of the HR function is probably on the board and his or her power is derived from professionalism and perceived contribution to the business.

Although insightful and relevant at the time this model does not express the complexities of the HR role as later ones do.

Kathleen Monks (1992)

The four types of practitioner identified by Monks following research in 97 organizations in Ireland extended those developed by Tyson and Fell:

1. *Traditional/administrative* – in this model the personnel practitioners have mainly a support role with the focus on administrative matters, record-keeping and adherence to rules and regulations.
2. *Traditional/industrial relations* – personnel practitioners concentrate on industrial relations, giving their other functions lower priority.
3. *Innovative/professional* – personnel specialists are professional and expert. They aim to remove traditional practices and replace them with improved human resource planning, recruitment and development, and reward policies and practices.

4. *Innovative/sophisticated* – personnel specialists are on the board, take part in integrating HR and business strategies, and are recognized as making an important contribution to organizational success. They develop and deliver sophisticated services in each of the main HR areas.

John Storey (1992a)

Storey's model suggests a two-dimensional map: interventionary/non-interventionary and strategic/tactical, as illustrated in Figure 4.1. From this he identifies four roles:

1. *Change masters* (interventionary/strategic), which is close to the HRM model.
2. *Advisers* (non-interventionary/strategic) who act as internal consultants, leaving much of HR practice to line managers.
3. *Regulators* (interventionary/tactical) who are 'managers of discontent' concerned with formulating and monitoring employment rules.
4. *Handmaidens* (non-interventionary/tactical) who merely provide a service to meet the demands of line managers.

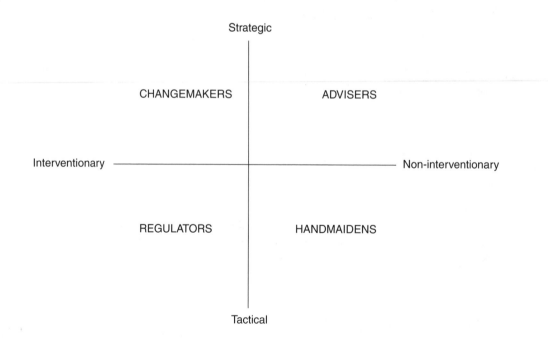

Figure 4.1 Types of personnel management (*Source*: Storey, 1992a)

Paul Reilly (2000)

The different roles that practitioners can play as described by Reilly are illustrated in Figure 4.2. He suggests that it is the 'strategist/integrator' who is most likely to make the longest-term strategic contribution. The 'administrator/controller' is likely to make a largely tactical short-term contribution, while the 'adviser/consultant' falls between the two.

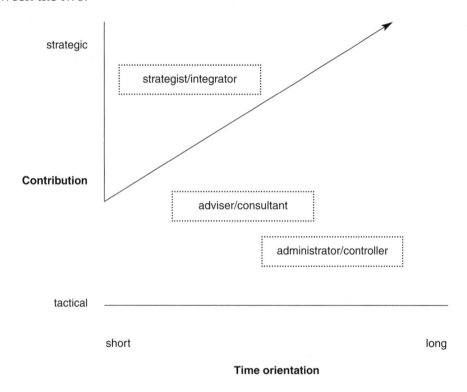

Figure 4.2   The changing role of the HR practitioner (*Source*: Reilly, 2000)

Dave Ulrich and Wayne Brockbank (2005a and 2005b)

In 1997 Dave Ulrich produced his model in which he suggested that as champions of competitiveness in creating and delivering value, HR professionals carry out the roles of strategic partners, administrative experts, employee champions and change agents. The response to this formulation concentrated on the business partner role. Ulrich, in conjunction with Brockbank, reformulated the 1997 model in 2005, listing the following roles:

- *Employee advocate* – focuses on the needs of today's employees through listening, understanding and empathizing.
- *Human capital developer* – in the role of managing and developing human capital (individuals and teams), focuses on preparing employees to be successful in the future.
- *Functional expert* – concerned with the HR practices that are central to HR value, acting with insight on the basis of the body of knowledge they possess. Some are delivered through administrative efficiency (such as technology or process design), and others through policies, menus and interventions. Necessary to distinguish between the foundation HR practices – recruitment, learning and development, rewards, etc – and the emerging HR practices such as communications, work process and organization design, and executive leadership development.
- *Strategic partner* – consists of multiple dimensions: business expert, change agent, strategic HR planner, knowledge manager and consultant, combining them to align HR systems to help accomplish the organization's vision and mission, helping managers to get things done, and disseminating learning across the organization.
- *Leader* – leading the HR function, collaborating with other functions and providing leadership to them, setting and enhancing the standards for strategic thinking and ensuring corporate governance.

Ulrich and Brockbank (2005b) explained that the revised formulation is in response to the changes in HR roles they have observed recently. They commented on the importance of the employee advocate role, noting that HR professionals spend on average about 19 per cent of their time on employee relations issues and that caring for, listening to and responding to employees remains a centrepiece of HR work. They noted that as a profession, HR possesses a body of knowledge that allows HR people to act with insight. Functional expertise enables them to create menus of choice for their business and thus identify options that are consistent with business needs rather than those that are merely ones they are able to provide. The additional heading of 'human capital developer' was introduced because of the increased emphasis on viewing people as critical assets and to recognize the significance of HR's role in developing the workforce. The concept of strategic partner remains broadly the same as before, but the additional heading of 'HR leader' has been introduced to highlight the importance of leadership by HR specialists of their own function – 'before they can develop other leaders, HR professionals must exhibit the leadership skills they expect in others'.

The 2005 Ulrich and Brockbank model focuses on the multifaceted role of HR people. It serves to correct the impression that Ulrich was simply focusing on them as business partners. This has had the unfortunate effect of implying that that was their only worthwhile function and has led to undue emphasis on this aspect of their role, important though it is, rather than a significant service delivery role. However, Ulrich cannot be blamed for this. In 1998 he gave equal emphasis to the need for administrative efficiency.

GAINING SUPPORT AND COMMITMENT

HR practitioners mainly get results by persuasion based on credibility and expertise. As Guest and Hoque (1994) note: 'By exerting influence, HR managers help to shape the framework of HR policy and practice.' Although line managers may make the day-to-day decisions, influencing skills are necessary for HR specialists. But there is a constant danger of HR professionals being so overcome by the beauty and truth of their bright idea that they expect everyone else – management and employees alike – to fall for it immediately. This is not how it is. Management and employees can create blockages and barriers and their support and commitment needs to be gained, which is not always easy.

Blockages and barriers within management

Managers will block or erect barriers to what the HR function believes to be progress if they are not persuaded that it will benefit both the organization and themselves at an acceptable cost (money and their time and trouble).

Blockages and barriers from employees

Employees will block or set up barriers to 'progress' or innovations if they feel they conflict with their own interests. They are likely, with reason, to be cynical about protestations that what is good for the organization will always be good for them.

Gaining support from top management

The support of top management is achievable by processes of marketing the HR function and persuasion. Boards and senior managers, like anyone else, are more likely to be persuaded to take a course of action if:

- it can be demonstrated that it will meet both the needs of the organization and their own personal needs;

- the proposal is based on a persuasive and realistic business case that spells out the benefits and the costs and, as far as possible, is justified either in added value terms (ie the income generated by the proposal will significantly exceed the cost of implementing it), and/or on the basis of a return on investment (ie the cost of the investment, say in training, is justified by the financial returns in such terms as increased productivity);
- there is proof that the innovation has already worked well within the organization (perhaps as a pilot scheme) or represents 'good practice', which is likely to be transferable to the organization;
- it can be shown that the proposal will increase the business's competitive edge, for example enlarging the skill base or multi-skilling to ensure that it can achieve competitive advantage through innovation and/or reducing time-to-market;
- it can be implemented without too much trouble, for example not taking up a lot of managers' time, or not meeting with strong opposition from line managers, employees or trade unions (it is as well to check the likely reaction before launching a proposal);
- it will add to the reputation of the company by showing that it is a 'world class' organization, ie what it does is as good as, if not better than, the world leaders in the sector in which the business operates (a promise that publicity will be achieved through articles in professional journals, press releases and conference presentations, will help);
- it will enhance the 'employer brand' of the company by making it a 'best place to work';
- the proposal is brief, to the point and well argued – it should take no more than five minutes to present orally and should be summarized in writing on the proverbial one side of one sheet of paper (supplementary details can be included in appendices).

Gaining the support and commitment of front line managers

This can sometimes be more difficult than gaining the support of top management. Front line managers can be cynical or realistic about innovation – they have seen it all before and/or they believe it won't work (sometimes with good reason). Innovations pushed down from the top can easily fail.

Gaining line management support requires providing an answer to the question, 'What's in it for me'? in terms of how the innovation will help them to achieve better results without imposing unacceptable additional burdens on them. New employment practices that take up precious time and involve paperwork will be treated with particular suspicion. Many line managers, often from bitter experience, resent the bureaucracy that can surround and, indeed, engulf systems favoured by HR people, such as traditional performance appraisal schemes.

Obtaining support requires market research and networking – getting around to talk to managers about their needs and testing new ideas to obtain reactions. The aim is to build up a body of information that will indicate approaches that are likely to be most acceptable, and therefore will most probably work, or at least to suggest areas where particular efforts will need to be made to persuade and educate line management. It is also useful to form 'strategic alliances' with influential managers who are enthusiastic about the innovation and will not only lend it vocal support but will also co-operate in pilot-testing it.

On the principle that 'nothing succeeds like success', support for new HR practices can often be achieved by demonstrating that it has worked well elsewhere in the organization.

Gaining commitment will be easier if managers have been consulted and know that their opinions have been listened to and acted upon. It is even better to involve them as members of project teams or task forces in developing the new process or system. This is the way to achieve ownership and therefore commitment.

Gaining the support and commitment of employees

When it comes to new employment practices, employees generally react in exactly the same way as managers: they will tend to resist change, wanting to know, 'What's in it for us?' They also want to know the hidden agenda – why is the company really wanting to introduce a performance management process? Will it simply be used as a means of gaining evidence for disciplinary proceedings? Or is it even going to provide the information required to select people for redundancy? As far as possible this kind of question needs to be answered in advance.

Sounding out employee opinion can be conducted through attitude surveys or focus groups. The latter method involves getting groups of people together to discuss (to 'focus' on) various issues and propositions. A well-run focus group can generate valid information on employees' feelings about and reaction to an initiative.

Employee commitment is also more likely if they are kept well informed of what is proposed, why it has been proposed and how it will affect them. It will be further enhanced if they participate in the development of the new employment practice and if they know that their contributions have been welcomed and acted upon.

ETHICAL CONSIDERATIONS

HR specialists are concerned with ethical standards in three ways: their conduct as professionals, the values that govern their behaviour, and the ethical standards of their firms.

Professional conduct

The CIPD Code of Professional Conduct states that:

> In the public interest and in the pursuit of its objects, the Chartered Institute of Personnel and Development is committed to the highest possible standards of professional conduct and competency. To this end members:
>
> - are required to exercise integrity, honesty, diligence and appropriate behaviour in all their business, professional and related personal activities;
> - must act within the law and must not encourage, assist or act in collusion with employees, employers or others who may be engaged in unlawful conduct.

Values

HR professionals are part of management. They are not there to act as surrogate representatives of the interests of employees. But there will be occasions when in their professional capacity HR specialists should speak out and oppose plans or actions that are clearly at variance with the values of the organization. And they should do their best to influence changes in those values where they feel they are necessary. They must not tolerate injustice or inequality of opportunity. If redundancies are inevitable as a result of business-led 'slimming down' or 'taking costs out of the business' processes, they must ensure that the organization takes whatever steps it can to mitigate detrimental effects by, for example, relying primarily on natural wastage and voluntary redundancy or, if people have to go involuntarily, doing whatever they can to help them find other jobs (outplacement).

HR specialists may often find themselves acting within a support function in a hard-nosed, entrepreneurial environment. But this does not mean that they can remain unconcerned about developing and helping to uphold the core values of the organization in line with their own values on how people should be managed. These may not always be reconcilable, and if this is strongly the case, the HR professional may have to make a choice on whether he or she can remain with the organization.

Ethical standards in the firm

More and more companies are, rightly, developing and publishing value statements and codes of ethics. The focus on such codes was encouraged by the Cadbury Report on corporate governance, which in 1992 recommended that companies should adopt one.

An ethics code may include the guiding principles the organization follows in conducting its business and relating to its stakeholders – employees, customers, shareholders (or other providers of finance), suppliers, and society in general. A code will also summarize the ethical standards expected of employees. These may include conflicts of interest, the giving and receiving of gifts, confidentiality, environmental pollution, health and safety, equal opportunities, managing diversity, sexual harassment, moonlighting and political activity.

As suggested by Pickard (1995), HR practitioners can contribute to enhancing awareness of ethical issues by:

- deploying professional expertise to develop and communicate an ethics policy and field the response to it, holding training sessions to help people think through the issues and monitoring the policy;
- contributing to the formation of company strategy, especially touching on mission and values;
- setting an example through professional conduct, on issues such as fairness, equal treatment and confidentiality.

PROFESSIONALISM IN HRM

If the term is used loosely, HR specialists are 'professional' because they display expertise in doing their work. A professional occupation such as medicine or law could, however, be defined as one that gives members of its association exclusive rights to practise their profession. A profession is not so much an occupation as a means of controlling an occupation. Human resource management is obviously not in this category.

The nature of professional work was best defined by the Hayes Committee (1972) as follows:

> Work done by the professional is usually distinguished by its reference to a framework of fundamental concepts linked with experience rather than by impromptu reaction to events or the application of laid down procedures. Such a high level of distinctive

competence reflects the skilful application of specialized education, training and experience. This should be accompanied by a sense of responsibility and an acceptance of recognized standards.

A 'profession' may be identified on the basis of the following criteria:

- skills based on theoretical knowledge;
- the provision of training and education;
- a test of the competence of members administered by a professional body;
- a formal professional organization that has the power to regulate entry to the profession;
- a professional code of conduct.

By these standards an institution such as the CIPD carries out most of the functions of a professional body.

Another approach to the definition of a profession is to emphasize the service ethic – the professional is there to serve others. This, however, leads to confusion when applied to HR specialists. Whom do they serve? The organization and its values, or the people in the organization and their needs? (Organizational values and personal needs do not necessarily coincide.) As Tyson and Fell (1986) have commented:

> In recent years the personnel manager seems to be encouraged to make the line manager his (sic) client, while trying simultaneously to represent wider social standards, and to possess a sense of service to employees. This results in confusion and difficulty for the personnel executive.

In the face of this difficulty, the question has to be asked, why bother? The answer was suggested by Watson (1977), who asserted that the adoption of a professional image by personnel managers is a strategic response to their felt lack of authority. They are in an ambiguous situation and sometimes feel they need all the help they can get to clarify and, indeed, strengthen their authority and influence.

If a profession is defined rigidly as a body of people who possess a particular area of competence, who control entry so that only members of the association can practise in that area, who unequivocally adopt the 'service ethic' and who are recognized by themselves and others as belonging to a profession, then HR practitioners are not strictly working in a profession. This is the case even when a professional institution like the CIPD exists with the objective of acting as a professional body in the full sense of the word, an aim that it does its best to fulfil.

On the basis of their research, Guest and Horwood (1981) expressed their doubts about the professional model of personnel management as follows:

The (research) data also highlights the range of career types in personnel management. Given the diversity of personnel roles and organizational contexts, this is surely something to be welcomed. It is tempting but wrong to view personnel managers as homogeneous. Their different backgrounds and fields of operations raise doubts about the value of a professional model and of any attempt to view personnel problems as amenable to solution through a primary focus on professionalism.

However, a broader definition of professionalism as the practice of specific skills based upon a defined body of knowledge in accordance with recognized standards of behaviour would entitle the practice of HRM to be regarded as a profession.

The debate continues, but it is an academic one. What matters is that HR 'professionals' need expertise and have to use it responsibly. In other words, they should act professionally but do not have to be members of a professional association to do so. Such associations, however, have an important part to play in setting and improving professional standards.

If this definition is accepted, then those who do practise specific HRM skills based upon a defined body of knowledge in accordance with recognized standards of behaviour can be regarded as members of a profession.

AMBIGUITIES IN THE ROLE OF HR PRACTITIONERS

The activities and roles of HR specialists and the demands made upon them as described above appear to be quite clear cut but, in Thurley's (1981) words, HR practitioners can be 'specialists in ambiguity'. This may arise because their role is ill-defined (they are unsure of where they stand), their status is not fully recognized, or top management and line managers have equivocal views about their value to the organization.

Ambiguity in the role of HR people can result in confusion between ideals and reality. Tyson and Fell (1986) see a contrast between the ideologies and actual realities of organizational life to which HR managers, 'as organization men or women', have to conform.

This ambiguity is reflected in the comments that have been made about the role of the HR function. For example, Mackay and Torrington (1986) suggested that: 'Personnel management is never identified with management interests, as it becomes ineffective when not able to understand and articulate the aspirations of the workforce.' In complete contrast, Tyson and Fell (1986) believe that:

> Classical personnel management has not been granted a position in decision-making circles because it has frequently not earned one. It has not been concerned with the totality of the organization but often with issues that have not only been parochial but esoteric to boot.

The debate on HRM versus personnel management has been generated by, but has also contributed to this ambiguity. HRM is management-oriented, and sees people as a key resource to be used to further the objectives of the business. Traditional personnel management, however, has tended to be more people-oriented, taking the view that if their needs are satisfied, the organization as well as its members will benefit. HR professionals can find themselves being pulled in both directions. It does not make their life any easier.

CONFLICT IN THE HR CONTRIBUTION

One of the questions HR practitioners sometimes have to ask themselves is, 'Who is the client – the company or the employee?' HR professionals may have to walk a fine line between serving the company that pays their salary and serving individual employees. They may be involved in counselling employees over work problems. This can only be carried out successfully if the employee trusts the HR practitioner to maintain confidentiality. But something might be revealed which is of interest to management and that places the counsellor in a dilemma – to betray or not to betray the trust? There is no pat answer to this question, but the existence of a code of professional conduct, a set of values and a company ethical code can provide guidance.

HR specialists, as Thurley (1981) put it, often 'work against the grain'. Their values may be different from those of line managers and this is a potential cause of conflict. But conflict is inevitable in organizations that are pluralistic societies, the members of which have different frames of reference and interests, particularly self-interest. Management may have their own priorities: 'Increase shareholder value', 'Keep the City happy', 'Innovate', 'Get the work done'. Employees might have a completely different set: 'Pay me well and equitably', 'Give me security', 'Provide good working conditions', 'Treat me fairly'. HR specialists, as noted above, may find themselves somewhere in the middle.

Conflicts in the HR contribution can arise in the following ways:

● *A clash of values* – line managers may simply regard their workers as factors of production to be used, exploited and dispensed with in accordance with organizational imperatives.

- *Different priorities* – management's priority may be to add value – make more out of less – and if this involves getting rid of people, that's too bad. HR people may recognize the need to add value but not at the expense of employees.
- *Freedom versus control* – line managers may want the freedom to get on with things their own way, interpreting company policies to meet their needs; the thrust for devolution has encouraged such feelings. But HR specialists will be concerned about the achievement of a consistent and equitable approach to managing people and implementing HR policies. They will also be concerned with the attainment of a proper degree of compliance to employment and health and safety law. They may be given the responsibility for exercising control, and conflict is likely if they use this authority too rigidly.
- *Disputes* – if unions are recognized, HR specialists may be involved in conflict during the process of resolution. Even when there are no unions, there may be conflict with individuals or groups of employees about the settlement of grievances.

As Follett (1924) wrote, there is the possibility that conflict can be creative if an integrative approach is used to settle it. This means clarifying priorities, policies and roles, using agreed procedures to deal with grievances and disputes, bringing differences of interpretation out into the open and achieving consensus through a solution that recognizes the interests of both parties – a win-win process. Resolving conflict by the sheer exercise of power (win-lose) will only lead to further conflict. Resolving conflict by compromise may lead to both parties being dissatisfied (lose-lose).

THE COMPETENCIES REQUIRED BY HR PROFESSIONALS

A competency framework for HR professionals is set out in Table 4.1.

An alternative formulation, as shown in Table 4.2, established by research conducted at the University of Michigan Business School (Brockbank *et al*, 1999) shows the key competency areas (domains) and their components are set out in Table 4.2.

The CIPD professional standards

The CIPD has produced the following list of competencies required by its professional members:

- *Personal drive and effectiveness.* The existence of a positive 'can do' mentality, anxious to find ways round obstacles and willing to exploit all the available resources to accomplish objectives.

Table 4.1 Competency framework for HR professionals

Business and cultural awareness	Understands: (1) the business environment, the competitive pressures the organization faces and the drivers of high performance, (2) the business' key activities and processes and how these affect business strategies, (3) the culture (core values and norms) of the business, (4) how HR policies and practices impact on business performance, and puts this to good use.
Strategic capability	(1) Seeks involvement in business strategy formulation and contributes to the development of the strategy, (2) contributes to the development for the business of a clear vision and a set of integrated values, (3) develops and implements coherent HR strategies which are aligned to the business strategy and integrated with one another, (4) understands the importance of human capital measurement, introduces measurement systems and ensures that good use is made of them.
Organizational effectiveness	(1) Contributes to the analysis and diagnosis of people issues and proposes practical solutions, (2) helps to develop resource capability by ensuring that the business has the skilled, committed and engaged workforce it needs, (3) helps to develop process capability by influencing the design of work systems to make the best use of people, (4) contributes to the development of knowledge management processes.
Internal consultancy	(1) Carries out the analysis and diagnosis of people issues and proposes practical solutions, (2) adopts interventionist style to meet client needs, acts as a catalyst, facilitator and expert as required, (uses process consultancy approaches to resolve people problems, (4) coaches clients to deal with their own problems, transfers skills.
Service delivery	(1) Anticipates requirements and sets up and operates appropriate services, (2) provides efficient and cost-effective services in each HR area; (3) responds promptly and efficiently to requests for HR services, help and advice, (4) promotes the empowerment of line managers to make HR decisions but provides guidance as required.
Continuous professional development	(1) Continually develops professional knowledge and skills, (2) benchmarks good HR practice, (3) keeps in touch with new HR concepts, practices and techniques, (keeps up-to-date with HR research and its practical implications.

Table 4.2 Key competency areas (*Source*: Brockbank *et al*, 1999)

Competency domain	Components
1 Personal credibility	Live the firm's values, maintain relationships founded on trust, act with an 'attitude' (a point of view about how the business can win, backing up opinion with evidence).
2 Ability to manage change	Drive change: ability to diagnose problems, build relationships with clients, articulate a vision, set a leadership agenda, solve problems, and implement goals.
3 Ability to manage culture	Act as 'keepers of the culture', identify the culture required to meet the firm's business strategy, frames culture in a way that excites employees, translates desired culture into specific behaviours, encourages executives to behave consistently with the desired culture.
4 Delivery of human resource practices	Expert in speciality, able to deliver state-of-the-art innovative HR practices in such areas as recruitment, employee development, compensation and communication.
5 Understanding of the business	Strategy, organization, competitors, finance, marketing, sales, operations and IT.

- *People management and leadership.* The motivation of others (whether subordinates, seniors or project team members) towards the achievement of shared goals, not through the application of formal authority but rather by personal role modelling, the establishment of professional credibility, and the creation of reciprocal trust.
- *Professional competence.* Possession of the professional skills and technical capabilities associated with successful achievement in personnel and development.
- *Adding value through people.* A desire not only to concentrate on tasks, but rather to select meaningful outputs which will produce added-value outcomes for the organization, or eliminate/reduce the existence of performance inhibitors, whilst simultaneously complying with all legal and ethical considerations.
- *Continuing learning.* Commitment to continuous improvement and change by the application of self-managed learning techniques, supplemented where appropriate by deliberate planned exposure to external learning sources (mentoring, coaching, etc).
- *Thinking and applied resourcefulness.* Application of a systematic approach to situational analysis, development of convincing, business-focused action plans, and

(where appropriate) the deployment of intuitive/creative thinking to generate innovative solutions and proactively seize opportunities.

- *'Customer' focus.* Concern for the perceptions of personnel's customers, including (principally) the central directorate of the organization, a willingness to solicit and act upon 'customer' feedback as one of the foundations for performance improvement.
- *Strategic capability.* The capacity to create an achievable vision for the future, to foresee longer-term developments, to envisage options (and their probable consequences), to select sound courses of action, to rise above the day-to-day detail, to challenge the *status quo.*
- *Influencing and interpersonal skills.* The ability to transmit information to others, especially in written (report) form, both persuasively and cogently; display of listening, comprehension and understanding skills, plus sensitivity to the emotional, attitudinal and political aspects of corporate life.

An important competency that the CIPD has omitted from this list is service delivery, ie the capacity to provide effective levels of service that meet the needs of internal customers. Ultimately, this is what HR professionals are there to do, bearing in mind that the services they provide will be concerned with the development and implementation of value-adding and integrated HR strategies as well as operational services.

HR professionals as 'thinking performers'

The CIPD has stated that:

> All personnel and development specialists must be thinking performers. That is, their central task is to be knowledgeable and competent in their various fields and to be able to move beyond compliance to provide a critique of organizational policies and procedures and to advise on how organizations should develop in the future.

This concept can be interpreted as meaning that HR professionals have to think carefully about what they are doing in the context of their organization and within the framework of a recognized body of knowledge, and they have to perform effectively in the sense of delivering advice, guidance and services which will help the organization to achieve its strategic goals. Legge (1995) made a similar point when she referred to HRM as a process of 'thinking pragmatism'.

5

Role of the front-line manager

Front-line managers are crucial to the success of HR policies and practices. This chapter starts with an analysis of their role generally and their people management responsibilities particularly. It continues with an examination of the respective roles of HR and line management and a discussion of the line manager's role in implementing HR. The chapter concludes with suggestions on how to improve front-line managers as people managers.

THE BASIC ROLE

Front-line managers as defined by Hutchinson and Purcell (2003) are managers who are responsible for a work group to a higher level of management hierarchy, and are placed in the lower layers of the management hierarchy, normally at the first level. They tend to have employees reporting to them who themselves do not have any management or supervisory responsibility and are responsible for the day-to-day running of their work rather than strategic matters. The roles of such managers typically include a combination of the following activities:

- people management;
- managing operational costs;

- providing technical expertise;
- organizing, such as planning work allocation and rotas;
- monitoring work processes;
- checking quality;
- dealing with customers/clients;
- measuring operational performance.

Hutchinson and Purcell noted that in all the 12 organizations in which they conducted their research, the most common people management activity handled by front-line managers was absence management. This could include not just monitoring absence and lateness but also phoning (and even visiting) absent staff at home, conducting back-to-work interviews, counselling staff and conducting disciplinary hearings. Other people management activities were coaching and development, performance appraisal, involvement and communication (thus providing a vital link between team members and more senior managers), and discipline and grievances. In many organizations, recruitment and selection was also carried out by line managers, often in conjunction with HR. Thus in all these organizations front-line managers were carrying out activities that traditionally had been the bread and butter of personnel or HR departments. These people-management duties were larger and encompassed more responsibilities than the traditional supervisory role.

THE LINE MANAGER AND PEOPLE MANAGEMENT

The CIPD research on employee well-being and the psychological contract (Guest and Conway, 2005) established that too many line managers are failing to motivate and improve the performance of the people they manage. Under half of respondents to the CIPD survey reported that they were regularly motivated by their line manager, only 45 per cent were happy with the level of feedback they received and just 37 per cent said that their manager helped them to improve their performance. This suggests that the organizations concerned were failing to get managers to understand their role in motivating people and were also failing to manage performance as effectively as they might. As the report emphasizes, 'One of the biggest challenges for HR is to support line managers in managing and developing their people and this means that the respective roles of line and HR managers need to be understood.'

THE RESPECTIVE ROLES OF HR AND LINE MANAGEMENT

It has been the accepted tradition of HR management that HR specialists are there to provide support and services to line managers, not to usurp the latter's role of 'getting things done through people' – their responsibility for managing their own HR affairs. In practice, the HR function has frequently had the role of ensuring that HR policies are implemented consistently throughout the organization, as well as the more recent onerous responsibility for ensuring that both the letter and the spirit of employment law are implemented consistently. The latter responsibility has often been seen as a process of ensuring that the organization does not get involved in tedious, time-wasting and often expensive employment tribunal proceedings.

Carrying out this role has often led to the HR function 'policing' line management, which can be a cause of tension and ambiguity. To avoid this, HR specialists may have to adopt a reasonably light touch: providing advice rather than issuing dicta, except when a manager is clearly contravening the law or when his or her actions are likely to lead to an avoidable dispute or an employment tribunal case that the organization will probably lose.

It has also frequently been the case that, in spite of paying lip-service to the principle that 'line managers must manage', HR departments have usurped the line managers' true role of being involved in key decisions concerning the recruitment, development and remuneration of their people, thus diminishing the managers' capacity to manage their key resource effectively. This situation has arisen most frequently in large bureaucratic organizations and/or those with a powerful centralized HR function. It still exists in some quarters, but as decentralization and devolution increase and organizations are finding that they are having to operate more flexibly, it is becoming less common.

It is necessary to reconcile what might be called the 'functional control' aspects of an HR specialist's role (achieving the consistent application of policies and acting as the guardian of the organization's values concerning people) and the role of providing services, support and, as necessary, guidance to managers, without issuing commands or relieving them of their responsibilities. However, the distinction between giving advice and telling people what to do, or between providing help and taking over can be blurred, and the relationship is one that has to be developed and nurtured with great care. The most appropriate line for HR specialists to take is that of emphasizing that they are there to help line managers achieve their objectives through their people, not to do their job for them.

In practice, however, some line managers may be only too glad to let the HR department do its people management job for them, especially the less pleasant aspects like handling discipline and grievance problems. A delicate balance has therefore to be achieved between providing help and advice when it is clearly needed and creating a 'dependency culture' that discourages managers from thinking and acting for themselves on people matters for which they are responsible. Managers will not learn about dealing with people if they are over-dependent on HR specialists. The latter therefore have to stand off sometimes and say, in effect, 'That's your problem.'

How HR and the line work together

Research into HR management and the line conducted by the IPD (Hutchinson and Wood, 1995) produced the following findings:

- Most organizations reported a trend towards greater line management responsibility for HR management without it causing any significant tension between HR and the line.
- Devolution offered positive opportunities for the HR function to become involved in strategic, proactive and internal consultancy roles because they were less involved in day-to-day operational HR activities.
- Both HR and line management were involved in operational HR activities. Line managers were more heavily involved in recruitment, selection and training decisions and in handling discipline issues and grievances. HR were still largely responsible for such matters as analysing training needs, running internal courses and pay and benefits.
- There is an underlying concern that line managers are not sufficiently competent to carry out their new roles. This may be for a number of reasons including lack of training, pressures of work, because managers have been promoted for their technical rather than managerial skills, or because they are used to referring certain issues to the HR department.
- Some HR specialists also have difficulty in adopting their new roles because they do not have the right skills (such as an understanding of the business) or because they see devolution as a threat to their own job security.
- Other problems over devolution include uncertainty on the part of line managers about the role of the HR function, lack of commitment by line managers to performing their new roles, and achieving the right balance between providing line managers with as much freedom as possible and the need to retain core controls and direction.

The conclusions reached by the researchers were that:

If line managers are to take an effective greater responsibility for HR management activities then, from the outset, the rules and responsibilities of personnel and line managers must be clearly defined and understood. Support is needed from the personnel department in terms of providing a procedural framework, advice and guidance on all personnel management matters, and in terms of training line managers so they have the appropriate skills and knowledge to carry out their new duties.

The research conducted by Hope-Hailey *et al* (1998) in eight UK-based organizations revealed that all of them were shifting responsibility for people management down the line. In practice, this often meant that responsibility for decision-making on HR issues had been devolved to line managers, but that the HR function continued to be responsible for operational functions such as recruitment and pay systems. As they commented: 'There seemed to be little indication that this move had reduced in any way the level of necessary bureaucracy associated with the implementation of personnel policies and procedures.' However, they noted that 'personnel was no longer seen as a rule maker or enforcer, but it was still regarded – in part – as an administrative function'. With reference to the activities of the HR functions in these organizations, the research established that there was 'more emphasis on achieving behavioural change through a more "nuts and bolts" systems approach rather than large scale organizational development activities'.

THE LINE MANAGER'S ROLE IN IMPLEMENTING HR POLICIES

HR can initiate new policies and practices but it is the line that has the main responsibility for implementing them. In other words, 'HR proposes but the line disposes.' If line managers are not disposed favourably towards what HR wants them to do they won't do it, or if compelled to, they will be half-hearted about it. As pointed out by Purcell *et al* (2003), high levels of organizational performance are not achieved simply by having a range of well-conceived HR policies and practices in place. What makes the difference is how these policies and practices are implemented. That is where the role of line managers in people management is crucial: 'The way line managers implement and enact policies, show leadership in dealing with employees and in exercising control come through as a major issue.' Purcell *et al* noted that dealing with people is perhaps the aspect of their work in which line managers can exercise the greatest amount of discretion. If they use their discretion not to put HR's ideas into practice, the result is that the rhetoric is unlikely to be converted into reality. Performance management schemes often fail because of the reluctance of managers to carry out reviews. It is, as Purcell *et al* point out, line managers who bring HR policies to life.

A further factor affecting the role of line management is their ability to do the HR tasks assigned to them. People-centred activities such as defining roles, interviewing, reviewing performance, providing feedback, coaching and identifying learning and development needs all require special skills. Some managers have them, many don't. Performance-related pay schemes sometimes fail because of untrained line managers.

Further research and analysis at Bath University (Hutchinson and Purcell, 2003) confirmed that: 'The role of line managers in bringing policy to life and in leading was one of the most important of all factors in explaining the difference between success and mediocrity in people management.'

HOW TO IMPROVE FRONT-LINE MANAGERS AS PEOPLE MANAGERS

The following suggestions were made by Hutchinson and Purcell (2003) on how to improve the quality of front-line managers in people management:

- Front-line managers need time to carry out their people management duties, which are often superseded by other management duties.
- They need to be carefully selected with much more attention being paid to the behavioural competencies required.
- They need the support of strong organizational values concerning leadership and people management.
- They need a good working relationship with their own managers.
- They need to receive sufficient skills training to enable them to perform their people management activities, such as performance management.

6

International HRM

INTERNATIONAL HRM DEFINED

International human resource management is the process of employing, developing and rewarding people in international or global organizations. It involves the world-wide management of people, not just the management of expatriates.

An international firm is one in which operations take place in subsidiaries overseas, which rely on the business expertise or manufacturing capacity of the parent company. International firms may be highly centralized with tight controls. A multi-national firm is one in which a number of businesses in different countries are managed as a whole from the centre. The degree of autonomy they have will vary. Global firms offer products or services that are rationalized and standardized to enable production or provision to be carried out locally in a cost-efficient way. Their subsidiaries are not subject to rigid control except over the quality and presentation of the product or service. They rely on the technical know-how of the parent company, but carry out their own manufacturing, service delivery or distribution activities.

ISSUES IN INTERNATIONAL HRM

Bartlett and Goshal (1991) argue that the main issue for multinational companies is the need to manage the challenges of global efficiency and multinational flexibility – 'the ability of an organization to manage the risks and exploit the opportunities that arise from the diversity and volatility of the global environment'. The dilemma facing all multinational corporations is that of achieving a balance between international consistency and local autonomy. Laurent (1986) commented that:

> In order to build, maintain and develop the corporate identity, multinational organizations need to strive for consistency in their ways of managing people on a worldwide basis. Yet, and in order to be effective locally, they also need to adapt those ways to the specific cultural requirements of different societies. While the global nature of business may call for increased consistency, the variety of cultural environments may be calling for differentiation.

International HRM involves a number of issues not present when the activities of the firm are confined to one country. These issues comprise the variety of international organizational models that exist, the extent to which HRM policy and practice should vary in different countries (convergence or divergence), the problems of managing in different cultures and environments, and the approaches used to select, deploy, develop and reward expatriates who could be nationals of the parent company or 'third-country nationals' (TCNs) – nationals of countries other than the parent company who work abroad in subsidiaries of that company.

INTERNATIONAL ORGANIZATIONAL MODELS

Four international organizational models have been identified by Bartlett and Goshal (1993):

1. *Decentralized federation* in which each national unit is managed as a separate entity that seeks to optimize its performance in the local environment. This is the traditional multinational corporation.
2. *Coordinated federation* in which the centre develops sophisticated management systems enabling it to maintain overall control, although scope is given to local management to adopt practices that recognize local market conditions.
3. *Centralized hub* in which the focus is on the global market rather than on local markets. Such organizations are truly global rather than multinational, which is the case when adopting a federated approach.
4. *Transnational* in which the corporation develops multi-dimensional strategic capabilities directed towards competing globally but also allows local responsiveness to market requirements.

Perkins and Hendry (1999) argue that notwithstanding this fourfold model, international firms seem to be polarizing around two organizational approaches: 1) regionalization, where local customer service is important; and 2) global business streams, which involve setting up centrally controlled business segments that deal with a related range of products worldwide.

CONVERGENCE AND DIVERGENCE

An issue facing all international firms is the extent to which their HR policies should either 'converge' worldwide to be basically the same in each location, or 'diverge' to be differentiated in response to local requirements. There is a natural tendency for managerial traditions in the parent company to shape the nature of key decisions, but there are strong arguments for giving as much local autonomy as possible in order to ensure that local requirements are sufficiently taken into account.

As noted by Adler and Ghader (1990), organizations have to follow very different HRM policies and practices according to the relevant stage of international corporate evolution: domestic, international, multinational and global. Harris and Brewster (1999) refer to this as 'the global/local dilemma', the issue being the extent to which operating units across the world are to be differentiated and at the same time integrated, controlled and coordinated. They suggest that the alternative strategies are the global approach in which the company's culture predominates and HRM is centralized and relatively standardized (an 'ethnocentric' policy), or the decentralized approach in which HRM responsibility is devolved to subsidiaries. They state that the factors affecting choice are:

- the extent to which there are well-defined local norms;
- the degree to which an operating unit is embedded in the local environment;
- the strength of the flow of resources – finance, information and people – between the parent and the subsidiary;
- the orientation of the parent to control;
- the nature of the industry – the extent to which it is primarily a domestic industry at local level;
- the specific organizational competences including HRM that are critical for achieving competitive advantage in a global environment.

Brewster (2004) believes that convergence may be increasing as a result of the power of the markets, the importance of cost, quality and productivity pressures, the emergence of transaction cost economies and the development of like-minded international cadres. The widespread practice of benchmarking 'best practice' may have contributed to convergence.

However, Brewster considers that European firms at least are so locked into their respective national institutional settings that no common model is likely to emerge in the foreseeable future. Since HR systems reflect national institutional contexts and cultures, they do not respond readily to the imperatives of technology or the market. Managers in each country operate within a national institutional context and share a set of cultural assumptions. Neither institutions nor cultures change quickly and rarely in ways that are the same as other countries. As Hofstede (1980) points out, it follows that managers in one country behave in a way that is noticeably different from managers in other countries.

Brewster (2004) concludes on the basis of his research that there is some convergence in Europe in the general direction of developments (directional convergence) such as the decreasing size of the HR function, increases in training and development and the increasing provision of information about strategy and finances. But there is little evidence of final convergence in the sense of companies becoming more alike in the way in which they manage their human resources.

Developing an international approach

Laurent (1986) proposes that a truly international approach to human resource management would require the following steps:

1. An explicit recognition by the parent organization that its own peculiar ways of managing human resources reflect some of the assumptions and values of its home culture.
2. An explicit recognition by the parent organization that its peculiar ways are neither universally better nor worse than others, but are different and likely to exhibit strengths and weaknesses, particularly abroad.
3. An explicit recognition by the parent organization that its foreign subsidiaries may have other preferred ways of managing people that are neither intrinsically better nor worse, but could possibly be more effective locally.
4. Willingness from headquarters not only to acknowledge cultural differences, but also to take action in order to make them discussable and therefore useable.
5. The building of a genuine belief by all parties that more creative and effective ways of managing people could be developed as a result of cross-cultural learning.

CULTURAL DIVERSITY

Cultural and environmental diversity is a key issue in international HRM. As Haley (1999) remarks:

In cultures where people are emphasized, it is the quality of interpersonal relationships which is important. In cultures where ideologies are emphasized, sharing common beliefs is more important than group membership. In cultures where action is emphasized, what is done is more important than what is said.

Hofstede (1980) emphasizes that there are a number of cultural dimensions that affect international operations. His framework has been adapted by Bento and Ferreira (1992) to produce the following cultural dualities:

- equality versus inequality;
- certainty versus uncertainty;
- controllability versus uncontrollability;
- individualism versus collectivism;
- materialistic versus personalization.

Sparrow and Hiltrop (1997) note the following HR areas that may be affected by national culture:

- decisions on what makes an effective manager;
- giving face-to-face feedback;
- readiness to accept international assignments;
- pay systems and different concepts of social justice;
- approaches to organizational structuring and strategic dynamics.

Harris *et al* (2003) provide the following instance of cultural differences:

A performance management system based on openness between manager and subordinate, each explaining plainly how they feel the other has done well or badly in the job, may work in some European countries, but is unlikely to fit with the greater hierarchical assumptions and 'loss of face' fears of some of the Pacific countries.

Sparrow (1999a) gives examples of different approaches to managerial qualities. The Anglo-Saxon sees management as something separate and definable, based on general and transferable skills, especially interpersonal skills. In Germany, an entirely opposite view is adopted: value is placed on entrepreneurial skills, technical competence, functional expertise and creativity, and managers rely more on formal authority than in other European countries. In France, management is seen as an intellectually demanding task and management development systems are elitist.

Brewster (1999) comments that the 'universalistic' approach to HRM prevalent in the USA is rejected in Europe where the basic functions of HRM are given different weights between countries and are carried out differently. If a convergent and therefore universalistic approach is adopted by a US international company, it might be difficult to get it accepted in Europe. Divergences to respect cultural differences may be more appropriate if the full potential of the overseas company is to be realized.

THINK GLOBALLY AND ACT LOCALLY

The cultural differences mentioned above have produced the slogan 'think globally and act locally'. This means that an international balancing act is required, which leads to the fundamental assumption made by Bartlett and Ghoshal (1991) that: 'Balancing the needs of co-ordination, control and autonomy and maintaining the appropriate balance are critical to the success of the multinational company.'

Ulrich (1998) suggests that to achieve this balancing act, there are six capabilities that enable firms to integrate and concentrate international activities and also separate and adopt local activities:

1. being able to determine core activities and non-core activities;
2. achieving consistency while allowing flexibility;
3. building global brand equity while honouring local customs;
4. obtaining leverage (bigger is better) while achieving focus (smaller is better);
5. sharing learning and creating new knowledge;
6. engendering a global perspective while ensuring local accountability.

INTERNATIONAL HR POLICIES

International HR policies will deal with the extent to which there should be convergence or divergence in the HR practices adopted in overseas subsidiaries or units. These will have to take account of differences in employment law, the character of the labour market, different employee relations processes and any cultural differences in the ways in which people are treated.

MANAGING EXPATRIATES

The management of expatriates is a major factor determining success or failure in an international business. Expatriates are expensive; they can cost three or four times as much as the employment of the same individual at home. They are difficult to manage because of the problems associated with adapting to and working in unfamiliar environments, concerns about their development and careers, difficulties encountered when they re-enter their parent company after an overseas assignment, and how they should be remunerated. Policies to address all these issues are required, as described below.

Resourcing policies

The challenge is that of resourcing international operations with people of the right calibre. As Perkins (1997) points out, it is necessary for businesses to 'remain competitive with their employment offering in the market place, to attract and retain high quality staff with worldwide capabilities'.

Policies are required on the employment of local nationals and the use of expatriates for long periods or shorter assignments. The advantages of employing local nationals are that they:

- are familiar with local markets, the local communities, the cultural setting and the local economy;
- speak the local language and are culturally assimilated;
- can take a long-term view and contribute for a long period (as distinct from expatriates who are likely to take a short-term perspective);
- do not take the patronizing (neo-colonial) attitude that expatriates sometimes adopt.

Expatriates (nationals of the parent company or third-country nationals) may be required to provide the experience and expertise that local nationals lack, at least for the time being. But there is much to be said for a long-term resourcing policy that states that the aim is to fill all or the great majority of posts with local people. Parent companies who staff their overseas subsidiaries with local nationals always have the scope to 'parachute in' specialist staff to deal with particular issues such as the start-up of a new product or service.

Recruitment and selection policies

Policies for recruitment and selection should deal with specifying requirements, providing realistic previews and preparation for overseas assignments.

Role specifications

Role specifications should take note of the behaviours required for those who work internationally. Leblanc (2001) suggested that they should be able to:

- recognize the diversity of overseas countries;
- accept differences between countries as a fact and adjust to these differences effectively;
- tolerate and adjust to local conditions;
- cope in the long term with a large variety of foreign contexts;
- manage local operations and personnel abroad effectively;
- gain acceptance as a representative of one's company abroad;
- obtain and interpret information about foreign national contexts (institutions, legislations, practices, market specifics, etc);
- inform and communicate effectively with a foreign environment about the home company's policies;
- take into account the foreign environment when negotiating contracts and partnerships;
- identify and accept adjustments to basic product specifications in order to meet the needs of the foreign market;
- develop elements of a common framework for company strategies, policies and operations;
- accept that the practices that will operate best in an overseas environment will not necessarily be the same as the company's 'home' practices.

Realistic previews

At interviews for candidates from outside the organization, and when talking to internal staff about the possibility of an overseas assignment, it is advisable to have a policy of providing a realistic preview of the job. The preview should provide information on the overseas operation, any special features of the work, what will need to be done to adjust to local conditions, career progression overseas, re-entry policy on completion of the assignment, pay, and special benefits such as home leave and children's education.

Preparation policy

The preparation policy for overseas assignments should include the provision of cultural familiarization for the country(ies) in which the expatriate will work (sometimes called 'acculturization'), the preferred approach to leading and working in international teams, and the business and HR policies that will apply.

Training

Tarique and Calligiri (1995) propose that the following steps should be taken to design a training programme for expatriates:

1. Identify the type of global assignment, eg technical, functional, tactical, developmental or strategic/executive.
2. Conduct a cross-cultural training needs analysis covering organizational analysis and requirements, assignment analysis of key tasks and individual analysis of skills.
3. Establish training goals and measures – cognitive (eg understanding the role of cultural values and norms) and affective (modifying perception about culture and increasing confidence in dealing with individual behaviours to form adaptive behaviours such as interpersonal skills).
4. Develop the programme – the content should cover both general and specific cultural orientation; a variety of methods should be used.
5. Evaluate training given.

Assimilation and review policies

Assimilation policies will provide for the adaptation of expatriates to overseas posts and their progress in them to be monitored and reviewed. This may take the form of conventional performance management processes, but additional information may be provided on potential and the ability of individuals to cope with overseas conditions. Where a number of expatriates are employed it is customary for someone at headquarters to have the responsibility of looking after them.

Re-entry policies

Re-entry policies should be designed to minimize the problems that can arise when expatriates return to their parent company after an overseas posting. They want to be assured that they will be given a position appropriate to their qualifications, and they will be concerned about their careers, suspecting that their overseas experience will not be taken into account. Policies should allow time for expatriates to adjust. The provision of mentors or counsellors is desirable.

Pay and allowances policies

The factors that are likely to impact on the design of reward systems as suggested by Bradley et al (1999) are the corporate culture of the multinational enterprise, expatriate and local labour markets, local cultural sensitivities and legal and institutional factors. They refer to the choice that has to be made between seeking internal consistency by developing common reward policies in order to facilitate the movement of employees across borders and preserve internal equity, and responding to pressures to conform to local practices. But they point out that: 'Studies of cultural differences suggest that reward system design and management need to be tailored to local values to enhance the performance of overseas operations.' As Sparrow (1999b) asserts: 'Differences in international reward are not just a consequence of cultural differences, but also of differences in international influences, national business systems and the role and competence of managers in the sphere of HRM.'

The policy of most organizations is to ensure that expatriates are no worse off because they have been posted abroad. In practice, various additional allowances or payments, such as hardship allowances, mean that they are usually better off financially than if they had stayed at home. The basic choice is whether to adopt a home-based or host-based policy for expatriates.

Home-based pay

The home-based pay approach aims to ensure that the value of the salary of expatriates is the same as in their home country. The home-base salary may be a notional one for long-term assignments (ie the salary which it is assumed would be paid to expatriates were they employed in a job of equivalent level at the parent company). For shorter-term assignments it may be the actual salary of the individual. The notional or actual home-base salary is used as the foundation upon which the total remuneration package is built. This is sometimes called the 'build-up' or 'balance sheet' approach.

The salary 'build-up' starts with the actual or notional home-base salary. To it is added a cost of living adjustment, which is applied to 'spendable income' – the portion of salary that would be used at home for everyday living. It usually excludes income tax, social security, pensions and insurance and can exclude discretionary expenditure on major purchases or holidays on the grounds that these do not constitute day-to-day living expenses.

The expatriate's salary would then consist of the actual or notional home-base salary plus the cost of living adjustment. In addition, it may be necessary to adjust salaries to take account of the host country's tax regime in order to achieve tax equalization. Moves of less than a year that might give rise to double taxation require particular attention.

Some or all of the following allowances may be added to this salary:

- 'incentive to work abroad' premium;
- hardship and location;

- housing and utilities;
- school fees;
- 'rest and recuperation' leave.

Host-based pay

The host-based pay approach provides expatriates with salaries and benefits such as company cars and holidays that are in line with those given to nationals of the host country in similar jobs. This method ensures equity between expatriates and host country nationals. It is adopted by companies using the so-called 'market rate' system, which ensures that the salaries of expatriates match the market levels of pay in the host country.

Companies using the host-based approach commonly pay additional allowances such as school fees, accommodation and medical insurance. They may also fund long-term benefits like social security, life assurance and pensions from home.

The host-based method is certainly equitable from the viewpoint of local nationals, and it can be less expensive than home-based pay. But it may be much less attractive as an inducement for employees to work abroad, especially in unpleasant locations, and it can be difficult to collect market rate data locally to provide a basis for setting pay levels.

Part II

Human resource management processes

Human resource management processes are those concerned with the development of HR strategies (strategic HRM), policies and practices that affect all aspects of HR and employment management. This part also covers other processes that affect most aspects of HRM, namely competency-based approaches, knowledge management and role and competency analysis.

7

Strategic HRM

An important defining characteristic of human resource management is that it is strategic. This characteristic is expressed by the concept of strategic HRM – an integrated approach to the development of HR strategies that enable the organization to achieve its goals. To understand the notion of strategic HRM it is necessary to appreciate the concept of strategy upon which it is based, and this is considered in the first section of the chapter. This leads into a definition of the concept of strategic HRM followed by expositions of its aims and approaches.

THE CONCEPT OF STRATEGY

Strategy has been defined by Johnson and Scholes (1993) as: 'The direction and scope of an organization over the longer term, which ideally matches its resources to its changing environment, and in particular, to its markets, customers and clients to meet stakeholder expectations.'

Strategy determines the direction in which the organization is going in relation to its environment. It is the process of defining intentions (*strategic intent*) and allocating or matching resources to opportunities and needs (*resource-based strategy*). Business strategy is concerned with achieving *competitive advantage*. The effective development and implementation of strategy depends on the *strategic capability* of the organization's managers. As expressed in the Professional Standards of the CIPD, this means the capacity to create an achievable vision for the future, to foresee longer-term developments, to envisage options (and their probable consequences), to select sound courses of action, to rise above the day-to-day detail, to challenge the *status quo*. Strategy is expressed in *strategic goals* and developed and implemented in *strategic plans* through the process of *strategic management*. Strategy is about implementation, which includes the management of change, as well as planning. An important aspect of strategy is the need to achieve *strategic fit*. This is used in three senses:

1. matching the organization's capabilities and resources to the opportunities available in the external environment;
2. matching one area of strategy, eg human resource management, to the business strategy; and
3. ensuring that different aspects of a strategy area cohere and are mutually supportive.

The concept of strategy is not a straightforward one. There are many different theories about what it is and how it works. Mintzberg *et al* (1988) suggest that strategy can have a number of meanings, namely:

●   *A plan*, or something equivalent – a direction, a guide, a course of action.
●   *A pattern*, that is, consistency in behaviour over time.
●   *A perspective*, an organization's fundamental way of doing things.
●   *A ploy*, a specific 'manoeuvre' intended to outwit an opponent or a competitor.

The formulation of corporate strategy can be defined as a process for developing and defining a sense of direction. It has often been described as a logical, step-by-step affair, the outcome of which is a formal written statement that provides a definitive guide to the organization's long-term intentions. Many people still believe that this is the case, but it is a misrepresentation of reality. In practice the formulation of strategy is never as rational and linear a process as some writers describe it or as some managers attempt to make it.

Mintzberg (1987) believes that strategy formulation is not necessarily rational and continuous. In theory, he says, strategy is a systematic process: first we think, then we act; we formulate then we implement. But we also 'act in order to think'. In practice, 'a realized strategy can emerge in response to an evolving situation' and the strategic planner is often 'a pattern organizer, a learner if you like, who manages a process in which strategies and visions can emerge as well as be deliberately conceived'. He has emphasized the concept of 'emergent strategies', and a key aspect of this process is the production of something that is new to the organization even if it is not developed as logically as the traditional corporate planners believed to be appropriate.

Tyson (1997) confirms that:

- strategy has always been emergent and flexible – it is always 'about to be', it never exists at the present time;
- strategy is not only realized by formal statements but also comes about by actions and reactions;
- strategy is a description of a future-oriented action that is always directed towards change;
- the management process itself conditions the strategies that emerge.

STRATEGIC HRM DEFINED

Strategic HRM is an approach to making decisions on the intentions and plans of the organization in the shape of the policies, programmes and practices concerning the employment relationship, resourcing, learning and development, performance management, reward, and employee relations. The concept of strategic HRM is derived from the concepts of HRM and strategy. It takes the HRM model with its focus on strategy, integration and coherence and adds to that the key notions of strategy, namely, strategic intent, resource-based strategy, competitive advantage, strategic capability and strategic fit.

Strategic HRM and HR strategies

Strategic HRM is an approach to the strategic management of human resources in accordance with the intentions of the organization on the future direction it wants to take. What emerges from this process is a stream of decisions over time that form the pattern adopted by the organization for managing its human resources and which define the areas in which specific HR strategies need to be developed. These focus on the decisions of the organization on what needs to be done and what needs to be changed in particular areas of people management.

The meaning of strategic HRM

According to Hendry and Pettigrew (1986), strategic HRM has four meanings:

1. the use of planning;
2. a coherent approach to the design and management of personnel systems based on an employment policy and manpower strategy and often underpinned by a 'philosophy';
3. matching HRM activities and policies to some explicit business strategy;
4. seeing the people of the organization as a 'strategic resource' for the achievement of 'competitive advantage'.

Purcell (2001) draws attention to the implications for strategic HRM of the concept of strategy as an emerging rather than a deliberate process:

> Big strategies in HRM are most unlikely to come, *ex cathedra*, from the board as a fully formed, written strategy or planning paper. Strategy is much more intuitive and often only 'visible' after the event, seen as 'emerging patterns of action'. This is especially the case when most of the strategy, as in HRM, is to do with internal implementation and performance strategies, not exclusively to do with external market ploys.

Strategic HRM as an integrated process

Strategic HRM is essentially an integrated process that aims to achieve 'strategic fit'. A strategic HRM approach produces HR strategies that are integrated vertically with the business strategy and are ideally an integral part of that strategy, contributing to the business planning process as it happens. Walker (1992) defines strategic HRM as 'the means of aligning the management of human resources with the strategic content of the business'. Vertical integration is necessary to provide congruence between business and human resource strategy so that the latter supports the accomplishment of the former and, indeed, helps to define it. Strategic HRM is also about horizontal integration, which aims to ensure that the different elements of the HR strategy fit together and are mutually supportive.

AIMS OF STRATEGIC HRM

The fundamental aim of strategic HRM is to generate a perspective on the way in which critical issues relating to people can be addressed. It enables strategic decisions to be made that have a major and long-term impact on the behaviour and success of the organization by ensuring that the organization has the skilled, committed and well-motivated employees it needs to achieve sustained competitive advantage. Its rationale is the advantage of having an agreed and understood basis for developing approaches to people management in the longer term by providing a sense of direction in an often turbulent environment. As Dyer and Holder (1998) remark, strategic HRM should provide 'unifying frameworks which are at once broad, contingency based and integrative'.

When examining the aims of strategic HRM it is necessary to consider the need for HR strategy to take into account the interests of all the stakeholders in the organization, employees in general as well as owners and management. In Storey's (1989) terms, 'soft strategic HRM' will place greater emphasis on the human relations aspect of people management, stressing continuous development, communication, involvement, security of employment, the quality of working life and work-life balance. Ethical considerations will be important. 'Hard strategic HRM' on the other hand will emphasize the yield to be obtained by investing in human resources in the interests of the business. This is also the philosophy of human capital management.

Strategic HRM should attempt to achieve a proper balance between the hard and soft elements. All organizations exist to achieve a purpose and they must ensure that they have the resources required to do so, and that they use them effectively. But they should also take into account the human considerations contained in the concept of soft strategic HRM. In the words of Quinn Mills (1983) they should plan with people in mind, taking into account the needs and aspirations of all the members of the organization. The problem is that hard considerations in many businesses will come first, leaving soft ones some way behind.

APPROACHES TO STRATEGIC HRM

Strategic HRM adopts an overall resource-based philosophy, as described below. Within this framework there are three possible approaches, namely, high-performance management (high-performance working), high-commitment management and high-involvement management.

Resource-based strategic HRM

A resource-based approach to strategic HRM focuses on satisfying the human capital requirements of the organization. The notion of resource-based strategic HRM is based on the ideas of Penrose (1959), who wrote that the firm is 'an administrative organization and a collection of productive resources'. It was developed by Hamel and Prahalad (1989), who declared that competitive advantage is obtained if a firm can obtain and develop human resources that enable it to learn faster and apply its learning more effectively than its rivals. Barney (1991) states that sustained competitive advantage stems from the acquisition and effective use of bundles of distinctive resources that competitors cannot imitate. As Purcell et al (2003) suggest, the values and HR policies of an organization constitute an important non-imitable resource. This is achieved by ensuring that:

- the firm has higher quality people than its competitors;
- the unique intellectual capital possessed by the business is developed and nurtured;
- organizational learning is encouraged;
- organization-specific values and a culture exist which 'bind the organization together (and) gives it focus'.

The aim of a resource-based approach is to improve resource capability – achieving strategic fit between resources and opportunities and obtaining added value from the effective deployment of resources. In line with human capital theory, resource-based theory emphasizes that investment in people adds to their value to the firm. Resource-based strategy, as Barney (1991) indicates, can develop strategic capability and produce what Boxall and Purcell (2003) refer to as 'human resource advantage'.

The high-performance management approach

High-performance working involves the development of a number of interrelated processes which together make an impact on the performance of the firm through its people in such areas as productivity, quality, levels of customer service, growth, profits and, ultimately, the delivery of increased shareholder value. This is achieved by 'enhancing the skills and engaging the enthusiasm of employees' (Stevens, 1998). According to Stevens, the starting point is leadership, vision and benchmarking to create a sense of momentum and direction. Progress must be measured constantly. He suggests that the main drivers, support systems and culture are:

- decentralized, devolved decision-making made by those closest to the customer – so as constantly to renew and improve the offer to customers;
- development of people capacities through learning at all levels, with particular emphasis on self-management and team capabilities – to enable and support performance improvement and organizational potential;
- performance, operational and people management processes aligned to organizational objectives – to build trust, enthusiasm and commitment to the direction taken by the organization;
- fair treatment for those who leave the organization as it changes, and engagement with the needs of the community outside the organization – this is an important component of trust and commitment-based relationships both within and outside the organization.

High-performance management practices include rigorous recruitment and selection procedures, extensive and relevant learning and development activities, incentive pay systems and performance management processes.

The strategy may be expressed as a drive to develop a performance culture in an organization. In the box below is an example of the high-performance strategy formulated by the Corporation of London.

The fundamental business need the strategy should meet is to develop and maintain a high performance culture. The characteristics of such a culture are:

- a clear line of sight exists between the strategic aims of the authority and those of its departments and its staff at all levels;
- management defines what it requires in the shape of performance improvements, sets goals for success and monitors performance to ensure that the goals are achieved;
- leadership from the top, which engenders a shared belief in the importance of continuing improvement;
- focus on promoting positive attitudes that result in a committed and motivated workforce;
- performance management processes aligned to the authority's objectives to ensure that people are engaged in achieving agreed goals and standards;
- capacities of people developed through learning at all levels to support performance improvement;
- people provided with opportunities to make full use of their skills and abilities;
- people valued and rewarded according to their contribution.

The high-commitment management model

One of the underpinning characteristics of HRM is its emphasis on the importance of enhancing mutual commitment (Walton, 1985b). High-commitment management has been described by Wood (1996) as:

> A form of management which is aimed at eliciting a commitment so that behaviour is primarily self-regulated rather than controlled by sanctions and pressures external to the individual, and relations within the organization are based on high levels of trust.

The approaches to creating a high-commitment organization as defined by Beer *et al* (1984) and Walton (1985b) are:

- the development of career ladders and emphasis on trainability and commitment as highly valued characteristics of employees at all levels in the organization;
- a high level of functional flexibility with the abandonment of potentially rigid job descriptions;
- the reduction of hierarchies and the ending of status differentials;
- a heavy reliance on team structure for disseminating information (team briefing), structuring work (team working) and problem solving (quality circles).

Wood and Albanese (1995) added to this list:

- job design as something management consciously does in order to provide jobs that have a considerable level of intrinsic satisfaction;
- a policy of no compulsory lay-offs or redundancies and permanent employment guarantees, with the possible use of temporary workers to cushion fluctuations in the demand for labour;
- new forms of assessment and payment systems and, more specifically, merit pay and profit sharing;
- a high involvement of employees in the management of quality.

Approaches to achieving commitment are described in Chapter 19.

High-involvement management

This approach involves treating employees as partners in the enterprise whose interests are respected and who have a voice on matters that concern them. It is concerned with communication and involvement. The aim is to create a climate in which a continuing dialogue between managers and the members of their teams take place to define expectations and share information on the organization's mission, values and objectives. This establishes mutual understanding of what *is* to be achieved and a framework for managing and developing people to ensure that it *will* be achieved.

The following high-involvement work practices have been identified by Pil and McDuffie (1999):

- 'on-line' work teams;
- 'off-line' employee involvement activities and problem-solving groups;
- job rotation;
- suggestion programmes;
- decentralization of quality efforts.

IMPLEMENTING STRATEGIC HRM

The implementation of strategic HRM is carried out within the framework of the approaches described above. The overarching imperative will be to achieve human resource advantage. A high-performance approach will emphasize the importance of creating and maintaining a performance culture, and both high-commitment and high-involvement management will contribute to the development of a committed and engaged workforce. Strategic HRM involves the formulation and implementation of specific strategies in each area of HRM as described in the next two chapters.

8

HR strategies

Strategic HRM leads to the formulation of HR strategies. In this chapter:

- HR strategies are defined;
- the purpose of HR strategies is examined;
- the distinction is made between strategic HRM and HR strategies;
- types of HR strategies are described with examples;
- criteria for an effective HR strategy are given.

HR STRATEGIES DEFINED

HR strategies set out what the organization intends to do about the different aspects of its human resource management policies and practices. They will be integrated with the business strategy and each other. HR strategies are described by Dyer and Reeves (1995) as 'internally consistent bundles of human resource practices', and in the words of Boxall (1996), they provide 'a framework of critical ends and means'. Richardson and Thompson (1999) suggest that:

> A strategy, whether it is an HR strategy or any other kind of management strategy must have two key elements: there must be strategic objectives (ie things the strategy is supposed to achieve), and there must be a plan of action (ie the means by which it is proposed that the objectives will be met.

PURPOSE

The purpose of HR strategies is to guide HRM development and implementation programmes. They provide a means of communicating to all concerned the intentions of the organization about how its human resources will be managed. They provide the basis for strategic plans and enable the organization to measure progress and evaluate outcomes against objectives. HR strategies provide visions for the future but they are also vehicles that define the actions required and how the vision should be realized. As Gratton (2000) commented: 'There is no great strategy, only great execution.'

THE DISTINCTION BETWEEN STRATEGIC HRM AND HR STRATEGIES

Strategic HRM as described in the last chapter is the process that results in the formulation of HR strategies. The terms 'strategic HRM' and 'HR strategy' are often used interchangeably, but a distinction can be made between them.

Strategic HRM can be regarded as a general approach underpinned by a philosophy to the strategic management of human resources in accordance with the intentions of the organization on the future direction it wants to take. What emerges from this process is a stream of decisions over time that form the pattern adopted by the organization for managing its human resources and define the areas in which specific HR strategies need to be developed. HR strategies will focus on the intentions of the organization on what needs to be done and what needs to be changed.

TYPES OF HR STRATEGIES

Because all organizations are different, all HR strategies are different. Research into HR strategy conducted by Armstrong and Long (1994) and Armstrong and Baron (2002) revealed many variations. Some strategies are simply very general declarations of intent; others go into much more detail. But two basic types of HR strategies can be identified: 1) overarching strategies; and 2) specific strategies relating to the different aspects of human resource management.

Overarching HR strategies

Overarching strategies describe the general intentions of the organization about how people should be managed and developed, what steps should be taken to ensure that the organization can attract and retain the people it needs, and ensure so far as possible that employees are committed, motivated and engaged. They are likely to be expressed as broad-brush statements of aims and purpose that set the scene for more specific strategies. They are concerned with overall organizational effectiveness – achieving human resource advantage by, as Boxall and Purcell (2003) explain, employing 'better people in organizations with better process', developing high-performance work systems and generally creating a great place to work.

The following are some examples of overarching HR strategy statements.

Aegon

'*The Human Resources Integrated Approach* aims to ensure that from whatever angle staff now look at the elements of pay management, performance, career development and reward, they are consistent and linked.'

B&Q

'Enhance employee commitment and minimize the loss of B&Q's best people. Position B&Q as one of the best employers in the UK.'

Egg

'The major factor influencing HR strategy was the need to attract, maintain and retain the right people to deliver it. The aim was to introduce a system that complemented the business, that reflected the way we wanted to treat our customers – treating our people the same. What we would do for our customers we would also do for our people. We wanted to make an impact on the culture – the way people do business.' (*HR Director*)

GlaxoSmithKline

'We want GSK to be a place where the best people do their best work.'

An insurance company

'Without the people in this business we don't have anything to deliver. We are driven to getting the people issues right in order to deliver the strategy. To a great extent it's the people that create and implement the strategy on behalf of the organization. We put people very much at the front of our strategic thought process. If we have the right people, the right training, the right qualifications and the right sort of culture then we can deliver our strategy. We cannot do it otherwise.' (*Chief Executive*)

Lands' End

'Based on the principle that staff who are enjoying themselves, are being supported and developed, and who feel fulfilled and respected at work, will provide the best service to customers.'

Pilkington Optronics

'The business strategy defines what has to be done to achieve success and that HR strategy must complement it, bearing in mind that one of the critical success factors for the company is its ability to attract and retain the best people. HR strategy must be in line with what is best in industry.'

A public utility

'The only HR strategy you really need is the tangible expression of values and the implementation of values... unless you get the human resource values right you can forget all the rest'. (*Managing Director*)

A manufacturing company

'The HR strategy is to stimulate changes on a broad front aimed ultimately at achieving competitive advantage through the efforts of our people. In an industry of fast followers, those who learn quickest will be the winners.' (*HR Director*)

A retail stores group

'The biggest challenge will be to maintain (our) competitive advantage and to do that we need to maintain and continue to attract very high calibre people. The key differentiator on anything any company does is fundamentally the people, and I think that people tend to forget that they are the most important asset. Money is easy to get hold of, good people are not. All we do in terms of training and manpower planning is directly linked to business improvement.' (*Managing Director*)

Specific HR strategies

Specific HR strategies set out what the organization intends to do in areas such as:

- *Talent management* – how the organization intends to 'win the war for talent'.
- *Continuous improvement* – providing for focused and continuous incremental innovation sustained over a period of time.

- *Knowledge management* – creating, acquiring, capturing, sharing and using knowledge to enhance learning and performance.
- *Resourcing* – attracting and retaining high quality people.
- *Learning and developing* – providing an environment in which employees are encouraged to learn and develop.
- *Reward* – defining what the organization wants to do in the longer term to develop and implement reward policies, practices and processes that will further the achievement of its business goals and meet the needs of its stakeholders.
- *Employee relations* – defining the intentions of the organization about what needs to be done and what needs to be changed in the ways in which the organization manages its relationships with employees and their trade unions.

The following are some examples of specific HR strategies.

The Children's Society

- Implement the rewards strategy of the Society to support the corporate plan and secure the recruitment, retention and motivation of staff to deliver its business objectives.
- Manage the development of the human resources information system to secure productivity improvements in administrative processes.
- Introduce improved performance management processes for managers and staff of the Society.
- Implement training and development which supports the business objectives of the Society and improves the quality of work with children and young people.

Diageo

There are three broad strands to the 'Organization and People Strategy':

1. *Reward and recognition*: use recognition and reward programmes to stimulate outstanding team and individual performance contributions.
2. *Talent management*: drive the attraction, retention and professional growth of a deep pool of diverse, talented employees.
3. *Organizational effectiveness*: ensure that the business adapts its organization to maximize employee contribution and deliver performance goals.

It provides direction to the company's talent, operational effectiveness and performance and reward agendas. The company's underlying thinking is that the people strategy is not for the human resource function to own but is the responsibility of the whole organization, hence the title 'Organization and People Strategy'.

A government agency

The key components of the HR strategy are:

- Investing in people – improving the level of intellectual capital.
- Performance management – integrating the values contained in the HR strategy into performance management processes and ensuring that reviews concentrate on how well people are performing those values.
- Job design – a key component concerned with how jobs are designed and how they relate to the whole business.
- The reward system – in developing rewards strategies, taking into account that this is a very hard driven business.

HR strategies for higher education institutions (The Higher Education Funding Council)

1. Address recruitment and retention difficulties in a targeted and cost-effective manner.
2. Meet specific staff development and training objectives that not only equip staff to meet their current needs but also prepare them for future changes, such as using new technologies for learning and teaching. This would include management development.
3. Develop equal opportunity targets with programmes to implement good practice throughout an institution. This would include ensuring equal pay for work of equal value, using institution-wide systems of job evaluation. This could involve institutions working collectively – regionally or nationally.
4. Carry out regular reviews of staffing needs, reflecting changes in market demands and technology. The reviews would consider overall numbers and the balance of different categories of staff.
5. Conduct annual performance reviews of all staff, based on open and objective criteria, with reward connected to the performance of individuals including, where appropriate, their contribution to teams.
6. Take action to tackle poor performance.

A local authority

The focus is on the organization of excellence. The strategy is broken down into eight sections: employee relations, recruitment and retention, training, performance management, pay and benefits, health and safety, absence management and equal opportunities.

CRITERIA FOR AN EFFECTIVE HR STRATEGY

An effective HR strategy is one that works in the sense that it achieves what it sets out to achieve. In particular, it:

- will satisfy business needs;
- is founded on detailed analysis and study, not just wishful thinking;
- can be turned into actionable programmes that anticipate implementation requirements and problems;
- is coherent and integrated, being composed of components that fit with and support each other;
- takes account of the needs of line managers and employees generally as well as those of the organization and its other stakeholders. As Boxall and Purcell (2003) emphasize: 'HR planning should aim to meet the needs of the key stakeholder groups involved in people management in the firm.'

Here is a comment from a chief executive (Peabody Trust) on what makes a good HR strategy:

A good strategy is one which actually makes people feel valued. It makes them knowledgeable about the organization and makes them feel clear about where they sit as a group, or team, or individual. It must show them how what they do either together or individually fits into that strategy. Importantly, it should indicate how people are going to be rewarded for their contribution and how they might be developed and grow in the organization.

9

Developing and implementing HR strategies

There is an ever-present risk that the concept of strategic HRM can become somewhat nebulous – nice to have but hard to realize. The danger of creating a rhetoric/reality gap is acute. Broad and often bland statements of strategic intent can be readily produced. What is much more difficult is to turn them into realistic plans that are then implemented effectively. Strategic HRM is more about getting things done than thinking about them. It leads to the formulation of HR strategies that first define what an organization intends to do in order to attain defined goals in overall human resource management policy and in particular areas of HR process and practice, and secondly set out how they will be implemented.

Difficult though it may be, a strategic approach is desirable in order to give a sense of direction and purpose and as a basis for the development of relevant and coherent HR policies and practices.

This chapter starts by giving general consideration to the development process, setting out various propositions and describing the levels of strategic decision-making. Reference is also made to the existence of strategic options and choices. This provides the background against which the approaches to formulating and implementing HR strategies are described.

PROPOSITIONS ABOUT THE DEVELOPMENT PROCESS

The following propositions about the formulation of HR strategy have been drawn up by Boxall (1993) from the literature:

- the strategy formation process is complex, and excessively rationalistic models that advocate formalistic linkages between strategic planning and HR planning are not particularly helpful to our understanding of it;
- business strategy may be an important influence on HR strategy but it is only one of several factors;
- implicit (if not explicit) in the mix of factors that influence the shape of HR strategies is a set of historical compromises and trade-offs from stakeholders.

It is also necessary to stress that coherent and integrated HR strategies are only likely to be developed if the top team understands and acts upon the strategic imperatives associated with the employment, development and motivation of people. This will be achieved more effectively if there is an HR director who is playing an active and respected role as a business partner. A further consideration is that the effective implementation of HR strategies depends on the involvement, commitment and cooperation of line managers and staff generally. Finally, there is too often a wide gap between the rhetoric of strategic HRM and the reality of its impact, as Gratton *et al* (1999) emphasize. Good intentions can too easily be subverted by the harsh realities of organizational life. For example, strategic objectives such as increasing commitment by providing more security and offering training to increase employability may have to be abandoned or at least modified because of the short-term demands made on the business to increase shareholder value.

The development process as described below takes place at different levels and involves analysing options and making choices. A methodology is required for the process that can be conducted by means of a strategic review. The methodology can be applied in three different ways. One of the most important aims in the development programme will be to align the HR strategy to the organizational culture and the business strategy by achieving vertical integration or fit.

LEVELS OF STRATEGIC DECISION-MAKING

Ideally, the formulation of HR strategies is conceived as a process, which is closely aligned to the formulation of business strategies. HR strategy can influence as well as be influenced by business strategy. In reality, however, HR strategies are more likely to flow from business strategies, which will be dominated by product/market and financial considerations. But there is still room for HR to make a useful, even essential contribution at the stage when business strategies are conceived, for example by focusing on resource issues. This contribution may be more significant if strategy formulation is an emergent or evolutionary process – HR strategic issues will then be dealt with as they arise during the course of formulating and implementing the corporate strategy.

A distinction is made by Purcell (1989) between:

- *'upstream' first-order decisions*, which are concerned with the long-term direction of the enterprise or the scope of its activities;
- *'downstream' second-order decisions*, which are concerned with internal operating procedures and how the firm is organized to achieve its goals;
- *'downstream' third-order decisions*, which are concerned with choices on human resource structures and approaches and are strategic in the sense that they establish the basic parameters of employee relations management in the firm.

It can indeed be argued that HR strategies, like other functional strategies such as product development, manufacturing and the introduction of new technology, will be developed within the context of the overall business strategy, but this need not imply that HR strategies come third in the pecking order. Observations made by Armstrong and Long (1994) during research into the strategy formulation processes of 10 large UK organizations suggested that there were only two levels of strategy formulation: 1) the corporate strategy relating to the vision and mission of the organization but often expressed in terms of marketing and financial objectives; 2) the specific strategies within the corporate strategy concerning product-market development, acquisitions and divestments, human resources, finance, new technology, organization, and such overall aspects of management as quality, flexibility, productivity, innovation and cost reduction.

STRATEGIC OPTIONS AND CHOICES

The process of developing HR strategies involves generating strategic HRM options and then making appropriate strategic choices. It has been noted by Cappelli (1999) that: 'The choice of practices that an employer pursues is heavily contingent on a number of factors at the organizational level, including their own business and production strategies, support of HR policies, and co-operative labour relations.' The process of developing HR strategies involves the adoption of a contingent approach in generating strategic HRM options and then making appropriate strategic choices. There is seldom if ever one right way forward.

Choices should relate to but also anticipate the critical needs of the business. They should be founded on detailed analysis and study, not just wishful thinking, and should incorporate the experienced and collective judgement of top management about the organizational requirements while also taking into account the needs of line managers and employees generally. The emerging strategies should anticipate the problems of implementation that may arise if line managers are not committed to the strategy and/or lack the skills and time to play their part, and the strategies should be capable of being turned into actionable programmes.

APPROACHES TO HR STRATEGY DEVELOPMENT

The starting point of HR strategy development is the alignment of HR strategy to the business strategy and the organizational culture – the achievement of vertical integration. This provides the necessary framework for the three approaches to the development of HR strategies that have been identified by Delery and Doty (1996) as the 'universalistic', the 'contingency' and the 'configurational'. Richardson and Thompson (1999) redefined the first two approaches as best practice and best fit, and retained the word 'configurational', meaning the use of 'bundles', as the third approach.

Aligning HR strategy

A fundamental requirement in developing HR strategy is that it should be aligned to the business strategy (vertical integration) and should fit the organizational culture. Everything else flows from this process of alignment.

Integration with the business strategy

The key business issues that may impact on HR strategies include:

- intentions concerning growth or retrenchment, acquisitions, mergers, divestments, diversification, product/market development;
- proposals on increasing competitive advantage through innovation leading to product/service differentiation, productivity gains, improved quality/customer service, cost reduction (downsizing);

● the felt need to develop a more positive, performance-oriented culture and any other culture management imperatives associated with changes in the philosophies of the organization in such areas as gaining commitment, mutuality, communications, involvement, devolution and teamworking.

Business strategies may be influenced by HR factors, although not excessively so. HR strategies are concerned with making business strategies work. But the business strategy must take into account key HR opportunities and constraints.

Wright and Snell (1998) suggest that seeking fit requires knowledge of the skills and behaviour needed to implement the strategy, knowledge of the HRM practices necessary to elicit those skills and behaviours, and the ability quickly to implement the desired system of HRM practices.

A framework for aligning HR and business strategies is provided by a competitive strategy approach that relates the different HR strategies to the firm's competitive strategies, including those listed by Porter (1985). An illustration of how this might be expressed is given in Table 9.1.

Culture fit

HR strategies need to be congruent with the existing culture of the organization, or designed to produce cultural change in specified directions. This will be a necessary factor in the formulation stage but could be a vital factor when it comes to implementation. In effect, if what is proposed is in line with 'the way we do things around here', then it will be more readily accepted. However, in the more likely event that it changes 'the way we do things around here', then careful attention has to be given to the real problems that may occur in the process of trying to embed the new initiative in the organization.

The best practice approach

This approach is based on the assumption that there is a set of best HRM practices and that adopting them will inevitably lead to superior organizational performance. Four definitions of best practice are given in Table 9.2.

The 'best practice' rubric has been attacked by a number of commentators. Cappelli and Crocker-Hefter (1996) comment that the notion of a single set of best practices has been overstated: 'There are examples in virtually every industry of firms that have very distinctive management practices... Distinctive human resource practices shape the core competencies that determine how firms compete.'

Purcell (1999) has also criticized the best practice or universalist view by pointing out the inconsistency between a belief in best practice and the resource-based view

Table 9.1 Linking HR and competitive strategies

Competitive Strategy	HR Strategy		
	Resourcing	**HR Development**	**Reward**
Achieve competitive advantage through innovation	Recruit and retain high quality people with innovative skills and a good track record in innovation.	Develop strategic capability and provide encouragement and facilities for enhancing innovative skills and enhancing the intellectual capital of the organization.	Provide financial incentives and rewards and recognition for successful innovations.
Achieve competitive advantage through quality	Use sophisticated selection procedures to recruit people who are likely to deliver quality and high levels of customer service.	Encourage the development of a learning organization, develop and implement knowledge management processes, support total quality and customer care initiatives with focused training.	Link rewards to quality performance and the achievement of high standards of customer service.
Achieve competitive advantage through cost-leadership	Develop core/ periphery employment structures; recruit people who are likely to add value; if unavoidable, plan and manage downsizing humanely	Provide training designed to improve productivity; inaugurate just-in-time training that is closely linked to immediate business needs and can generate measurable improvements in cost-effectiveness.	Review all reward practices to ensure that they provide value for money and do not lead to unnecessary expenditure.
Achieve competitive advantage by employing people who are better than those employed by competitors	Use sophisticated recruitment and selection procedures based on a rigorous analysis of the special capabilities required by the organization.	Develop organizational learning processes; encourage self-managed learning through the use of personal development plans as part of a performance management process.	Develop performance management processes which enable both financial and non-financial rewards to be related to competence and skills; ensure that pay levels are competitive.

Table 9.2 HRM best practices

Guest (1999a)	Patterson *et al* (1997)	Pfeffer (1994)	US Department of Labor (1993)
• Selection and the careful use of selection tests to identify those with potential to make a contribution • Training, and in particular a recognition that training is an on-going activity • Job design to ensure flexibility, commitment and motivation, including steps to ensure that employees have the responsibility and autonomy fully to use their knowledge and skills. • Communication to ensure that a two-way process keeps everyone fully informed • Employee share ownership programmes to increase employees' awareness of the implications of their actions, for the financial performance of the firm.	• Sophisticated selection and recruitment processes • Sophisticated induction programmes • Sophisticated training • Coherent appraisal systems • Flexibility of workforce skills • Job variety on shop floor • Use of formal teams • Frequent and comprehensive communication to workforce • Use of quality improvement teams • Harmonized terms and conditions • Basic pay higher than competition • Use of incentive schemes	• Employment security • Selective hiring • Self-managed teams • High compensation contingent on performance • Training to provide a skilled and motivated workforce • Reduction of status differentials • Sharing information	• Careful and extensive systems for recruitment, selection and training • Formal systems for sharing information with employees • Clear job design • High-level participation processes • Monitoring of attitudes • Performance appraisals • Properly functioning grievance procedures • Promotion and compensation schemes that provide for the recognition and reward of high-performing employees

which focuses on the intangible assets, including HR, that allow the firm to do better than its competitors. He asks how can 'the universalism of best practice be squared with the view that only some resources and routines are important and valuable by being rare and imperfectly imitable?' The danger, as Legge (1995) points out, is that of 'mechanistically matching strategy with HRM policies and practices'.

In accordance with contingency theory, which emphasizes the importance of interactions between organizations and their environments so that what organizations do is dependent on the context in which they operate, it is difficult to accept that there is any such thing as universal best practice. What works well in one organization will not necessarily work well in another because it may not fit its strategy, culture, management style, technology or working practices. As Becker *et al* (1997) remark, 'Organizational high-performance work systems are highly idiosyncratic and must be tailored carefully to each firm's individual situation to achieve optimum results.' But knowledge of best practice can inform decisions on what practices are most likely to fit the needs of the organization as long as it is understood *why* it is best practice. And Becker and Gerhart (1996) argue that the idea of best practice might be more appropriate for identifying the principles underlying the choice of practices, as opposed to the practices themselves.

The best fit approach

The best fit approach emphasizes the importance of ensuring that HR strategies are appropriate to the circumstances of the organization, including its culture, operational processes and external environment. HR strategies have to take account of the particular needs of both the organization and its people. For the reasons given above, it is accepted by most commentators that 'best fit' is more important than 'best practice'. There can be no universal prescriptions for HRM policies and practices. It all depends. This is not to say that 'good practice', or 'leading edge practice' ie practice that does well in one successful environment, should be ignored. 'Benchmarking' (comparing what the organization does with what is done elsewhere) is a valuable way of identifying areas for innovation or development that are practised to good effect elsewhere by leading companies. But having learnt about what works and, ideally, what does not work in comparable organizations, it is up to the firm to decide what may be relevant in general terms and what lessons can be learnt that can be adapted to fit its particular strategic and operational requirements. The starting point should be an analysis of the business needs of the firm within its context (culture, structure, technology and processes). This may indicate clearly what has to be done. Thereafter, it may be useful to pick and mix various 'best practice' ingredients, and develop an approach that applies those that are appropriate in a way that is aligned to the identified business needs.

But there are problems with the best fit approach, as stated by Purcell (1999):

> Meanwhile, the search for a contingency or matching model of HRM is also limited by the impossibility of modelling all the contingent variables, the difficulty of showing their interconnection, and the way in which changes in one variable have an impact on others.

In Purcell's view, organizations should be less concerned with best fit and best practice and much more sensitive to processes of organizational change so that they can 'avoid being trapped in the logic of rational choice'.

The configurational approach (bundling)

As Richardson and Thompson (1999) comment, 'A strategy's success turns on combining "vertical" or external fit and "horizontal" or internal fit.' They conclude that a firm with bundles of HR practices should have a higher level of performance, provided it also achieves high levels of fit with its competitive strategy. Emphasis is given to the importance of 'bundling' – the development and implementation of several HR practices together so that they are interrelated and therefore complement and reinforce each other. This is the process of horizontal integration, which is also referred to as the adoption of a 'configurational mode' (Delery and Doty, 1996) or the use of 'complementarities' (MacDuffie, 1995), who explained the concept of bundling as follows:

> Implicit in the notion of a 'bundle' is the idea that practices within bundles are interrelated and internally consistent, and that 'more is better' with respect to the impact on performance, because of the overlapping and mutually reinforcing effect of multiple practices.

Dyer and Reeves (1995) note that: 'The logic in favour of bundling is straightforward… Since employee performance is a function of both ability and motivation, it makes sense to have practices aimed at enhancing both.' Thus there are several ways in which employees can acquire needed skills (such as careful selection and training) and multiple incentives to enhance motivation (different forms of financial and non-financial rewards). A study by Dyer and Reeves (1995) of various models listing HR practices which create a link between HRM and business performance found that the activities appearing in most of the models were involvement, careful selection, extensive training and contingent compensation.

The aim of bundling is to achieve coherence, which is one of the four 'meanings' of strategic HRM defined by Hendry and Pettigrew (1986). Coherence exists when a mutually reinforcing set of HR policies and practices have been developed that jointly contribute to the attainment of the organization's strategies for matching resources to organizational needs, improving performance and quality and, in commercial enterprises, achieving competitive advantage.

The process of bundling HR strategies (horizontal integration or fit) is an important aspect of the concept of strategic HRM. In a sense, strategic HRM is holistic; it is concerned with the organization as a total entity and addresses what needs to be done across the organization as a whole in order to enable it to achieve its corporate strategic objectives. It is not interested in isolated programmes and techniques, or in the *ad hoc* development of HR practices.

In their discussion of the four policy areas of HRM (employee influence, human resource management flow, reward systems and work systems) Beer *et al* (1984) suggested that this framework can stimulate managers to plan how to accomplish the major HRM tasks 'in a unified, coherent manner rather than in a disjointed approach based on some combination of past practice, accident and ad hoc response to outside pressures'.

The problem with the bundling approach is that of deciding which is the best way to relate different practices together. There is no evidence that one bundle is generally better than another, although the use of performance management practices and competence frameworks are two ways that are typically adopted to provide for coherence across a range of HR activities. *Pace* the findings of MacDuffie, there is no conclusive proof that in the UK bundling has actually improved performance.

METHODOLOGY FOR STRATEGY DEVELOPMENT

A methodology for formulating HR strategies was developed by Dyer and Holder (1998) as follows:

1. *Assess feasibility* – from an HR point of view, feasibility depends on whether the numbers and types of key people required to make the proposal succeed can be obtained on a timely basis and at a reasonable cost, and whether the behavioural expectations assumed by the strategy are realistic (eg retention rates and productivity levels).
2. *Determine desirability* – examine the implications of strategy in terms of sacrosanct HR policies (eg, a strategy of rapid retrenchment would have to be called into question by a company with a full employment policy).

3. *Determine goals* – these indicate the main issues to be worked on and they derive primarily from the content of the business strategy. For example, a strategy to become a lower-cost producer would require the reduction of labour costs. This in turn translates into two types of HR goals: higher performance standards (contribution) and reduced headcounts (composition).

4. *Decide means of achieving goals* – the general rule is that the closer the external and internal fit, the better the strategy, consistent with the need to adapt flexibly to change. External fit refers to the degree of consistency between HR goals on the one hand and the exigencies of the underlying business strategy and relevant environmental conditions on the other. Internal fit measures the extent to which HR means follow from the HR goals and other relevant environmental conditions, as well as the degree of coherence or synergy among the various HR means.

But many different routes may be followed when formulating HR strategies – there is no one right way. On the basis of their research in 30 well-known companies, Tyson and Witcher (1994) commented that: 'The different approaches to strategy formation reflect different ways to manage change and different ways to bring the people part of the business into line with business goals.'

In developing HR strategies, process may be as important as content. Tyson and Witcher (1994) also noted from their research that: 'The process of formulating HR strategy was often as important as the content of the strategy ultimately agreed. It was argued that by working through strategic issues and highlighting points of tension, new ideas emerged and a consensus over goals was found.'

Although HR strategies can and will emerge over a period of time, there is much to be said for adopting a systematic approach by conducting a strategic review.

CONDUCTING A STRATEGIC REVIEW

A strategic review systematically assesses strategy requirements in the light of an analysis of present and future business and people needs. Such a review provides answers to three basic questions:

1. Where are we now?
2. Where do we want to be in one, two or three years' time?
3. How are we going to get there?

The stages of a strategic review are illustrated in Figure 9.1.

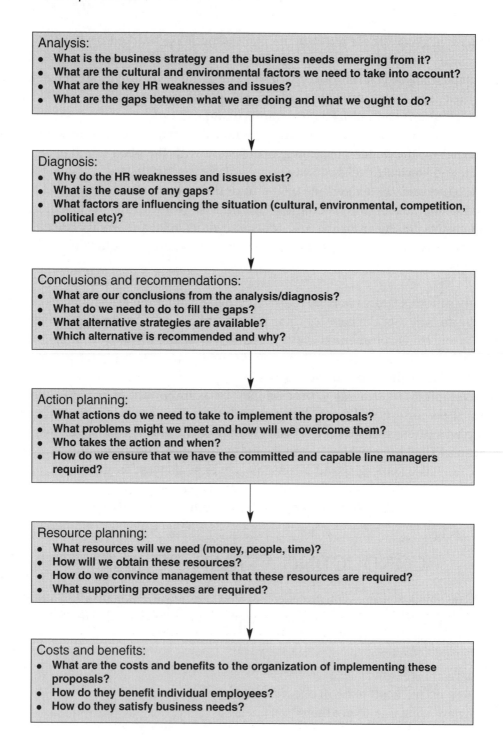

Figure 9.1 Strategic review sequence

SETTING OUT THE STRATEGY

A strategic review can provide the basis for setting out the strategy. There is no standard model for doing this, but the following headings are typical.

1. *Basis*
   - business needs in terms of the key elements of the business strategy;
   - analysis of business and environmental factors (SWOT/PESTLE);
   - cultural factors – possible helps or hindrances to implementation.
2. *Content* – details of the proposed HR strategy.
3. *Rationale* – the business case for the strategy against the background of business needs and environmental/cultural factors.
4. *Implementation plan*
   - action programme;
   - responsibility for each stage;
   - resources required;
   - proposed arrangements for communication, consultation, involvement and training;
   - project management arrangements.
5. *Costs and benefits analysis* – an assessment of the resource implications of the plan (costs, people and facilities) and the benefits that will accrue, for the organization as a whole, for line managers and for individual employees (so far as possible these benefits should be quantified in value-added terms).

IMPLEMENTING HR STRATEGIES

Getting HR strategies into action is not easy even if they have been developed by means of a systematic review and set out within a clear framework. Because strategies tend to be expressed as abstractions, they must be translated into programmes with clearly stated objectives and deliverables. The term 'strategic HRM' has been devalued in some quarters, sometimes to mean no more than a few generalized ideas about HR policies, at other times to describe a short-term plan, for example, to increase the retention rate of graduates. It must be emphasized that HR strategies are not just *ad hoc* programmes, policies, or plans concerning HR issues that the HR department happens to feel are important. Piecemeal initiatives do not constitute strategy.

The problem, as noted by Gratton *et al* (1999), is that too often there is a gap between what the strategy states will be achieved and what actually happens to it. As they put it:

One principal strand that has run through this entire book is the disjunction between rhetoric and reality in the area of human resource management, between HRM theory and HRM practice, between what the HR function says it is doing and how that practice is perceived by employees, and between what senior management believes to be the role of the HR function, and the role it actually plays.

The factors identified by Gratton *et al* that contributed to creating this gap include:

- the tendency of employees in diverse organizations only to accept initiatives they perceive to be relevant to their own areas;
- the tendency of long-serving employees to cling to the *status quo*;
- complex or ambiguous initiatives may not be understood by employees or will be perceived differently by them, especially in large, diverse organizations;
- it is more difficult to gain acceptance of non-routine initiatives;
- employees will be hostile to initiatives if they are believed to be in conflict with the organization's identity, eg downsizing in a culture of 'job-for-life';
- the initiative is seen as a threat;
- inconsistencies between corporate strategies and values;
- the extent to which senior management is trusted;
- the perceived fairness of the initiative;
- the extent to which existing processes could help to embed the initiative;
- a bureaucratic culture that leads to inertia.

Barriers to the implementation of HR strategies

Each of the factors listed by Gratton *et al* can create barriers to the successful implementation of HR strategies. Other major barriers include failure to understand the strategic needs of the business, inadequate assessment of the environmental and cultural factors that affect the content of the strategies, and the development of ill-conceived and irrelevant initiatives, possibly because they are current fads or because there has been a poorly digested analysis of best practice that does not fit the organization's requirements. These problems are compounded when insufficient attention is paid to practical implementation problems, the important role of line managers in implementing strategies, and the need to have established supporting processes for the initiative (eg, performance management to support performance pay).

Overcoming the barriers

To overcome these barriers it is necessary to:

- conduct a rigorous preliminary analysis of needs and requirements;
- formulate the strategy;
- enlist support for the strategy;
- assess barriers and deal with them;
- prepare action plans;
- project-manage implementation;
- follow up and evaluate progress so that remedial action can be taken as necessary.

10

HRM policies

WHAT HUMAN RESOURCE POLICIES ARE

HR policies are continuing guidelines on the approach the organization intends to adopt in managing its people. They define the philosophies and values of the organization on how people should be treated, and from these are derived the principles upon which managers are expected to act when dealing with HR matters. HR policies therefore serve as reference points when employment practices (described in Chapter 57) are being developed, and when decisions are being made about people. They help to define 'the way things are done around here'.

HR policies should be distinguished from procedures, as discussed in Chapter 58. A policy provides generalized guidance on the approach adopted by the organization, and therefore its employees, concerning various aspects of employment. A procedure spells out precisely what action should be taken in line with the policy.

WHY HAVE HR POLICIES

HR or employment policies help to ensure that when dealing with matters concerning people, an approach in line with corporate values is adopted throughout the organization. They serve as the basis for enacting values – converting espoused values into values in use. They provide frameworks within which consistent decisions are made, and promote equity in the way in which people are treated. Because they provide guidance on what managers should do in particular circumstances they facilitate empowerment, devolution and delegation. While they should fit the corporate culture, they can also help to shape it.

DO POLICIES NEED TO BE FORMALIZED?

All organizations have HR policies. Some, however, exist implicitly as a philosophy of management and an attitude to employees that is expressed in the way in which HR issues are handled; for example, the introduction of new technology. The advantage of explicit policies in terms of consistency and understanding may appear to be obvious, but there are disadvantages: written policies can be inflexible, constrictive, platitudinous or all three. To a degree, policies have often to be expressed in abstract terms, and managers do not care for abstractions. But they do prefer to know where they stand – people like structure – and formalized HR policies can provide the guidelines they need.

Formalized HR policies can be used in induction, team leader and management training to help participants understand the philosophies and values of the organization, and how they are expected to behave within that context. They are a means for defining the employment relationship and the psychological contract (see Chapters 15 and 16).

Although written policies are important, their value is reduced if they are not backed up by a supportive culture. This particularly applies to work-life balance policies.

HR POLICY AREAS

HR policies can be expressed as overall statements of the values of the organization. The main points that can be included in an overall policy statement and specific policy areas are set out below.

Overall policy

The overall policy defines how the organization fulfils its social responsibilities for its employees and sets out its attitudes towards them. It is an expression of its values or beliefs about how people should be treated. Peters and Waterman (1982) wrote that if they were asked for one all-purpose bit of advice for management, one truth that they could distil from all their research on what makes an organization excellent, it would be, 'Figure out your value system. Decide what the organization stands for.' Selznick (1957) emphasized the key role of values in organizations, when he wrote 'The formation of an institution is marked by the making of value commitments, that is, choices which fix the assumptions of policy makers as to the nature of the enterprise, its distinctive aims, methods and roles.'

The values expressed in an overall statement of HR policies may explicitly or implicitly refer to the following concepts:

- *Equity:* treating employees fairly and justly by adopting an 'even handed' approach. This includes protecting individuals from any unfair decisions made by their managers, providing equal opportunities for employment and promotion, and operating an equitable payment system.
- *Consideration:* taking account of individual circumstances when making decisions that affect the prospects, security or self-respect of employees.
- *Organizational learning:* a belief in the need to promote the learning and development of all the members of the organization by providing the processes and support required.
- *Performance through people:* the importance attached to developing a performance culture and to continuous improvement; the significance of performance management as a means of defining and agreeing mutual expectations; the provision of fair feedback to people on how well they are performing.
- *Work-life balance:* striving to provide employment practices that enable people to balance their work and personal obligations.
- *Quality of working life:* consciously and continually aiming to improve the quality of working life. This involves increasing the sense of satisfaction people obtain from their work by, so far as possible, reducing monotony, increasing variety, autonomy and responsibility, and avoiding placing people under too much stress.
- *Working conditions:* providing healthy, safe and so far as practicable pleasant working conditions.

These values are espoused by many organizations in one form or another, but to what extent are they practised when making 'business-led' decisions, which can of course be highly detrimental to employees if, for example, they lead to redundancy? One of the dilemmas facing all those who formulate HR policies is, how can we pursue business-led policies focusing on business success, and also fulfil our obligations to employees in such terms as equity, consideration, work-life balance, quality of working life and working conditions? To argue, as some do, that HR strategies should be entirely business-led seems to imply that human considerations are unimportant. Organizations have obligations to all their stakeholders, not just their owners.

It may be difficult to express these policies in anything but generalized terms, but employers are increasingly having to recognize that they are subject to external as well as internal pressures, which act as constraints on the extent to which they can disregard the higher standards of behaviour towards their employees that are expected of them.

Specific policies

The specific policies should cover the following areas as described below: equal opportunity, managing diversity, age and employment, promotion, work-life balance, employee development, reward, involvement and participation, employee relations, new technology, health and safety, discipline, grievances, redundancy, sexual harassment, bullying, substance abuse, smoking, AIDS, and e-mails.

Equal opportunity

The equal opportunity policy should spell out the organization's determination to give equal opportunities to all, irrespective of sex, race, creed, disability, age or marital status. The policy should also deal with the extent to which the organization wants to take 'affirmative action' to redress imbalances between numbers employed according to sex or race, or to differences in the levels of qualifications and skills they have achieved.

The policy could be set out as follows:

1. We are an equal opportunity employer. This means that we do not permit direct or indirect discrimination against any employee on the grounds of race, nationality, sex, sexual orientation, disability, religion, marital status or age.
2. Direct discrimination takes place when a person is treated less favourably than others are, or would be, treated in similar circumstances.
3. Indirect discrimination takes place when, whether intentionally or not, a condition is applied that adversely affects a considerable proportion of people of one race, nationality, sex, sexual orientation, religion or marital status, those with disabilities, or older employees.
4. The firm will ensure that equal opportunity principles are applied in all its HR policies, and in particular to the procedures relating to the recruitment, training, development and promotion of its employees.
5. Where appropriate and where permissible under the relevant legislation and codes of practice, employees of under-represented groups will be given positive training and encouragement to achieve equal opportunity.

Managing diversity

A policy on managing diversity recognizes that there are differences among employees and that these differences, if properly managed, will enable work to be done more efficiently and effectively. It does not focus exclusively on issues of discrimination, but instead concentrates on recognizing the differences between people. As Kandola and Fullerton (1994) express it, the concept of managing diversity 'is founded on the premise that harnessing these differences will create a productive environment in which everyone will feel valued, where their talents are fully utilized, and in which organizational goals are met'.

Managing diversity is a concept that recognizes the benefits to be gained from differences. It differs from equal opportunity, which aims to legislate against discrimination, assumes that people should be assimilated into the organization, and often relies on affirmative action.

A management of diversity policy could:

- acknowledge cultural and individual differences in the workplace;
- state that the organization values the different qualities people bring to their jobs;
- emphasize the need to eliminate bias in such areas as selection, promotion, performance assessment, pay and learning opportunities;
- focus attention on individual differences rather than group differences.

Age and employment

The policy on age and employment should take into account the following facts as listed by the CIPD:

- Age is a poor predictor of job performance.
- It is misleading to equate physical and mental ability with age.
- More of the population are living active, healthy lives as they get older.

The policy should define the approach the organization adopts to engaging, promoting and training older employees. It should emphasize that the only criterion for selection or promotion should be ability to do the job; and for training, the belief that the employee will benefit, irrespective of age. The policy should also state that age requirements should not be set out in external or internal job advertisements.

Promotion

A promotion policy could state the organization's intention to promote from within wherever this is appropriate as a means of satisfying its requirements for high quality staff. The policy could, however, recognize that there will be occasions when the organization's present and future needs can only be met by recruitment from outside. The point could be made that a vigorous organization needs infusions of fresh blood from time to time if it is not to stagnate. In addition, the policy might state that employees will be encouraged to apply for internally advertised jobs, and will not be held back from promotion by their managers, however reluctant the latter may be to lose them.

Work-life balance

Work-life balance policies define how the organization intends to allow employees greater flexibility in their working patterns so that they can balance what they do at work with the responsibilities and interests they have outside work. The policy will indicate how flexible work practices can be developed and implemented. It will emphasize that the numbers of hours worked must not be treated as a criterion for assessing performance. It will set out guidelines on specific arrangements that can be made, such as flexible hours, compressed working week, term-time working contracts, working at home, special leave for parents and carers, career breaks and various kinds of child care.

Employee development

The employee development policy could express the organization's commitment to the continuous development of the skills and abilities of employees in order to maximize their contribution and to give them the opportunity to enhance their skills, realize their potential, advance their careers and increase their employability both within and outside the organization.

Reward

The reward policy could cover such matters as:

- providing an equitable pay system;
- equal pay for work of equal value;
- paying for performance, competence, skill or contribution;
- sharing in the success of the organization (gain sharing or profit sharing);
- the relationship between levels of pay in the organization and market rates;
- the provision of employee benefits, including flexible benefits if appropriate;
- the importance attached to the non-financial rewards resulting from recognition, accomplishment, autonomy, and the opportunity to develop.

Involvement and participation

The involvement and participation (employee voice policy) should spell out the organization's belief in giving employees an opportunity to have a say in matters that affect them. It should define the mechanisms for employee voice, such as joint consultation and suggestion schemes.

Employee relations

The employee relations policy will set out the organization's approach to the rights of employees to have their interests represented to management through trade unions, staff associations or some other form of representative system. It will also cover the basis upon which the organization works with trade unions, for example, emphasizing that this should be regarded as a partnership.

New technology

A new technology policy statement could state that there will be consultation about the introduction of new technology, and the steps that would be taken by the organization to minimize the risk of compulsory redundancy or adversely affect other terms and conditions or working arrangements.

Health and safety

Health and safety policies cover how the organization intends to provide healthy and safe places and systems of work (see Chapter 55).

Discipline

The disciplinary policy should state that employees have the right to know what is expected of them and what could happen if they infringe the organization's rules. It would also make the point that, in handling disciplinary cases, the organization will treat employees in accordance with the principles of natural justice.

Grievances

The policy on grievances could state that employees have the right to raise their grievances with their manager, to be accompanied by a representative if they so wish, and to appeal to a higher level if they feel that their grievance has not been resolved satisfactorily.

Redundancy

The redundancy policy could state that it is the organization's intention to use its best endeavours to avoid involuntary redundancy through its redeployment and retraining procedures. However, if redundancy is unavoidable those affected will be given fair and equitable treatment, the maximum amount of warning, and every help that can be provided by the organization to obtain suitable alternative work.

Sexual harassment

The sexual harassment policy should state that:

1. Sexual harassment will not be tolerated.
2. Employees subjected to sexual harassment will be given advice, support and counselling as required.
3. Every attempt will be made to resolve the problem informally with the person complained against.
4. Assistance will be given to the employee to complain formally if informal discussions fail.
5. A special process will be available for hearing complaints about sexual harassment. This will provide for employees to bring their complaint to someone of their own sex if they so wish.
6. Complaints will be handled sensitively and with due respect for the rights of both the complainant and the accused.
7. Sexual harassment is regarded as gross industrial misconduct and, if proved, makes the individual liable for instant dismissal. Less severe penalties may be reserved for minor cases but there will always be a warning that repetition will result in dismissal.

Bullying

An anti-bullying policy will state that bullying will not be tolerated by the organization and that those who persist in bullying their staff will be subject to disciplinary action, which could be severe in particularly bad cases. The policy will make it clear that individuals who are being bullied should have the rights to discuss the problem with a management representative or a member of the HR function, and to make a complaint. The policy should emphasize that if a complaint is received it will be thoroughly investigated.

Substance abuse

A substance abuse policy could include assurances that:

- Employees identified as having substance abuse problems will be offered advice and help.
- Any reasonable absence from work necessary to receive treatment will be granted under the organization's sickness scheme provided that there is full cooperation from the employee.
- An opportunity will be given to the employee to discuss the matter once it has become evident or suspected that work performance is being affected by substance-related problems.
- The employee has the right to be accompanied by a friend or employee representative in any such discussion.
- Agencies will be recommended to which the employee can go for help if necessary.
- Employment rights will be safeguarded during any reasonable period of treatment.

Smoking

The smoking policy would define no-smoking rules including where, if at all, smoking is permitted.

AIDS

An AIDS policy could include the following points:

- The risks of infection in most workplaces are negligible.
- Where the occupation involves blood contact, as in hospitals, doctors' surgeries and laboratories, the special precautions advised by the Health and Safety Commission will be implemented.
- Employees who know that they are infected with AIDS will not be obliged to disclose the fact to the company, but if they do, the fact will remain completely confidential.
- There will be no discrimination against anyone with or at risk of acquiring AIDS.
- Employees infected by HIV or suffering from AIDS will be treated no differently from anyone else suffering a severe illness.

E-mails

The policy on e-mails could state that the sending or downloading of offensive e-mails is prohibited, and that those sending or downloading such messages will be subject to normal disciplinary procedures. They may also prohibit any browsing or downloading of material not related to the business, although this can be difficult to enforce. Some companies have always believed that reasonable use of the telephone is acceptable, and that policy may be extended to e-mails.

If it is decided that employees' e-mails should be monitored to check on excessive or unacceptable use, then this should be included in an e-mail policy which would therefore be part of the contractual arrangements. A policy statement could be included to the effect that 'The company reserves the right to access and monitor all e-mail messages created, sent, received or stored on the company's system'.

FORMULATING HR POLICIES

The following steps should be taken to formulate and implement HR policies:

1. Gain understanding of the corporate culture and its core values.
2. Analyse existing policies, written and unwritten. HR policies will exist in any organization, even if they are implicit rather than expressed formally.
3. Analyse external influences. HR policies are subject to the influence of UK employment legislation, European Community Employment Regulations, and the official codes of practice issued by bodies in the UK such as ACAS (Advisory, Conciliation and Arbitration Service), the EOC (Equal Opportunities Commission), the CRR (Commission on Racial Relations) and the Health and Safety Executive. The codes of practice issued by relevant professional institutions, such as the CIPD, should also be consulted.
4. Assess any areas where new policies are needed or existing policies are inadequate.
5. Check with managers, preferably starting at the top, on their views about HR policies and where they think they could be improved.
6. Seek the views of employees about the HR policies, especially the extent to which they are inherently fair and equitable and are implemented fairly and consistently. Consider doing this through an attitude survey.
7. Seek the views of union representatives.
8. Analyse the information obtained in the first seven steps and prepare draft policies.

9. Consult, discuss and agree policies with management and union representatives.

10. Communicate the policies, with guidance notes on their implementation as required (although they should be as self-explanatory as possible). Supplement this communication with training.

IMPLEMENTING HR POLICIES

The aim will be to implement policies fairly and consistently. Line managers have a key role in doing this. As pointed out by Purcell *et al* (2003), 'there is a need for HR policies to be designed for and focused on front line managers'. It is they who will be largely responsible for policy implementation. Members of the HR can give guidance, but it is line managers who are on the spot and have to make decisions about people. The role of HR is to communicate and interpret the policies, convince line managers that they are necessary, and provide training and support that will equip managers to implement them. As Purcell *et al* emphasize, it is line managers who bring HR policies to life.

11

Competency-based HRM

Competency-based HRM is about using the concept of competency and the results of competency analysis to inform and improve the processes of performance management, recruitment and selection, employee development and employee reward. The language has dominated much of HR thinking and practice in recent years.

The concept of competency has achieved this degree of prominence because it is essentially about performance. Mansfield (1999) defines competency as 'an underlying characteristic of a person that results in effective or superior performance'. Rankin (2002) describes competencies as 'definitions of skills and behaviours that organizations expect their staff to practice in their work' and explains that:

> Competencies represent the language of performance. They can articulate both the expected outcomes from an individual's efforts and the manner in which these activities are carried out. Because everyone in the organization can learn to speak this language, competencies provide a common, universally understood means of describing expected performance in many different contexts.

Competency-based HR is primarily based on the concepts of behavioural and technical competencies as defined in the first section of this chapter. But it is also associated with the use of National and Scottish Vocational qualifications (NVQs/SNVQs) as also examined in the first section. The next five sections of the chapter concentrate on the application and use of behavioural and technical competencies under the following headings:

- competency frameworks;
- reasons for using competencies;
- use of competencies;
- guidelines on the development of competency frameworks;
- keys to success in using competencies.

The final section describes the associated concept of emotional intelligence.

TYPES OF COMPETENCIES

The three types of competencies are behavioural competencies, technical competencies and NVQs and SNVQs.

Behavioural competencies

Behavioural competencies define behavioural expectations, ie the type of behaviour required to deliver results under such headings as teamworking, communication, leadership and decision-making. They are sometimes known as 'soft skills'. Behavioural competencies are usually set out in a competency framework.

The behavioural competency approach was first advocated by McClelland (1973). He recommended the use of criterion-referenced assessment. Criterion referencing or validation is the process of analysing the key aspects of behaviour that differentiate between effective and less effective performance.

But the leading figure in defining and popularizing the concept of competency in the USA and elsewhere was Boyatzis (1982). He conducted research that established that there was no single factor but a range of factors that differentiated successful from less successful performance. These factors included personal qualities, motives, experience and behavioural characteristics. Boyatzis defined competency as: 'capacity that exists in a person that leads to behaviour that meets the job demands within the parameters of the organizational environment and that, in turn, brings about desired results'.

The 'clusters' of competencies he identified were goal and action management, directing subordinates, human resource management and leadership. He made a distinction between threshold competencies, which are the basic competencies required to do a job, and performance competences, which differentiate between high and low performance.

Technical competencies

Technical competencies define what people have to know and be able to do (knowledge and skills) to carry out their roles effectively. They are related to either generic roles (groups of similar jobs), or individual roles (as 'role-specific competencies').

The term 'technical competency' has been adopted fairly recently to avoid the confusion that existed between the terms 'competency' and 'competence'. Competency, as mentioned above, is about behaviours, while competence as defined by Woodruffe (1990) is: 'A work-related concept which refers to areas of work at which the person is competent. Competent people at work are those who meet their performance expectations.' Competences are sometimes known as 'hard skills'. The terms technical competencies and competences are closely related although the latter has a particular and more limited meaning when applied to NVQs/SNVQs, as discussed below.

NVQ/SNVQ competences

The concept of competence was conceived in the UK as a fundamental part of the process of developing standards for NVQs/SNVQs. These specify minimum standards for the achievement of set tasks and activities expressed in ways that can be observed and assessed with a view to certification. An element of competence in NVQ language is a description of something that people in given work areas should be able to do. They are assessed on being competent or not yet competent. No attempt is made to assess the degree of competence.

COMPETENCY FRAMEWORKS

A competency framework contains definitions of all the behavioural competencies used in the whole or part of an organization. It provides the basis for the use of competencies in such areas as recruitment, employee development and reward. The 2003/4 *Competency and Emotional Intelligence* survey established that the 49 frameworks reviewed had a total of 553 competency headings. Presumably, many of these overlapped. The most common number of competencies was eight.

Competency headings

The competency headings included in the frameworks of 20 per cent or more of the organizations responding to the survey are shown in Table 11.1. The first seven of these are used in over 50 per cent of the respondents.

Table 11.1 Incidence of different competency headings

Competency heading	Summary definition	% used
Team orientation	The ability to work co-operatively and flexibly with other members of the team with a full understanding of the role to be played as a team member.	85
Communication	The ability to communicate clearly and persuasively, orally or in writing.	73
People management	The ability to manage and develop people and gain their trust and cooperation to achieve results.	67
Customer focus	The exercise of unceasing care in looking after the interests of external and internal customers to ensure that their wants, needs and expectations are met or exceeded.	65
Results orientation	The desire to get things done well and the ability to set and meet challenging goals, create own measures of excellence and constantly seek ways of improving performance.	59
Problem-solving	The capacity to analyse situations, diagnose problems, identify the key issues, establish and evaluate alternative courses of action and produce a logical, practical and acceptable solution.	57
Planning and organizing	The ability to decide on courses of action, ensuring that the resources required to implement the action will be available and scheduling the programme of work required to achieve a defined end-result.	51
Technical skills	Possession of the knowledge, understanding and expertise required to carry out the work effectively.	49
Leadership	The capacity to inspire individuals to give of their best to achieve a desired result and to maintain effective relationships with individuals and the team as a whole.	43
Business awareness	The capacity continually to identify and explore business opportunities, understand the business needs and priorities of of the organization and constantly to seek methods of ensuring that the organization becomes more business-like.	37
Decision-making	The capacity to make sound and practical decisions which deal effectively with the issues and are based on thorough analysis and diagnosis.	37
Change-orientation	The ability to manage and accept change.	33

continued

Table 11.1 *continued*

Developing others	The desire and capacity to foster the development of members of his or her team, providing feedback, support, encouragement and coaching.	33
Influence and persuasion	The ability to convince others to agree on or to take a course of action.	33
Initiative	The capacity to take action independently and to assume responsibility for one's actions.	29
Interpersonal skills	The ability to create and maintain open and constructive relationships with others, to respond helpfully to their requests and to be sensitive to their needs.	29
Strategic orientation	The capacity to take a long-term and visionary view of the direction to be followed in the future.	29
Creativity	The ability to originate new practices, concepts and ideas.	26
Information management	The capacity to originate and use information effectively.	26
Quality focus	The focus on delivering quality and continuous improvement.	24
Self-confidence and assertiveness	Belief in oneself and standing up for one's own rights.	24
Self-development	Managing one's own learning and development.	22
Managing	Managing resources, people, programmes and projects.	20

REASONS FOR USING COMPETENCIES

The two prime reasons for organizations to use competencies, as established by Miller *et al* (2001) were first, that the application of competencies to appraisal, training and other personnel processes will help to increase the performance of employees; and second, that competencies provide a means of articulating corporate values so that their requirements can be embodied in HR practices and be readily understood by individuals and teams within the organization. Other reasons include the use of competencies as a means of achieving cultural change and of raising skill levels.

COVERAGE OF COMPETENCIES

The Miller *et al* research found that employers adopted different approaches to the parts of the workforce covered by competencies:

- 22 per cent covered the whole workforce with a single set or framework of core competencies (modified in a further 10 per cent of employers by the incorporation of additional behavioural competencies for managers and other staff);
- 48 per cent confined competencies to specific work groups, functions or departments;
- 20 per cent have a core competency framework that covers all staff in respect of behavioural competencies, alongside sets of technical/functional or departments.

Subsequent research (Rankin, 2002) found that:

- 25 per cent of employers using behavioural competencies had a core framework;
- 19 per cent supplemented the core framework with additional competencies for single groups such as managers.

The 'menu' approach

Rankin notes that 21 per cent of respondents adopted a 'menu' approach. This enables competencies to be selected that are relevant to generic or individual roles. Approaches vary. Some organizations provide guidelines on the number of competencies to be selected (eg four to eight) and others combine their core framework with a menu so that users are required to select the organization-wide core competencies and add a number of optional ones.

Role-specific competencies

Role-specific competencies are also used by some organizations for generic or individual roles. These may be incorporated in a role profile in addition to information about the key output or result areas of the role. This approach is likely to be adopted by employers who use competencies in their performance management processes, but role-specific competencies also provide the basis for person specifications used in recruitment and for the preparation of individual learning programmes.

Graded competencies

A further, although less common, application of competencies is in graded career or job family structures (career or job families consist of jobs in a function or occupation such as marketing, operations, finance, IT, HR, administration or support services, which are related through the activities carried out and the basic knowledge and skills required, but in which the levels of responsibility, knowledge, skill or competence needed differ). In such families, the successive levels in each family are defined in terms of competencies as well as the key activities carried out. (Career and job family structures are described in Chapter 46.)

USE OF COMPETENCIES

The *Competency and Emotional Intelligence* 2003/4 survey found that 95 per cent of respondents used behavioural competencies and 66 per cent used technical competencies. It was noted that because the latter deal with specific activities and tasks they inevitably result in different sets of competencies for groups of related roles, functions or activities. The top four uses of competencies were:

1. Performance management – 89 per cent.
2. Training and development – 85 per cent.
3. Selection – 85 per cent.
4. Recruitment – 81 per cent.

Only 35 per cent of organizations link competencies to reward. The ways in which these competencies are used are described below.

Performance management

Competencies in performance management are used to ensure that performance reviews do not simply focus on outcomes but also consider the behavioural aspects of how the work is carried out that determine those outcomes. Performance reviews conducted on this basis are used to inform personal improvement and development plans and other learning and development initiatives.

As noted by *Competency and Emotional Intelligence* (2003/4): 'Increasingly, employers are extending their performance management systems to assess not only objectives but also qualitative aspects of the job.' The alternative approaches are: 1) the assessment has to be made by reference to the whole set of core competencies in the framework; or 2) the manager and the individual carry out a joint assessment of the latter's performance and agree on the competencies to be assessed, selecting those most relevant to the role. The joint assessments may be guided by examples known as 'behavioural indicators' of how the competency may be demonstrated in the employee's day-to-day work and in some cases the assessment is linked to defined levels of competency (see Chapter 33 for further details of how this process works).

Learning and development

Role profiles, which are either generic (covering a range of similar jobs) or individual (role-specific), can include statements of the technical competencies required. These can be used as the basis for assessing the levels of competency achieved by individuals and so identifying their learning and development needs.

Career family grade structures (see Chapter 46) can define the competencies required at each level in a career family. These definitions provide a career map showing the competencies people need to develop in order to progress their career.

Competencies are also used in development centres (see Chapter 40), which help participants build up their understanding of the competencies they require now and in the future so that they can plan their own self-directed learning programmes.

Recruitment and selection

The language of competencies is used in many organizations as a basis for the person specification, which is set out under competency headings as developed through role analysis. The competencies defined for a role are used as the framework for recruitment and selection.

A competencies approach can help to identify which selection techniques such as psychological testing are most likely to produce useful evidence. It provides the information required to conduct a structured interview in which questions can focus on particular competency areas to establish the extent to which candidates meet the specification as set out in competency terms.

In assessment centres, competency frameworks are used to define the competency dimensions that distinguish high performance. This indicates what exercises or simulations are required and the assessment processes that should be used.

Reward management

In the 1990s, when the competency movement came to the fore, the notion of linking pay to competencies – competency-related pay – emerged. But it has never taken off; only 8 per cent of the respondents to the e-reward 2004 survey of contingent pay used it. However, more recently, the concept of contribution-related pay has emerged, which provides for people to be rewarded according to both the results they achieve and their level of competence, and the e-reward 2004 survey established that 33 per cent of respondents had introduced it.

Another application of competencies in reward management is that of career family grade and pay structures.

DEVELOPING A COMPETENCY FRAMEWORK

The language used in competency frameworks should be clear and jargon-free. Without clear language and examples it can be difficult to assess the level of competency achieved. When defining competencies, especially when they are used for performance management or competency-related pay, it is essential to ensure that they can be assessed. They must not be vague or overlap with other competencies and they must specify clearly the sort of behaviour that is expected and the level of technical or functional skills (competencies) required to meet acceptable standards. As Rankin (2002) suggests, it is helpful to address the user directly ('you will...') and give clear and brief examples of how the competency needs to be performed.

Developing a behavioural competency framework that fits the culture and purpose of the organization and provides a sound basis for a number of key HR processes is not an undertaking to be taken lightly. It requires a lot of hard work, much of it concerned with involving staff and communicating with them to achieve understanding and buy-in. The steps required are described below.

Step 1. Programme launch

Decide on the purpose of the framework and the HR processes for where it will be used. Make out a business case for its development, setting out the benefits to the organization in such areas as improved performance, better selection outcomes, more focused performance management, employee development and reward processes. Prepare a project plan that includes an assessment of the resources required and the costs.

Step 2. Involvement and communication

Involve line managers and employees in the design of the framework (stages 3 and 4) by setting up a task force. Communicate the objectives of the exercise to staff.

Step 3. Framework design – competency list

First, get the task force to draw up a list of the core competencies and values of the business – what it should be good at doing and the values it believes should influence behaviour. This provides a foundation for an analysis of the competencies required by people in the organization. The aim is to identify and define the behaviours that contribute to the achievement of organizational success, and there should be a powerful link between these people competencies and the organization's core competencies (more guidance on defining competencies is provided in Chapter 13).

The production of the list may be done by brainstorming. The list should be compared with examples of other competency frameworks. The purpose of this comparison is not to replicate other lists. It is essential to produce a competency framework that fits and reflects the organization's own culture, values, core competencies and operations. But referring to other lists will help to clarify the conclusions reached in the initial analysis and serve to check that all relevant areas of competency have been included. When identifying competencies care must be taken to avoid bias because of sex or race.

Step 4. Framework design – definition of competencies

Care needs to be exercised to ensure that definitions are clear and unambiguous and that they will serve their intended purpose. If, for example, one of the purposes is to provide criteria for conducting performance reviews, then it is necessary to be certain that the way the competency is defined, together with supporting examples, will enable fair assessments to be made. The following four questions have been produced by Mirabile (1998) to test the extent to which a competency is valid and can be used:

1. Can you describe the competency in terms that others understand and agree with?
2. Can you observe it being demonstrated or failing to be demonstrated?
3. Can you measure it?
4. Can you influence it in some way, eg by training, coaching or some other method of development?

It is also important at this stage to ensure that definitions are not biased.

Step 5. Define uses of competency framework

Define exactly how it is intended the competency framework should be used, covering such applications as performance management, recruitment, learning and development, and reward.

Step 6. Test the framework

Test the framework by gauging the reactions of a balanced selection of line managers and other employees to ensure that they understand it and believe that it is relevant to their roles. Also pilot test the framework in live situations for each of its proposed applications.

Step 7. Finalize the framework

Amend the framework as necessary following the tests and prepare notes for guidance on how it should be used.

Step 8. Communicate

Let everyone know the outcome of the project – what the framework is, how it will be used and how people will benefit. Group briefings and any other suitable means should be used.

Step 9. Train

Give line managers and HR staff training in how to use the framework.

Step 10. Monitor and evaluate

Monitor and evaluate the use of the framework and amend it as required.

DEFINING TECHNICAL COMPETENCIES

Technical competencies are most often produced for generic roles within job families or functions, although they can be defined for individual roles as 'role-specific competencies'. They are not usually part of a behaviour-based competency framework, although of course the two are closely linked when considering and assessing role demands and requirements. Guidelines on defining technical competencies are provided in Chapter 13.

KEYS TO SUCCESS IN USING COMPETENCIES

The keys to success in using competencies are:

- frameworks should not be over-complex;
- there should not be too many headings in a framework – seven or eight will often suffice;
- the language used should be clear and jargon-free;
- competencies must be selected and defined in ways that ensure they can be assessed by managers – the use of 'behavioural indicators' is helpful;
- frameworks should be regularly updated.

EMOTIONAL INTELLIGENCE

Goleman (1995) has defined emotional intelligence as: 'The capacity for recognizing our own feelings and that of others, for motivating ourselves, for managing emotions well in ourselves as well as others.' The four components of emotional intelligence are:

1. *Self-management* – the ability to control or redirect disruptive impulses and moods and regulate your own behaviour coupled with a propensity to pursue goals with energy and persistence. The six competencies associated with this component are self-control, trustworthiness and integrity, initiative, adaptability – comfort with ambiguity, openness to change and strong desire to achieve.
2. *Self-awareness* – the ability to recognize and understand your moods, emotions and drives as well as their effect on others. This is linked to three competencies: self-confidence, realistic self-assessment and emotional self-awareness.
3. *Social awareness* – the ability to understand the emotional makeup of other people and skill in treating people according to their emotional reactions. This is linked to six competencies: empathy, expertise in building and retaining talent, organizational awareness, cross-cultural sensitivity, valuing diversity and service to clients and customers.
4. *Social skills* – proficiency in managing relationships and building networks to get the desired result from others and reach personal goals, and the ability to find common ground and build rapport. The five competencies associated with this component are: leadership, effectiveness in leading change, conflict management, influence/communication, and expertise in building and leading teams.

According to Goleman it is not enough to have a high IQ (intelligence quotient); emotional intelligence is also required.

In 1998 Goleman defined emotional intelligence in a way that encompasses many of the areas covered by typical competency frameworks. Miller *et al* (2001) found that one-third of employers covered by their survey had consciously included emotional intelligence-type factors such as interpersonal skills in their frameworks.

Dulewicz and Higgs (1999) have produced a detailed analysis of how the emotional intelligence elements of self-awareness, emotional management, empathy, relationships, communication and personal style correspond to competencies such as sensitivity, flexibility, adaptability, resilience, impact, listening, leadership, persuasiveness, motivating others, energy, decisiveness and achievement motivation. They conclude that there are distinct associations between competency modes and elements of emotional intelligence.

As noted by Miller *et al* (2001), a quarter of the employers they surveyed have provided or funded training that is based on emotional intelligence. The most common areas are in leadership skills, people management skills and teamworking. The application of emotional intelligence concepts to management development is dealt with in Chapter 40.

12

Knowledge management

Knowledge management is concerned with storing and sharing the wisdom, understanding and expertise accumulated in an organization about its processes, techniques and operations. It treats knowledge as a key resource. As Ulrich (1998) comments, 'Knowledge has become a direct competitive advantage for companies selling ideas and relationships.' There is nothing new about knowledge management. Hansen *et al* (1999) remark that 'For hundreds of years, owners of family businesses have passed on their commercial wisdom to children, master craftsmen have painstakingly taught their trades to apprentices, and workers have exchanged ideas and know-how on the job.' But they also remark that, 'As the foundation of industrialized economies has shifted from natural resources to intellectual assets, executives have been compelled to examine the knowledge underlying their business and how that knowledge is used.'

Knowledge management deals as much with people and how they acquire, exchange and disseminate knowledge as with information technology. That is why it has become an important area for HR practitioners, who are in a strong position to exert influence in this aspect of people management. Scarborough *et al* (1999) believe that they should have 'the ability to analyse the different types of knowledge deployed by the organization... [and] to relate such knowledge to issues of organizational design, career patterns and employment security.'

The concept of knowledge management is closely associated with intellectual capital theory as described in Chapter 2 in that it refers to the notions of human, social and organizational or structural capital. It is also linked to the concepts of organizational learning and the learning organization as discussed in Chapter 36. Knowledge management is considered in this chapter under the following headings:

- definition of the process of knowledge management;
- the concept of knowledge;
- types of knowledge;
- the purpose and significance of knowledge management;
- approaches to knowledge management;
- knowledge management issues;
- the contribution of HR to knowledge management.

KNOWLEDGE MANAGEMENT DEFINED

Knowledge management is 'any process or practice of creating, acquiring, capturing, sharing and using knowledge, wherever it resides, to enhance learning and performance in organizations' (Scarborough *et al*, 1999). They suggest that it focuses on the development of firm-specific knowledge and skills that are the result of organizational learning processes. Knowledge management is concerned with both stocks and flows of knowledge. Stocks included expertise and encoded knowledge in computer systems. Flows represent the ways in which knowledge is transferred from people to people or from people to a knowledge database. Knowledge management has also been defined by Tan (2000) as: 'The process of systematically and actively managing and leveraging the stores of knowledge in an organization'.

Knowledge management involves transforming knowledge resources by identifying relevant information and then disseminating it so that learning can take place. Knowledge management strategies promote the sharing of knowledge by linking people with people, and by linking them to information so that they learn from documented experiences.

Knowledge can be stored in databanks and found in presentations, reports, libraries, policy documents and manuals. It can be moved around the organization through information systems and by traditional methods such as meetings, workshops, courses, 'master classes', written publications, videos and tapes. The intranet provides an additional and very effective medium for communicating knowledge.

THE CONCEPT OF KNOWLEDGE

A distinction was made by Ryle (1949) between 'knowing how' and 'knowing that'. Knowing how is the ability of a person to perform tasks, and knowing that is holding pieces of knowledge in one's mind.

Blackler (1995) notes that 'Knowledge is multifaceted and complex, being both situated and abstract, implicit and explicit, distributed and individual, physical and mental, developing and static, verbal and encoded. He categorizes forms of knowledge as:

- *embedded* in technologies, rules and organizational procedures;
- *encultured* as collective understandings, stories, values and beliefs;
- *embodied* into the practical activity-based competencies and skills of key members of the organization (ie practical knowledge or 'know-how');
- *embraced* as the conceptual understanding and cognitive skills of key members (ie conceptual knowledge or 'know-how').

Nonaka (1991) suggests that knowledge is held either by individuals or collectively. In Blackler's terms, embodied or embraced knowledge is individual and embedded, and cultural knowledge is collective.

It can be argued (Scarborough and Carter, 2000) that knowledge emerges from the collective experience of work and is shared between members of a particular group or community.

It is useful to distinguish between data, information and knowledge:

- *data* consists of the basic facts – the building blocks for information and knowledge;
- *information* is data that have been processed in a way which is meaningful to individuals, it is available to anyone entitled to gain access to it; as Drucker (1988) wrote, 'information is data endowed with meaning and purpose';
- *knowledge* is information put to productive use; it is personal and often intangible and it can be elusive – the task of tying it down, encoding it and distributing it is tricky.

Explicit and tacit knowledge

Nonaka (1991) and Nonaka and Takeuchi (1995) stated that knowledge is either explicit or tacit. Explicit knowledge can be codified: it is recorded and available, and is held in databases, in corporate intranets and intellectual property portfolios.

Tacit knowledge exists in people's minds. It is difficult to articulate in writing and is acquired through personal experience. As suggested by Hansen *et al* (1999), it includes scientific or technological expertise, operational know-how, insights about an industry, and business judgement. The main challenge in knowledge management is how to turn tacit knowledge into explicit knowledge.

THE PURPOSE AND SIGNIFICANCE OF KNOWLEDGE MANAGEMENT

As explained by Blake (1998), the purpose of knowledge management is to capture a company's collective expertise and distribute it to 'wherever it can achieve the biggest payoff'. This is in accordance with the resource-based view of the firm which, as argued by Grant (1991), suggests that the source of competitive advantage lies within the firm (ie in its people and their knowledge), not in how it positions itself in the market. Trussler (1998) comments that 'the capability to gather, lever, and use knowledge effectively will become a major source of competitive advantage in many businesses over the next few years'. A successful company is a knowledge-creating company.

Knowledge management is about getting knowledge from those who have it to those who need it in order to improve organizational effectiveness. In the information age, knowledge rather than physical assets or financial resources is the key to competitiveness. In essence, as pointed out by Mecklenberg *et al* (1999), 'Knowledge management allows companies to capture, apply and generate value from their employees' creativity and expertise'.

APPROACHES TO KNOWLEDGE MANAGEMENT

The codification and personalization approaches

Two approaches to knowledge management have been identified by Hansen *et al* (1999):

1. *The codification strategy* – knowledge is carefully codified and stored in databases where it can be accessed and used easily by anyone in the organization. Knowledge is explicit and is codified using a 'people-to-document' approach. This strategy is therefore document driven. Knowledge is extracted from the person who developed it, made independent of that person and re-used for

various purposes. It will be stored in some form of electronic repository for people to use. This allows many people to search for and retrieve codified knowledge without having to contact the person who originally developed it. This strategy relies largely on information technology to manage databases and also on the use of the intranet.

2. *The personalization strategy* – knowledge is closely tied to the person who has developed it and is shared mainly through direct person-to-person contacts. This is a 'person-to-person' approach which involves sharing tacit knowledge. The exchange is achieved by creating networks and encouraging face-to-face communication between individuals and teams by means of informal conferences, workshops, brainstorming and one-to-one sessions.

Hansen *et al* state that the choice of strategy should be contingent on the organization; what it does, how it does it, and its culture. Thus consultancies such as Ernst & Young, using knowledge to deal with recurring problems, may rely mainly on codification so that recorded solutions to similar problems are easily retrievable. Strategy consultancy firms such as McKinsey or Bains, however, will rely mainly on a personalization strategy to help them to tackle the high-level strategic problems they are presented with, which demand the provision of creative, analytically rigorous advice. They need to channel individual expertise, and they find and develop people who are able to use a person-to-person knowledge-sharing approach effectively. In this sort of firm, directors or experts can be established who can be approached by consultants by telephone, e-mail or personal contact.

The research conducted by Hansen *et al* established that companies which use knowledge effectively pursue one strategy predominantly and use the second strategy to support the first. Those who try to excel at both strategies risk failing at both.

The knowledge-creating company

In the opinion of Nonaka and Takeuchi (1995), a core competitive activity of organizations is knowledge creation – 'an organic, fluid and socially constructed process in which different knowledges are blended to produce innovative outcomes that are predicted or predictable'. Fundamental to knowledge creation is the blending of tacit and explicit knowledge through processes of socialization (tacit to tacit), externalization (tacit to explicit), internalization (explicit to tacit) and combination (explicit to explicit).

The resource-based approach

Scarborough and Carter (2000) describe knowledge management as 'the attempt by management to actively create, communicate and exploit knowledge as a resource for the organization'. They suggest that this attempt has technical, social and economic components:

- In technical terms knowledge management involves centralizing knowledge that is currently scattered across the organization and codifying tacit forms of knowledge.
- In social and political terms, knowledge management involves collectivizing knowledge so that it is no longer the exclusive property of individuals or groups.
- In economic terms, knowledge management is a response by organizations to the need to intensify their creation and exploitation of knowledge.

KNOWLEDGE MANAGEMENT SYSTEMS

A survey of 431 US and European firms by Ruggles (1998) found that the following systems were used:

- Creating an intranet (47 per cent).
- Creating 'data warehouses', large physical databases that hold information from a wide variety of sources (33 per cent).
- Using decision support systems which combine data analysis and sophisticated models to support non-routine decision making (33 per cent).
- Using 'groupware', information communication technologies such as e-mail or Lotus Notes discussion bases, to encourage collaboration between people to share knowledge (33 per cent).
- Creating networks and communities of interest or practice of knowledge workers to share knowledge (24 per cent).
- Mapping sources of internal expertise by, for example, producing 'expert yellow pages' and directories of communities (18 per cent).

KNOWLEDGE MANAGEMENT ISSUES

The various approaches referred to above do not provide easy answers. The issues that need to be addressed in developing knowledge management processes are discussed below.

The pace of change

One of the main issues in knowledge management is how to keep up with the pace of change and identify what knowledge needs to be captured and shared.

Relating knowledge management strategy to business strategy

As Hansen *et al* (1999) show, it is not knowledge *per se* but the way it is applied to strategic objectives that is the critical ingredient in competitiveness. They point out that 'competitive strategy must drive knowledge management strategy', and that managements have to answer the question: 'How does knowledge that resides in the company add value for customers?' Mecklenberg *et al* (1999) argue that organizations should 'start with the business value of what they gather. If it doesn't generate value, drop it.'

Technology and people

Technology may be central to companies adopting a codification strategy but for those following a personalization strategy, IT is best used in a supportive role. As Hansen *et al* (1999) comment:

> In the codification model, managers need to implement a system that is much like a traditional library – it must contain a large cache of documents and include search engines that allow people to find and use the documents they need. In the personalization model, it's more important to have a system that allows people to find other people.

Scarborough *et al* (1999) suggest that 'technology should be viewed more as a means of communication and less as a means of storing knowledge'. Knowledge management is more about people than technology. As research by Davenport (1996) established, managers get two-thirds of their information from face-to-face or telephone conversations.

There is a limit to how much tacit knowledge can be codified. In organizations relying more on tacit than explicit knowledge, a person-to-person approach works best, and IT can only support this process; it cannot replace it.

The significance of process and social capital and culture

A preoccupation with technology may mean that too little attention is paid to the processes (social, technological and organizational) through which knowledge combines and interacts in different ways (Blackler, 1995). The key process is the interactions between people. This constitutes the social capital of an organization, ie the 'network of relationships [that] constitute a valuable resource for the conduct of social affairs' (Nahpiet and Ghoshal, 1998). Social networks can be particularly important in ensuring that knowledge is shared. What is also required is another aspect of social capital: trust. People will not be willing to share knowledge with those whom they do not trust.

The culture of the company may inhibit knowledge sharing. The norm may be for people to keep knowledge to themselves as much as they can because 'knowledge is power'. An open culture will encourage people to share their ideas and knowledge.

Knowledge workers

Knowledge workers as defined by Drucker (1993) are individuals who have high levels of education and specialist skills combined with the ability to apply these skills to identify and solve problems. As Argyris (1991) points out: 'The nuts and bolts of management... increasingly consists of guiding and integrating the autonomous but interconnected work of highly skilled people.' Knowledge management is about the management and motivation of knowledge workers who create knowledge and will be the key players in sharing it.

THE CONTRIBUTION OF HR TO KNOWLEDGE MANAGEMENT

HR can make an important contribution to knowledge management simply because knowledge is shared between people; it is not just a matter of capturing explicit knowledge through the use of information technology. The role of HR is to ensure that the organization has the intellectual capital it needs. The resource-based view of the firm emphasizes, in the words of Cappelli and Crocker-Hefter (1996), that 'distinctive human resource practices help to create unique competencies that differentiate products and services and, in turn, drive competitiveness'.

Ten ways in which HR can contribute

The main ways in which HR can contribute to knowledge management are summarized below and described in more detail in the rest of this section.

1. Help to develop an open culture in which the values and norms emphasize the importance of sharing knowledge.
2. Promote a climate of commitment and trust.

3. Advise on the design and development of organizations which facilitate knowledge sharing through networks and communities of practice (groups of people who share common concerns about aspects of their work), and teamwork.

4. Advise on resourcing policies and provide resourcing services which ensure that valued employees who can contribute to knowledge creation and sharing are attracted and retained.

5. Advise on methods of motivating people to share knowledge and rewarding those who do so.

6. Help in the development of performance management processes which focus on the development and sharing of knowledge.

7. Develop processes of organizational and individual learning which will generate and assist in disseminating knowledge.

8. Set up and organize workshops, conferences, seminars and symposia which enable knowledge to be shared on a person-to-person basis.

9. In conjunction with IT, develop systems for capturing and, as far as possible, codifying explicit and tacit knowledge.

10. Generally, promote the cause of knowledge management with senior managers to encourage them to exert leadership and support knowledge management initiatives.

Culture development

An open culture is one in which as Schein (1985) suggests, people contribute out of a sense of commitment and solidarity. Relationships are characterized by mutuality and trust. In such a culture, organizations place a high priority on mutual support, collaboration and creativity, and on constructive relationships. There is no 'quick fix' way in which a closed culture where these priorities do not exist can be converted into an open culture. Long-established cultures are difficult to change. HR can encourage management to develop purpose and value statements which spell out that an important aim of the organization is to achieve competitive advantage by developing and effectively using unique resources of knowledge and expertise, and that to achieve the aim, sharing knowledge is core value. Such statements may be rhetoric but they can be converted into reality through the various processes described below.

Promote a climate of commitment and trust

Gaining commitment is a matter of trying to get everyone to identify with the purpose and values of the organization, which will include processes for developing and sharing knowledge. Commitment can be enhanced by developing a strategy which will include the implementation of communication, education and training programmes, initiatives to increase involvement and 'ownership', and the introduction of performance and reward processes.

Developing a high-trust organization means creating trust between management and employees as a basis for encouraging trust between individual employees or groups of employees. People are more likely to trust management if its actions are fair, equitable, consistent and transparent, and if it keeps its word.

It is difficult although not impossible to develop trust between management and employees. But it is not possible to make individual employees trust one another, and such trust is important if knowledge is to be shared. Developing a climate of trust in the organization helps, otherwise it is a matter of developing social capital in the sense of putting people into positions where they have to work together, and encouraging interaction and networking so that individuals recognize the value of sharing knowledge because it helps achieve common and accepted aims. This process can be helped by team-building activities. Trust may also be enhanced if knowledge is exchanged as a matter of course in forums, conferences etc. Dialogue occurs between people who want to connect and are given opportunities to do so in a collaborative, creative and adaptive culture.

Organization design and development

HR can contribute to effective knowledge management by advising on the design of process-based organizations in which the focus is on horizontal processes that cut across organizational boundaries. Such organizations rely largely on networking and cross-functional or inter-disciplinary project teams or task forces, and knowledge-sharing is an essential part of the operation. Attention is paid to identifying and encouraging 'communities of practice' which, as defined by Wenger and Snyder (2000), are 'groups of people informally bound together by shared expertise and a passion for joint enterprise'. They are seen as important because it is within such communities that much of the organization's tacit knowledge is created and shared.

The role definitions that emerge from organization design activities should emphasize knowledge-sharing as both an accountability (a key result area) and a competency (an expected mode of behaviour). Thus it can become an accepted part of the fabric and therefore the culture of the organization.

Organizational development activities can focus on team-building in communities with an emphasis on processes of interaction, communication and participation. The aims would be to develop a 'sharing' culture.

Resourcing

HR contributes to enhancing knowledge management processes by advising on how to attract and retain people with the required skills and abilities, including those who are likely to exhibit the behaviours needed in a knowledge-sharing culture. This means devising competency frameworks for recruitment and development purposes which include knowledge-sharing as a key behaviour. Such a competency could be defined as 'The disposition to share knowledge fully and willingly with other members of the community'. Questions would be asked at the interview stage on the approach adopted by candidates to sharing knowledge in their present organization. Other questions along the lines of the one given below could be put to test candidates on their views:

> This organization relies to a considerable extent on achieving success through the development of new products and techniques. We believe that it is important to ensure that the knowledge generated by such developments is spread around the business as widely as possible to those who might put it to good use. What part do you think you could play as an individual in this process?

Posing this sort of question at the interview stage helps to define expectations as part of the psychological contract.

Assessment centres can also include exercises and tests designed to test the disposition and ability of individuals to share knowledge.

Retaining knowledge workers is a matter of providing a supportive workplace environment and motivating them through both tangible and intangible rewards as discussed below.

Motivation

A study by Tampoe (1993) identified four key motivators for knowledge workers:

1. Personal growth – the opportunity for individuals to fully realize their potential.
2. Occupational autonomy – a work environment in which knowledge workers can achieve the task assigned to them.
3. Task achievement – a sense of accomplishment from producing work that is of high quality and relevance to the organization.
4. Money rewards – an income that is a just reward for their contribution to corporate success and that symbolizes their contribution to that success.

Hansen *et al* (1999) state that in their 'codification model', managers need to develop a system that encourages people to write down what they know and to get these documents into the electronics depository. They believe that real incentives – not just enticements – are required to get people to take these steps. In companies following the personalization model, rewards for sharing knowledge directly with other people may have to be different. Direct financial rewards for contributing to the codification and sharing of knowledge may often be inappropriate, but this could be a subject for discussion in a performance review as part of a performance management process.

Performance management

The promotion and development of performance management processes by HR can make an important contribution to knowledge management, by providing for behavioural expectations which are related to knowledge-sharing to be defined, and ensuring that actual behaviours are reviewed and, where appropriate, rewarded by financial or non-financial means. Performance management reviews can identify weaknesses and development needs in this aspect and initiate personal development plans which are designed to meet these needs.

One starting point for the process could be the cascading of corporate core values for knowledge-sharing to individuals, so that they understand what they are expected to do to support those core values. As mentioned earlier, knowledge-sharing can be included as an element of a competency framework, and the desired behaviour would be spelt out and reviewed. For example, positive indicators such as those listed below could be used as a basis for agreeing competency requirements and assessing the extent to which they are met. The following are examples of positive behaviour in meeting competency expectations for knowledge-sharing:

- is eager to share knowledge with colleagues;
- takes positive steps to set up group meetings to exchange relevant information and knowledge;
- builds networks which provide for knowledge sharing;
- ensures as appropriate that knowledge is captured, codified, recorded and disseminated through the intranet and/or other means of communication.

Hansen *et al* mention that at Ernst & Young, consultants are evaluated at performance reviews along five dimensions, one of which is their 'contribution to and utilization of the knowledge asset of the firm'. At Bain, partners are evaluated each year on a variety of dimensions, including how much direct help they have given colleagues.

In a 360-degree feedback process (see Chapter 34), one of the dimensions for an assessment by colleagues and direct reports could be the extent to which an individual shares knowledge.

Organizational and individual learning

Organizational learning takes place when people learn collaboratively (Hoyle, 1995). It involves accumulating, analysing and utilizing knowledge resources which contribute to the achievement of business objectives. Knowledge management approaches as described in the chapter can make a major contribution to the enhancement of learning in an organization. Practices associated with creating the right environment for sharing knowledge will in particular promote organizational learning by creating a 'rich landscape of learning and development opportunities' (Kessels, 1996).

The concept of a learning organization (see Chapter 36) is also relevant. As defined by Miller and Stewart (1999), one of the characteristics of such an organization is that 'there are well-defined processes for defining, creating, capturing, sharing and acting on knowledge'. And Garvin (1993) postulates that learning organizations 'transfer knowledge quickly and efficiently throughout the organization by means of formal training programmes linked to implementation'.

Organizational learning, however, is based on individual learning, and the significance of knowledge management and the techniques available to support it can be learnt in formal training sessions or monitoring programmes designed and facilitated by the HR function.

Workshops and conferences etc

HR can play an important part in knowledge management by setting up and facilitating workshops, conferences, seminars and forums in which members exchange information and ideas, discuss what they have learnt and agree on what use can be made of the knowledge they have acquired. Apart from their value in disseminating knowledge, such gatherings can help to develop an environment in which knowledge-sharing is accepted as a natural and continuing activity.

Working with IT

Knowledge management is neither the preserve of the IT function nor that of HR. The two functions need to work together. IT ensures that knowledge is recorded and made acceptable through means such as the intranet. HR collaborates by providing means for tacit knowledge to be collected and, where feasible, codified.

Promoting the cause

Some organizations such as ICL have appointed a 'knowledge programme director' to develop corporate knowledge assets. Others have relied upon IT or business teams. But HR can make a major contribution not only in the specific activities referred to above, but also in generally promoting the cause of knowledge management, emphasizing to senior management at every opportunity the importance of developing a culture in which the significance of knowledge management is recognized.

13

Analysing roles, competencies and skills

Role analysis is a fundamental HR process. It provides the information needed to produce role profiles and for use in recruitment, learning and development, performance management and job evaluation. For reasons given below, the terms 'role analysis' and 'role profile' are rapidly replacing the terms 'job analysis' and 'job description'. However, role analysis uses basically the same techniques as job analysis and many features of role profiles are found in more traditional job descriptions. Job analysis is also still used to provide the data for job evaluation, as explained in Chapter 44.

In this chapter, role analysis is covered first and the chapter continues with descriptions of the associated techniques of competency and skills analysis.

ROLE ANALYSIS

Role analysis defined

Role analysis is the process of finding out what people are expected to achieve when carrying out their work and the competencies and skills they need to meet these expectations.

Role profiles

The result of role analysis is a role profile, which defines the outcomes role holders are expected to deliver in terms of key result areas or accountabilities. It also lists the competencies required to perform effectively in the role – what role holders need to know and be able to do. Profiles can be individual or generic (covering similar roles).

Roles and jobs

If it is used in its strictest sense, the term 'role' refers to the part people play in their work – the emphasis is on their behaviour. For example, a role profile may stress the need for flexibility. In this sense, a role can be distinguished from a job, which consists of a group of prescribed tasks/activities to be carried out or duties to be performed.

Job analysis defines those tasks or duties in order to produce a *job description*. This is usually prescriptive and inflexible. It spells out exactly what job holders are required to do. It gives people the opportunity to say: 'It's not in my job description', meaning that they only feel they have to do the tasks listed there.

Increasingly, the practice is to refer to roles, role analysis and role profiles rather than to jobs, job analysis and job descriptions. The latter are no longer in favour because they tend to be prescriptive, restrict flexibility and do not focus on outcomes or the competencies needed to achieve them. Role profiles are preferred because they are concerned with performance, results, and knowledge and skill requirements and are therefore in accord with the present-day emphasis on high-performance working, outcomes and competencies.

Purpose of role analysis

Role analysis aims to produce the following information about a role for use in recruitment, performance management and learning and development evaluation:

- *Overall purpose* – why the role exists and, in essence, what the role holder is expected to contribute.
- *Organization* – to whom the role holder reports and who reports to the role holder.
- *Key result areas or accountabilities* – what the role holder is required to achieve in each of the main elements of the role.
- *Competency requirements* – the specific technical competencies attached to the role; what the role holder is expected to know and to be able to do.

For job evaluation purposes, the role will also be analysed in terms of the factors used in the job evaluation scheme.

Role analysis may be carried out by HR or other trained people acting as role analysts. But line managers can also carry out role analysis in conjunction with individual members of their teams as an important part of their performance management responsibilities (see Chapter 33).

Approach to role analysis by specialized role analysts

The essence of role analysis is the application of systematic methods to the collection of the information required to produce a role profile under the headings set out above. The steps required to collect this information are:

1. Obtain documents such as the organization structure, existing job descriptions (treat these with caution, they are likely to be out of date), and procedure or training manuals that give information about the job.
2. Ask managers for fundamental information concerning the overall purpose of the role, the key result areas and the technical competencies required.
3. Ask the role holders similar questions about their roles.

The methods that can be used are interviews, questionnaires or observation.

Interviews

To obtain the full flavour of a role, it is best to interview role holders and check the findings with their managers or team leaders. The aim of the interview is to obtain all the relevant facts about the role to provide the information required for a role profile. It is helpful to use a checklist when conducting the interview. Elaborate checklists are not necessary; they only confuse people. The basic questions to be answered are:

1. What is the title of your role?
2. To whom are you responsible?
3. Who is responsible to you? (An organization chart is helpful.)
4. What is the main purpose of your role, ie in overall terms, what are you expected to do?
5. What are the key activities you have to carry out in your role? Try to group them under no more than 10 headings.
6. What are the results you are expected to achieve in each of those key activities?
7. What are you expected to know to be able to carry out your role?
8. What skills should you have to carry out your role?

The answers to these questions may need to be sorted out – they can often result in a mass of jumbled information that has to be analysed so that the various activities can be distinguished and refined to seven or eight key areas.

The advantages of the interviewing method are that it is flexible, can provide in-depth information and is easy to organize and prepare. It is therefore the most common approach. But interviewing can be time-consuming, which is why in large role analysis exercises, questionnaires as described below may be used to provide advance information about the job. This speeds up the interviewing process or even replaces the interview altogether, although this means that much of the 'flavour' of the job – ie what it is really like – may be lost.

Questionnaire

Questionnaires about their roles can be completed by role holders and approved by the role holder's manager or team leader. They are helpful when a large number of roles have to be covered. They can also save interviewing time by recording purely factual information and by enabling the analyst to structure questions in advance to cover areas that need to be explored in greater depth. The simpler the questionnaire the better. It need only cover the eight questions listed above.

The advantage of questionnaires is that they can produce information quickly and cheaply for a large number of jobs. But a substantial sample is needed, and the construction of a questionnaire is a skilled job that should only be carried out on the basis of some preliminary fieldwork. It is highly advisable to pilot test questionnaires before launching into a full-scale exercise. The accuracy of the results also depends on the willingness and ability of job holders to complete questionnaires. Many people find it difficult to express themselves in writing about their work.

Observation

Observation means studying role holders at work, noting what they do, how they do it, and how much time it takes. This method is most appropriate for routine administrative or manual roles, but it is seldom used because of the time it takes.

Role analysis as part of a performance management process

As explained in more detail in Chapter 33, the basis of performance planning and review processes is provided by a role profile. To develop a role profile it is necessary for the line manager and the individual to get together and agree the key result areas and competencies. The questions are similar to those that would be put by a role analyst, but for line managers can be limited to the following:

- What do you think are the most important things you have to do?
- What do you believe you are expected to achieve in each of these areas?
- How will you – or anyone else – know whether or not you have achieved them?
- What do you have to know and be able to do to perform effectively in these areas?
- What knowledge and skills in terms of qualifications, technical and procedural knowledge, problem-solving, planning and communication skills, etc do role holders need to carry out the role effectively?

This process requires some skill, which needs to be developed by training followed by practice. It is an area in which HR specialists can usefully coach and follow-up on a one-to-one basis after an initial training session.

Role profile content

Role profiles are set out under the following headings:

- *Role title.*
- *Department.*
- *Responsible to.*
- *Responsible to role holder.*
- *Purpose of the role* – defined in one reasonably succinct sentence that defines why the role exists in terms of the overall contribution the role holder makes.
- *Key result areas* – if at all possible these should be limited to seven or eight, certainly not more than 10. Each key result area should be defined in a single sentence beginning with an active verb (eg, identify, develop, support), which provides a positive indication of what has to be done and eliminates unnecessary wording. Describe the object of the verb (what is done) as succinctly as possible, for example: test new systems, post cash to the nominal and sales ledgers, schedule production, ensure that management accounts are produced, prepare marketing plans. State briefly the purpose of the activity in terms of outputs or standards to be achieved, for example: test new systems to ensure they meet agreed systems specifications, post cash to the nominal and sales ledgers in order to provide up-to-date and accurate financial information, schedule production in order to meet output and delivery targets, ensure that management accounts are produced that provide the required level of information to management and individual managers on financial performance against budget and on any variances, prepare marketing plans that support the achievement of the marketing strategies of the enterprise, are realistic, and provide clear guidance on the actions to be taken by the development, production, marketing and sales departments.

- *Need to know* – the knowledge required overall or in specific key result areas of the business and its competitors and customers, techniques, processes, procedures or products.
- *Need to be able to do* – the skills required in each area of activity.
- *Expected behaviour* – the behaviours particularly expected of the role holder (behavioural competencies), which may be extracted from the organization's competency framework.

An example of a role profile is given in Figure 13.1.

Role title: Database administrator

Department: Information systems

Purpose of role: Responsible for the development and support of databases and their underlying environment.

Key result areas
- ➤ Identify database requirements for all projects that require data management in order to meet the needs of internal customers.
- ➤ Develop project plans collaboratively with colleagues to deliver against their database needs.
- ➤ Support underlying database infrastructure.
- ➤ Liaise with system and software providers to obtain product information and support.
- ➤ Manage project resources (people and equipment) within predefined budget and criteria, as agreed with line manager and originating department.
- ➤ Allocate work to and supervise contractors on day-to-day basis.
- ➤ Ensure security of the underlying database infrastructure through adherence to established protocols and to develop additional security protocols where needed.

Need to know
- ➤ Oracle database administration.
- ➤ Operation of Designer 2000 and oracle forms SQL/PLSQL, Unix administration, shell programming.

Able to:
- ➤ Analyse and choose between options where the solution is not always obvious.
- ➤ Develop project plans and organize own workload on a timescale of 1–2 months.
- ➤ Adapt to rapidly changing needs and priorities without losing sight of overall plans and priorities.
- ➤ Interpret budgets in order to manage resources effectively within them.
- ➤ Negotiate with suppliers.
- ➤ Keep abreast of technical developments and trends, bring these into day-to-day work when feasible and build them into new project developments.

Behavioural competencies
- ➤ Aim to get things done well and set and meet challenging goals, create own measures of excellence and constantly seek ways of improving performance.
- ➤ Analyse information from range of sources and develop effective solutions/recommendations.
- ➤ Communicate clearly and persuasively, orally or in writing, dealing with technical issues in a non-technical manner.
- ➤ Work participatively on projects with technical and non-technical colleagues.
- ➤ Develop positive relationships with colleagues as the supplier of an internal service.

Figure 13.1   Example of a role profile

COMPETENCY ANALYSIS

Competency analysis uses behavioural analysis to establish the behavioural dimensions that affect role performance and produce competency frameworks. Functional analysis or a version of it can be used to define technical competencies.

Analysing behavioural competencies

There are six approaches to behavioural competency analysis. In ascending order of complexity these are:

1. expert opinion;
2. structured interview;
3. workshops;
4. critical-incident technique;
5. repertory grid analysis;
6. job competency assessment.

Expert opinion

The basic, crudest and least satisfactory method is for an 'expert' member of the HR department, possibly in discussion with other 'experts' from the same department, to draw up a list from their own understanding of 'what counts' coupled with an analysis of other published lists, such as those given in Chapter 11.

This is unsatisfactory because the likelihood of the competencies being appropriate, realistic and measurable in the absence of detailed analysis, is fairly remote. The list tends to be bland and, because line managers and job holders have not been involved, unacceptable.

Structured interview

This method begins with a list of competencies drawn up by 'experts' and proceeds by subjecting a number of role holders to a structured interview. The interviewer starts by identifying the key result areas of the role and goes on to analyse the behavioural characteristics that distinguish performers at different levels of competence.

The basic question is: 'What are the positive or negative indicators of behaviour that are conducive or non-conducive to achieving high levels of performance?' These may be analysed under such headings as:

- personal drive (achievement motivation);
- impact on results;
- analytical power;
- strategic thinking;
- creative thinking (ability to innovate);
- decisiveness;
- commercial judgement;
- team management and leadership;
- interpersonal relationships;
- ability to communicate;
- ability to adapt and cope with change and pressure;
- ability to plan and control projects.

In each area instances will be sought which illustrate effective or less effective behaviour.

One of the problems with this approach is that it relies too much on the ability of the expert to draw out information from interviewees. It is also undesirable to use a deductive approach, which pre-empts the analysis with a prepared list of competency headings. It is far better to do this by means of an inductive approach that starts from specific types of behaviour and then groups them under competence headings. This can be done in a workshop by analysing positive and negative indicators to gain an understanding of the competence dimensions of an occupation or job, as described below.

Workshops

Workshops bring a group of people together who have 'expert' knowledge or experience of the role – managers and role holders as appropriate – with a facilitator, usually but not necessarily a member of the HR department or an outside consultant.

The members of the workshop begin by getting agreement to the overall purpose of the role and its key result areas. They then develop examples of effective and less effective behaviour for each area, which are recorded on flipcharts. For example, one of the key result areas for a divisional HR director might be human resource planning, defined as: *Prepares forecasts of human resource requirements and plans for the acquisition, retention and effective utilization of employees, which ensure that the company's needs for people are met.*

The positive indicators for this competence area could include:

- seeks involvement in business strategy formulation;

- contributes to business planning by taking a strategic view of longer-term human resource issues that are likely to affect business strategy;
- networks with senior management colleagues to understand and respond to the human resource planning issues they raise;
- suggests practical ways to improve the use of human resources, for example the introduction of annual hours.

Negative indicators could include:

- takes a narrow view of HR planning – does not seem to be interested in or understand the wider business context;
- lacks the determination to overcome problems and deliver forecasts;
- fails to anticipate skills shortages, for example unable to meet the multiskilling requirements implicit in the new computer integrated manufacturing system;
- does not seem to talk the same language as line management colleagues – fails to understand their requirements;
- slow in responding to requests for help.

When the positive and negative indicators have been agreed the next step is to distil the competency dimensions that can be inferred from the lists. In this example they could be:

- strategic capability;
- business understanding;
- achievement motivation;
- interpersonal skills;
- communication skills;
- consultancy skills.

These dimensions might also be reflected in the analysis of other areas of competency so that, progressively, a picture of the competencies is built up that is linked to actual behaviour in the workplace.

The facilitator's job is to prompt, help the group to analyse its findings and assist generally in the production of a set of competence dimensions that can be illustrated by behaviour-based examples. The facilitator may have some ideas about the sort of headings that may emerge from this process, but should not try to influence the group to come to a conclusion that it has not worked out for itself, albeit with some assistance from the facilitator.

Workshops can use the critical incident or repertory grid techniques, as described below.

Critical-incident technique

The critical-incident technique is a means of eliciting data about effective or less effective behaviour that is related to examples of actual events – critical incidents. The technique is used with groups of job holders and/or their managers or other 'experts' (sometimes, less effectively, with individuals) as follows:

- Explain what the technique is and what it is used for, ie, 'to assess what constitutes good or poor performance by analysing events that have been observed to have a noticeably successful or unsuccessful outcome, thus providing more factual and "real" information than by simply listing tasks and guessing performance requirements'.
- Agree and list the key result in the role to be analysed. To save time, the analyst can establish these prior to the meeting but it is necessary to ensure that they are agreed provisionally by the group, which can be told that the list may well be amended in the light of the forthcoming analysis.
- Take each area of the role in turn and ask the group for examples of critical incidents. If, for instance, one of the job responsibilities is dealing with customers, the following request could be made: 'I want you to tell me about a particular occasion at work which involved you – or that you observed – in dealing with a customer. Think about what the circumstances were, for example who took part, what the customer asked for, what you or the other member of the staff did and what the outcome was.'
- Collect information about the critical incident under the following headings: what the circumstances were; what the individual did; the outcome of what the individual did.
- Record this information on a flipchart.
- Continue this process for each key result area.
- Refer to the flipchart and analyse each incident by obtaining ratings of the recorded behaviour on a scale such as 1 for least effective to 5 for most effective.
- Discuss these ratings to get initial definitions of effective and ineffective performance for each of the key result areas.
- Refine these definitions as necessary after the meeting – it can be difficult to get a group to produce finished definitions.
- Produce the final analysis, which can list the competencies required and include performance indicators or standards of performance for each key result area.

Repertory grid

Like the critical incident technique, the repertory grid can be used to identify the dimensions that distinguish good from poor standards of performance. The technique is based on Kelly's (1955) personal construct theory. Personal constructs are the ways in which we view the world. They are personal because they are highly individual and they influence the way we behave or view other people's behaviour. The aspects of the role to which these 'constructs' or judgements apply are called 'elements'.

To elicit judgements, a group of people are asked to concentrate on certain elements, which are the tasks carried out by role holders, and develop constructs about these elements. This enables them to define the qualities that indicate the essential requirements for successful performance.

The procedure followed by the analyst is known as the 'triadic method of elicitation' (a sort of three-card trick) and involves the following steps:

1. Identify the tasks or elements of the role to be subjected to repertory grid analysis. This is done by one of the other forms of job analysis, eg interviewing.
2. List the tasks on cards.
3. Draw three cards at random from the pack and ask the members of the group to nominate which of the three tasks is the odd one out from the point of view of the qualities and characteristics needed to perform it.
4. Probe to obtain more specific definitions of these qualities or characteristics in the form of expected behaviour. If, for example, a characteristic has been described as the 'ability to plan and organize', ask questions such as: 'What sort of behaviour or actions indicate that someone is planning effectively?' or, 'How can we tell if someone is not organizing his or her work particularly well?'
5. Draw three more cards from the pack and repeat steps 3 and 4.
6. Repeat this process until all the cards have been analysed and there do not appear to be any more constructs left to be identified.
7. List the constructs and ask the group members to rate each task on every quality, using a six or seven point scale.
8. Collect and analyse the scores in order to assess their relative importance. This can be done statistically, as described by Markham (1987).

Like the critical-incident technique, repertory grid analysis helps people to articulate their views by reference to specific examples. An additional advantage is that the repertory grid makes it easier for them to identify the behavioural characteristics or competencies required in a job by limiting the area of comparison through the triadic technique.

Although a full statistical analysis of the outcome of a repertory grid exercise is helpful, the most important results that can be obtained are the descriptions of what constitute good or poor performance in each element of the job.

Both the repertory grid and the critical incident techniques require a skilled analyst who can probe and draw out the descriptions of job characteristics. They are quite detailed and time-consuming, but even if the full process is not followed, much of the methodology is of use in a less elaborate approach to competency analysis.

Choice of approach

Workshops are probably the best approach. They get people involved and do not rely on 'expert' opinion. Critical incident or repertory grid techniques are more sophisticated but they take more time and expertise to run.

Analysing technical competencies (functional analysis)

The approach to the definition of technical competencies differs from that used for behavioural competencies. As technical competencies are in effect competences, a functional analysis process can be used. This methodology was originally developed by Mansfield and Mitchell (1986) and Fine (1988). In essence, functional analysis focuses on the *outcomes* of work performance. Note that the analysis is not simply concerned with *outputs* in the form of quantifiable results but deals with the broader results that have to be achieved by role holders. An outcome could be a satisfied customer, a more highly motivated subordinate or a better-functioning team. Functional analysis deals with processes such as developing staff, providing feedback and monitoring performance as well as tasks. As described by Miller *et al* (2001) it starts with an analysis of the roles fulfilled by an individual in order to arrive at a description of the separate components or 'units' of performance that make up that role. The resulting units consist of performance criteria, described in terms of outcomes, and a description of the knowledge and skill requirements that underpin successful performance.

Functional analysis is the method used to define competence-based standards for NVQs/SNVQs.

SKILLS ANALYSIS

Skills analysis determines the skills required to achieve an acceptable standard of performance. It is mainly used for technical, craft, manual and office jobs to provide the basis for devising learning and training programmes. Skills analysis starts from a broad job analysis but goes into details of not only what job holders have to do but also the particular abilities and skills they need to do it. Skills analysis techniques are described below.

Job breakdown

The job breakdown technique analyses a job into separate operations, processes, or tasks, which can be used as the elements of an instruction sequence. A job breakdown analysis is recorded in a standard format of three columns:

1. *The stage column* in which the different steps in the job are described – most semi-skilled jobs can easily be broken down into their constituent parts.
2. *The instruction column* in which a note is made against each step of how the task should be done. This, in effect, describes what has to be learnt by the trainee.
3. *The key points column* in which any special points such as quality standards or safety instructions are noted against each step so that they can be emphasized to a trainee learning the job.

Manual skills analysis

Manual skills analysis is a technique developed from work study. It isolates for instructional purposes the skills and knowledge employed by experienced workers in performing tasks that require manual dexterity. It is used to analyse short-cycle, repetitive operations such as assembly tasks and other similar factory work.

The hand, finger and other body movements of experienced operatives are observed and recorded in detail as they carry out their work. The analysis concentrates on the tricky parts of the job which, while presenting no difficulty to the experienced operative, have to be analysed in depth before they can be taught to trainees. Not only are the hand movements recorded, but particulars are also noted of the cues (visual and other senses) that the operative absorbs when performing the tasks. Explanatory comments are added when necessary.

Task analysis

Task analysis is a systematic analysis of the behaviour required to carry out a task with a view to identifying areas of difficulty and the appropriate training techniques and learning aids necessary for successful instruction. It can be used for all types of jobs but is specifically relevant to administrative tasks.

The analytical approach used in task analysis is similar to those adopted in the job breakdown and manual skills analysis techniques. The results of the analysis are usually recorded in a standard format of four columns as follows:

1. *Task* – a brief description of each element.
2. *Level of importance* – the relative significance of each task to the successful performance of the role.

3. *Degree of difficulty* – the level of skill or knowledge required to perform each task.
4. *Training method* – the instructional techniques, practice and experience required.

Faults analysis

Faults analysis is the process of analysing the typical faults that occur when performing a task, especially the more costly faults. It is carried out when the incidence of faults is high. A study is made of the job and, by questioning workers and team leaders, the most commonly occurring faults are identified. A faults specification is then produced, which provides trainees with information on what faults can be made, how they can be recognized, what causes them, what effect they have, who is responsible for them, what action the trainees should take when a particular fault occurs, and how a fault can be prevented from recurring.

Job learning analysis

Job learning analysis, as described by Pearn and Kandola (1993), concentrates on the inputs and process rather than the content of the job. It analyses nine learning skills that contribute to satisfactory performance. A learning skill is one used to increase other skills or knowledge and represents broad categories of job behaviour that need to be learnt. The learning skills are the following:

1. physical skills requiring practice and repetition to get right;
2. complex procedures or sequences of activity that are memorized or followed with the aid of written material such as manuals;
3. non-verbal information such as sight, sound, smell, taste and touch, which is used to check, assess or discriminate, and which usually takes practice to get right;
4. memorizing facts or information;
5. ordering, prioritizing and planning, which refer to the degree to which a role holder has any responsibility for and flexibility in determining the way a particular activity is performed;
6. looking ahead and anticipating;
7. diagnosing, analysing and problem-solving, with or without help;
8. interpreting or using written manuals and other sources of information such as diagrams or charts;
9. adapting to new ideas and systems.

In conducting a job learning analysis interview, the interviewer obtains information on the main aims and principal activities of the job and then, using question cards for each of the nine learning skills, analyses each activity in more depth, recording responses and obtaining as many examples as possible under each heading.

Part III

Work and employment

This part of the handbook is concerned with the factors affecting employment in organizations. It explores the nature of work, the employment relationship and the important concept of the psychological contract.

14

The nature of work

In this chapter the nature of work is explored – what it is, the various theories about work, the organizational factors that affect it and attitudes towards work.

WHAT IS WORK?

Work is the exertion of effort and the application of knowledge and skills to achieve a purpose. Most people work to earn a living – to make money. But they also work because of the other satisfactions it brings, such as doing something worthwhile, a sense of achievement, prestige, recognition, the opportunity to use and develop abilities, the scope to exercise power, and companionship. Within organizations, the nature of the work carried out by individuals and what they feel about it are governed by the employment relationship as discussed in Chapter 15 and the psychological contract as considered in Chapter 16.

In this chapter the various theories of work are summarized in the first section. The following sections deal with the organizational factors that affect work such as the 'lean' and 'flexible' organization, changes in the pattern of working, unemployment, careers and attitudes to work.

THEORIES ABOUT WORK

The theories about work described in this section consist of labour process theory, agency theory and exchange theory. The concept of the pluralist and unitarist frame of reference is also considered.

Labour process theory

Labour process theory was originally formulated by Karl Marx (translated in 1976). His thesis was that surplus is appropriated from labour by paying it less than the value it adds to the labour process. Capitalists therefore design the labour process to secure the extraction of surplus value. The human capacity to produce is subordinated to the exploitative demands of the capitalist, which is an alien power confronting the worker who becomes a 'crippled monstrosity by furthering his skill as if in a forcing house through the suppression of a whole world of productive drives and inclinations'.

Considerably later, a version of labour process theory was set out by Braverman (1974). His view was that the application of modern management techniques, in combination with mechanization and automation, secures the real subordination of labour and de-skilling of work in the office as well as the shop-floor. He stated that the removal of all forms of control from the worker is 'the ideal towards which management tends, and in pursuit of which it uses every productive innovation shaped by science'. He saw this as essentially the application of 'Taylorism' (ie F. W Taylor's concept of scientific management, meaning the use of systematic observation and measurement, task specialism and, in effect, the reduction of workers to the level of efficiently functioning machines).

Braverman's notion of labour process theory has been criticized as being simplistic by subsequent commentators such as Littler and Salaman (1982) who argue that there are numerous determinants in the control of the labour process. And Friedman (1977) believes that Braverman's version neglects the diverse and sophisticated character of management control as it responds not only to technological advances but also to changes in the degree and intensity of worker resistance and new product and labour market conditions. Storey (1995) has commented that 'the labour process bandwagon... is now holed and patched beyond repair'.

But more recent commentators such as Newton and Findlay (1996) believe that labour process theory explains how managements have at their disposal a range of mechanisms through which control is exercised: 'Job performance and its assessment is at the heart of the labour process.' Managements, according to Newton and Findlay, are constantly seeking ways to improve the effectiveness of control mechanisms to achieve compliance. They 'try to squeeze the last drop of surplus value' out of their labour.

Agency theory

Agency or principal agent theory indicates that principals (owners and managers) have to develop ways of monitoring and controlling the activities of their agents (staff). Agency theory suggests that principals may have problems in ensuring that agents do what they are told. It is necessary to clear up ambiguities by setting objectives and monitoring performance to ensure that objectives are achieved.

Agency theory has been criticized by Gomez-Mejia and Balkin (1992) as 'managerialist'. As Armstrong (1996) wrote: 'It looks at the employment relationship purely from management's point of view and regards employees as objects to be motivated by the carrot and stick. It is a dismal theory, which suggests that people cannot be trusted.'

Exchange theory

Exchange theory sets out to explain organizational behaviour in terms of the rewards and costs incurred in the interaction between employers and employees. There are four concepts:

- *Rewards* – payoffs that satisfy needs emerging from the interactions between individuals and their organizations.
- *Costs* – fatigue, stress, anxiety, punishments and the value of rewards that people have lost because of lack of opportunity.
- *Outcomes* – rewards minus costs: if positive, the interaction yields a 'profit' and this is satisfactory as long as it exceeds the minimum level of expectation.
- *Level of comparisons* – people evaluate the outcome of an interaction against the profit they are foregoing elsewhere.

Unitary and pluralist frames of reference

One of the often expressed aims of human resource management is to increase the commitment of people to the organization by getting them to share its views and values and integrate their own work objectives with those of the organization. This concept adopts a unitary frame of reference; in other words, as expressed by Gennard and Judge (1997), organizations are assumed to be 'harmonious and integrated, all employees sharing the organisational goals and working as members of one team'.

Alternatively, the pluralist perspective as expressed by Cyert and March (1963) sees organizations as coalitions of interest groups and recognizes the legitimacy of different interests and values. Organizational development programmes, which, amongst other things, aim to increase commitment and teamwork, adopt a unitary framework. But it can be argued that this is a managerialist assumption and that the legitimate interests of the other members of a pluralist society – the stakeholders – will have their own interests, which should be respected.

ORGANIZATIONAL FACTORS AFFECTING WORK

The nature of work changes as organizations change in response to new demands and environmental pressures. Business-process engineering, downsizing and delayering all have significant effects on the type of work carried out, on feelings of security and on the career opportunities available in organizations. Three of the most important factors – the 'lean' organization, the changing role of the process worker and the flexible firm – are discussed below.

The lean organization

The term 'lean production' was popularized by Womack and Jones (1970) in *The Machine That Changed the World*. But the drive for leaner methods of working was confined initially to the car industry. In the classic case of Toyota, one of the pioneers of lean production, or more loosely, 'world class manufacturing', seven forms of waste were identified, which had to be eliminated. These were overproduction, waiting, transporting, over-processing, inventories, moving, and making defective parts or products. Lean production aims to add value by minimizing waste in terms of materials, time, space and people. Production systems associated with leanness include just-in-time, supply chain management, material resources planning and zero defects/right first time. Business process re-engineering programmes often accompany drives for leaner methods of working and total quality management approaches are used to support drives for greater levels of customer satisfaction and service.

The concept of 'leanness' has since been extended to non-manufacturing organizations. This can often be number driven and is implemented by means of a reduction in headcounts (downsizing) and a reduction in the number of levels of management and supervision (delayering). But there is no standard model of what a lean organization looks like. According to the report on the research conducted by the Institute of Personnel and Development (IPD) on lean and responsive organizations (IPD,

1998b), firms select from a menu the methods that meet their particular business needs. These include, other than delayering or the negative approach of downsizing, positive steps such as:

- team-based work organizations;
- shop-floor empowerment and problem-solving practices;
- quality built in, not inspected in;
- emphasis on horizontal business processes rather than vertical structures;
- partnership relationships with suppliers;
- cross-functional management and development teams;
- responsiveness to customer demand;
- human resource management policies aimed at high motivation and commitment and including communication programmes and participation in decision-making.

The IPD report emphasizes that qualitative change through people is a major feature of lean working but that the issue is not just that of launching change. The key requirement is to sustain it. The report also noted that HR practitioners can play a number of important roles in the process of managing change. These include that of supporter, interpreter, champion, monitor, resourcer, and anticipator of potential problems.

A question posed by Purcell et al (1998) was: 'Are lean organizations usually mean organizations?' But they commented that the IPD research did not indicate that leaner methods of work have positive implications for employees. The evidence suggested that the impact on people is often negative, particularly when restructuring means downsizing and re-engineering. Employees work longer hours, stress rises, career opportunities are reduced and morale and motivation fall. They also made the point that it is clear that many initiatives fail because they do not take into account the people implications, and that the first and most significant barrier was middle management resistance.

The changing role of the process worker

A report published on a research project into process working by the Institute of Employment Studies (Giles et al 1997) revealed that management structures designed in response to technological advances and competitive pressures are transforming the role of process workers.

Increasing automation and the application of new technologies to the production process mean that low-skilled manual jobs continue to disappear, and that process workers are becoming progressively less involved in manual operating tasks. Instead, they are being given more responsibility for the processes they work on, while being expected to become more customer and business oriented and, in many cases, to carry out simple engineering and maintenance tasks.

The flexible firm

The concept of the 'flexible firm' was originated by Atkinson (1984) who claimed that there is a growing trend for firms to seek various forms of structural and operational flexibility. The three kinds of flexibility areas follow:

- *Functional flexibility* is sought so that employees can be redeployed quickly and smoothly between activities and tasks. Functional flexibility may require multi-skilling – craft workers who possess and can apply a number of skills covering, for example, both mechanical and electrical engineering, or manufacturing and maintenance activities.
- *Numerical flexibility* is sought so that the number of employees can be quickly and easily increased or decreased in line with even short-term changes in the level of demand for labour.
- *Financial flexibility* provides for pay levels to reflect the state of supply and demand in the external labour market and also means the use of flexible pay systems that facilitate either functional or numerical flexibility.

The new structure in the flexible firm involves the break-up of the labour force into increasingly peripheral, and therefore numerically flexible, groups of workers clustered around a numerically stable core group that will conduct the organization's key, firm-specific activities. At the core, the focus is on functional flexibility. Shifting to the periphery, numerical flexibility becomes more important. As the market grows, the periphery expands to take up slack; as growth slows, the periphery contracts. At the core, only tasks and responsibilities change; the workers here are insulated from medium-term fluctuations in the market and can therefore enjoy job security, whereas those in the periphery are exposed to them.

CHANGING PATTERNS OF WORK

The most important developments over the past decade have been a consider-able increase in the use of part-timers, a marked propensity for organizations to subcontract work and to outsource services, and a greater requirement for specialists (knowledge workers) and professionals in organizations. Teleworking has increased (working at home with a computer terminal link to the firm) and call centre work has expanded.

Under the pressures to be competitive and to achieve 'cost leadership', organizations are not only 'downsizing' but are also engaging people on short-term contracts and make no pretence that they are there to provide careers. They want specific contributions to achieving organizational goals now and, so far as people are concerned, they may let the future take care of itself, believing that they can purchase the talent required as and when necessary. This may be short-sighted, but it is the way many businesses now operate.

When preparing and implementing human resource plans, HR practitioners need to be aware of these factors and trends within the context of their internal and external environments. A further factor that affects the way in which the labour market operates, and therefore human resource planning decisions, is unemployment.

In general there is far less security in employment today, and the old tradition of the life-long career is no longer so much in evidence. Employers are less likely to be committed to their employees. At the same time, employees tend to be less committed to their employers and more committed to their careers, which they may perceive are likely to progress better if they change jobs rather than remain with their present employer. They are concerned with their employability, and are determined to extract as much value as possible from their present employment to provide for their future elsewhere.

The Economic and Social Research Council and the Tomorrow Project (2005) reported that, today, more than 5 million people, almost a fifth of employees, spend some time working at home or on the move. The report predicts the rise of the 'mobile worker', moving – laptop and mobile in tow – between office, home, airport lounge or motorway service station as the needs of a job demand. As stated in the report:

> Individuals at work will not necessarily see themselves as working from home. They could equally be working from the office. But they will be on the move from place to place... There will be a shift from personalized space to personalized time and the boundaries between work and leisure time will be less distinct.

The report says that managers will have to find new ways to control these mobile workers, possibly based on capturing workers' hearts and minds to create a culture of hard work even at a distance.

UNEMPLOYMENT

Economists are unable to agree on the causes of or cures for unemployment (or anything else, it seems). The essence of the Keynesian explanation is that firms demand too little labour because individuals demand too few goods. The classical view was that unemployment was voluntary and could be cleared by natural market forces. The neo-classical theory is that there is a natural rate of unemployment, which reflects a given rate of technology, individual preferences and endowments. With flexible wages in a competitive labour market, wages adjust to clear the market and any unemployment that remains is voluntary. The latter view was that held by Milton Friedman and strongly influenced government policy in the early 1980s, but without success. There is, of course, no simple explanation of unemployment and no simple solution.

ATTITUDES TO WORK

The IPD research into employee motivation and the psychological contract (Guest *et al*, 1996; Guest and Conway, 1997) obtained the following responses from the people they surveyed:

- Work remains a central interest in the lives of most people.
- If they won the lottery, 39 per cent would quit work, but most of the others would continue working.
- Asked to cite the three most important things they look for in a job, 70 per cent of respondents cited pay, 62 per cent wanted interesting and varied work and only 22 per cent were looking for job security.
- 35 per cent claimed that they were putting in so much effort that they could not work any harder and a further 34 per cent claimed they were working very hard.

JOB-RELATED WELL-BEING

The 2004 Workplace Employee Relations Survey (WERS, 2005) covering 700,000 workplaces and 22.5 million employees surveyed 21,624 employees in workplaces employing more than 10 people on how they felt at work. The results are summarized in Table 14.1.

This does not present an unduly gloomy picture. The percentage of people feeling either tense or calm some, more or all of the time was much the same. An equal

Table 14.1   Feelings at work (WERS, 2005)

The job makes you feel:	All of the time %	Most of the time %	Some of the time %	Occasionally %	Never %
Tense	4	15	42	27	12
Calm	3	30	29	27	11
Relaxed	2	10	35	32	21
Worried	2	10	35	32	21
Uneasy	2	8	28	33	29
Content	5	33	30	22	11

number of people were never relaxed or worried, and rather more were never uneasy. Sixty-nine per cent were content all, most or part of the time. The WERS survey also revealed that job-related well-being was higher in small organizations and work-places than in large ones, higher among union members, fell with increased education and is U-shaped with regard to age (ie higher amongst younger and older employees than amongst the middle-aged).

15

The employment relationship

This chapter explores the nature of the employment relationship and the creation of a climate of trust within that relationship.

THE EMPLOYMENT RELATIONSHIP DEFINED

The term employment relationship describes the interconnections that exist between employers and employees in the workplace. These may be formal, eg contracts of employment, procedural agreements. Or they may be informal, in the shape of the psychological contract, which expresses certain assumptions and expectations about what managers and employer have to offer and are willing to deliver (Kessler and Undy, 1996). They can have an individual dimension, which refers to individual contracts and expectations, or a collective dimension, which refers to relationships between management and trade unions, staff associations or members of joint consultative bodies such as works councils.

NATURE OF THE EMPLOYMENT RELATIONSHIP

The dimensions of the employment relationship as described by Kessler and Undy (1996) are shown in Figure 15.1.

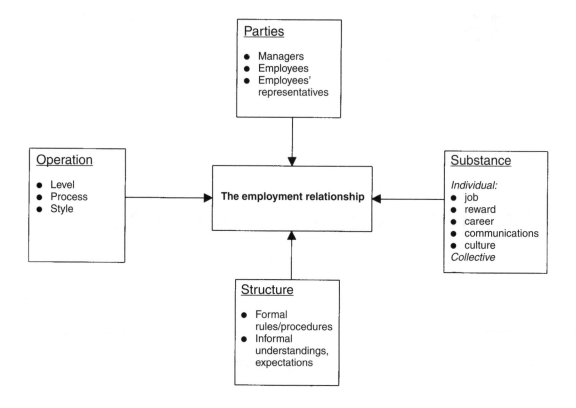

Figure 15.1   Dimensions of the employment relationship

(*Source:* S Kessler and R Undy, *The New Employment Relationship: Examining the psychological contract*, Institute of Personnel and Development, London, 1996)

The parties are managers, employees and employee representatives. The 'substance' incorporates the job, reward and career of individuals and the communications and culture of the organization as it affects them. It can also include collective agreements and joint employee relations machinery (works councils and the like). The formal dimensions include rules and procedures, and the informal aspect covers understanding, expectations and assumptions. Finally, the employment relationship exists at different levels in the organization (management to employees generally, and managers to individual employees and their representatives or groups of people). The operation of the relationship will also be affected by processes such as communications and consultation, and by the management style prevailing throughout the organization or adopted by individual managers.

BASIS OF THE EMPLOYMENT RELATIONSHIP

The starting point of the employment relationship is an undertaking by an employee to provide skill and effort to the employer in return for which the employer provides the employee with a salary or a wage. Initially the relationship is founded on a legal contract. This may be a written contract but the absence of such a contract does not mean that no contractual relationship exists. Employers and employees still have certain implied legal rights and obligations. The employer's obligations include the duty to pay salary or wages, to provide a safe workplace, to act in good faith towards the employee and not to act in such a way as to undermine the trust and confidence of the employment relationship. The employee has corresponding obligations, which include obedience, competence, honesty and loyalty.

An important factor to remember about the employment relationship is that, generally, it is the employer who has the power to dictate the contractual terms unless they have been fixed by collective bargaining. Individuals, except when they are much in demand, have little scope to vary the terms of the contract imposed upon them by employers.

DEFINING THE EMPLOYMENT RELATIONSHIP

Two types of contracts defining the employment relationship have been distinguished by Macneil (1985) and Rousseau and Wade-Benzoni (1994):

- *Transactional contracts* have well-described terms of exchange, which are usually expressed financially. They are of limited duration, with specified performance requirements.
- *Relational contracts* are less well defined with more abstract terms and refer to an open-ended membership of the organization. Performance requirements attached to this continuing membership are incomplete or ambiguous.

However, the employment relationships can also be expressed in terms of a *psychological contract*, which, according to Guzzo and Noonan (1994), has both transactional and relational qualities. The concept of a psychological contract expresses the view that at its most basic level the employment relationship consists of a unique combination of beliefs held by an individual and his or her employer about what they expect of one another. This concept is discussed in more detail in Chapter 16.

SIGNIFICANCE OF THE EMPLOYMENT RELATIONSHIP CONCEPT

The concept of the employment relationship is significant to HR specialists because it governs much of what organizations need to be aware of in developing and applying HR processes, policies and procedures. These need to be considered in terms of what they will or will not contribute to furthering a productive and rewarding employment relationship between all the parties concerned.

CHANGES IN THE EMPLOYMENT RELATIONSHIP

As noted by Gallie *et al* (1998) in their analysis of the outcome of their 'employment in Britain' research programme, while there have been shifts in the ways in which people are employed: 'The evidence for a major change in the nature of the employment relationship was much less convincing.' But they did note the following characteristics of employment as revealed by the survey:

- New forms of management, often based explicitly or implicitly on HRM principles and emphasizing individual contracts rather than collective bargaining.
- There was some increase in task discretion but there was no evidence of a significant decline in managerial control; indeed, in some important respects control was intensified.
- Supervisory activity was still important.
- Integrative forms of management policy were centred on non-manual employees.
- The great majority of employees continued to attach a high level of importance to the intrinsically motivating aspects of work.
- The higher the level of skill, the more people were involved with their work.
- The raising of skill levels and the granting of increased discretion to employers are key factors in improving the quality of work experience.
- High levels of commitment to the organization can reduce absenteeism and labour turnover but there was no evidence that organizational commitment 'added anything over and above other organizational and task characteristics with regard to the quality of work performance'.

MANAGING THE EMPLOYMENT RELATIONSHIP

The dynamic and often nebulous nature of the employment relationship increases the difficulty of managing it. The problem is compounded because of the multiplicity of factors that influence the contract: the culture of the organization; the prevailing management style; the values, espoused and practised, of top management; the existence or non-existence of a climate of trust; day-to-day interactions between employees and line managers; and the HR policies and practices of the business.

The latter are particularly important. The nature of the employment relationship is strongly influenced by HR actions. These cover all aspects of HR management. But how people are treated in such areas as recruitment, performance reviews, promotion, career development, reward, involvement and participation, grievance handling, disciplinary procedures and redundancy will be particularly important. How people are required to carry out their work (including flexibility and multi-skilling), how performance expectations are expressed and communicated, how work is organized and how people are managed will also make a significant impact on the employment relationship. HR specialists can contribute to the development of a positive and productive employment relationship in the following ways:

- *during recruitment interviews* – presenting the unfavourable as well as the favourable aspects of a job in a 'realistic job preview';
- in *induction programmes* – communicating to new starters the organization's personnel policies and procedures and its core values, indicating to them the standards of performance expected in such areas as quality and customer service, and spelling out requirements for flexibility;
- by issuing and updating *employee handbooks* that reinforce the messages delivered in induction programmes;
- by encouraging the development of *performance management* processes that ensure that performance expectations are agreed and reviewed regularly;
- by encouraging the use of *personal development plans* that spell out how continuous improvement of performance can be achieved, mainly by self-managed learning;
- by using *learning and development programmes* to underpin core values and define performance expectations;
- by ensuring through *manager and team leader training* that managers and team leaders understand their role in managing the employment relationship through such processes as performance management and team leadership;
- by encouraging the maximum amount of *contact* between managers and team leaders and their team members to achieve mutual understanding of expectations and to provide a means of two-way communications;
- by adopting a general policy of *transparency* – ensuring that in all matters that affect them, employees know what is happening, why it is happening and the impact it will make on their employment, development and prospects;

- by developing *HR procedures* covering grievance handling, discipline, equal opportunities, promotion and redundancy and ensuring that they are implemented fairly and consistently;
- developing and communicating *HR policies* covering the major areas of employment, development, reward and employee relations;
- by ensuring that the *reward system* is developed and managed to achieve equity, fairness and consistency in all aspects of pay and benefits;
- generally, by advising on *employee relations procedures*, processes and issues that further good collective relationships.

These approaches to managing the employment relationship cover all aspects of people management. It is important to remember, however, that this is a continuous process. The effective management of the relationship means ensuring that values are upheld and that a transparent, consistent and fair approach is adopted in dealing with all aspects of employment.

TRUST AND THE EMPLOYMENT RELATIONSHIP

The IPD suggested in its statement *People Make the Difference* (1994) that building trust is the only basis upon which commitment can be generated. The IPD commented that: 'In too many organizations inconsistency between what is said and what is done undermines trust, generates employee cynicism and provides evidence of contradictions in management thinking.'

It has also been suggested by Herriot *et al* (1998) that trust should be regarded as social capital – the fund of goodwill in any social group that enables people within it to collaborate with one another. Thompson (1998) sees trust as a 'unique human resource capability that helps the organization fulfil its competitive advantage' – a core competency that leads to high business performance. Thus there is a business need to develop a climate of trust, as there is a business need to introduce effective pay-for-contribution processes, which are built on trust.

The meaning of trust

Trust, as defined by the Oxford English Dictionary, is a firm belief that a person may be relied on. An alternative definition has been provided by Shaw (1997) to the effect that trust is the 'belief that those on whom we depend will meet our expectations of them'. These expectations are dependent on 'our assessment of another's responsibility to meet our needs'.

A climate of trust

A high-trust organization has been described by Fox (1973) as follows:

> Organizational participants share certain ends or values; bear towards each other a diffuse sense of long-term obligations; offer each other spontaneous support without narrowly calculating the cost or anticipating any short-term reciprocation; communicate honestly and freely; are ready to repose their fortunes in each other's hands; and give each other the benefit of any doubt that may arise with respect to goodwill or motivation.

This ideal state may seldom, if ever, be attained, but it does represent a picture of an effective organization in which, as Thompson (1998) notes, trust 'is an outcome of good management'.

When do employees trust management?

Management is more likely to be trusted by employees when the latter:

- believe that the management means what it says;
- observe that management does what it says it is going to do – suiting the action to the word;
- know from experience that management, in the words of David Guest (Guest and Conway, 1998), 'delivers the deal – it keeps its word and fulfils its side of the bargain';
- feel they are treated fairly, equitable and consistently.

Developing a high-trust organization

As Thompson (1998) comments, a number of writers have generally concluded that trust is 'not something that can, or should, be directly managed'. He cites Sako (1994) who wrote that: 'Trust is a cultural norm which can rarely be created intentionally because attempts to create trust in a calculative manner would destroy the effective basis of trust.'

It may not be possible to 'manage' trust but, as Thompson argues, trust is an outcome of good management. It is created and maintained by managerial behaviour and by the development of better mutual understanding of expectations – employers of employees, and employees of employers. But Herriot et al (1998) point out that issues of trust are not in the end to do with managing people or processes, but are more about relationships and mutual support through change.

Clearly, the sort of behaviour that is most likely to engender trust is when management is honest with people, keeps its word (delivers the deal) and practises what it preaches. Organizations that espouse core values ('people are our greatest asset') and then proceed to ignore them will be low-trust organizations.

More specifically, trust will be developed if management acts fairly, equitably and consistently, if a policy of transparency is implemented, if intentions and the reasons for proposals or decisions are communicated both to employees generally and to individuals, if there is full involvement in developing HR processes, and if mutual expectations are agreed through performance management.

Failure to meet these criteria, wholly or in part, is perhaps the main reason why so many performance-related pay schemes have not lived up to expectations. The starting point is to understand and apply the principles of distributive and procedural justice.

Justice

To treat people justly is to deal with them fairly and equitably. Leventhal (1980), following Adams (1965), distinguished between distributive and procedural justice.

Distributive justice refers to how rewards are distributed. People will feel that they have been treated justly in this respect if they believe that rewards have been distributed in accordance with their contributions, that they receive what was promised to them and that they get what they need.

Procedural justice refers to the ways in which managerial decisions are made and HR procedures are managed. People will feel that they have been treated justly if management's decisions and procedures are fair, consistent, transparent, non-discriminatory and properly consider the views and needs of employees.

Renewing trust

As suggested by Herriot *et al* (1998), if trust is lost, a four-step programme is required for its renewal:

1. admission by top management that it has paid insufficient attention in the past to employees' diverse needs;
2. a limited process of contracting whereby a particular transition to a different way of working for a group of employees is done in a form that takes individual needs into account;

3. establishing 'knowledge-based' trust, which is based not on a specific transactional deal but on a developing perception of trustworthiness;
4. achieving trust based on identification in which each party empathizes with each other's needs and therefore takes them on board themselves (although this final state is seldom reached in practice).

16

The psychological contract

The employment relationship, as described in Chapter 15, is a fundamental feature of all aspects of people management. At its most basic level, the employment relationship consists of a unique combination of beliefs held by an individual and his or her employer about what they expect of one another. This is the psychological contract, and to manage the employment relationship effectively it is necessary to understand what the psychological contract is, how it is formed and its significance.

THE PSYCHOLOGICAL CONTRACT DEFINED

Fundamentally, the psychological contract expresses the combination of beliefs held by an individual and his or her employer about what they expect of one another. It can be described as the set of reciprocal but unarticulated expectations that exist between individual employees and their employers. As defined by Schein (1965): 'The notion of a psychological contract implies that there is an unwritten set of expectations operating at all times between every member of an organization and the various managers and others in that organization.'

This definition was amplified by Rousseau and Wade-Benzoni (1994) who stated that:

Psychological contracts refer to beliefs that individuals hold regarding promises made, accepted and relied upon between themselves and another. (In the case of organizations, these parties include an employee, client, manager, and/or organization as a whole.) Because psychological contracts represent how people *interpret* promises and commitments, both parties in the same employment relationship (employer and employee) can have different views regarding specific terms.

Sparrow (1999b) defined the psychological contract as:

an open-ended agreement about what the individual and the organization expect to give and receive in return from the employment relationship... psychological contracts represent a dynamic and reciprocal deal... New expectations are added over time as perceptions about the employer's commitment evolve. These unwritten individual contracts are therefore concerned with the social and emotional aspects of the exchange between employer and employee.

Within organizations, as Katz and Kahn (1966) pointed out, every role is basically a set of behavioural expectations. These expectations are often implicit – they are not defined in the employment contract. Basic models of motivation such as expectancy theory (Vroom, 1964) and operant conditioning (Skinner, 1974) maintain that employees behave in ways they expect will produce positive outcomes. But they do not necessarily know what to expect. As Rousseau and Greller (1994) comment:

The ideal contract in employment would detail expectations of both employee and employer. Typical contracts, however, are incomplete due to bounded rationality, which limits individual information seeking, and to a changing organizational environment that makes it impossible to specify all conditions up front. Both employee and employer are left to fill up the blanks.

The notion of bounded rationality expresses the belief that while people often try to act rationally, the extent to which they do so is limited by their emotional reactions to the situation they are in.

Employees may expect to be treated fairly as human beings, to be provided with work that uses their abilities, to be rewarded equitably in accordance with their contribution, to be able to display competence, to have opportunities for further growth, to know what is expected of them and to be given feedback (preferably positive) on how they are doing. Employers may expect employees to do their best on behalf of the organization – 'to put themselves out for the company' – to be fully committed to its values, to be compliant and loyal, and to enhance the image of the organization with its customers and suppliers. Sometimes these assumptions are justified – often they are not. Mutual misunderstandings can cause friction and stress and lead to recriminations and poor performance, or to a termination of the employment relationship.

To summarize, in the words of Guest and Conway (1998), the psychological contract lacks many of the characteristics of the formal contract: 'It is not generally written down, it is somewhat blurred at the edges, and it cannot be enforced in a court or tribunal.' They believe that: 'The psychological contract is best seen as a metaphor; a word or phrase borrowed from another context which helps us make sense of our experience. The psychological contract is a way of interpreting the state of the employment relationship and helping to plot significant changes.'

THE SIGNIFICANCE OF THE PSYCHOLOGICAL CONTRACT

As suggested by Spindler (1994): 'A psychological contract creates emotions and attitudes which form and control behaviour.' The significance of the psychological contract was further explained by Sims (1994) as follows: 'A balanced psychological contract is necessary for a continuing, harmonious relationship between the employee and the organization. However, the violation of the psychological contract can signal to the participants that the parties no longer share (or never shared) a common set of values or goals.'

The concept highlights the fact that employee/employer expectations take the form of unarticulated assumptions. Disappointments on the part of management as well as employees may therefore be inevitable. These disappointments can, however, be alleviated if managements appreciate that one of their key roles is to manage expectations, which means clarifying what they believe employees should achieve, the competencies they should possess and the values they should uphold. And this is a matter not just of articulating and stipulating these requirements but of discussing and agreeing them with individuals and teams.

The psychological contract governs the continuing development of the employment relationship, which is constantly evolving over time. But how the contract is developing and the impact it makes may not be fully understood by any of the parties involved. Spindler (1994) comments that: 'In a psychological contract the rights and obligations of the parties have not been articulated, much less agreed to. The parties do not express their expectations and, in fact, may be quite incapable of doing so.'

People who have no clear idea about what they expect may, if such unexpressed expectations have not been fulfilled, have no clear idea why they have been disappointed. But they will be aware that something does not feel right. And a company staffed by 'cheated' individuals who expect more than they get is heading for trouble.

The importance of the psychological contract was emphasized by Schein (1965) who suggested that the extent to which people work effectively and are committed to the organization depends on:

- the degree to which their own expectations of what the organization will provide to them and what they owe the organization in return match that organization's expectations of what it will give and get in return;
- the nature of *what is actually to be exchanged* (assuming there is some agreement) – money in exchange for time at work; social need satisfaction and security in exchange for hard work and loyalty; opportunities for self-actualization and challenging work in exchange for high productivity, high-quality work, and creative effort in the service of organizational goals; or various combinations of these and other things.

The research conducted by Guest and Conway (2002) led to the conclusion that 'The management of the psychological contract as Schalk and Rousseau (2001) suggest, is a core task of management and acknowledged as such by many senior HR and employment relations managers, and shows that it has a positive association with a range of outcomes within the employment relationship and is a useful way of conceptualising that relationship.'

THE NATURE OF THE PSYCHOLOGICAL CONTRACT

A psychological contract is a system of beliefs that may not have been articulated. It encompasses the actions employees believe are expected of them and what response they expect in return from their employer. As described by Guest *et al* (1996): 'It is concerned with assumptions, expectations, promises and mutual obligations.' It creates attitudes and emotions that form and govern behaviour. A psychological contract is implicit. It is also dynamic – it develops over time as experience accumulates, employment conditions change and employees re-evaluate their expectations.

The psychological contract may provide some indication of the answers to the two fundamental employment relationship questions that individuals pose: 'What can I reasonably expect from the organization?' and 'What should I reasonably be expected to contribute in return?' But it is unlikely that the psychological contract and therefore the employment relationship will ever be fully understood by either party.

The aspects of the employment relationship covered by the psychological contract will include, from the employee's point of view:

- how they are treated in terms of fairness, equity and consistency;
- security of employment;
- scope to demonstrate competence;
- career expectations and the opportunity to develop skills;
- involvement and influence;
- trust in the management of the organization to keep their promises;
- safe working environment.

From the employer's point of view, the psychological contract covers such aspects of the employment relationship as:

- competence;
- effort;
- compliance;
- commitment;
- loyalty.

As Guest *et al* (1996) point out:

> While employees may want what they have always wanted – security, a career, fair rewards, interesting work and so on – employers no longer feel able or obliged to provide these. Instead, they have been demanding more of their employees in terms of greater input and tolerance of uncertainty and change, while providing less in return, in particular less security and more limited career prospects.

An operational model of the psychological contract

An operational model of the psychological contract as formulated by Guest *et al* (1996) suggests that the core of the contract can be measured in terms of fairness of treatment, trust, and the extent to which the explicit deal or contract is perceived to be delivered. The full model is illustrated in Figure 16.1.

HOW PSYCHOLOGICAL CONTRACTS DEVELOP

Psychological contracts are not developed by means of a single transaction. There are many contract makers who exert influence over the whole duration of an employee's involvement with an organization. As Spindler (1994) comments:

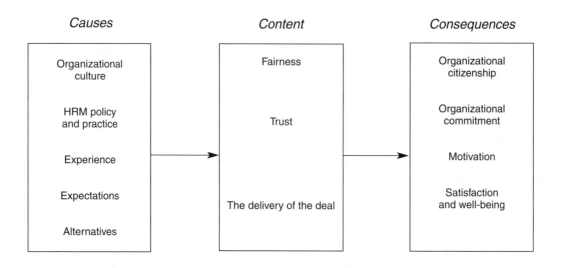

Figure 16.1 A model of the psychological contract

(*Source:* D Guest, N Conway, R Briner and M Dickman, *The State of the Psychological Contract in Employment: Issues in people management*, Institute of Personnel and Development, London, 1996)

> Every day we create relationships by means other than formal contracts... As individuals form relationships they necessarily bring their accumulated experience and developed personalities with them. In ways unknown to them, what they expect from the relationship reflects the sum total of their conscious and unconscious learning to date.

The problem with psychological contracts is that employees are often unclear about what they want from the organization or what they can contribute to it. Some employees are equally unclear about what they expect from their employees.

Because of these factors, and because a psychological contract is essentially implicit, it is likely to develop in an unplanned way with unforeseen consequences. Anything that management does or is perceived as doing that affects the interests of employees will modify the psychological contract. Similarly the actual or perceived behaviour of employees, individually or collectively, will affect an employer's concept of the contract.

THE CHANGING NATURE OF THE PSYCHOLOGICAL CONTRACT

Many commentators have delivered warnings about changes to the psychological contract that are not all advantageous to employees. And the nature of the psychological contract is changing in many organizations in response to changes in their external and internal environments. This is largely because of the impact of global competition and the effect this has had on how businesses operate, including moves into 'lean' forms of operation.

The psychological contract has not been an issue in the past because usually it did not change much. This is no longer the case because:

- business organizations are neither stable nor long-lived – uncertainty prevails, job security is no longer on offer by employers who are less anxious to maintain a stable workforce – as Mirvis and Hall (1994) point out, organizations are making continued employment explicitly contingent on the fit between people's competences and business needs;
- flexibility, adaptability and speed of response are all-important and individual roles may be subject to constant change – continuity and predictability are no longer available for employees;
- leaner organizations mean that careers may mainly develop laterally – expectations that progress will be made by promotion through the hierarchy are no longer so valid;
- leaner organizations may make greater demands on employees and are less likely to tolerate people who no longer precisely fit their requirements.

But, more positively, some organizations are realizing that steps have to be taken to increase mutuality and to provide scope for lateral career development and improvement in knowledge and skills through opportunities for learning. They recognize that because they can no longer guarantee long-term employment they have the responsibility to help people to continue to develop their careers if they have to move on. In other words they take steps to improve employability. Even those that have fully embraced the 'core–periphery' concept may recognize that they still need to obtain the commitment of their core employees and pay attention to their continuous development, although in most organizations the emphasis is likely to be on self-development.

Kissler (1994) summed up the differences between old and new employment contracts as follows:

Old	New
Relationship is pre-determined and imposed	Relationship is mutual and negotiated
You are who you work for and what you do	You are defined by multiple roles, many external to the organization
Loyalty is defined by performance	Loyalty is defined by output and quality
Leaving is treason	People and skills only needed when required
Employees who do what they are told will work until retirement	Long-term employment is unlikely; expect and prepare for multiple relationships

The following ways in which psychological contracts are changing have been suggested by Hiltrop (1995):

From	To
Imposed relationship (compliance, command and control)	Mutual relationship (commitment, participation and involvement)
Permanent employment relationship	Variable employment relationship – people and skills only obtained or retained when required
Focus on promotion	Focus on lateral career development
Finite job duties	Multiple roles
Meet job requirements	Add value
Emphasis on job security and loyalty to company	Emphasis on employability and loyalty to own career and skills
Training provided by organization	Opportunities for self-managed learning

Hiltrop suggests that a new psychological contract is emerging – one that is more situational and short term and which assumes that each party is much less dependent on the other for survival and growth. He believes that in its most naked form, the new contract could be defined as follows:

> There is no job security. The employee will be employed as long as he or she adds value to the organization, and is personally responsible for finding new ways to add value. In return, the employee has the right to demand interesting and important work, has the freedom and resources to perform it well, receives pay that reflects his or her contribution, and gets the experience and training needed to be employable here or elsewhere.

But this could hardly be called a balanced contract. To what extent do employees in general have 'the right to demand interesting and important work'? Employers still call the shots, except when dealing with the special cases of people who are much in demand and in short supply. In Britain, as Mant (1996) pointed out, 'people often really are regarded as merely "resources" to be acquired or divested according to short-term economic circumstances'. It is the employer who has the power to dictate contractual terms unless they have been fixed by collective bargaining. Individuals, except when they are highly sought after, have little scope to vary the terms of the contract imposed upon them by employers.

Perhaps one of the most important trends in the employment relationship as expressed by the psychological contract is that employees are now being required to bear risks that were previously carried by the organization. As Elliott (1996) notes: 'The most profound change in the labour market over the past two decades has been the massive shift in power from employee to employer. This has not only meant that workers have had their rights eroded, but also that much of the risk involved in a business has been shifted from capital to labour.'

THE STATE OF THE PSYCHOLOGICAL CONTRACT

But the dire warnings about the state of the psychological contract referred to above were not borne out by three research projects commissioned by the Institute of Personnel and Development. The research conducted by Guest *et al* (1996) established that the psychological contract (defined in terms of workers' judgements of fairness, trust and organizational delivery of 'the deal') was in better shape than many pundits suggest. A follow-up survey (Guest and Conway, 1997) found that a very high proportion of employees (90 per cent) believe that on balance they are fairly treated by their employers and 79 per cent say they trust management 'a lot' or 'somewhat' to keep its promises. Job security is not a major concern – 86 per cent feel very or fairly secure in their jobs. A majority (62 per cent) believe that management and workers are on the same side and only 18 per cent disagree. However, job satisfaction was only moderate (38 per cent express high satisfaction, but 22 per cent express low satisfaction), although commitment to the organization was high (49 per cent felt 'a lot' and 36 per cent 'some' loyalty to their organization).

A further survey (Guest and Conway, 1998) established that:

- there had been no significant changes in attitudes and behaviour since the previous survey;
- workers continue to believe that they are fairly treated – 67 per cent report fair treatment by management and 64 per cent say that they get a fair day's pay for a fair day's work;
- the number of progressive HRM practices in place is the key determinant of whether workers believe they are fairly treated, because they exert a major influence on work attitudes;
- people report that home is for relaxation, work is for challenge;
- feelings of security remain high – 88 per cent felt very or fairly secure in their jobs;
- people still expect a career – 60 per cent believe that their employer has made a career promise and of these, 65 per cent think that management has largely kept its promise (these feelings are more prevalent amongst younger workers).

The overall conclusion of the researchers in 1998 was that 'the psychological contract is very healthy'. On the whole, management is seen as fair, trustworthy and likely to keep its promises. The key influences on a healthy psychological contract are the use of progressive human resource practices, scope for direct participation at work and working in a smaller organization.

DEVELOPING AND MAINTAINING A POSITIVE PSYCHOLOGICAL CONTRACT

As Guest *et al* (1996) point out: 'A positive psychological contract is worth taking seriously because it is strongly linked to higher commitment to the organization, higher employee satisfaction and better employment relations. Again this reinforces the benefits of pursuing a set of progressive HRM practices.' They also emphasize the importance of a high-involvement climate and suggest in particular that HRM practices such as the provision of opportunities for learning, training and development, focus on job security, promotion and careers, minimizing status differentials, fair reward systems and comprehensive communication and involvement processes will all contribute to a positive psychological contract.

Steps taken to manage the employment relationship as specified in Chapter 15 will also help to form a positive psychological contract. These include:

- defining expectations during recruitment and induction programmes;
- communicating and agreeing expectations as part of the continuing dialogue implicit in good performance management practices;
- adopting a policy of transparency on company policies and procedures and on management's proposals and decisions as they affect people;
- generally treating people as stakeholders, relying on consensus and cooperation rather than control and coercion.

STATE OF THE PSYCHOLOGICAL CONTRACT 2004

The 2004 Workplace Employee Relations Survey (WERS, 2005) covering 700,000 workplaces and 22.5 million employees, surveyed 21,624 employees in workplaces employing more than 10 people about their level of job satisfaction. The results are shown in Table 16.1.

Table 16.1 Job satisfaction (WERS, 2005)

	Very satisfied %	Satisfied %	Neither %	Dissatisfied %	Very dissatisfied %
Sense of achievement	18	52	19	8	3
Scope for using initiative	20	52	19	8	3
Influence over job	12	15	28	11	3
Training	11	40	26	16	7
Pay	4	31	26	28	13
Job security	13	50	22	11	5
Work itself	17	55	19	7	3
Involvement in decision-making	8	30	39	17	6

The only area in which there was more dissatisfaction than satisfaction was pay. A higher proportion than might have been expected (72 per cent) were satisfied or very satisfied with the work itself, and equally high percentages were satisfied with regard to having a sense of achievement and scope for using initiative.

People will feel that they have been treated justly if management's decisions and procedures are fair, consistent, transparent and non-discriminatory, and properly consider the views and needs of employees.

Part IV

Organizational behaviour

People perform their roles within complex systems called organizations. The study of organizational behaviour is concerned with how people within organizations act, individually or in groups, and how organizations function, in terms of their structure and processes. All managers and HR specialists are in the business of influencing behaviour in directions that will meet business needs. An understanding of organizational processes and skills in the analysis and diagnosis of patterns of organizational behaviour are therefore important. As Nadler and Tushman (1980) have said:

> The manager needs to be able to understand the patterns of behaviour that are observed to predict in what direction behaviour will move (particularly in the light of managerial action), and to use this knowledge to control behaviour over the course of time. Effective managerial action requires that the manager be able to diagnose the system he or she is working in.

The purpose of this part of the book is to outline a basic set of concepts and to provide analytical tools which will enable HR specialists to diagnose organizational behaviour and to take appropriate actions. This purpose is achieved by initially (Chapter 17) providing a general analysis of the characteristics of individuals at work. The concepts of individual motivation, job satisfaction, commitment and job engagement are then explored in Chapters 18 and 19 before reviewing generally in Chapter 20 the ways in which organizations function – formal and informal structures – and how people work together in groups. The cultural factors that affect organizational behaviour are then examined in Chapter 21.

17

Characteristics of people

To manage people effectively, it is necessary to understand the factors that affect how people behave at work. This means taking into account the fundamental characteristics of people as examined in this chapter under the following headings:

- individual differences – as affected by people's abilities, intelligence, personality, background and culture, gender and race;
- attitudes – causes and manifestations;
- influences on behaviour – personality and attitudes;
- attribution theory – how we make judgements about people;
- orientation – the approaches people adopt to work;
- roles – the parts people play in carrying out their work.

INDIVIDUAL DIFFERENCES

The management of people would be much easier if everyone were the same, but they are, of course, different because of their ability, intelligence, personality, background and culture (the environment in which they were brought up), as discussed below. Gender, race and disability are additional factors to be taken into account. Importantly, the needs and wants of individuals will also differ, often fundamentally, and this affects their motivation, as described in the next chapter.

The headings under which personal characteristics can vary have been classified by Mischel (1981) as follows:

- *competencies* – abilities and skills;
- *constructs* – the conceptual framework which governs how people perceive their environment;
- *expectations* – what people have learned to expect about their own and others' behaviour;
- *values* – what people believe to be important;
- *self-regulatory plans* – the goals people set themselves and the plans they make to achieve them.

Environmental or situational variables include the type of work individuals carry out; the culture, climate and management style in the organization, the social group within which individuals work; and the 'reference groups' that individuals use for comparative purposes (eg comparing conditions of work between one category of employee and another).

Ability

Ability is the quality that makes an action possible. Abilities have been analysed by Burt (1954) and Vernon (1961). They classified them into two major groups:

- V:ed – standing for verbal, numerical, memory and reasoning abilities;
- K:m – standing for spatial and mechanical abilities, as well as perceptual (memory) and motor skills relating to physical operations such as eye/hand coordination and mental dexterity.

They also suggested that overriding these abilities there is a 'g' or general intelligence factor which accounts for most variations in performance.
   Alternative classifications have been produced by

- Thurstone (1940) – spatial ability, perceptual speed, numerical ability, verbal meaning, memory, verbal fluency and inductive reasoning;
- Gagne (1977) – intellectual skills, cognitive (understanding and learning) skills, verbal and motor skills;
- Argyle (1989) – judgement, creativity and social skills.

Intelligence

Intelligence has been defined as:

- 'the capacity to solve problems, apply principles, make inferences and perceive relationships' (Argyle, 1989);
- 'the capacity for abstract thinking and reasoning with a range of different contents and media' (Toplis *et al* 1991);
- 'the capacity to process information' (Makin *et al*, 1996);
- 'what is measured by intelligence tests' (Wright and Taylor, 1970).

The last, tautological definition is not facetious. As an operational definition, it can be related to the specific aspects of reasoning, inference, cognition (ie knowing, conceiving) and perception (ie understanding, recognition) that intelligence tests attempt to measure.

General intelligence, as noted above, consists of a number of mental abilities that enable a person to succeed at a wide variety of intellectual tasks that use the faculties of knowing and reasoning. The mathematical technique of factor analysis has been used to identify the constituents of intelligence, such as Thurstone's (1940) multiple factors listed above. But there is no general agreement among psychologists as to what these factors are or, indeed, whether there is such a thing as general intelligence.

An alternative approach to the analysis of intelligence was put forward by Guilford (1967), who distinguished five types of mental operation: thinking, remembering, divergent production (problem-solving which leads to unexpected and original solutions), convergent production (problem-solving which leads to the one, correct solution) and evaluating.

Personality

Definition

As defined by Toplis *et al* (1991), the term personality is all-embracing in terms of the individual's behaviour and the way it is organized and coordinated when he or she interacts with the environment. Personality can be described in terms of traits or types.

The trait concept of personality

Personality can be defined as the relatively stable and enduring aspects of individuals that distinguish them from other people. This is the 'trait' concept, traits being predispositions to behave in certain ways in a variety of different situations. The assumption that people are consistent in the ways they express these traits is the basis for making predictions about their future behaviour. We all attribute traits to people in an attempt to understand why they behave in the way they do. As Chell (1987) says: 'This cognitive process gives a sense of order to what might otherwise appear to be senseless uncoordinated behaviours. Traits may therefore be thought of as classification systems, used by individuals to understand other people's and their own behaviour.'

The so-called big five personality traits as defined by Deary and Matthews (1993) are:

- *neuroticism* – anxiety, depression, hostility, self-consciousness, impulsiveness, vulnerability;
- *extraversion* – warmth, gregariousness, assertiveness, activity, excitement seeking, positive emotions;
- *openness* – feelings, actions, ideas, values;
- *agreeableness* – trust, straightforwardness, altruism, compliance, modesty, tender-mindedness;
- *conscientiousness* – competence, order, dutifulness, achievement-striving, self-discipline, deliberation.

A widely used instrument for assessing traits is Cattell's (1963) 16PF test. But the trait theory of personality has been attacked by people such as Mischel (1981), Chell (1985) and Harre (1979). The main criticisms have been as follows:

- People do not necessarily express the same trait across different situations or even the same trait in the same situation. Different people may exhibit consistency in some traits and considerable variability in others.
- Classical trait theory as formulated by Cattell (1963) assumes that the manifestation of trait behaviour is independent of the situations and the persons with whom the individual is interacting – this assumption is questionable, given that trait behaviour usually manifests itself in response to specific situations.
- Trait attributions are a product of language – they are devices for speaking about people and are not generally described in terms of behaviour.

Type theories of personality

Type theory identifies a number of types of personality that can be used to categorize people and may form the basis of a personality test. The types may be linked to descriptions of various traits.

One of the most widely used type theories is that of Jung (1923). He identified four major preferences of people:

- relating to other people – extraversion or introversion;
- gathering information – sensing (dealing with facts that can be objectively veri-fied) or intuitive (generating information through insight);
- using information – thinking (emphasizing logical analysis as the basis for deci-sion-making) or feeling (making decisions based on internal values and beliefs);
- making decisions – perceiving (collecting all the relevant information before making a decision) or judging (resolving the issue without waiting for a large quantity of data).

This theory of personality forms the basis of personality tests such as the Myers-Briggs Types Indicator.

Eysenck (1953) identified three personality traits: extroversion/introversion, neuroticism and psychoticism, and classified people as stable or unstable extroverts or introverts. For example, a stable introvert is passive, careful, controlled and thoughtful, while a stable extrovert is lively, outgoing, responsive and sociable.

As Makin *et al* (1996) comment, studies using types to predict work-related behav-iours are less common and may be difficult to interpret: 'In general it would be fair to say that their level of predictability is similar to that for trait measures.'

The influence of background

Individual differences may be a function of people's background, which will include the environment and culture in which they have been brought up and now exist. Levinson (1978) suggested that 'individual life structure' is shaped by three types of external event:

- the socio-cultural environment;
- the roles they play and the relationships they have;
- the opportunities and constraints that enable or inhibit them to express and develop their personality.

Differences arising from gender, race or disability

It is futile, dangerous and invidious to make assumptions about inherent differences between people because of their sex, race or degree of disability. *If* there are differ-ences in behaviour at work, these are more likely to arise from environmental and cultural factors than from differences in fundamental personal characteristics. The work environment undoubtedly influences feelings and behaviour for each of these categories. Research cited by Arnold *et al* (1991) established that working women as a whole 'experienced more daily stress, marital dissatisfaction, and ageing worries, and were less likely to show overt anger than either housewives or men'. Ethnic minorities may find that the selection process is biased against them, promotion prospects are low and that they are subject to other overt or subtle forms of discrimination. The behaviour of people with disabilities can also be affected by the fact that they are not given equal opportunities. There is, of course, legislation against discrimination in each of those areas but this cannot prevent the more covert forms of prejudice.

ATTITUDES

An attitude can broadly be defined as a settled mode of thinking. Attitudes are evaluative. As described by Makin *et al* (1996), 'Any attitude contains an assessment of whether the object to which it refers is liked or disliked.' Attitudes are developed through experience but they are less stable than traits and can change as new experiences are gained or influences absorbed. Within organizations they are affected by cultural factors (values and norms), the behaviour of management (management style), policies such as those concerned with pay, recognition, promotion and the quality of working life, and the influence of the 'reference group' (the group with whom people identify).

INFLUENCES ON BEHAVIOUR AT WORK

Factors affecting behaviour

Behaviour at work is dependent on both the personal characteristics of individuals (personality and attitudes) and the situation in which they are working. These factors interact, and this theory of behaviour is sometimes called interactionism. It is because of this process of interaction and because there are so many variables in personal characteristics and situations that behaviour is difficult to analyse and predict. It is generally assumed that attitudes determine behaviour, but there is not such a direct link as most people suppose. As Arnold *et al* (1991) comment, research evidence has shown that: 'People's avowed feelings and beliefs about someone or something seemed only loosely related to how they behaved towards it.'

Behaviour will be influenced by the perceptions of individuals about the situation they are in. The term *psychological climate* has been coined by James and Sells (1981) to describe how people's perceptions of the situation give it psychological significance and meaning. They suggested that the key environmental variables are:

- role characteristics such as role ambiguity and conflict (see the last section in this chapter);
- job characteristics such as autonomy and challenge;
- leader behaviours, including goal emphasis and work facilitation;
- work group characteristics, including cooperation and friendliness;
- organizational policies that directly affect individuals, such as the reward system.

ATTRIBUTION THEORY – HOW WE MAKE JUDGEMENTS ABOUT PEOPLE

The ways in which we perceive and make judgements about people at work are explained by attribution theory, which concerns the assignment of causes to events. We make an attribution when we perceive and describe other people's actions and try to discover why they behaved in the way they did. We can also make attributions about our own behaviour. Heider (1958) has pointed out that: 'In everyday life we form ideas about other people and about social situations. We interpret other people's actions and we predict what they will do under certain circumstances.'

In attributing causes to people's actions we distinguish between what is in the person's power to achieve and the effect of environmental influence. A personal cause, whether someone does well or badly, may, for example, be the amount of effort displayed, while a situational cause may be the extreme difficulty of the task. Kelley (1967) has suggested that there are four criteria that we apply to decide whether behaviour is attributable to personal rather than external (situational) causes:

- *distinctiveness* – the behaviour can be distinguished from the behaviour of other people in similar situations;
- *consensus* – if other people agree that the behaviour is governed by some personal characteristic;
- *consistency over time* – whether the behaviour is repeated;
- *consistency over modality* (ie the manner in which things are done) – whether or not the behaviour is repeated in different situations.

Attribution theory is also concerned with the way in which people attribute success or failure to themselves. Research by Weiner (1974) and others has indicated that when people with high achievement needs have been successful, they ascribe this to internal factors such as ability and effort. High achievers tend to attribute failure to lack of effort and not lack of ability. Low achievers tend not to link success with effort but to ascribe their failures to lack of ability.

ORIENTATION TO WORK

Orientation theory examines the factors that are instrumental, ie serve as a means, in directing people's choices about work. An orientation is a central organizing principle that underlies people's attempts to make sense of their lives. In relation to work, as defined by Guest (1984): 'An orientation is a persisting tendency to seek certain goals and rewards from work which exists independently of the nature of the work and the work content.' The orientation approach stresses the role of the social environment factor as a key factor affecting motivation.

Orientation theory is primarily developed from fieldwork carried out by sociologists rather than from laboratory work conducted by psychologists. Goldthorpe *et al* (1968) studied skilled and semi-skilled workers in Luton, and, in their findings, they stressed the importance of instrumental orientation, that is, a view of work as a means to an end, a context in which to earn money to purchase goods and leisure. According to Goldthorpe, the 'affluent' worker interviewed by the research team valued work largely for extrinsic reasons.

In their research carried out with blue-collar workers in Peterborough, Blackburn and Mann (1979) found a wider range of orientations. They suggested that different ones could come into play with varying degrees of force in different situations. The fact that workers, in practice, had little choice about what they did contributed to this diversity – their orientations were affected by the choice or lack of choice presented to them and this meant that they might be forced to accept alternative orientations.

But Blackburn and Mann confirmed that pay was a key preference area, the top preferences being:

1. pay;
2. security;
3. workmates;
4. intrinsic job satisfaction;
5. autonomy.

They commented that: 'An obsession with wages clearly emerged... A concern to minimize unpleasant work was also widespread.' Surprisingly, perhaps, they also revealed that the most persistent preference of all was for outside work, 'a fairly clear desire for a combination of fresh air and freedom'.

ROLES

When faced with any situation, eg carrying out a job, people have to enact a role in order to manage that situation. This is sometimes called the 'situation-act model'. As described by Chell (1985), the model indicates that: 'The person must act within situations: situations are rule-governed and how a person behaves is often prescribed by these socially acquired rules. The person thus adopts a suitable role in order to perform effectively within the situation.'

At work, the term *role* describes the part to be played by individuals in fulfilling their job requirements. Roles therefore indicate the specific forms of behaviour required to carry out a particular task or the group of tasks contained in a *position* or job. Work role profiles primarily define the requirements in terms of the ways tasks are carried out rather than the tasks themselves. They may refer to broad aspects of behaviour, especially with regard to working with others and styles of management. A distinction can therefore be made between a *job description*, which simply lists the main tasks an individual has to carry out, and a *role profile*, which is more concerned with the behavioural aspects of the work and the outcomes the individual in the role is expected to achieve. The concept of a role emphasizes the fact that people at work are, in a sense, always acting a part; they are not simply reciting the lines but interpreting them in terms of their own perceptions of how they should behave in relation to the context in which they work, especially with regard to their interactions with other people and their discretionary behaviour.

Role theory, as formulated by Katz and Kahn (1966) states that the role individuals occupy at work – and elsewhere – exists in relation to other people – their *role set*. These people have expectations about the individuals' role, and if they live up to these expectations they will have successfully performed the role. Performance in a role is a product of the situation individuals are in (the organizational context and the direction or influence exercised from above or elsewhere in the organization) and their own skills, competences, attitudes and personality. Situational factors are important, but the role individuals perform can both shape and reflect their personalities. Stress and inadequate performance result when roles are ambiguous, incompatible, or in conflict with one another.

Role ambiguity

When individuals are unclear about what their role is, what is expected of them, or how they are getting on, they may become insecure or lose confidence in themselves.

Role incompatibility

Stress and poor performance may be caused by roles having incompatible elements, as when there is a clash between what other people expect from the role and what individuals believe is expected of them.

Role conflict

Role conflict results when, even if roles are clearly defined and there is no incompatibility between expectations, individuals have to carry out two antagonistic roles. For example, conflict can exist between the roles of individuals at work and their roles at home.

IMPLICATIONS FOR HR SPECIALISTS

The main implications for HR specialists of the factors that affect individuals at work are as follows:

- *Individual differences* – when designing jobs, preparing learning programmes, assessing and counselling staff, developing reward systems and dealing with grievances and disciplinary problems, it is necessary to remember that all people are different. This may seem obvious but it is remarkable how many people ignore it. What fulfils one person may not fulfil another. Abilities, aptitudes and intelligence differ widely and particular care needs to be taken in fitting the right people into the right jobs and giving them the right training. Personalities and attitudes also differ. It is important to focus on how to manage diversity as described in Chapter 57. This should take account of individual differences, which will include any issues arising from the employment of women, people from different ethnic groups, those with disabilities and older people.
- *Personalities* should not be judged simplistically in terms of stereotyped traits. People are complex and they change, and account has to be taken of this. The problem for HR specialists and managers in general is that, while they have to accept and understand these differences and take full account of them, they have ultimately to proceed on the basis of fitting them to the requirements of the situation, which are essentially what the organization needs to achieve. There is always a limit to the extent to which an organization, which relies on collective effort to achieve its goals, can adjust itself to the specific needs of individuals. But the organization has to appreciate that the pressures it makes on people can result in stress and therefore become counter-productive.

- *Judgements about people* (attribution theory) – we all ascribe motives to other people and attempt to establish the causes of their behaviour. We must be careful, however, not to make simplistic judgements about causality (ie what has motivated someone's behaviour) – for ourselves as well as in respect of others – especially when we are assessing performance.
- *Orientation theory* – the significance of orientation theory is that it stresses the importance of the effect of environmental factors on the motivation to work.
- *Role theory* – role theory helps us to understand the need to clarify with individuals what is expected of them in behavioural and outcome terms and to ensure when designing roles that they do not contain any incompatible elements. We must also be aware of the potential for role conflict so that steps can be taken to minimize stress.

18

Motivation

All organizations are concerned with what should be done to achieve sustained high levels of performance through people. This means giving close attention to how individuals can best be motivated through such means as incentives, rewards, leadership and, importantly, the work they do and the organization context within which they carry out that work. The aim is to develop motivation processes and a work environment that will help to ensure that individuals deliver results in accordance with the expectations of management.

Motivation theory examines the process of motivation. It explains why people at work behave in the way they do in terms of their efforts and the directions they are taking. It describes what organizations can do to encourage people to apply their efforts and abilities in ways that will further the achievement of the organization's goals as well as satisfying their own needs. It is also concerned with job satisfaction – the factors that create it and its impact on performance.

In understanding and applying motivation theory, the aim is to obtain added value through people in the sense that the value of their output exceeds the cost of generating it. This can be achieved through discretionary effort. In most if not all roles there is scope for individuals to decide how much effort they want to exert. They can do just enough to get away with it, or they can throw themselves into their work and deliver added value. Discretionary effort can be a key component in organizational performance.

Unfortunately, approaches to motivation are too often underpinned by simplistic assumptions about how it works. The process of motivation is much more complex than many people believe. People have different needs, establish different goals to satisfy those needs and take different actions to achieve those goals. It is wrong to assume that one approach to motivation fits all. That is why the assumptions underlying belief in the virtues of performance-related pay as a means of providing a motivational incentive are simplistic. Motivational practices are most likely to function effectively if they are based on proper understanding of what is involved. This chapter therefore covers the following:

- the process of motivation;
- the various theories of motivation which explain and amplify the basic process;
- the practical implications of motivation theory;
- job satisfaction.

THE PROCESS OF MOTIVATION

What is motivation? A motive is a reason for doing something. Motivation is concerned with the factors that influence people to behave in certain ways. The three components of motivation as listed by Arnold *et al* (1991) are:

- *direction* – what a person is trying to do;
- *effort* – how hard a person is trying;
- *persistence* – how long a person keeps on trying.

Motivating other people is about getting them to move in the direction you want them to go in order to achieve a result. Motivating yourself is about setting the direction independently and then taking a course of action which will ensure that you get there. Motivation can be described as goal-directed behaviour. People are motivated when they expect that a course of action is likely to lead to the attainment of a goal and a valued reward – one that satisfies their needs.

Well-motivated people are those with clearly defined goals who take action that they expect will achieve those goals. Such people may be self-motivated, and as long as this means they are going in the right direction to achieve what they are there to achieve, then this is the best form of motivation. Most people, however, need to be motivated to a greater or lesser degree. The organization as a whole can provide the context within which high levels of motivation can be achieved by providing incentives and rewards, satisfying work, and opportunities for learning and growth. But managers still have a major part to play in using their motivating skills to get people to give of their best, and to make good use of the motivational processes provided by the organization. To do this it is necessary to understand the process of motivation – how it works and the different types of motivation that exist.

A needs-related model of the process of motivation is shown in Figure 18.1. This suggests that motivation is initiated by the conscious or unconscious recognition of unsatisfied needs. These needs create wants, which are desires to achieve or obtain something. Goals are then established which it is believed will satisfy these needs and wants and a behaviour pathway is selected which it is expected will achieve the goal. If the goal is achieved, the need will be satisfied and the behaviour is likely to be repeated the next time a similar need emerges. If the goal is not achieved, the same action is less likely to be repeated. This process of repeating successful behaviour or actions is called reinforcement or the law of effect (Hull, 1951). It has, however, been criticised by Allport (1954) as ignoring the influence of expectations and therefore constituting 'hedonism of the past'.

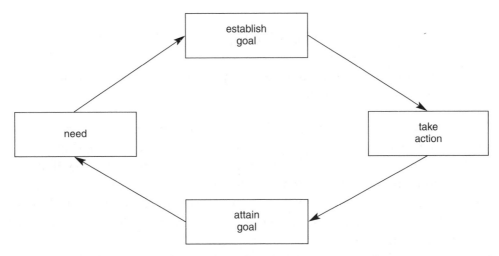

Figure 18.1   The process of motivation

TYPES OF MOTIVATION

Motivation at work can take place in two ways. First, people can motivate themselves by seeking, finding and carrying out work (or being given work) that satisfies their needs or at least leads them to expect that their goals will be achieved. Secondly, people can be motivated by management through such methods as pay, promotion, praise, etc.

There are two types of motivation as originally identified by Herzberg *et al* (1957):

- *Intrinsic motivation* – the self-generated factors that influence people to behave in a particular way or to move in a particular direction. These factors include responsibility (feeling that the work is important and having control over one's own resources), autonomy (freedom to act), scope to use and develop skills and abilities, interesting and challenging work and opportunities for advancement.
- *Extrinsic motivation* – what is done to or for people to motivate them. This includes rewards, such as increased pay, praise, or promotion, and punishments, such as disciplinary action, withholding pay, or criticism.

Extrinsic motivators can have an immediate and powerful effect, but it will not necessarily last long. The intrinsic motivators, which are concerned with the 'quality of working life' (a phrase and movement that emerged from this concept), are likely to have a deeper and longer-term effect because they are inherent in individuals and not imposed from outside.

MOTIVATION THEORY

Approaches to motivation are underpinned by motivation theory. The most influential theories are classified as follows:

- *Instrumentality theory*, which states that rewards or punishments (carrots or sticks) serve as the means of ensuring that people behave or act in desired ways.
- *Content theory*, which focuses on the content of motivation. It states that motivation is essentially about taking action to satisfy needs, and identifies the main needs that influence behaviour. Needs theory was originated by Maslow (1954), and in their two-factor model, Herzberg *et al* (1957) listed needs which they termed 'satisfiers'.
- *Process theory*, which focuses on the psychological processes which affect motivation, by reference to expectations (Vroom, 1964), goals (Latham and Locke, 1979) and perceptions of equity (Adams, 1965).

These are summarized in Table 18.1 on page 256.

INSTRUMENTALITY THEORY

'Instrumentality' is the belief that if we do one thing it will lead to another. In its crudest form, instrumentality theory states that people only work for money.

The theory emerged in the second half of the nineteenth century with its emphasis on the need to rationalize work and on economic outcomes. It assumes that a person will be motivated to work if rewards and penalties are tied directly to his or her performance, thus the awards are contingent upon effective performance. Instrumentality theory has its roots in Taylorism, ie the scientific management methods of F W Taylor (1911), who wrote: 'It is impossible, through any long period of time, to get workmen to work much harder than the average men around them unless they are assured a large and permanent increase in their pay.'

This theory is based on the principle of reinforcement as influenced by Skinner's (1974) concept of conditioning – the theory that people can be 'conditioned' to act in certain ways if they are rewarded for behaving as required. It is also called the law of effect. Motivation using this approach has been, and still is, widely adopted and can be successful in some circumstances. But it is based exclusively on a system of external controls and fails to recognize a number of other human needs. It also fails to appreciate the fact that the formal control system can be seriously affected by the informal relationship existing between workers.

CONTENT (NEEDS) THEORY

The basis of this theory is the belief that the content of motivation consists of needs. An unsatisfied need creates tension and a state of disequilibrium. To restore the balance, a goal that will satisfy the need is identified, and a behaviour pathway that will lead to the achievement of the goal is selected. All behaviour is therefore motivated by unsatisfied needs.

Not all needs are equally important for a person at any one time – some may provide a much more powerful drive towards a goal than others, depending on the individual's background and present situation. Complexity is further increased because there is no simple relationship between needs and goals. The same need can be satisfied by a number of different goals and the stronger the need and the longer its duration, the broader the range of possible goals. At the same time, one goal may satisfy a number of needs – a new car provides transport as well as an opportunity to impress the neighbours.

Needs theory was developed originally by Maslow (1954), who postulated the concept of a hierarchy of needs which he believed were fundamental to the personality. Herzberg *et al's* (1957) two-factor model (see page 262) cannot strictly be classified as needs theory but he did identify a number of fundamental needs.

Table 18.1 Summary of motivation theories

Category	Type	Theorist(s)	Summary of theory	Implications
Instrumentality	Taylorism	Taylor	If we do one thing it leads to another. People will be motivated to work if rewards and punishments are directly related to their performance	Basis of crude attempts to motivate people by incentives. Often used as the implied rationale for performance-related pay although this is seldom an effective motivator
Content (needs) theory	Hierarchy of needs	Maslow	A hierarchy of five needs exist: physiological, safety, social, esteem, self-fulfilment. Needs at a higher level only emerge when a lower need is satisfied	Focuses attention on the various needs that motivate people and the notion that a satisfied need is no longer a motivator. The concept of a hierarchy has no practical significance
Two-factor model	Satisfiers/ dissatisfiers	Herzberg	Two groups of factors affect job satisfaction: (1) those intrinsic to the job (intrinsic motivators or satisfiers) such as achievement, recognition, the work itself, responsibility and growth; (2) those extrinsic to the job (extrinsic motivators or hygiene factors) such as pay and working conditions	Identifies a number of fundamental needs, ie achievement, recognition, advancement, autonomy and the work itself. Strongly influences approaches to job design (job enrichment). Drew attention to the concept of intrinsic and extrinsic motivation and the fact that intrinsic motivation mainly derived from the work itself will have a longer-lasting effect. Therefore underpins the proposition that reward systems should provide for both financial and non-financial rewards

continued

Table 18.1 *continued*

Process/ cognitive theory	Expectancy theory	Vroom, Porter and Lawler	Motivation and performance are influenced by: (1) the perceived link between effort and performance, (2) the perceived link between performance and outcomes, and (3) the significance (valence) of the outcome to the person. Effort (motivation) depends on the likelihood that rewards will follow effort and that the reward is worthwhile	The key theory informing approaches to rewards, ie that there must be a link between effort and reward (line of sight), the reward should be achievable and should be worthwhile
	Goal theory	Latham and Locke	Motivation and performance will improve if people have difficult but agreed goals and receive feedback	Provides the rationale for performance management processes, goal setting and feedback
	Equity theory	Adams	People are better motivated if treated equitably	Need to develop equitable reward and employment practices

In addition, Alderfer (1972) developed his ERG theory, which refers to the need for existence, relatedness and growth. Maslow's theory has been most influential.

Maslow's hierarchy of needs

The most famous classification of needs is the one formulated by Maslow (1954). He suggested that there are five major need categories which apply to people in general, starting from the fundamental physiological needs and leading through a hierarchy of safety, social and esteem needs to the need for self-fulfilment, the highest need of all. Maslow's hierarchy is as follows:

1. *Physiological* – the need for oxygen, food, water and sex.

2. *Safety* – the need for protection against danger and the deprivation of physiological needs.
3. *Social* – the need for love, affection and acceptance as belonging to a group.
4. *Esteem* – the need to have a stable, firmly based, high evaluation of oneself (self-esteem) and to have the respect of others (prestige). These needs may be classified into two subsidiary sets: first, the desire for achievement, for adequacy, for confidence in the face of the world, and for independence and freedom, and, second, the desire for reputation or status defined as respect or esteem from other people, and manifested by recognition, attention, importance, or appreciation.
5. *Self-fulfilment (self-actualization)* – the need to develop potentialities and skills, to become what one believes one is capable of becoming.

Maslow's theory of motivation states that when a lower need is satisfied, the next highest becomes dominant and the individual's attention is turned to satisfying this higher need. The need for self-fulfilment, however, can never be satisfied. He said that 'man is a wanting animal'; only an unsatisfied need can motivate behaviour and the dominant need is the prime motivator of behaviour. Psychological development takes place as people move up the hierarchy of needs, but this is not necessarily a straightforward progression. The lower needs still exist, even if temporarily dormant as motivators, and individuals constantly return to previously satisfied needs.

One of the implications of Maslow's theory is that the higher-order needs for esteem and self-fulfilment provide the greatest impetus to motivation – they grow in strength when they are satisfied, while the lower needs decline in strength on satisfaction. But the jobs people do will not necessarily satisfy their needs, especially when they are routine or deskilled.

Maslow's needs hierarchy has an intuitive appeal and has been very influential. But it has not been verified by empirical research and it has been criticized for its apparent rigidity – different people may have different priorities and it is difficult to accept that people's needs progress steadily up the hierarchy. In fact, Maslow himself expressed doubts about the validity of a strictly ordered hierarchy.

PROCESS THEORY

In process theory, the emphasis is on the psychological processes or forces that affect motivation, as well as on basic needs. It is also known as cognitive theory because it is concerned with people's perceptions of their working environment and the ways in which they interpret and understand it. According to Guest (1992a), process theory provides a much more relevant approach to motivation than the theories of Maslow and Herzberg, which, he suggests, have been shown by extensive research to be wrong.

Process or cognitive theory can certainly be more useful to managers than needs theory because it provides more realistic guidance on motivation techniques. The processes are:

- expectations (expectancy theory);
- goal achievement (goal theory);
- feelings about equity (equity theory).

Expectancy theory

The concept of expectancy was originally contained in the valency–instrumentality–expectancy (VIE) theory which was formulated by Vroom (1964). Valency stands for value, instrumentality is the belief that if we do one thing it will lead to another, and expectancy is the probability that action or effort will lead to an outcome. This concept of expectancy was defined in more detail by Vroom as follows:

> Where an individual chooses between alternatives which involve uncertain outcomes, it seems clear that his behaviour is affected not only by his preferences among these outcomes but also by the degree to which he believes these outcomes to be possible. An expectancy is defined as a momentary belief concerning the likelihood that a particular act will be followed by a particular outcome. Expectancies may be described in terms of their strength. Maximal strength is indicated by subjective certainty that the act will be followed by the outcome, while minimal (or zero) strength is indicated by subjective certainty that the act will not be followed by the outcome.

The strength of expectations may be based on past experiences (reinforcement), but individuals are frequently presented with new situations – a change in job, payment system, or working conditions imposed by management – where past experience is not an adequate guide to the implications of the change. In these circumstances, motivation may be reduced.

Motivation is only likely when a clearly perceived and usable relationship exists between performance and outcome, and the outcome is seen as a means of satisfying needs. This explains why extrinsic financial motivation – for example, an incentive or bonus scheme – works only if the link between effort and reward is clear (in the words of Lawler (1990) there is a 'line of sight') and the value of the reward is worth the effort. It also explains why intrinsic motivation arising from the work itself can be more powerful than extrinsic motivation. Intrinsic motivation outcomes are more under the control of individuals, who can place greater reliance on their past experiences to indicate the extent to which positive and advantageous results are likely to be obtained by their behaviour.

This theory was developed by Porter and Lawler (1968) into a model, illustrated in Figure 18.2, which follows Vroom's ideas by suggesting that there are two factors determining the effort people put into their jobs:

1. the value of the rewards to individuals in so far as they satisfy their needs for security, social esteem, autonomy, and self-actualization;
2. the probability that rewards depend on effort, as perceived by individuals – in other words, their expectations about the relationships between effort and reward.

Thus, the greater the value of a set of awards and the higher the probability that receiving each of these rewards depends upon effort, the greater the effort that will be put forth in a given situation.

But, as Porter and Lawler emphasize, mere effort is not enough. It has to be effective effort if it is to produce the desired performance. The two variables additional to effort which affect task achievement are:

● *ability* – individual characteristics such as intelligence, manual skills, know-how;
● *role perceptions* – what the individual wants to do or thinks he or she is required to do. These are good from the viewpoint of the organization if they correspond with what it thinks the individual ought to be doing. They are poor if the views of the individual and the organization do not coincide.

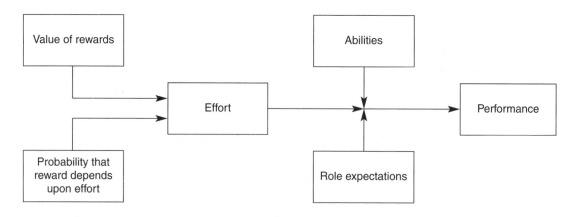

Figure 18.2 Motivation model (Porter and Lawler, 1968)

Goal theory

Goal theory as developed by Latham and Locke (1979) states that motivation and performance are higher when individuals are set specific goals, when goals are difficult but accepted, and when there is a feedback on performance. Participation in goal setting is important as a means of getting agreement to the setting of higher goals. Difficult goals must be agreed and their achievement reinforced by guidance and advice. Finally, feedback is vital in maintaining motivation, particularly towards the achievement of even higher goals.

Erez and Zidon (1984) emphasized the need for acceptance of and commitment to goals. They found that, as long as they are agreed, demanding goals lead to better performance than easy ones. Erez (1977) also emphasized the importance of feedback. As Robertson *et al* (1992) point out:

> Goals inform individuals to achieve particular levels of performance, in order for them to direct and evaluate their actions; while performance feedback allows the individual to track how well he or she has been doing in relation to the goal, so that, if necessary, adjustments in effort, direction or possibly task strategies can be made.

Goal theory is in line with the 1960s concept of management by objectives. The latter approach, however, often failed because it was tackled bureaucratically without gaining the real support of those involved and, importantly, without ensuring that managers were aware of the significance of the processes of agreement, reinforcement and feedback, and were skilled in practising them.

Goal theory, however, plays a key part in the performance management process which was evolved from the largely discredited management-by-objectives approach. Performance management is dealt with in Part VII.

Equity theory

Equity theory is concerned with the perceptions people have about how they are being treated compared with others. To be dealt with equitably is to be treated fairly in comparison with another group of people (a reference group) or a relevant other person. Equity involves feelings and perceptions and is always a comparative process. It is not synonymous with equality, which means treating everyone the same, since this would be inequitable if they deserve to be treated differently.

Equity theory states, in effect, that people will be better motivated if they are treated equitably and demotivated if they are treated inequitably. It explains only one aspect of the process of motivation and job satisfaction, although it may be significant in terms of morale.

As suggested by Adams (1965), there are two forms of equity: distributive equity, which is concerned with the fairness with which people feel they are rewarded in accordance with their contribution and in comparison with others; and procedural equity, or procedural justice, which is concerned with the perceptions employees have about the fairness with which procedures in such areas as performance appraisal, promotion and discipline are being operated.

Interpersonal factors are closely linked to feelings about procedural fairness. Five factors that contribute to perceptions of procedural fairness have been identified by Tyler and Bies (1990). These are:

1. adequate considerations of an employee's viewpoint;
2. suppression of personal bias towards the employee;
3. applying criteria consistently across employees;
4. providing early feedback to employees concerning the outcome of decisions;
5. providing employees with an adequate explanation of the decision made.

HERZBERG'S TWO-FACTOR MODEL

The two-factor model of satisfiers and dissatisfiers was developed by Herzberg *et al* (1957) following an investigation into the sources of job satisfaction and dissatisfaction of accountants and engineers. It was assumed that people have the capacity to report accurately the conditions that made them satisfied and dissatisfied with their jobs. Accordingly, the subjects were asked to tell their interviewers about the times during which they felt exceptionally good and exceptionally bad about their jobs and how long their feelings persisted. It was found that the accounts of 'good' periods most frequently concerned the content of the job, particularly achievement, recognition, advancement, autonomy, responsibility, and the work itself. On the other hand, accounts of 'bad' periods most frequently concerned the context of the job. Company policy and administration, supervision, salary and working conditions more frequently appeared in these accounts than in those told about 'good' periods. The main implications of this research, according to Herzberg, are that:

> The wants of employees divide into two groups. One group revolves around the need to develop in one's occupation as a source of personal growth. The second group operates as an essential base to the first and is associated with fair treatment in compensation, supervision, working conditions and administrative practices. The fulfilment of the needs of the second group does not motivate the individual to high levels of job satisfaction and to extra performance on the job. All we can expect from satisfying this second group of needs is the prevention of dissatisfaction and poor job performance.

These groups form the two factors in Herzberg's model: one consists of the satisfiers or motivators, because they are seen to be effective in motivating the individual to superior performance and effort. The other consists of the dissatisfiers, which essentially describe the environment and serve primarily to prevent job dissatisfaction, while having little effect on positive job attitudes. The latter were named the hygiene factors in the medical use of the term, meaning preventive and environmental.

Reservations about Herzberg's theory

Herzberg's two-factor model has been attacked. The research method has been criticized because no attempt was made to measure the relationship between satisfaction and performance. It has been suggested that the two-factor nature of the theory is an inevitable result of the questioning method used by the interviewers. It has also been suggested that wide and unwarranted inferences have been drawn from small and specialized samples and that there is no evidence to suggest that the satisfiers do improve productivity.

In spite of these criticisms (or perhaps because of them, as they are all from academics), the Herzberg theory continues to thrive; partly because for the layman it is easy to understand and seems to be based on 'real-life' rather than academic abstraction, and partly because it fits in well with the highly respected ideas of Maslow (1954) and McGregor (1960) in its emphasis on the positive value of the intrinsic motivating factors. It is also in accord with a fundamental belief in the dignity of labour and the Protestant ethic – that work is good in itself. As a result, Herzberg had immense influence on the job enrichment movement, which sought to design jobs in a way that would maximize the opportunities to obtain intrinsic satisfaction from work and thus improve the quality of working life. His emphasis on the distinction between intrinsic and extrinsic motivation is also important.

THE RELATIONSHIP BETWEEN MOTIVATION, JOB SATISFACTION AND MONEY

The basic requirements for job satisfaction may include comparatively higher pay, an equitable payment system, real opportunities for promotion, considerate and participative management, a reasonable degree of social interaction at work, interesting and varied tasks and a high degree of autonomy: control over work pace and work methods. The degree of satisfaction obtained by individuals, however, depends largely upon their own needs and expectations, and the working environment.

JOB SATISFACTION

The term 'job satisfaction' refers to the attitudes and feelings people have about their work. Positive and favourable attitudes towards the job indicate job satisfaction. Negative and unfavourable attitudes towards the job indicate job dissatisfaction.

Morale is often defined as being equivalent to job satisfaction. Thus Guion (1958) defines morale as 'the extent to which an individual's needs are satisfied and the extent to which the individual perceives that satisfaction as stemming from his (*sic*) total work situation'. Other definitions stress the group aspects of morale. Gilmer (1961) suggests that morale 'is a feeling of being accepted by and belonging to a group of employees through adherence to common goals'. He distinguishes between morale as a group variable, related to the degree to which group members feel attracted to their group and desire to remain a member of it, and job attitude as an individual variable related to the feelings employees have about their job.

Factors affecting job satisfaction

The level of job satisfaction is affected by intrinsic and extrinsic motivating factors, the quality of supervision, social relationships with the work group and the degree to which individuals succeed or fail in their work. Purcell *et al* (2003) believe that discretionary behaviour which helps the firm to be successful is most likely to happen when employees are well motivated and feel committed to the organization and when the job gives them high levels of satisfaction. Their research found that the key factors affecting job satisfaction were career opportunities, job influence, teamwork and job challenge.

Job satisfaction and performance

It is a commonly held and a seemingly not unreasonable belief that an increase in job satisfaction will result in improved performance. But research has not established any strongly positive connection between satisfaction and performance. A review of the extensive literature on this subject by Brayfield and Crockett (1955) concluded that there was little evidence of any simple or appreciable relationship between employee attitudes and their performance. An updated review of their analysis by Vroom (1964) covered 20 studies, in each of which one or more measures of job satisfaction or employee attitudes was correlated with one or more criteria of performance. The median correlation of all these studies was 0.14, which is not high enough to suggest a marked relationship between satisfaction and performance. Brayfield and Crockett concluded that:

Productivity is seldom a goal in itself but a means to goal attainment. Therefore we might expect high satisfaction and high productivity to occur together when productivity is perceived as a path to certain important goals and when these goals are achieved. Under such conditions, satisfaction and productivity might be unrelated or even negatively related.

It can be argued that it is not job satisfaction that produces high performance but high performance that produces job satisfaction, and that a satisfied worker is not necessarily a productive worker and a high producer is not necessarily a satisfied worker. People are motivated to achieve certain goals and will be satisfied if they achieve these goals through improved performance. They may be even more satisfied if they are then rewarded by extrinsic recognition or an intrinsic sense of achievement. This suggests that performance improvements can be achieved by giving people the opportunity to perform, ensuring that they have the knowledge and skill required to perform, and rewarding them by financial or non-financial means when they do perform. It can also be argued that some people may be complacently satisfied with their job and will not be inspired to work harder or better. They may find other ways to satisfy their needs.

Measuring job satisfaction

The level of job satisfaction can be measured by the use of attitude surveys. There are four methods of conducting them:

1. *By the use of structured questionnaires.* These can be issued to all or a sample of employees. The questionnaires may be standardized ones, such as the Brayfield and Rothe Index of Job Satisfaction, or they may be developed specially for the organization. The advantage of using standardized questionnaires is that they have been thoroughly tested and in many cases norms are available against which results can be compared. Benchmarking can be carried out with other organizations, possibly using the services provided by the Saratoga Institute. Additional questions especially relevant to the company can be added to the standard list. A tailor-made questionnaire can be used to highlight particular issues, but it may be advisable to obtain professional help from an experienced psychologist, who can carry out the skilled work of drafting and pilot-testing the questionnaire and interpreting the results. Questionnaires have the advantage of being relatively cheap to administer and analyse, especially when there are large numbers involved. An example of a questionnaire is given in the Appendix.
2. *By the use of interviews.* These may be 'open-ended' or depth interviews in which the discussion is allowed to range quite freely. Or they may be semi-structured in

that there is a checklist of points to be covered, although the aim of the inter-viewer should be to allow discussion to flow around the points so that the frank and open views of the individual are obtained. Alternatively, and more rarely, interviews can be highly structured so that they become no more than the spoken application of a questionnaire. Individual interviews are to be preferred because they are more likely to be revealing, but they are expensive and time-consuming and not so easy to analyse. Discussions through 'focus groups' (ie groups of employees convened to focus their attention on particular issues) are a quicker way of reaching a large number of people, but the results are not so easy to quan-tify and some people may have difficulty in expressing their views in public.

3. *By a combination of questionnaire and interview.* This is the ideal approach because it combines the quantitative data from the questionnaire with the qualitative data from the interviews. It is always advisable to accompany questionnaires with some depth interviews, even if time permits only a limited sample. An alterna-tive approach is to administer the questionnaire to a group of people and then discuss the reactions to each question with the group. This ensures that a quanti-fied analysis is possible but enables the group, or at least some members of it, to express their feelings more fully.

4. *By the use of focus groups.* A focus group is a representative sample of employees whose attitudes and opinions are sought on issues concerning the organization and their work. The essential features of a focus group are that it is structured, informed, constructive and confidential.

Assessing results

It is an interesting fact that when people are asked directly if they are satisfied with their job, many will say that on the whole they are. This can be regardless of the work being done and in spite of strongly held grievances. The possible reason for this phenomenon is that while most people are willing to admit to having grievances – in fact, if invited to complain, they will complain – they may be reluctant to admit, even to themselves, to being dissatisfied with a job that they have no immediate intention of leaving. Many employees have become reconciled to their work, even if they do not like some aspects of it, and have no real desire to do anything else. So they are, in a sense, satisfied enough to continue, even if they have complaints. Finally, many people are satisfied with their job overall, although they may grumble about some aspects of it.

Overall measures of satisfaction do not, therefore, always reveal anything really interesting. It is more important to look at particular aspects of satisfaction or dissat-isfaction to decide whether or not anything needs to be done. In these circumstances, the questionnaire will indicate only a line to be followed up. It will not provide the answers, hence the advantage of individual meetings or focus group discussions to explore in depth any issue raised.

MOTIVATION AND MONEY

Money, in the form of pay or some other sort of remuneration, is the most obvious extrinsic reward. Money provides the carrot that most people want.

Doubts have been cast by Herzberg *et al* (1957) on the effectiveness of money because, they claimed, while the lack of it can cause dissatisfaction, its provision does not result in lasting satisfaction. There is something in this, especially for people on fixed salaries or rates of pay who do not benefit directly from an incentive scheme. They may feel good when they get an increase; apart from the extra money, it is a highly tangible form of recognition and an effective means of helping people to feel that they are valued. But this feeling of euphoria can rapidly die away. Other dissatisfactions from Herzberg's list of hygiene factors, such as working conditions or the quality of management, can loom larger in some people's minds when they fail to get the satisfaction they need from the work itself. However, it must be re-emphasized that different people have different needs and wants and Herzberg's two-factor theory has not been validated. Some will be much more motivated by money than others. What cannot be assumed is that money motivates everyone in the sameway and to the same extent. Thus it is naive to think that the introduction of a performance-related pay (PRP) scheme will miraculously transform everyone overnight into well-motivated, high-performing individuals.

Nevertheless, money provides the means to achieve a number of different ends. It is a powerful force because it is linked directly or indirectly to the satisfaction of many needs. It clearly satisfies basic needs for survival and security, if it is coming in regularly. It can also satisfy the need for self-esteem (as noted above, it is a visible mark of appreciation) and status – money can set you in a grade apart from your fellows and can buy you things they cannot to build up your prestige. Money satisfies the less desirable but still prevalent drives of acquisitiveness and cupidity.

Money may in itself have no intrinsic meaning, but it acquires significant motivating power because it comes to symbolize so many intangible goals. It acts as a symbol in different ways for different people, and for the same person at different times. As noted by Goldthorpe *et al* (1968) from their research into the 'affluent worker', pay is the dominant factor in the choice of employer and considerations of pay seem most powerful in binding people to their present job.

Do financial incentives motivate people? The answer is yes, for those people who are strongly motivated by money and whose expectations that they will receive a financial reward are high. But less confident employees may not respond to incentives that they do not expect to achieve. It can also be argued that extrinsic rewards may erode intrinsic interest – people who work just for money could find their tasks less pleasurable and may not, therefore, do them so well. What we do know is that a multiplicity of factors are involved in performance improvements and many of those factors are interdependent.

Money can therefore provide positive motivation in the right circumstances, not only because people need and want money but also because it serves as a highly tangible means of recognition. It can also be argued that money may be an important factor in attracting people to organizations and is one of the factors that will influence their retention. But badly designed and managed pay systems can demotivate. Another researcher in this area was Jaques (1961), who emphasized the need for such systems to be perceived as being fair and equitable. In other words, the reward should be clearly related to effort or level of responsibility and people should not receive less money than they deserve compared with their fellow workers. Jaques called this the 'felt-fair' principle.

MOTIVATION STRATEGIES

The factors that affect motivational strategies and the contribution that HR can make to achieving higher levels of motivation are summarized in Table 18.2.

Table 18.2 Motivation strategies

Factors affecting motivation strategies	The HR contribution
• The complexity of the process of motivation means that simplistic approaches based on instrumentality theory are unlikely to be successful	• Avoid the trap of developing or supporting strategies that offer prescriptions for motivation based on a simplistic view of the process or fail to recognize individual differences
• People are more likely to be motivated if they work in an environment in which they are valued for what they are and what they do. This means paying attention to the basic need for recognition	• Encourage the development of performance management processes which provide opportunities to agree expectations and give positive feedback on accomplishments • Develop reward systems which provide opportunities for both financial and non-financial rewards to recognize achievements. Bear in mind, however, that financial rewards systems are not necessarily appropriate and the lessons of expectancy, goal and equity theory need to be taken into account in designing and operating them
• The need for work which provides people with the means to achieve their goals, a reasonable degree of autonomy, and scope for the use of skills and competencies should be recognized	• Advise on processes for the design of jobs which take account of the factors affecting the motivation to work, providing for job enrichment in the shape of variety, decision-making responsibility and as much control as possible in carrying out the work
• The need for the opportunity to grow by developing abilities and careers.	• Provide facilities and opportunities for learning through such means as personal development planning processes as well as more formal training • Develop career planning processes
• The cultural environment of the organization in the shape of its values and norms will influence the impact of any attempts to motivate people by direct or indirect means	• Advise on the development of a culture which supports processes of valuing and rewarding employees
• Motivation will be enhanced by leadership which sets the direction, encourages and stimulates achievement, and provides support to employees in their efforts to reach goals and improve their performance generally	• Devise competency frameworks which focus on leadership qualities and the behaviours expected of managers and team leaders • Ensure that leadership potential is identified through performance management and assessment centres • Provide guidance and training to develop leadership qualities

19

Organizational commitment and engagement

In this chapter the topics of organizational commitment and job engagement are examined. They are important because independently or in association with one another, they can significantly affect organizational performance. But there is some confusion about their respective meanings, and the chapter starts by examining these.

THE CONCEPTS OF COMMITMENT AND ENGAGEMENT

Commitment and engagement are closely related concepts. In fact, some people use the terms interchangeably or refer to engagement as an alternative, more up-to-date and, maybe, a more sophisticated term for commitment. The various definitions available of commitment and engagement do not help. *The Oxford English Dictionary* states that someone is committed when they are morally dedicated (to doctrine or cause), while someone is engaged when they are employed busily.

The meaning of organizational commitment

As defined by Porter *et al* (1974), commitment refers to attachment and loyalty. It is the relative strength of the individual's identification with, and involvement in, a particular organization. It consists of three factors:

1. A strong desire to remain a member of the organization.
2. A strong belief in, and acceptance of, the values and goals of the organization.
3. A readiness to exert considerable effort on behalf of the organization.

An alternative, although closely related, definition of commitment emphasizes the importance of behaviour in creating commitment. As Salancik (1977) put it: 'Commitment is a state of being in which an individual becomes bound by his (sic) actions to beliefs that sustain his activities and his own involvement.' Three features of behaviour are important in binding individuals to their acts: the visibility of the acts, the extent to which the outcomes are irrevocable, and the degree to which the person undertakes the action voluntarily. Commitment, according to Salancik, can be increased and harnessed 'to obtain support for organizational ends and interests' through such ploys as participation in decisions about actions.

The meaning of engagement

As defined by Chiumento (2004):

> Engagement is a positive, two-way, relationship between an employee and their organization. Both parties are aware of their own and the other's needs, and the way they support each other to fulfil those needs. Engaged employees and organizations will go the extra mile for each other because they see the mutual benefit of investing in their relationship.

The Royal Bank of Scotland (2005) defines engagement as the state of emotional and intellectual commitment to the group and lists its components as satisfaction (how much I like working here), commitment (how much I want to be here) and performance (how much I want to and actually do in achieving results).

The Hay Group, as reported by Thompson (2002), refers to their concept of 'engaged performance' which is 'about understanding why working for a particular organization is attractive to different kinds of individuals... And which looks at the hearts and mind reasons why people work for you'.

The Institute of Employment Studies (Bevan *et al*, 1997) defines engagement as: 'A positive attitude held by the employee towards the organization and its values. An engaged employee is aware of business context, and works closely with colleagues to improve performance within the job for the benefit of the organization.'

These all overlap with the traditional definition of commitment as being concerned with attachment to the organization. There is no reason why this should not be the case – the two concepts are after all closely connected – but there is some value in distinguishing between commitment to the organization and commitment to the job, and treating the former as organizational commitment and the latter as job engagement.

Many people are more committed to their work than the organization that provides the work, for example researchers in universities or research establishments. Others take a transient view of their organization as a stepping stone in their career that provides them with the sort of experience they want but to which they feel no particular loyalty. If the organization wants people in the latter categories to work harder and better, it may well want to focus on the work they provide and opportunities for development they offer and place less emphasis on organizational commitment. If the organization wants to concentrate more on retention, loyalty and people putting themselves out for the organization rather than themselves, then policies to encourage commitment come to the fore. Best of all, it is recognized that both commitment and engagement need attention but that different approaches may be necessary although they can be mutually supportive – increased commitment to the organization can produce higher levels of job engagement; more job engagement can increase commitment to the organization. The rest of this chapter is devoted to exploring both concepts.

ORGANIZATIONAL COMMITMENT

The concept of organizational commitment plays an important part in HRM philosophy. As Guest (1987) has suggested, HRM policies are designed to 'maximise organizational integration, employee commitment, flexibility and quality of work'. The next five sections of this chapter consider the meaning and significance of organizational commitment, the problems associated with the concept, factors affecting commitment, developing a commitment strategy, and measuring commitment.

Organizational commitment is the relative strength of the individual's identification with, and involvement in, a particular organization. It consists of three factors:

- a strong desire to remain a member of the organization;
- a strong belief in, and acceptance of, the values and goals of the organization;
- a readiness to exert considerable effort on behalf of the organization.

An alternative, although closely related, definition of commitment emphasizes the importance of behaviour in creating commitment. As Salancik (1977) put it, 'Commitment is a state of being in which an individual becomes bound by his actions to beliefs that sustain his activities and his own involvement.' Three features of behaviour are important in binding individuals to their acts: the visibility of the acts, the extent to which the outcomes are irrevocable, and the degree to which the person undertakes the action voluntarily. Commitment, according to Salancik, can be increased and harnessed 'to obtain support for organizational ends and interests' through such ploys as participation in decisions about actions.

The significance of organizational commitment

There have been two schools of thought about commitment. One, the 'from control to commitment' school, was led by Walton (1985a and b), who saw commitment strategy as a more rewarding approach to human resource management, in contrast to the traditional control strategy. The other, 'Japanese/excellence' school, is represented by writers such as Pascale and Athos (1981) and Peters and Waterman (1982), who looked at the Japanese model and related the achievement of excellence to getting the wholehearted commitment of the workforce to the organization.

From control to commitment

The importance of commitment was highlighted by Walton (1985a and b). His theme was that improved performance would result if the organization moved away from the traditional control-oriented approach to workforce management, which relies upon establishing order, exercising control and 'achieving efficiency in the application of the workforce'. He proposed that this approach should be replaced by a commitment strategy. Workers respond best – and most creatively – not when they are tightly controlled by management, placed in narrowly defined jobs, and treated like an unwelcome necessity, but instead when they are given broader responsibilities, encouraged to contribute and helped to achieve satisfaction in their work. Walton (1985b) suggested that in the new commitment-based approach:

> Jobs are designed to be broader than before, to combine planning and implementation, and to include efforts to upgrade operations, not just to maintain them. Individual responsibilities are expected to change as conditions change, and teams, not individuals, often are the organizational units accountable for performance. With management hierarchies relatively flat and differences in status minimized, control and lateral coordination depend on shared goals. And expertise rather than formal position determines influence.

Put like this, a commitment strategy may sound idealistic but does not appear to be a crude attempt to manipulate people to accept management's values and goals, as some have suggested. In fact, Walton does not describe it as being instrumental in this manner. His prescription is for a broad HRM approach to the ways in which people are treated, jobs are designed and organizations are managed. He believes that the aim should be to develop 'mutuality', a state that exists when management and employees are interdependent and both benefit from this interdependency.

The Japanese/excellence school

Attempts made to explain the secret of Japanese business success in the 1970s by such writers as Ouchi (1981) and Pascale and Athos (1981) led to the theory that the best way to motivate people is to get their full commitment to the values of the organization by leadership and involvement. This might be called the 'hearts and minds' approach to motivation, and among other things it popularized such devices as quality circles.

The baton was taken up by Peters and Waterman (1982) and their imitators later in the 1980s. This approach to excellence was summed up by Peters and Austin (1985) when they wrote, again somewhat idealistically, 'Trust people and treat them like adults, enthuse them by lively and imaginative leadership, develop and demonstrate an obsession for quality, make them feel they own the business, and your workforce will respond with total commitment.'

Problems with the concept of commitment

A number of commentators have raised questions about the concept of commitment. These relate to three main problem areas: first, its unitary frame of reference; second, commitment as an inhibitor of flexibility; and third, whether high commitment does in practice result in improved organizational performance.

Unitary frame of reference

A comment frequently made about the concept of commitment is that it is too simplistic in adopting a unitary frame of reference; in other words, it assumes unrealistically that an organization consists of people with shared interests. It has been suggested by people like Cyert and March (1963), Mangham (1979) and Mintzberg (1983a) that an organization is really a coalition of interest groups, where political processes are an inevitable part of everyday life. The pluralistic perspective recognizes the legitimacy of different interests and values, and therefore asks the question 'Commitment to what?' Thus, as Coopey and Hartley (1991) put it, 'commitment is not an all-or-nothing affair (though many managers might like it to be) but a question of multiple or competing commitments for the individual'.

Legge (1989) also raises this question in her discussion of strong culture as a key requirement of HRM through 'a shared set of managerially sanctioned values'.

However, values concerned with performance, quality, service, equal opportunity and innovation are not necessarily wrong because they are managerial values. But it is not unreasonable to believe that pursuing a value such as innovation could work against the interests of employees by, for example, resulting in redundancies. And it would be quite reasonable for any employee, encouraged to behave in accordance with a value supported by management, to ask 'What's in it for me?' It can also be argued that the imposition of management's values on employees without their having any part to play in discussing and agreeing them is a form of coercion.

Commitment and flexibility

It was pointed out by Coopey and Hartley (1991) that 'The problem for a unitarist notion of organizational commitment is that it fosters a conformist approach which not only fails to reflect organizational reality, but can be narrowing and limiting for the organization.' They argue that if employees are expected and encouraged to commit themselves tightly to a single set of values and goals they will not be able to cope with the ambiguities and uncertainties that are endemic in organizational life in times of change. Conformity to 'imposed' values will inhibit creative problem solving, and high commitment to present courses of action will increase both resistance to change and the stress that invariably occurs when change takes place.

If commitment is related to tightly defined plans then this will become a real problem. To avoid it, the emphasis should be on overall strategic directions. These would be communicated to employees with the proviso that changing circumstances will require their amendment. In the meantime, however, everyone can at least be informed in general terms where the organization is heading and, more specifically, the part they are expected to play in helping the organization to get there. And if they can be involved in the decision making processes on matters that affect them (which include management's values for performance, quality and customer service), so much the better.

Values need not necessarily be restrictive. They can be defined in ways that allow for freedom of choice within broad guidelines. In fact, the values themselves can refer to such processes as flexibility, innovation and responsiveness to change. Thus, far from inhibiting creative problem solving, they can encourage it.

The impact of high commitment

A belief in the positive value of commitment has been confidently expressed by Walton (1985b): 'Underlying all these (human resource) policies is a management philosophy, often embedded in a published statement, that acknowledges the legitimate claims of a company's multiple stakeholders – owners, employees, customers and the public. At the centre of this philosophy is a belief that eliciting employee commitment will lead to enhanced performance. The evidence shows this belief to be well founded.' However, a review by Guest (1991) of the mainly North American literature, reinforced by the limited UK research available, led him to the conclusion that 'High organizational commitment is associated with lower labour turnover and absence, but there is no clear link to performance.'

It is probably wise not to expect too much from commitment as a means of making a direct and immediate impact on performance. It is not the same as motivation. Commitment is a wider concept, and tends to be more stable over a period of time and less responsive to transitory aspects of an employee's job, hence the importance of the concept of job engagement, which is immediate. It is possible to be dissatisfied with a particular feature of a job while retaining a reasonably high level of commitment to the organization as a whole.

In relating commitment to motivation it is useful to distinguish, as do Buchanan and Huczynski (1985), three perspectives:

- The goals towards which people aim. From this perspective, goals such as the good of the company, or effective performance at work, may provide a degree of motivation for some employees, who could be regarded as committed in so far as they feel they own the goals.
- The process by which goals and objectives at work are selected, which is quite distinct from the way in which commitment arises within individuals.
- The social process of motivating others to perform effectively. From this viewpoint, strategies aimed at increasing motivation also affect commitment. It may be true to say that, where commitment is present, motivation is likely to be strong, particularly if a long term view is taken of effective performance.

It is reasonable to believe that strong commitment to work is likely to result in conscientious and self-directed application to do the job, regular attendance, nominal supervision and a high level of effort. Commitment to the organization will certainly be related to the intention to stay – in other words, loyalty to the company.

Factors affecting commitment

Kochan and Dyer (1993) have indicated that the factors affecting the level of commitment in what they call mutual commitment firms are as follows:

- *Strategic level:*
  - supportive business strategies;
  - top management value commitment;
  - effective voice for HR in strategy making and governance.
- *Functional (human resource policy) level:*
  - staffing based on employment stabilization;
  - investment in training and development;
  - contingent compensation that reinforces cooperation, participation and contribution.
- *Workplace level:*
  - selection based on high standards'
  - broad task design and teamwork'
  - employee involvement in problem solving'
  - climate of cooperation and trust.

The research carried out by Purcell *et al* (2003) established that the key policy and practice factors influencing levels of commitment were:

- received training last year;
- are satisfied with career opportunities;
- are satisfied with the performance appraisal system;
- think managers are good in people management (leadership);
- find their work challenging;
- think their form helps them achieve a work-life balance;
- are satisfied with communication or company performance.

Developing a commitment strategy

A commitment strategy will be based on the high commitment model described in Chapter 7. It will aim to develop commitment using, as appropriate, approaches such as those described below. When formulating the strategy, account should be taken of the reservations expressed earlier in this chapter, and too much should not be expected from it. The aim will be to increase identification with the organization, develop feelings of loyalty among its employees, provide a context within which motivation and therefore performance will increase, and reduce employee turnover.

Steps to create commitment will be concerned with both strategic goals and values. They may include initiatives to increase involvement and 'ownership', communication, leadership development, developing a sense of excitement in the job, and developing various HR policy and practice initiatives.

Developing ownership

A sense of belonging is enhanced if there is a feeling of 'ownership' among employees, not just in the literal sense of owning shares (although this can help) but in the sense of believing they are genuinely accepted by management as key stakeholders in the organization. This concept of 'ownership' extends to participating in decisions on new developments and changes in working practices that affect the individuals concerned. They should be involved in making those decisions, and feel that their ideas have been listened to and that they have contributed to the outcome.

Communication programmes

It may seem to be strikingly obvious that commitment will only be gained if people understand what they are expected to commit to, but managements too often fail to pay sufficient attention to delivering the message in terms that recognize that the frame of reference for those who receive it is likely to be quite different from their own. Management's expectations will not necessarily coincide with those of employees. Pluralism prevails. And in delivering the message, the use of different and complementary channels of communication such as newsletters, briefing groups, videos and notice boards is often neglected.

Leadership development

Commitment is enhanced if managers can gain the confidence and respect of their teams, and development programmes to improve the quality of leadership should form an important part of any strategy for increasing commitment. Management training can also be focused on increasing the competence of managers in specific areas of their responsibility for gaining commitment, such as performance management.

INFLUENCES ON COMMITMENT AND EMPLOYEE SATISFACTION

An IRS survey (IRS, 2004) established that the following were the top five influences on employee satisfaction and commitment and employee satisfaction:

1. Relationship with manager – 63 per cent.
2. Relationship with colleagues – 60 per cent.

3. Quality of line management – 62 per cent.
4. Recognition of contribution – 56 per cent.
5. Leadership: visibility and confidence – 55 per cent.

The survey also obtained examples from organizations of what they were doing to increase commitment:

- Bacardi-Martini – focus groups, team briefings, consultation with union, joint consultative committee, attitude surveys, road shows.
- Eversheds – 'have your say' communication sessions involving all employees, key business discussions.
- Lefarge Cement – joint partnership training courses with managers and trade union representatives, regular business updates, bonus scheme linked to jointly agreed performance indicators, team development workshops.
- North Herts District Council – introduction of staff consultation forums, new policies for complaints resolution and dignity at work.
- West Bromwich Building Society – various focus groups, social club, away-days by department.
- Yorkshire Water – active and comprehensive communications, involvement in business planning, face-to-face meetings with directors, consultation on change, celebration of business success, rewards and recognition.

Developing HR practices that enhance organizational commitment

The policies and practices that may contribute to the increase of commitment are training, career planning, performance management, work-life balance policies and job design.

The HR function can play a major part in developing a high commitment organization. The ten steps it can take are:

- Advise on methods of communicating the values and aims of management and the achievements of the organization, so that employees are more likely to identify with it as one they are proud to work for.
- Emphasize to management that commitment is a two-way process; employees cannot be expected to be committed to the organization unless management demonstrates that it is committed to them and recognizes their contribution as stakeholders.
- Impress on management the need to develop a climate of trust by being honest with people, treating them fairly, justly and consistently, keeping its word, and

showing willingness to listen to the comments and suggestions made by employees during processes of consultation and participation.

- Develop a positive psychological contract (see Chapter 16) by treating people as stakeholders, relying on consensus and cooperation rather than control and coercion, and focusing on the provision of opportunities for learning, development and career progression.
- Advise on and assist in the establishment of partnership agreements with trade unions which emphasize unity of purpose, common approaches to working together and the importance of giving employees a voice in matters that concern them.
- Recommend and take part in the achievement of single status for all employees (often included in a partnership agreement) so that there is no longer an 'us and them' culture.
- Encourage management to declare a policy of employment security, and ensure that steps are taken to avoid involuntary redundancies.
- Develop performance management processes that provide for the alignment of organizational and individual objectives.
- Advise on means of increasing employee identification with the company through rewards related to organizational performance (profit sharing or gain-sharing) or employee share ownership schemes.
- Develop 'job engagement' (identification of employees with the job they are doing) through job design processes that aim to create higher levels of job satisfaction (job enrichment).

ENGAGEMENT

Engagement takes place when people are committed to their work. They are interested, indeed excited, about what they do. Job engagement can exist even when individuals are not committed to the organization, except in so far as it gives them the opportunity and scope to perform and to develop their skills and potential. They may be more attached to the type of work they carry out than to the organization that provides that work, especially if they are knowledge workers.

Enhancing job engagement starts with job design or 'role development' as discussed in Chapter 23. This will focus on the provision of:

- *interest and challenge* – the degree to which the work is interesting in itself and creates demanding goals to people;
- *variety* – the extent to which the activities in the job call for a selection of skills and abilities;

- *autonomy* – the freedom and independence the job holder has, including discretion to make decisions, exercise choice, schedule the work and decide on the procedures to carry it out, and the job holder's personal responsibility for outcomes;
- *task identity* – the degree to which the job requires completion of a whole and identifiable piece of work;
- *task significance* – the extent to which the job contributes to a significant end result and has a substantial impact on the lives and work of other people.

All these factors are affected by the organization structure, the system of work and the quality of leadership. The latter is vital. The degree to which jobs provide variety, autonomy, task identity and task significance depends more on the way in which job holders are managed and led than any formal process of job design. Managers and team leaders often have considerable discretion on how they allocate work, and the extent to which they delegate. They can provide feedback that recognizes the contribution of people, and they can spell out the significance of the work they do.

The Hay Group has developed a model for what they call 'engaged performance', which is made up of six elements, and is summarized in Table 19.1.

Table 19.1   The Hay Group model of engaged performance

1 Inspiration/values	4 Tangible rewards
<ul><li>reputation of organization</li><li>organizational values and behaviours</li><li>quality of leadership</li><li>risk sharing</li><li>recognition</li><li>communication</li></ul>	<ul><li>competitive pay</li><li>good benefits</li><li>incentives for higher performance</li><li>ownership potential</li><li>recognition awards</li><li>fairness of reward</li></ul>
2 Quality of work	5 Work–life balance
<ul><li>perception of the value of the work</li><li>challenge/interest</li><li>opportunities for achievement</li><li>freedom and autonomy</li><li>workload</li><li>quality of work relationship</li></ul>	<ul><li>supportive environment</li><li>recognition of life cycle needs/flexibility</li><li>security of income</li><li>social support</li></ul>
3 Enabling environment	6 Future growth/opportunity
<ul><li>physical environment</li><li>tools and equipment</li><li>job training (current position)</li><li>information and processes</li><li>safety/personal security</li></ul>	<ul><li>learning and development beyond current job</li><li>career advancement opportunities</li><li>performance improvement and feedback</li></ul>

20

How organizations function

BASIC CONSIDERATIONS

The two factors that determine how an organization functions in relation to its internal and external environment are its structure and the processes that operate within it. Organizations are also affected by the culture they develop, that is, the values and norms that affect behaviour (see Chapter 21).

Much has been written to explain how organizations function and the first part of this chapter summarizes the various theories of organization. These theories provide the background to the last three sections of the chapter which deal with organization structure, types of organizations and organizational processes.

ORGANIZATION THEORIES

The classical school

The classical or scientific management school, as represented by Fayol (1916), Taylor (1911) and Urwick (1947), believed in control, order and formality. Organizations need to minimize the opportunity for unfortunate and uncontrollable informal relations, leaving room only for the formal ones.

The bureaucratic model

The bureaucratic model of organization as described by Perrow (1980) is a way of expressing how organizations function as machines and can therefore be associated with some of the ideas generated by the classical school. It is based on the work of Max Weber (1946) who coined the term 'bureaucracy' as a label for a type of formal organization in which impersonality and rationality are developed to the highest degree. Bureaucracy, as he conceived it, was the most efficient form of organization because it is coldly logical and because personalized relationships and non-rational, emotional considerations do not get in its way.

The human relations school

The classical, and by implication, the bureaucratic model were first challenged by Barnard (1938). He emphasized the importance of the informal organization – the network of informal roles and relationships which, for better or worse, strongly influences the way the formal structure operates. He wrote: 'Formal organizations come out of and are necessary to informal organizations: but when formal organizations come into operation, they create and require informal organizations.' More recently, Child (1977) has pointed out that it is misleading to talk about a clear distinction between the formal and the informal organization. Formality and informality can be designed into structure.

Roethlisberger and Dickson (1939) reported on the Hawthorne studies – which highlighted the importance of informal groups and decent, humane leadership.

The behavioural science school

In the 1960s the focus shifted completely to the behaviour of people in organizations. Behavioural scientists such as Argyris (1957), Herzberg et al (1957), McGregor (1960) and Likert (1961) adopted a humanistic point of view which is concerned with what people can contribute and how they can best be motivated.

- *Argyris* believed that individuals should be given the opportunity to feel that they have a high degree of control over setting their own goals and over defining the paths to these goals.
- *Herzberg* suggested that improvements in organization design must centre on the individual job as the positive source of motivation. If individuals feel that the job is stretching them, they will be moved to perform it well.
- *McGregor* developed his theory of integration (theory Y) which emphasizes the importance of recognizing the needs of both the organization and the individual

and creating conditions that will reconcile these needs so that members of the organization can work together for its success and share in its rewards.

- *Likert* stated that effective organizations function by means of supportive relationships which, if fostered, will build and maintain people's sense of personal worth and importance.

The concepts of these and other behavioural scientists provided the impetus for the organization development (OD) movement as described in Chapter 22.

The systems school

Another important insight into how organizations function was provided by Miller and Rice (1967) who stated that organizations should be treated as open systems which are continually dependent upon and influenced by their environments. The basic characteristic of the enterprise as an open system is that it transforms inputs into outputs within its environment.

As Katz and Kahn (1966) wrote: 'Systems theory is basically concerned with problems of relationship, of structure and of interdependence.' As a result, there is a considerable emphasis on the concept of transactions across boundaries – between the system and its environment and between the different parts of the system. This open and dynamic approach avoided the error of the classical, bureaucratic and human relations theorists, who thought of organizations as closed systems and analysed their problems with reference to their internal structures and processes of interaction, without taking account either of external influences and the changes they impose or of the technology in the organization.

The socio-technical model

The concept of the organization as a system was extended by the Tavistock Institute researchers into the socio-technical model of organizations. The basic principle of this model is that in any system of organization, technical or task aspects are interrelated with the human or social aspects. The emphasis is on interrelationships between, on the one hand, the technical processes of transformation carried out within the organization, and, on the other, the organization of work groups and the management structures of the enterprise. This approach avoided the humanistic generalizations of the behavioural scientists without falling into the trap of treating the organization as a machine.

The contingency school

The contingency school consists of writers such as Burns and Stalker (1961), Woodward (1965) and Lawrence and Lorsch (1976) who have analysed a variety of organizations and concluded that their structures and methods of operation are a function of the circumstances in which they exist. They do not subscribe to the view that there is one best way of designing an organization or that simplistic classifications of organizations as formal or informal, bureaucratic or non-bureaucratic are helpful. They are against those who see organizations as mutually opposed social systems (what Burns and Stalker refer to as the 'Manichean world of the Hawthorne studies') that set up formal against informal organizations. They disagree with those who impose rigid principles of organization irrespective of the technology or environmental conditions.

More recent contributions to understanding how organizations function

Kotter (1995) developed the following overall framework for examining organizations:

- key organizational processes – the major information gathering, communication, decision-making, matter/energy transporting and matter/energy converting actions of the organization's employees and machines;
- external environment – an organization's 'task' environment includes suppliers, markets and competitors; the wider environment includes factors such as public attitudes, economic and political systems, laws etc;
- employees and other tangible assets – people, plant, and equipment;
- formal organizational requirements – systems designed to regulate the actions of employees (and machines);
- the social system – culture (values and norms) and relationships between employees in terms of power, affiliation and trust;
- technology – the major techniques people use while engaged in organizational processes and that are programmed into machines;
- the dominant coalition – the objectives, strategies, personal characteristics and internal relationships of those who oversee the organization as a whole and control its basic policy making.

Mintzberg (1983b) analysed organizations into five broad types or configurations:

- *simple structures*, which are dominated by the top of the organization with centralized decision making;
- *machine bureaucracy*, which is characterized by the standardization of work processes and the extensive reliance on systems;
- *professional bureaucracy*, where the standardization of skills provides the prime coordinating mechanism;
- *divisionalized structures*, in which authority is drawn down from the top and activities are grouped together into units which are then managed according to their standardized outputs;
- *adhocracies*, where power is decentralized selectively to constellations of work that are free to coordinate within and between themselves by mutual adjustments.

Drucker (1988) points out that organizations have established, through the development of new technology and the extended use of knowledge workers, 'that whole layers of management neither make decisions nor lead. Instead, their main, if not their only, function, is to serve as relays – human boosters for the faint, unfocused signals that pass for communications in the traditional pre-information organization'.

Pascale (1990) believes that the new organizational paradigm functions as follows:

- *from* the image of organizations as machines, with the emphasis on concrete strategy, structure and systems, *to* the idea of organizations as organisms, with the emphasis on the 'soft' dimensions – style, staff and shared values;
- *from* a hierarchical model, with step-by-step problem solving, *to* a network model, with parallel nodes of intelligence which surround problems until they are eliminated;
- *from* the status-driven view that managers think and workers do as they are told, *to* a view of managers as 'facilitators', with workers empowered to initiate improvements and change;
- *from* an emphasis on 'vertical tasks' within functional units, *to* an emphasis on 'horizontal tasks' and collaboration across units;
- *from* a focus on 'content' and the prescribed use of specific tools and techniques, *to* a focus on 'process' and a holistic synthesis of techniques;
- *from* the military model *to* a commitment model.

Handy (1989) describes two types of organization: the 'shamrock' and the federal.

The shamrock organization consists of three elements: 1) the core workers (the central leaf of the shamrock) – professionals, technicians and managers; 2) the contractual fringe – contract workers; and 3) the flexible labour force consisting of temporary staff.

The federal organization takes the process of decentralization one stage further by establishing every key operational, manufacturing or service provision activity as a distinct, federated unit.

ORGANIZATION STRUCTURE

Each of the members of the various schools was, in effect, commenting on the factors affecting organization structure as considered below.

Organization structure defined

All organizations have some form of more or less formalized structure which has been defined by Child (1977) as comprising 'all the tangible and regularly occurring features which help to shape their members' behaviour'. Structures incorporate a network of roles and relationships and are there to help in the process of ensuring that collective effort is explicitly organized to achieve specified ends.

Organizations vary in their complexity, but it is always necessary to divide the overall management task into a variety of activities, to allocate these activities to the different parts of the organization and to establish means of controlling, coordinating and integrating them.

The structure of an organization can be regarded as a framework for getting things done. It consists of units, functions, divisions, departments and formally constituted work teams into which activities related to particular processes, projects, products, markets, customers, geographical areas or professional disciplines are grouped together. The structure indicates who is accountable for directing, coordinating and carrying out these activities and defines management hierarchies – the 'chain of command' – thus spelling out, broadly, who is responsible to whom for what at each level in the organization.

Organization charts

Structures are usually described in the form of an organization chart. This places individuals in boxes that denote their job and their position in the hierarchy and traces the direct lines of authority (command and control) through the management hierarchies.

Organization charts are vertical in their nature and therefore misrepresent reality. They do not give any indication of the horizontal and diagonal relationships that exist within the framework between people in different units or departments, and do not recognize the fact that within any one hierarchy, commands and control information do not travel all the way down and up the structure as the chart implies. In practice, information jumps (especially computer-generated information) and managers or team leaders will interact with people at levels below those immediately beneath them.

Organization charts have their uses as means of defining – simplistically – who does what and hierarchical lines of authority. But even if backed up by organization manuals (which no one reads and which are, in any case, out of date as soon as they are produced), they cannot convey how the organization really works. They may, for example, lead to definitions of jobs – what people are expected to do – but they cannot convey the roles these people carry out in the organization; the parts they play in interacting with others and the ways in which, like actors, they interpret the parts they are given.

TYPES OF ORGANIZATION

The basic types of organization are described below.

Line and staff

The line and staff organization was the type favoured by the classical theorists. Although the term is not so much used today, except when referring to line managers, it still describes many structures. The line hierarchy in the structure consists of functions and managers who are directly concerned in achieving the primary purposes of the organization, for example manufacturing and selling or directing the organization as a whole. 'Staff' in functions such as finance, personnel and engineering provide services to the line to enable them to get on with their job.

Divisionalized organizations

The process of divisionalization, as first described by Sloan (1963) on the basis of his experience in running General Motors, involves structuring the organization into separate divisions, each concerned with discrete manufacturing, sales, distribution or service functions, or with serving a particular market. At group headquarters, functional departments may exist in such areas as finance, planning, personnel, legal and engineering to provide services to the divisions and, importantly, to exercise a degree of functional control over their activities. The amount of control exercised will depend on the extent to which the organization has decided to decentralize authority to strategic business units positioned close to the markets they serve.

Decentralized organizations

Some organizations, especially conglomerates, decentralize most of their activities and retain only a skeleton headquarters staff to deal with financial control matters, strategic planning, legal issues and sometimes, but not always, personnel issues, especially those concerned with senior management on an across the group basis (recruitment, development and remuneration).

Matrix organizations

Matrix organizations are project based. Development, design or construction projects will be controlled by project directors or managers, or, in the case of a consultancy, assignments will be conducted by project leaders. Project managers will have no permanent staff except, possibly, some administrative/secretarial support. They will draw the members of their project teams from discipline groups, each of which will be headed up by a director or manager who is responsible on a continuing basis for resourcing the group, developing and managing its members and ensuring that they are assigned as fully as possible to project teams. These individuals are assigned to a project team and they will be responsible to the team leader for delivering the required results, but they will continue to be accountable generally to the head of their discipline for their overall performance and contribution.

Flexible organizations

Flexible organizations may conform broadly to the Mintzberg (1983b) category of an adhocracy in the sense that they are capable of adapting quickly to new demands and operate fluidly. They may be organized along the lines of Handy's (1989) 'shamrock' with core workers carrying out the fundamental and continuing activities of the organization and contract workers and temporary staff being employed as required. This is also called a core–periphery organization. An organization may adopt a policy of numerical flexibility, which means that the number of employees can be quickly increased or decreased in line with changes in activity levels. The different types of flexibility as defined by Atkinson (1984) are described in Chapter 14.

The process-based organization

A process-based organization is one in which the focus is on horizontal processes that cut across organizational boundaries. Traditional organization structures consist of a range of functions operating semi-independently and each with its own, usually extended, management hierarchy. Functions acted as vertical 'chimneys' with boundaries between what they did and what happened next door. Continuity of work between functions and the coordination of activities were prejudiced. Attention was focused on vertical relationships and authority-based management – the 'command and control' structure. Horizontal processes received relatively little attention. It was, for example, not recognized that meeting the needs of customers by systems of order processing could only be carried out satisfactorily if the flow of work from sales through manufacturing to distribution was treated as a continuous process and not as three distinct parcels of activity. Another horizontal process that drew attention to the need to reconsider how organizations should be structured was total quality. This is not a top-down system. It cuts across the boundaries separating organizational units to ensure that quality is built into the organization's products and services. Business process re-engineering exercises have also demonstrated the need for businesses to integrate functionally separated tasks into unified horizontal work processes.

The result, as indicated by Ghoshal and Bartlett (1993), has been that:

> ... managers are beginning to deal with their organizations in different ways. Rather than seeing them as a hierarchy of static roles, they think of them as a portfolio of dynamic processes. They see core organizational processes that overlay and often dominate the vertical, authority-based processes of the hierarchical structure.

In a process-based organization there will still be designated functions for, say, manufacturing, sales and distribution. But the emphasis will be on how these areas work together on multi-functional projects to deal with new demands such as product/market development. Teams will jointly consider ways of responding to customer requirements. Quality and continuous improvement will be regarded as a common responsibility shared between managers and staff from each function. The overriding objective will be to maintain a smooth flow of work between functions and to achieve synergy by pooling resources from different functions in task forces or project teams.

ORGANIZATIONAL PROCESSES

The structure of an organization as described in an organization chart does not give any real indication of how it functions. To understand this, it is necessary to consider the various processes that take place within the structural framework: those of group behaviour, teamwork, leadership, power, politics and conflict, interaction and networking and communications.

Group behaviour

Organizations consist of groups of people working together. Interactions take place within and between groups and the degree to which these processes are formalized varies according to the organizational context. To understand and influence organizational behaviour, it is necessary to appreciate how groups behave. In particular, this means considering the nature of:

- formal and informal groups;
- the processes that take place within groups;
- channels of communication;
- task and maintenance functions;
- group ideology and cohesion;
- the concept of a reference group and its impact on group members;
- the factors that make for group effectiveness;
- the stages of group development;
- group identification.

Formal groups

Formal groups are set up by organizations to achieve a defined purpose. People are brought together with the necessary skills to carry out the tasks and a system exists for directing, coordinating and controlling the group's activities. The structure, composition and size of the group will depend largely on the nature of the task, although tradition, organizational culture and management style may exert considerable influence. The more routine or clearly defined the task is, the more structured the group will be. In a highly structured group the leader will have a positive role and may well adopt an authoritarian style. The role of each member of the group will be precise and a hierarchy of authority is likely to exist. The more ambiguous the task, the more difficult it will be to structure the group. The leader's role is more likely to be supportive – he or she will tend to concentrate on encouragement and coordination rather than on issuing orders. The group will operate in a more democratic way and individual roles will be fluid and less clearly defined.

Informal groups

Informal groups are set up by people in organizations who have some affinity for one another. It could be said that formal groups satisfy the needs of the organization while informal groups satisfy the needs of their members. One of the main aims of organization design and development should be to ensure, so far as possible, that the basis upon which activities are grouped together and the way in which groups are allowed or encouraged to behave satisfy both these needs. The values and norms established by informal groups can work against the organization. This was first clearly established in the Hawthorne studies, which revealed that groups could regulate their own behaviour and output levels irrespective of what management wanted. An understanding of the processes that take place within groups can, however, help to make them work for, rather than against, what the organization needs.

Group processes

As mentioned above, the way in which groups function is affected by the task and by the norms in the organization. An additional factor is size. There is a greater diversity of talent, skills and knowledge in a large group, but individuals find it more difficult to make their presence felt. According to Handy (1981), for best participation and for highest all-round involvement, the optimum size is between five and seven. But to achieve the requisite breadth of knowledge the group may have to be considerably larger, and this makes greater demands on the skills of the leader in getting participation. The term 'group dynamics' is sometimes used loosely to describe the ways in which group members interact, but properly it refers to the work of Lewin (1947). This was mainly concerned with the improvement of group processes through various forms of training, eg T-groups, team building and interactive skills training. The main processes that take place in groups as described below are interaction, task and maintenance functions, group ideology, group cohesion, group development and identification.

Channels of communication

Three basic channels of communication within groups were identified by Leavitt (1951) and are illustrated in Figure 20.1.

The characteristics of these different groups are as follows:

- *Wheel groups*, where the task is straightforward, work faster, need fewer messages to solve problems and make fewer errors than circle groups, but they are inflexible if the task changes.

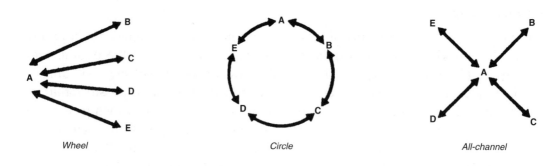

Figure 20.1 Channels of communication within groups

- *Circle groups* are faster in solving complex problems than wheel groups.
- *All-channel groups* are the most flexible and function well in complex, open-ended situations.

The level of satisfaction for individuals is lowest in the circle group, fairly high in the all-channel group and mixed in the wheel group, where the leader is more satisfied than the outlying members.

Task and maintenance functions

The following functions need to be carried out in groups:

- *task* – initiating, information seeking, diagnosing, opinion-seeking, evaluating, decision-managing;
- *maintenance* – encouraging, compromising, peace-keeping, clarifying, summarizing, standard-setting.

It is the job of the group leader or leaders to ensure that these functions operate effectively. Leaderless groups can work, but only in special circumstances. A leader is almost essential – whether official or self-appointed. The style adopted by a leader affects the way the group operates. If the leader is respected, this will increase group cohesiveness and its ability to get things done. An inappropriately authoritarian style creates tension and resentment. An over-permissive style means that respect for the leader diminishes and the group does not function so effectively.

Group ideology

In the course of interacting and carrying out its task and maintenance functions, the group develops an ideology which affects the attitudes and actions of its members and the degree of satisfaction which they feel.

Group cohesion

If the group ideology is strong and individual members identify closely with the group, it will become increasingly cohesive. Group norms or implicit rules will be evolved, which define what is acceptable behaviour and what is not. The impact of group cohesion can, however, result in negative as well as positive results. Janis's (1972) study of the decision-making processes of US foreign policy groups established that a cohesive group of individuals, sharing a common fate, exerts a strong pressure towards conformity. He coined the term 'group think' to describe the exaggeration of irrational tendencies that appears to occur in groups and argued that a group setting can magnify weakness of judgement.

To be 'one of us' is not always a good thing in management circles. A sturdy spirit of independence, even a maverick tendency, may be more conducive to correct decision-making. Team-working is a good thing, but so is flexibility and independent judgement. These need not be incompatible with team membership, but could be if there is too much emphasis on cohesion and conformity within the group.

Reference group

A reference group consists of the group of people with whom an individual identifies. This means that the group's norms are accepted and if in doubt about what to do or say, reference is made to these norms or to other group members before action is taken. Most people in organizations belong to a reference group and this can significantly affect the ways in which they behave.

Impact on group members

The reference group will also affect individual behaviour. This may be through overt pressure to conform or by more subtle processes. Acceptance of group norms commonly goes through two stages – compliance and internalization. Initially, a group member complies in order not to be rejected by the group, although he or she may behave differently when away from the group. Progressively, however, the individual accepts the norm whether with the group or not – the group norm has been internalized. As noted by Chell (1987), pressure on members to conform can cause problems when:

- there is incompatibility between a member's personal goals and those of the group;
- there is no sense of pride from being a member of the group;
- the member is not fully integrated with the group;
- the price of conformity is too high.

Group development

Tuckman (1965) has identified four stages of group development:

1. *forming*, when there is anxiety, dependence on the leader and testing to find out the nature of the situation and the task, and what behaviour is acceptable;
2. *storming*, where there is conflict, emotional resistance to the demands of the task, resistance to control and even rebellion against the leader;
3. *norming*, when group cohesion is developed, norms emerge, views are exchanged openly, mutual support and cooperation increase and the group acquires a sense of its identity;
4. *performing*, when interpersonal problems are resolved, roles are flexible and functional, there are constructive attempts to complete tasks and energy is available for effective work.

Identification

Individuals will identify with their groups if they like the other members, approve of the purpose and work of the group and wish to be associated with the standing of the group in the organization. Identification will be more complex if the standing of the group is good.

Teamwork

Definition of a team

As defined by Katzenbach and Smith (1993):

> A team is a small number of people with complementary skills who are committed to a common purpose, performance goals and approach for which they hold themselves mutually accountable.

Characteristics of effective teams

The characteristics of teams as described by Katzenbach and Smith are:

- Teams are the basic units of performance for most organizations. They meld together the skills, experiences and insights of several people.
- Teamwork applies to the whole organization as well as specific teams. It represents 'a set of values that encourage behaviours such as listening and responding co-operatively to points of view expressed by others, giving others the benefit of the doubt, providing support to those who need it and recognising the interests and achievements of others'.
- Teams are created and energized by significant performance challenges.
- Teams outperform individuals acting alone or in large organizational groupings, especially when performance requires multiple skills, judgements and experiences.
- Teams are flexible and responsive to changing events and demands. They can adjust their approach to new information and challenges with greater speed, accuracy and effectiveness than can individuals caught in the web of larger organizational conventions.
- High-performance teams invest much time and effort exploring, shaping and agreeing on a purpose that belongs to them, both collectively and individually. They are characterized by a deep sense of commitment to their growth and success.

Dysfunctional teams

The specification set out above is somewhat idealistic. Teams do not always work like that. They can fail to function effectively in the following ways:

- The atmosphere can be strained and over-formalized.
- Either there is too much discussion that gets nowhere or discussion is inhibited by dominant members of the team.
- Team members do not really understand what they are there to do and the objectives or standards they are expected to achieve.
- People don't listen to one another.
- Disagreements are frequent and often relate to personalities and differences of opinion rather than a reasoned discussion of alternative points of view.
- Decisions are not made jointly by team members.
- There is evidence of open personal attacks or hidden personal animosities.
- People do not feel free to express their opinions.
- Individual team members opt out or are allowed to opt out, leaving the others to do the work.

- There is little flexibility in the way in which team members operate – people tend to use a limited range of skills or specific tasks, and there is little evidence of multi-skilling.
- The team leader dominates the team; more attention is given to who takes control rather than to getting the work done.
- The team determines its own standards and norms, which may not be in accord with the standards and norms of the organization.

Team roles

The different types of roles played by team members have been defined by Belbin (1981) as follows:

- *chairmen* who control the way the team operates;
- *shapers* who specify the ways the team should work;
- *company workers* who turn proposals into practical work procedures;
- *plants* who produce ideas and strategies;
- *resource investigators* who explore the availability of resources, ideas and developments outside the team;
- *monitor-evaluators* who analyse problems and evaluate ideas;
- *team workers* who provide support to team members, improve team communications and foster team spirit;
- *completer-finishers* who maintain a sense of urgency in the team.

An alternative classification of roles has been developed by Margerison and McCann (1986). The eight roles are:

- *reporter-advisor:* gathers information and expresses it in an easily understandable form;
- *creator-innovator:* enjoys thinking up new ideas and ways of doing things;
- *explorer-promoter:* takes up ideas and promotes them to others;
- *assessor-developer:* takes ideas and makes them work in practice;
- *thruster-organizer:* gets things done, emphasizing targets, deadlines and budgets;
- *concluder-producer:* sets up plans and standard systems to ensure outputs are achieved;
- *controller-inspector:* concerned with the details and adhering to rules and regulations;
- *upholder-maintainer:* provides guidance and help in meeting standards.

According to Margerison and McCann, a balanced team needs members with preferences for each of these eight roles.

Leadership, power, politics and conflict

The main processes that affect how organizations function are leadership, power, politics and conflict.

Leadership

Leadership can be defined as the ability to persuade others willingly to behave differently. The function of team leaders is to achieve the task set for them with the help of the group. Leaders and their groups are therefore interdependent.

Leaders have two main roles. First, they must achieve the task. Secondly, they have to maintain effective relationships between themselves and the group and the individuals in it – effective in the sense that they are conducive to achieving the task. As Adair (1973) pointed out, in fulfilling their roles, leaders have to satisfy the following needs:

1. *Task needs.* The group exists to achieve a common purpose or task. The leader's role is to ensure that this purpose is fulfilled. If it is not, they will lose the confidence of the group and the result will be frustration, disenchantment, criticism and, possibly, the ultimate disintegration of the group.
2. *Group maintenance needs.* To achieve its objectives, the group needs to be held together. The leader's job is to build up and maintain team spirit and morale.
3. *Individual needs.* Individuals have their own needs, which they expect to be satisfied at work. The leader's task is to be aware of these needs so that where necessary they can take steps to harmonize them with the needs of the task and the group.

These three needs are interdependent. The leader's actions in one area affect both the others; thus successful achievement of the task is essential if the group is to be held together and its members motivated to give their best effort to the job. Action directed at meeting group or individual needs must be related to the needs of the task. It is impossible to consider individuals in isolation from the group or to consider the group without referring to the individuals within it. If any need is neglected, one of the others will suffer and the leader will be less successful.

The kind of leadership exercised will be related to the nature of the task and the people being led. It will also depend on the environment and, of course, on the actual leader. Analysing the qualities of leadership in terms of intelligence, initiative, self-assurance and so on has only limited value. The qualities required may be different in different situations. It is more useful to adopt a contingency approach and take account of the variables leaders have to deal with; especially the task, the group and their own position relative to the group.

Power

Organizations exist to get things done and in the process of doing this, people or groups exercise power. Directly or indirectly, the use of power in influencing behaviour is a pervading feature of organizations, whether it is exerted by managers, specialists, informal groups or trade union officials.

Power is the capacity to secure the dominance of one's goals or values over others. Four different types of power have been identified by French and Raven (1959):

- *reward power* – derived from the belief of individuals that compliance brings rewards; the ability to distribute rewards contributes considerably to an executive's power;
- *coercive power* – making it plain that non-compliance will bring punishment;
- *expert power* – exercised by people who are popular or admired and with whom the less powerful can identify;
- *legitimized power* – power conferred by the position in an organization held by an executive.

Politics

Power and politics are inextricably mixed, and in any organization there will inevitably be people who want to achieve their satisfaction by acquiring power, legitimately or illegitimately. Kakabadse (1983) defines politics as 'a process, that of influencing individuals and groups of people to your point of view, where you cannot rely on authority'.

Organizations consist of individuals who, while they are ostensibly there to achieve a common purpose, are, at the same time, driven by their own needs to achieve their own goals. Effective management is the process of harmonizing individual endeavour and ambition to the common good. Some individuals genuinely believe that using political means to achieve their goals will benefit the organization as well as themselves. Others rationalize this belief. Yet others unashamedly pursue their own ends.

Conflict

Conflict is inevitable in organizations because they function by means of adjustments and compromises among competitive elements in their structure and membership. Conflict also arises when there is change, because it may be seen as a threat to be challenged or resisted, or when there is frustration – this may produce an aggressive reaction; fight rather than flight. Conflict is not to be deplored. It is an inevitable result of progress and change and it can and should be used constructively.

Conflict between individuals raises fewer problems than conflict between groups. Individuals can act independently and resolve their differences. Members of groups may have to accept the norms, goals and values of their group. The individual's loyalty will usually be to his or her own group if it is in conflict with others.

Interaction and networking

Interactions between people criss-cross the organization, creating networks for getting things done and exchanging information, which is not catered for in the formal structure. 'Networking' is an increasingly important process in flexible and delayered organizations where more fluid interactions across the structure are required between individuals and teams. Individuals can often get much more done by networking than by going through formal channels. At least this means that they can canvass opinion and enlist support to promote their projects or ideas and to share their knowledge.

People also get things done in organizations by creating alliances – getting agreement on a course of action with other people and joining forces to get things done.

Communications

The communications processes used in organizations have a marked effect on how they function, especially if they take place through the network, which can then turn into the 'grapevine'. E-mails in intranets encourage the instant flow of information (and sometimes produce information overload) but may inhibit face-to-face interactions, which are often the best ways of getting things done.

21

Organizational culture

This chapter starts with definitions of organizational culture and the associated concept of organizational climate. The notion of management style as a way of describing how managers behave within the culture of their organizations is also defined. The chapter continues with comments on the significance of the concept to organizations and how culture develops. The components of culture and methods of analysing and describing culture and the climate are then considered. The chapter concludes with a review of approaches to supporting or changing cultures.

DEFINITIONS

Organizational culture

Organizational or corporate culture is the pattern of values, norms, beliefs, attitudes and assumptions that may not have been articulated but shape the ways in which people behave and things get done. Values refer to what is believed to be important about how people and the organizations behave. Norms are the unwritten rules of behaviour.

The definition emphasizes that organizational culture is concerned with abstractions such as values and norms which pervade the whole or part of an organization.

They may not be defined, discussed or even noticed. Put another way, culture can be regarded as a 'code word for the subjective side of organizational life' (Meyerson and Martin, 1987). Nevertheless, culture can have a significant influence on people's behaviour.

The following are some other definitions of culture:

> The culture of an organization refers to the unique configuration of norms, values, beliefs and ways of behaving that characterize the manner in which groups and individuals combine to get things done.
>
> *Eldridge and Crombie (1974)*

> Culture is a system of informal rules that spells out how people are to behave most of the time.
>
> *Deal and Kennedy (1982)*

> Culture is the commonly held beliefs, attitudes and values that exist in an organization. Put more simply, culture is 'the way we do things around here'.
>
> *Furnham and Gunter (1993)*

> A system of shared values and beliefs about what is important, what behaviours are important and about feelings and relationships internally and externally.
>
> *Purcell et al (2003)*

Summing up the various definitions of culture, Furnham and Gunter (1993) list, amongst others, the following areas of agreement on the concept:

- It is difficult to define (often a pointless exercise).
- It is multi-dimensional, with many different components at different levels.
- It is not particularly dynamic, and ever changing (being relatively stable over short periods of time).
- It takes time to establish and therefore time to change a corporate culture.

Problems with the concept

Furnham and Gunter refer to a number of problems with the concept, including:

- how to categorize culture (what terminology to use);
- when and why corporate culture should be changed and how this takes place;
- what is the healthiest, most optimal or desirable culture.

They also point out that it is dangerous to treat culture as an objective entity 'as if everyone in the world would be able to observe the same phenomenon, whereas this is patently not the case'.

Organizational climate

The term organizational climate is sometimes confused with organizational culture and there has been much debate on what distinguishes the concept of climate from that of culture. In his analysis of this issue, Denison (1996) believed that *culture* refers to the deep structure of organizations, which is rooted in the values, beliefs and assumptions held by organizational members. In contrast, *climate* refers to those aspects of the environment that are consciously perceived by organizational members. Rousseau (1988) stated that climate is a perception and is descriptive. Perceptions are sensations or realizations experienced by an individual. Descriptions are what a person reports of these sensations.

The debate about the meanings of these terms can become academic. It is easiest to regard organizational climate as how people perceive (see and feel about) the culture existing in their organization. As defined by French *et al* (1985), it is 'the relatively persistent set of perceptions held by organization members concerning the characteristics and quality of organizational culture'. They distinguish between the actual situations (ie culture) and the perception of it (climate).

THE SIGNIFICANCE OF CULTURE

As Furnham and Gunter (1993) suggest:

> Culture represents the 'social glue' and generates a 'we-feeling', thus counteracting processes of differentiations which are an unavoidable part of organizational life. Organizational culture offers a shared system of meanings which is the basis for communications and mutual understanding. If these functions are not fulfilled in a satisfactory way, culture may significantly reduce the efficiency of an organization.

Purcell *et al* (2005) found in their previous research (2003) that in some organizations there was a certain something – christened the 'big idea' – that seemed to give them a competitive edge. The big idea consisted of a few words or statements that very clearly summed up the organization, what it was about and what it was like to work there. In turn this enabled the organization to manage its corporate culture and establish a set of shared values, which recognized and reinforced the sort of organization it wanted to be. Thus it was able to establish a strong shared culture within which particular practices that encouraged better performance would be embedded and flourish.

HOW ORGANIZATIONAL CULTURE DEVELOPS

The values and norms that are the basis of culture are formed in four ways. First, culture is formed by the leaders in the organization, especially those who have shaped it in the past. Schein (1990) indicates that people identify with visionary leaders – how they behave and what they expect. They note what such leaders pay attention to and treat them as role models. Second, as Schein also points out, culture is formed around critical incidents – important events from which lessons are learnt about desirable or undesirable behaviour. Third, as proposed by Furnham and Gunter (1993), culture develops from the need to maintain effective working relationships among organization members, and this establishes values and expectations. Finally, culture is influenced by the organization's environment. The external environment may be relatively dynamic or unchanging.

Culture is learned over a period of time. Schein (1984) stated that there are two ways in which this learning takes place. First, the trauma model, in which members of the organization learn to cope with some threat by the erection of defence mechanisms. Second, the positive reinforcement model, where things that seem to work become embedded and entrenched. Learning takes place as people adapt to and cope with external pressures, and as they develop successful approaches and mechanisms to handle the internal challenges, processes and technologies in their organization.

Where culture has developed over long periods of time and has become firmly embedded, it may be difficult to change quickly, if at all, unless a traumatic event occurs.

THE DIVERSITY OF CULTURE

The development process described above may result in a culture that characterizes the whole organization. But there may be different cultures within organizations. For example, the culture of an outward-looking marketing department may be substantially different from that of an internally focused manufacturing function. There may be some common organizational values or norms, but in some respects these will vary between different work environments.

THE COMPONENTS OF CULTURE

Organizational culture can be described in terms of values, norms, artefacts and leadership or management style.

Values

Schiffman and Kanuk (1994) state that: 'Values help to determine what we think is right or wrong, what is important and what is desirable.'

Values are beliefs in what is best or good for the organization and what should or ought to happen. The 'value set' of an organization may only be recognized at top level, or it may be shared throughout the business, in which case it could be described as value driven.

The stronger the values, the more they will influence behaviour. This does not depend upon their having been articulated. Implicit values that are deeply embedded in the culture of an organization and are reinforced by the behaviour of management can be highly influential, while espoused values that are idealistic and are not reflected in managerial behaviour may have little or no effect. It is 'values in use', values that drive desirable behaviour, that are important.

Some of the most typical areas in which values can be expressed, implicitly or explicitly, are:

- performance;
- competence;
- competitiveness;
- innovation;
- quality;
- customer service;
- teamwork;
- care and consideration for people.

Values are translated into reality (enacted) through *norms* and *artefacts* as described below. They may also be expressed through the media of language (organizational jargon), rituals, stories and myths.

Norms

Norms are the unwritten rules of behaviour, the 'rules of the game' that provide informal guidelines on how to behave. Norms tell people what they are supposed to be doing, saying, believing, even wearing. They are never expressed in writing – if they were, they would be policies or procedures. They are passed on by word of mouth or behaviour and can be enforced by the reactions of people if they are violated. They can exert very powerful pressure on behaviour because of these reactions – we control others by the way we react to them.

Norms refer to such aspects of behaviour as:

- how managers treat the members of their teams (management style) and how the latter relate to their managers;
- the prevailing work ethic, eg 'work hard, play hard', 'come in early, stay late', 'if you cannot finish your work during business hours you are obviously inefficient', 'look busy at all times', 'look relaxed at all times';
- status – how much importance is attached to it; the existence or lack of obvious status symbols;
- ambition – naked ambition is expected and approved of, or a more subtle approach is the norm;
- performance – exacting performance standards are general; the highest praise that can be given in the organization is to be referred to as very professional;
- power – recognized as a way of life; executed by political means, dependent on expertise and ability rather than position; concentrated at the top; shared at different levels in different parts of the organization;
- politics – rife throughout the organization and treated as normal behaviour; not accepted as overt behaviour;
- loyalty – expected, a cradle to grave approach to careers; discounted, the emphasis is on results and contribution in the short term;
- anger – openly expressed; hidden, but expressed through other, possibly political, means;
- approachability – managers are expected to be approachable and visible; everything happens behind closed doors;
- formality – a cool, formal approach is the norm; forenames are/are not used at all levels; there are unwritten but clearly understood rules about dress.

Artefacts

Artefacts are the visible and tangible aspects of an organization that people hear, see or feel. Artefacts can include such things as the working environment, the tone and language used in letters or memoranda, the manner in which people address each other at meetings or over the telephone, the welcome (or lack of welcome) given to visitors and the way in which telephonists deal with outside calls. Artefacts can be very revealing.

Leadership style

Leadership style, often called management style, describes the approach managers use to deal with people in their teams. There are many styles of leadership, and leaders can be classified in extremes as follows:

- *Charismatic/non-charismatic*. Charismatic leaders rely on their personality, their inspirational qualities and their 'aura'. They are visionary leaders who are achievement-oriented, calculated risk-takers and good communicators. Non-charismatic leaders rely mainly on their know-how (authority goes to the person who knows), their quiet confidence and their cool, analytical approach to dealing with problems.
- *Autocratic-democratic*. Autocratic leaders impose their decisions, using their position to force people to do as they are told. Democratic leaders encourage people to participate and involve themselves in decision-taking.
- *Enabler-controller*. Enablers inspire people with their vision of the future and empower them to accomplish team goals. Controllers manipulate people to obtain their compliance.
- *Transactional-transformational*. Transactional leaders trade money, jobs and security for compliance. Transformational leaders motivate people to strive for higher-level goals.

Most managers adopt an approach somewhere between the extremes. Some will vary it according to the situation or their feelings at the time, others will stick to the same style whatever happens. A good case can be made for using an appropriate style according to the situation, but it is undesirable to be inconsistent in the style used in similar situations. Every manager has his or her own style but this will be influenced by the organizational culture, which may produce a prevailing management style that represents the behavioural norm for managers that is generally expected and adopted.

CLASSIFYING ORGANIZATIONAL CULTURE

There have been many attempts to classify or categorize organizational culture as a basis for the analysis of cultures in organizations and for taking action to support or change them. Most of these classifications are expressed in four dimensions and some of the best-known ones are summarized below.

Harrison

Harrison (1972) categorized what he called 'organization ideologies'. These are:

- *power-orientated* – competitive, responsive to personality rather than expertise;
- *people-orientated* – consensual, management control rejected;
- *task-orientated* – focus on competency, dynamic;
- *role-orientated* – focus on legality, legitimacy and bureaucracy.

Handy

Handy (1981) based his typology on Harrison's classification, although Handy preferred the word 'culture' to 'ideology' as culture conveyed more of the feeling of a pervasive way of life or set of norms. His four types of culture are:

- The *power culture* is one with a central power source that exercises control. There are few rules or procedures and the atmosphere is competitive, power-orientated and political.
- The *role culture* is one in which work is controlled by procedures and rules and the role, or job description, is more important than the person who fills it. Power is associated with positions, not people.
- The *task culture* is one in which the aim is to bring together the right people and let them get on with it. Influence is based more on expert power than on position or personal power. The culture is adaptable and teamwork is important.
- The *person culture* is one in which the individual is the central point. The organization exists only to serve and assist the individuals in it.

Schein

Schein (1985) identified the following four cultures:

- The *power culture* is one in which leadership resides in a few and rests on their ability and which tends to be entrepreneurial.
- The *role culture* is one in which power is balanced between the leader and the bureaucratic structure. The environment is likely to be stable and roles and rules are clearly defined.
- The *achievement culture* is one in which personal motivation and commitment are stressed and action, excitement and impact are valued.
- The *support culture* is one in which people contribute out of a sense of commitment and solidarity. Relationships are characterized by mutuality and trust.

Williams, Dobson and Walters

Williams *et al* (1989) redefined the four categories listed by Harrison and Handy as follows:

- *Power orientation* – organizations try to dominate their environment and those exercising power strive to maintain absolute control over subordinates.
- *Role orientation* emphasizes legality, legitimacy and responsibility. Hierarchy and status are important.
- *Task orientation* focuses on task accomplishment. Authority is based on appropriate knowledge and competence.
- *People orientation* – the organization exists primarily to serve the needs of its members. Individuals are expected to influence each other through example and helpfulness.

ASSESSING ORGANIZATIONAL CULTURE

A number of instruments exist for assessing organizational culture. This is not easy because culture is concerned with both subjective beliefs and unconscious assumptions (which might be difficult to measure), and with observed phenomena such as behavioural norms and artefacts. Two of the better-known instruments are summarized below.

Organizational ideology questionnaire (Harrison, 1972)

This questionnaire deals with the four orientations referred to earlier (power, role, task, self). The questionnaire is completed by ranking statements according to views on what is closest to the organization's actual position. Statements include:

- A good boss is strong, decisive and firm but fair.
- A good subordinate is compliant, hard-working and loyal.
- People who do well in the organization are shrewd and competitive, with a strong need for power.
- The basis of task assignment is the personal needs and judgements of those in authority.
- Decisions are made by people with the most knowledge and expertise about the problem.

Organizational culture inventory (Cooke and Lafferty, 1989)

This instrument assesses organizational culture under 12 headings:

1. *Humanistic-helpful* – organizations managed in a participative and person-centred way.
2. *Affiliative* – organizations that place a high priority on constructive relationships.
3. *Approval* – organizations in which conflicts are avoided and interpersonal relationships are pleasant – at least superficially.
4. *Conventional* – conservative, traditional and bureaucratically controlled organizations.
5. *Dependent* – hierarchically controlled and non-participative organizations.
6. *Avoidance* – organizations that fail to reward success but punish mistakes.
7. *Oppositional* – organizations in which confrontation prevails and negativism is rewarded.
8. *Power* – organizations structured on the basis of the authority inherent in members' positions.
9. *Competitive* – a culture in which winning is valued and members are rewarded for out-performing one another.
10. *Competence/perfectionist* – organizations in which perfectionism, persistence and hard work are valued.
11. *Achievement* – organizations that do things well and value members who set and accomplish challenging but realistic goals.
12. *Self-actualization* – organizations that value creativity, quality over quantity, and both task accomplishment and individual growth.

MEASURING ORGANIZATIONAL CLIMATE

Organizational climate measures attempts to assess organizations in terms of dimensions that are thought to capture or describe perceptions about the climate. Perceptions about climate can be measured by questionnaires such as that developed by Litwin and Stringer (1968) which covers eight categories:

1. *Structure* – feelings about constraints and freedom to act and the degree of formality or informality in the working atmosphere.
2. *Responsibility* – the feeling of being trusted to carry out important work.
3. *Risk* – the sense of riskiness and challenge in the job and in the organization; the relative emphasis on taking calculated risks or playing it safe.
4. *Warmth* – the existence of friendly and informal social groups.

5. *Support* – the perceived helpfulness of managers and co-workers; the emphasis (or lack of emphasis) on mutual support.
6. *Standards* – the perceived importance of implicit and explicit goals and performance standards; the emphasis on doing a good job; the challenge represented in personal and team goals.
7. *Conflict* – the feeling that managers and other workers want to hear different opinions; the emphasis on getting problems out into the open rather than smoothing them over or ignoring them.
8. *Identity* – the feeling that you belong to a company; that you are a valuable member of a working team.

A review of a number of questionnaires was carried out by Koys and De Cotiis (1991), which produced the following eight typical dimensions:

- *autonomy* – the perception of self-determination with respect to work procedures, goals and priorities;
- *cohesion* – the perception of togetherness or sharing within the organization setting, including the willingness of members to provide material risk;
- *trust* – the perception of freedom to communicate openly with members at higher organizational levels about sensitive or personal issues, with the expectation that the integrity of such communications will not be violated;
- *resource* – the perception of time demands with respect to task competition and performance standards;
- *support* – the perception of the degree to which superiors tolerate members' behaviour, including willingness to let members learn from their mistakes without fear of reprisal;
- *recognition* – the perception that members' contributions to the organization are acknowledged;
- *fairness* – the perception that organizational policies are non-arbitrary or capricious;
- *innovation* – the perception that change and creativity are encouraged, including risk-taking into new areas where the member has little or no prior experience.

APPROPRIATE CULTURES

It could be argued that a 'good' culture exerts a positive influence on organizational behaviour. It could help to create a 'high-performance' culture, one that will produce a high level of business performance. As described by Furnham and Gunter (1993), 'a good culture is consistent in its components and shared amongst organizational members, and it makes the organization unique, thus differentiating it from other organizations'.

However, a high-performance culture means little more than any culture that will produce a high level of business performance. The attributes of cultures vary tremendously by context. The qualities of a high-performance culture for an established retail chain, a growing service business and a consumer products company that is losing market share may be very different. Further, in addition to context differences, all cultures evolve over time. Cultures that are 'good' in one set of circumstances or period of time may be dysfunctional in different circumstances or different times.

Because culture is developed and manifests itself in different ways in different organizations, it is not possible to say that one culture is better than another, only that it is dissimilar in certain ways. There is no such thing as an ideal culture, only an appropriate culture. This means that there can be no universal prescription for managing culture, although there are certain approaches that can be helpful, as described in the next section.

SUPPORTING AND CHANGING CULTURES

While it may not be possible to define an ideal structure or to prescribe how it can be developed, it can at least be stated with confidence that embedded cultures exert considerable influence on organizational behaviour and therefore performance. If there is an appropriate and effective culture it would be desirable to take steps to support or reinforce it. If the culture is inappropriate, attempts should be made to determine what needs to be changed and to develop and implement plans for change.

Culture analysis

In either case, the first step is to analyse the existing culture. This can be done through questionnaires, surveys and discussions in focus groups or workshops. It is often helpful to involve people in analysing the outcome of surveys, getting them to produce a diagnosis of the cultural issues facing the organization and participate in the development and implementation of plans and programmes to deal with any issues. This could form part of an organizational development programme as described in Chapter 24. Groups can analyse the culture through the use of measurement instruments. Extra dimensions can be established by the use of group exercises such as 'rules of the club' (participants brainstorm the 'rules' or norms that govern behaviour) or 'shield' (participants design a shield, often quartered, which illustrates major cultural features of the organization). Joint exercises like this can lead to discussions on appropriate values, which are much more likely to be 'owned' by people if they have helped to create them rather than having them imposed from above.

While involvement is highly desirable, there will be situations when management has to carry out the analysis and determine the actions required without the initial participation of employees. But the latter should be kept informed and brought into discussion on developments as soon as possible.

Culture support and reinforcement

Culture support and reinforcement programmes aim to preserve and underpin what is good and functional about the present culture. Schein (1985) has suggested that the most powerful primary mechanisms for culture embedding and reinforcement are:

- what leaders pay attention to, measure and control;
- leaders' reactions to critical incidents and crises;
- deliberate role modelling, teaching and coaching by leaders;
- criteria for allocation of rewards and status;
- criteria for recruitment, selection, promotion and commitment.

Other means of underpinning the culture are:

- re-affirming existing values;
- operationalizing values through actions designed, for example, to implement total quality and customer care programmes, to provide financial and non-financial rewards for expected behaviour, to improve productivity, to promote and reward good teamwork, to develop a learning organization (see Chapter 36);
- using the value set as headings for reviewing individual and team performance – emphasizing that people are expected to uphold the values;
- ensuring that induction procedures cover core values and how people are expected to achieve them;
- reinforcing induction training on further training courses set up as part of a continuous development programme.

Culture change

Focus

In theory, culture change programmes start with an analysis of the existing culture. The desired culture is then defined, which leads to the identification of a 'culture gap' that needs to be filled. This analysis can identify behavioural expectations so that development and reward processes can be used to define and reinforce them. In real life, it is not quite as simple as that.

A comprehensive change programme may be a fundamental part of an organizational transformation programme as described in Chapter 24. But culture change programmes can focus on particular aspects of the culture, for example performance, commitment, quality, customer service, teamwork, organizational learning. In each case the underpinning values would need to be defined. It would probably be necessary to prioritize by deciding which areas need the most urgent attention. There is a limit to how much can be done at once except in crisis conditions.

Levers for change

Having identified what needs to be done, and the priorities, the next step is to consider what levers for change exist and how they can be used. The levers could include, as appropriate:

- *performance* – performance-related or contribution-related pay schemes; performance management processes; gainsharing; leadership training, skills development;
- *commitment* – communication, participation and involvement programmes; developing a climate of cooperation and trust; clarifying the psychological contract;
- *quality* – total quality and continuous improvement programmes;
- *customer service* – customer care programmes;
- *teamwork* – team building; team performance management; team rewards;
- *organizational learning* – taking steps to enhance intellectual capital and the organization's resource-based capability by developing a learning organization;
- *values* – gaining understanding, acceptance and commitment through involvement in defining values, performance management processes and employee development interventions.

Change management

The effectiveness of culture change programmes largely depends on the quality of change management processes. These are described in Chapter 24.

Part V

Organization, design and development

This part is concerned with the practical applications of organizational behaviour theory. It starts by looking at the processes of organizational design and development and then deals with job and role development.

22

Organization design

The management of people in organizations constantly raises questions such as 'Who does what?', 'How should activities be grouped together?', 'What lines and means of communication need to be established?', 'How should people be helped to understand their roles in relation to the objectives of the organization and the roles of their colleagues?', 'Are we doing everything that we ought to be doing and nothing that we ought not to be doing?' and 'Have we got too many unnecessary layers of management in the organization?'

These are questions involving people which must concern HR practitioners in their capacity of helping the business to make the best use of its people. HR specialists should be able to contribute to the processes of organization design or redesign as described below because of their understanding of the factors affecting organizational behaviour and because they are in a position to take an overall view of how the business is organized, which it is difficult for the heads of other functional departments to obtain.

THE PROCESS OF ORGANIZING

The process of organizing can be described as the design, development and maintenance of a system of coordinated activities in which individuals and groups of people work cooperatively under leadership towards commonly understood and accepted goals. The key word in that definition is 'system'. Organizations are systems which, as affected by their environment, have a structure which has both formal and informal elements.

The process of organizing may involve the grand design or redesign of the total structure, but most frequently it is concerned with the organization of particular functions and activities and the basis upon which the relationships between them are managed.

Organizations are not static things. Changes are constantly taking place in the business itself, in the environment in which the business operates, and in the people who work in the business. There is no such thing as an 'ideal' organization. The most that can be done is to optimize the processes involved, remembering that whatever structure evolves it will be contingent on the environmental circumstances of the organization, and one of the aims of organization is to achieve the 'best fit' between the structure and these circumstances.

An important point to bear in mind is that organizations consist of people working more or less cooperatively together. Inevitably, and especially at managerial levels, the organization may have to be adjusted to fit the particular strengths and attributes of the people available. The result may not conform to the ideal, but it is more likely to work than a structure that ignores the human element. It is always desirable to have an ideal structure in mind, but it is equally desirable to modify it to meet particular circumstances, as long as there is awareness of the potential problems that may arise. This may seem an obvious point, but it is frequently ignored by management consultants and others who adopt a doctrinaire approach to organization, often with disastrous results.

AIM

Bearing in mind the need to take an empirical and contingent approach to organizing, as suggested above, the aim of organization design could be defined as being to *optimize* the arrangements for conducting the affairs of the business. To do this it is necessary, as far as circumstances allow, to:

- clarify the overall purposes of the organization – the strategic thrusts that govern what it does and how it functions;
- define as precisely as possible the key activities required to achieve that purpose;
- group these activities logically together to avoid unnecessary overlap or duplication;

- provide for the integration of activities and the achievement of cooperative effort and teamwork in pursuit of a common purpose;
- build flexibility into the system so that organizational arrangements can adapt quickly to new situations and challenges;
- provide for the rapid communication of information throughout the organization;
- define the role and function of each organizational unit so that all concerned know how it plays its part in achieving the overall purpose;
- clarify individual roles, accountabilities and authorities;
- design jobs to make the best use of the skills and capacities of the job holders and to provide them with high levels of intrinsic motivation (job design is considered in Chapter 23);
- plan and implement organization development activities to ensure that the various processes within the organization operate in a manner that contributes to organizational effectiveness;
- set up teams and project groups as required to be responsible for specific processing, development, professional or administrative activities or for the conduct of projects.

CONDUCTING ORGANIZATION REVIEWS

Organization reviews are conducted in the following stages:

1. An *analysis*, as described below, of the existing arrangements and the factors that may affect the organization now and in the future.
2. A *diagnosis* of what needs to be done to improve the way in which the organization is structured and functions.
3. A *plan* to implement any revisions to the structure emerging from the diagnosis, possibly in phases. The plan may include longer-term considerations about the structure and the type of managers and employees who will be required to operate within it.
4. *Implementation* of the plan.

ORGANIZATION ANALYSIS

The starting point for an organization review is an analysis of the existing circumstances, structure and processes of the organization and an assessment of the strategic issues that might affect it in the future. This covers:

- The *external environment*. The economic, market and competitive factors that may affect the organization. Plans for product-market development will be significant.
- The *internal environment*. The mission, values, organization climate, management style, technology and processes of the organization as they affect the way it functions and should be structured to carry out those functions. Technological developments in such areas as cellular manufacturing may be particularly important as well as the introduction of new processes such as just-in-time or the development of an entirely new computer system.
- *Strategic issues and objectives*. As a background to the study it is necessary to identify the strategic issues facing the organization and its objectives. These may be considered under such headings as growth, competition and market position and standing. Issues concerning the availability of the required human, financial and physical resources would also have to be considered.
- *Activities*. Activity analysis establishes what work is done and what needs to be done in the organization to achieve its objectives within its environment. The analysis should cover what is and is not being done, who is doing it and where, and how much is being done. An answer is necessary to the key questions: 'Are all the activities required properly catered for?', 'Are there any unnecessary activities being carried out, ie those that do not need to be done at all or those that could be conducted more economically and efficiently by external contractors or providers?'
- *Structure*. The analysis of structure covers how activities are grouped together, the number of levels in the hierarchy, the extent to which authority is decentralized to divisions and strategic business units (SBUs), where functions such as finance, personnel and research and development are placed in the structure (eg as central functions or integrated into divisions or SBUs) and the relationships that exist between different units and functions (with particular attention being given to the way in which they communicate and cooperate with one another). Attention would be paid to such issues as the logic of the way in which activities are grouped and decentralized, the span of control managers (the number of separate functions or people they are directly responsible for), any overlap between functions or gaps leading to the neglect of certain activities, and the existence of unnecessary departments, units, functions or layers of management.

ORGANIZATION DIAGNOSIS

The diagnosis should be based on the analysis and an agreement by those concerned with what the aims of the organization should be. The present arrangements can be considered against these aims and future requirements to assess the extent to which they meet them or fall short.

It is worth repeating that there are no absolute standards against which an organization structure can be judged. There is never one right way of organizing anything and there are no absolute principles that govern organizational choice. The fashion for delayering organizations has much to commend it, but it can go too far, leaving units and individuals adrift without any clear guidance on where they fit into the structure and how they should work with one another, and making the management task of coordinating activities more difficult.

Organization guidelines

There are no 'rules' or 'principles' of organization but there are certain guidelines that are worth bearing in mind in an organization study. These are:

- *Allocation of work*. The work that has to be done should be defined and allocated to functions, units, departments, work teams, project groups and individual positions. Related activities should be grouped together, but the emphasis should be on process rather than hierarchy, taking into account the need to manage processes that involve a number of different work units or teams.
- *Differentiation and integration*. It is necessary to differentiate between the different activities that have to be carried out, but it is equally necessary to ensure that these activities are integrated so that everyone in the organization is working towards the same goals.
- *Teamwork*. Jobs should be defined and roles described in ways that facilitate and underline the importance of teamwork. Areas where cooperation is required should be emphasized. The organization should be designed and operated across departmental or functional boundaries. Wherever possible, self-managing teams should be set up and given the maximum amount of responsibility to run their own affairs, including planning, budgeting and exercising quality control. Networking should be encouraged in the sense of people communicating openly and informally with one another as the need arises. It is recognized that these informal processes can be more productive than rigidly 'working through channels' as set out in the organization chart.
- *Flexibility*. The organization structure should be flexible enough to respond quickly to change, challenge and uncertainty. Flexibility should be enhanced by the creation of core groups and by using part-time, temporary and contract workers to handle extra demands. At top management level and elsewhere, a collegiate approach to team operation should be considered in which people

share responsibility and are expected to work with their colleagues in areas outside their primary function or skill.

- *Role clarification.* People should be clear about their roles as individuals and as members of a team. They should know what they will be held accountable for and be given every opportunity to use their abilities in achieving objectives to which they have agreed and are committed. Role profiles should define key result areas but should not act as straitjackets, restricting initiative and unduly limiting responsibility.
- *Decentralization.* Authority to make decisions should be delegated as close to the scene of action as possible. Profit centres should be set up as strategic business units which operate close to their markets and with a considerable degree of autonomy. A multiproduct or market business should develop a federal organization with each federated entity running its own affairs, although they will be linked together by the overall business strategy.
- *Delayering.* Organizations should be 'flattened' by removing superfluous layers of management and supervision in order to promote flexibility, facilitate swifter communication, increase responsiveness, enable people to be given more responsibility as individuals or teams and reduce costs.

Organization design leads into organization planning.

ORGANIZATION PLANNING

Organization planning is the process of converting the analysis into the design. It determines structure, relationships, roles, human resource requirements and the lines along which changes should be implemented. There is no one best design. There is always a choice between alternatives. Logical analysis will help in the evaluation of the alternatives but Mary Parker Follet's (1924) law of the situation will have to prevail. The final choice will be contingent upon the present and future circumstances of the organization. It will be strongly influenced by personal and human considerations – the inclinations of top management, the strengths and weaknesses of management generally, the availability of people to staff the new organization and the need to take account of the feelings of those who will be exposed to change. Cold logic may sometimes have to override these considerations. If it does, then it must be deliberate and the consequences must be appreciated and allowed for when planning the implementation of the new organization.

It may have to be accepted that a logical regrouping of activities cannot be introduced in the short term because no one with the experience is available to manage the new activities, or because capable individuals are so firmly entrenched in one area that to uproot them would cause serious damage to their morale and would reduce the overall effectiveness of the new organization.

The worst sin that organization designers can commit is that of imposing their own ideology on the organization. Their job is to be eclectic in their knowledge, sensitive in their analysis of the situation and deliberate in their approach to the evaluation of alternatives.

Having planned the organization and defined structures, relationships and roles, it is necessary to consider how the new organization should be implemented. It may be advisable to stage implementation over a number of phases, especially if new people have to be found and trained.

RESPONSIBILITY FOR ORGANIZATION DESIGN

Organization design may be carried out by line management with or without the help of members of the HR function acting as internal consultants, or it may be done by outside consultants. HR management should always be involved because organization design is essentially about people and the work they do. The advantage of using outside consultants is that an independent and dispassionate view is obtained. They can cut through internal organizational pressures, politics and constraints and bring experience of other organizational problems they have dealt with. Sometimes, regrettably, major changes can be obtained only by outside intervention. But there is a danger of consultants suggesting theoretically ideal organizations that do not take sufficient account of the problems of making them work with existing people. They do not have to live with their solutions, as do line and HR managers. If outside consultants are used, it is essential to involve people from within the organization so they can ensure that they are able to implement the proposals smoothly.

23

Job design and role development

JOBS AND ROLES

A *job* consists of a related set of tasks that are carried out by a person to fulfil a purpose. It can be regarded as a unit in an organization structure that remains unchanged whoever is in the job. A job in this sense is a fixed entity, part of a machine that can be 'designed' like any other part of a machine. Routine or machine-controlled jobs do indeed exist in most organizations but, increasingly, the work carried out by people is not mechanistic. What is done, how it is done and the results achieved depend more and more on the capabilities and motivation of individuals and their interactions with one another and their customers or suppliers.

The rigidity inherent in the notion of a job is not in accord with the realities of organizational life for many people. A flexible approach is often required to use and develop their skills in order to respond swiftly to the new demands they face every day.

The concept of a *role* conveys these realities more than that of a *job*. Essentially, a role is the part people play in carrying out their work. *Individual roles* are those carried out by one person. *Generic roles* are those in which essentially similar activities are carried out by a number of people. They may cover a whole occupation. A role can be described in behavioural terms – given certain expectations, this is how the person needs to behave to meet them. A role profile will not spell out the tasks to be carried out but will instead indicate expectations in the form of outputs and outcomes and competency requirements in the shape of the inputs of skill and behaviours required to fulfil these expectations. The definition may be broad. It will not be prescriptive. Scope will be allowed for people to use their skills in accordance with their interpretation of the situation. Encouragement will be given for them both to grow in their roles and to grow their roles by developing their competencies and by extending the range of their responsibilities so that their contributions exceed expectations. The need for flexibility will also be recognised.

Roles are therefore more about people than jobs and this means that the extent to which a role can be 'designed' may be limited or even non-existent where flexibility and growth are important. This may apply particularly to knowledge workers.

There are, however, certain considerations that affect the ways in which roles can be developed in order to increase satisfaction with the work and to encourage growth. These considerations can also apply to jobs and this chapter therefore starts with a general review of the factors that affect job design and that are also relevant to role building. Attention is then directed to approaches to job design, which include the notion of job enrichment. Consideration is next given to the characteristics of team roles and what can be done to set up and maintain effective self-managed teams and high-performance work design. Finally, the focus is on roles and how they can be *developed* rather than designed in today's flexible organizations on the basis of an understanding of what role holders are expected to achieve, the scope they have to go beyond these basic expectations and the capabilities they need to carry out and extend their role.

FACTORS AFFECTING JOB DESIGN

The content of jobs is affected by the purpose of the organization or the organizational unit, the particular demands that achieving that purpose makes on the people involved, the structure of the organization, the processes and activities carried out in the organization, the technology of the organization, the changes that are taking place in that technology and the environment in which the organization operates. Job design has therefore to be considered within the context of organizational design, as described in Chapter 22, but it must also take into account the following factors:

- the process of intrinsic motivation;
- the characteristics of task structure;
- the motivating characteristics of jobs;
- the significance of the job characteristics model;
- providing intrinsic motivation.

The process of intrinsic motivation

The case for using job design techniques is based on the premise that effective performance and genuine satisfaction in work follow mainly from the intrinsic content of the job. This is related to the fundamental concept that people are motivated when they are provided with the means to achieve their goals. Work provides the means to earn money, which as an extrinsic reward satisfies basic needs and is instrumental in providing ways of satisfying higher-level needs. But work also provides intrinsic rewards, which are under the direct control of the worker.

Characteristics of task structure

Job design requires the assembly of a number of tasks into a job or a group of jobs. An individual may carry out one main task, which consists of a number of interrelated elements or functions. Or task functions may be allocated to a team working closely together in a manufacturing 'cell' or customer service unit, or strung along an assembly line. In more complex jobs, individuals may carry out a variety of connected tasks, each with a number of functions, or these tasks may be allocated to a team of workers or divided between them. In the latter case, the tasks may require a variety of skills, which have to be possessed by all members of the team (multi-skilling) in order to work flexibly.

Complexity in a job may be a reflection of the number and variety of tasks to be carried out, the different skills or competences to be used, the range and scope of the decisions that have to be made, or the difficulty of predicting the outcome of decisions.

The internal structure of each task consists of three elements: planning (deciding on the course of action, its timing and the resources required), executing (carrying out the plan), and controlling (monitoring performance and progress and taking corrective action when required). A completely integrated job includes all these elements for each of the tasks involved. The worker, or group of workers, having been given objectives in terms of output, quality and cost targets, decides on how the work is to be done, assembles the resources, performs the work, and monitors output, quality and cost standards. Responsibility in a job is measured by the amount of authority someone has to do all these things.

Motivating characteristics of jobs

The ideal arrangement from the point of view of intrinsic motivation is to provide for fully integrated jobs containing all three task elements. In practice, management and team leaders are often entirely responsible for planning and control, leaving the worker responsible for execution. To a degree, this is inevitable, but one of the aims of job design is often to extend the responsibility of workers into the functions of planning and control. This can involve empowerment – giving individuals and teams more responsibility for decision making and ensuring that they have the training, support and guidance to exercise that responsibility properly.

The job characteristics model

A useful perspective on the factors affecting job design and motivation is provided by Hackman and Oldham's (1974) job characteristics model. They suggest that the 'critical psychological states' of 'experienced meaningfulness of work, experienced responsibility for outcomes of work and knowledge of the actual outcomes of work' strongly influence motivation, job satisfaction and performance.

As Robertson *et al* (1992) point out: 'This element of the model is based on the notion of personal reward and reinforcement… Reinforcement is obtained when a person becomes aware (knowledge of results) that he or she has been responsible for (experienced responsibility) and good performance on a task that he or she cares about (experienced meaningfulness).'

Providing intrinsic motivation

Three characteristics have been distinguished by Lawler (1969) as being required in jobs if they are to be intrinsically motivating:

- *Feedback* – individuals must receive meaningful feedback about their performance, preferably by evaluating their own performance and defining the feedback. This implies that they should ideally work on a complete product, or a significant part of it that can be seen as a whole.
- *Use of abilities* – the job must be perceived by individuals as requiring them to use abilities they value in order to perform the job effectively.
- *Self-control* – individuals must feel that they have a high degree of self-control over setting their own goals and over defining the paths to these goals.

JOB DESIGN

Job design has been defined by Davis (1966) as: 'The specification of the contents, methods, and relationships of jobs in order to satisfy technological and organizational requirements as well as the social and personal requirements of the job holder'.

Job design has two aims: first, to satisfy the requirements of the organization for productivity, operational efficiency and quality of product or service, and second, to satisfy the needs of the individual for interest, challenge and accomplishment, thus providing for 'job engagement' – commitment to carrying out the job well. Clearly, these aims are interrelated and the overall objective of job design is to integrate the needs of the individual with those of the organization.

The process of job design starts, as described in Chapter 13, from an analysis of what work needs to be done – the tasks that have to be carried out if the purpose of the organization or an organizational unit is to be achieved. The job designer can then consider how the jobs can be set up to provide the maximum degree of intrinsic motivation for those who have to carry them out with a view to improving performance and productivity. Consideration has also to be given to another important aim of job design: to fulfil the social responsibilities of the organization to the people who work in it by improving the quality of working life, an aim which, as stated in Wilson's (1973) report on this subject, 'depends upon both efficiency of performance and satisfaction of the worker'. The outcome of job design may be a job description, as explained in Chapter 13, although as noted in that chapter, the emphasis today is more on roles and the development of role profiles.

Principles of job design

Robertson and Smith (1985) suggest the following five principles of job design:

- To influence skill variety, provide opportunities for people to do several tasks and combine tasks.
- To influence task identity, combine tasks and form natural work units.
- To influence task significance, form natural work units and inform people of the importance of their work.
- To influence autonomy, give people responsibility for determining their own working systems.
- To influence feedback, establish good relationships and open feedback channels.

Turner and Lawrence (1965) identified six important characteristics, which they called 'requisite task characteristics', namely: variety, autonomy, required interactions, optional interactions, knowledge and skill, and responsibility. And Cooper (1973) outlined four conceptually distinct job dimensions: variety, discretion, contribution and goal characteristics.

An integrated view suggests that the following motivating characteristics are of prime importance in job design:

- autonomy, discretion, self-control and responsibility;
- variety;
- use of abilities;
- feedback;
- belief that the task is significant.

These are the bases of the approach used in job enrichment, as described later in this chapter.

Approaches to job design

The main job design approaches are:

- *Job rotation*, which comprises the movement of employees from one task to another to reduce monotony by increasing variety.
- *Job enlargement*, which means combining previously fragmented tasks into one job, again to increase the variety and meaning of repetitive work.
- *Job enrichment*, which goes beyond job enlargement to add greater autonomy and responsibility to a job and is based on the job characteristics approach.
- *Self-managing teams (autonomous work groups)* – these are self-regulating teams who work largely without direct supervision. The philosophy on which this technique is based is a logical extension of job enrichment.
- *High-performance work design*, which concentrates on setting up working groups in environments where high levels of performance are required.

Of these five approaches, it is generally recognized that, although job rotation and job enlargement have their uses in developing skills and relieving monotony, they do not go to the root of the requirements for intrinsic motivation and for meeting the various motivating characteristics of jobs as described above. These are best satisfied by using, as appropriate, job enrichment, autonomous work groups or high-performance work design.

JOB ENRICHMENT

Job enrichment aims to maximize the interest and challenge of work by providing the employee with a job that has these characteristics:

- It is a complete piece of work in the sense that the worker can identify a series of tasks or activities that end in a recognizable and definable product.

- It affords the employee as much variety, decision-making responsibility and control as possible in carrying out the work.
- It provides direct feedback through the work itself on how well the employee is doing his or her job.

Job enrichment as proposed by Herzberg (1968) is not just increasing the number or variety of tasks; nor is it the provision of opportunities for job rotation. It is claimed by supporters of job enrichment that these approaches may relieve boredom, but they do not result in positive increases in motivation.

SELF-MANAGING TEAMS

A self-managing team or autonomous work group is allocated an overall task and given discretion over how the work is done. This provides for intrinsic motivation by giving people autonomy and the means to control their work, which will include feedback information. The basis of the autonomous work group approach to job design is socio-technical systems theory, which suggests that the best results are obtained if grouping is such that workers are primarily related to each other by way of task performance and task interdependence. As Emery (1980) has stated:

> In designing a social system to efficiently operate a modern capital-intensive plant the key problem is that of creating self-managing groups to man the interface with the technical system.

A self-managing team:

- enlarges individual jobs to include a wider range of operative skills (multi-skilling);
- decides on methods of work and the planning, scheduling and control of work;
- distributes tasks itself among its members.

The advocates of self-managing teams or autonomous work groups claim that this approach offers a more comprehensive view of organizations than the rather simplistic individual motivation theories that underpin job rotation, enlargement and enrichment. Be that as it may, the strength of this system is that it does take account of the social or group factors and the technology as well as the individual motivators.

HIGH-PERFORMANCE WORK DESIGN

High-performance work design, as described by Buchanan (1987), requires the following steps:

- Management clearly defines what it needs in the form of new technology or methods of production and the results expected from its introduction.
- Multi-skilling is encouraged – that is, job demarcation lines are eliminated as far as possible and encouragement and training are provided for employees to acquire new skills.
- Equipment that can be used flexibly is selected and is laid out to allow freedom of movement and vision.
- Self-managed teams or autonomous working groups are established, each with around a dozen members and with full 'back-to-back' responsibility for product assembly and testing, fault-finding and some maintenance.
- Managers and team leaders adopt a supportive rather than an autocratic style (this is the most difficult part of the system to introduce).
- Support systems are provided for kit-marshalling and material supply, which help the teams to function effectively as productive units.
- Management sets goals and standards for success.
- The new system is introduced with great care by means of involvement and communication programmes.
- Thorough training is carried out on the basis of an assessment of training needs.
- The payment system is specially designed with employee participation to fit their needs as well as those of management.
- Payment may be related to team performance (team pay), but with skill-based pay for individuals.
- In some cases, a 'peer performance review' process may be used which involves team members assessing one another's performance as well as the performance of the team as a whole.

ROLE DEVELOPMENT

Job design as described above takes place when a new job is created or an existing job is substantially changed, often following a reorganization. But the part people play in carrying out their jobs – their roles – can evolve over time as people grow into them and grow with them, and as incremental changes take place in the scope of the work and the degree to which individuals are free to act (their autonomy). Roles will be developed as people develop in them, responding to opportunities and changing demands, acquiring new skills and developing competencies.

Role development is a continuous process which takes place in the context of day to day work, and it is therefore a matter between managers and the members of their teams. It involves agreeing definitions of key results areas and competency requirements as they evolve. When these change – as they probably will in all except the most routine jobs – it is desirable to achieve mutual understanding of new expectations. The forces should be on role flexibility – giving people the chance to develop their roles by making better and extended use of their skills and capabilities.

The process of understanding how roles are developing and agreeing the implications can take place within the framework of performance management as described in Part VII, where the performance agreement, which is updated regularly, spells out the outcomes (key result areas) and the competency requirements. It is necessary to ensure that managers, team leaders and employees generally acquire the skills necessary to define roles within the performance management framework, taking into account the principles of job design set out earlier in this chapter. Ways in which role profiles can be set out are described in Chapter 13.

24

Organizational development, change and transformation

This chapter starts with a definition and critical review of the overall concept of organizational development (OD). Approaches to change management are then examined. These have sometimes been treated as an aspect of organizational development, but in fact they are used in any organization that is concerned with the effective introduction of changed structures, policies or practices. They therefore exist in their own right. The chapter continues with a discussion of organizational transformation principles and practice which are an extension of change management methodology into comprehensive programmes for managing fundamental changes to the culture and operations of an organization. The final section of the chapter deals with specific approaches to organizational development or change, namely: team building, culture change management, total quality management, continual improvement processes, business process re-engineering and performance management.

WHAT IS ORGANIZATIONAL DEVELOPMENT?

Organizational development is concerned with the planning and implementation of programmes designed to enhance the effectiveness with which an organization functions and responds to change. Overall, the aim is to adopt a planned and coherent approach to improving organizational effectiveness. An effective organization can be defined broadly as one that achieves its purpose by meeting the wants and needs of its stakeholders, matching its resources to opportunities, adapting flexibly to environmental changes and creating a culture that promotes commitment, creativity, shared values and mutual trust.

Organizational development is concerned with process, not structure or systems – with the way things are done rather than what is done. Process refers to the ways in which people act and interact. It is about the roles they play on a continuing basis to deal with events and situations involving other people and to adapt to changing circumstances.

Organizational development is an all-embracing term for the approaches described in this chapter to changing processes, culture and behaviour in the organization. The changes may take place within the framework of an overall programme of organization development (OD). Within this programme, or taking place as separate activities, one or more of the following approaches may be used.

- organization development (OD);
- change management;
- team building;
- culture change or management;
- total quality management;
- continuous improvement;
- business process re-engineering;
- performance management;
- organizational transformation.

ORGANIZATION DEVELOPMENT

Defined

Organization development (OD) has been defined by French and Bell (1990) as:

A planned systematic process in which applied behavioural science principles and practices are introduced into an ongoing organization towards the goals of effecting organizational improvement, greater organizational competence, and greater organizational effectiveness. The focus is on organizations and their improvement or, to put it another way, *total systems change*. The orientation is on action – achieving desired results as a result of planned activities.

The classic and ambitious approach to OD was described by Bennis (1960) as follows: 'Organization development (OD) is a response to change, a complex educational strategy intended to change the beliefs, attitudes, values, and structure of organizations so that they can better adapt to new technologies, markets, and challenges, and the dizzying rate of change itself.'

A short history of OD

Origins of OD

The origin of OD can be traced to the work of Kurt Lewin (1947, 1951), who developed the concept of group dynamics (the phrase was first coined in 1939). Group dynamics is concerned with the ways in which groups evolve and how people in groups behave and interact. Lewin founded the Research Centre for Group Dynamics in 1945 and out of this emerged the process of 'T-group' or sensitivity training, in which participants in an unstructured group learn from their own interaction and the evolving dynamics of the group. T-group laboratory training became one of the fundamental OD processes. Lewin also pioneered action research approaches.

The formative years of OD

During the 1950s and 1960s behavioural scientists such as Argyris, Beckhard, Bennis, Blake, McGregor, Schein, Shepart and Tannenbaum developed the concepts and approaches that together represented 'OD'. They defined the scope, purpose and philosophy of OD, methods of conducting OD 'interventions', approaches to 'process consulting' and methodologies such as action research and survey feedback.

OD – the glory years

The later 1960s and the 1970s were the days when behavioural science reigned and OD was seen, at least by behavioural scientists, as the answer to the problem of improving organizational effectiveness. Comprehensive programmes using the various approaches described below were introduced in a number of American businesses such as General Motors and Corning Glass and a few UK companies such as ICI. US research quoted by French and Bell (1990) found that positive impacts were made in between 70 and 80 per cent of the cases studied.

OD in decline

Doubt about the validity of OD as a concept was first expressed in the 1970s. Kahn

(1974) wrote that: 'It is not a concept, at least not in the scientific sense of the word: it is not precisely defined; it is not reducible to specific, uniform, observable behaviour.'

A typical criticism of OD was made later by McLean (1981) who wrote that: 'There seems to be a growing awareness of the inappropriateness of some of the fundamental values, stances, models and prescriptions inherited from the 1960s. Writers are facing up to the naivete of early beliefs and theories in what might be termed a climate of sobriety and new realism.'

New approaches to improving organizational effectiveness

During the 1980s and 1990s the focus shifted from OD as a behavioural science concept to a number of other approaches. Some of these, such as organizational transformation, are not entirely dissimilar to OD. Others, such as team building, change management and culture change or management, are built on some of the basic ideas developed by writers on organization development and OD practitioners. Yet other approaches, such as total quality management, continuous improvement, business process re-engineering and performance management, could be described as holistic processes that attempt to improve overall organizational effectiveness from a particular perspective. The tendency now is to rely more on specific interventions such as performance management, team pay or total quality management, than on all-embracing but somewhat nebulous OD programmes which were often owned by the HR department and its consultants, and not by line management.

Characteristics of the traditional approach to OD

OD concentrated on how things are done as well as what they do. It was a form of applied behavioural science that was concerned with system-wide change. The organization was considered as a total system and the emphasis was on the interrelationships, interactions and interdependencies of different aspects of how systems operate as they transform inputs and outputs and use feedback mechanisms for self-regulation. OD practitioners talked about 'the client system' – meaning that they were dealing with the total organizational system.

OD as originally conceived was based upon the following assumptions and values:

- Most individuals are driven by the need for personal growth and development as long as their environment is both supportive and challenging.
- The work team, especially at the informal level, has great significance for feelings of satisfaction and the dynamics of such teams have a powerful effect on the behaviour of their members.

- OD programmes aimed to improve the quality of working life of all members of the organization.
- Organizations can be more effective if they learn to diagnose their own strengths and weaknesses.
- But managers often do not know what is wrong and need special help in diagnosing problems, although the outside 'process consultant' ensures that decision making remains in the hands of the client.

The three main features of OD programmes were:

- They were managed, or at least strongly supported, from the top but often made use of third parties or 'change agents' to diagnose problems and to manage change by various kinds of planned activity or 'intervention'.
- The plans for organization development were based upon a systematic analysis and diagnosis of the circumstances of the organization and the changes and problems affecting it.
- They used behavioural science knowledge and aimed to improve the way the organization copes in times of change through such processes as interaction, communications, participation, planning and conflict.

The activities that may be incorporated in a traditional OD programme are summarized below.

- *Action research*. This is an approach developed by Lewin (1947) which takes the form of systematically collecting data from people about process issues and feeds it back in order to identify problems and their likely causes so that action can be taken cooperatively by the people involved to deal with the problem. The essential elements of action research are data collection, diagnosis, feedback, action planning, action and evaluation.
- *Survey feedback*. This is a variety of action research in which data are systematically collected about the system and then fed back to groups to analyse and interpret as the basis for preparing action plans. The techniques of survey feedback include the use of attitude surveys and workshops to feed back results and discuss implications.
- *Interventions*. The term 'intervention' in OD refers to core structured activities involving clients and consultants. The activities can take the form of action research, survey feedback or any of those mentioned below. Argyris (1970) summed up the three primary tasks of the OD practitioner or interventionist as being to:

- generate and help clients to generate valid information that they can understand about their problems;
- create opportunities for clients to search effectively for solutions to their problems, to make free choices;
- create conditions for internal commitment to their choices and opportunities for the continual monitoring of the action taken.

- *Process consultation*. As described by Schein (1969), this involves helping clients to generate and analyse information that they can understand and, following a thorough diagnosis, act upon. The information will relate to organizational processes such as inter-group relations, interpersonal relations and communications. The job of the process consultant was defined by Schein as being to 'help the organization to solve its own problems by making it aware of organizational processes, of the consequences of these processes, and of the mechanisms by which they can be changed'.

- *Team-building interventions* as discussed later in this chapter. These deal with permanent work teams or those set up to deal with projects or to solve particular problems. Interventions are directed towards the analysis of the effectiveness of team processes such as problem solving, decision making and interpersonal relationships, a diagnosis and discussion of the issues and joint consideration of the actions required to improve effectiveness.

- *Inter-group conflict interventions*. As developed by Blake *et al* (1964), these aim to improve inter-group relations by getting groups to share their perceptions of one another and to analyse what they have learned about themselves and the other group. The groups involved meet each other to share what they have learnt, to agree on the issues to be resolved and the actions required.

- *Personal interventions*. These include sensitivity training laboratories (T-groups), transactional analysis and, more recently, neuro-linguistic programming (NLP). Another approach is behaviour modelling, which is based on Bandura's (1977) social learning theory. This states that for people to engage successfully in a behaviour they 1) must perceive a link between the behaviour and certain outcomes, 2) must desire those outcomes (this is termed 'positive valence'), and 3) must believe they can do it (termed 'self-efficacy'). Behaviour-modelling training involves getting a group to identify the problem and develop and practise the skills required by looking at DVDs showing what skills can be applied, role playing, practising the use of skills on the job and discussing how well they have been applied.

Use of OD

The decline of traditional OD, as described above, has been partly caused by disenchantment with the jargon used by consultants and the unfulfilled expectations of significant improvements in organizational effectiveness. There was also a reaction in the hard-nosed 1980s against the perceived softness of the messages preached by the behavioural scientists. Managements in the later 1980s and 1990s wanted more specific prescriptions which would impact on processes they believed to be important as means of improving performance, such as total quality management, business process re-engineering and performance management. The need to manage change to processes, systems or culture was still recognized as long as it was results driven, rather than activity centred. Team-building activities in the new process-based organizations were also regarded favourably as long as they were directed towards measurable improvements in the shorter term. It was also recognized that organizations were often compelled to transform themselves in the face of massive challenges and external pressures, and traditional OD approaches would not make a sufficient or speedy impact. A survey of the views of chief executives about organizational development, (IPD, 1999a) found that a large proportion of them are expecting greater team contributions, more sophisticated people management practices and processes for managing knowledge. As the IPD commented, 'HR has a pivotal role in developing the behaviours and culture to support the delivery of these strategies.'

CHANGE MANAGEMENT

The change process

Conceptually, the change process starts with an awareness of the need for change. An analysis of this situation and the factors that have created it leads to a diagnosis of their distinctive characteristics and an indication of the direction in which action needs to be taken. Possible courses of action can then be identified and evaluated and a choice made of the preferred action.

It is then necessary to decide how to get from here to there. Managing change during this transition state is a critical phase in the change process. It is here that the problems of introducing change emerge and have to be managed. These problems can include resistance to change, low stability, high levels of stress, misdirected energy, conflict and loss of momentum. Hence the need to do everything possible to anticipate reactions and likely impediments to the introduction of change.

The installation stage can also be painful. When planning change there is a tendency for people to think that it will be an entirely logical and linear process of going from A to B. It is not like that at all. As described by Pettigrew and Whipp (1991), the implementation of change is an 'iterative, cumulative and reformulation-in-use process'.

To manage change, it is first necessary to understand the types of change and why people resist change. It is important to bear in mind that while those wanting change need to be constant about ends, they have to be flexible about means. This requires them to come to an understanding of the various models of change that have been developed. In the light of an understanding of these models they will be better equipped to make use of the guidelines for change set out at the end of this section.

Types of change

There are two main types of change: strategic and operational.

Strategic change

Strategic change is concerned with organizational transformation as described in the last section of this chapter. It deals with broad, long-term and organization-wide issues. It is about moving to a future state, which has been defined generally in terms of strategic vision and scope. It will cover the purpose and mission of the organization, its corporate philosophy on such matters as growth, quality, innovation and values concerning people, the customer needs served and the technologies employed. This overall definition leads to specifications of competitive positioning and strategic goals for achieving and maintaining competitive advantage and for product-market development. These goals are supported by policies concerning marketing, sales, manufacturing, product and process development, finance and human resource management.

Strategic change takes place within the context of the external competitive, economic and social environment, and the organization's internal resources, capabilities, culture, structure and systems. Its successful implementation requires thorough analysis and understanding of these factors in the formulation and planning stages. The ultimate achievement of sustainable competitive advantage relies on the qualities defined by Pettigrew and Whipp (1991), namely: 'The capacity of the firm to identify and understand the competitive forces in play and how they change over time, linked to the competence of a business to mobilize and manage the resources necessary for the chosen competitive response through time.'

Strategic change, however, should not be treated simplistically as a linear process of getting from A to B which can be planned and executed as a logical sequence of events. Pettigrew and Whipp (1991) issued the following warning based on their research into competitiveness and managing change in the motor, financial services, insurance and publishing industries:

> The process by which strategic changes are made seldom moves directly through neat, successive stages of analysis, choice and implementation. Changes in the firm's environment persistently threaten the course and logic of strategic changes: dilemma abounds... We conclude that one of the defining features of the process, in so far as management action is concerned, is ambiguity; seldom is there an easily isolated logic to strategic change. Instead, that process may derive its motive force from an amalgam of economic, personal and political imperatives. Their introduction through time requires that those responsible for managing that process make continual assessments, repeated choices and multiple adjustments.

Operational change

Operational change relates to new systems, procedures, structures or technology which will have an immediate effect on working arrangements within a part of the organization. But their impact on people can be more significant than broader strategic change and they have to be handled just as carefully.

Resistance to change

Why people resist change

People resist change because it is seen as a threat to familiar patterns of behaviour as well as to status and financial rewards. Joan Woodward (1968) made this point clearly:

> When we talk about resistance to change we tend to imply that management is always rational in changing its direction, and that employees are stupid, emotional or irrational in not responding in the way they should. But if an individual is going to be worse off, explicitly or implicitly, when the proposed changes have been made, any resistance is entirely rational in terms of his own best interest. The interests of the organization and the individual do not always coincide.

Specifically, the main reasons for resisting change are as follows:

● *The shock of the new* – people are suspicious of anything which they perceive will upset their established routines, methods of working or conditions of employment. They do not want to lose the security of what is familiar to them. They may not believe statements by management that the change is for their benefit as well as that of the organization; sometimes with good reason. They may feel that management has ulterior motives and, sometimes, the louder the protestations of managements, the less they will be believed.

- *Economic fears* – loss of money, threats to job security.
- *Inconvenience* – the change will make life more difficult.
- *Uncertainty* – change can be worrying because of uncertainty about its likely impact.
- *Symbolic fears* – a small change that may affect some treasured symbol, such as a separate office or a reserved parking space, may symbolize big ones, especially when employees are uncertain about how extensive the programme of change will be.
- *Threat to interpersonal relationships* – anything that disrupts the customary social relationships and standards of the group will be resisted.
- *Threat to status or skill* – the change is perceived as reducing the status of individuals or as de-skilling them.
- *Competence fears* – concern about the ability to cope with new demands or to acquire new skills.

Overcoming resistance to change

Resistance to change can be difficult to overcome even when it is not detrimental to those concerned. But the attempt must be made. The first step is to analyse the potential impact of change by considering how it will affect people in their jobs. The analysis should indicate which aspects of the proposed change may be supported generally or by specified individuals and which aspects may be resisted. So far as possible, the potentially hostile or negative reactions of people should be identified, taking into account all the possible reasons for resisting change listed above. It is necessary to try to understand the likely feelings and fears of those affected so that unnecessary worries can be relieved and, as far as possible, ambiguities can be resolved. In making this analysis, the individual introducing the change, who is sometimes called the 'change agent', should recognize that new ideas are likely to be suspect and should make ample provision for the discussion of reactions to proposals to ensure complete understanding of them.

Involvement in the change process gives people the chance to raise and resolve their concerns and make suggestions about the form of the change and how it should be introduced. The aim is to get 'ownership' – a feeling amongst people that the change is something that they are happy to live with because they have been involved in its planning and introduction – it has become *their* change.

Communications about the proposed change should be carefully prepared and worded so that unnecessary fears are allayed. All the available channels as described in Chapter 54 should be used, but face-to-face communications direct from managers to individuals or through a team briefing system are best.

Change models

The best-known change models are those developed by Lewin (1951) and Beckhard (1969). But other important contributions to an understanding of the mechanisms for change have been made by Thurley (1979), Quinn (1980), Nadler and Tushman (1980), Bandura (1986) and Beer *et al* (1990).

Lewin

The basic mechanisms for managing change, according to Lewin (1951), are as follows:

- *Unfreezing* – altering the present stable equilibrium which supports existing behaviours and attitudes. This process must take account of the inherent threats that change presents to people and the need to motivate those affected to attain the natural state of equilibrium by accepting change.
- *Changing* – developing new responses based on new information.
- *Refreezing* – stabilizing the change by introducing the new responses into the personalities of those concerned.

Lewin also suggested a methodology for analysing change which he called 'field force analysis'. This involves:

- analysing the restraining or driving forces that will affect the transition to the future state; these restraining forces will include the reactions of those who see change as unnecessary or as constituting a threat;
- assessing which of the driving or restraining forces are critical;
- taking steps both to increase the critical driving forces and to decrease the critical restraining forces.

Beckhard

According to Beckhard (1969), a change programme should incorporate the following processes:

- setting goals and defining the future state or organizational conditions desired after the change;

- diagnosing the present condition in relation to these goals;
- defining the transition state activities and commitments required to meet the future state;
- developing strategies and action plans for managing this transition in the light of an analysis of the factors likely to affect the introduction of change.

Thurley

Thurley (1979) described the following five approaches to managing change:

- *Directive* – the imposition of change in crisis situations or when other methods have failed. This is done by the exercise of managerial power without consultation.
- *Bargained* – this approach recognizes that power is shared between the employer and the employed and that change requires negotiation, compromise and agreement before being implemented.
- *'Hearts and minds'* – an all-embracing thrust to change the attitudes, values and beliefs of the whole workforce. This 'normative' approach (ie one that starts from a definition of what management thinks is right or 'normal') seeks 'commitment' and 'shared vision' but does not necessarily include involvement or participation.
- *Analytical* – a theoretical approach to the change process using models of change such as those described above. It proceeds sequentially from the analysis and diagnosis of the situation, through the setting of objectives, the design of the change process, the evaluation of the results and, finally, the determination of the objectives for the next stage in the change process. This is the rational and logical approach much favoured by consultants – external and internal. But change seldom proceeds as smoothly as this model would suggest. Emotions, power politics and external pressures mean that the rational approach, although it might be the right way to start, is difficult to sustain.
- *Action-based* – this recognizes that the way managers behave in practice bears little resemblance to the analytical, theoretical model. The distinction between managerial thought and managerial action blurs in practice to the point of invisibility. What managers think is what they do. Real life therefore often results in a 'ready, aim, fire' approach to change management. This typical approach to change starts with a broad belief that some sort of problem exists, although it may not be well defined. The identification of possible solutions, often on a trial and error basis, leads to a clarification of the nature of the problem and a shared understanding of a possible optimal solution, or at least a framework within which solutions can be discovered.

Quinn

According to Quinn (1980), the approach to strategic change is characterized as a process of artfully blending 'formal analysis, behavioural techniques and power politics to bring about cohesive step-by-step movement towards ends which were initially conceived, but which are constantly refined and reshaped as new information appears. Their integrating methodology can best be described as "logical incrementation".' Quinn emphasizes that it is necessary to:

- create awareness and commitment incrementally;
- broaden political support;
- manage coalitions;
- empower champions.

Nadler and Tushman

The guidelines produced by Nadler and Tushman (1980) on implementing change were:

- *Motivate* in order to achieve changes in behaviour by individuals.
- *Manage the transition* by making organizational arrangements designed to assure that control is maintained during and after the transition, and by developing and communicating a clear image of the future.
- *Shape the political dynamics of change* so that power centres develop that support the change rather than block it.
- *Build in stability* of structures and processes to serve as anchors for people to hold on to. Organizations and individuals can only stand so much uncertainty and turbulence (hence the emphasis by Quinn (1980) on the need for an incremental approach).

Bandura

The ways in which people change were described by Bandura (1986) as follows:

1. People make conscious choices about their behaviours.
2. The information people use to make their choices comes from their environment.
3. Their choices are based upon:
   - the things that are important to them;
   - the views they have about their own abilities to behave in certain ways;

  – the consequences they think will accrue to whatever behaviour they decide to engage in.

For those concerned in change management, the implications of this theory are that:

- the tighter the link between a particular behaviour and a particular outcome, the more likely it is that we will engage in that behaviour;
- the more desirable the outcome, the more likely it is that we will engage in behaviour that we believe will lead to it;
- the more confident we are that we can actually assume a new behaviour, the more likely we are to try it.

To change people's behaviour, therefore, we have first to change the environment within which they work, secondly, convince them that the new behaviour is something they can accomplish (training is important) and, thirdly, persuade them that it will lead to an outcome that they will value. None of these steps is easy.

Beer, Eisenstat and Spector

Michael Beer (1990) and his colleagues suggested in a seminal *Harvard Business Review* article, 'Why change programs don't produce change', that most such programmes are guided by a theory of change that is fundamentally flawed. This theory states that changes in attitudes lead to changes in behaviour. 'According to this model, change is like a conversion experience. Once people "get religion", changes in their behaviour will surely follow.' They believe that this theory gets the change process exactly backwards:

> In fact, individual behaviour is powerfully shaped by the organizational roles people play. The most effective way to change behaviour, therefore, is to put people into a new organizational context, which imposes new roles, responsibilities and relationships on them. This creates a situation that in a sense 'forces' new attitudes and behaviour on people.

They prescribe six steps to effective change, which concentrate on what they call 'task alignment' – reorganizing employees' roles, responsibilities and relationships to solve specific business problems in small units where goals and tasks can be clearly defined. The aim of following the overlapping steps is to build a self-reinforcing cycle of commitment, coordination and competence. The steps are:

1. Mobilize commitment to change through the joint analysis of problems.
2. Develop a shared vision of how to organize and manage to achieve goals such as competitiveness.
3. Foster consensus for the new vision, competence to enact it, and cohesion to move it along.
4. Spread revitalization to all departments without pushing it from the top – don't force the issue, let each department find its own way to the new organization.
5. Institutionalize revitalization through formal policies, systems and structures.
6. Monitor and adjust strategies in response to problems in the revitalization process.

Guidelines for change management

- The achievement of sustainable change requires strong commitment and visionary leadership from the top.
- Understanding is necessary of the culture of the organization and the levers for change that are most likely to be effective in that culture.
- Those concerned with managing change at all levels should have the temperament and leadership skills appropriate to the circumstances of the organization and its change strategies.
- It is important to build a working environment that is conducive to change. This means developing the firm as a 'learning organization'.
- People support what they help to create. Commitment to change is improved if those affected by change are allowed to participate as fully as possible in planning and implementing it. The aim should be to get them to 'own' the change as something they want and will be glad to live with.
- The reward system should encourage innovation and recognize success in achieving change.
- Change will always involve failure as well as success. The failures must be expected and learned from.
- Hard evidence and data on the need for change are the most powerful tools for its achievement, but establishing the need for change is easier than deciding how to satisfy it.
- It is easier to change behaviour by changing processes, structure and systems than to change attitudes or the corporate culture.
- There are always people in organizations who can act as champions of change. They will welcome the challenges and opportunities that change can provide. They are the ones to be chosen as change agents.

- Resistance to change is inevitable if the individuals concerned feel that they are going to be worse off – implicitly or explicitly. The inept management of change will produce that reaction.
- In an age of global competition, technological innovation, turbulence, discontinuity, even chaos, change is inevitable and necessary. The organization must do all it can to explain why change is essential and how it will affect everyone. Moreover, every effort must be made to protect the interests of those affected by change.

ORGANIZATIONAL TRANSFORMATION

Defined

Transformation, according to Webster's Dictionary, is: 'A change in the shape, structure, nature of something'. Organizational transformation is the process of ensuring that an organization can develop and implement major change programmes that will ensure that it responds strategically to new demands and continues to function effectively in the dynamic environment in which it operates. Organizational transformation activities may involve radical changes to the structure, culture and processes of the organization – the way it looks at the world. This may be in response to competitive pressures, mergers, acquisitions, investments, disinvestments, changes in technology, product lines, markets, cost reduction exercises and decisions to downsize or outsource work. Transformational change may be forced on an organization by investors or government decisions. It may be initiated by a new chief executive and top management team with a remit to 'turn round' the business.

Transformational change means that significant and far-reaching developments are planned and implemented in corporate structures and organization-wide processes. The change is neither incremental (bit by bit) nor transactional (concerned solely with systems and procedures). Transactional change, according to Pascale (1990), is merely concerned with the alteration of ways in which the organization does business and people interact with one another on a day-to-day basis, and 'is effective when what you want is more of what you've already got'. He advocates a 'discontinuous improvement in capability' and this he describes as transformation.

The distinction between organizational transformation and organization development

Organizational transformation programmes are business-led. They focus on what needs to be done to ensure that the business performs more effectively in adding value, especially for its owners, and achieving competitive advantage. They will be concerned with building strategic capability and improving the ways in which the business reaches its goals. This means considering what needs to be done to ensure that people work and interact well, but they are not dominated by the concepts of behavioural science, as was the case in traditional OD interventions.

Types of transformational change

The four types of transformational change as identified by Beckhard (1989) are:

- *a change in what drives the organization* – for example, a change from being production-driven to being market-driven would be transformational;
- *a fundamental change in the relationships between or among organizational parts* – for example, decentralization;
- *a major change in the ways of doing work* – for example, the introduction of new technology such as computer-integrated manufacturing;
- *a basic, cultural change in norms, values or research systems* – for example, developing a customer-focused culture.

Transformation through leadership

Transformation programmes are led from the top within the organization. They do not rely on an external 'change agent' as did traditional OD interventions, although specialist external advice might be obtained on aspects of the transformation such as strategic planning, reorganization or developing new reward processes.

The prerequisite for a successful programme is the presence of a transformational leader who, as defined by Burns (1978), motivates others to strive for higher-order goals rather than merely short-term interest. Transformational leaders go beyond dealing with day-to-day management problems; they commit people to action and focus on the development of new levels of awareness of where the futur lies, and commitment to achieving that future. Burns contrasts transformational leaders with transactional leaders who operate by building up a network of interpersonal transactions in a stable situation and who enlist compliance rather than commitment through the reward system and the exercise of authority and power. Transactional leaders may be good at dealing with here-and-now problems but they will not provide the vision required to transform the future.

Managing the transition

The transition from where the organization is to where the organization wants to be is the critical part of a transformation programme. It is during the transition period of getting from here to there that change takes place. Transition management starts from a definition of the future state and a diagnosis of the present state. It is then necessary to define what has to be done to achieve the transformation. This means deciding on the new processes, systems, procedures, structures, products and markets to be developed. Having defined these, the work can be programmed and the resources required (people, money, equipment and time) can be defined. The plan for managing the transition should include provisions for involving people in the process and for communicating to them about what is happening, why it is happening and how it will affect them. Clearly the aims are to get as many people as possible committed to the change.

The transformation programme

The eight steps required to transform an organization have been summed up by Kotter (1995) as follows:

1. *Establishing a sense of urgency*
    – Examining market and competitive realities
    – Identifying and discussing crises, potential crises, or major opportunities
2. *Forming a powerful guiding coalition*
    – Assembling a group with enough power to lead the change effort
    – Encouraging the group to work together as a team
3. *Creating a vision*
    – Creating a vision to help direct the change effort
    – Developing strategies for achieving that vision
4. *Communicating the vision*
    – Using every vehicle possible to communicate the new vision and strategies
    – Teaching new behaviours by the example of the guiding coalition
5. *Empowering others to act on the vision*
    – Getting rid of obstacles to change
    – Changing systems or structures that seriously undermine the vision
    – Encouraging risk taking and non-traditional ideas, activities and actions
6. *Planning for and creating short-term wins*
    – Planning for visible performance improvement
    – Creating those improvements
    – Recognizing and rewarding employees involved in the improvements

7. *Consolidating improvements and producing still more change*
   - Using increased credibility to change systems, structures and policies that don't fit the vision
   - Hiring, promoting and developing employees who can implement the vision
   - Reinvigorating the process with new projects, themes and change agents
8. *Institutionalizing new approaches*
   - Articulating the connections between the new behaviours and corporate success
   - Developing the means to ensure leadership development and succession.

The role of HR in organizational transformation

HR can and should play a key role in organizational transition and transformation programmes. It can provide help and guidance in analysis and diagnosis, highlighting the people issues that will fundamentally affect the success of the programme. HR can advise on resourcing the programme and planning and implementing the vital training, reward, communications and involvement aspects of the process. It can anticipate people problems and deal with them before they become serious. If the programme does involve restructuring and downsizing, HR can advise on how this should be done humanely and with the minimum disruption to people's lives.

DEVELOPMENT AND CHANGE PROCESSES

Team building

Team-building activities aim to improve and develop the effectiveness of a group of people who work (permanently or temporarily) together. This improvement may be defined in terms of outputs, for example the speed and quality of the decisions and actions produced by the team. It may also be defined in more nebulous terms, such as the quality of relationships or greater cooperation. The activities in team-building programmes can:

- increase awareness of the social processes that take place within teams;
- develop the interactive or interpersonal skills that enable individuals to function effectively as team members;
- increase the overall effectiveness with which teams operate in the organization.

To be effective, team-building programmes should be directly relevant to the responsibilities of the participants and be seen as relevant by all participants. They need to support business objectives, fit in with practical working arrangements and reflect the values the organization wishes to promote. Approaches such as action learning, group dynamics, group exercises, interactive skills training, interactive video, role-playing and simulation can be used. Team-building training is often based on either Belbin or Margerison and McCann classifications of team roles as listed in Chapter 20.

Outdoor learning (outdoor-based development) is another good method of providing team-building training. It can offer a closer approximation to reality than other forms of training. Participants tend to behave more normally and, paradoxically, it is precisely because the tasks are unrelated to work activities and are relatively simple that they highlight the processes involved in teamwork and provide a good basis for identifying how these processes can be improved.

Total quality management

Total quality management is an intensive, long-term effort directed at the creation and maintenance of the high standards of product quality and services expected by customers. As such, it can operate as a major influence in developing the culture and processes of the organization. The object is significantly to increase the awareness of all employees that quality is vital to the organization's success and their future. The business must be transformed into an entity that exists to deliver value to customers by satisfying their needs.

Continuous improvement

Continuous improvement is a management philosophy that contends that things can be done better. Continuous improvement is defined by Bessant *et al* (1994) as 'a company-wide process of focused and continuous incremental innovation sustained over a period of time'. The key words in this definition are:

- *Focused* – continuous improvement addresses specific issues where the effectiveness of operations and processes needs to be improved, where higher quality products or services should be provided and, importantly, where the levels of customer service and satisfaction need to be enhanced.
- *Continuous* – the search for improvement is never-ending; it is not a one-off campaign to deal with isolated problems.
- *Incremental* – continuous improvement is not about making sudden quantum leaps in response to crisis situations; it is about adopting a steady, step-by-step approach to improving the ways in which the organization goes about doing things.

- *Innovation* – continuous improvement is concerned with developing new ideas and approaches to deal with new and sometimes old problems and requirements.

Business process re-engineering

Business process re-engineering as a panacea emerged in the 1990s. It examines processes horizontally in organizations to establish how they can be integrated more effectively and streamlined. Re-engineering exercises can provide an overall approach to developing an organization but they often promise more than they achieve and they have been criticized because they pay insufficient attention to the human element.

Performance management

Performance management as a holistic – all-embracing – process for managing performance throughout an organization is one of the most commonly used instruments for improving organizational effectiveness. It is described in Part VII.

Part VI

People resourcing

PEOPLE RESOURCING DEFINED

People resourcing is concerned with ensuring that the organization obtains and retains the human capital it needs and employs them productively. It is also about those aspects of employment practice that are concerned with welcoming people to the organization and, if there is no alternative, releasing them. It is a key part of the HRM process.

PEOPLE RESOURCING AND HRM

HRM is fundamentally about matching human resources to the strategic and operational needs of the organization and ensuring the full utilization of those resources. It is concerned not only with obtaining and keeping the number and quality of staff required but also with selecting and promoting people who 'fit' the culture and the strategic requirements of the organization.

HRM places more emphasis than traditional personnel management on finding people whose attitudes and behaviour are likely to be congruent with what management believes to be appropriate and conducive to success. In the words of Townley (1989), organizations are concentrating more on 'the attitudinal and behavioural characteristics of employees'. This tendency has its dangers. Innovative and adaptive organizations need non-conformists, even mavericks, who can 'buck the system'. If managers recruit people 'in their own image' there is the risk of staffing the organization with conformist clones and of perpetuating a dysfunctional culture – one that may have been successful in the past but is no longer appropriate (nothing fails like success).

The HRM approach to resourcing therefore emphasizes that matching resources to organizational requirements does not simply mean maintaining the status quo and perpetuating a moribund culture. It can and often does mean radical changes in thinking about the competencies required in the future to achieve sustainable growth and to achieve cultural change. HRM resourcing policies address two fundamental questions:

1. *What kind of people do we need to compete effectively, now and in the foreseeable future?*
2. *What do we have to do to attract, develop and keep these people?*

Integrating business and resourcing strategies

The philosophy behind the HRM approach to resourcing is that it is people who implement the strategic plan. As Quinn Mills (1983) has put it, the process is one of 'planning with people in mind'.

The integration of business and resourcing strategies is based on an understanding of the direction in which the organization is going and of the resulting human resource needs in terms of:

- *numbers required in relation to projected activity levels;*
- *skills required on the basis of technological and product/market developments and strategies to enhance quality or reduce costs;*
- *the impact of organizational restructuring as a result of rationalization, decentralization, delayering, mergers, product or market development, or the introduction of new technology – for example, cellular manufacturing;*
- *plans for changing the culture of the organization in such areas as ability to deliver, performance standards, quality, customer service, team working and flexibility which indicate the need for people with different attitudes, beliefs and personal characteristics.*

These factors will be strongly influenced by the type of business strategies adopted by the organization and the sort of business it is in. These may be expressed in such terms as the Boston Consulting Group's classification of businesses as wild cat, star, cash cow or dog; or Miles and Snow's (1978) typology of defender, prospector and analyser organizations.

Resourcing strategies exist to provide the people and skills required to support the business strategy, but they should also contribute to the formulation of that strategy. HR directors have an obligation to point out to their colleagues the human resource opportunities and constraints that will affect the achievement of strategic plans. In mergers or acquisitions, for example, the ability of management within the company to handle the new situation and the quality of management in the new business will be important considerations.

PLAN

This part deals with the following aspects of employee resourcing:

- *human resource planning;*
- *talent management;*
- *recruitment;*
- *selection interviewing;*
- *selection testing;*
- *introduction to the organization;*
- *release from the organization.*

25

Human resource planning

THE ROLE OF HUMAN RESOURCE PLANNING

Definition

Human resource planning determines the human resources required by the organization to achieve its strategic goals. As defined by Bulla and Scott (1994) it is 'the process for ensuring that the human resource requirements of an organization are identified and plans are made for satisfying those requirements'. Human resource planning is based on the belief that people are an organization's most important strategic resource. It is generally concerned with matching resources to business needs in the longer term, although it will sometimes address shorter term requirements. It addresses human resource needs both in quantitative and qualitative terms, which means answering two basic questions: first, how many people, and second, what sort of people? Human resource planning also looks at broader issues relating to the ways in which people are employed and developed in order to improve organizational effectiveness. It can therefore play an important part in strategic human resource management.

Human resource planning and business planning

Conceptually, human resource planning should be an integral part of business planning. The strategic planning process should define projected changes in the scale and types of activities carried out by the organization. It should identify the core competences the organization needs to achieve its goals and therefore its skill requirements. But there are often limitations to the extent to which such plans are made, and indeed the clarity of the plans, and these may restrict the feasibility of developing integrated human resource plans that flow from them.

In so far as there are articulated strategic business plans, human resource planning interprets them in terms of people requirements. But it may influence the business strategy by drawing attention to ways in which people could be developed and deployed more effectively to further the achievement of business goals as well as focusing on any problems that might have to be resolved in order to ensure that the people required will be available and will be capable of making the necessary contribution. As Quinn Mills (1983) indicates, human resource planning is 'a decision-making process that combines three important activities: (1) identifying and acquiring the right number of people with the proper skills, (2) motivating them to achieve high performance, and (3) creating interactive links between business objectives and people-planning activities'. In situations where a clear business strategy does not exist, human resource planning may have to rely more on making broad assumptions about the need for people in the future, based on some form of scenario planning. Alternatively, the planning process could focus on specific areas of activity within the organization where it is possible to forecast likely future people requirements in terms of numbers and skills; for example, scientists in a product development division.

Hard and soft human resource planning

A distinction can be made between 'hard' and 'soft' human resource planning. The former is based on quantitative analysis in order to ensure that the right number of the right sort of people are available when needed. Soft human resource planning is concerned with ensuring the availability of people with the right type of attitudes and motivation who are committed to the organization and engaged in their work, and behave accordingly. It is based on assessments of the requirement for these qualities, and measurements of the extent to which they exist, by the use of staff surveys, the analysis of the outcomes of performance management reviews and opinions generated by focus groups.

These assessments and analyses can result in plans for improving the work environment, providing opportunities to develop skills and careers and adopting a 'total reward' approach which focuses on non-financial 'relational' rewards as well as the financial 'transactional' rewards. They can also lead to the creation of a high commitment management strategy which incorporates such approaches as creating functional flexibility, designing jobs to provide intrinsic motivation, emphasizing team working, de-emphasizing hierarchies and status differentials, increasing employment security, rewarding people on the basis of organizational performance, and enacting organization-specific values and a culture that bind the organization together and give it focus. As described by Marchington and Wilkinson (1996), soft human resource planning 'is more explicitly focused on creating and shaping the culture of the organization so that there is a clear integration between corporate goals and employee values, beliefs and behaviours'. But as they point out, the soft version becomes virtually synonymous with the whole subject of human resource management.

Human resource planning and manpower planning

Human resource planning is indeed concerned with broader issues about the employment of people than the traditional quantitative approaches of manpower planning. Such approaches, as Liff (2000) comments, derive from a rational top-down view of planning in which well tested quantitative techniques are applied to long term assessments of supply and demand. She notes that 'there has been a shift from reconciling numbers of employees available with predictable stable jobs, towards a greater concern with skills, their development and deployment'.

Limitations of human resource planning

Human resource planning is said to consist of three clear steps:

- Forecasting future people needs (demand forecasting).
- Forecasting the future availability of people (supply forecasting).
- Drawing up plans to match supply to demand.

But as Casson (1978) pointed out, this conventional wisdom represents human resource planning as an 'all-embracing, policy-making activity producing, on a rolling basis, precise forecasts using technically sophisticated and highly integrated planning systems'. He suggests that it is better regarded as, first, a regular monitoring activity, through which human resource stocks and flows and their relationship to business needs can be better understood, assessed and controlled, problems highlighted and a base established from which to respond to unforeseen events; and second, an investigatory activity by which the human resource implications of particular problems and change situations can be explored and the effects of alternative policies and actions investigated.

He points out that the spurious precision of quantified staffing level plans 'has little value when reconciled with the complex and frequently changing nature of manpower, the business and the external environment'. The typical concept of human resource planning as a matter of forecasting the long term demand and supply of people fails because the ability to make these estimates must be severely limited by the difficulty of predicting the influence of external events. There is a risk, in the words of Heller (1972), that 'Sensible anticipation gets converted into foolish numbers, and their validity depends on large, loose assumptions.'

Human resource planning today is more likely to concentrate on what skills will be needed in the future, and may do no more than provide a broad indication of the numbers required in the longer term, although in some circumstances it might involve making short term forecasts when it is possible to predict activity levels and skills requirements with a reasonable degree of accuracy. Such predictions will often be based on broad scenarios rather than on specific supply and demand forecasts.

The incidence of and rationale for human resource planning

Although the notion of human resource planning is well established in the HRM vocabulary, it does not seem to be commonly practised as a key HR activity. As Rothwell (1995) suggests, 'Apart from isolated examples, there has been little research evidence of increased use or of its success.' She explains the gap between theory and practice as arising from:

- the impact of change and the difficulty of predicting the future – 'the need for planning may be in inverse proportion to its feasibility';
- the 'shifting kaleidoscope' of policy priorities and strategies within organizations;
- the distrust displayed by many managers of theory or planning – they often prefer pragmatic adaptation to conceptualization;
- the lack of evidence that human resource planning works.

Be that as it may, it is difficult to reject out of hand the belief that some attempt should be made broadly to forecast future human resource requirements as a basis for planning and action. Heller refers to 'sensible anticipation', and perhaps this is what human resource planning is really about, bearing in mind that major changes in the operations of an organization can usually be foreseen. If that is the case, it does make sense to keep track of developments so that the organization is in a better position to deal with resourcing problems in good time.

On the basis of research conducted by the Institute for Employment Studies, Reilly

(1999) has suggested a number of reasons why organizations choose to engage in some form of human resource planning. These fall into the following three groups.

- *Planning for substantive reasons:* that is, to have a practical effect by optimizing the use of resources and/or making them more flexible, acquiring and nurturing skills that take time to develop, identifying potential problems and minimizing the chances of making a bad decision.
- *Planning because of the process benefits* which involves understanding the present in order to confront the future, challenging assumptions and liberating thinking, making explicit decisions which can later be challenged, standing back and providing an overview, and ensuring that long term thinking is not driven out by short term focus.
- *Planning for organizational reasons* which involves communicating plans so as to obtain support/adherence to them, linking HR plans to business plans so as to influence them, (re)gaining corporate control over operating units, and coordinating and integrating organizational decision making and actions.

The organizational context of human resource planning

Human resource planning takes place within the context of the organization. The extent to which it is used, and the approach adopted, will be contingent on the extent to which management recognizes that success depends on forecasting future people requirements and implementing plans to satisfy those requirements. The approach will also be affected by the degree to which it is possible to make accurate forecasts. Organizations operating in turbulent environments in which future activity levels are difficult to predict may rely on *ad hoc* and short term measures to recruit and keep people. However, even these businesses may benefit from those aspects of human resource planning that are concerned with policies for attracting and retaining key staff.

The labour market context

The context for obtaining the people required will be the labour markets in which the organization is operating which are, first, the internal labour market – the stocks and flows of people within the organization who can be promoted, trained, or redeployed to meet future needs – and second, the external labour market – the external local, regional, national and international markets from which different sorts of people can be recruited. There are usually a number of markets, and the labour supply in these markets may vary considerably. Likely shortages will need to be identified so that steps can be taken to deal with them, for example by developing a more attractive 'employment proposition'.

As part of the human resource planning process, an organization may have to formulate 'make or buy' policy decisions. A 'make' policy means that the organization prefers to recruit people at a junior level or as trainees, and rely mainly on promotion from within and training programmes to meet future needs. A 'buy' policy means that more reliance will be placed on recruiting from outside – 'bringing fresh blood into the organization'. In practice, organizations tend to mix the two choices together to varying degrees, depending on the situation of the firm and the type of people involved. A highly entrepreneurial company operating in turbulent conditions, or one which has just started up, will probably rely almost entirely on external recruitment. When dealing with knowledge workers, there may be little choice – they tend to be much more mobile, and resourcing strategy may have to recognize that external recruitment will be the main source of supply. Management consultancies typically fall into this category. Firms that can predict people requirements fairly accurately may rely more on developing their own staff once they have been recruited.

AIMS OF HUMAN RESOURCE PLANNING

The aims of human resource planning in any organization will depend largely on its context but in general terms, the typical aims might be to:

- attract and retain the number of people required with the appropriate skills, expertise and competencies;
- anticipate the problems of potential surpluses or deficits of people;
- develop a well trained and flexible workforce, thus contributing to the organization's ability to adapt to an uncertain and changing environment;
- reduces dependence on external recruitment when key skills are in short supply by formulating retention, as well as employee development strategies;
- improve the utilization of people by introducing more flexible systems of work.

THE PROCESS OF HUMAN RESOURCE PLANNING

The process of human resource planning as illustrated in Figure 25.1 is not necessarily a linear one, starting with the business strategy and flowing logically through to resourcing, flexibility and retention plans. It may, as Hendry (1995) suggests, be circular rather than linear, with the process starting anywhere in the cycle. For example, scenario planning may impact on resourcing strategy which in turn may influence the business strategy. Alternatively, the starting point could be demand and supply forecasts which form the basis for the resourcing strategy. The analysis of labour turnover may feed into the supply forecast, but it could also lead directly to the development of retention plans.

It cannot be assumed that there will be a well articulated business plan as a basis for the HR plans. The business strategy may be evolutionary rather than deliberate; it may be fragmented, intuitive and incremental. Resourcing decisions may be based on scenarios riddled with assumptions that may or may not be correct and cannot be tested. Resourcing strategy may be equally vague, or based on unproven beliefs about the future. It may contain statements, about for example building the skills base, that are little more than rhetoric.

There is much to be said for a systematic approach to developing resourcing strategy, scenario planning, demand and supply forecasting and labour turnover analysis as discussed in the rest of this chapter. But because of the factors mentioned above, there will often be reservations about the extent to which this process can be formalized. What may emerge is simply a broad statement of intent, although this could be sufficient to guide resourcing practice generally and would be better than nothing at all. The degree to which human resource planning can be carried out systematically will depend on the nature of the organization. If the future is fairly predictable, then formal planning might be appropriate. If it is not, the approach to human resource planning might have to rely on broad scenarios rather than precise forecasts.

These processes are summarized below.

- *Business strategic plans:* defining future activity levels and initiatives demanding new skills.
- *Resourcing strategy:* planning to achieve competitive advantage by developing intellectual capital – employing more capable people than rivals, ensuring that they develop organization specific knowledge and skills, and taking steps to become an 'employer of choice'.
- *Scenario planning:* assessing in broad terms where the organization is going in its environment and the implications for human resource requirements.
- *Demand/supply forecasting:* estimating the future demand for people (numbers and skills), and assessing the number of people likely to be available from within and outside the organization.
- *Labour turnover analysis:* analysing actual labour turnover figures and trends as an input to supply forecasts.

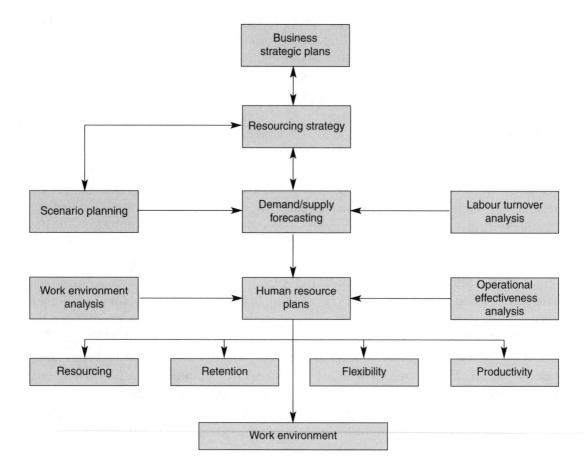

Figure 25.1 The process of human resource planning

- *Work environment analysis:* analysing the environment in which people work in terms of the scope it provides for them to use and develop their skills and achieve job satisfaction.
- *Operational effectiveness analysis:* analysing productivity, the utilization of people and the scope for increasing flexibility to respond to new and changing demands.

RESOURCING STRATEGY

Objective

The objective of HRM resourcing strategy, as expressed by Keep (1989), is 'To obtain the right basic material in the form of a workforce endowed with the appropriate qualities, skills, knowledge and potential for future training. The selection and recruitment of workers best suited to meeting the needs of the organization ought to form a core activity upon which most other HRM policies geared towards development and motivation could be built.'

The concept that the strategic capability of a firm depends on its resource capability in the shape of people (resource based strategy, as explained in Chapter 7) provides the rationale for resourcing strategy. The aim of this strategy is therefore to ensure that a firm achieves competitive advantage by employing more capable people than its rivals. These people will have a wider and deeper range of skills, and behave in ways that maximize their contribution. The organization attracts such people by being 'the employer of choice'. It retains them by providing better opportunities and rewards than others, and by developing a positive psychological contract which increases commitment and creates mutual trust. Furthermore, the organization deploys its people in ways that maximize the added value they supply.

Checklist

The resourcing strategy should attempt to provide answers to the following questions:

- In the light of the business plan, how many people are we likely to need in each of our key operational or functional areas in the short and longer term?
- What skills are we likely to need in the future?
- Will we be able to meet the needs from our existing resources?
- If not, where will we be able to find them?
- What do we need to do to develop or extend our skills base?
- What should we do about identifying people with potential and developing their abilities?
- Do we have a problem in attracting or retaining key staff? If so, what do we need to do about it?
- Is there scope to make better use of people by increasing employment flexibility?
- Is there any danger of downsizing? If so, how are we going to deal with it?

The components of resourcing strategy

These are:

- *Resourcing plans:* preparing plans for finding people from within the organization and/or for training programmes to help people learn new skills. If needs cannot be satisfied from within the organization, preparing longer term plans for meeting them by attracting high quality candidates as the 'employer of choice'.
- *Flexibility plans:* planning for increased flexibility in the use of human resources to enable the organization to make the best use of people and adapt swiftly to changing circumstances.
- *Retention plans:* preparing plans for retaining the people the organization needs.

Resourcing strategy provides the basis for these plans within the framework of business needs. It will, however, be more strongly based if it is underpinned by a process of scenario planning.

SCENARIO PLANNING

Scenario planning is sometimes described as a formal strategic planning technique, but it can also be regarded as an informal approach to thinking about the future in broad terms, based upon an analysis of likely changes in the internal and external environment.

A scenario can be defined as 'an imagined sequence of future events' (*Oxford English Dictionary*). Scenario planning is simply a more or less formalized process for establishing a view about any changes that can be foreseen to the scale and type of activities in the organization and to its structure, and for identifying any external environmental changes that are likely to affect it. The aim is to obtain a better understanding of the possible situations that may have to be dealt with in the future. It is described by Reilly (1999) as follows: 'Scenario planning tries to open minds to a range of possibilities that organizations may have to confront. These possibilities are then ordered to produce a series of internally consistent pictures of alternative futures… It is an intellectual process that seeks to identify issues and examine the possible consequences of events.'

The creation of a scenario involves making broad assessments of likely internal developments – the direction in which the organization is going and the implications this has on people requirements. The assessments may have to be made in the absence of any articulated business plan, and thus involve questioning top managment and key line managers on how they see the future, and asking them to interpret what this means in terms of their human resource needs. Assessments also have to be made on likely changes in the external environment as it may affect the labour market.

ESTIMATING FUTURE HUMAN RESOURCE REQUIREMENTS

Scenario planning is in some situations as far as it is possible to go in estimating future people requirements, but where it is feasible and appropriate, attempts can be made to produce demand and supply forecasts, and to determine what action needs to be taken if the forecasts indicate the possibility of a human resource deficit or surplus.

Demand forecasting

Demand forecasting is the process of estimating the future numbers of people required and the likely skills and competences they will need. The ideal basis of the forecast is an annual budget and longer term business plan, translated into activity levels for each function and department, or decisions on 'downsizing'. In a manufacturing company the sales budget would be translated into a manufacturing plan giving the numbers and types of products to be made in each period. From this information the number of hours to be worked by each skill category to make the quota for each period would be computed.

Details are required of any plans or projects that would result in demands for additional employees or different skills: for example setting up a new regional organization, creating a new sales department, carrying out a major project or developing new products or services. So far as possible, plans should also be reviewed that could result in rationalization, and possibly downsizing, as a result of a cost reduction drive, a business process re-engineering exercise, new technology leading to increased productivity, or a merger or acquisition.

The demand forecasting techniques that can be used to produce quantitative estimates of future requirements are described below.

Managerial or expert judgement

This is the most typical method of forecasting and may be linked to some form of scenario planning. It simply requires managers or specialists to sit down, think about future workloads, and decide how many people are needed. This can be no more than guesswork unless there is reliable evidence available of forecast increases in activity levels or new demands for skills.

Ratio trend analysis

This is carried out by studying past ratios between, say, the number of direct (production) workers and indirect (support) workers in a manufacturing plant, and forecasting future ratios, having made some allowance for changes in organization or methods. Activity level forecasts are then used to determine (in this example) direct labour requirements, and the forecast ratio of indirects to directs would be used to calculate the number of indirect workers needed.

Work study techniques

Work study techniques can be used when it is possible to apply work measurement to calculate how long operations should take and the number of people required. Work study techniques for direct workers can be combined with ratio trend analysis to calculate the number of indirect workers needed.

Forecasting skill and competence requirements

Forecasting skill requirements is largely a matter of managerial judgement. This judgement should, however, be exercised on the basis of a careful analysis of the impact of projected product market developments and the introduction of new technology, either information technology or computerized manufacturing.

Supply forecasting

Supply forecasting measures the number of people likely to be available from within and outside the organization, having allowed for attrition (labour wastage and retirements), absenteeism, internal movements and promotions, and changes in hours and other conditions of work. The forecast will be based on:

- an analysis of existing human resources in terms of numbers in each occupation, skills and potential;
- forecast losses to existing resources through attrition (the analysis of labour wastage as described in the next main section of this chapter is an important aspect of human resource planning because it provides the basis for plans to improve retention rates);

- forecast changes to existing resources through internal promotions;
- effect of changing conditions of work and absenteeism;
- sources of supply from within the organization;
- sources of supply from outside the organization in the national and local labour markets.

Mathematical modelling techniques aided by computers can help in the preparation of supply forecasts in situations where comprehensive and reliable data on stocks and flows can be provided. As this is rarely the case, they are seldom used.

Analysing demand and supply forecasts

The demand and supply forecasts can then be analysed to determine whether there are any deficits or surpluses. This provides the basis for recruitment, retention, and if unavoidable downsizing, plans. Computerized planning models can be used for this purpose. It is, however, not essential to rely on a software planning package. The basic forecasting calculations can be carried out with a spreadsheet that sets out and calculates the number required for each occupation where plans need to be made, as in the following example:

1.	Number currently employed	70
2.	Annual wastage rate based on past records	10 per cent
3.	Expected losses during the year	7
4.	Balance at end year	63
5.	Number required at end year	75
6.	Number to be obtained during year (5–4)	12

LABOUR TURNOVER

The analysis of the numbers of people leaving the organization (labour turnover or wastage) provides data for use in supply forecasting, so that calculations can be made on the number of people lost who may have to be replaced. More importantly, however, the analysis of the numbers of leavers and the reasons why they leave provides information that will indicate whether any action is required to improve retention rates. It can prompt further investigations to establish underlying causes and identify remedies.

In this section, consideration is given to the following aspects of labour turnover:

- its significance;
- methods of measurement;
- the reasons for turnover;
- what it costs;
- its incidence;
- how to benchmark rates of turnover.

The significance of labour turnover

The point was made by IRS (2000) that 'rates of labour turnover provide a graphic illustration of the turbulence within an organization. High rates of attrition can destabilize a business and demotivate those who attempt to maintain levels of service and output against a background of vacant posts, inexperienced staff and general discontent.' Obviously recruitment, induction and training costs all rise with an increase in labour turnover. As the CIPD (2000) has commented, 'Turnover may be a function of negative job attitudes, low job satisfaction, combined with an ability to secure employment elsewhere, ie the state of the labour market. On the other hand, turnover is a normal part of organizational functioning, and while excessively high turnover may be dysfunctional, a certain level of turnover is to be expected and can be beneficial to an organization.'

Methods of measurement

There are a number of ways of measuring labour turnover, as described below.

The labour turnover index

The labour turnover index (sometimes referred to as the employee or labour wastage index) is the traditional formula for measuring wastage. It has been described by the CIPD (2000) as the 'crude wastage method'. It is calculated as follows:

$$\frac{\text{Number of leavers in a specified period (usually 1 year)} \times 100}{\text{Average number of employees during the same period}}$$

This method is commonly used because it is easy to calculate and to understand. For human resource planning purposes, it is a simple matter to work out that if a company wants to increase its workforce by 50 people from 150 to 200, and the labour turnover rate is 20 per cent (leading to a loss of 30 people), then if this trend continues, the company would have to recruit 90 employees during the following year in order to increase and to hold the workforce at 200 in that year (50 extra employees, plus 40 to replace the 20 per cent wastage of the average 200 employees employed). It can also be used to make comparisons with other organizations which will typically adopt this method.

This wastage formula may be simple to use but it can be misleading. The main objection to the measurement of turnover in terms of the proportion of those who leave in a given period is that the figure may be inflated by the high turnover of a relatively small proportion of the workforce, especially in times of heavy recruitment. Thus, a company employing 150 people might have had an annual wastage rate of 20 per cent, meaning that 30 jobs had become vacant during the year, but this could have been spread throughout the company, covering all occupations and long as well as short service employees. Alternatively, it could have been restricted to a small sector of the workforce – only 20 jobs might have been affected, although each of these had to be filled 10 times during the year. These are totally different situations, and unless they are understood, inaccurate forecasts would be made of future requirements and inappropriate actions would be taken to deal with the problem. The turnover index is also suspect if the average number of employees upon which the percentage is based is unrepresentative of recent trends because of considerable increases or decreases during the period in the numbers employed. When assembling and analysing labour turnover figures, it is important to obtain information on the incidence for different categories of employee, especially those who are most difficult to attract and retain, such as knowledge or highly skilled workers.

Survival rate

A method of analysing turnover that is particularly useful for human resource planners is the survival rate: the proportion of employees engaged within a certain period who remain with the organization after so many months or years of service. Thus, an analysis of trainees who have completed their training might show that after two years, 10 of the original cohort of 20 trainees are still with the company, a survival rate of 50 per cent.

The distribution of losses for each entry group, or cohort, can be plotted in the form of a 'survival curve' as shown in Figure 25.2. The basic shape of this curve has been found to be similar in many situations, although it has been observed that the peak of the curve may occur further along the time scale and/or may be lower when it relates to more highly skilled or trained entry cohorts. Table 25.1 tells human resource planners that unless they do something about the situation, they will have to allow for half the number of recruits in any one year to be lost over the next five years. Thus, to ensure that 50 trained staff in five years' time, 100 people would have to be engaged this year. Stark figures like this can prompt action, especially when the costs of recruitment and induction are taken into account.

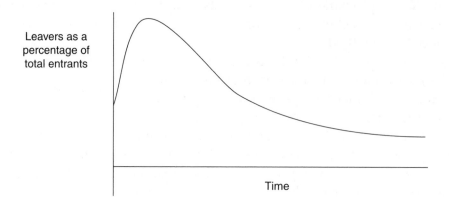

Figure 25.2 A survival curve

Table 25.1 Survival rate analysis

Entry Cohort	Original strength	Number surviving to end of year after engagement				
		Year 1	Year 2	Year 3	Year 4	Year 5
A	40	35	28	26	22	20
B	32	25	24	19	18	17
C	48	39	33	30	25	23
D	38	32	27	24	22	19
E	42	36	30	26	23	21
Total	200	167	142	125	110	100
Average survival rate	100%	83%	71%	62%	55%	50%

Half-life index

A simpler concept derived from survival rate analysis is the half-life index, which is defined as the time taken for a group or cohort of starters to reduce to half its original size through wastage (five years in the above example). Comparisons can then be made for successive entry years or between different groups of employees, in order to show where action may have to be taken to counter undesirable wastage trends.

Stability index

The stability index is considered by many to be an improvement on the turnover index. The formula is:

$$\frac{\text{Number with 1 year's service or more} \times 100}{\text{Number employed 1 year ago}}$$

This index provides an indication of the tendency for longer service employees to remain with the company, and therefore shows the degree to which there is continuity of employment. But this too can be misleading because the index will not reveal the vastly different situations that exist in a company or department with a high proportion of long serving employees, in comparison with one where the majority of employees are short service.

Length of service analysis

This disadvantage of the stability index can be partly overcome if an analysis is also made of the average length of service of people who leave, as in Table 25.2. This analysis is still fairly crude, because it deals only with those who leave. A more refined analysis would compare for each service category the numbers leaving with the numbers employed. If, in the example shown, the total numbers employed with fewer than three months' service were 100 and the total with more than five years were also 100, the proportion of leavers in each category would be 28 per cent and 11 per cent respectively – more revealing figures, especially if previous periods could be analysed to reveal adverse trends.

Choice of measurement

It is difficult to avoid using the conventional employee (labour) turnover index as the easiest and most familiar of all methods of measurement, but it needs to be supplemented with some measure of stability. An analysis of turnover or wastage as part of

Table 25.2 Leavers by length of service

Occupation	Leavers by length of service						Total number leaving	Average number employed	Index of labour turnover %
	Less than 3 months	3–6 months	6 months –1 year	1–2 years	3–5 years	5 or more years			
A	5	4	3	3	2	3	20	220	10
B	15	12	10	6	3	4	50	250	20
C	8	6	5	4	3	4	30	100	30
Totals	28	22	18	13	8	11	100	550	18

a human resource planning exercise requires detailed information on the length of service of leavers, to identify problem areas and to provide a foundation for supply forecasts.

Reasons for turnover

An analysis of the reasons for leaving derived from exit interviews will provide useful information on which to base retention plans. Exit interviews aim to establish why people are leaving, not to persuade them to stay. The reasons for leaving can be classified under the following headings:

- more pay;
- better prospects (career move);
- more security;
- more opportunity to develop skills;
- better working conditions;
- poor relationships with manager/team leader;
- poor relationship with colleagues;
- bullying or harassment;
- personal – pregnancy, illness, moving away from area etc.

Exit interviews should aim to elicit opinions on any specific reasons for dissatisfaction under any of the above non-personal headings. Some leavers will be forthcoming, others will not. It is up to the interviewer to probe skilfully and sensitively to establish reasons for dissatisfaction or unhappiness, so that where those feelings are justified, something can be done about them. Judgement is required to sort out genuine complaints from unjustified or exaggerated ones. An analysis of reasons should take place and trends be noted. General issues can be addressed by reviewing employment and reward policies and practices. Issues affecting particular managers should also be tackled. This may be difficult if it is a behavioural matter, such as bullying, but if there is a build-up of information that suggests this may be the case, the problem cannot be ignored.

However, exit interviews are not completely reliable, and it is desirable to gain a more comprehensive picture of the views of existing employees through attitude surveys (see Chapter 53).

The cost of labour turnover

Labour turnover can be costly. The following factors should be considered:

- leaving costs – payroll costs and personnel administration of leaver;
- direct cost of recruiting replacements (advertising, interviewing, testing etc);
- opportunity cost of time spent by HR and line managers in recruitment;
- direct cost of introducing replacements (induction course, cost of induction manuals etc);
- opportunity cost of time spent by HR and managers in introducing new starters;
- direct cost of training replacements in the necessary skills;
- opportunity cost of time spent by line managers and other staff in providing training;
- loss of the input from those leaving before they are replaced in terms of contribution, output, sales, customer satisfaction and support etc;
- loss arising from reduced input from new starters until they are fully trained.

The CIPD 2005 Recruitment, Retention and Turnover survey established that the average cost per leaver was £4,625. This is a typical figure, and the calculation of the costs of labour turnover in an organization can produce alarming sums if labour turnover is high, especially among managers and knowledge workers. The information can be used by HR as a powerful argument in support of changes in employment and reward policies.

The incidence of labour turnover

The labour turnover rate for all employees as revealed by the CIPD 2005 UK survey was 15.7 per cent. The turnover of different categories of employees were: staff 31.1 per cent, manual workers 16.7 per cent, secretarial and administrative staff 16.7 per cent and professional staff and managers 9.1 per cent.

Benchmarking labour turnover

Labour turnover rates provide a valuable means of benchmarking the effectiveness of HR policies and practices in organizations. They do not tell the whole story, but if turnover is significantly higher than in comparable organizations, this should stimulate action to investigate why this is the case and to do something about it.

Benchmarking can be carried out by networking with other organizations, possibly forming a 'club' to exchange information regularly. There are also a number of benchmarking agencies as listed by the IRS (2000), and the European Foundation for Quality Management (EFQM) survey which uses the internet. National sources of data include the government's Labour Force and Learning and Training at Work surveys, and the annual survey of labour turnover conducted by the CIPD.

ACTION PLANNING

Action plans are derived from broad resourcing strategies and more detailed analysis of demand and supply factors. However, the plans often have to be short term and flexible because of the difficulty of making firm predictions about human resource requirements in times of rapid change. Plans need to be prepared in the areas of resourcing, flexibility and downsizing, as described below.

The resourcing plan

This needs to consider approaches to obtaining people from within the organization, to recruiting them externally, and to attracting high quality candidates (becoming 'the employer of choice').

Internal resourcing

The first step is to analyse the availability of suitable people from within the organization, by reference to assessments of potential and a skills database. The latter should contain a regularly updated list of employees with the sort of skills needed by the organization. Decisions are then made on what steps should be taken to promote, redeploy, and as necessary provide additional experience and training to, eligible staff. Plans can also be made to make better use of existing employees, which may include flexibility arrangements as discussed later, or home working.

The recruitment plan

This will incorporate:

- the numbers and types of employees required to make up any deficits, when they are needed;
- the likely sources of candidates – schools, colleges of further education, universities, advertising, the internet etc;
- plans for tapping alternative sources, such as part-timers, or widening the recruitment net to include, for example, more women re-entering the labour market;
- how the recruitment programme will be conducted.

Employer of choice plans

The recruitment plan should include plans for attracting good candidates by ensuring that the organization will become an 'employer of choice'. This could be achieved by such means as generally improving the image of the company as an employer (the employer brand) and by offering:

- better remuneration packages;
- more opportunities for learning, development and careers;
- enhanced future employability because of the reputation of the organization as one that employs and develops high quality people, well as the learning opportunities it provides;
- employment conditions which address work–life balance issues by, for example, adapting working hours and arrangements and leave policies, and providing child care facilities or vouchers to meet the needs of those with domestic responsibilities;
- better facilities and scope for knowledge workers, such as research and development scientists or engineers or IT specialists;
- 'golden hellos' (sums of money paid upfront to recruits);
- generous relocation payments.

Flexibility plan

The aims of the flexibility plan should be to:

- provide for greater operational flexibility;
- improve the utilization of employees' skills and capacities;
- reduce employment costs;
- help to achieve downsizing smoothly and in a way which avoids the need for compulsory redundancies;
- increase productivity.

The plan can be based on a radical look at traditional employment patterns. This means identifying the scope for using alternatives to full-time permanent staff, which could include increasing the number of part-timers, job sharing, the expansion of home working or teleworking, or employing more temporary workers. The two main new trends in temporary working are first, to establish permanent staffing levels to meet minimum or normal levels of demand and rely on temporary staff to cover peaks, and second, to develop a 'two-tier' workforce in order to provide greater job security for the core workers, by employing a certain percentage of temporary staff at the periphery. Consideration can also be given to making more use of subcontractors or outsourcing work, and to the introduction of more flexible working arrangements.

Use of part-time workers

The advantages of using part-time workers are as follows:

- more scope for flexing hours worked;
- better utilization of plant and equipment by, for example, the introduction of a 'twilight shift';
- lower unit labour costs because overtime levels for full-time workers are reduced;
- higher productivity on repetitive work because part-time workers can give more attention to their work during their shorter working day.

The disadvantages are:

- part-timers are generally less willing to undertake afternoon or evening work, may find it more difficult to vary their hours of work, and may be less mobile;
- rates of labour turnover may be higher among part-timers;
- part-timers may be less committed than full-time employees.

It should be remembered that the Part-time Regulations 1999 require that part-timers should not be treated less favourably than full-time workers, and should be paid pro rata.

Job sharing

Job sharing is an arrangement whereby two employees share the work of one full-time position, dividing pay and benefits between them according to the time each works. Job sharing can involve splitting days or weeks, or less frequently working alternate weeks. The advantages of job sharing include reduced employee turnover and absenteeism because it suits the needs of individuals. Greater continuity results because if one-half of the job sharing team is ill or leaves, the sharer will continue working for at least half the time. Job sharing also means that a wider employment pool can be tapped, of those who cannot work full-time but want permanent employment. The disadvantages are the administrative costs involved and the risk of responsibility being divided.

Home working and teleworking

Home-based employees can be employed in such jobs as consultants, analysts, designers, programmers or various kinds of administrative work. The advantages of these arrangements are:

- flexibility to respond rapidly to fluctuations in demand;
- reduced overheads;
- lower employment costs if the home workers are self-employed (care, however, has to be taken to ensure that they are regarded as self-employed for income tax and national insurance purposes).

Teleworking involves people working at home with a terminal which is linked to the main company or networked with other outworkers. Its aim is to achieve greater flexibility, rapid access to skills and the retention of skilled employees who would otherwise be lost to the company. Teleworkers can be used in a number of functions such as marketing, finance and IT. The arrangement does, however, depend for its success on the involvement and education of all employees (full-time and teleworkers), the careful selection and training of teleworkers, allocating adequate resources to them and monitoring the operation of the system.

Subcontracting

Subcontracting enables:

- resources to be concentrated on core business activities;
- employment costs to be reduced;
- flexibility and productivity to be increased;
- job security for core employees to be enhanced.

The potential drawbacks include:

- The legal status of subcontractors. This has to be clarified for income tax, national insurance and employment legislation purposes.
- The degree to which subcontractors will be able to meet delivery and quality requirements – it may be more difficult to control their work.
- Negative reactions from employees and trade unions who prefer work to be kept within the company.

The decision on how much work can be subcontracted is mainly an operational one, but the flexibility plan should cover the implications of subcontracting on employment levels and employee relations.

Flexible hour arrangements

Flexible hour arrangements can be included in the flexibility plan in one or more of the following ways:

- Flexible daily hours. These may follow an agreed pattern day by day according to typical or expected work loads (eg flexitime systems).
- Flexible weekly hours, providing for longer weekly hours to be worked at certain peak periods during the year.
- Flexible daily and weekly hours: varying daily or weekly hours or a combination of both to match the input of hours to achieve the required output. Such working times, unlike daily or weekly arrangements, may fluctuate between a minimum and a maximum.
- Compressed working weeks in which employees work fewer than the five standard days.
- Annual hours: scheduling employee hours on the basis of the number of hours to be worked, with provisions for the increase or reduction of hours in any given period, according to the demand for goods or services.

Overtime arrangements

A flexibility plan can contain proposals to reduce overtime costs by the use of flexible hours, new shift arrangements (as for twilight shifts), time off in lieu and overtime limitation agreements. The reduction of overtime is often catered for in formal productivity deals which include a quid pro quo in the form of increased pay for the elimination of overtime payments and the introduction of flexible work patterns.

Shift working arrangements

These can be introduced or modified to meet demand requirements, reduce overtime or provide for better plant or equipment utilization.

The downsizing plan

If all else fails, it may be necessary to deal with unacceptable employment costs or surplus numbers of employees by what has euphemistically come to be known as 'downsizing'. The downsizing plan should be based on the timing of reductions and forecasts of the extent to which these can be achieved by natural wastage or voluntary redundancy. The plan should set out:

- the total number of people who have to go, and when and where this needs to take place;
- arrangements for informing and consulting with employees and their trade unions;
- a forecast of the number of losses that can be taken up by natural wastage;
- any financial or other inducements to encourage voluntary redundancy;
- a forecast of the likely numbers who will volunteer to leave;
- a forecast of the balance of employees, if any, who will have to be made redundant (the plan should, of course, aim to avoid this through natural wastage and voluntary redundancy);
- the redundancy terms;
- any financial inducements to be offered to key employees whom the company wishes to retain;
- any arrangements for retraining employees and finding them work elsewhere in the organization;
- the steps to be taken to help redundant employees find new jobs by counselling, contacting other employers or offering the services of outplacement consultants;
- the arrangements for telling individual employees about the redundancies and how they are affected, and for keeping the trade unions informed.

THE CONTRIBUTION OF HR TO HUMAN RESOURCE PLANNING

Human resource planning, in the broader meaning of the term, is one of the fundamental strategic roles of the HR function. HR can make a major contribution to developing the resource capability of the firm and therefore its strategic capability by systematically reviewing the firm's strategic objectives and by ensuring that plans are made that will ensure that the human resources are available to meet those objectives. Thus HR is focusing on the acquisition and development of the human capital required by the organization.

To make this contribution, heads of HR and their colleagues in the HR function need to:

● ensure that they are aware of the strategic plans of the business, and can provide advice on the human resource implications of those plans;
● point out to management the strengths and weaknesses of the human resources of the organization, and the opportunities and threats they present, so that these can be considered when developing business plans;
● be capable of scenario planning in the sense that they can identify future issues concerning the acquisition, retention and employment of people, and advise on methods of addressing those issues;
● understand the extent to which quantitative assessments of the future demand for and supply of people may be feasible and useful, and know the methods that can be used to prepare such forecasts;
● be aware of the scope to deal with future requirements by introducing various forms of flexibility;
● be capable of preparing relevant and practical resourcing plans and strategies for retaining people, based upon an understanding of the internal and external environment of the organization, and the implications of analyses of labour turnover.

26

Talent management

Talent management consisting of talent planning and development is a relatively new concept, only emerging in the 2000s. It derives from the phrase 'the war for talent', which originated in the late 1990s as a means of highlighting the problems that organizations were having in attracting and retaining talented people. However O'Reilly and Pfeffer (2000) point out that: 'Companies that adopt a "talent war" mindset may place too much value on outsiders and downplay the talent already in the company.' The approach should be one that emphasizes the ability of everyone to succeed and thereby 'achieve extraordinary results with ordinary people'. And Pfeffer (2001) warns that the war for talent is the wrong metaphor because it overlooks the extent to which teams of people will often operate more effectively than mere collections of individuals.

There is nothing new about the various approaches contained in the concept of talent management – attraction, retention, motivation and engagement, development, and succession planning. But they are bundled together to produce a more coherent whole that can be a vehicle for the development and implementation of coordinated and mutually supporting approaches that help the organization to get and to keep the talented people it needs. It is closely associated with the notion of creating 'a best place to work', which has again become prominent in the 2000s.

In this chapter talent management is dealt with under the following headings:

- talent management defined;
- the elements of talent management;
- creating a 'best place to work';
- attraction policies;
- retention policies;
- career management (career and succession planning) policy and practice;
- talent management for knowledge workers;
- conclusions – the practice of talent management.

TALENT MANAGEMENT DEFINED

Talent management is the use of an integrated set of activities to ensure that the organization attracts, retains, motivates and develops the talented people it needs now and in the future. The aim is to secure the flow of talent, bearing in mind that talent is a major corporate resource.

It is sometimes assumed that talent management is only concerned with key people – the high flyers. For example, Smilansky (2005) states that it is 'aimed at improving the calibre, availability and flexible utilization of exceptionally capable (high potential) employees who can have a disproportionate impact on business performance'. But everyone in an organization has talent, even if some have more talent than others. Talent management processes should not be limited to the favoured few. This point was made by deLong and Vijayaraghavan (2003) when they suggested that the unsung heroes of corporate performance are the capable, steady performers.

THE ELEMENTS OF TALENT MANAGEMENT

The elements of talent management and their interrelationships are shown in Figure 26.1.

Talent management starts with the business strategy and what it signifies in terms of the talented people required by the organization. Ultimately, its aim is to develop and maintain a talent pool consisting of a skilled, engaged and committed workforce. Its elements are described below.

The resourcing strategy

The business plan provides the basis for human resource planning, which defines

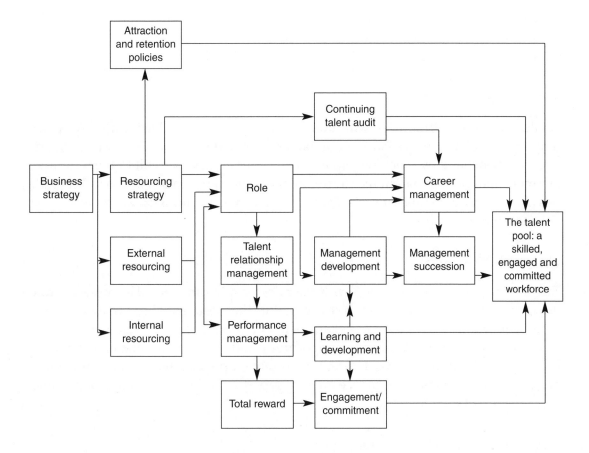

Figure 26.1 The elements of talent management

human capital requirements and leads to attraction and retention policies and programmes for internal resourcing (identifying talent within the organization and developing and promoting it).

Attraction and retention policies and programmes

These policies and programmes describe the approach to ensuring that the organization both gets and keeps the talent it needs. Attraction policies lead to programmes for external resourcing (recruitment and selection of people from outside the organization). Retention policies are designed to ensure that people remain as committed members of the organization. The outcome of these policies is a talent flow that creates and maintains the talent pool. Both attraction and retention policies as discussed in greater detail later in this chapter will be included amongst the steps required to make the organization 'a great place to work', also considered in the next main section of this chapter.

Talent audit

A talent audit identifies those with potential and provides the basis for career planning and development – ensuring that talented people have the sequence of experience supplemented by coaching and learning programmes that will fit them to carry out more demanding roles in the future. Talent audits can also be used to indicate the possible danger of talented people leaving (risk analysis) and what action may need to be taken to retain them.

Role development

Talent management is concerned with the roles people carry out. This involves role development – ensuring that roles provide the responsibility, challenge and autonomy required to create role engagement and motivation. It also involves taking steps to ensure that people have the opportunity and are given the encouragement to learn and develop in their roles. Talent management policies also focus on role flexibility – giving people the chance to develop their roles by making better and extended use of their talents.

Talent relationship management

Talent relationship management is the process of building effective relationships with people in their roles. It is concerned generally with creating a great place to work (see later), but particularly it is about treating individual employees fairly, recognizing their value, giving them a voice and providing opportunities for growth. The aim is to achieve 'talent engagement', ensuring that people are committed to their work and the organization. As Sears (2003) points out, it is 'better to build an existing relationship rather than try to create a new one when someone leaves'.

Performance management

Performance management processes provide a means of building relationships with people, identifying talent and potential, planning learning and development activities and making the most of the talent possessed by the organization. Line managers can be asked to carry out separate 'risk analyses' for any key staff to assess the likelihood of their leaving. Properly carried out, performance management is a means of increasing the engagement and motivation of people by providing positive feedback and recognition. This is part of a total reward system.

Total reward

Total reward strategies (see Chapter 43), which provide for both financial and non-financial rewards, can contribute to the engagement and commitment of talented people by demonstrating that they are valued for their contribution and by operating fairly and consistently. Paying competitive rates will affect the ability of organizations to attract and retain people, but there is a limit to the extent to which companies can compete with the 'pull of the market' as Cappelli (2000) points out. Retention or loyalty bonuses (golden handcuffs) are used by some companies, but again, as stressed by Cappelli there is a limit to their effectiveness as bribes. If talented people want to go they will go.

Learning and development

Learning and development policies and programmes are essential components in the process of developing talent – ensuring that people acquire and enhance the skills and competencies they need. Policies should be formulated by reference to 'employee success profiles', which are described in terms of competencies and define the qualities that need to be developed. Employee success profiles can be incorporated in role profiles.

Learning and development activities are also important means of developing managers and gaining the engagement and commitment of talented staff by giving them opportunities to grow in their present roles and to progress to higher-level roles.

Career management

Career management consists of the processes of career planning and management succession. Career planning shapes the progression of individuals within an organization in accordance with assessments of organizational needs, defined employee success profiles and the performance, potential and preferences of individual members of the enterprise.

Management succession planning takes place to ensure that, as far as possible, the organization has the managers it requires to meet future business needs. Career management is dealt with in more detail in the last section of this chapter.

CREATING A GREAT PLACE TO WORK

Ensuring that the organization is perceived as being 'a great place to work' means that it becomes an 'employer of choice', ie one for whom people want to work. There is a desire to join the organization and once there, to want to stay. Employees are committed to the organization and engaged in the work they do. To acquire a national, even a local reputation as a good employer takes time. But it's worth the effort.

On the basis of their longitudinal research in 12 companies, Purcell *et al* (2003) concluded that:

> What seems to be happening is that successful firms are able to meet people's needs both for a good job and to work 'in a great place'. They create good work and a conducive working environment. In this way they become an 'employer of choice'. People will want to work there because their individual needs are met – for a good job with prospects linked to training, appraisal, and working with a good boss who listens and gives some autonomy but helps with coaching and guidance.

The criteria used by the *Sunday Times* in identifying the '100 Best Companies to Work For', 2005 were:

- leadership at senior management level;
- my manager – local management on a day-to-day basis;
- personal growth – opportunities to learn, grow and be challenged;
- well-being – balanced work-life issues;
- my team – immediate colleagues;
- giving something back – to society and the local community;
- my company – the way it treats staff;
- fair deal – pay and benefits.

The factors used in the *Financial Times* 2005 best workplaces report were:

- have a range of management practices that help staff to feel valued, productive and listened to;
- support at home – step in when people are suffering from personal problems;
- maintain a balance between work and family;
- effective employee development programme;
- staff trusted to do their jobs properly.

Creating a great place to work starts with developing the image of the organization so that it is recognized as one that achieves results, delivers quality products and services, behaves ethically and provides good conditions of employment. Organizations with a clear vision and a set of integrated and enacted values are likely to project themselves as being well worth working for.

ATTRACTION STRATEGIES

The overall strategy should be to become an employer of choice. As Scarborough and Elias (2002) put it: 'The recruitment of key individuals who will contribute significantly to the value-creating capacity of the firm is crucial to success.' The aims are to establish the brand image of the organization – how others perceive it (employee branding), to become an employer of choice, and to target recruitment and selection to obtain the sort of people the organization needs.

Employer branding

Employer branding is the creation of a brand image of the organization for prospective employees. It will be influenced by the reputation of the organization as a business or provider of services as well as its reputation as an employer. As described by Alan Reed, Founder and Chief Executive of Reed Executive plc, in 2001: 'Employer branding is the concept of applying to the recruitment process the same marketing coherence used in the management of customers.' He suggests that the approaches required to develop an employer brand are:

- analyse what ideal candidates need and want and take this into account in deciding what should be offered and how it should be offered;
- establish how far the core values of the organization support the creation of an attractive brand and ensure that these are incorporated in the presentation of the brand as long as they are 'values in use' (lived by members of the organization) rather than simply espoused;
- define the features of the brand on the basis of an examination and review of each of the areas that affect the perceptions of people about the organization as 'a great place to work' – the way people are treated, the provision of a fair deal, opportunities for growth, work-life balance, leadership, the quality of management, involvement with colleagues and how and why the organization is successful;

- benchmark the approaches of other organizations (the *Sunday Times* list of the 100 best companies to work for is useful) to obtain ideas about what can be done to enhance the brand;
- be honest and realistic.

Employer of choice

The aim is to become an 'employer of choice', a place where people prefer to work. This means developing what Sears (2003) calls 'a value proposition', which communicates what the organization can offer its employees as a 'great place to work'. The factors that contribute to being an employer of choice are the provision of:

- interesting and rewarding work;
- opportunities for learning, development and career progression;
- a reasonable degree of security;
- enhanced future employability because of the reputation of the organization as one that employs and develops high quality people, as well as the learning opportunities it provides;
- better facilities and scope for knowledge workers, eg research and development scientists or engineers and IT specialists;
- employment conditions that satisfy work-life balance needs;
- a reward system that recognizes and values contribution and provides competitive pay and benefits.

This all adds up to an employee value proposition which, as a means of attracting and retaining high potential employees, recognizes that they will be looking for strong values and expecting to be well managed, to have freedom and autonomy, high job challenge and career opportunities. A powerful method of retention is simply to ensure that people feel they are valued.

Targeted recruitment and selection

The first step is to identify what sort of people the organization needs with regard to their qualifications and experience and the extent to which they are likely to fit the culture of the organization – its values and norms. This involves analysing and assessing work requirements and defining what cultural fit means. The most important characteristics of those who are already thriving – what separates successful from unsuccessful employees – should be determined so that others like them can be recruited. Attitudes to work, careers and the company are important; behaviour can be influenced later as people become familiar with the culture so long as their attitudes are right. As Leary-Joyce (2004) says: 'Recruit for attitude, induct for culture.'

RETENTION STRATEGIES

The turnover of key employees can have a disproportionate impact on the business and the people organizations wish to retain are probably the ones most likely to leave. Reed (2001) claims that:

> Every worker is five minutes away from handing in his or her notice, and 150 working hours away from walking out of the door to a better offer. There is no such thing as a 'job for life' and today's workers have few qualms about leaving employers for greener pastures... The average permanent job in the UK lasts six years.

Concerted action is required to retain talented people, but there are limits to what any organization can do. It is also necessary to encourage the greatest contribution from existing talent and to value them accordingly.

Factors affecting retention

Retention strategies should be based on an understanding of the factors that affect them. For early career employees (30 years and under) career advancement is significant. For mid-career employees (age 31–50) the ability to manage their careers and satisfaction from their work are important. Late career employees (over 50) will be interested in security. It is also the case that a younger workforce will change jobs and employers more often than an older workforce, and workforces with a lot of part-timers are less stable than those with predominately full-time staff. The specific factors that affect retention are:

- company image;
- recruitment, selection and deployment;
- leadership – 'employees join companies and leave managers';
- learning opportunities;
- performance recognition and rewards.

A study of high flyers by Holbeche (1998) found that the factors that aided the retention and motivation of high performers included providing challenge and achievement opportunities (eg assignments), mentors, realistic self-assessment and feedback processes.

Basis of the strategy

A retention strategy takes into account the particular retention issues the organization is facing and sets out ways in which these issues can be dealt with. This may mean accepting the reality, as mentioned by Cappelli (2000), that the market, not the company will ultimately determine the movement of employees. Cappelli believes that it may be difficult to counter the pull of the market – 'you can't shield your people from attractive opportunities and aggressive recruiters', and suggests that: 'The old goal of HR management – to minimize overall employee turnover – needs to be replaced by a new goal: to influence who leaves and when.' This, as proposed by Bevan *et al* (1997), could be based on risk analysis to quantify the seriousness of losing key people, or of key posts becoming vacant.

Risk analysis

Risk analysis can be carried out initially by identifying potential risk areas – the key people who may leave and, for each of them as individuals or groups, estimating:

- the likelihood of this occurring;
- how serious the effects of a loss would be on the business;
- the ease with which a replacement could be made and the replacement costs.

Each of the estimates could be expressed on a scale, say: very high, high, medium, low, very low. An overview of the ratings under each heading could then indicate where action may need to be taken to retain key people or groups of people.

Analysis of reasons for leaving

Risk analysis provides specific information on areas for concern. More generally, some indication of the reasons for leaving and therefore where action needs to be taken may be provided by exit interviews, but they are fallible. More reliance can be placed on the results of attitude or opinion surveys to identify any areas of dissatisfaction. The retention plan should propose actions that would focus on each of the areas in which lack of commitment and dissatisfaction can arise.

Areas for action

Depending on the outcome of the risk analysis and the overall assessment of reasons for leaving, the possible actions that can be taken are as follows:

- Deal with uncompetitive, inequitable or unfair pay systems. But as Cappelli (2000) points out, there is a limit to the extent to which people can be bribed to stay. Remember that while money might attract, you can't buy love – it is often other things that get people to stay (how they are treated).
- Design jobs to maximize skill variety, task significance, autonomy, control over their work and feedback, and ensure that they provide opportunities for learning and growth. Some roles can be 'customized' to meet the needs of particular individuals.
- Develop commitment to the work (job engagement) not only through job design but also by organizing work around projects with which people can identify more readily than the company as a whole.
- Encourage the development of social ties within the company. In the words of Cappelli (2000), 'loyalty to companies may be disappearing but loyalty to colleagues is not'.
- Ensure that selection and promotion procedures match the capacities of individuals to the demands of the work they have to do. Rapid turnover can result simply from poor selection or promotion decisions.
- Reduce the losses of people who cannot adjust to their new job – the 'induction crisis' – by giving them proper training and support when they join the organization.
- Take steps to improve work-life balance by developing policies including flexible working that recognize the needs of employees outside work.
- Eliminate as far as possible unpleasant working conditions or the imposition of too much stress on employees.
- Select, brief and train managers and team leaders so that they appreciate the positive contribution they can make to improving retention by the ways in which they lead their teams. Bear in mind that people often leave their managers rather than their organization.

CAREER MANAGEMENT

Career management defined

Career management is concerned with providing opportunities for people to progress and develop their careers and ensuring that the organization has the flow of talent it needs. The elements of career management are the provision of learning and development opportunities, career planning and management succession planning.

Aims

For employees, the aims of career management policies are first, to give individuals the guidance, support and encouragement they need if they are to fulfil their potential and achieve a successful career with the organization in tune with their talents and aspirations. Secondly, the aim is to provide men and women of promise with a sequence of learning activities and experience that will equip them for whatever level of responsibility they have the ability to reach.

For the organization, the aim of career management is to meet the objectives of its talent management policies, which are to ensure that there is a talent flow that creates and maintains the required talent pool.

Career management calls for an approach that explicitly takes into account both organizational needs and employee interests. As described by Hirsh and Carter (2002), it encompasses recruitment, personal development plans, lateral moves, special assignments at home or abroad, development positions, career bridges, lateral moves, and support for employees who want to develop. It calls for creativity in identifying ways to provide development opportunities and enhance employee loyalty.

Career dynamics

Career planning should be based on an understanding of career dynamics. This is concerned with how careers progress – the ways in which people move through their careers either upwards when they are promoted, or by enlarging or enriching their roles to take on greater responsibilities or make more use of their skills and abilities. The three stages of career progression – expanding, establishing and maturing – are illustrated in Figure 26.2. This also shows how individuals progress or fail to progress at different rates through these stages.

The process of career management

The process of career management is illustrated in Figure 26.3.

Career management policies

The organization needs to decide on the extent to which it 'makes or buys' talented people. Should it grow its own talent (a promotion from within policy) or should it rely on external recruitment (bringing 'fresh blood' into the organization)? The policy may be to recruit potentially high performers who will be good at their present job and are rewarded accordingly. If they are really good, they will be promoted and the enterprise will get what it wants. Deliberately to train managers for a future that may

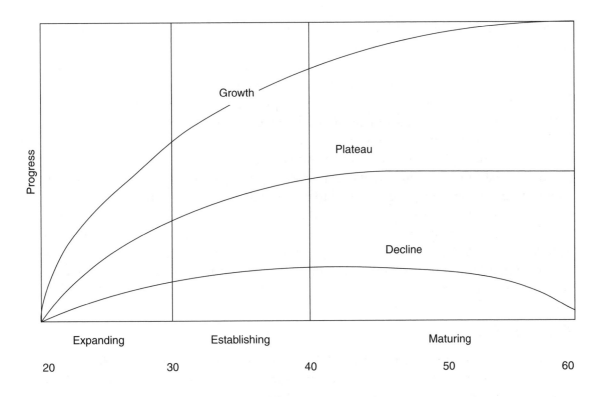

Figure 26.2 Career progression curves

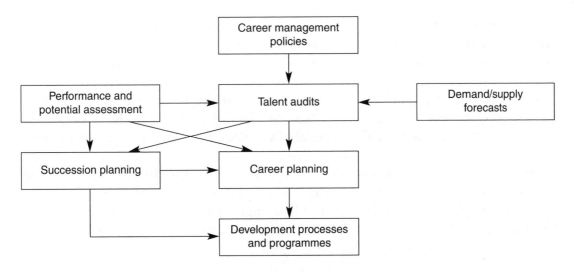

Figure 26.3 The process of career management

never happen is considered a waste of time. In contrast and less frequently, employers who believe in long-term career planning develop structured approaches to career management. These include elaborate reviews of performance and potential, assessment centres to identify talent or confirm that it is there, 'high-flyer' schemes, and planned job moves in line with a predetermined programme.

There may also be policies for dealing with the 'plateaued' manager who has got so far but will get no further. Some managers in this position may be reconciled to reaching the end of the 'rat race' but continue to work effectively. Others will become bored, frustrated and unproductive, especially rising stars on the wane. The policy may be to provide for steps to be taken to reshape their careers so that they still have challenging work at the same level, even if this does not involve promotion up the hierarchy. Alternatively, the policy may need to recognize that some managers will have to be encouraged to start new careers elsewhere. In the latter case, career counselling advice should be provided, possibly through 'outplacement' consultants who provide such a service.

Talent audits

These review the stocks of talent available and the flows required by reference to demand and supply forecasts and performance and potential assessments. They provide the basis for succession and career planning.

Performance and potential assessments

The aim of performance and potential assessment is to identify training and development needs, provide guidance on possible directions in which an individual's career might go, and indicate who has potential for promotion. This information can be obtained from performance management processes, as described in Part VII.

Assessment of potential can be carried out formally by managers following a performance review. They may be asked to identify people who have very high potential, some potential, or no potential at all. They may also be asked to indicate when individuals will be ready for promotion and how far they are likely to get. The problem with this sort of assessment is that managers find it difficult to forecast the future for the people they are reviewing – good performance in the current job does not guarantee that individuals will be able to cope with wider responsibilities, especially if this involves moving into management. And managers may not necessarily be aware of the qualities required for longer-term promotion. But the organization does need information on those with potential and assessors should be encouraged in their comments section at least to indicate that this is someone who is not only performing well in the present job but may well perform well in higher-level jobs.

This information can identify those who may be nominated to attend development centres (see Chapter 40), which can be used to establish potential and discuss career plans.

Demand and supply forecasts

Demand and supply forecasts are provided by the use of human resource planning and modelling techniques (see Chapter 25). In larger organizations, modelling is a particularly fruitful method to use because it allows for sensitivity analysis of the impact of different assumptions about the future (answering 'What if?' questions).

Expert systems, as described in Chapter 59, can also be used where this is an extensive database on flows, attribute requirements (person specifications), and performance and potential assessments. Such systems can establish relationships between the opportunities and the personal attributes they demand, so that careers advisers can take a set of personal attributes and identify the most appropriate available opportunities. At the career planning stage, they can also identify people with the correct abilities and skills for particular jobs and provide information on the career management programmes required to ensure that attributes and jobs are matched and careers progress at an appropriate rate. Career management systems such as ExecuGROW (Control Data) have been specially developed for this purpose.

There is a limit, however, to sophistication. There are so many variables and unpredictable changes in both supply and demand factors that it may be possible to conduct only an annual check to see what the relationship is between the numbers of managers who will definitely retire over the next four or five years and the numbers at the next level who have the potential to succeed them. If this comparison reveals a serious imbalance, then steps can be taken to reduce or even eliminate the deficit, or to consider other types of deployment for those who are unlikely to progress.

Succession planning

Succession planning is the process of assessing and auditing the talent in the organization in order to answer three fundamental questions:

1. Are there enough potential successors available – a supply of people coming through who can take key roles in the longer term?
2. Are they good enough?
3. Do they have the right skills and attributes for the future?

Succession planning is based on the information supplied by talent audits, supply and demand forecasts and performance and potential reviews. In some large organizations in which demand and supply forecasts can be made accurately, highly formalized succession planning processes exist based on the sort of management succession schedule illustrated in Figure 26.4.

MANAGEMENT SUCCESSION SCHEDULE					Department	Director/manager:		
Existing managers						Potential successors		
Name	Position	Due for replacement	Rating		If promotable, to what position and when?	Names: 1st and 2nd choice	Positions	When
			Performance	Potential				

Figure 26.4   Management succession schedule

However, Hirsh (2000) points out that the focus of succession planning has shifted from identifying successors for posts towards providing for the development of those successors by creating 'talent pools'. This is because it is difficult in the changeable environment in which most organizations exist to predict succession requirements. There is also the problem of making reliable assessments of potential or 'promotability'. Another issue raised by Hirsh is that organizations fear that too much talk of 'careers' gives employees unrealistic expectations of promotion. It can be difficult to talk about the future in a volatile business. 'The result has been that many managers feel no one wants to talk about their career prospects and the organization would secretly like them to stay just where they are. This situation leads to frustration and demotivation.'

Career planning

Career planning uses all the information provided by the organization's assessments of requirements, the assessments of performance, and potential and management succession plans, and translates it into the form of individual career development programmes and general arrangements for management development, career counselling and mentoring.

It is possible to define career progression in terms of what people are required to know and be able to do to carry out work at progressive levels of responsibility or contribution. These levels can be described as competency bands. For each band, the experience and training needed to achieve the competency level would be defined in order to produce a career map incorporating 'aiming points' for individuals, as illustrated in Figure 26.5, who would be made aware of the competency levels they must reach in order to achieve progress in their careers. This would help them to plan their own development, although support and guidance should be provided by their managers, HR specialists and, if they exist, management development advisers or mentors. The provision of additional experience and training could be arranged as appropriate, but it would be important to clarify what individual employees need to do for themselves if they want to progress within the organization.

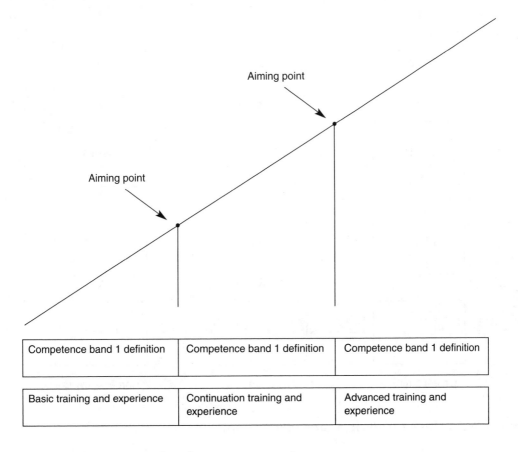

Figure 26.5 Competence band career progression system

Career family grade structures, as described in Chapter 46, can define levels of competency in each career family and show career paths upwards within families or between families, as illustrated in Figure 26.6.

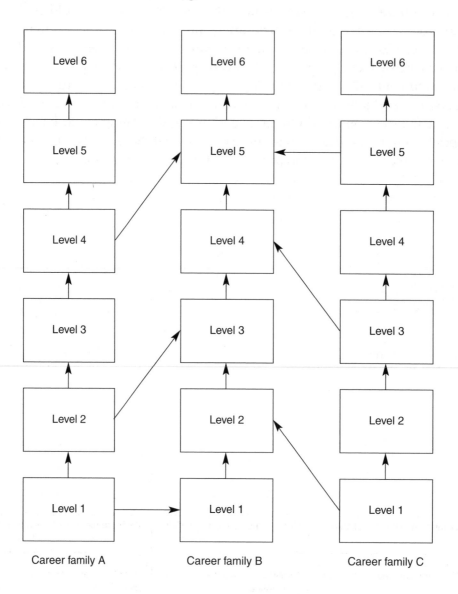

Figure 26.6 Career paths in a career family structure

Formal career planning along these lines may be the ideal, but as noted by Hirsh *et al* (2000), there has been a shift from managed career moves to more open internal job markets. The process of internal job application has become the main way in which employees manage their careers.

TALENT MANAGEMENT FOR KNOWLEDGE WORKERS

Knowledge workers are defined as workers whose skills or knowledge are inextricably linked with the product or service of their employing organizations. The term therefore embraces such diverse groups as lawyers, accountants, software designers, web designers, academics, marketers and media workers. More and more work is being defined by some kind of knowledge element. According to Swart and Kinnie (2004) the effective management of knowledge workers presents organizations with a number of dilemmas. Choices have to be made between the retention of knowledge and knowledge workers, and the desire of knowledge workers to increase their employability. Tension also exists between the need to develop organization-specific knowledge and the wish of knowledge workers to develop transferable knowledge. The firm may want to appropriate the value of that knowledge, but workers may want to retain ownership of their knowledge.

Swart and Kinnie argue that understanding of these dilemmas is improved by a greater appreciation of where professional workers get their primary source of identification – is it from their profession, the organization that employs them, the team or the client? Their loyalty may be to their professional mission rather than their employer. Professional research staff or academics may be committed to achieving professional status and recognition above any forms of performance recognition that the employing organization might be able to offer.

TALENT MANAGEMENT IN PRACTICE

As described in this chapter talent management consists of a wide range of activities. Organizations differ hugely in the ways in which they manage their talent. Some aim to integrate all or most of these activities, others concentrate on one or two such as talent audits and succession planning. Centrica provides an example of a comprehensive approach, illustrated in Figure 26.7.

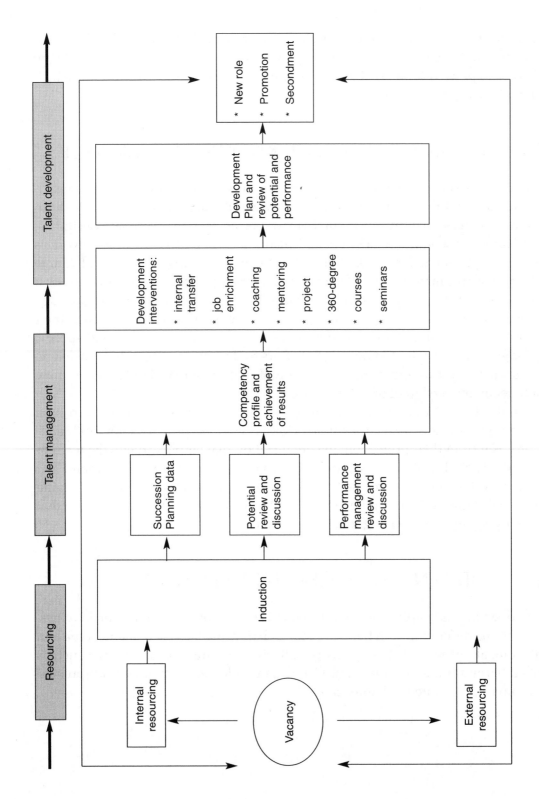

Figure 26.7 Talent acquisition and development at Centrica

27

Recruitment and selection

THE RECRUITMENT AND SELECTION PROCESS

The overall aim of the recruitment and selection process should be to obtain at minimum cost the number and quality of employees required to satisfy the human resource needs of the company. The three stages of recruitment and selection dealt with in this chapter are:

1. *defining requirements* – preparing job descriptions and specifications; deciding terms and conditions of employment;
2. *attracting candidates* – reviewing and evaluating alternative sources of applicants, inside and outside the company, advertising, using agencies and consultants;
3. *selecting candidates* – sifting applications, interviewing, testing, assessing candidates, assessment centres, offering employment, obtaining references; preparing contracts of employment.

Selection interviewing and selection testing are dealt with in Chapters 28 and 29.

DEFINING REQUIREMENTS

The number and categories of people required should be specified in the recruitment programme, which is derived from the human resource plan. In addition, there will be demands for replacements or for new jobs to be filled, and these demands should be checked to ensure that they are justified. It may be particularly necessary to check on the need for a replacement or the level or type of employee that is specified. Requirements for particular positions are set out in the form of role profiles and person specifications. These provide the basic information required to draft advertisements, brief agencies or recruitment consultants, and assess candidates. A role profile listing competence, skill, educational and experience requirements produces the job criteria against which candidates will be assessed at the interview or by means of psychological tests.

Role profiles for recruitment purposes

Role profiles, as described in Chapter 13, define the overall purpose of the role, its reporting relationships and key result areas. They may also include a list of the competencies required. These will be technical competencies (knowledge and skills) and any specific behavioural competencies attached to the role. The latter would be selected from the organization's competency framework and modified as required to fit the demands made on role holders. For recruiting purposes, the profile is extended to include information on terms and conditions (pay, benefits, hours of work), special requirements such as mobility, travelling or unsocial hours, and training, development and career opportunities. The recruitment role profile provides the basis for a person specification.

Person specifications

A person specification, also known as a recruitment, personnel or job specification, defines the education, training, qualifications and experience. The technical competencies as set out in the role profile may also be included.

A person specification can be set out under the following headings:

- *technical competencies* – what the individual needs to know and be able to do to carry out the role, including any special aptitudes or skills required;
- *behavioural and attitudinal requirements* – the types of behaviours required for successful performance in the role will be related to the core values and competency framework of the organization to ensure that cultural fit is achieved when selecting people. But role-specific information is also needed, which should be developed by analysing the characteristics of existing employees who are carrying out their roles effectively. By defining behavioural requirements it is

possible to elicit information about attitudinal requirements, ie what sort of attitudes are likely to result in appropriate behaviours and successful performance.

- *qualifications and training* – the professional, technical or academic qualifications required, or the training that the candidate should have undertaken;
- *experience* – in particular, categories of work or organizations; the types of achievements and activities that would be likely to predict success;
- *specific demands* – where the role holder will be expected to achieve in specified areas, eg develop new markets, improve sales, or introduce new systems;
- *organizational fit* – the corporate culture (eg formal or informal) and the need for candidates to be able to work within it;
- *special requirements* – travelling, unsocial hours, mobility, etc;
- *meeting candidate expectations* – the extent to which the organization can meet candidates' expectations in terms of career opportunities, training, security etc.

The behavioural and attitudinal parts of the person specification are used as the basis for structured interviews (see Chapter 28). As reported by *Competency and Emotional Intelligence* (2004), Britannia Building Society recruits on the basis of the candidates' attitudes first, and skills and abilities second. Developing the process involved mapping the Society's values to its core competencies, identifying the sort of competency-based questions that should be asked by interviewers, defining the typical types of responses that candidates might make, and tracking those back to the values.

A role profile (see Chapter 12) will set out output expectations and competency requirements for interviewing purposes (competency-based recruitment is considered in more detail below). But more information may be required to provide the complete picture for advertising and briefing candidates on terms and conditions and career prospects. An example of a person specification is given in Figure 27.1.

The biggest danger to be avoided at this stage is that of overstating the competencies and qualifications required. It is natural to go for the best, but setting an unrealistically high level for candidates increases the problems of attracting them, and results in dissatisfaction when they find their talents are not being used. Understating requirements can be equally dangerous, but it happens much less frequently. The best approach is to distinguish between essential and desirable requirements.

When the requirements have been agreed, they should be analysed under suitable headings. There are various ways of doing this. A basic approach is to set out and define the essential or desirable requirements under the key headings of competencies, qualifications and training and experience. Additional information can be provided on specific demands. It is necessary to spell out separately the terms and conditions of the job.

---

1. *Technical competencies:*

   ● *Essential in:*
     - all aspects of recruitment including test administration;
     - interviewing techniques;
     - job analysis;
     - inputting data to computers;
     - administering fairly complex paperwork processes.
   ● *Desirable in:*
     - administering OPQ test;
     - job evaluation;
     - counselling techniques;
     - conducting training sessions.

2. *Behavioural competencies:*

   ● able to relate well to others and use interpersonal skills to achieve desired objectives;
   ● able to influence the behaviour and decisions of people on matters concerning recruitment and other personnel or individual issues;
   ● able to cope with change, to be flexible and to handle uncertainty;
   ● able to make sense of issues, identify and solve problems and 'think on one's feet';
   ● focus on achieving results;
   ● able to maintain appropriately directed energy and stamina, to exercise self-control and to learn new behaviours;
   ● able to communicate well, orally and on paper.

3. *Qualifications/experience:*
   ● Graduate Member of the Chartered Institute of Personnel and Development plus relevant experience in each aspect of the work.

Figure 27.1 Person specification for an HR officer

Alternatively, there are the traditional classification schemes although, these are no longer so popular. The most familiar are the seven-point plan developed by Rodger (1952) and the fivefold grading system produced by Munro Fraser (1954).

The seven-point plan

The seven-point plan covers:

1. *physical make-up* – health, physique, appearance, bearing and speech;
2. *attainments* – education, qualifications, experience;
3. *general intelligence* – fundamental intellectual capacity;
4. *special aptitudes* – mechanical, manual dexterity, facility in the use of words or figures;

5. *interests* – intellectual, practical, constructional, physically active, social, artistic;
6. *disposition* – acceptability, influence over others, steadiness, dependability, self-reliance;
7. *circumstances* – domestic circumstances, occupations of family.

The fivefold grading system

The fivefold grading system covers:

1. *impact on others* – physical make-up, appearance, speech and manner;
2. *acquired qualifications* – education, vocational training, work experience;
3. *innate abilities* – natural quickness of comprehension and aptitude for learning;
4. *motivation* – the kinds of goals set by the individual, his or her consistency and determination in following them up, and success in achieving them;
5. *adjustment* – emotional stability, ability to stand up to stress and ability to get on with people.

Choice of system

Of these two systems, the seven-point plan has the longer pedigree. The fivefold grading scheme is simpler, in some ways, and places more emphasis on the dynamic aspects of the applicant's career. Both can provide a good framework for interviewing, but increasingly, interviewers are using a competency-based approach.

Using a competency-based approach

A competency-based approach means that the competencies defined for a role are used as the framework for the selection process. As described by Taylor (2002): 'A competency approach is person-based rather than job-based. The starting point is thus not an analysis of jobs but an analysis of people and what attributes account for their effective and superior performance.' Roberts (1997) suggests that:

> The benefit of taking a competencies approach is that people can identify and isolate the key characteristics which would be used as the basis for selection, and that those characteristics will be described in terms which both can understand and agree... . The competencies therefore become a fundamental part of the selection process.

A competencies approach can help to identify which selection techniques, such as psychological testing or assessment centres, are most likely to produce useful evidence. It provides the information required to conduct a structured interview in which questions can focus on particular competency areas to establish the extent to which candidates meet the specification as set out in competency terms.

The advantages of a competency-based approach have been summarized by Wood and Payne (1998) as follows:

- It increases the accuracy of predictions about suitability.
- It facilitates a closer match between the person's attributes and the demands of the job.
- It helps to prevent interviewers making 'snap' judgements.
- It can underpin the whole range of recruitment techniques – application forms, interviews, tests and assessment centres.

The framework can be defined in terms of technical or work-based competencies, which refer to expectations of what people have to be able to do if they are going to achieve the results required in the job. It can also include definitions of required behavioural competencies, which refer to the personal characteristics and behaviour required for successful performance in such areas as interpersonal skills, leadership, personal drive, communication skills, team membership and analytical ability.

The competencies used for recruitment and selection purposes should meet the following criteria:

- They should focus on areas in which candidates will have demonstrated their competency in their working or academic life – eg leadership, teamwork, initiative.
- They are likely to predict successful job performance, eg achievement motivation.
- They can be assessed in a targeted behavioural event interview in which, for example, if team management is a key competence area, candidates can be asked to give examples of how they have successfully built a team and got it into action.
- They can be used as criteria in an assessment centre (see below).

A competency approach along these lines can provide the most effective means of identifying suitable candidates as part of a systematic selection process.

ATTRACTING CANDIDATES

Attracting candidates is primarily a matter of identifying, evaluating and using the most appropriate sources of applicants. However, in cases where difficulties in attracting or retaining candidates are being met or anticipated, it may be necessary to carry out a preliminary study of the factors that are likely to attract or repel candidates – the strengths and weaknesses of the organization as an employer.

Analysis of recruitment strengths and weaknesses

The analysis of strengths and weaknesses should cover such matters as the national or local reputation of the organization, pay, employee benefits and working conditions, the intrinsic interest of the job, security of employment, opportunities for education and training, career prospects, and the location of the office or plant. These need to be compared with the competition in order that a list of what are, in effect, selling points can be drawn up as in a marketing exercise, in which the preferences of potential customers are compared with the features of the product in order that those aspects that are likely to provide the most appeal to the customers can be emphasized. Candidates are, in a sense, selling themselves, but they are also buying what the organization has to offer. If, in the latter sense, the labour market is a buyer's market, then the company that is selling itself to candidates must study their needs in relation to what it can provide.

The aim of the study might be to prepare a better image of the organization (the employer brand) for use in advertisements, brochures or interviews. Or it might have the more con- structive aim of showing where the organization needs to improve as an employer if it is to attract more or better candidates *and* to retain those selected. The study could make use of an attitude survey to obtain the views of existing employees. One such survey mounted by the writer in an engineering company wishing to attract science graduates established that the main concern of the graduates was that they would be able to use and develop the knowledge they had gained at university. As a result, special brochures were written for each major discipline giving technical case histories of the sort of work graduates carried out. These avoided the purple passages used in some brochures (which the survey established were distinctly off-putting to most students) and proved to be a most useful recruitment aid. Strong measures were also taken to ensure that research managers made proper use of the graduates they recruited.

Sources of candidates

First consideration should be given to internal candidates, although some organizations with powerful equal opportunity policies (often local authorities) insist that all internal candidates should apply for vacancies on the same footing as external candidates. If there are no people available within the organization the main sources of candidates, as described below, are advertising, the internet, and outsourcing to consultants or agencies.

ADVERTISING

Advertising is the most obvious method of attracting candidates. Nevertheless, the first question to ask is whether an advertisement is really justified. This means looking at the alternative sources mentioned above and confirming, preferably on the basis of experience, that they will not do. Consideration should be given as to whether it might be better to use an agency or a selection consultant. When making the choice, refer to the three criteria of cost, speed and the likelihood of providing good candidates. The objectives of an advertisement should be to:

- *attract attention* – it must compete for the interest of potential candidates against other employers;
- *create and maintain interest* – it has to communicate in an attractive and interesting way information about the job, the company, the terms and conditions of employment and the qualifications required;
- *stimulate action* – the message needs to be conveyed in a manner that will not only focus people's eyes on the advertisement but also encourage them to read to the end, as well as prompt a sufficient number of replies from good candidates.

To achieve these aims, it is necessary to carry out the actions set out below.

Analyse the requirement, likely sources and job features

First it is necessary to establish how many jobs have to be filled and by when. Then turn to the job description and person specification to obtain information on responsibilities, qualifications and experience required.

The next step is to consider where suitable candidates are likely to come from; the companies, jobs or education establishments they are in; and the parts of the country where they can be found.

Finally, define the terms and conditions of the job (pay and benefits) and think about what about the job or the organization is likely to attract good candidates so that the most can be made of these factors in the advertisement. Consider also what might put them off, for example the location of the job, in order that objections can be anticipated. Analyse previous successes or failures to establish what does or does not work.

Decide who does what

When planning a campaign or recruiting key people, there is much to be said for using an advertising agency. An agency can provide expertise in producing eye-catching headlines and writing good copy. It can devise an attractive house style and prepare layouts that make the most of the text, the logo and any 'white space' round the advertisement. Moreover, it can advise on ways of achieving visual impact by the use of illustrations and special typographical features. Finally, an agency can advise on media, help in response analysis and take up the burden of placing advertisements.

The following steps should be taken when choosing an advertising agency:

- Check its experience in handling recruitment advertising.
- See examples of its work.
- Check with clients on the level of service provided.
- Meet the staff who will work on the advertisements.
- Check the fee structure.
- Discuss methods of working.

Write the copy

A recruitment advertisement should start with a compelling headline and then contain information on:

- the organization;
- the job;
- the person required – qualifications, experience etc;
- the pay and benefits offered;
- the location;
- the action to be taken.

The headline is all-important. The simplest and most obvious approach is to set out the job title in bold type. To gain attention, it is advisable to quote the salary (if it is worth quoting) and to put 'plus car' if a company car is provided. Salaries and cars are major attractions and should be stated clearly. Applicants are rightly suspicious of clauses such as 'salary will be commensurate with age and experience' or 'salary negotiable'. This usually means either that the salary is so low that the company is afraid to reveal it, or that salary policies are so incoherent that the company has no idea what to offer until someone tells them what he or she wants.

The name of the company should be given. Do not use box numbers – if you want to remain anonymous, use a consultant. Add any selling points, such as growth or diversification, and any other areas of interest to potential candidates, such as career prospects. The essential features of the job should be conveyed by giving a brief description of what the job holder will do and, as far as space permits, the scope and scale of activities. Create interest in the job but do not oversell it.

The qualifications and experience required should be stated as factually as possible. There is no point in overstating requirements and seldom any point in specifying exactly how much experience is wanted. This will vary from candidate to candidate, and the other details about the job and the rate of pay should provide them with enough information about the sort of experience required. Be careful about including a string of personal qualities such as drive, determination and initiative. These have no real meaning to candidates. Phrases such as 'proven track record' and 'successful experience' are equally meaningless. No one will admit to not having either of them.

The advertisement should end with information on how the candidate should apply. 'Brief but comprehensive details' is a good phrase. Candidates can be asked to write, but useful alternatives are to ask them to telephone or to come along for an informal chat at a suitable venue.

Remember that the Sex Discrimination Act 1975 makes it unlawful to discriminate in an advertisement by favouring either sex, the only exceptions being a few jobs that can be done only by one sex. Advertisements must therefore avoid sexist job titles such as 'salesman' or 'stewardess'. They must refer to a neutral title such as 'sales representative', or amplify the description to cover both sexes by stating 'steward or stewardess'. It is accepted, however, that certain job titles are unisex and therefore non-discriminatory. These include director, manager, executive and officer. It is best to avoid any reference to the sex of the candidate by using neutral or unisex titles and referring only to the 'candidate' or the 'applicant'. Otherwise you must specify 'man or woman' or 'he or she'.

The Race Relations Act 1976 has similar provisions, making unlawful an advertisement that discriminates against any particular race. As long as race is never mentioned or even implied in an advertisement, you should have no problem in keeping within the law.

Choose type of advertisement

The main types of advertisement are the following:

- Classified/run-on, in which copy is run on, with no white space in or around the advertisement and no paragraph spacing or indentation. They are cheap but suitable only for junior or routine jobs.

- Classified/semi-display, in which the headings can be set in capitals, paragraphs can be indented and white space is allowed round the advertisement. They are fairly cheap, and semi-display can be much more effective than run-on advertisements.
- Full display, which are bordered and in which any typeface and illustrations can be used. They can be expensive but obviously make the most impact for managerial, technical and professional jobs.

Plan the media

An advertising agency can advise on the choice of media (press, radio, television) and its cost. *British Rates and Data* (BRAD) can be consulted to give the costs of advertising in particular media.

The so-called 'quality papers' are best for managerial, professional and technical jobs. The popular press, especially evening papers, can be used to reach staff such as sales representatives and technicians. Local papers are obviously best for recruiting office staff and manual workers. Professional and trade journals can reach your audience directly, but results can be erratic and it may be advisable to use them to supplement a national campaign.

Avoid Saturdays and be cautious about repeating advertisements in the same medium. Diminishing returns can set in rapidly.

Evaluate the response

Measure response to provide guidance on the relative cost-effectiveness of different media. Cost per reply is the best ratio.

Successful recruitment advertisements

To summarize, a panel of creative experts (IRS, 2004f) made the following suggestions on what makes a recruitment advertisement successful:

- Do the groundwork – consider and analyse the recruiter's potential audience and the perceptions of existing employees.
- Prepare a thorough brief for the advertising agency, which expresses clearly the employer's idea of what to feed into the creative process – get the views of the employing manager on what is the strong selling point for the post.
- Have 'a good idea' behind the advertisement that contains a promise of a potential benefit for a jobseeker – there has to be a unique selling proposition.

- Remember that self-selection on the part of potential candidates is an important aim that can be achieved through careful presentation of information about the job and the success criteria.
- Ensure that the core information about the vacancy is included – a specification of the qualifications, experience, skills and attributes required, who jobseekers will be working for, where they will be working, and how much they will be earning. Consider providing enough hard data about the role to attract interest and then direct them to the corporate website where more information can be obtained.
- Project a realistic picture of the job, otherwise the result might be retention problems.
- Develop and communicate an employer brand that conveys a clear and positive image of the organization to attract job seekers and, incidentally but importantly, retain existing members of staff. Do not rely on the strength of the consumer brand in the market place – it is necessary to develop an employer brand that will communicate the fact that the organization offers a positive and rewarding employment experience.
- Consider the online approach (job boards, corporate websites) but remember that there will be a lot of potential candidates, especially older ones, who may not use the web and can best be attracted by traditional media. A multimedia approach may therefore be necessary.
- Bear in mind the considerable costs of media advertising (up to £17,000 for a fairly modest advertisement in *The Guardian*).
- Select an agency that fits the organization's culture, goals and values.
- Take care to act in accordance with equal opportunities and anti-discrimination legislation (sex, race, religion, marital status, disability and age). The Equal Opportunities Commission (1994) recommends that: 'Each advertisement needs to be considered as a whole in terms of the job advertised, the words used in the job description and the message that the advertiser is attempting to portray through the addition of an illustration.'
- Monitor the effectiveness of advertisements to establish which approach produced the best results.

E-RECRUITMENT

E-recruitment or online recruitment uses web-based tools such as a firm's public internet site or its own intranet to recruit staff. The processes of e-recruitment consist of attracting, screening and tracking applicants, selecting, and offering jobs or rejecting candidates. It has been estimated by Cappelli (2001) that it costs only about one-twentieth as much to hire someone online, if that is the only method used, as it does to hire the same person through traditional methods.

Advantages

E-recruitment not only saves costs but also enables organizations to provide much more information to applicants, which can easily be updated. There is more scope to present the 'employment proposition' in terms that increase the attractiveness of the company as a place in which to work.

The options available for online selection include self-assessments, online screening and psychometric testing online. Online tests can be standardized and scored easily.

Usage

An IRS (2004a) survey established that 84 per cent of employers made some use of electronic recruitment. It was noted by IRS that the internet is now a fundamental part of the recruitment process. At the very least, employers are utilizing the internet and e-mail systems to communicate with candidates and support their existing hiring practices. Many organizations also use their corporate website.

The IRS survey found that organizations have made a strategic decision to cut the costs of their recruitment processes and get better value for money, and have turned to the internet to achieve this. However, a significant proportion of users still encounter problems with the use of e-recruitment, generally receiving too many unsuitable candidates. Some organizations address this through the use of self-selection tools such as a self-selection questionnaire to discourage unsuitable applicants. IRS comments that this approach means that: 'Subtly and sensitively, organizations can let candidates know that this may not be the role for them, while maintaining their goodwill and self-esteem.'

Some organizations use 'job boards' to advertise vacancies (a job board is an internet site that hosts recruitment advertisements from a range of employers), often as a portal to their corporate website. Most companies are prepared to communicate with candidates by e-mail about their applications.

The IRS survey established that almost all private sector firms using e-recruiting accepted CVs. Organizations in the public sector were more likely to despatch application forms by e-mail.

The National Online Recruitment Survey (2003) found that the average online job seeker is 33 years old with more than 11 years' work experience; he or she has been with the same employer for more than four years, and has visited more than five online sites in a quest for new employment.

An IRS (2004a) survey of recruitment methods for managers established that the top three methods of recruitment, based on the quality of the applications received, were the use of commercial employment agencies (32 per cent), advertising in specialist journals (23 per cent), and national newspaper advertising (22 per cent). Only 3 per cent rated e-recruiting as the best method, although 56 per cent used it. The favourite method of recruitment remains interviewing (53 per cent) followed by assessment centres (23 per cent).

Typical approach

A typical approach is to advertise the vacancy on an online recruitment site. This will provide job details and information about the company together with an online application form. A job seeker returns the completed application electronically and computer software reviews the application forms for an initial match with the organisation's requirements. For example, a job offer for a business development manager in a computer firm might specify the following competencies as a basis for matching on the site against a CV, or by the employer against details provided by the candidate for each of the competence areas:

- Minimum 10 years' business and sales experience in the computer, networking or communications industry.
- Good exposure to the network consulting world, within UK.
- Formal sales training very desirable.
- Self-motivated to succeed in position.
- Ability to lead and manage small group of sales personnel.
- Strong organizational and prioritization skills.
- Ability to drive opportunities to closure.

Sites

The main types of online recruitment sites are:

- *Job sites* – these are operated by specialized firms and can contain over 100,000 vacancies with 6 or 7 million 'hits' a month. Companies pay to have their jobs listed on the sites, which are not usually linked to agencies.
- *Agency sites* – are run by established recruitment agencies. Candidates register online but may be expected to discuss their details in person before their details are forwarded to a prospective employer.
- *Media sites* – which may simply contain a copy of an advertisement appearing in the press, but may include an external description of the vacancy and the company and provide a link to the company's website.

OUTSOURCING RECRUITMENT

There is much to be said for outsourcing recruitment – getting agencies or consultants to carry out at least the preliminary work of submitting suitable candidates or drawing up a short list. It costs money, but it can save a lot of time and trouble.

Using agencies

Most private agencies deal with secretarial and office staff. They are usually quick and effective but quite expensive. Agencies can charge a fee of 15 per cent or more of the first year's salary for finding someone. It can be cheaper to advertise, especially when the company is in a buyer's market. Shop around to find the agency that suits the organization's needs at a reasonable cost.

Agencies should be briefed carefully on what is wanted. They produce unsuitable candidates from time to time but the risk is reduced if they are clear about your requirements.

Using recruitment consultants

Recruitment consultants generally advertise, interview and produce a short list. They provide expertise and reduce workload. The organization can be anonymous if it wishes. Most recruitment consultants charge a fee based on a percentage of the basic salary for the job, usually ranging from 15 to 20 per cent.

The following steps should be taken when choosing a recruitment consultant:

- Check reputation with other users.
- Look at the advertisements of the various firms in order to obtain an idea of the quality of a consultancy and the type and level of jobs with which it deals.
- Check on special expertise – the large accountancy firms, for example, are obviously skilled in recruiting accountants.
- Meet the consultant who will work on the assignment to assess his or her quality.
- Compare fees, although the differences are likely to be small, and the other considerations are usually more important.

When using recruitment consultants it is necessary to:

- agree terms of reference;
- brief them on the organization, where the job fits in, why the appointment is to be made, terms and conditions and any special requirements;

- give them every assistance in defining the job and the person specification, including any special demands that will be made on the successful candidate in the shape of what he or she will be expected to achieve – they will do much better if they have comprehensive knowledge of what is required and what type of person is most likely to fit well into the organization;
- check carefully the proposed programme and the draft text of the advertisement;
- clarify the arrangements for interviewing and short-listing;
- clarify the basis upon which fees and expenses will be charged;
- ensure that arrangements are made to deal directly with the consultant who will handle the assignment.

Using executive search consultants

Use an executive search consultant, or 'head-hunter', for senior jobs where there are only a limited number of suitable people and a direct lead to them is wanted. They are not cheap. Head-hunters charge a fee of 30 to 50 per cent or so of the first year's salary, but they can be quite cost-effective.

Executive search consultants first approach their own contacts in the industry or profession concerned. The good ones have an extensive range of contacts and their own data bank. They will also have researchers who will identify suitable people who may fit the specification or can provide a lead to someone else who may be suitable. The more numerous the contacts, the better the executive search consultant.

When a number of potentially suitable and interested people have been assembled, a fairly relaxed and informal meeting takes place and the consultant forwards a short list with full reports on candidates to the client.

There are some good and some not-so-good executive search consultants. Do not use one unless a reliable recommendation is obtained.

EDUCATIONAL AND TRAINING ESTABLISHMENTS

Many jobs can, of course, be filled by school leavers. For some organizations the major source of recruits for training schemes will be universities and training establishments as well as schools. Graduate recruitment is a major annual exercise for some companies, which go to great efforts to produce glossy brochures, visit campuses on the 'milk run' and use elaborate sifting and selection procedures to vet candidates, including 'biodata' and assessment centres, as described later in this chapter, and the internet.

APPLICATION FORMS

Application forms set out the information on a candidate in a standardized format. They provide a structured basis for drawing up short lists, the interview itself and for the subsequent actions in offering an appointment and in setting up personnel records. An example of a form is given in Figure 27.2.

The following suggestions have been made by Pioro and Baum (2005) on how to use application forms more effectively:

- Decide what the criteria for selection are and how these will be assessed by use of the application form.
- Keep questions clear, relevant and non-discriminatory.
- Ask for only the bare minimum of personal details.
- Widen your pool of applicants by offering different options and guidance for completing and viewing application forms.
- Develop a consistent and effective sifting process.
- Use a team of sifters from a range of backgrounds to represent the diversity of your candidates.
- Review how effective you have been at the end of the process and once the successful candidates are in their roles.

SIFTING APPLICATIONS

When the vacancy or vacancies have been advertised and a fair number of replies received, the typical sequence of steps required to process and sift applications is as follows:

1. List the applications on a control sheet, setting out name, date the application was received and the actions taken (reject, hold, interview, short list, offer).
2. Send a standard acknowledgement letter to each applicant unless an instant decision can be made to interview or reject.
3. The applicant may be asked to complete and return an application form to supplement a letter or CV which may be on paper or in electronic format. This ensures that all applicants are considered on the same basis – it can be very difficult to plough through a pile of letters, often ill-written and badly organized. Even CVs may be difficult to sift, although their quality is likely to be higher if the applicant has been receiving advice from an 'outplacement' consultant, ie one who specializes in finding people jobs. However, to save time, trouble, expense and irritation, many recruiters prefer to make a decision on the initial letter plus

APPLICATION FORM			
Surname:		First name:	
Address:			
Tel: (home)	Tel: (work)	e-mail (personal)	
Position applied for:			
Education			

Education

Dates		Name of secondary school, college or university	Main subjects taken	Qualifications
From	To			

Specialized training received

Other qualifications and skills (including languages, keyboard skills, current driving licence etc

Employment history
(give details of all positions held since completing full-time education, start with your present or most recent position and work back)

Dates		Name of employer, address and nature of business including any service in the armed forces	Position and summary of main duties	Starting and leaving rate of pay	Reasons for leaving or wanting to leave
From	To				

Figure 27.2 Example of an application form (compressed)

Add any comments you wish to make to support your application

I confirm that the information given on this application form is correct

Signature of
applicant .... Date ....

Figure 27.2 *continued*

CV, where it is quite clear that an applicant meets or does not meet the specification, rather than ask for a form. It is generally advisable for more senior jobs to ask for a CV.

4. Compare the applications with the key criteria in the job specification and sort them initially into three categories: possible, marginal and unsuitable.

5. Scrutinize the possibles again to draw up a short list for interview. This scrutiny could be carried out by the personnel or employment specialist and, preferably, the manager. The numbers on the short list should ideally be between four and eight. Fewer than four leaves relatively little choice (although such a limitation may be forced on you if an insufficient number of good applications have been received). More than eight will mean that too much time is spent on interviewing and there is a danger of diminishing returns setting in.

6. Draw up an interviewing programme. The time you should allow for the interview will vary according to the complexity of the job. For a fairly routine job, 30 minutes or so should suffice. For a more senior job, 60 minutes or more is required. It is best not to schedule too many interviews in a day – if you try to carry out more than five or six exacting interviews you will quickly run out of steam and do neither the interviewee nor your company any justice. It is advisable to leave about 15 minutes between interviews to write up notes and prepare for the next one.

7. Invite the candidates to interview, using a standard letter where large numbers are involved. At this stage, candidates should be asked to complete an

application form, if they have not already done so. There is much to be said at this stage for sending candidates some details of the organization and the job so that you do not have to spend too much time going through this information at the interview.

8. Review the remaining possibles and marginals and decide if any are to be held in reserve. Send reserves a standard 'holding' letter and send the others a standard rejection letter. The latter should thank candidates for the interest shown and inform them briefly, but not too brusquely, that they have not been successful. A typical reject letter might read as follows:

> Since writing to you on… we have given careful consideration to your application for the above position. I regret to inform you, however, that we have decided not to ask you to attend for an interview. We should like to thank you for the interest you have shown.

The process described above should be controlled by an applicant tracking system (ATS) as part of a computerized recruitment control process.

Biodata

A highly structured method of sifting applications is provided by the use of biodata. These are items of biographical data which are criterion based (ie they relate to established criteria in such terms as qualifications and experience which indicate that individuals are likely to be suitable). These are objectively scored and, by measurements of past achievements, predict future behaviour.

The items of biodata consist of demographic details (sex, age, family circumstances), education and professional qualifications, previous employment history and work experience, positions of responsibility outside work, leisure interests and career/job motivation. These items are weighted according to their relative importance as predictors, and a range of scores is allocated to each one. The biodata questionnaire (essentially a detailed application form) obtains information on each item, which is then scored.

Biodata are most useful when a large number of applicants are received for a limited number of posts. Cut-off scores can then be determined, based on previous experience. These scores would indicate who should be accepted for the next stage of the selection process and who should be rejected, but they would allow for some possible candidates to be held until the final cut-off score can be fixed after the first batch of applicants have been screened.

Biodata criteria and predictors are selected by job and functional analysis, which produces a list of competences. The validity of these items as predictors and the weighting to be given to them are established by analysing the biodata of existing employees who are grouped into high or low performers. Weights are allocated to items according to the discriminating power of the response.

Biodata questionnaires and scoring keys are usually developed for specific jobs in an organization. Their validity compares reasonably well with other selection instruments, but they need to be developed and validated with great care and they are only applicable when large groups of applicants have to be screened.

Electronic CVs

Electronic CVs are associated with internet recruiting. Computers can read CVs by means of high-grade, high-speed scanners using optical character recognition (OCR) software. CVs are scanned and converted into basic text format. The system's artificial intelligence reads the text and extracts key data such as personal details, skills, educational qualifications, previous employers and jobs, and relevant dates. Search criteria are created listing mandatory and preferred requirements such as qualifications, companies in which applicants have worked and jobs held. The system carries out an analysis of the CVs against these criteria, lists the candidates that satisfy all the mandatory requirements and ranks them by the number of these requirements each one meets. The recruiter can then use this ranking as a short list or can tighten the search criteria to produce a shorter list. Essentially, the computer is looking for the same key words as human recruiters, but it can carry out this task more systematically and faster, cross-referencing skills. Any recruiter knows the problem of dealing with a large number of applications and trying, often against the odds, to extract a sensible short list.

SELECTION METHODS

The main selection methods are the interview, assessment centres and tests. The various types of interviews and assessment centres are described in the next two sections of this chapter. Interviewing techniques are dealt with separately in Chapter 28. Tests are described in Chapter 29. Another and much more dubious method, used by a few firms in the UK and more extensively in the rest of Europe, is graphology.

TYPES OF INTERVIEWS

Individual interviews

The individual interview is the most familiar method of selection. It involves face-to-face discussion and provides the best opportunity for the establishment of close contact – rapport – between the interviewer and the candidate. If only one interviewer is used, there is more scope for a biased or superficial decision, and this is one reason for using a second interviewer or an interviewing panel.

Interviewing panels

Two or more people gathered together to interview one candidate may be described as an interviewing panel. The most typical situation is that in which a personnel manager and line managers see the candidate at the same time. This has the advantage of enabling information to be shared and reducing overlaps. The interviewers can discuss their joint impressions of the candidate's behaviour at the interview and modify or enlarge any superficial judgements.

Selection boards

Selection boards are more formal and, usually, larger interviewing panels, convened by an official body because there are a number of parties interested in the selection decision. Their only advantage is that they enable a number of different people to have a look at the applicants and compare notes on the spot. The disadvantages are that the questions tend to be unplanned and delivered at random, the prejudices of a dominating member of the board can overwhelm the judgements of the other members, and the candidates are unable to do justice to themselves because they are seldom allowed to expand. Selection boards tend to favour the confident and articulate candidate, but in doing so they may miss the underlying weaknesses of a superficially impressive individual. They can also underestimate the qualities of those who happen to be less effective in front of a formidable board, although they would be fully competent in the less formal or less artificial situations that would face them in the job.

ASSESSMENT CENTRES

A more comprehensive approach to selection is provided by the use of assessment centres. These incorporate a range of assessment techniques and typically have the following features:

- The focus of the centre is on behaviour.
- Exercises are used to capture and simulate the key dimensions of the job. These include one-to-one role-plays and group exercises. It is assumed that performance in these simulations predicts behaviour on the job.
- Interviews and tests will be used in addition to group exercises.
- Performance is measured in several dimensions in terms of the competencies required to achieve the target level of performance in a particular job or at a particular level in the organization.
- Several candidates or participants are assessed together to allow interaction and to make the experience more open and participative.
- Several assessors or observers are used in order to increase the objectivity of assessments. Involving senior managers is desirable to ensure that they 'own' the process. Assessors must be carefully trained.

Assessment centres provide good opportunities for indicating the extent to which candidates match the culture of the organization. This will be established by observation of their behaviour in different but typical situations, and by the range of the tests and structured interviews that are part of the proceedings. Assessment centres also give candidates a better feel for the organization and its values so that they can decide for themselves whether or not they are likely to fit.

A well-conducted assessment centre can achieve a better forecast of future performance and progress than judgements made by line or even personnel managers in the normal, unskilled way.

GRAPHOLOGY

Graphology can be defined as the study of the social structure of a human being through his or her writing. Its use in selection is to draw conclusions about a candidate's personality from his or her handwriting as a basis for making predictions about future performance in a role. The use of graphology as a selection aid is extensive on the Continent but relatively uncommon in the UK – Fowler (1991a) quotes research findings that indicate that only between 0.5 and 1.0 per cent of employers use it in the UK. This very small proportion may be attributed to the suspicion the great majority of recruiters have that graphology is in some way spurious and using it as a predictor will be a waste of time and money. In an extensive review of the research literature, Fowler (1991a) established that some studies had indicated a predictive validity coefficient in the range of 0.1 to 0.3, although zero results have also been obtained. These are low figures, which achieve only a poor level of validity. Fowler's conclusion was that clues about personality characteristics may be deduced by skilled graphologists but that the use of graphology as a single or standard predictor cannot be recommended. He also suspects that, for some people, the real attraction of graphology is that it can be used without the subject's knowledge.

CHOICE OF SELECTION METHODS

There is a choice between the main selection methods. What Cook (1993) refers to as the classic trio consists of application forms, interviews and references. These can be supplemented or replaced by biodata, assessment centres and, as described in Chapter 29, psychological tests. It has been demonstrated again and again that interviews are an inefficient method of predicting success in a job. Smart (1983), for example, claims that only 94 out of 1,000 interviewees respond honestly in conventional interviews. Validity studies such as those quoted by Taylor (1998), as illustrated in Figure 27.3, produce equally dubious figures for conventional interviews and indicate that assessment centres, psychometric tests, biodata and structured interviews are more accurate methods of selection. For good and not so good reasons, organizations will retain interviews as the main method of selection where assessment centres are inappropriate. But there is a very powerful case for structuring the interview and a strong case for supplementing it with tests. The more evidence that can be produced to help in making crucial selection decisions, the better.

IMPROVING THE EFFECTIVENESS OF RECRUITMENT AND SELECTION

An HRM approach can be adopted to recruitment, which involves taking much more care in matching people to the requirements of the organization as a whole as well as to the particular needs of the job. And these requirements will include commitment and ability to work effectively as a member of a team.

Examples of this approach in Japanese companies in the UK include the establishment of the Nissan plant in Washington and Kumatsu in Newcastle. As described by Townley (1989), both followed a conscious recruitment policy with rigorous selection procedures. Aptitude tests, personality questionnaires and group exercises were used and the initial pre-screening device was a detailed 'biodata'-type questionnaire, which enabled the qualifications and work history of candidates to be assessed and rated systematically. Subsequent testing of those who successfully completed the first stage was designed to assess individual attitudes as well as aptitude and ability. As

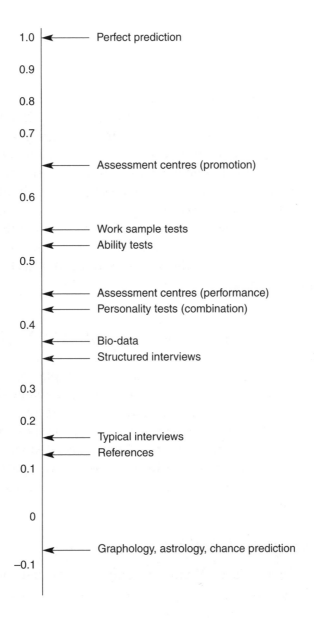

Figure 27.3 Accuracy of some methods of selection

(Reproduced with permission from Stephen Taylor (1998) *Employee Resourcing*, Institute of Personnel and Development)

Wickens (1987) said of the steps taken at Nissan to achieve commitment and team working: 'It is something which develops because management genuinely believes in it and acts accordingly – and recruits or promotes people who have the same belief.'

The need for a more sophisticated approach to recruitment along these lines is characteristic of HRM. The first requirement is to take great care in specifying the competences and behavioural characteristics required of employees. The second is to use a wider range of methods to identify candidates who match the specification. As noted earlier in this chapter, the predictive quality of the traditional interview is very limited. At the very least, structured interviewing techniques should be adopted as described in Chapter 28. Wherever possible, psychological tests should be used to extend the data obtained from the interview. Well-planned and administered assessment centres are the best predictors of success in a job, but they are only practical for a limited number of more complex or demanding jobs or for selecting graduates and entrants to training programmes.

REFERENCES, QUALIFICATIONS AND OFFERS

After the interviewing and testing procedure has been completed, a provisional decision to make an offer by telephone or in writing can be made. This is normally 'subject to satisfactory references' and the candidate should, of course, be told that these will be taken up. If there is more than one eligible candidate for a job it may be advisable to hold one or two people in reserve. Applicants often withdraw, especially those whose only purpose in applying for the job was to carry out a 'test marketing' operation, or to obtain a lever with which to persuade their present employers to value them more highly.

References – purpose and method

The purpose of a reference is to obtain in confidence factual information about a prospective employee and opinions about his or her character and suitability for a job.

The factual information is straightforward and essential. It is simply necessary to confirm the nature of the previous job, the period of time in employment, the reason for leaving (if relevant), the salary or rate of pay and, possibly, the attendance record.

Opinions about character and suitability are less reliable and should be treated with caution. The reason is obvious. Previous or present employers who give references tend to avoid highly detrimental remarks either out of charity or because they think anything they say or write may be construed as slanderous or libellous (references are, in fact, privileged as long as they are given without malice and are factually correct).

Personal referees are, of course, entirely useless. All they prove is that the applicant has at least one or two friends.

Written references save time, especially if they are standardized. They may take the form of an invitation to write a letter confirming the employment record and commenting on the applicant's character in general. If brief details about the job are included (these may be an extract from the advertisement – they should certainly not be an over-elaborate job description), previous employers can be asked to express their views about the suitability of the individual for the job. But this is asking a lot. Unless the job and companies are identical, how well can existing or ex-employers judge the suitability of someone they may not know particularly well for another job in a different environment?

More factual answers may be obtained if a standard form is provided for the employer to complete. The questions asked on this form could include:

- What was the period of employment?
- What was the job title?
- What work was carried out?
- What was the rate of pay or salary?
- How many days' absence over the last 12 months?
- Would you re-employ (if not, why not)?

Telephone references may be used as an alternative or in addition to written references. The great advantage of a telephone conversation is that people are more likely to give an honest opinion orally than if they have to commit themselves in writing. It may also save time to use the telephone.

Employer references are necessary to check on the facts given by the prospective employee. Opinions have to be treated with more caution. A very glowing reference may arouse suspicion, and it is worth comparing it with a reference from another employer (two employment references are desirable in any case). Poor or grudging references must create some alarm, if only because they are so infrequent. But allowance should be made for prejudice and a check should be made, by telephone if possible.

References – legal aspects

The key legal points that should be considered when asking for or giving references are:

- Once the decision has been made to make an offer, the letter should state that 'this is a provisional offer subject to references satisfactory to the company being received'.
- It has been generally held that there is no common law duty on an employer to provide references for a serving or past employee unless there is a term to that effect in the employment contract. But it has been ruled (*Spring* v *Guardian Assurance* 1994) that there might be a 'contractual duty' to provide a reference where it is 'natural practice' to require a reference from a previous employer before offering employment, and where the employee could not expect to enter that type of employment without a reference.
- If a reference contains a false or unsubstantiated statement that damages the reputation of the individual, action for damages may result.
- It is possible to succeed in a claim for damages if it can be shown that the reference provided was negligent because, if the facts had been checked, they would have been found to be groundless.
- Referees have a legal liability to the prospective employer not to give a reference that contains 'material factors' which were known to be untrue. If an employer appointed someone on the basis of a reference and found that the employee was unsuitable in respect of a material factor given in that reference, the employer can initiate legal action alleging 'deceit'. Employers can try to protect themselves by adding the phrase 'without legal responsibility' to any references given, but this does not provide a certain defence.

Qualifications

It has been estimated by the CIPD (2005c) that one in eight candidates exaggerate or falsify their qualifications. One in four companies had to withdraw a job offer because of CV fraud in 2004, and a similar number sacked someone for the same offence. If a qualification is a necessary requirement for the job, it is always worth checking with the university or college concerned, or asking the candidate to produce evidence in the shape of a certificate or diploma.

FINAL STAGES

Confirming the offer

The final stage in the selection procedure is to confirm the offer of employment after satisfactory references have been obtained, and the applicant has passed the medical examination required for pension and life assurance purposes or because a certain standard of physical fitness is required for the work. The contract of employment should also be prepared at this stage.

Contracts of employment

The basic information that should be included in a written contract of employment varies according to the level of job. Contracts of employment are dealt with in Chapter 57.

Follow-up

It is essential to follow up newly engaged employees to ensure that they have settled in and to check on how well they are doing. If there are any problems, it is much better to identify them at an early stage rather than allowing them to fester.

Following up is also important as a means of checking on the selection procedure. If by any chance a mistake has been made, it is useful to find out how it happened so that the selection procedure can be improved. Misfits can be attributed to a number of causes; for example, inadequate job description or specification, poor sourcing of candidates, weak advertising, poor interviewing techniques, inappropriate or invalidated tests, or prejudice on the part of the selector. If any of these are identified, steps can be taken to prevent their recurrence.

28

Selection interviewing

The techniques and skills of selection interviewing are described in this chapter under the following headings:

- purpose;
- advantages and disadvantages of interviews;
- nature of an interview;
- interviewing arrangements;
- preparation;
- timing;
- planning and structuring interviews;
- interviewing approaches;
- interview techniques – starting and finishing;
- interviewing techniques – asking questions;
- selection interviewing skills;
- coming to a conclusion;
- dos and don'ts of selection interviewing.

PURPOSE

The purpose of the selection interview is to obtain and assess information about a candidate which will enable a valid prediction to be made of his or her future performance in the job in comparison with the predictions made for any other candidates. Interviewing therefore involves processing and evaluating evidence about the capabilities of a candidate in relation to the person specification. Some of the evidence will be on the application form, but the aim of the interview is to supplement this data with the more detailed or specific information about competencies, attitudes, experience and personal characteristics that can be obtained in a face-to-face meeting. Such a meeting also provides an opportunity for judgements by the interviewer on whether the individual will 'fit' the organization, and by both parties as to how they would get on together. Although these judgements are entirely subjective and are often biased or prejudiced, it has to be recognized that they will be made.

In particular, selection interviews aim to provide answers to these questions:

- *Can* individuals do the job – are they competent?
- *Will* individuals do the job – are they well motivated?
- *How* will individuals fit into the organization?

The interview forms a major part of the 'classic trio' of selection techniques, the other two being the application form and references. Further evidence may be obtained from psychological tests as described in Chapter 29 but, in spite of the well-publicized inadequacies of interviews as reliable means of predicting success in a job, they are still an inevitable part of a selection procedure for most people. This chapter focuses on the advantages and disadvantages of interviews, the nature of an interview and methods of carrying out effective interviews, effective in that they provide reliable and valid predictions.

ADVANTAGES AND DISADVANTAGES OF INTERVIEWS

The advantages of interviews as a method of selection are that they:

- provide opportunities for interviewers to ask probing questions about the candidate's experience and to explore the extent to which the candidate's competences match those specified for the job;
- enable interviewers to describe the job (a 'realistic job preview') and the organization in more detail, suggesting some of the terms of the psychological contract;
- provide opportunities for candidates to ask questions about the job and to clarify issues concerning training, career prospects, the organization and terms and conditions of employment;

- enable a face-to-face encounter to take place so that the interviewer can make an assessment of how the candidate would fit into the organization and what he or she would be like to work with;
- give the candidate the same opportunity to assess the organization, the interviewer and the job.

The disadvantages of interviews are that they:

- can lack validity as a means of making sound predictions of performance, and lack reliability in the sense of measuring the same things for different candidates;
- rely on the skill of the interviewer; but many people are poor at interviewing, although most think that they are good at it;
- do not necessarily assess competence in meeting the demands of the particular job;
- can lead to biased and subjective judgements by interviewers.

However, these disadvantages can be alleviated if not entirely removed, first, by using a structured approach that focuses on the competences and attitudes required for successful performance and, secondly, by training interviewers. The use of another opinion or other opinions can also help to reduce bias, especially if the same structured approach is adopted by all the interviewers.

THE NATURE OF AN INTERVIEW

An interview can be described as a conversation with a purpose. It is a conversation because candidates should be induced to talk freely with their interviewers about themselves, their experience and their careers. But the conversation has to be planned, directed and controlled to achieve the main purpose of the interview, which is to make an accurate prediction of the candidate's future performance in the job for which he or she is being considered.

However, interviews also provide a valuable opportunity for an exchange of information, which will enable both parties to make a decision: to offer or not to offer a job; to accept or not to accept the offer. It may be better for the candidates to 'de-select' themselves at this stage if they do not like what they hear about the job or the company rather than take on a disagreeable job. Interviews are often used to give the candidates a favourable impression of the organization and the job. But this must be realistic – a 'realistic job preview' will spell out any special demands that will be made on the successful applicant in terms of the standards they will be expected to achieve, the hours they may have to work, the travelling they have to do and any requirement for mobility in the UK or abroad. Clearly, if these are onerous, it will be necessary to convince good candidates that the rewards will be commensurate with the requirements. If poor candidates are put off, so much the better.

Good interviewers know what they are looking for and how to set about finding it. They have a method for recording their analyses of candidates against a set of assessment criteria, which will be spelt out in a person specification.

INTERVIEWING ARRANGEMENTS

The interviewing arrangements will depend partly on the procedure being used, which may consist of individual interviews, an interviewing panel, a selection board or some form of assessment centre, sometimes referred to as a group selection procedure. In most cases, however, the arrangements for the interviews should conform broadly to the following pattern:

- The candidate who has applied in writing or by telephone should be told where and when to come and for whom to ask. The interview time should be arranged to fit in with the time it will take to get to the company. It may be necessary to adjust times for those who cannot get away during working hours. If the company is difficult to find, a map should be sent with details of public transport. The receptionist or security guard should be told who is coming. Candidates are impressed to find that they are expected
- Applicants should have somewhere quiet and comfortable in which to wait for the interview, with reading material available and access to cloakroom facilities.
- The interviewers or interviewing panel should have been well briefed on the programme. Interviewing rooms should have been booked and arrangements made, as necessary, for welcoming candidates, for escorting them to interviews, for meals and for a conducted tour round the company.
- Comfortable private rooms should be provided for interviews with little, if any, distractions around them. Interviewers should preferably not sit behind their desks, as this creates a psychological barrier.
- During the interview or interviews, some time, but not too much, should be allowed to tell candidates about the company and the job and to discuss with them conditions of employment. Negotiations about pay and other benefits may take place after a provisional offer has been made, but it is as well to prepare the ground during the interviewing stage.
- Candidates should be told what the next step will be at the end of the interview. They may be asked at this stage if they have any objections to references being taken up.

● Follow-up studies should be carried out, comparing the performance of successful candidates in their jobs with the prediction made at the selection stage. These studies should be used to validate the selection procedure and to check on the capabilities of interviewers.

Briefing interviewers

When making arrangements for an interview it is essential that the people who are going to conduct the interview are properly briefed on the job and the procedures they should use. There is everything to be said for including training in interviewing techniques as an automatic part of the training programmes for managers and team leaders.

It is particularly important that everyone is fully aware of the provisions of the Sex, Race and Disability Discrimination Acts. It is essential that any form of prejudiced behaviour or any prejudiced judgements are eliminated completely from the interview and the ensuing discussion. Even the faintest hint of a sexist or racist remark must be totally avoided. When recording a decision following an interview it is also essential to spell out the reasons why someone was rejected, making it clear that this was absolutely on the grounds of their qualifications for the job and had nothing to do with their sex, race or disability.

Ethical considerations

Another important consideration in planning and executing a recruitment programme is to behave ethically towards candidates. They have the right to be treated with consideration and this includes acknowledging replies and informing them of the outcome of their application without undue delay.

Planning the interview programme

It is best to leave some time, say 15 minutes, between interviews to allow for comments to be made. There is a limit to how many interviews can be conducted in a day without running out of steam, and holding more than six demanding interviews of, say, one hour each in a day is unwise. Even with less demanding half-hour interviews it is preferable to limit the number to eight or so in a day.

PREPARATION

Careful preparation is essential and this means a careful study of the person specification and the candidate's application form and/or CV. It is necessary at this stage to identify those features of the applicant that do not fully match the specification so that these can be probed more deeply during the interview. It can be assumed that the candidate is only being considered because there is a reasonable match, but it is most unlikely that this match will be perfect. It is also necessary to establish if there are any gaps in the job history or items that require further explanation.

There are three fundamental questions that need to be answered at this stage:

- What are the criteria to be used in selecting the candidate – these may be classified as essential or desirable and will refer to the experience, qualifications, and competency and skill requirements as set out in the person specification.
- What more do I need to find out at the interview to ensure that the candidate meets the essential selection criteria?
- What further information do I need to obtain at the interview to ensure that I have an accurate picture of how well the candidate meets the criteria?

The preparation should include making notes of the specific questions the interviewer needs to ask to establish the relevance of the candidate's experience and the extent to which he or she has the skills, knowledge, levels of competency and attitudes required. These may be quite detailed if a highly structured approach is being adopted as described below – it is essential to probe during an interview to establish what the candidate really can do and has achieved. Applicants will generally aim to make the most of themselves and this can lead to exaggerated, even false, claims about their experience and capabilities.

TIMING

The length of time allowed for an interview will be related to the seniority and complexity of the job. For relatively routine jobs, 20 to 30 minutes may suffice. For more demanding jobs, up to an hour may be necessary. Interviews should rarely, if ever, exceed an hour.

PLANNING AND STRUCTURING INTERVIEWS

The problem with interviews is that they are often inadequate as predictors of performance – an hour's interview may not cover the essential points unless it is carefully planned and, sadly, the general standard of interviewing is low. This is not simply a result of many people using poor interviewing techniques (eg they talk rather than listen). More importantly, it is a result of not carrying out a proper analysis of the competencies required, with the result that interviewers do not know the information they need to obtain from the candidate as a basis for structuring the interview.

There are a number of methods of conducting interviews. At their worst, interviewers adopt an entirely unstructured approach, which involves asking random questions that are not based on any understanding of what they are looking for. At best, they are clearly structured and related to a thorough analysis of role requirements in terms of skills and competencies.

Generally, an interview can be divided into five parts:

1. the welcome and introductory remarks;
2. the major part concerned with obtaining information about the candidate to assess against the person specification;
3. the provision of information to candidates about the organization and the job;.
4. answering questions from the candidate;
5. closing the interview with an indication of the next step.

The bulk of the time – at least 80 per cent – should be allocated to obtaining information from the candidate. The introduction and conclusion should be brief, though friendly.

The two traditional ways of planning an interview are to adopt a biographical approach or to follow the assessment headings in, for example, the seven-point plan. These approaches are sometimes classified as 'unstructured interviews' in contrast to the 'structured interview', which is generally regarded as best practice. The latter term usually has the special meaning of referring to interviews that are structured around situational-based or behavioural-based questions, focusing on one or other or both. The common element is that the questions are prepared in advance and are related to the role analysis and person specification in terms of the things candidates will be expected to do and/or the behaviour they will be expected to demonstrate. But it could be argued that a biographical or assessment heading approach is 'structured', although they may not relate so specifically to identified role requirements. A further but less common variety of structured interview is psychometric-based. All these approaches are examined below.

INTERVIEWING APPROACHES

The biographical interview

The traditional biographical interview either starts at the beginning (education) and goes on in sequence to the end (the current or last job or the most recent educational experience), or proceeds in the opposite direction, starting with the present job and going backwards to the first job and the candidate's education or training. Many interviewers prefer to go backwards with experienced candidates, spending most time on the present or recent jobs, giving progressively less attention to the earlier experience, and only touching on education lightly.

There is no one best sequence to follow but it is important to decide in advance which to adopt. It is also important to get the balance right. You should concentrate most on recent experience and not dwell too much on the distant past. You should allow time not only to the candidate to talk about his or her career but also to ask probing questions as necessary. You should certainly not spend too much time at the beginning of the interview talking about the company and the job. It is highly desirable to issue that information in advance to save interview time and simply encourage the candidate to ask questions at the end of the interview (the quality of the questions can indicate something about the quality of the candidate).

This form of plan is logical but it will not produce the desired information unless interviewers are absolutely clear about what they are looking for and are prepared with questions that will elicit the data they need to make a selection decision.

Interview planned by reference to a person specification

The person specification as described in Chapter 27 provides a sound basis for a structured interview. The aim is to obtain information under each of the main headings to indicate the extent to which the candidate matches the specification. Typical headings are:

- *knowledge, skills and expertise* – what the candidate is expected to know and be able to do as a result of experience, education and training (work-based competencies), for example, technical or professional knowledge, numeracy, manual skills, and experience at the appropriate level in carrying out relevant work;
- *personal qualities* – how the candidate will be expected to behave in carrying out the job, such as working with other people, exercising leadership, influencing people, communicating (eg report writing, making presentations) achieving results, decision-making, taking the initiative, and being self-reliant (behavioural competencies);
- *qualifications* – essential academic or professional qualifications.

A 'person specification' setting out such requirements can be sent to candidates (or posted on an online recruitment site). The applicant is asked to respond with information on how they believe they match these requirements. This approach can make it much easier to sift applications.

Interviews planned by reference to assessment headings

Assessment headings such as those described in Chapter 27 can be used. They define a number of areas in which information can be generated and assessed in a broadly comparable way. But as Edenborough (1994) points out, they do not provide any clear indication of which items of the data collected are likely to predict success in a job.

Structured situational-based interviews

In a situational-based interview (sometimes described as a critical-incident interview) the focus is on a number of situations or incidents in which behaviour can be regarded as being particularly indicative of subsequent performance. A typical situation is described and candidates are asked how they would deal with it. Follow-up questions are asked to explore the response in more detail, thus gaining a better understanding of how candidates might tackle similar problems.

Situational-based questions ask candidates how they would handle a hypothetical situation that resembles one they may encounter in the job. For example, a sales assistant might be asked how he or she would react to rudeness from a customer. Situational questions can provide some insight into how applicants might respond to particular job demands and have the advantage of being work-related. They can also provide candidates with some insight into the sort of problems they might meet in the job. But, because they are hypothetical and can necessarily only cover a limited number of areas, they cannot be relied on by themselves. They could indicate that candidates understand how they might handle one type of situation in theory but not that they would be able to handle similar or other situations in practice.

An example of part of a situation-based set of questions is given in Figure 28.1.

Structured behavioural (competency) based interviews

In a behavioural-based interview (sometimes referred to as a criterion-referenced interview) the interviewer progresses through a series of questions, each based on a criterion, which could be a behavioural competency or a competence in the form of a fundamental skill, capability or aptitude that is required to achieve an acceptable level of performance in the job. These will have been defined by job or competency analysis as described in Chapter 13 and will form the basis of a person specification. The aim is to collect evidence about relevant aspects of experience in using skills and competencies on the assumption that such evidence of past performance and

---

LISTENING

Sometimes a customer won't say directly what they want and you have to listen to the messages behind the words. Tell me about a time when you were able to help the sale along.

- Why was the customer reluctant to say what was wanted?
- How did you check that you really did understand?
- How did you show that it was OK for the customer to have the concerns shown in the hidden message?
- Did you actually do a deal that day?
- Is the customer still on your books?
- Had others experienced difficulty with that particular customer?

Figure 28.1 Part of a critical-incident interview for sales people

(Source: R Edenborough (1994) *Using Psychometrics*, Kogan Page)

behaviour is the best predictor of future performance and behaviour as long as the criteria are appropriate in relation to the specified demands of the job.

Behavioural-based questions ask candidates to describe how they dealt with particular situations they have come across in their past experience. In effect they are asked to indicate how they behaved in response to a problem and how well that behaviour worked. Questions are structured around the key competencies identified for the role. The definitions of these competencies should identify what is regarded as effective behaviour as a basis for evaluating answers. A list of questions can be drawn up in advance to cover the key competencies set out in the person specification. For instance, if one of these competencies is concerned with behaviour as a team member, questions such as: 'Can you tell me about any occasions when you have persuaded your fellow team members to do something which at first they didn't really want to do?' An example of a set of behavioural questions is given in Figure 28.2.

Behavioural-based interviews can provide a clear and relevant framework. But preparing for them takes time and interviewers need to be trained in the technique. A fully behavioural or criterion-referenced structure is probably most appropriate for jobs that have to be filled frequently. But even with one-off jobs, the technique of having a set of competency-referenced questions to ask, which will be applied consistently to all candidates, will improve the reliability of the prediction.

Structured psychometric interviews

Another type of structured interview consists of entirely predetermined questions as

---

PRACTICAL CREATIVITY
The ability to originate and realize effective solutions to everyday problems

1. Tell me about a time when you used previous experience to solve a problem new to you.

2. Do you ever make things, perhaps in your spare time, out of all sorts of odds and ends? (if necessary) Tell me what you have done.

3. Tell me about a time when you got a piece of equipment or a new system to work when other people were struggling with it.

4. Have you ever found an entirely new use for a hand or power tool? Do you often do that sort of thing? Tell me more.

5. Do people come to you to help solve problems? (if so) Tell me about a problem you have solved recently.

Figure 28.2   Behavioural-based interview set

(Source: R Edenborough (1994) *Using Psychometrics*, Kogan Page)

in a psychometric test (see Chapter 29). There is no scope to follow through questions as in the other types of structured interviews referred to above. Responses to the questions are coded so that results can be analysed and compared. The aim is to obtain consistency between different interviews and interviewers. A typical question would be: 'Have you ever been in a situation where you have had to get someone to do something against their will?'; *(if yes)* 'Please give me a recent example.' This is a highly structured approach and, because of the research and training required, it is probably only feasible when large numbers of candidates have to be interviewed.

Choice of approach

The more the approach can be structured by the use of situational or behavioural-based questions, the better. If the criteria have been properly researched, much more insight will be obtained about candidates' capabilities by reference to analysed and specified role requirements. It is still useful, however, to review candidates' sequence of experience and the responsibilities exercised in successive jobs. It may be important, for example, to establish the extent to which the career of candidates has progressed smoothly or why there have been gaps between successive jobs. It is useful to know what responsibilities candidates have had in recent jobs and the extent to which this experience is useful and relevant. Candidates should also be given the chance to highlight their achievements. This review provides a framework within which more specific questions that refer to behavioural criteria or critical incidents can be asked. It was noted by Latham *et al* (1980) that interviews using this technique produced reasonably reliable and consistent assessments. A typical interview may include about 10 or more, depending on the job, pre-prepared behavioural event or 'situational' questions.

INTERVIEW TECHNIQUES – STARTING AND FINISHING

You should start interviews by putting candidates at their ease. You want them to provide you with information and they are not going to talk freely and openly if they are given a cool reception.

In the closing stages of the interview candidates should be asked if they have anything they wish to add in support of their application. They should also be given the opportunity to ask questions. At the end of the interview the candidate should be thanked and given information about the next stage. If some time is likely to elapse before a decision is made, the candidate should be informed accordingly so as not to be left on tenterhooks. It is normally better not to announce the final decision during the interview. It may be advisable to obtain references and, in any case, time is required to reflect on the information received.

INTERVIEWING TECHNIQUES – ASKING QUESTIONS

The interviewee should be encouraged to do most of the talking – one of the besetting sins of poor interviewers is that they talk too much. The interviewer's job is to draw the candidate out, at the same time ensuring that the information required is obtained. To this end it is desirable to ask a number of open-ended questions – questions that cannot be answered by yes or no and that promote a full response. But a good interviewer will have an armoury of other types of questions to be asked as appropriate, as described below.

Open questions

Open questions are the best ones to use to get candidates to talk – to encourage a full response. Single-word answers are seldom illuminating. It is a good idea to begin the interview with one or two open questions, thus helping candidates to settle in.

Open questions or phrases inviting a response can be phrased as follows:

- I'd like you to tell me about the sort of work you are doing in your present job.
- What do you know about…?
- Could you give me some examples of…?

- In what ways do you think your experience fits you to do the job for which you have applied?
- How have you tackled…?
- What have been the most challenging aspects of your job?
- Please tell me about some of the interesting things you have been doing at work recently.

Open questions can give you a lot of useful information but you may not get exactly what you want, and answers can go into too much detail. For example, the question: 'What has been the main feature of your work in recent months?' may result in a one-word reply – 'marketing'. Or it may produce a lengthy explanation that takes up too much time. Replies to open questions can get bogged down in too much detail, or miss out some key points. They can come to a sudden halt or lose their way. You need to ensure that you get all the facts, keep the flow going and maintain control. Remember that you are in charge. Hence the value of probing, closed and the other types of questions which are discussed below.

Probing questions

Probing questions are used to get further details or to ensure that you are getting all the facts. You ask them when answers have been too generalized or when you suspect that there may be some more relevant information that candidates have not disclosed. A candidate may claim to have done something and it may be useful to find out more about exactly what contribution was made. Poor interviewers tend to let general and uninformative answers pass by without probing for further details, simply because they are sticking rigidly to a predetermined list of open questions. Skilled interviewers are able to flex their approach to ensure they get the facts while still keeping control to ensure that the interview is completed on time. A candidate could say to you something like: 'I was involved in a major business process re-engineering exercise that produced significant improvements in the flow of work through the factory.' This statement conveys nothing about what the candidate actually did. You have to ask probing questions such as:

- What was your precise role in this project?
- What exactly was the contribution you made to its success?
- What knowledge and skills were you able to apply to the project?
- Were you responsible for monitoring progress?
- Did you prepare the final recommendations in full or in part? If in part, which part?

The following are some other examples of probing questions:

- You've informed me that you have had experience in.... Could you tell me more about what you did?
- Could you describe in more detail the equipment you use?

Closed questions

Closed questions aim to clarify a point of fact. The expected reply will be an explicit single word or brief sentence. In a sense, a closed question acts as a probe but produces a succinct factual statement without going into detail. When you ask a closed question you intend to find out:

- what the candidate has or has not done – 'What did you do then?'
- why something took place – 'Why did that happen?'
- when something took place – 'When did that happen?'
- how something happened – 'How did that situation arise?'
- where something happened – 'Where were you at the time?'
- who took part – 'Who else was involved?'

Hypothetical questions

Hypothetical questions are used in structured situational-based interviews to put a situation to candidates and ask them how they would respond. They can be prepared in advance to test how candidates would approach a typical problem. Such questions may be phrased: 'What do you think you would do if...?' When such questions lie well within the candidate's expertise and experience, the answers can be illuminating. But it could be unfair to ask candidates to say how they would deal with a problem without knowing more about the context in which the problem arose. It can also be argued that what candidates say they would do and what they actually do could be quite different. Hypothetical questions can produce hypothetical answers. The best data upon which judgements about candidates can be made are what they have actually done or achieved. You need to find out if they have successfully dealt with the sort of issues and problems they may be faced with if they join your organization.

Behavioural event questions

Behavioural event questions as used in behavioural-based structured interviews aim to get candidates to tell you how they would behave in situations that have been identified as critical to successful job performance. The assumption upon which such questions are based is that past behaviour in dealing with or reacting to events is the best predictor of future behaviour.

The following are some typical behavioural event questions:

- Could you give an instance when you persuaded others to take an unusual course of action?
- Could you describe an occasion when you completed a project or task in the face of great difficulties?
- Could you describe any contribution you have made as a member of a team in achieving an unusually successful result?
- Could you give an instance when you took the lead in a difficult situation in getting something worthwhile done?

Capability questions

Capability questions aim to establish what candidates know, the skills they possess and use and their competencies – what they are capable of doing. They can be open, probing or closed but they will always be focused as precisely as possible on the contents of the person specification referring to knowledge, skills and competencies. Capability questions are used in behavioural-based structured interviews.

Capability questions should therefore be explicit – focused on what candidates must know and be able to do. Their purpose is to obtain from candidates evidence that shows the extent to which they meet the specification in each of its key areas. Because time is always limited, it is best to concentrate on the most important aspects of the work. And it is always best to prepare the questions in advance.

The sort of capability questions you can ask are:

- What do you know about…?
- How did you gain this knowledge?
- What are the key skills you are expected to use in your work?
- How would your present employer rate the level of skill you have reached in…?
- Could you please tell me exactly what sort and how much experience you have had in…?
- Could you tell me more about what you have actually been doing in this aspect of your work?
- Can you give me any examples of the sort of work you have done that would qualify you to do this job?
- What are the most typical problems you have to deal with?
- Would you tell me about any instances when you have had to deal with an unexpected problem or a crisis?

Questions about motivation

The degree to which candidates are motivated is a personal quality to which it is usually necessary to give special attention if it is to be properly assessed. This is best achieved by inference rather than direct questions. 'How well are you motivated?' is a leading question that will usually produce the response: 'Highly.'

You can make inferences about the level of motivation of candidates by asking questions about:

- Their career – replies to such questions as 'Why did you decide to move on from there?' can give an indication of the extent to which they have been well motivated in progressing their career.
- Achievements – not just 'What did you achieve?' but 'How did you achieve it?' and 'What difficulties did you overcome?'
- Triumphing over disadvantages – candidates who have done well in spite of an unpromising upbringing and relatively poor education may be more highly motivated than those with all the advantages that upbringing and education can bestow, but who have not made good use of these advantages.
- Spare time interests – don't accept at its face value a reply to a question about spare time interests that, for example, reveals that a candidate collects stamps. Find out if the candidate is well motivated enough to pursue the interest with determination and to achieve something in the process. Simply sticking stamps in an album is not evidence of motivation. Becoming a recognized expert on 19th-century stamps issued in Mexico is.

Continuity questions

Continuity questions aim to keep the flow going in an interview and encourage candidates to enlarge on what they have told you, within limits. Here are some examples of continuity questions:

- What happened next?
- What did you do then?
- Can we talk about your next job?
- Can we move on now to…?
- Could you tell me more about…?

It has been said that to keep the conversation going during an interview the best thing an interviewer can do is to make encouraging grunts at appropriate moments. There is more to interviewing than that, but single words or phrases like 'good', 'fine', 'that's interesting', 'carry on' can help things along.

Play-back questions

Play-back questions test your understanding of what candidates have said by putting to them a statement of what it appears they have told you, and asking them if they agree or disagree with your version. For example, you could say: 'As I understand it, you resigned from your last position because you disagreed with your boss on a number of fundamental issues – have I got that right?' The answer might simply be yes to this closed question, in which case you might probe to find out more about what happened. Or the candidate may reply 'not exactly', in which case you ask for the full story.

Career questions

As mentioned earlier, questions about the career history of candidates can provide some insight into motivation as well as establishing how they have progressed in acquiring useful and relevant knowledge, skills and experience. You can ask such questions as:

- What did you learn from that new job?
- What different skills had you to use when you were promoted?
- Why did you leave that job?
- What happened after you left that job?
- In what ways do you think this job will advance your career?

Focused work questions

These are questions designed to tell you more about particular aspects of the candidate's work history, such as:

- How many days' absence from work did you have last year?
- How many times were you late last year?
- Have you been absent from work for any medical reason not shown on your application form?
- Have you a clean driving licence? (For those whose work will involve driving.)

Questions about outside interests

You should not spend much time asking people with work experience about their outside interests or hobbies. It is seldom relevant, although, as mentioned earlier, it can give some insight into how well motivated candidates are if the depth and vigour with which the interest is pursued is explored.

Active interests and offices held at school, colleges or universities can, however, provide some insight into the attributes of candidates in the absence of any work history except, possibly, vacation jobs. If, for example, a student has been on a long back-pack trip, some information can be obtained about the student's initiative, motivation and determination if the journey has been particularly adventurous.

Unhelpful questions

There are two types of questions that are unhelpful:

- *Multiple questions* such as 'What skills do you use most frequently in your job? Are they technical skills, leadership skills, team-working skills or communicating skills?' will only confuse candidates. You will probably get a partial or misleading reply. Ask only one question at a time.
- *Leading questions* that indicate the reply you expect are also unhelpful. If you ask a question such as: 'That's what you think, isn't it?' you will get the reply: 'Yes, I do.' If you ask a question such as: 'I take it that you don't really believe that….?', you will get the reply: 'No, I don't.' Neither of these replies will get you anywhere.

Questions to be avoided

Avoid any questions that could be construed as being biased on the grounds of sex, race or disability. Don't ask:

- Who is going to look after the children? This is no concern of yours, although it is reasonable to ask if the hours of work pose any problems.
- Are you planning to have any more children?
- Would it worry you being a member of an ethnic minority here?
- With your disability, do you think you can cope with the job?

Ten useful questions

The following are 10 useful questions from which you can select any that are particularly relevant in an interview you are conducting:

- What are the most important aspects of your present job?
- What do you think have been your most notable achievements in your career to date?
- What sort of problems have you successfully solved recently in your job?
- What have you learned from your present job?
- What has been your experience in...?
- What do you know about...?
- What is your approach to handling...?
- What particularly interests you in this job and why?
- Now you have heard more about the job, would you please tell me which aspects of your experience are most relevant?
- Is there anything else about your career that hasn't come out yet in this interview but that you think I ought to hear?

SELECTION INTERVIEWING SKILLS

Establishing rapport

Establishing rapport means establishing a good relationship with candidates – getting on their wavelength, putting them at ease, encouraging them to respond and generally being friendly. This is not just a question of being 'nice' to candidates. If you achieve rapport you are more likely to get them to talk freely about both their strengths and their weaknesses.

Good rapport is created by the way in which you greet candidates, how you start the interview and how you put your questions and respond to replies. Questions should not be posed aggressively or imply that you are criticizing some aspect of the candidate's career. Some people like the idea of 'stress' interviews, but they are always counter-productive. Candidates clam up and gain a negative impression of you and the organization.

When responding to answers you should be appreciative, not critical: 'Thank you, that was very helpful; now can we go on to...?', not 'Well, that didn't show you in a good light, did it?'

Body language can also be important. If you maintain natural eye contact, avoid slumping in your seat, nod and make encouraging comments when appropriate, you will establish better rapport and get more out of the interview

Listening

If an interview is a conversation with a purpose, as it should be, listening skills are important. You need not only to hear but also to understand what candidates are saying. When interviewing, you must concentrate on what candidates are telling you. Summarizing at regular intervals forces you to listen because you have to pay attention to what they have been saying in order to get the gist of their replies. If you play back to candidates your understanding of what they have told you for them to confirm or amend, it will ensure that you have fully comprehended the messages they are delivering.

Maintaining continuity

So far as possible, link your questions to a candidate's last reply so that the interview progresses logically and a cumulative set of data is built up. You can put bridging questions to candidates such as: 'Thank you, that was an interesting summary of what you have been doing in that aspect of your work. Now, could you tell me something about your other key responsibilities?'

Keeping control

You want candidates to talk, but not too much. When preparing for the interview, you should have drawn up an agenda and you must try to stick to it. Don't cut candidates short too brutally but say something like: 'Thank you, I've got a good picture of that, now what about…?'

Focus on specifics as much as you can. If candidates ramble on a bit, ask a pointed question (a 'probe' question) that asks for an example illustrating the particular aspect of their work that you are considering.

Note taking

You won't remember everything that candidates tell you. It is useful to take notes of the key points they make, discreetly, but not surreptitiously. However, don't put candidates off by frowning or tut-tutting when you are making a negative note.

It may be helpful to ask candidates if they would mind if you take notes. They can't really object but will appreciate the fact that they have been asked.

COMING TO A CONCLUSION

It is essential not to be beguiled by a pleasant, articulate and confident interviewee who is in fact surface without substance in the shape of a good track record. Beware of the 'halo' effect that occurs when one or two good points are seized upon, leading to the neglect of negative indicators. The opposite 'horns' effect should also be avoided.

Individual candidates should be assessed against the criteria. These could be set under the headings of competence/skills, qualifications, experience, and overall suitability. Ratings can be given against each heading, for example: very acceptable, acceptable, marginally acceptable, unacceptable. The person specification should indicate which of the requirements are essential and which are only desirable. Clearly, to be considered for the job, candidates have to be acceptable or, perhaps stretching a point, marginally acceptable, in all the essential requirements. Next, compare your assessment of each of the candidates against one another. You can then make a conclusion on those preferred by reference to their assessments under each heading.

In the end, your decision between qualified candidates may well be judgemental. There may be one outstanding candidate, but quite often there are two or three. In these circumstances you have to come to a balanced view on which one is more likely to fit the job and the organization *and* have potential for a long-term career, if thi is possible. Don't, however, settle for second best in desperation. It is better to try again.

Remember to make and keep notes of the reasons for your choice and why candidates have been rejected. These together with the applications should be kept for at least six months just in case your decision is challenged as being discriminatory.

DOS AND DON'TS OF SELECTION INTERVIEWING

To conclude, here is a summary of the dos and don'ts of selection interviewing:

Do

- give yourself sufficient time;
- plan the interview so you can structure it properly;
- create the right atmosphere;
- establish an easy and informal relationship – start with open questions;
- encourage the candidate to talk;
- cover the ground as planned, ensuring that you complete a prepared agenda and maintain continuity;
- analyse the candidate's career to reveal strengths, weaknesses and patterns of interest;
- ask clear, unambiguous questions;
- get examples and instances of the successful application of knowledge, skills and the effective use of capabilities;

- make judgements on the basis of the factual information you have obtained about candidates' experience and attributes in relation to the person specification;
- keep control over the content and timing of the interview.

Don't

- attempt too many interviews in a row;
- fall into the halo or horns effect trap;
- start the interview unprepared;
- plunge too quickly into demanding (probe) questions;
- ask multiple or leading questions;
- pay too much attention to isolated strengths or weaknesses;
- allow candidates to gloss over important facts;
- talk too much or allow candidates to ramble on;
- allow your prejudices to get the better of your capacity to make objective judgements.

29

Selection tests

Selection tests are used to provide more valid and reliable evidence of levels of intelligence, personality characteristics, abilities, aptitudes and attainments than can be obtained from an interview. This chapter is mainly concerned with psychological tests of intelligence or personality as defined below, but it also refers to the principal tests of ability etc that can be used.

PSYCHOLOGICAL TESTS: DEFINITION

As defined by Smith and Robertson (1986), a psychological test is:

> A carefully chosen, systematic and standardised procedure for evolving a sample of responses from candidates which can be used to assess one or more of their psychological characteristics with those of a representative sample of an appropriate population.

PURPOSE OF PSYCHOLOGICAL TESTS

Psychological tests are measuring instruments, which is why they are often referred to as psychometric tests. Psychometric literally means 'mental measurement'.

The purpose of a psychological test is to provide an objective means of measuring individual abilities or characteristics. They are used to enable selectors to gain a greater understanding of individuals so that they can predict the extent to which they will be successful in a job.

CHARACTERISTICS OF A GOOD TEST

A good test is one that provides valid data that enable reliable predictions of behaviour to be made, and therefore assist in the process of making objective and reasoned decisions when selecting people for jobs. It will be based on thorough research that has produced standardized criteria that have been derived by using the same measure to test a number of representative people to produce a set of 'norms'. The test should be capable of being objectively scored by reference to the normal or average performance of the group.

The characteristics of a good test are:

- It is *sensitive* measuring instrument that discriminates well between subjects.
- It has been *standardized* on a representative and sizeable sample of the population for which it is intended so that any individual's score can be interpreted in relation to that of others.
- It is *reliable* in the sense that it always measures the same thing. A test aimed at measuring a particular characteristic, such as intelligence, should measure the same characteristic when applied to different people at the same or a different time, or to the same person at different times.
- It is *valid* in the sense that it measures the characteristic that the test is intended to measure. Thus, an intelligence test should measure intelligence (however defined) and not simply verbal facility. A test meant to predict success in a job or in passing examinations should produce reasonably convincing (statistically significant) predictions.

There are five types of validity:

- *Predictive validity* – the extent to which the test correctly predicts future behaviour. To establish predictive validity it is necessary to conduct extensive research over a period of time. It is also necessary to have accurate measures of performance so that the prediction can be compared with actual behaviour.
- *Concurrent validity* – the extent to which a test score differentiates individuals in relation to a criterion or standard of performance external to the test. This means comparing the test scores of high and low performances as indicated by the criteria and establishing the degree to which the test indicates who should fit into the high or low performance groups.

- *Content validity* – the extent to which the test is clearly related to the characteristics of the job or role for which it is being used as a measuring instrument.
- *Face validity* – the extent to which it is felt that the test 'looks' right, ie is measuring what it is supposed to measure.
- *Construct validity* – the extent to which the test measures a particular construct or characteristic. As Edenborough (1994) suggests, construct validity is in effect concerned with looking at the test itself. If it is meant to measure numerical reasoning, is that what it measures?

Measuring validity

A criterion-related approach is used to assess validity. This means selecting criteria against which the validity of the test can be measured. These criteria must reflect 'true' performance at work as accurately as possible. This may be difficult and Smith and Robertson (1986) emphasize that a single criterion is inadequate. Multiple criteria should be used. The extent to which criteria can be contaminated by other factors should also be considered and it should be remembered that criteria are dynamic – they will change over time.

Validity can be expressed as a coefficient of correlation in which 1.0 would equal perfect correlation between test results and subsequent behaviour, while 0.0 would equal no relationship between the test and performance. The following rule of thumb guide on whether a validity coefficient is big enough was produced by Smith (1984):

over 0.5 excellent
0.40-0.49 good
0.30-0.39 acceptable
less than 0.30 poor

On this basis, only ability tests, biodata and (according to Smith's figures) personality questionnaires reach acceptable levels of validity.

TYPES OF TEST

The main types of selection test as described below are intelligence, personality, ability, aptitude and attainment tests.

A distinction can be made between psychometric tests and psychometric questionnaires. As explained by Toplis *et al* (1991), a psychometric test such as one on mental ability has correct answers so that the higher the score, the better the performance. Psychometric questionnaires such as personality tests assess habitual performance and measure personality characteristics, interests, values or behaviour. With questionnaires, a high or low score signifies the extent to which a person has a certain quality and the appropriateness of the replies depends on the particular qualities required in the job to be filled.

Intelligence tests

Tests of intelligence such as Raven's Progressive Matrices measure general intelligence (termed 'g' by Spearman (1927), one of the pioneers of intelligence testing). Intelligence is defined by Toplis *et al* (1991) as 'the capacity for abstract thinking and reasoning'. The difficulty with intelligence tests is that they have to be based on a theory of what constitutes intelligence and then have to derive a series of verbal and non-verbal instruments for measuring the different factors or constituents of intelligence. But intelligence is a highly complex concept and the variety of theories about intelligence and the consequent variations in the test instruments or batteries available make the choice of an intelligence test a difficult one.

For general selection purposes, an intelligence test that can be administered to a group of candidates is the best, especially if it has been properly validated, and it is possible to relate test scores to 'norms' in such a way as to indicate how the individual taking the test compares with the rest of the population, in general or in a specific area.

Personality tests

Personality tests attempt to assess the personality of candidates in order to make predictions about their likely behaviour in a role. Personality is an all-embracing and imprecise term that refers to the behaviour of individuals and the way it is organized and coordinated when they interact with the environment. There are many different theories of personality and, consequently, many different types of personality tests. These include self-report personality questionnaires and other questionnaires that measure interests, values or work behaviour.

One of the most generally accepted ways of classifying personality is the five-factor model. As summarized by McCrae and Costa (1989), this model defines the key personality characteristics. These 'big five', as Roberts (1997) calls them, are:

- *extraversion/introversion* – gregarious, outgoing, assertive, talkative and active (extraversion); or reserved, inward-looking, diffident, quiet, restrained (introversion);
- *emotional stability* – resilient, independent, confident, relaxed; or apprehensive, dependent, under-confident, tense;

- *agreeableness* – courteous, cooperative, likeable, tolerant; or rude, uncooperative, hostile, intolerant;
- *conscientiousness* – hard-working, persevering, careful, reliable; or lazy, dilettante, careless, expedient;
- *openness to experience* – curious, imaginative, willingness to learn, broad-minded; or blinkered, unimaginative, complacent, narrow-minded.

Research cited by Roberts (1997) has indicated that these factors are valid predictors of work performance and that one factor in particular, 'conscientiousness', was very effective.

Self-report personality questionnaires are the ones most commonly used. They usually adopt a 'trait' approach, defining a trait as a fairly independent but enduring characteristic of behaviour that all people display but to differing degrees. Trait theorists identify examples of common behaviour, devise scales to measure these, and then obtain ratings on these behaviours by people who know each other well. These observations are analysed statistically, using the factor analysis technique to identify distinct traits and to indicate how associated groups of traits might be grouped loosely into 'personality types'.

'Interest' questionnaires are sometimes used to supplement personality tests. They assess the preferences of respondents for particular types of occupation and are therefore most applicable to vocational guidance, but can be helpful when selecting apprentices and trainees.

'Value' questionnaires attempt to assess beliefs about what is 'desirable or good' or what is 'undesirable or bad'. The questionnaires measure the relative prominence of such values as conformity, independence, achievement, decisiveness, orderliness and goal-orientation.

Specific work behaviour questionnaires cover behaviours such as leadership or selling.

Personality questionnaires were shown to have the low validity coefficient of 0.15 on the basis of research conducted by Schmitt *et al* (1984). But as Saville and Sik (1992) point out, this was based on a rag-bag of tests, many developed for clinical use and some using 'projective' techniques such as the Rorschach inkblots test, the interpretation of which relies on a clinician's judgement and is therefore quite out of place in a modern selection procedure. Smith's (1988) studies based on modern self-report questionnaires revealed an average validity coefficient of 0.39, which is reasonably high.

A vigorous attack was launched on personality tests by Blinkorn and Johnson (1990). They commented: 'We see precious little evidence of personality tests predicting job performance.' But Fletcher (1991) responded: 'Like any other selection procedure, they (psychometric tests) can be used well or badly. But it would be foolish to dismiss all the evidence of the value of personality assessment in selection on the basis of some misuse. Certainly the majority of applied psychologists feel the balance of the evidence supports the use of personality inventories.' Personality tests can provide interesting supplementary information about candidates that is free from the biased reactions that frequently occur in face-to-face interviews. But they have to be used with great care. The tests should have been developed by a reputable psychologist or test agency on the basis of extensive research and field testing and they must meet the specific needs of the user. Advice should be sought from a member of the British Psychological Society on what tests are likely to be appropriate.

Ability tests

Ability tests measure job-related characteristics such as number, verbal, perceptual or mechanical ability.

Aptitude tests

Aptitude tests are job-specific tests that are designed to predict the potential an individual has to perform tasks within a job. They can cover such areas as clerical aptitude, numerical aptitude, mechanical aptitude and dexterity.

Aptitude tests should be properly validated. The usual procedure is to determine the aptitudes required by means of job and skills analysis. A standard test or a test battery is then obtained from a test agency. Alternatively, a special test is devised by or for the organization. The test is then given to employees already working on the job and the results compared with a criterion, usually managers' or team leaders' ratings. If the correlation between test and criterion is sufficiently high, the test is then given to applicants. To validate the test further, a follow-up study of the job performance of the applicants selected by the test is usually carried out. This is a lengthy procedure, but without it no real confidence can be attached to the results of any aptitude test. Many do-it-yourself tests are worse than useless because they have not been properly validated.

Attainment tests

Attainment tests measure abilities or skills that have already been acquired by training or experience. A typing test is the most typical example. It is easy to find out how many words a minute a typist can type and compare that with the standard required for the job.

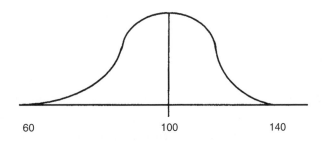

60   100   140

Figure 29.1 A normal curve

INTERPRETING TEST RESULTS

The two main methods of interpreting test results are the use of norms and the normal curve.

Norms

Tests can be interpreted in terms of how an individual's results compare with the scores achieved by a group on whom the task was standardized – the norm or reference group. A normative score is read from a norms table. The most common scale indicates the proportion of the reference who scored less than the individual. Thus if someone scored at the 70th percentile in a test, that person's score would be better than 65 per cent of the reference group.

The normal curve

The normal curve describes the relationship between a set of observations and measures and the frequency of their occurrence. It indicates, as illustrated in Figure 29.1, that on many things that can be measured on a scale, a few people will produce extremely high or low scores and there will be a large proportion of people in the middle.

The most important characteristic of the normal curve is that it is symmetrical – there are an equal number of cases on either side of the mean, the central axis. The normal curve is a way of expressing how scores will typically be distributed; for example, that 60 per cent of the population are likely to get scores between x and y, 15 per cent are likely to get scores below x and 15 per cent are likely to get more than y.

CHOOSING TESTS

It is essential to choose tests that meet the four criteria of sensitivity, standardization, reliability and validity. It is very difficult to achieve the standards required if an organization tries to develop its own test batteries unless it employs a qualified psychologist or obtains professional advice from a member of the British Psychological Society. This organization, with the support of the reputable test suppliers, exercises rigorous control over who can use what tests and the standard of training required and given. Particular care should be taken when selecting personality tests – there are a lot of charlatans about.

Do-it-yourself tests are always suspect unless they have been properly validated and realistic norms have been established. Generally speaking, it is best to avoid using them.

THE USE OF TESTS IN A SELECTION PROCEDURE

Tests are often used as part of a selection procedure for occupations where a large number of recruits are required, and where it is not possible to rely entirely on examination results or information about previous experience as the basis for predicting future performance. In these circumstances it is economical to develop and administer the tests, and a sufficient number of cases can be built up for the essential validation exercise. Tests usually form part of an assessment centre procedure.

Intelligence tests are particularly helpful in situations where intelligence is a key factor, but there is no other reliable method of measuring it. It may, incidentally, be as important to use an intelligence test to keep out applicants who are too intelligent for the job as to use one to guarantee a minimal level of intelligence.

Aptitude and attainment tests are most useful for jobs where specific and measurable skills are required, such as typing or computer programming. Personality tests are potentially of greatest value in jobs such as selling where 'personality' is important, and where it is not too difficult to obtain quantifiable criteria for validation purposes.

It is essential to evaluate all tests by comparing the results at the interview stage with later achievements. To be statistically significant, these evaluations should be carried out over a reasonable period of time and cover as large a number of candidates as possible.

In some situations a battery of tests may be used, including various types of intelligence, aptitude and personality tests. These may be a standard battery supplied by a test agency, or a custom-built battery may be developed. The biggest pitfall to avoid is adding extra tests just for the sake of it, without ensuring that they make a proper contribution to the success of the predictions for which the battery is being used.

The six criteria for the use of psychological tests produced by the IPD (1997a) are:

1. Everyone responsible for the application of tests including evaluation, interpretation and feedback should be trained at least to the level of competence recommended by the British Psychological Society.
2. Potential test users should satisfy themselves that it is appropriate to use tests at all before incorporating tests into their decision-making processes.
3. Users must satisfy themselves that any tests they decide to use actively measure factors which are directly relevant to the employment situation.
4. Users must satisfy themselves that all tests they use should have been rigorously developed and that claims about their reliability, validity and effectiveness are supported by statistical evidence (*The Data Protection Act 1998 is relevant here. If candidates are selected on the basis of a test they have the right to know the rationale for the selection decision.*)
5. Care must be taken to provide equality of opportunity among all individuals required to take tests.
6. The results of single tests should not be used as the sole basis for decision-making. This is particularly relevant with regard to personality tests.

30

Introduction to the organization

It is important to ensure that care is taken over introducing people to the organization through effective induction arrangements as described in this chapter.

INDUCTION DEFINED

Induction is the process of receiving and welcoming employees when they first join a company and giving them the basic information they need to settle down quickly and happily and start work. Induction has four aims:

- to smooth the preliminary stages when everything is likely to be strange and unfamiliar to the starter;
- to establish quickly a favourable attitude to the company in the mind of the new employee so that he or she is more likely to stay;
- to obtain effective output from the new employee in the shortest possible time;
- to reduce the likelihood of the employee leaving quickly.

WHY TAKING CARE ABOUT INDUCTION IS IMPORTANT

Induction is important for the reasons given below.

Reducing the cost and inconvenience of early leavers

As pointed out by Fowler (1996), employees are far more likely to resign during their first months after joining the organization. The costs can include:

- recruitment costs of replacement;
- induction costs (training etc);
- costs of temporary agency replacement;
- cost of extra supervision and error correction;
- gap between the employee's value to the company and the cost of the employee's pay and benefits.

These costs can be considerable. The cost for a professional employee could be 75 per cent of annual salary. For a support worker the cost could easily reach 50 per cent of pay. If 15 out of 100 staff paid an average of £12,500 a year leave during the year, the total cost could amount to £90,000 – 7.5 per cent of the payroll. It is worth making an effort to reduce that cost. First impressions are important, as are the impact of the first four weeks of employment. Giving more attention to induction pays off.

Increasing commitment

A committed employee is one who identifies with the organization, wants to stay with it and is prepared to work hard on behalf of the organization. The first step in achieving commitment is to present the organization as one that is worth working for and to ensure that this first impression is reinforced during the first weeks of employment.

Clarifying the psychological contract

The psychological contract, as described in Chapter 16, consists of implicit, unwritten beliefs and assumptions about how employees are expected to behave and what responses they can expect from their employer. It is concerned with norms, values and attitudes. The psychological contract provides the basis for the employment relationship, and the more this can be clarified from the outset, the better. Induction arrangements can indicate what the organization expects in terms of behavioural norms and the values that employees should uphold. Induction provides an opportunity to inform people of 'the way things are done around here' so that misapprehensions are reduced even if they cannot be eliminated.

Accelerating progress up the learning curve

New employees will be on a learning curve – they will take time to reach the required level of performance. Clearly, the length of the learning curve and rates of learning vary, but it is important to provide for it to take place in a planned and systematic manner from the first day to maximize individual contributions as quickly as possible.

Socialization

New employees are likely to settle in more quickly and enjoy working for the organization if the process of socialization takes place smoothly. The social aspects of work – relationships with colleagues – are very important for many people. The extent to which employees can directly influence the quality of socialization may often be limited, but it is a feature of introduction to the organization to which they should pay attention, as far as this is possible, during the induction arrangements described below, which are concerned with reception, documentation, initial briefing, introduction to the workplace, formal induction courses and formal and informal training activities.

RECEPTION

Most people suffer from some feelings of trepidation when they start a new job. However outwardly confident they may appear, they may well be asking themselves such questions as: What will the company be like? How will my boss behave to me? Will I get on with the other workers? Will I be able to do the job?

These questions may not be answered immediately, but at least general fears may be alleviated by ensuring that the first contacts are friendly and helpful.

The following checklist for reception is recommended by Fowler (1996):

- Ensure that the person whom the starter first meets (ie the receptionist, personnel assistant or supervisor) knows of their pending arrival and what to do next.

- Set a reporting time, which will avoid the risk of the starter turning up before the reception or office staff arrive.
- Train reception staff in the need for friendly and efficient helpfulness towards new starters.
- If the new starter has to go to another location immediately after reporting, provide a guide, unless the route to the other location is very straightforward.
- Avoid keeping the new starter waiting; steady, unhurried, guided activity is an excellent antidote to first-day nerves.

DOCUMENTATION

The new employee will be asked to hand over the P45 income tax form from the previous employer. A variety of documents may then be issued to employees, including safety rules and safety literature, a company rule book containing details of disciplinary and grievance procedures and an employee handbook as described below.

The employee handbook

An employee handbook is useful for this purpose. It need not be too glossy, but it should convey clearly and simply what new staff need to know under the following headings:

- a brief description of the company – its history, products, organization and management;
- basic conditions of employment – hours of work, holidays, pension scheme, insurance;
- pay – scales, when paid and how, deductions, queries;
- sickness – notification of absence, certificates, pay;
- leave of absence;
- company rules;
- disciplinary procedure;
- capability procedure;
- grievance procedure;
- promotion procedure;
- union and joint consultation arrangements;
- education and training facilities;
- health and safety arrangements;
- medical and first-aid facilities;

- restaurant and canteen facilities;
- social and welfare arrangements;
- telephone calls and correspondence;
- rules for using e-mail;
- travelling and subsistence expenses.

If the organization is not large enough to justify a printed handbook, the least that can be done is to prepare a typed summary of this information.

COMPANY INDUCTION – INITIAL BRIEFING

Company induction procedures, however, should not rely on the printed word. The member of the HR department or other individual who is looking after new employees should run through the main points with each individual or, when larger numbers are being taken on, with groups of people. In this way, a more personal touch is provided and queries can be answered.

When the initial briefing has been completed, new employees should be taken to their place of work and introduced to their manager or team leader for the departmental induction programme. Alternatively, they may go straight to a training school and join the department later.

INTRODUCTION TO THE WORKPLACE

New starters will be concerned about who they are going to work for (their immediate manager or team leader), who they are going to work with, what work they are going to do on their first day, and the geographical layout of their place of work (location of entrances, exits, lavatories, restrooms and the canteen).

Some of this information may be provided by a member of the HR department, or an assistant in the new employee's place of work. But the most important source of information is the immediate manager, supervisor or team leader.

The departmental induction programme should, wherever possible, start with the departmental manager, not the immediate team leader. The manager may give only a general welcome and a brief description of the work of the department before handing new employees over to their team leaders for the more detailed induction. But it is important for the manager to be involved at this stage so that he or she is not seen as a remote figure by the new employee. And at least this means that the starter will not be simply a name or a number to the manager.

The detailed induction is probably best carried out by the immediate team leader, who should have five main aims:

- to put the new employee at ease;
- to interest the employee in the job and the organization;
- to provide basic information about working arrangements;
- to indicate the standards of performance and behaviour expected from the employee;
- to tell the employee about training arrangements and how he or she can progress in the company.

The team leader should introduce new starters to their fellow team members. It is best to get one member of the team to act as a guide or 'starter's friend'. As Fowler suggests, there is much to be said for these initial guides to be people who have not been long with the organization. As relative newcomers they are likely to remember all the small points that were a source of worry to them when they started work, and so help new employees to settle in quickly.

FORMAL INDUCTION COURSES

Reason for

Formal induction courses can provide for recruits to be assembled in groups so that a number of people can be given consistent and comprehensive information at the same time, which may not be forthcoming if reliance is placed solely on supervisors. A formal course is an opportunity to deliver messages about the organization, its products and services, its mission and values, using a range of media such as videos and other visual aids that would not be available within departments. But formal induction courses cannot replace informal induction arrangements at the workplace, where the most important need – settling people well – can best be satisfied.

Arrangements

Decisions will have to be made about who attends and when. It is normal to mix people from different departments but less common to have people from widely different levels on the same course. In practice, managers and senior professional staff are often dealt with individually.

Ideally, induction courses should take place as soon as possible after starting. If there are sufficient new employees available, this could be half the first day or a half or whole day during the first week. If a lot of information is to be conveyed, supplementary half or one-day courses may be held later. However, the course may have to be delayed until sufficient numbers of new starters are available. If such delays are unavoidable, it is essential to ensure that key information is provided on the first day by personnel and the departmental supervisor. Organizations with branches or a number of different locations often hold formal induction courses at headquarters, which helps employees to feel that they are part of the total business and gives an opportunity to convey information about the role of head office.

Content

The content of formal induction courses may be selected according to the needs of the organization from the following list of subject areas:

- *information about the organization* – its products/services, structure, mission and core values;
- *learning arrangements and opportunities* – formal training, self-managed learning, personal development plans;
- *performance management processes* – how they work and the parts people play;
- *health and safety* – occupational health, prevention of injuries and accidents, protective clothing, basic safety rules;
- *conditions of service* – hours, holidays, leave, sick pay arrangements, maternity/paternity leave;
- *pay and benefits* – arrangements for paying salaries or wages, the pay structure, allowances, details of performance, competence- or skill-based pay schemes, details of profit sharing, gainsharing or share ownership arrangements, pension and life or medical insurance schemes;
- *policies, procedures and working arrangements* – equal opportunities policies, rules regarding sexual and racial harassment and bullying, disciplinary and grievance procedures, no-smoking arrangements;
- *trade unions and employee involvement* – trade union membership and recognition, consultative systems, agreements, suggestion schemes.

ON-THE-JOB INDUCTION TRAINING

Most new starters other than those on formal training schemes will learn on the job, although this may be supplemented with special off-the-job courses to develop particular skills or knowledge. On-the-job training can be haphazard, inefficient and wasteful. A planned, systematic approach is very desirable. This can incorporate:

- job or skills analysis to prepare a learning specification;
- an initial assessment of what the new starter needs to learn;
- the use of designated colleagues to act as guides and mentors – these individuals should be trained in how to carry out this role;
- coaching by team leaders or specially appointed and trained departmental trainers;
- special assignments.

These on-the-job arrangements can be supplemented by self-managed learning arrangements, e-learning and by providing advice on learning opportunities.

31

Release from the organization

GENERAL CONSIDERATIONS

The employment relationship may be ended voluntarily by someone moving elsewhere. Or it may finish at the end of a career on retirement. Increasingly, however, people are having to go involuntarily. Organizations are becoming mean as well as lean. They are terminating the relationship through redundancy and they are tightening up disciplinary procedures to handle not only cases of misconduct but also those of incapability – as judged by the employer. Resourcing policies and practices concerning release from the organization have also to cover voluntary turnover and retirement.

Causes of redundancy

Redundancy, like the poor which it helps to create, has always been with us. At one time, however, it was mainly a result of adverse trading conditions, especially during times of recession. This is, of course, still a major cause of redundancy, exacerbated by the pressures of global competition and international recession. But the drive for competitive advantage has forced organizations to 'take cost out of the business' – a euphemism for getting rid of people, employment costs being the ones on which companies focus, as they are usually the largest element in their cost structures. The result has been delayering (eliminating what are deemed to be unnecessary layers of management and supervision) and 'downsizing' (another euphemism) or even 'right-sizing' (a yet more egregious euphemism).

The introduction of new technology has contributed hugely to the reduction in the number of semi-skilled or unskilled people in offices and on the shop floor. But the thrust for productivity (more from less) and added value (increasing the income derived from the expenditure on people) has led to more use of such indices as added value per £ of employment costs to measure business performance with regard to the utilization of its 'human resources' (the use of human resources in this connection implies a measure of exploitation). Business process re-engineering techniques are deployed as instruments for downsizing. Benchmarking to establish which organizations are in fact doing more with less (and if so how they do it) is another popular way of preparing the case for 'downsizing'.

Setting higher performance standards

The pressure for improved performance to meet more intense global competition explains why many organizations are setting higher standards for employees and are not retaining those who do not meet those standards. This may be done through disciplinary procedures, but performance management processes are being used to identify under-performers. Properly administered, such processes will emphasize positive improvement and development plans but they will inevitably highlight weaknesses and, if these are not overcome, disciplinary proceedings may be invoked.

Voluntary release

Of course, people also leave organizations voluntarily to further their careers, get more money, move away from the district or because they are fed up with the way they feel they have been treated. They may also take early retirement (although this is sometimes involuntary) or volunteer for redundancy (under pressure or because they are being rewarded financially for doing so).

Managing organizational release – the role of the HR function

The HR function is usually given the task of managing organizational release and, in its involuntary form, this is perhaps the most distasteful, onerous and stressful of all the activities with which HR people get involved. In effect, the function is being asked to go into reverse. Having spent a lot of positive effort on employees' resourcing and development, it is now being placed in what appears to be an entirely negative position. HR people are indeed acting, however unwillingly, as the agents of the management who made the 'downsizing' decisions or want to 'let someone go' (there are more euphemisms in this area of management than the rest of the areas put together). Being placed in this often invidious position means that there are ethical and professional considerations to be taken into account, as discussed below.

A more positive aspect of the function's involvement in organizational release is the part HR people can play in easing retirement and analysing the reasons given by employees for leaving the organization so that action can be taken to correct organizational shortcomings.

Ethical and professional considerations

HR professionals may have no choice about taking part in a 'downsizing' exercise – that is, if they wish to remain with the organization. But they can and should make an important contribution to managing the process in order to minimize the distress and trauma that badly handled redundancies can create, or the distress and bad feeling that unfair or uncouth disciplinary practices can engender. They can press for policies and actions that will minimize, even if they cannot eliminate, involuntary redundancy. They can emphasize the need to handle redundancies sensitively, advising line managers on the approach they adopt, helping them to communicate the decision to employees, advising generally on communication within and outside the organization and laying on counselling and outplacement services. Professionally, they should ensure that there are proper redundancy procedures (including those relating to consultation) which are in line with codes of practice and legal requirements, and they must see that these practices are followed.

Similarly, a professional approach to discipline means that HR specialists should ensure that there are disciplinary procedures which conform to codes of practice and take into account legal implications. They have to communicate these procedures to line managers, provide training in how they are applied and advise on their use. Ethically, personnel professionals should do their best to see that people are treated fairly in accordance with the principles of natural justice.

Career dynamics

Career dynamics is the term used to describe how careers progress within organizations or over a working life. As long ago as 1984 Charles Handy forecast that many more people would not be working in organizations. Instead there would be an increase in the number of outworkers and subcontractors facilitated by information technology. He also predicted that there would be more requirements for specialists and professionals (knowledge workers) within organizations. In later books (eg *The Empty Raincoat*, 1994) he developed his concept of a portfolio career – people changing their careers several times during their working lives, either because they have been forced to leave their jobs or because they have seized new opportunities.

The national culture has changed too. High levels of unemployment seem set to continue, more people are working for themselves (often because they have to) and short-term contracts are becoming more common, especially in the public sector. Some commentators believe that organizations are no longer in the business of providing 'life-long careers' as they slim down, delayer and rely on a small core of workers. Clearly, this is taking place in some companies, but employees do not all necessarily see it this way. The IPD 1995 survey established that 46 per cent of their respondents viewed their current job as a long-term one in which they intended to stay. However, 16 per cent saw their present job as part of a career or profession that would probably take them to different companies and 15 per cent saw their job as one they would leave as it was not part of their career.

Organizational release activities

Against this background, organizational release activities as described in this chapter deal with redundancy, outplacement, dismissal, voluntary turnover and retirement.

REDUNDANCY

'Downsizing' is one of the most demanding areas of people management with which HR professionals can become involved. Their responsibilities, as discussed below, are to:

- plan ahead to achieve downsizing without involuntary redundancy;
- advise on and implement other methods of reducing numbers or avoiding redundancy;
- encourage voluntary redundancy if other methods fail;
- develop and apply a proper redundancy procedure;
- deal with payment arrangements for releasing employees;
- advise on methods of handling redundancies and take part as necessary to ensure that they are well managed.

HR specialists should also be involved in organizing outplacement services as described in the next section of this chapter.

Plan ahead

Planning ahead means anticipating future reductions in people needs and allowing natural wastage to take effect. A forecast is needed of the amount by which the workforce has to be reduced and the likely losses through employee turnover. Recruitment can then be frozen at the right moment to allow the surplus to be absorbed by wastage.

The problem is that forecasts are often difficult to make, and in periods of high unemployment, natural wastage rates are likely to be reduced. It is possible therefore to overestimate the extent to which they will achieve the required reduction in numbers. It is best to be pessimistic about the time it will take to absorb future losses and apply the freeze earlier rather than later.

Ideally, steps should be taken to transfer people to other, more secure jobs and retrain them where possible.

Use other methods to avoid redundancy

The other methods that can be used to avoid or at least minimize redundancy include, in order or severity:

- calling in outside work;
- withdrawing all subcontracted labour;
- reducing or preferably eliminating overtime;
- developing worksharing: two people doing one job on alternate days or splitting the day between them;
- reducing the number of part-timers, remembering that they also have employment rights;
- temporary lay-offs.

Voluntary redundancy

Asking for volunteers – with a suitable pay-off – is one way of relieving the number of compulsory redundancies. The amount needed to persuade people to go is a matter of judgement. It clearly has to be more than the statutory minimum, although one inducement for employees to leave early may be the belief that they will get another job more easily than if they hang on until the last moment. Help can be provided to place them elsewhere.

One of the disadvantages of voluntary redundancy is that the wrong people might go, ie good workers who are best able to find other work. It is sometimes necessary to go into reverse and offer them a special loyalty bonus if they agree to stay on.

Outplacement

Outplacement is the process of helping redundant employees to find other work or start new careers. It may involve counselling, which can be provided by firms who specialize in this area.

Redundancy procedure

If you are forced to resort to redundancy, the problems will be reduced if there is an established procedure to follow. This procedure should have three aims:

- to treat employees as fairly as possible;
- to reduce hardship as much as possible;
- to protect management's ability to run the business effectively.

These aims are not always compatible. Management will want to retain its key and more effective workers. Trade unions, on the other hand, may want to adopt the principle of last in, first out, irrespective of the value of each employee to the company. An example of a procedure is given in Chapter 58.

Handling redundancy

The first step is to ensure that the redundancy selection policy has been applied fairly. It is also necessary to make certain that the legal requirements for consultation have been met. The information to be presented at any consultative meetings will need to cover the reasons for the redundancy, what steps the company has taken or will take to minimize the problem and the redundancy pay arrangements. An indication should also be given of the time scale. The basis for selecting people for redundancy as set out in the redundancy policy should be confirmed.

It will then be necessary to make a general announcement if it is a large-scale redundancy or inform a unit or department if it is on a smaller scale. It is best if the announcement is made in person by an executive or manager who is known to the individuals concerned. It should let everyone know about the difficulties the organization has been facing and the steps that have been taken to overcome them. The announcement should also indicate in general how the redundancy will take place, including arrangements for individuals to be informed (as soon as possible after the general announcement), payment arrangements and, importantly, help to those affected in finding work through outplacement counselling or a 'job shop'.

If it is a fairly large redundancy, the media will have to be informed, but only after the internal announcement. A press release will need to be prepared, again indicating why the redundancy is taking place and how the company intends to tackle it.

The next step is to inform those affected. It is very important to ensure that everything possible is done to ensure that the interviews with those who are to be made redundant are handled sensitively. Managers should be given guidance and, possibly, training on how to deal with what is sometimes called (another euphemism) a 'release interview'. It may well be advisable for a member of the personnel function to be present at all interviews, although it is best for the line manager to conduct them. Advance information should be obtained on the reasons why individuals were selected and how they may react. Their personal circumstances should also be checked in case there are any special circumstances with which the interviewer should be familiar.

The interview itself should explain as gently as possible why the individual has been selected for redundancy and how it will affect him or her (payment, timing etc). Time should be allowed to describe the help that the organization will provide to find another job and to get initial reactions from the individual which may provide guidance on the next steps.

OUTPLACEMENT

Outplacement is about helping redundant employees to find alternative work. It involves assisting individuals to cope with the trauma of redundancy through counselling, helping them to redefine their career and employment objectives and then providing them with knowledgeable but sensitive guidance on how to attain those objectives.

Job shops

Help may be provided by the organization on an individual basis, but in larger-scale redundancies 'job shops' can be set up. The people who staff these scour the travel-to-work area seeking job opportunities for those who are being made redundant. This is often done by telephone. Further help may be given by matching people to suitable jobs, arranging interviews, training in CV preparation and interview techniques. Job shops are sometimes staffed by members of the personnel function (the writer successfully organized one in an aerospace firm some years ago). Alternatively, the organization may ask a firm of outplacement consultants to set up and run the job shop and provide any other counselling or training services that may be required.

Outplacement consultancy services

As described by Eggert (1991), the outplacement process usually takes place along the following lines:

- initial counselling – gaining biographical data and discussing immediate issues of concern;
- achievement list – clients write up all the achievements they can think of to do with their career;
- skills inventory – clients develop from the achievement list a personal portfolio of saleable skills;
- personal statement – clients develop a personal statement in 20 to 30 words about what is being presented to the job market;
- personal success inventory – those recent or appropriate successes that can be quantified and which support the personal profile;
- three jobs – identification of three possible types of job that can be searched for;
- psychological assessment – development of a personality profile with a psychologist;
- development and agreement of a CV (see below);
- identify job market opportunities;
- practice interview;
- plan job search campaign.

CVs

CVs provide the basic information for job searching and an outplacement consultant will guide individuals on how to write their CVs. The traditional CV uses what Eggert (1991) calls the 'tombstone' approach because it reads like an obituary. It sets out personal details and education and employment history in chronological order.

Outplacement consultants prefer what they call the 'achievement CV' which is structured on the principle of a sales brochure, providing information in simple, positive statements sequenced for the reader's convenience. The CV lists the most important areas of experience in reverse chronological order and sets out for each position a list of achievements beginning with such words as 'set up', 'developed', 'introduced', 'increased', 'reduced' and 'established'. This is designed to generate the thought in the reader's mind that 'if the individual can do it for them, he or she will be able to do it for us'. The career achievement history is followed by details of professional qualifications and education, and personal information.

Selecting an outplacement consultant

There are some highly reputable outplacement consultants around; there are also some cowboys. It is advisable only to use firms that follow a code of practice such as that produced by the CIPD or the Career Development and Outplacement Association.

DISMISSAL

The legal framework

The legal framework is provided by employment statutory and case law relating to unfair dismissal. Under current UK employment legislation, an employee who has been employed for one year or more has the right not to be unfairly dismissed. Complaints by an employee that he or she has been unfairly dismissed are heard by employment tribunals.

Definition of dismissal

Legally, dismissal takes place when:

- the employer terminates the employee's contract with or without notice – a contract can be terminated as a result of a demotion or transfer as well as dismissal;
- the employee terminates the contract (resigns) with or without notice by reason of the employer's behaviour in the sense that the employer's conduct was such that the employee could not be expected to carry on – this is termed 'constructive dismissal';
- the employee is employed under a fixed-term contract of one year or more which is not renewed by the employer when it expires;
- an employee resigns while under notice following dismissal;
- an employee is unreasonably refused work after pregnancy.

Fundamental questions

The legislation lays down that employment tribunals should obtain answers to two fundamental questions when dealing with unfair dismissal cases:

1. Was there sufficient reason for the dismissal, ie was it fair or unfair?
2. Did the employer act reasonably in the circumstances?

Fair dismissal

Dismissals may be held by an employment tribunal to be fair if the principal reason was one of the following:

- incapability, which covers the employee's skill, aptitude, health and physical or mental qualities;
- misconduct;
- failure to have qualifications relevant to the job;
- a legal factor that prevents the employee from continuing work;
- redundancy – where this has taken place in accordance with a customary or agreed redundancy procedure;
- the employee broke or repudiated his or her contract by going on strike – as long as he or she was not singled out for this treatment, ie all striking employees were treated alike and no selective re-engagement took place;
- the employee was taking part in an unofficial strike or some other form of industrial action;
- some other substantial reason of a kind that would justify the dismissal of an employee holding the position that the employee held.

Unfair dismissal

Dismissals may be unfair if:

- the employer has failed to show that the principal reason was one of the admissible reasons as stated above, or if the dismissal was not reasonable in the circumstances (see below);
- a constructive dismissal has taken place;
- they are in breach of a customary or agreed redundancy procedure, and there are no valid reasons for departing from that procedure.

The onus of proof is on employers to show that they had acted reasonably in treating the reason for dismissal as sufficient. The employment tribunal is required, in considering the circumstances, to take into account the size and administrative resources of the employer's undertaking.

Reasonable in the circumstances

Even if the employer can show to a tribunal that there was good reason to dismiss the employee (ie if it clearly fell into one of the categories listed above, and the degree of incapability or misconduct was sufficient to justify dismissal), the tribunal still has to decide whether or not the employer acted in a reasonable way at the time of dismissal. The principles defining 'reasonable' behaviour on the part of an employer are as follows:

- Employees should be informed of the nature of the complaint against them.
- The employee should be given the chance to explain.
- The employee should be given the opportunity to improve, except in particularly gross cases of incapability or misconduct.
- Employees should be allowed to appeal.
- The employee should be warned of the consequences in the shape of dismissal if specified improvements do not take place.
- The employer's decision to dismiss should be based on sufficient evidence.
- The employer should take any mitigating circumstances into account.
- The employer should act in good faith.
- The offence or misbehaviour should merit the penalty of dismissal rather than some lesser penalty.

A good disciplinary procedure (see the example in Chapter 58) will include arrangements for informal and formal warnings and provisions to ensure that the other aspects of discipline are handled reasonably.

Remedies

Employment tribunals that find that a dismissal was unfair can make an order for reinstatement or re-engagement and state the terms on which this should take place. The tribunal can consider the possibility of compensation for unfair dismissal, but only after the possibility of reinstatement or re-engagement has been examined.

Approach to handling disciplinary cases

The approach should be governed by the following three principles of natural justice:

1. Individuals should know the standards of performance they are expected to achieve and the rules to which they are expected to conform.
2. They should be given a clear indication of where they are failing or what rules have been broken.
3. Except in cases of gross misconduct, they should be given an opportunity to improve before disciplinary action is taken.

There should be a disciplinary procedure which is understood and applied by all managers and team leaders. The procedure should provide for the following three-stage approach before disciplinary action is taken:

1. informal oral warnings;
2. formal oral warnings, which, in serious cases, may also be made in writing – these warnings should set out the nature of the offence and the likely consequences of further offences;
3. final written warnings, which should contain a statement that any recurrence would lead to suspension, dismissal or some other penalty.

The procedure should provide for employees to be accompanied by a colleague or employee representative at any hearing. There should also be an appeal system and a list of offences that constitute gross misconduct and may therefore lead to instant dismissal. Managers and supervisors should be told what authority they have to take disciplinary action. It is advisable to have all final warnings and actions approved by a higher authority. In cases of gross misconduct, team leaders and junior managers should be given the right to suspend, if higher authority is not immediately available, but not to dismiss. The importance of obtaining and recording the facts should be emphasized. Managers should always have a colleague with them when issuing a formal warning and should make a note to file of what was said on the spot.

VOLUNTARY LEAVERS

When people leave of their own volition, two actions may be taken: conducting exit interviews and analysing reasons for turnover as described in Chapter 25.

RETIREMENT

Retirement is a major change and should be prepared for. Retirement policies need to specify:

- when people are due to retire;
- the circumstances, if any, in which they can work on beyond their normal retirement date;
- the provision of pre-retirement training;
- the provision of advice to people about to retire.

Pre-retirement training can cover such matters as finance, insurance, State pension rights, health, working either for money or in a voluntary organization during retirement and sources of advice and help. The latter can be supplied by such charities as Help the Aged and Age Concern.

Part VII

Performance management

Performance management processes have become prominent in recent years as means of providing a more integrated and continuous approach to the management of performance than was provided by previous isolated and often inadequate merit rating or performance appraisal schemes. Performance management is based on the principle of management by agreement or contract rather than management by command. It emphasizes development and the initiation of self-managed learning plans as well as the integration of individual and corporate objectives. It can, in fact, play a major role in providing for an integrated and coherent range of human resource management processes which are mutually supportive and contribute as a whole to improving organizational effectiveness.

In this part, Chapter 32 covers the fundamental concepts of performance management. The practice of performance management is described in Chapter 33 and the part is completed in Chapter 34 by a review of the process of 360-degree feedback as a multi-source method of assessing performance.

32

The basis of performance management

In this chapter the nature, aims, characteristics, concerns and guiding principles of performance management are described. In addition, the differences between performance appraisal and performance management are examined and reference is made to the views of a selection of practitioners on performance management.

PERFORMANCE MANAGEMENT DEFINED

Performance management can be defined as a systematic process for improving organizational performance by developing the performance of individuals and teams. It is a means of getting better results by understanding and managing performance within an agreed framework of planned goals, standards and competency requirements. Processes exist for establishing shared understanding about what is to be achieved, and for managing and developing people in a way that increases the probability that it *will* be achieved in the short and longer term. It focuses people on doing the right things by clarifying their goals. It is owned and driven by line management.

AIMS OF PERFORMANCE MANAGEMENT

The overall aim of performance management is to establish a high performance culture in which individuals and teams take responsibility for the continuous improvement of business processes and for their own skills and contributions within a framework provided by effective leadership.

Specifically, performance management is about aligning individual objectives to organizational objectives and ensuring that individuals uphold corporate core values. It provides for expectations to be defined and agreed in terms of role responsibilities and accountabilities (expected to do), skills (expected to have) and behaviours (expected to be). The aim is to develop the capacity of people to meet and exceed expectations and to achieve their full potential to the benefit of themselves and the organization. Importantly, performance management is concerned with ensuring that the support and guidance people need to develop and improve are readily available.

The following are the aims of performance management as expressed by a variety of organizations (source IRS, 2003):

- Empowering, motivating and rewarding employees to do their best. *Armstrong World Industries*
- Focusing employee's tasks on the right things and doing them right. Aligning everyone's individual goals to the goals of the organization. *Eli Lilly & Co*
- Proactively managing and resourcing performance against agreed accountabilities and objectives. *ICI Paints*
- The process and behaviours by which managers manage the performance of their people to deliver a high-achieving organization. *Standard Chartered Bank*
- Maximizing the potential of individuals and teams to benefit themselves and the organization, focusing on achievement of their objectives. *West Bromwich Building Society*

CHARACTERISTICS OF PERFORMANCE MANAGEMENT

Performance management is a planned process of which the primary elements are agreement, measurement, feedback, positive reinforcement and dialogue. It is concerned with measuring outputs in the shape of delivered performance compared with expectations expressed as objectives. In this respect, it focuses on targets, standards and performance measures or indicators. It is based on the agreement of role requirements, objectives and performance improvement and personal development plans. It provides the setting for ongoing dialogues about performance that involves the joint and continuing review of achievements against objectives, requirements and plans.

But it is also concerned with inputs and values. The inputs are the knowledge, skills and behaviours required to produce the expected results. Developmental needs are identified by defining these requirements and assessing the extent to which the expected levels of performance have been achieved through the effective use of knowledge and skills and through appropriate behaviour that upholds core values.

Performance management is a continuous and flexible process, which involves managers and those whom they manage acting as partners within a framework that sets out how they can best work together to achieve the required results. It is based on the principle of management by contract and agreement rather than management by command. It relies on consensus and co-operation rather than control or coercion.

Performance management focuses on future performance planning and improvement rather than on retrospective performance appraisal. It functions as a continuous and evolutionary process, in which performance improves over time. It provides the basis for regular and frequent dialogues between managers and individuals about performance and development needs. It is mainly concerned with individual performance but it can also be applied to teams. The emphasis is on development, although performance management is an important part of the reward system through the provision of feedback and recognition and the identification of opportunities for growth. It may be associated with performance or contribution-related pay, but its developmental aspects are much more important.

UNDERSTANDING PERFORMANCE MANAGEMENT

There are five issues that need to be considered to obtain a full understanding of performance management:

1. the meaning of performance;
2. the significance of values;
3. the meaning of alignment;
4. managing expectations;
5. the significance of discretionary behaviour.

The meaning of performance

Performance is often defined simply in output terms – the achievement of quantified objectives. But performance is a matter not only of what people achieve but how they achieve it. *The Oxford English Dictionary* confirms this by including the phrase 'carrying out' in its definition of performance: 'The accomplishment, execution, carrying out, working out of anything ordered or undertaken.' High performance results from appropriate behaviour, especially discretionary behaviour, and the effective use of the required knowledge, skills and competencies. Performance management must examine how results are attained because this provides the information necessary to consider what needs to be done to improve those results.

The concept of performance has been expressed by Brumbrach (1988) as follows:

> Performance means both behaviours and results. Behaviours emanate from the performer and transform performance from abstraction to action. Not just the instruments for results, behaviours are also outcomes in their own right – the product of mental and physical effort applied to tasks – and can be judged apart from results.

This definition of performance leads to the conclusion that when managing performance both inputs (behaviour) and outputs (results) need to be considered. It is not a question of simply considering the achievement of targets, as used to happen in 'management by objectives' schemes. Competency factors need to be included in the process. This is the so-called 'mixed model' of performance management, which covers the achievement of expected levels of competence as well as objective setting and review.

Performance management and values

Performance is about upholding the values of the organization – 'living the values' (an approach to which much importance is attached at Standard Chartered Bank). This is an aspect of behaviour but it focuses on what people do to realize core values such as concern for quality, concern for people, concern for equal opportunity and operating ethically. It means converting espoused values into values in use: ensuring that the rhetoric becomes reality.

The meaning of alignment

One of the most fundamental purposes of performance management is to align individual and organizational objectives. This means that everything people do at work leads to outcomes that further the achievement of organizational goals. This purpose was well expressed by Fletcher (1993), who wrote:

> The real concept of performance management is associated with an approach to creating a shared vision of the purpose and aims of the organization, helping each employee understand and recognize their part in contributing to them, and in so doing, manage and enhance the performance of both individuals and the organization.

Alignment can be attained by a cascading process so that objectives flow down from the top and at each level team or individual objectives are defined in the light of higher-level goals. But it should also be a bottom-up process, individuals and teams being given the opportunity to formulate their own goals within the framework provided by the defined overall purpose, strategy and values of the organization. Objectives should be *agreed* not set, and this agreement should be reached through the open dialogues that take place between managers and individuals throughout the year. In other words, this needs to be seen as a partnership in which responsibility is shared and mutual expectations are defined.

Managing expectations

Performance management is essentially about the management of expectations. It creates a shared understanding of what is required to improve performance and how this will be achieved by clarifying and agreeing what people are expected to do and how they are expected to behave. It uses these agreements as the basis for measurement and review, and the preparation of plans for performance improvement and development.

Performance management and discretionary behaviour

Performance management is concerned with the encouragement of productive discretionary behaviour. As defined by Purcell and his team at Bath University, School of Management (2003): 'Discretionary behaviour refers to the choices that people make about how they carry out their work and the amount of effort, care, innovation and productive behaviour they display.' Purcell and his team, while researching the relationship between HR practice and business performance, noted that 'the experience of success seen in performance outcomes helps reinforce positive attitudes'.

GUIDING PRINCIPLES OF PERFORMANCE MANAGEMENT

Egan (1995) proposes the following guiding principles for performance management:

Most employees want direction, freedom to get their work done, and encouragement not control. The performance management system should be a control system only by exception. The solution is to make it a collaborative development system, in two ways. First, the entire performance management process – coaching, counselling, feedback, tracking, recognition, and so forth – should encourage development. Ideally, team members grow and develop through these interactions. Second, when managers and team members ask what they need to be able to do to do bigger and better things, they move to strategic development.

PERFORMANCE APPRAISAL AND PERFORMANCE MANAGEMENT

It is sometimes assumed that performance appraisal is the same thing as performance management. But there are significant differences. Performance appraisal can be defined as the formal assessment and rating of individuals by their managers at, usually, an annual review meeting. In contrast, performance management is a continuous and much wider, more comprehensive and more natural process of management that clarifies mutual expectations, emphasizes the support role of managers who are expected to act as coaches rather than judges, and focuses on the future.

Performance appraisal has been discredited because too often it has been operated as a top-down and largely bureaucratic system owned by the HR department rather than by line managers. It has been perceived by many commentators such as Townley (1989) as solely a means of exercising managerial control. Performance appraisal tended to be backward looking, concentrating on what had gone wrong, rather than looking forward to future development needs. Performance appraisal schemes existed in isolation. There was little or no link between them and the needs of the business. Line managers have frequently rejected performance appraisal schemes as being time-consuming and irrelevant. Employees have resented the superficial nature with which appraisals have been conducted by managers who lack the skills required, tend to be biased and are simply going through the motions. As Armstrong and Murlis (1998) assert, performance appraisal too often degenerated into 'a dishonest annual ritual'. The differences between them as summed up by Armstrong and Baron (2004) are set out in Table 32.1.

VIEWS ON PERFORMANCE MANAGEMENT

The research conducted by the CIPD in 2003 (Armstrong and Baron, 2004) elicited the following views from practitioners about performance management:

Table 32.1 Performance appraisal compared with performance management

Performance appraisal	Performance management
Top-down assessment	Joint process through dialogue
Annual appraisal meeting	Continuous review with one or more formal reviews
Use of ratings	Ratings less common
Monolithic system	Flexible process
Focus on quantified objectives	Focus on values and behaviours as well as objectives
Often linked to pay	Less likely to be a direct link to pay
Bureaucratic – complex paperwork	Documentation kept to a minimum
Owned by the HR department	Owned by line managers

- We expect line managers to recognize it (performance management) as a useful contribution to the management of their teams rather than a chore. (*Centrica*)
- Managing performance is about coaching, guiding, motivating and rewarding colleagues to help unleash potential and improve organizational performance. Where it works well it is built on excellent leadership and high quality coaching relationships between managers and teams. (*Halifax BOS*)
- Performance management is designed to ensure that what we do is guided by our values and is relevant to the purposes of the organization. (*Scottish Parliament*)

The research conducted by the CIPD in 1997 (Armstrong and Baron, 1998) obtained the following additional views from practitioners about performance management:

- A management tool which helps managers to manage.
- Driven by corporate purpose and values.
- To obtain solutions that work.
- Only interested in things you can do something about and get a visible improvement.
- Focus on changing behaviour rather than paperwork.
- It's about how we manage people – it's not a system.

- Performance management is what managers do: a natural process of management.
- Based on accepted principles but operates flexibly.
- Focus on development not pay.
- Success depends on what the organization is and needs to be in its performance culture.

The processes of performance management are described in the next chapter.

33

The process of performance management

PERFORMANCE MANAGEMENT AS A PROCESS

Performance management should be regarded as a flexible process, not as a 'system'. The use of the term 'system' implies a rigid, standardized and bureaucratic approach that is inconsistent with the concept of performance management as a flexible and evolutionary, albeit coherent, process that is applied by managers working with their teams in accordance with the circumstances in which they operate. As such, it involves managers and those whom they manage acting as partners, but within a framework that sets out how they can best work together.

PERFORMANCE MANAGEMENT AS A CYCLE

Performance management can be described as a continuous self-renewing cycle, as illustrated in Figure 33.1.

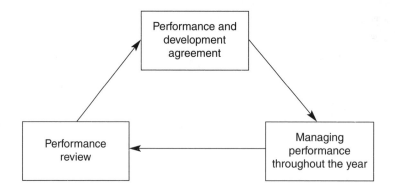

Figure 33.1   The performance management cycle

This chapter deals with each of these parts of the cycle as follows:

- *Planning:* concluding a performance and development agreement.
- *Acting:* managing performance throughout the year.
- *Reviewing:* assessing progress and achievements so that action plans can be prepared and agreed and, in many schemes, performance can be rated.

Consideration is also given to managing under-performers, and approaches to introducing performance management are considered at the end of the chapter.

PERFORMANCE AGREEMENTS

Performance agreements form the basis for development, assessment and feedback in the performance management process. They define expectations in the form of a role profile that sets out role requirements in terms of key result areas and the competencies required for effective performance. The role profile provides the basis for agreeing objectives and methods of measuring performance and assessing the level of competency reached. The performance agreement incorporates any performance improvement plans that may be necessary, and a personal development plan. It describes what individuals are expected to do but also indicates what support they will receive from their manager.

Performance agreements emerge from the analysis of role requirements and the performance review. An assessment of past performance leads to an analysis of future requirements. The two processes can take place at the same meeting.

Defining role requirements

The foundation for performance management is a role profile that defines the role in terms of the key results expected, what role holders need to know and be able to do (competencies), and how they are expected to behave in terms of behavioural competencies and upholding the organization's core values. Role profiles need to be updated every time a formal performance agreement is developed. Guidelines on preparing role profiles and an example are given in Chapter 13.

Objectives

Objectives describe something that has to be accomplished. Objective setting that results in an agreement on what the role holder has to achieve is an important part of the performance management processes of defining and managing expectations, and forms the point of reference for performance reviews.

Types of objectives

The different types of objectives are:

- *On-going role or work objectives* – all roles have built-in objectives that may be expressed as key result areas in a role profile.
- *Targets* – these define the quantifiable results to be attained as measured in such terms as output, throughput, income, sales, levels of service delivery, cost reduction, reduction of reject rates.
- *Tasks/projects* – objectives can be set for the completion of tasks or projects by a specified date or to achieve an interim result.
- *Behaviour* – behavioural expectations are often set out generally in competency frameworks but they may also be defined individually under the framework headings. Competency frameworks may deal with areas of behaviour associated with core values, for example teamwork, but they often convert the aspirations contained in value statements into more specific examples of desirable and undesirable behaviour, which can help in planning and reviewing performance.

Criteria for objectives

Many organizations use the following 'SMART' mnemonic to summarize the criteria for objectives:

S   = *Specific/stretching* – clear, unambiguous, straightforward, understandable and challenging.

M   = *Measurable* – quantity, quality, time, money.

A   = *Achievable* – challenging but within the reach of a competent and committed person.

R   = *Relevant* – relevant to the objectives of the organization so that the goal of the individual is aligned to corporate goals.

T   = *Time framed* – to be completed within an agreed time scale.

Measuring performance in achieving objectives

Measurement is an important concept in performance management. It is the basis for providing and generating feedback, it identifies where things are going well to provide the foundations for building further success, and it indicates where things are not going so well, so that corrective action can be taken.

Measuring performance is relatively easy for those who are responsible for achieving quantified targets, for example sales. It is more difficult in the case of knowledge workers, for example scientists. But this difficulty is alleviated if a distinction is made between the two forms of results – outputs and outcomes.

An output is a result that can be measured quantifiably, while an outcome is a visible effect that is the result of effort but cannot necessarily be measured in quantified terms.

There are components in all jobs that are difficult to measure quantifiably as outputs. But all jobs produce outcomes even if they are not quantified. It is therefore often necessary to measure performance by reference to what outcomes have been attained in comparison with what outcomes were expected, and the outcomes may be expressed in qualitative terms as a standard or level of competency to be attained. That is why it is important when agreeing objectives to answer the question: 'How will we know that this objective has been achieved?' The answer needs to be expressed in the form: 'Because such and such will have happened.' The 'such and such' will be defined either as outputs in such forms as meeting or exceeding a quantified target, completing a project or task satisfactorily ('satisfactory' having been defined), or as outcomes in such forms as reaching an agreed standard of performance, or delivering an agreed level of service.

However, when assessing performance it is also necessary to consider inputs in the shape of the degree of knowledge and skill attained and behaviour that is demonstrably in line with the standards set out in competency frameworks and statements of core values. Behaviour cannot be measured quantitatively but it can be assessed against definitions of what constitutes good and not so good behaviour, and the evidence that can be used to make that assessment can be identified.

Use of performance measures

The CIPD survey of performance management in 2003 (Armstrong and Baron, 2004) revealed that in order of importance, the following performance measures were used by the respondents:

1. Achievement of objectives.
2. Competence.
3. Quality.
4. Contribution to team.
5. Customer care.
6. Working relationships.
7. Productivity.
8. Flexibility.
9. Skills/learning targets.
10. Aligning personal objectives with organizational goals.
11. Business awareness.
12. Financial awareness.

Performance planning

The performance planning part of the performance management sequence involves agreement between the manager and the individual on what the latter needs to do to achieve objectives, raise standards, improve performance and develop the required competencies. It also establishes priorities – the key aspects of the job to which attention has to be given. The aim is to ensure that the meaning of the objectives, performance standards and competencies as they apply to everyday work is understood. They are the basis for converting aims into action.

Agreement is also reached at this stage on how performance will be measured and the evidence that will be used to establish levels of competence. It is important that these measures and evidence requirements should be identified and fully agreed now because they will be used by individuals as well as managers to monitor and demonstrate achievements.

Personal development planning

A personal development plan provides a learning action plan for which individuals are responsible with the support of their managers and the organization. It may include formal training but, more importantly, it will incorporate a wider set of learning and development activities such as self-managed learning, coaching, mentoring, project work, job enlargement and job enrichment. If multi-source assessment (360-degree feedback) is practised in the organization this will be used to discuss development needs.

The development plan records the actions agreed to improve performance and to develop knowledge, skills and capabilities. It is likely to focus on development in the current job – to improve the ability to perform it well and also, importantly, to enable individuals to take on wider responsibilities, extending their capacity to undertake a broader role. This plan therefore contributes to the achievement of a policy of continuous development that is predicated on the belief that everyone is capable of learning more and doing better in their jobs. But the plan will also contribute to enhancing the potential of individuals to carry out higher-level jobs.

MANAGING PERFORMANCE THROUGHOUT THE YEAR

Perhaps one of the most important concepts of performance management is that it is a continuous process that reflects normal good management practices of setting direction, monitoring and measuring performance and taking action accordingly. Performance management should not be imposed on managers as something 'special' they have to do. It should instead be treated as a natural function that all good managers carry out.

This approach contrasts with that used in conventional performance appraisal systems, which were usually built around an annual event, the formal review, which tended to dwell on the past. This was carried out at the behest of the personnel department, often perfunctorily, and then forgotten. Managers proceeded to manage without any further reference to the outcome of the review and the appraisal form was buried in the personnel record system.

To ensure that a performance management culture is built and maintained, performance management has to have the active support and encouragement of top management who must make it clear that it is regarded as a vital means of achieving sustained organizational success. They must emphasize that performance management is what managers are expected to do and that their performance as managers will be measured by reference to the extent to which they do it conscientiously and well. Importantly, the rhetoric supporting performance management must be converted into reality by the deeds as well as the words of the people who have the ultimate responsibility for running the business.

The sequence of performance management activities as described in this chapter does no more than provide a framework within which managers, individuals and teams work together in whatever ways best suit them to gain better understanding of what is to be done, how it is to be done and what has been achieved. This framework and the philosophy that supports it can form the basis for training newly appointed or would-be managers in this key area of their responsibilities. It can also help in improving the performance of managers who are not up to standard in this respect.

A formal, often annual, review is still an important part of a performance management framework but it is not the most important part. Equal, if not more, prominence is given to the performance agreement and the continuous process of performance management.

REVIEWING PERFORMANCE

Although performance management is a continuous process it is still necessary to have a formal review once or twice yearly. This provides a focal point for the consideration of key performance and development issues. This performance review meeting is the means through which the five primary performance management elements of agreement, measurement, feedback, positive reinforcement and dialogue can be put to good use.

The review should be rooted in the reality of the employee's performance. It is concrete, not abstract and it allows managers and individuals to take a positive look together at how performance can become better in the future and how any problems in meeting performance standards and achieving objectives can be resolved. Individuals should be encouraged to assess their own performance and become active agents for change in improving their results. Managers should be encouraged to adopt their proper enabling role: coaching and providing support and guidance.

There should be no surprises in a formal review if performance issues have been dealt with as they should have been – as they arise during the year. Traditional appraisals are often no more than an analysis of where those involved are now, and where they have come from. This static and historical approach is not what performance management is about. The true role of performance management is to look forward to what needs to be done by people to achieve the purpose of the job, to meet new challenges, to make even better use of their knowledge, skills and abilities, to develop their capabilities by establishing a self-managed learning agenda, and to reach agreement on any areas where performance needs to be improved and how that improvement should take place. This process also helps managers to improve their ability to lead, guide and develop the individuals and teams for whom they are responsible.

The most common practice is to have one annual review (65 per cent of respondents to the 2003 CIPD survey). Twice-yearly reviews were held by 27 per cent of the respondents. These reviews led directly into the conclusion of a performance agreement (at the same meeting or later). It can be argued that formal reviews are unnecessary and that it is better to conduct informal reviews as part of normal good management practice to be carried out as and when required. Such informal reviews are valuable as part of the continuing process of performance management (managing performance throughout the year, as discussed in the previous chapter). But there is everything to be said for an annual or half-yearly review that sums up the conclusions reached at earlier reviews and provides a firm foundation for a new performance agreement and a framework for reviewing performance informally, whenever appropriate.

Criteria for assessing performance

The criteria for assessing performance should be balanced between:

- achievements in relation to objectives;
- the level of knowledge and skills possessed and applied (competences);
- behaviour in the job as it affects performance (competencies);
- the degree to which behaviour upholds the core values of the organization;
- day-to-day effectiveness.

The criteria should not be limited to a few quantified objectives, as has often been the case in traditional appraisal schemes. In many cases the most important consideration will be the job holders' day-to-day effectiveness in meeting the continuing performance standards associated with their key tasks. It may not be possible to agree meaningful new quantified targets for some jobs every year. Equal attention needs to be given to the behaviour that has produced the results as to the results themselves.

The review may be concluded with a performance rating (see page 512).

Conducting a performance review meeting

There are 12 golden rules for conducting performance review meetings.

1. *Be prepared*. Managers should prepare by referring to a list of agreed objectives and their notes on performance throughout the year. They should form views about the reasons for success or failure and decide where to give praise, which performance problems should be mentioned and what steps might be undertaken to overcome them. Thought should also be given to any changes that have taken place or are contemplated in the individual's role and to work and personal objectives for the next period. Individuals should also prepare in order

to identify achievements and problems, and to be ready to asses their own performance at the meeting. They should also note any points they wish to raise about their work and prospects.

2. *Work to a clear structure*. The meeting should be planned to cover all the points identified during preparation. Sufficient time should be allowed for a full discussion – hurried meetings will be ineffective. An hour or two is usually necessary to get maximum value from the review.

3. *Create the right atmosphere*. A successful meeting depends on creating an informal environment in which a full, frank but friendly exchange of views can take place. It is best to start with a fairly general discussion before getting into any detail.

4. *Provide good feedback*. Individuals need to know how they are getting on. Feedback should be based on factual evidence. It refers to results, events, critical incidents and significant behaviours that have affected performance in specific ways. The feedback should be presented in a manner that enables individuals to recognize and accept its factual nature – it should be a description of what has happened, not a judgement. Positive feedback should be given on the things that the individual did well in addition to areas for improvement. People are more likely to work at improving their performance and developing their skills if they feel empowered by the process.

5. *Use time productively*. The reviewer should test understanding, obtain information, and seek proposals and support. Time should be allowed for the individual to express his or her views fully and to respond to any comments made by the manager. The meeting should take the form of a dialogue between two interested and involved parties, both of whom are seeking a positive conclusion.

6. *Use praise*. If possible, managers should begin with praise for some specific achievement, but this should be sincere and deserved. Praise helps people to relax – everyone needs encouragement and appreciation.

7. *Let individuals do most of the talking*. This enables them to get things off their chest and helps them to feel that they are getting a fair hearing. Use open-ended questions (ie questions that invite the individual to think about what to reply rather than indicating the expected answer). This is to encourage people to expand.

8. *Invite self-assessment*. This is to see how things look from the individual's point of view and to provide a basis for discussion – many people underestimate themselves. Ask questions such as:

   – How well do you feel you have done?
   – What do you feel are your strengths?
   – What do you like most/least about your job?
   – Why do you think that project went well?
   – Why do you think you didn't meet that target?

9. *Discuss performance not personality.* Discussions on performance should be based on factual evidence, not opinion. Always refer to actual events or behaviour and to results compared with agreed performance measures. Individuals should be given plenty of scope to explain why something did or did not happen.
10. *Encourage analysis of performance.* Don't just hand out praise or blame. Analyse jointly and objectively why things went well or badly and what can be done to maintain a high standard or to avoid problems in the future.
11. *Don't deliver unexpected criticisms.* There should be no surprises. The discussion should only be concerned with events or behaviours that have been noted at the time they took place. Feedback on performance should be immediate. It should not wait until the end of the year. The purpose of the formal review is to reflect briefly on experiences during the review period and on this basis to look ahead.
12. *Agree measurable objectives and a plan of action.* The aim should be to end the review meeting on a positive note.

These golden rules may sound straightforward and obvious enough, but they will only function properly in a culture that supports this type of approach. Hence the importance of getting and keeping top management support and the need to take special care in developing and introducing the system and in training managers *and* their staff.

RATING PERFORMANCE

Most performance management schemes include some form of rating. This indicates the quality of performance or competence achieved or displayed by an employee by selecting the level on a scale that most closely corresponds with the view of the assessor on how well the individual has been doing. A rating scale is supposed to assist in making judgements and it enables those judgements to be categorized to inform performance or contribution pay decisions, or simply to produce an instant summary for the record of how well or not so well someone is doing.

The rationale for rating

There are four arguments for rating:

1. It recognizes the fact that we all form an overall view of the performance of the people who work for us and that it makes sense to express that view explicitly against a framework of reference rather than hiding it. Managers can thus be held to account for the ratings they make and be required to justify them.

2. It is useful to sum up judgements about people – indicating who are the exceptional performers or under-performers and who are the reliable core performers so that action can be taken (developmental or some form of reward).

3. It is impossible to have performance or contribution pay without ratings – there has to be a method that relates the size of an award to the level of individual achievement. However, this is not actually the case: many organizations with contribution or performance pay do not include ratings as part of the performance management process (23 per cent of the respondents to the e-reward 2005 survey).

4. It conveys a clear message to people on how they are doing and can motivate them to improve performance if they seek an answer to the question: 'What do I have to do to get a higher rating next time?'

Types of rating scales

Rating scales can be defined alphabetically (a, b, c, etc), or numerically (1, 2, 3, etc). Abbreviations or initials (ex for excellent, etc) are sometimes used in an attempt to disguise the hierarchical nature of the scale. The alphabetical or numerical points scale points may be described adjectivally, for example, a = excellent, b = good, c = satisfactory and d= unsatisfactory.

Alternatively, scale levels may be spelt out, as in the following example:

- *Exceptional performance:* exceeds expectations and consistently makes an outstanding contribution that significantly extends the impact and influence of the role.
- *Well-balanced performance:* meets objectives and requirements of the role, consistently performs in a thoroughly proficient manner.
- *Barely effective performance:* does not meet all objectives or role requirements of the role; significant performance improvements are needed.
- *Unacceptable performance:* fails to meet most objectives or requirements of the role; shows a lack of commitment to performance improvement, or a lack of ability, which has been discussed prior to the performance review.

The CIPD 2004c survey found that the majority of organizations had five levels. Some organizations are settling for three levels, but there is no evidence that any single approach is clearly superior to another, although the greater the number of levels the more is being asked of managers in the shape of discriminatory judgement. It does, however, seem to be preferable for level definitions to be positive rather than negative and for them to provide as much guidance as possible on the choice of ratings. It is equally important to ensure that level definitions are compatible with the culture of the organization and that close attention is given to ensuring that managers use them as consistently as possible.

Problems with rating

Ratings are largely subjective and it is difficult to achieve consistency between the ratings given by different managers (ways of achieving consistent judgements are discussed below). Because the notion of 'performance' is often unclear, subjectivity can increase. Even if objectivity is achieved, to sum up the total performance of a person with a single rating is a gross over-simplification of what may be a complex set of factors influencing that performance – to do this after a detailed discussion of strengths and weaknesses suggests that the rating will be a superficial and arbitrary judgement. To label people as 'average' or 'below average', or whatever equivalent terms are used, is both demeaning and demotivating.

The whole performance review meeting may be dominated by the fact that it will end with a rating, thus severely limiting the forward-looking and developmental focus of the meeting, which is all-important. This is particularly the case if the rating governs performance or contribution pay increases.

Achieving consistency in ratings

The problem with rating scales is that it is very difficult, if not impossible without very careful management, to ensure that a consistent approach is adopted by managers responsible for rating, and this means that performance or contribution pay decisions will be suspect. It is almost inevitable that some people will be more generous than others, while others will be harder on their staff. Some managers may be inconsistent in the distribution of ratings to their staff because they are indulging in favouritism or prejudice.

Ratings can, of course, be monitored and challenged if their distribution is significantly out of line, and computer-based systems have been introduced for this purpose in some organizations. But many managers want to do the best for their staff, either because they genuinely believe that they are better or because they are trying to curry favour. It can be difficult in these circumstances to challenge them.

The methods available for increasing consistency are described below.

Training

Training can take place in the form of 'consistency' workshops for managers who discuss how ratings can be justified objectively and test rating decisions on simulated performance review data. This can build a level of common understanding about rating levels.

Peer reviews

Groups of managers meet to review the pattern of each other's ratings and challenge unusual decisions or distributions. This process of moderation or calibration is time-consuming but is possibly the best way to achieve a reasonable degree of consistency, especially when the group members share some knowledge of the performances of each other's staff as internal customers.

Monitoring

The distribution of ratings is monitored by a central department, usually HR, which challenges any unusual patterns and identifies and questions what appear to be unwarrantable differences between departments' ratings.

Consistency at a price can also be achieved by forced distribution or ranking, as described later in this chapter.

Conclusions on ratings

Many organizations retain ratings because they perceive that the advantages outweigh the disadvantages. However, those businesses that want to emphasize the developmental aspect of performance management and play down, even eliminate, the performance pay element, will be convinced by the objections to rating and will dispense with them altogether, relying instead on overall analysis and assessment.

DEALING WITH UNDER-PERFORMERS

The improvement of performance is a fundamental part of the continuous process of performance management. The aim should be the positive one of maximizing high performance, although this involves taking steps to deal with under-performance. When managing under-performers, remember the advice given by Handy (1989) that this should be about 'applauding success and forgiving failure'. He suggests that mistakes should be used as an opportunity for learning – 'something only possible if the mistake is *truly* forgiven because otherwise the lesson is heard as a reprimand and not as an offer of help'.

When dealing with poor performers, note should be made of the following comments by Risher (2003): 'Poor performance is best seen as a problem in which the employer and management are both accountable. In fact, one can argue that it is unlikely to emerge if people are effectively managed.' This is another way of putting the old Army saying: 'There are no bad soldiers, only bad officers.'

Managing under-performers is therefore a positive process that is based on feedback throughout the year and looks forward to what can be done by individuals to overcome performance problems and, importantly, how managers can provide support and help.

The five basic steps required to manage under-performers are as follows.

1. *Identify and agree the problem.* Analyse the feedback and, as far as possible, obtain agreement from the individual on what the shortfall has been. Feedback may be provided by managers but it can in a sense be built into the job. This takes place when individuals are aware of their targets and standards, know what performance measures will be used and either receive feedback/control information automatically or have easy access to it. They will then be in a position to measure and assess their own performance and, if they are well-motivated and well-trained, take their own corrective actions. In other words, a self-regulating feedback mechanism exists. This is a situation that managers should endeavour to create on the grounds that prevention is better than cure.

2. *Establish the reason(s) for the shortfall.* When seeking the reasons for any shortfalls the manager should not crudely be trying to attach blame. The aim should be for the manager and the individual jointly to identify the facts that have contributed to the problem. It is on the basis of this factual analysis that decisions can be made on what to do about it by the individual, the manager, or the two of them working together.

    It is necessary first to identify any causes that are external to the job and outside the control of either the manager or the individual. Any factors that are within the control of the individual and/or the manager can then be considered. What needs to be determined is the extent to which the reason for the problem is because the individual:

    - did not receive adequate support or guidance from his or her manager;
    - did not fully understand what he or she was expected to do;
    - could not do it – ability;
    - did not know how to do it – skill;
    - would not do it – attitude.

3. *Decide and agree on the action required.* Action may be taken by the individual, the manager, or both parties. This could include:

- the individual taking steps to improve skills or change behaviour;
- the individual changing attitudes – the challenge is that people will not change their attitudes simply because they are told to do so; they can only be helped to understand that certain changes to their behaviour could be beneficial not only to the organization but also to themselves;
- the manager providing more support or guidance;
- the manager and the individual working jointly to clarify expectations;
- the manager and the individual working jointly to develop abilities and skills – this is a partnership in the sense that individuals will be expected to take steps to develop themselves, but managers can give help as required in the form of coaching, training and providing additional experience.

Whatever action is agreed, both parties must understand how they will know that it has succeeded. Feedback arrangements can be made but individuals should be encouraged to monitor their own performance and take further action as required.

4. *Resource the action*. Provide the coaching, training, guidance, experience or facilities required to enable agreed actions to happen.
5. *Monitor and provide feedback*. Both managers and individuals monitor performance, ensure that feedback is provided or obtained and analysed, and agree on any further actions that may be necessary.

INTRODUCING PERFORMANCE MANAGEMENT

The programme for introducing performance management should take into account the fact that one of the main reasons why it fails is that line managers are not interested, or they don't have the skills, or both. It is important to get buy-in from top management so that their leadership can encourage line managers to play their part. To ensure buy-in, the process has to be simple (not too much paper) and managers have to be convinced that the time they spend will pay off in terms of improved performance. The demanding skills of concluding performance agreements, setting objectives, assessing performance, giving feedback and coaching need to be developed by formal training supplemented by coaching and the use of mentors.

Excellent practical advice on introducing performance management or making substantial changes to an existing scheme was given by the respondents to the e-Reward 2005 survey. This is summarized below with quotations from respondents to illustrate their views.

Dos

The most frequently mentioned 'dos' in order of frequency were to:

- consult/involve;
- provide training;
- communicate (process and benefits);
- get buy-in from senior management;
- align and ensure relevance to organizational/business/stakeholder needs;
- keep it simple;
- get ownership from line managers;
- ensure clear purpose and processes;
- monitor and evaluate;
- align to culture;
- plan and prepare carefully;
- align with other HR processes;
- run a pilot scheme;
- clarify link to reward;
- treat as a business process;
- be realistic about the scale and pace of change;
- define performance expectations;
- make process mandatory.

Examples of comments

- You can never do enough training/coaching of both staff and line managers. You can never do too much communication on the new changes.
- Ensure the process is seen as a business one, not an HR process.
- Keep it simple and concentrate on the quality going into the process rather than the design of the process itself (although the design must be appropriate to the organization).
- Engage all managers in why it is important and ensure that they have the necessary understanding and skills to carry out the process. Get buy-in and tailor it to the specific needs of the organization. Get the support of key stakeholders such as the union from the start, and get them to work with you to sell the scheme. Agree the overall objectives and guiding principles with all concerned. Keep employees informed and ensure the message is consistent throughout.
- Understand clearly why you are doing it and the desired objectives. Engage others in the design of the scheme. Communicate purpose, etc clearly.

Don'ts

The most common 'don'ts' in order of frequency were:

- don't just make it a form-filling, paper-intensive exercise;
- don't make it too complicated;
- don't rush in a new system;
- don't underestimate the time it takes to introduce;
- don't keep changing the system;
- don't assume managers have the skills required;
- don't link to pay;
- don't blindly follow others;
- don't neglect communication, consultation and training;
- don't assume that everyone wants it.

Examples of comments

- Don't expect that staff will leap for joy at the prospect of another way they would see of criticizing them in their job. Start your change management process where you think the staff are, not where you've assumed they are.
- Don't assume that what seems obvious and logical to you, as an HR manager, will also seem logical to other managers and staff. Don't get caught up in HR-speak and become pedantic about the differences between 'performance management' and 'appraisals', or between a 'personal development/learning plan' and a 'training plan'. As HR professionals we may be able to argue eloquently the subtle differences and merits of each – for most people the distinction is absolutely meaningless!
- Don't just make it a form-filling exercise – you need to gain the belief from managers that the system is beneficial otherwise it won't work.
- Don't put in a lengthy complicated process – it will become a chore to do rather than a meaningful exercise.
- Don't make HR own the initiative – it is a business improvement model and one that the business needs to manage.
- Don't assume that managers have the requisite skills to manage performance fairly and equitably, embark upon such an initiative without clear goals and without the support of respected key players in the organization, set the wheels in motion until extensive briefings/training have been completed.
- Don't underestimate the amount of work involved!
- Don't expect it to work quickly. It takes a few years to embed performance management in the organization's ethos.

34

360-degree feedback

360-degree feedback is a relatively new feature of performance management, although interest is growing. The Institute of Personnel and Development 2003 survey (Armstrong and Baron, 2004) found that only 11 per cent of the organizations covered used it, but the e-reward 2005 survey established that 30 per cent did. This chapter starts with a definition of 360-degree feedback and goes on to describe how it is used and operated and to discuss its advantages and disadvantages and methods of introduction.

360-DEGREE FEEDBACK DEFINED

360-degree feedback has been defined by Ward (1995) as: 'The systematic collection and feedback of performance data on an individual or group derived from a number of the stakeholders on their performance.'

The data is usually fed back in the form of ratings against various performance dimensions. 360-degree feedback is also referred to as multi-source assessment or multi-rater feedback.

Performance data in a 360-degree feedback process, as shown in Figure 34.1, can be generated for individuals from the person to whom they report, their direct reports, their peers (who could be team members and/or colleagues in other parts of the organization) and their external and internal customers.

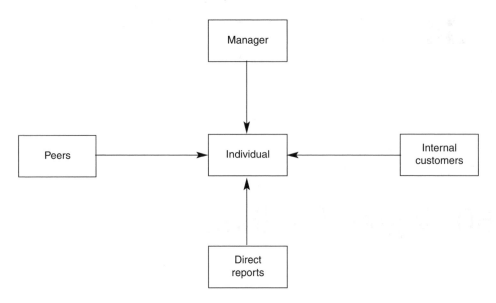

Figure 34.1 360-degree feedback model

The range of feedback could be extended to include other stakeholders – external customers, clients or suppliers (this is sometimes known as 540-degree feedback). A self-assessment process may also be incorporated using for comparison purposes the same criteria as the other generators of feedback.

Feedback can be initiated entirely by peers (in a team setting) or by both peers and team leaders. It can also take the form of 180-degree or upward feedback where this is given by subordinates to their managers. Feedback may be presented direct to individuals, or to their managers, or both. Expert counselling and coaching for individuals as a result of the feedback may be provided by a member of the HR department or by an outside consultant.

USE OF 360-DEGREE FEEDBACK

360-degree feedback is used for a number of purposes. Research conducted by the Ashridge Management Research Group (Handy *et al* 1996) found that typically, 360-degree feedback forms part of a self-development or management development programme. The 45 users covered by the survey fell into the following groups:

- 71 per cent used it solely to support learning and development;

- 23 per cent used it to support a number of HR processes such as appraisal, resourcing and succession planning;
- 6 per cent used it to support pay decisions.

A 1997 survey by the Performance Management Group (unpublished) of 22 organizations using 360-degree feedback found that:

- 77 per cent either disagreed or strongly disagreed with the statement that it is 'a personal development tool and should not be used for wider HR or organizational purposes';
- 81 per cent disagreed or strongly disagreed that 'the natural use of 360-degree feedback is to provide a basis for reward'.

The research conducted by Armstrong and Baron (1998) for the IPD also found that the 51 organizations covered by the research predominantly used 360-degree feedback to help in assessing development needs, and as a basis for performance coaching. Only one-fifth of the respondents used it to determine a performance grade or pay award.

RATIONALE FOR 360-DEGREE FEEDBACK

The main rationale for 360-degree feedback has been expressed by Turnow (1993) as follows:

> 360-degree activities are usually based on two key assumptions: (1) that awareness of any discrepancy between how we see ourselves and how others see us increases self-awareness, and (2) that enhanced self-awareness is a key to maximum performance as a leader, and thus becomes a foundation block for management and leadership development programmes.

London and Beatty (1993) have suggested that the justification for 360-degree feedback is as follows:

- 360-degree feedback can become a powerful organizational intervention to increase awareness of the importance of aligning leader behaviour, work unit results and customer expectations, as well as increasing employee participation in leadership development and work unit effectiveness.
- 360-degree feedback recognizes the complexity of management and the value of input from various sources – it is axiomatic that managers should not be assessing

behaviours they cannot observe, and the leadership behaviours of subordinates may not be known to their managers.

- 360-degree feedback calls attention to important performance dimensions which may hitherto have been neglected by the organization.

360-DEGREE FEEDBACK – METHODOLOGY

The questionnaire

360-degree feedback processes usually obtain data from questionnaires, which measure from different perspectives the behaviours of individuals against a list of competencies. In effect, they ask for an evaluation: 'how well does... do...?' The competency model may be one developed within the organization or the competency headings may be provided by the supplier of a questionnaire.

The dimensions may broadly refer to leadership, management and approaches to work. The headings used in the Performance Management Group's Orbit 360-degree questionnaire are:

- leadership;
- team player/manage people;
- self-management;
- communication;
- vision;
- organizational skills;
- decision making;
- expertise;
- drive;
- adaptability.

The leadership heading, for example, is defined as: 'Shares a clear vision and focuses on achieving it. Demonstrates commitment to the organization's mission. Provides a coherent sense of purpose and direction, both internally and externally, harnessing energy and enthusiasm of staff.'

Ratings

Ratings are given by the generators of the feedback on a scale against each heading. This may refer both to importance and performance, as in the PILAT questionnaire which asks those completing it to rate the importance of each item on a scale of 1 (not important) to 6 (essential), and performance on a scale of 1 (weak in this area) to 6 (outstanding).

Data processing

Questionnaires are normally processed with the help of software developed within the organization or, most commonly, provided by external suppliers. This enables the data collection and analysis to be completed swiftly, with the minimum of effort and in a way that facilitates graphical as well as numerical presentation.

Graphical presentation is preferable as a means of easing the process of assimilating the data. The simplest method is to produce a profile as illustrated in Figure 34.2.

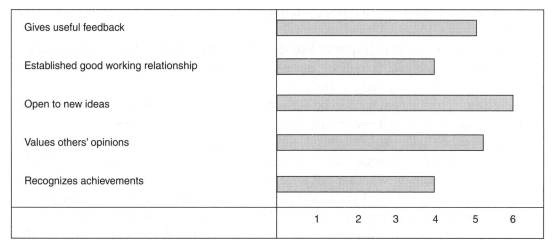

Figure 34.2 360-degree feedback profile

Some of the proprietary software presents feedback data in a much more elaborate form.

Feedback

The feedback is often anonymous and may be presented to the individual (most commonly), to the individual's manager (less common) or to both the individual and the manager. Some organizations do not arrange for feedback to be anonymous. Whether or not feedback is anonymous depends on the organization's culture – the more open the culture, the more likely is the source of feedback to be revealed.

Action

The action generated by the feedback will depend on the purposes of the process, ie development, appraisal or pay. If the purpose is primarily developmental, the action may be left to individuals as part of their personal development plans, but the planning process may be shared between individuals and their managers if they both have access to the information. Even if the data only goes to the individual, it can be discussed in a performance review meeting so that joint plans can be made, and there is much to be said for adopting this approach.

DEVELOPMENT AND IMPLEMENTATION

To develop and implement 360-degree feedback the following steps need to be taken:

1. *Define objectives* – it is important to define exactly what 360-degree feedback is expected to achieve. It will be necessary to spell out the extent to which it is concerned with personal development, appraisal or pay.
2. *Decide on recipients* – who is to be at the receiving end of feedback. This may be an indication of who will eventually be covered after a pilot scheme.
3. *Decide on who will give the feedback* – the individual's manager, direct reports, team members, other colleagues, internal and external customers. A decision will also have to be made on whether HR staff or outside consultants should take part in helping managers to make use of the feedback. A further decision will need to be made on whether or not the feedback should be anonymous (it usually is).
4. *Decide on the areas of work and behaviour* on which feedback will be given – this may be in line with an existing competency model or it may take the form of a list of headings for development. Clearly, the model should fit the culture, values and type of work carried out in the organization. But it might be decided that a list of headings or questions in a software package would be acceptable, at least to start with.
5. *Decide on the method of collecting the data* – the questionnaire could be designed in-house or a consultant's or software provider's questionnaire could be adopted, with the possible option of amending it later to produce better fit.
6. *Decide on data analysis and presentation* – again, the decision is on developing the software in-house or using a package. Most organizations installing 360-degree feedback do, in fact, purchase a package from a consultancy or software house. But the aim should be to keep it as simple as possible.
7. *Plan initial implementation programme* – it is desirable to pilot the process, preferably at top level or with all the managers in a function or department. The pilot

scheme will need to be launched with communications to those involved about the purpose of 360-degree feedback, how it will work and the part they will play. The aim is to spell out the benefits and, as far as possible, allay any fears. Training in giving and receiving feedback will also be necessary.

8. *Analyse outcome of pilot scheme* – the reactions of those taking part in a pilot scheme should be analysed and necessary changes made to the process, the communication package and the training.

9. *Plan and implement full programme* – this should include briefing, communicating, training and support from HR and, possibly, the external consultants.

10. *Monitor and evaluate* – maintain a particularly close watch on the initial implementation of feedback, but monitoring should continue. This is a process that can cause anxiety and stress, or produce little practical gain in terms of development and improved performance for a lot of effort.

360-DEGREE FEEDBACK – ADVANTAGES AND DISADVANTAGES

The survey conducted by the Performance Management Group in 1997 (unpublished) revealed that respondents believed the following benefits resulted from using 360-degree feedback:

- Individuals get a broader perspective of how they are perceived by others than previously possible.
- Increased awareness of and relevance of competencies.
- Increased awareness by senior management that they too have development needs.
- More reliable feedback to senior managers about their performance.
- Gaining acceptance of the principle of multiple stakeholders as a measure of performance.
- Encouraging more open feedback – new insights.
- Reinforcing the desired competencies of the business.
- Provided a clearer picture to senior management of individual's real worth (although there tended to be some 'halo'-effect syndromes).
- Clarified to employees critical performance aspects.
- Opens up feedback and gives people a more rounded view of performance than they had previously.
- Identifying key development areas for the individual, a department and the organization as a whole.

- Identify strengths that can be used to the best advantage of the business.
- A rounded view of an individual's/team's/the organization's performance and what its strengths and weaknesses are.
- It has raised the self-awareness of people managers of how they personally impact upon others – positively and negatively.
- It is supporting a climate of continuous improvement.
- It is starting to improve the climate/morale, as measured through our employee opinion survey.
- Focused agenda for development. Forced line managers to discuss development issues.
- Perception of feedback as more valid and objective, leading to acceptance of results and actions required.

But there may be problems. These include:

- people not giving frank or honest feedback;
- people being put under stress in receiving or giving feedback;
- lack of action following feedback;
- over-reliance on technology;
- too much bureaucracy.

These can all be minimized if not avoided completely by careful design, communication, training and follow-up.

360-DEGREE FEEDBACK – CRITERIA FOR SUCCESS

360-degree feedback is most likely to be successful when:

- it has the active support of top management who themselves take part in giving and receiving feedback and encourage everyone else to do the same;
- there is commitment everywhere else to the process based on briefing, training and an understanding of the benefits to individuals as well as the organization;
- there is real determination by all concerned to use feedback data as the basis for development;
- questionnaire items fit or reflect typical and significant aspects of behaviour;
- items covered in the questionnaire can be related to actual events experienced by the individual;
- comprehensive and well-delivered communication and training programmes are followed;

- no one feels threatened by the process – this is usually often achieved by making feedback anonymous and/or getting a third-party facilitator to deliver the feedback;
- feedback questionnaires are relatively easy to complete (not unduly complex or lengthy, with clear instructions);
- bureaucracy is minimized;
- 360-degree feedback is not limited to pay – its main purpose is developmental, not financial reward.

Part VIII

Human resource development

Human resource development (HRD) is concerned with the provision of learning, development and training opportunities in order to improve individual, team and organizational performance. HRD is essentially a business-led approach to developing people within a strategic framework.

This part considers human resource development under the following headings:

- *Strategic human resource development – definition, aims and activities.*
- *Organizational learning – the process of organizational learning and the concept of the learning organization.*
- *How people learn – a review of learning theory as it affects individual learning.*
- *Learning and development – how organizations make arrangements for appropriate learning and development to take place by various means, including training.*
- *E-learning – the use of electronic methods of supporting learning.*
- *Management development – improving the performance of managers, encouraging self-development and giving them opportunities for growth; the concept of emotional intelligence and its relevance to the development of effective managers.*
- *Formulating and implementing learning and development strategies.*

35

Strategic human resource development

STRATEGIC HRD DEFINED

Strategic human resource management was defined by Hall (1984) as: 'The identification of needed skills and active management of learning for the long range future in relation to explicit corporate and business strategy.' A later definition was provided by Walton (1999) as follows:

> Strategic human resource development involves introducing, eliminating, modifying, directing and guiding processes in such a way that all individuals and teams are equipped with the skills, knowledge and competences they require to undertake current and future tasks required by the organization.

As described by Harrison (2000), strategic HRD is 'development that arises from a clear vision about people's abilities and potential and operates within the overall strategic framework of the business'. Strategic HRD takes a broad and long-term view about how HRD policies and practices can support the achievement of business strategies. It is business-led and the learning and development strategies that are established as part of the overall strategic HRD approach flow from business strategies and have a positive role in helping to ensure that the business attains its goals.

STRATEGIC HRD AIMS

The fundamental aim of strategic HRD is to enhance resource capability in accordance with the belief that the human capital of an organization is a major source of competitive advantage. It is therefore about ensuring that the right quality people are available to meet present and future needs. This is achieved by producing a coherent and comprehensive framework for developing people.

The specific objectives of strategic HRD are to develop intellectual capital and promote organizational, team and individual learning by creating a learning culture – an environment in which employees are encouraged to learn and develop and in which knowledge is managed systematically.

Although strategic HRD is business-led, its policies have to take into account individual aspirations and needs. The importance of increasing employability outside as well as within the organization is an important HRD policy consideration.

COMPONENTS OF HRD

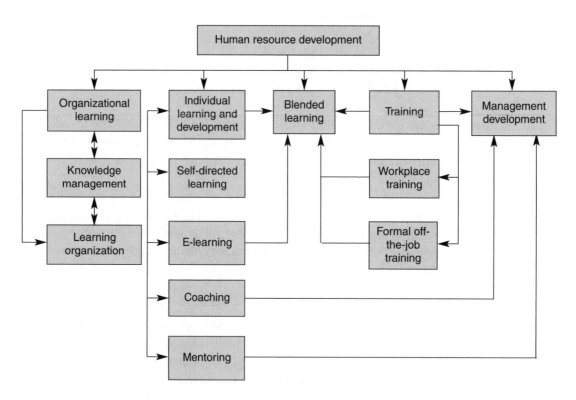

Figure 35.1 Components of human resource development

HRD AND HRM

HRD policies are closely associated with that aspect of HRM that is concerned with investing in people and developing the organization's human capital. As Keep (1989) says:

> One of the primary objectives of HRM is the creation of conditions whereby the latent potential of employees will be realized and their commitment to the causes of the organization secured. This latent potential is taken to include, not merely the capacity to acquire and utilize new skills and knowledge, but also a hitherto untapped wealth of ideas about how the organization's operations might be better ordered.

THE PROCESS OF LEARNING AND DEVELOPMENT

Learning and development was defined by the CIPD (2001) as follows:

> The organizational process of developing people involves the integration of learning and development processes, operations and relationships. Its most powerful outcomes for the business are to do with enhanced organizational effectiveness and sustainability. For the individual they are to do with enhanced personal competence, adaptability and employability. It is therefore a critical business process in for-profit or not-for-profit organizations.

The elements of this process are:

- *Learning* – defined by Bass and Vaughan (1966) as 'a relatively permanent change in behaviour that occurs as a result of practice or experience'.
- *Education* – the development of the knowledge, values and understanding required in all aspects of life rather than the knowledge and skills relating to particular areas of activity.
- *Development* – the growth or realization of a person's ability and potential through the provision of learning and educational experiences.
- *Training* – the planned and systematic modification of behaviour through learning events, programmes and instruction, which enable individuals to achieve the levels of knowledge, skill and competence needed to carry out their work effectively.

STRATEGIES FOR HRD

Strategic priorities

The strategic priorities for human resource development as defined by Harrison (2005) are to:

- raise awareness of the need for a learning culture that leads to continuous improvement;
- develop the competence of managers to become actively involved in learning that leads to knowledge creation;
- expand learning capacity throughout the organization;
- focus on all the organization's knowledge workers, not just the key personnel;
- harness e-learning to knowledge sharing and knowledge creation.

Development steps

The steps required to develop a learning and development strategy as described by Harrison (2005) are:

1. Agree on the strategy-making team.
2. Clarify organizational mission.
3. Explore core values.
4. Identify the strategic issues facing the organization.
5. Agree on strategy and strategic plan.

Models for the delivery of the strategy

Carter *et al* (2002) suggest that the following models are available to deliver HRD strategy:

- centralized – all learning and development activities are conducted and controlled from the centre;
- key account holder – a small corporate centre is responsible for career management and management development processes; key account holders are responsible to the centre for delivering learning and training in business units;
- devolved – all learning and development activities are devolved to business units;
- business partner – key account holders report to business unit;

- shared service – business units share common learning and development services and specify what they want to the corporate centre;
- outsourced – training outsourced to providers by corporate centre or business units;
- stakeholder – small corporate centre engages in transformational learning activities, separate shared service facilities are used, learning and development practitioners act as business partners and specialized learning is outsourced.

HUMAN RESOURCE DEVELOPMENT PHILOSOPHY

A human resource development philosophy could be expressed in the following terms:

We believe that:

- Human resource development makes a major contribution to the successful attainment of the organization's objectives and that investment in it benefits all the stakeholders of the organization.
- Human resource development plans and programmes should be integrated with and support the achievement of business and human resource strategies.
- Human resource development should always be performance-related – designed to achieve specified improvements in corporate, functional, team and individual performance, and make a major contribution to bottom-line results.
- Everyone in the organization should be encouraged and given the opportunity to learn – to develop their skills and knowledge to the maximum of their capacity.
- Personal development processes provide the framework for individual learning.
- While we recognize the need to invest in learning and development and to provide appropriate learning opportunities and facilities, the prime responsibility for development rests with the individual, who will be given the guidance and support of his or her manager and, as necessary, members of the HR department.

36

Organizational learning and the learning organization

Organizational learning theory is concerned with how learning takes place in organizations. It focuses on collective learning but takes into account the proposition made by Argyris (1992) that organizations do not perform the actions that produce the learning; it is individual members of the organization who behave in ways that lead to it, although organizations can create conditions which facilitate such learning. The concept of organizational learning as discussed in the first section of this chapter recognizes that the way in which this takes place is affected by the context of the organization and its culture.

The concept of a learning organization, which is often associated with that of organizational learning, has been defined by Scarborough and Carter (2000) as one 'that is able to discover what is effective by reframing its own experiences and learning from that process'. The notion of the learning organization is sometimes confused with the concept of organizational learning. However, Harrison (2002) points out that it is often assumed that 'the learning organization' and 'organizational learning' are synonymous processes, yet they are not.

ORGANIZATIONAL LEARNING

Organizational learning is defined by Easterby-Smith and Araujo (1999) as an 'efficient procedure to process, interpret and respond to both internal and external information of a predominantly explicit nature'. Organizational learning is concerned with the development of new knowledge or insights that have the potential to influence behaviour (Mabey and Salaman, 1995). It takes place within the wide institutional context of inter-organizational relationships (Geppert, 1996), and 'refers broadly to an organization's acquisition of understanding, know-how, techniques and practices of any kind and by any means' (Argyris and Schon, 1996). Organizational learning theory examines how in this context individual and team learning can be translated into an organizational resource and is therefore linked to processes of knowledge management (see Chapter 12).

Organizational learning has been defined by Marsick (1994) as a process of 'coordinated systems change, with mechanisms built in for individuals and groups to access, build and use organizational memory, structure and culture to develop long-term organizational capacity'.

It is emphasized by Harrison (2000) that organizational learning is not simply the sum of the learning of individuals and groups across the organization. She comments that: 'Many studies (see for example Argyris and Schon, 1996) have confirmed that without effective processes and systems linking individual and organizational learning, the one has no necessary counterpart with the other'.

Outcomes of organizational learning

Organizational learning outcomes contribute to the development of a firm's resource-based capability. This is in accordance with one of the basic principles of human resource management, namely that it is necessary to invest in people in order to develop the intellectual capital required by the organization and thus increase its stock of knowledge and skills. As stated by Ehrenberg and Smith (1994), human capital theory indicates that: 'The knowledge and skills a worker has – which comes from education and training, including the training that experience brings – generate productive capital'.

Pettigrew and Whipp (1991) believe that the focus of organizational learning should be on developing 'organizational capability'. This means paying attention to the intricate and often unnoticed or hidden learning that takes place and influences what occurs within the organization. 'Hidden learning' is acquired and developed in the normal course of work by people acting as individuals and, importantly, in groups or 'communities of practice' (Wenger and Snyder, 2000).

The process of organizational learning

Organizational learning can be characterized as an intricate three-stage process consisting of knowledge acquisition, dissemination and shared implementation (Dale, 1994). Knowledge may be acquired from direct experience, the experience of others or organizational memory.

Argyris (1992) suggests that organizational learning occurs under two conditions: first, when an organization achieves what is intended, and second, when a mismatch between intentions and outcomes is identified and corrected. He distinguishes between single-loop and double-loop learning. These two types of learning have been described by West (1996) as adaptive or generative learning.

Single-loop or adaptive learning is sequential, incremental and focused on issues and opportunities that are within the scope of the organization's activities. As described by Argyris (1992), organizations where single-loop learning is the norm define the 'governing variables' – what they expect to achieve in terms of targets and standards – and then monitor and review achievements, and take corrective action as necessary, thus completing the loop. Double-loop learning occurs when the monitoring process initiates action to redefine the 'governing variables' to meet the new situation, which may be imposed by the external environment. The organization has learnt something new about what has to be achieved in the light of changed circumstances, and can then decide how this should be achieved. This learning is converted into action. The process is illustrated in Figure 36.1.

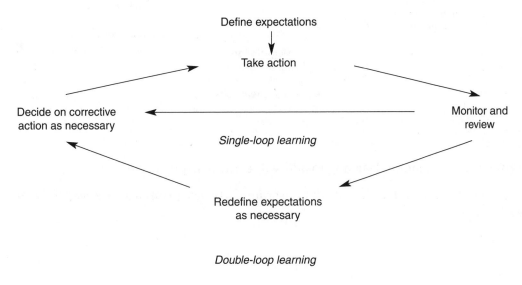

Figure 36.1 Single- and double-loop learning

Argyris believes that single-loop learning is appropriate for routine, repetitive issues – 'it helps get the everyday job done'. Double-loop learning is more relevant for complex, non-programmable issues. As Pickard (1997) points out, double-loop learning questions why the problem occurred in the first place, and tackles its root causes, rather than simply addressing its surface symptoms, as happens with single-loop learning.

Organizational learning takes place in a learning cycle as shown in Figure 36.2.

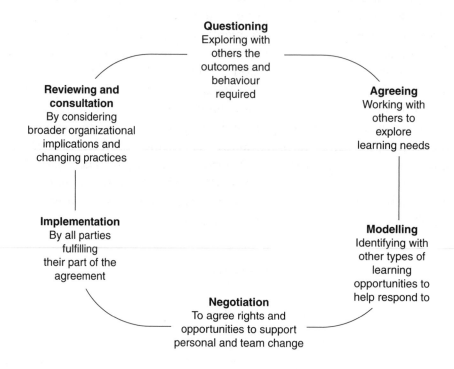

Figure 36.2 Managing learning to add value; the learning cycle

(*Source:* New Learning for New Work Consortium, *Managing Learning for Added Value*, IPD, 1999)

Principles of organizational learning

Harrison (1997) has defined five principles of organizational learning:

1. The need for a powerful and cohering vision of the organization to be communicated and maintained across the workforce in order to promote awareness of the need for strategic thinking at all levels.
2. The need to develop strategy in the context of a vision that is not only powerful but also open-ended and unambiguous. This will encourage a search for a wide rather than a narrow range of strategic options, will promote lateral thinking and will orient the knowledge creating activities of employees.
3. Within the framework of vision and goals, frequent dialogue, communication and conversations are major facilitators of organizational learning.
4. It is essential continuously to challenge people to re-examine what they take for granted.
5. It is essential to develop a conducive learning and innovation climate.

THE LEARNING ORGANIZATION

The philosophy underpinning the learning organization concept, as expressed by Garvin (1993), is that learning is an essential ingredient if organizations are to survive; that learning at operational, policy and strategic levels needs to be conscious, continuous and integrated; and that management is responsible for creating an emotional climate in which all staff can learn continuously.

Definition of a learning organization

Senge (1990), who created the term, described a learning organization as one 'where people continually expand their capacity to create the results they truly desire, where new and expansive patterns of thinking are nurtured, where collective aspiration is set free, and where people are continually learning how to learn together'.

There have been many other definitions of a learning organization, all of which are aspirational in the vein of Senge. Pedler *et al* (1991) state that a learning organization is one 'which facilitates the learning of all its members and continually transforms itself'. Wick and Leon (1995) refer to a learning organization as one that 'continually improves by rapidly creating and refining the capabilities required for future success'.

Garvin (1993) defines a learning organization as one which is 'skilled at creating, acquiring, and transferring knowledge, and at modifying its behaviour to reflect new knowledge and insights'. He believes that learning organizations ensure that they learn from experience, develop continuous improvement programmes, use systematic problem-solving techniques, and transfer knowledge quickly and efficiently throughout the organization by means of formal training programmes linked to implementation.

As Burgoyne (1994) has pointed out, learning organizations have to be able to adapt to their context and develop their people to match the context. Many individual jobs could be learnt by processes of 'natural discovery' rather than formula learning. His definition (1988a) of a learning organization is that it channels the career and life-planning activities of individual managers in a way that allows the organization to meet its strategic needs. This is done by encouraging the identification of individual needs, organic formulation of business strategy with inputs from training departments on current skills, and continual organizational review and learning from experience. In 1999 he suggested that a learning organization 'provides a healthy environment for natural learning'.

Key principles of the learning organization

Miller and Stewart (1999) propose the following key principles of the learning organization:

- learning and business strategy are closely linked;
- the organization consciously learns from business opportunities and threats;
- individuals, groups and the whole organization are not only learning but also learning how to learn;
- information systems and technology serve to support learning rather than control it;
- there are well-defined processes for defining, creating, capturing, sharing and acting on knowledge;
- these various systems and dimensions are balanced and managed as a whole.

Corporate universities provide one way of putting these principles into effect - they offer an educational experience tailored to the specific needs of the organization, the emphasis being on employees constantly engaging with learning and on educators designing courses that will continuously motivate them, usually and sometimes wholly in a virtual environment. The emphasis is on employees learning continuously and on transferring knowledge quickly.

Developing a learning organization

One approach to the development of a learning organization, as advocated by Senge (1990), is to focus on collective problem-solving within an organization using team learning and a 'soft systems' approach whereby all the possible causes of a problem are considered in order to define more clearly those which can be dealt with and those which are insoluble.

Garratt (1990) believes that managers have to develop learning abilities as individuals, and work and learn as teams. He advocates the use of development activities such as job enlargement, job enrichment, monitoring, and various forms of team and project-based work.

The learning organization and knowledge management

Learning organizations are very much concerned with developing and sharing the knowledge that is critical to their strategic success. The problem is that it is hard to capture tacit knowledge in the form of the deeply embedded amalgam of wisdom and know-how that competitors are unable to copy. Methods of sharing knowledge were described in Chapter 12. One approach, as advocated by Wenger and Snyder (2000), is to encourage the development of 'communities of practice' in which people with similar concerns exchange ideas and knowledge and discuss shared problems. Wenger and Snyder claim that a community of practice could be treated as a 'learning ecology' with a life of its own in which there is scope to reflect jointly on experience so that it can be converted into learning.

Scarborough and Carter (2000) suggest that although the concepts of the learning organization and organizational learning have offered some valuable insights into the way in which knowledge and learning are fostered by management practice, they have been overshadowed, at least in terms of practitioner interest, by the explosive growth of knowledge management activity. They comment that:

> This may be attributable to the problems of translating their (knowledge management and organizational learning) broad, holistic principles into practice. Knowledge management initiatives by contrast, are often more specifically targeted and can therefore be identified more closely with business needs.

Problems with the concept of the learning organization

The notion of the learning organization remains persuasive because of its 'rationality, human attractiveness and presumed potential to aid organizational effectiveness and advancement' (Harrison, 1997). But the concept has been criticized by Harrison

(2005) because, 'as usually defined, it suggests that organizations have a life of their own and are themselves capable of learning, which is not the case'. Scarborough *et al* (1999) argue that 'the dominant perspective (of the learning organization concept) is that of organization systems and design'. Little attention seems to be paid to what individuals want to learn or how they learn. The idea that individuals should be enabled to invest in their own development (a fundamental theme of human capital theory) seems to have escaped learning organization theorists, who are more inclined to focus on the imposition of learning by the organization, rather than creating a climate conducive to collaborative and self-managed learning.

Viewing organizations as learning systems is a limited notion. Argyris and Schon (1996) contend that organizations are products of visions, ideas, norms and beliefs so that their shape is much more fragile than the organization's material structure. People act as learning agents for the organization in ways that cannot easily be systematized. They are not only individual learners but also have the capacity to learn collaboratively (Hoyle, 1995). Organization learning theory analyses how this happens and leads to the belief that it is the culture and environment that are important, not the systems approach implied by the concept of the learning organization. Argyris and Schon (1996) refer to the practice-orientated and prescriptive literature of the learning organization, which is quite different from the concerns of organizational learning theorists about collaborative and informal learning processes within organizations.

The notion of a learning organization is somewhat nebulous. It incorporates miscellaneous ideas about human resource development, systematic training, action learning, organizational development and knowledge management, with an infusion of the precepts of total quality management. But they do not add up to a convincing whole. Easterby-Smith (1997) argues that attempts to create a single best-practice framework for understanding the learning organization are fundamentally flawed. Prescriptions from training specialists and management consultants abound but, as Sloman (1999) asserts, they often fail to recognize that learning is a continuous process, not a set of discrete training activities.

Burgoyne (1999), one of the earlier publicists for the idea of a learning organization, has admitted that there has been some confusion about the concept and that there have been substantial naiveties in most of the early thinking: 'The learning organization has not delivered its full potential or lived up to all our aspirations'. He also mentioned that after a decade of working with the notion of the learning organization there are distressingly few, if any, case studies of success with the idea on a large scale. He believes that the concept should be integrated with knowledge management initiatives so that different forms of knowledge can be linked, fed by organizational learning and used in adding value to goods and services. This, he states, will replace the 'soft' organizational development tools of the 1970s that were pressed hurriedly into service; 'The learning organization ran ahead of the methods available to implement it and into this vacuum were sucked traditional approaches such as teamworking, leadership and personal development.'

At least, however, the learning organization movement has helped to emphasize the importance of knowledge management as a practical proposition for promoting organizational learning. In added-value terms, this is likely to provide more benefit to organizations than pursuing the will-o'-the-wisp of the learning organization as originally conceived.

37

How people learn

An understanding of how people learn is necessary if learning is to take place effectively in an organization. The aims of this chapter are to:

- define the concept of learning;
- describe the process of learning;
- summarize the different ways in which people in general learn (learning theory);
- describe how individuals learn – their learning styles and 'learning to learn';
- examine the concept of the learning curve – how people achieve required skill levels;
- discuss the key topic of the motivation to learn;
- describe the practical implications of these theories, concepts and approaches;
- set out the conditions for effective learning.

LEARNING DEFINED

Learning has been defined by Kim (1993) as the process of 'increasing one's capacity to take action'. As explained by Reynolds *et al* (2002) it should be distinguished from training: 'Learning is the process by which a person acquires new knowledge, skills and capabilities whereas training is one of several responses an organization can take to promote learning.'

A distinction was also made between learning and development by Pedler *et al* (1989), who see learning as being concerned with an increase in knowledge or a higher degree of an existing skill, whereas development is more towards a different state of being or functioning. Argyris (1993) makes the point that 'Learning is not simply having a new insight or a new idea. Learning occurs when we take effective action, when we detect and correct error. How do you know when you know something? When you can produce what it is you claim to know.'

THE LEARNING PROCESS

A number of leading authorities on learning in organizations (Honey, 1998) have declared that 'learning is complex and various, covering all sorts of things such as knowledge, skills, insights, beliefs, values, attitudes and habits'. Individuals learn for themselves and learn from other people. They learn as members of teams and by interaction with their managers, co-workers and people outside the organization. People learn by doing and by instruction. The ways in which individuals learn differ, and the extent to which they learn depends largely on how well they are externally motivated or self-motivated.

The effectiveness of learning will be strongly influenced by the context in which it takes place. This includes the values of the organization. Is it truly believed that learning is important as a means of developing a high performance culture and achieving competitive advantage? Is this belief confirmed by actions that encourage and support learning? Is the approach to learning delivery in line with the belief of Birchall and Lyons (1995) that 'For effective learning to take place at the individual level it is essential to foster an environment where individuals are encouraged to take risks and experiment, where mistakes are tolerated, but where means exist for those involved to learn from their experiences'?

LEARNING THEORY

There are a number of learning theories, each of which focuses on different aspects of the learning process as applied to people in general. The main theories are concerned with:

- reinforcement;
- cognitive learning;
- experiential learning;
- social learning.

Reinforcement theory

Reinforcement theory is based on the work of Skinner (1974). It expresses the belief that changes in behaviour take place as a result of an individual's response to events or stimuli, and the ensuing consequences (rewards or punishments). Individuals can be 'conditioned' to repeat the behaviour by positive reinforcement in the form of feedback and knowledge of results.

Gagne (1977) later developed his stimulus-response theory, which relates the learning process to a number of factors, including reinforcement, namely:

- *Drive* – there must be a basic need or drive to learn.
- *Stimulus* – people must be stimulated by the learning process.
- *Response* – people must be helped by the learning process to develop appropriate responses; in other words, the knowledge, skills and attitudes that will lead to effective performance.
- *Reinforcement* – these responses need to be reinforced by feedback and experience until they are learnt.

Cognitive learning theory

Cognitive learning involves gaining knowledge and understanding by absorbing information in the form of principles, concepts and facts, and then internalizing it. Learners can be regarded as powerful information processing machines

Experiential learning theory

People are active agents of their own learning (Reynolds *et al* 2002). Experiential learning takes place when people learn from their experience by reflecting on it so that it can be understood and applied. Learning is therefore a personal 'construction' of meaning through experience. 'Constructivists' such as Rogers (1983) believe that experiential learning will be enhanced through facilitation – creating an environment in which people can be stimulated to think and act in ways that help them to make good use of their experience.

Social learning theory

Social learning theory states that effective learning requires social interaction. Wenger (1998) suggested that we all participate in 'communities of practice' (groups of people with shared expertise who work together) and that these are our primary sources of learning. Bandura (1977) views learning as a series of information processing steps set in train by social interactions.

LEARNING STYLES

Learning theories describe in general terms how people learn, but individual learners will have different styles – a preference for a particular approach to learning. The two most familiar classifications of learning styles are those produced by Kolb and by Honey and Mumford.

Kolb's learning style inventory

Kolb *et al* (1974) identified a learning cycle consisting of four stages as shown in Figure 37.1. He defined these stages as follows:

- *Concrete experience* – this can be planned or accidental.
- *Reflective observation* – this involves actively thinking about the experience and its significance.
- *Abstract conceptualization (theorizing)* – generalizing from experience in order to develop various concepts and ideas which can be applied when similar situations are encountered.
- *Active experimentation* – testing the concepts or ideas in new situations. This gives rise to a new concrete experience and the cycle begins again.

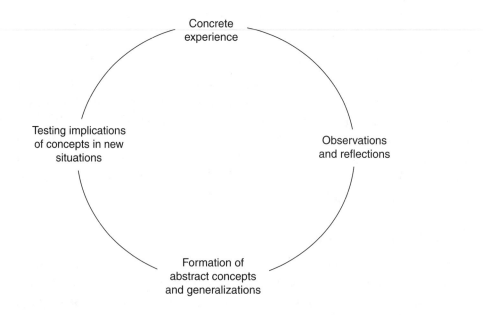

Figure 37.1 The Kolb learning cycle

The key to Kolb's model is that it is a simple description of how experience is translated into concepts which are then used to guide the choice of new experiences. To learn effectively, individuals must shift from being observers to participants, from direct involvement to a more objective analytical detachment. Every person has his or her own learning style, and one of the most important arts that trainers have to develop is to adjust their approaches to the learning styles of trainees. Trainers must acknowledge these learning styles rather than their own preferred approach.

Kolb also defined the following learning styles of trainees:

- *Accommodators* who learn by trial and error, combining the concrete experience and experimentation stages of the cycle.
- *Divergers* who prefer concrete to abstract learning situations, and reflection to active involvement. Such individuals have great imaginative ability, and can view a complete situation from different viewpoints.
- *Convergers* who prefer to experiment with ideas, considering them for their practical usefulness. Their main concern is whether the theory works in action, thus combining the abstract and experimental dimensions.
- *Assimilators* who like to create their own theoretical models and assimilate a number of disparate observations into an overall integrated explanation. Thus they veer towards the reflective and abstract dimensions.

The Honey and Mumford learning styles

Another analysis of learning styles was made by Honey and Mumford (1996). They identified four styles:

- *Activists* who involve themselves fully without bias in new experiences and revel in new challenges.
- *Reflectors* who stand back and observe new experiences from different angles. They collect data, reflect on it and then come to a conclusion.
- *Theorists* who adapt and apply their observations in the form of logical theories. They tend to be perfectionists.
- *Pragmatists* who are keen to try out new ideas, approaches and concepts to see if they work.

However, none of these four learning styles is exclusive. It is quite possible that one person could be both a reflector and a theorist, and someone else could be an activist/pragmatist, a reflector/pragmatist or even a theorist/pragmatist.

LEARNING TO LEARN

People learn all the time, and through doing so acquire knowledge, skills and insight. But they will learn more effectively if they 'learn how to learn'. As defined by Honey (1998), the process of learning to learn is the acquisition of knowledge, skills and insights about the learning process itself. The aims, as described by Honey, are to:

- provide a basis for organizing and planning learning;
- pinpoint precisely what has been learnt and what to do better or differently as a consequence;
- share what has been learnt with other people so that they benefit;
- check on the quality of what has been learnt;
- transfer what has been learnt and apply it in different circumstances;
- improve the learning process itself so that how people learn, not just what people learn, is given constant attention.

THE LEARNING CURVE

The concept of the learning curve refers to the time it takes an inexperienced person to reach the required level of performance in a job or a task. This is sometimes called the experienced worker's standard (ESW). The standard learning curve is shown in Figure 37.2, but rates of learning vary, depending on the effectiveness of the learning process, the experience and natural aptitude of the learner, and the latter's interest in learning. Both the time taken to reach the experienced worker's standard and the variable speed with which learning takes place at different times affect the shape of the curve, as shown in Figure 37.3.

Learning is often stepped, with one or more plateaux while further progress is halted. This may be because learners cannot continually increase their skills or speeds of work and need a pause to consolidate what they have already learnt. The existence of steps such as those shown in Figure 37.4 can be used when planning skills training, to provide deliberate reinforcement periods when newly acquired skills are practised in order to achieve the expected standards.

When a training module is being prepared which describes what has to be learnt and the training required to achieve the required levels of skill and speed, it is often desirable to proceed step by step, taking one task or part of a task at a time, reinforcing it and then progressively adding other parts, consolidating at each stage. This is called the progressive parts method of training.

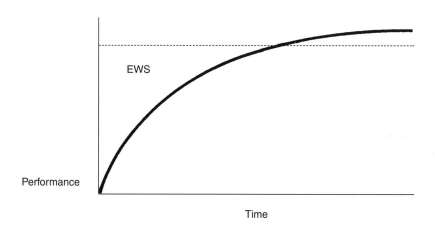

Figure 37.2   A standard learning curve

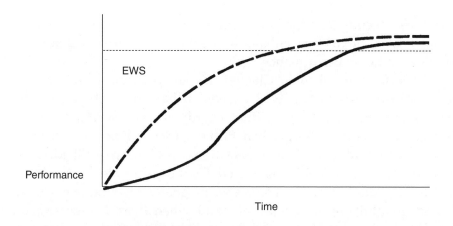

Figure 37.3   Different rates of learning

THE MOTIVATION TO LEARN

People will learn more effectively if they are motivated to learn. The motivation to learn can be defined as 'those factors that energise and direct behavioural patterns organized around a learning goal' (Rogers, 1996). As Reynolds *et al* (2002) comment, 'The disposition and commitment of the learner – their motivation to learn – is one of

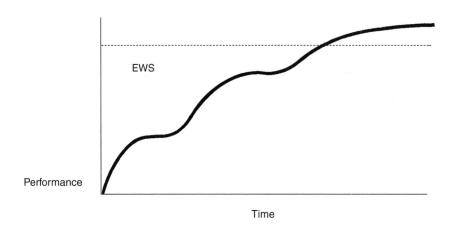

Figure 37.4 A stepped learning curve

the most critical factors affecting learning and training effectiveness. Under the right conditions, a strong disposition to learn, enhanced by solid experience and a positive attitude, can lead to exceptional performance.'

Two motivation theories (described in Chapter 18) are particularly relevant to learning. Expectancy theory states that goal-directed behaviour is driven by the expectation of achieving something the individual regards as desirable. If individuals feel that the outcome of learning is likely to benefit them, they will be more inclined to pursue it. When they find that their expectations have been fulfilled, their belief that learning is worthwhile will be reinforced. Goal theory states that motivation is higher when individuals aim to achieve specific goals, when these goals are accepted and, although difficult, are achievable, and when there is feedback on performance. Learning goals may be set for individuals (but to be effective as motivators they must be agreed), or individuals may set their own goals (self-directed learning).

THE IMPLICATIONS OF LEARNING THEORY AND CONCEPTS

The practical implications of the learning theories and concepts described above are summarized in Table 37.1.

Table 37.1 The implications of learning theory and concepts

Theory/concept	Content	Practical implications
The process of learning	Learning is complex and is achieved in many different ways. The context is important	Different learning needs require different learning methods, often in combination. Learning effectiveness depends on the extent to which the organization believes in learning and supports it
Reinforcement theory	Behaviours can be strengthened by reinforcing them with positive feedback (conditioning)	Reinforcement theory underpins training programmes concerned with developing skills through instruction. In these, the learner is conditioned to make a response and receives immediate feedback, and progress is made in incremental steps, each directed to a positive outcome
Cognitive learning theory	Learners acquire understanding which they internalize by being exposed to learning materials and by solving problems	The knowledge and understanding of learners can be enriched and internalized by presenting them with learning materials (eg e-learning). Case studies, projects and problem solving activities can also be used for this purpose. Self-directed learning, personal development planning activities and discovery learning processes with help from facilitators, coaches or mentors are underpinned by cognitive learning theory
Experiential learning theory	People learn by constructing meaning and developing their skills through experience	Learning through experience can be enhanced by encouraging learners to reflect on and make better use of what they learn through their own work and from other people. Self-directed learning and personal development planning activities with help from facilitators, coaches or mentors are also underpinned by experiential learning theory, as is action learning

continued

Table 37.1 *continued*

Social learning theory	Learning is most effective in a social setting. Individual understanding is shaped by active participation in real situations	Learning can be encouraged in communities of practice, and in project teams and networks
Learning styles	Every person has his or her own learning style	Learning programmes need to be adjusted to cope with different learning styles. Trainers have also to flex their methods. People will learn more effectively if they are helped to 'learn how to learn' by making the best use of their own style, but also by experimenting with other styles
The learning curve	The time required to reach an acceptable standard of skills or competence which varies between people. Learning may proceed in steps with plateaux, rather than being a continuous process	Recognize that progress may vary and may not be continuous. Enable learners to consolidate their learning, and introduce reinforcement periods in training programmes to recognize the existence of learning steps and plateaux
The motivation to learn	People need to be motivated to learn effectively	Learners should be helped to develop learning goals and to understand the benefits to them of achieving them. Performance management processes leading to personal development plans can provide a means of doing this

38

Learning and development

This chapter is about how organizations make arrangements for appropriate learning and development to take place by various means, including training. It is divided into three sections: learning, development and training.

The formulation and implementation of learning and development strategies is dealt with in Chapter 41.

LEARNING

Defined

Learning is the process by which a person acquires and develops new knowledge, skills, capabilities and attitudes. As Williams (1998) defined it, 'learning is goal directed, it is based on experience, it impacts behaviour and cognition, and the changes brought about are relatively stable'. Honey and Mumford (1996) explained that: 'Learning has happened when people can demonstrate that they know something that they did not know before (insights, realizations as well as facts) and when they can do something they could not do before (skills)'. Mumford and Gold (2004) emphasized that: 'Learning is both a process and an outcome concerned with knowledge, skills and insight.'

There are four types of learning:

1. *Instrumental learning* – learning how to do the job better once the basic standard of performance has been attained. Helped by learning on the job.
2. *Cognitive learning* – outcomes based on the enhancement of knowledge and understanding.
3. *Affective learning* – outcomes based on the development of attitudes or feelings rather than knowledge.
4. *Self-reflective learning* – developing new patterns of understanding, thinking and behaving and therefore creating new knowledge (Harrison, 2005).

Aim

The aim of the learning policies and programmes of an organization is to provide the skilled, knowledgeable and competent people required to meet its present and future needs. To achieve this aim it is necessary to ensure that learners are ready to learn, understand what they need to know and be able to do, and are able to take responsibility for their learning by making good use of the learning resources available, including the support and guidance of their line managers.

Philosophy

The philosophy of learning was expressed by Sloman (2003a) as follows:

> Interventions and activities that are intended to improve knowledge and skills will increasingly focus on the learner. Emphasis will shift to the individual learner (or team). And he or she will be encouraged to take more responsibility for his or her learning. Efforts will be made to develop a climate that supports effective and appropriate learning. Such interventions and activities will form part of an integrated approach to creating competitive advantage through people in the organization.

Learning and development

Learning is a continuous process that not only enhances existing capabilities but also leads to the development of the skills, knowledge and attitudes that prepare people for enlarged or higher-level responsibilities in the future.

Learning and training

The encouragement of learning makes use of a process model that is concerned with facilitating the learning activities of individuals and providing learning resources for them to use. Conversely, the provision of training involves the use of a content model, which means deciding in advance the knowledge and skills that need to be enhanced by training, planning the programme, deciding on training methods and presenting the content in a logical sequence through various forms of instruction. A distinction is made by Sloman (2003a) between learning that 'lies within the domain of the individual' and training that 'lies within the domain of the organization'. Today, the approach is to focus on individual learning and ensure that it takes place when required – ' just-for-you' and 'just-in-time' learning.

Conditions for effective learning

The conditions required for learning to be effective, as derived from the learning theories and concepts described in Chapter 37, are set out below.

Motivation to learn

Individuals must be motivated to learn. They should be aware that their present level of knowledge, skill or competence, or their existing attitude or behaviour, need to be developed or improved if they are to perform their work to their own and to others' satisfaction. They must, therefore, have a clear picture of the behaviour they should adopt. To be motivated, learners must gain satisfaction from learning. They are most capable of learning if it satisfies one or more of their needs. Conversely, the best learning programmes can fail if they are not seen as useful by those undertaking them.

Self-directed learning

Self-directed or self-managed learning involves encouraging individuals to take responsibility for their own learning needs, either to improve performance in their present job or to develop their potential and satisfy their career aspirations. It can be based on a process of recording achievement and action planning that involves individuals reviewing what they have learnt, what they have achieved, what their goals are, how they are going to achieve those goals and what new learning they need to acquire. The learning programme can be 'self-paced' in the sense that learners can decide for themselves up to a point the rate at which they work and are encouraged to measure their own progress and adjust the programme accordingly.

Self-directed learning is based on the principle that people learn and retain more if they find things out for themselves. But they still need to be given guidance on what to look for and help in finding it. Learners have to be encouraged to define, with whatever help they may require, what they need to know to perform their job effectively. They need to be provided with guidance on where they can get the material or information that will help them to learn and how to make good use of it. Personal development plans, as described later in this chapter, can provide a framework for this process. They also need support from their manager and the organization with the provision of coaching, mentoring and learning facilities, including e-learning.

Self-directed learning can also be described as self-reflective learning (Mezirow, 1985), which is the kind of learning that involves encouraging individuals to develop new patterns of understanding, thinking and behaving. It is a process which was described by Argyris (1992) as double-loop learning, which is based on an examination of the root causes of problems and can create a new learning loop that goes far deeper than the traditional learning loop provided by 'instrumental learning' (ie learning how to perform a job better) which tends only to focus on the surface symptoms of a problem.

Learning goals, direction and feedback

Effective learning is more likely to be achieved if learners have learning goals. They should have targets and standards of performance that they find acceptable and achievable and can use to judge their own progress. They should be encouraged and helped to set their own goals. The learning outcome must be clear.

Learners need a sense of direction and feedback on how they are doing. They should receive reinforcement of correct behaviour. Self-motivated individuals may provide much of this for themselves, but it is necessary to have a learning facilitator, eg a mentor, who is available to encourage and help when necessary. Learners usually need to know quickly how well they are doing. In a prolonged programme, intermediate steps are required in which learning can be reinforced. The content of the learning programme may therefore need to be broken down into small modules or elements, each with an objective.

Learning methods

The learning goals and the particular needs and learning style of the learner should indicate what learning method or methods should be used. Specific goals and understanding of individual needs help to select appropriate learning methods. It should not be assumed that a single learning method will do. A combination of methods is likely to produce better results. The use of a variety of methods, as long as they are all appropriate, helps learning by engaging the interest of learners.

Learning is 'personal, subjective and inseparable from activity' (Reynolds, 2004). It is an active, not a passive process. As far as possible, therefore, the learning process should be active, although this may take more time than passive methods in which the learner is at the receiving end of some form of training, eg instruction. The more complex the skill to be mastered, the more the learning methods need to be active. Learning requires time to assimilate, test and accept. This time should be provided in the learning programme.

Levels of learning

Different levels of learning exist and these need different methods and take different times. At the simplest level, learning requires direct physical responses, memorization and basic conditioning. At a higher level, learning involves adapting existing knowledge or skill to a new task or environment. At the next level, learning becomes a complex process when principles are identified in a range of practices or actions, when a series of isolated tasks have to be integrated, or when the process is about developing interpersonal skills. The most complex form of learning takes place when learning is concerned with the values and attitudes of people and groups. This is not only the most complex area, but also the most difficult.

Blending learning

Blending different but appropriate types of learning produces the best results.

Spectrum of learning – from informal to formal

There is a spectrum of learning as defined by Watkins and Marsick (1993), from informal to formal, as follows:

- unanticipated experiences and encounters that result in learning as an incidental by-product, which may or may not be consciously recognized;
- new job assignments and participation in teams, or other job-related challenges that provide for learning and self-development;
- self-initiated and self-planned experiences, including the use of media and seeking out a coach or mentor;
- total quality or improvement groups/active learning designed to promote continuous learning for continuous improvement;
- providing a framework for learning associated with personal development planning or career planning;
- the combination of less-structured with structured opportunities to learn from these experiences;
- designed programmes of mentoring, coaching or workplace learning;
- formal training programmes or courses involving instruction.

Informal learning

Informal learning is experiential learning. Most learning does not take place in formal training programmes. People can learn 70 per cent of what they know about their job informally, through processes not structured or sponsored by the organization.

A study by Eraut *et al* (1998) established that in organizations adopting a learner-centred perspective, formal education and training provided only a small part of what was learnt at work. Most of the learning described to the researchers was non-formal, neither clearly specified nor planned. It arose naturally from the challenges of work. Effective learning was, however, dependent on the employees' confidence, motivation and capability. Some formal training to develop skills (especially induction training) was usually provided, but learning from experience and other people at work predominated. Reynolds (2004) notes that:

> The simple act of observing more experienced colleagues can accelerate learning; conversing, swapping stories, co-operating on tasks and offering mutual support deepen and solidify the process... This kind of learning – often very informal in nature – is thought to be vastly more effective in building proficiency than more formalized training methods.

The advantages of informal learning are that:

- learning efforts are relevant and focused in the immediate environment;
- understanding can be achieved in incremental steps rather than in indigestible chunks;
- learners define how they will gain the knowledge they need – formal learning is more packaged;
- learners can readily put their learning into practice.

The disadvantages are that:

- it may be left to chance – some people will benefit, some won't;
- it can be unplanned and unsystematic, which means that it will not necessarily satisfy individual or organizational learning needs;
- learners may simply pick up bad habits.

Workplace learning

Informal learning occurs in the workplace and, as explained by Stern and Sommerlad (1999), this takes three forms:

1. *The workshop as a site for learning*. In this case, learning and working are spatially separated with some form of structured learning activity occurring off or near the job. This may be in a company training centre or a 'training island' on the shop floor where the production process is reproduced for trainees.

2. *The workplace as a learning environment*. In this approach, the workplace itself becomes an environment for learning. Various on-the-job training activities take place, which are structured to different degrees. Learning is intentional and planned, aimed at training employees by supporting, structuring and monitoring their learning.

3. *Learning and working are inextricably mixed*. In this case, learning is informal. It becomes an everyday part of the job and is built into routine tasks. Workers develop skills, knowledge and understanding through dealing with the challenges posed by the work. This can be described as continuous learning. As Zuboff (1988) put it: 'Learning is not something that requires time out from being engaged in productive activity; learning is the heart of productive activity.'

Formal learning

Formal learning is planned and systematic and involves the use of structured training programmes consisting of instruction and practice.

Informal and formal learning compared

A comparison between informal and formal learning is shown in Table 38.1.

Table 38.1   Characteristics of formal and informal learning

Informal	Formal
Highly relevant to individual needs	Relevant to some, not so relevant to others
Learners learn according to need	All learners learn the same thing
May be small gap between current and target knowledge	May be variable gaps between current and target knowledge
Learner decides how learning will occur	Trainer decides how learning will occur
Immediate applicability ('Just-in-time' learning)	Variable times, often distant
Learning readily transferable	Problems may occur in transferring learning to the workplace
Occurs in work setting	Often occurs in non-work setting

Learning programmes

Learning programmes are concerned with:

- defining the objectives of learning;
- creating an environment in which effective learning can take place (a learning culture);
- making use of blended learning approaches;
- adopting a systematic, planned and balanced approach to the delivery of learning;
- identifying learning and development needs;
- satisfying these needs by delivering blended different learning, development and training processes including e-learning;
- evaluating the effectiveness of those processes.

As mentioned earlier, learning is a continuous process and much of it arises from day-to-day experience in the workplace. But this learning may be haphazard, inappropriate and fail to meet the short and longer-term needs of either the individual or the organization. A *laissez-faire* approach by the organization could be highly unsatisfactory if it does not ensure that these needs are met by whatever means are available. Experiential learning will be enhanced if the climate in the organization is supportive, and an important aspect of a learning and development strategy will be creating such a climate, as discussed later in this chapter. But it will also be extended if individuals are helped to identify their own learning needs and provided with guidance on how they can be met using various means. As described below, the learning programme can concentrate on making the best use of workplace learning opportunities, ensuring that people are aware of what they need to learn and providing them with encouragement and support, agreeing learning contracts, and enhancing learning through coaching or mentoring. These activities should be used as part of a blended approach, which is discussed below.

Making the most of learning opportunities

Learning opportunities occur all the time and the challenge is to ensure that people make the most of them. Some will need no encouragement. Others will have to be helped. Line managers or team leaders have a crucial role in encouraging and supporting learning. They can do this within the relatively formal setting of a performance and development review. Or, better still, they can consciously promote learning from day-to-day events when they discuss how a task might be done, when they analyse information on outcomes with individuals, and when they ask individuals to tell them what they have learnt from an event and what it tells them about any additional learning required. But it is necessary to ensure that line managers are aware of the need to promote learning and have the will and the skills to do it.

Identifying and meeting learning needs

It is necessary to ensure that people are aware of what they need to learn to carry out their present role and to develop in the future. This starts with induction and involves the specification of learning programmes and the planning of learning events, with an emphasis on self-directed learning accompanied by a blend of other learning approaches as appropriate. It continues with performance and development reviews that identify learning needs and define how they will be met, again by self-managed learning as far as possible but making use of coaching, mentoring and formal training courses as required.

Learning contract

A learning contract is a formal agreement between the manager and the individual on what learning needs to take place, the objectives of such learning and what part the individual, the manager, the training department or a mentor will play in ensuring that learning happens. The partners to the contract agree on how the objectives will be achieved and their respective roles. It will spell out learning programmes and indicate what coaching, mentoring and formal training activities should be carried out. It is, in effect, a blueprint for learning. Learning contracts can be part of a personal development planning process, as described later in this chapter.

Coaching

The Industrial Society (1999) defines coaching as: 'The art of facilitating the enhanced performance, learning and development of others.' It takes the form of a personal (usually one-to-one) on-the-job approach to helping people develop their skills and levels of competence. Hirsh and Carter (2002) state that coaching is aimed at the rapid improvement of skills, behaviour and performance, usually for the present job. A structured and purposeful dialogue is at the heart of coaching. The coach uses feedback and brings an objective perspective. They noted that the boundaries between what a coach, mentor, counsellor or organization development consultant do are inevitably blurred – they all use similar skills.

The need for coaching may arise from formal or informal performance reviews but opportunities for coaching will emerge during normal day-to-day activities. Coaching as part of the normal process of management consists of:

- making people aware of how well they are performing by, for example, asking them questions to establish the extent to which they have thought through what they are doing;
- controlled delegation – ensuring that individuals not only know what is expected of them but also understand what they need to know and be able to do to complete the task satisfactorily; this gives managers an opportunity to provide guidance at the outset – guidance at a later stage may be seen as interference;
- using whatever situations may arise as opportunities to promote learning;
- encouraging people to look at higher-level problems and how they would tackle them.

A common framework used by coaches is the GROW model:

'G' is for the goal of coaching, which needs to be expressed in specific measurable terms that represent a meaningful step towards future development.
'R' is for the reality check – the process of eliciting as full a description as possible of what the person being coached needs to learn.
'O' is for option generation – the identification of as many solutions and actions as possible.
'W' is for wrapping up – when the coach ensures that the individual being coached is committed to action.

Coaching will be most effective when the coach understands that his or her role is to help people to learn and individuals are motivated to learn. They should be aware that their present level of knowledge or skill or their behaviour needs to be improved if they are going to perform their work satisfactorily. Individuals should be given guidance on what they should be learning and feedback on how they are doing and, because learning is an active not a passive process, they should be actively involved with their coach who should be constructive, building on strengths and experience.

Coaching may be informal but it has to be planned. It is not simply checking from time to time on what people are doing and then advising them on how to do it better. Nor is it occasionally telling people where they have gone wrong and throwing in a lecture for good measure. As far as possible, coaching should take place within the framework of a general plan of the areas and direction in which individuals will benefit from further development. Coaching plans can and should be incorporated into the personal development plans set out in a performance agreement.

Coaching should provide motivation, structure and effective feedback if managers have the required skills and commitment. As coaches, managers believe that people can succeed, that they can contribute to their success and that they can identify what people need to be able to do to improve their performance.

Mentoring

Mentoring is the process of using specially selected and trained individuals to provide guidance, pragmatic advice and continuing support, which will help the person or persons allocated to them to learn and develop. It has been defined by Clutterbuck (2004) as: 'Off-line help from one person to another in making significant transitions in knowledge, work or thinking.' Hirsh and Carter (2002) suggest that mentors prepare individuals to perform better in the future and groom them for higher and greater things, ie career advancement.

Mentoring can be defined as a method of helping people to learn, as distinct from coaching, which is a relatively directive means of increasing people's competence. It involves learning on the job, which must always be the best way of acquiring the particular skills and knowledge the job holder needs. Mentoring also complements formal training by providing those who benefit from it with individual guidance from experienced managers who are 'wise in the ways of the organization'.

Mentors provide people with:

- advice in drawing up self-development programmes or learning contracts;
- general help with learning programmes;
- guidance on how to acquire the necessary knowledge and skills to do a new job;
- advice on dealing with any administrative, technical or people problems individuals meet, especially in the early stages of their careers;
- information on 'the way things are done around here' – the corporate culture and its manifestations in the shape of core values and organizational behaviour (management style);
- coaching in specific skills;
- help in tackling projects – not by doing it for them, but by pointing them in the right direction: helping people to help themselves;
- a parental figure with whom individuals can discuss their aspirations and concerns and who will lend a sympathetic ear to their problems.

There are no standard mentoring procedures, although it is essential to select mentors who are likely to adopt the right non-directive but supportive help to the person or persons they are dealing with. They must then be carefully briefed and trained in their role.

Blended learning

Blended learning is defined by Sloman (2003b) as: 'An approach to training design that involves the use of a combination of delivery methods and in some cases learning methodology.' Schramm (2001) describes it as: 'The combination of different modes of delivery that take into account the learner's environment, motivation and learning styles with different theoretical approaches. This creates a multi-layered and richer palette of learning methods.' Blended learning aims to make the different parts of the learning mix complementary and mutually supportive in meeting learning needs.

Recognition of the need to blend learning avoids the pitfall of over-reliance on one approach. It means using conventional instruction, e-learning and self-directed learning as well as experiential learning. The aim is to inspire and motivate learners over extended periods of time and through an appropriate mix of inputs and outputs, individual and collaborative study, formal and informal processes, and a blend of face-to-face and virtual contact. Focus on the learner is achieved by taking special care to provide them with support and guidance from their managers, coaches and mentors and to complement this with the provision of e-learning material.

A blended programme might be planned for an individual using a mix of self-managed learning activities defined in a personal development plan, e-learning facilities, group action learning activities, coaching or mentoring, and instruction provided in an in-company course or externally. Generic training for groups of people might include e-learning, planned instruction programmes, planned experience, and selected external courses. Within a training course a complementary mix of different training activities might take place; for example a skills development course for managers or team leaders might include some instruction on basic principles but much more time would be spent on case studies, simulations, role-playing and other exercises.

DEVELOPMENT

Development is an unfolding process that enables people to progress from a present state of understanding and capability to a future state in which higher-level skills, knowledge and competencies are required. It takes the form of learning activities that prepare people to exercise wider or increased responsibilities. It does not concentrate on improving performance in the present job. Development has been defined by Harrison (2000) as: 'Learning experiences of any kind, whereby individuals and groups acquire enhanced knowledge, skills, values or behaviours. Its outcomes unfold through time, rather than immediately, and they tend to be long-lasting.'

In development programmes there is an emphasis on personal development planning and planned learning from experience. Use may be made of a 'corporate university'. Development can also focus on managers and take the form of action learning or outdoor learning. To maximize the impact of development a balanced approach is necessary, using a mix of learning methods as described in the previous section of this chapter.

Personal development planning

Personal development planning is carried out by individuals with guidance, encouragement and help from their managers as required. A personal development plan sets out the actions people propose to take to learn and to develop themselves. They take responsibility for formulating and implementing the plan, but they receive support from the organization and their managers in doing so. The purpose is to provide what Tamkin *et al* (1995) call a 'self-organized learning framework'.

Personal development planning consists of the following stages, as modelled in Figure 38.1:

1. *Analyse current situation and development needs.* This can be done as part of a performance management process.
2. *Set goals.* These could include improving performance in the current job, improving or acquiring skills, extending relevant knowledge, developing specified areas of competence, moving across or upwards in the organization, preparing for changes in the current role.
3. *Prepare action plan.* The action plan sets out what needs to be done and how it will be done under headings such as outcomes expected (learning objectives), the development activities, the responsibility for development (what individuals are expected to do and the support they will get from their manager, the HR department or other people), and timing. A variety of activities tuned to individual needs should be included in the plan, for example: observing what others do, project work, planned use of e-learning programmes and internal learning resource centres, working with a mentor, coaching by the line manager or team leader, experience in new tasks, guided reading, special assignments and action learning. Formal training to develop knowledge and skills may be part of the plan but it is not the most important part.
4. *Implement.* Take action as planned.

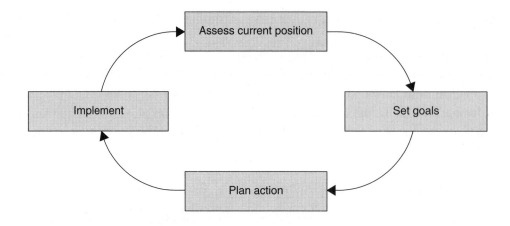

Figure 38.1 Stages in preparing and implementing a personal development plan

The plan can be expressed in the form of a *learning contract* as described earlier in this chapter.

Planned experience

Experiential learning can take place by planning a sequence of experience that meets a learning specification for acquiring knowledge and skills that will prepare people to take on increased responsibilities in the same or different functions and occupations. A programme is drawn up which sets down what people are expected to learn in each department or job in which they are given experience. This should spell out what they are expected to discover for themselves. A suitable person should be available to see that people in a development programme are given the right experience and opportunity to learn, and arrangements should be made to check progress. A good way of stimulating people to find out for themselves is to provide them with a list of questions to answer. It is essential, however, to follow up each segment of experience to check what has been learnt and, if necessary, modify the programme.

Planned experience used to be known as 'job rotation', but was often an inefficient and frustrating method of acquiring additional knowledge and skills. What has sometimes been referred to as the 'Cook's tour' method of moving trainees from department to department has incurred much justified criticism because of the time wasted by them in locations where no one knew what to do with them, or cared.

Corporate university

A corporate university is an institution set up and run by an organization, often with outside help, in which education and learning takes place. As Carter *et al* (2002) point out:

> The term 'corporate university' is interpreted in different ways. For some, it is specific and refers to the use of academic terminology to describe and raise the status of training and development and, perhaps, also implies a relationship with one or more 'real' conventional universities who co-design or accredit the company's programmes. For others, the term is interpreted more broadly as an umbrella that describes the creation and marketing of internal brands for all the learning and development opportunities an organization provides.

For example, BAe Systems operates a virtual university, which has a strategic partnership policy that allows them to co-design programmes with the help of conventional universities. In contrast, Lloyds TSB runs its training function just as though it were a university, with faculties for each development area, the aim being to align training and development with business strategy and use the concept as an internal brand, letting employees know that it is investing in them.

Action learning

Action learning, as developed by Revans (1971), is a method of helping managers develop their talents by exposing them to real problems. They are required to analyse them, formulate recommendations, and then take action. It accords with the belief that managers learn best by doing rather than being taught.

In 1989 Revans produced the following formula to describe his concept: L (learning) = P (programmed learning) + Q (questioning, insight). He suggests that the concept is based on six assumptions:

1. Experienced managers have a huge curiosity to know how other managers work.
2. We learn not as much when we are motivated to learn, as when we are motivated to learn something.
3. Learning about oneself is threatening and is resisted if it tends to change one's self-image. However, it is possible to reduce the external threat to a level that no longer acts as a total barrier to learning about oneself.
4. People learn only when they do something, and they learn more the more responsible they feel the task to be.

5. Learning is deepest when it involves the whole person – mind, values, body, emotions.
6. The learner knows better than anyone else what he or she has learnt. Nobody else has much chance of knowing.

A typical action learning programme brings together a group, or 'set' of four or five managers to solve the problem. They help and learn from each other, but an external consultant, or 'set adviser', sits in with them regularly. The project may last several months, and the set meets frequently, possibly one day a week. The adviser helps the members of the set to learn from one another and clarifies the process of action learning. This process involves change embedded in the web of relationships called 'the client system'. The web comprises at least three separate networks: the power network, the information network, and the motivational network (this is what Revans means by 'who can, who knows, and who cares'). The forces for change are already there within the client system and it is the adviser's role to point out the dynamics of this system as the work of diagnosis and implementation proceeds.

The group or set has to manage the project like any other project, deciding on objectives, planning resources, initiating action and monitoring progress. But all the time, with the help of their adviser, they are learning about the management processes involved as they actually happen.

Outdoor learning

Outdoor learning involves exposing individuals to various 'Outward Bound' type activities: sailing, mountain walking, rock climbing, canoeing, caving, etc. It means placing participants, operating in teams, under pressure to carry out physical activities that are completely unfamiliar to them. The rationale is that these tests are paradigms of the sort of challenges people have to meet at work, but their unfamiliar nature means that they can learn more about how they act under pressure as team leaders or team members. Outdoor learning involves a facilitator helping participants to learn individually and collectively from their experiences.

Impact of development – a balanced approach

A balanced approach is required to maximize the impact of development on engagement and performance. This is illustrated in Figure 38.2, adapted from Walker (2004).

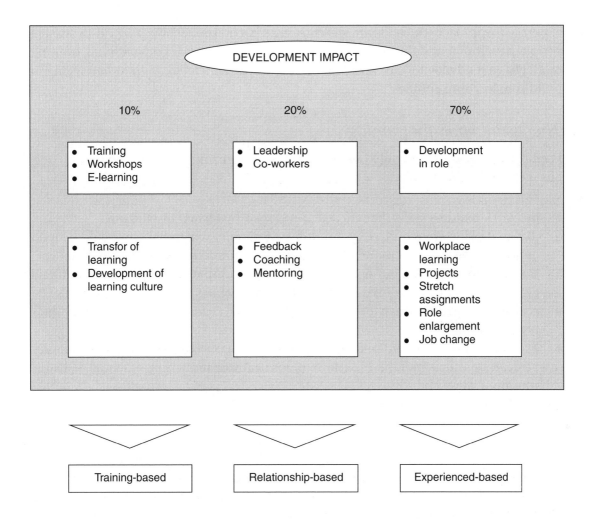

Figure 38.2 Impact of development

TRAINING

Training is the use of systematic and planned instruction activities to promote learning. The approach can be summarized in the phrase 'learner-based training'. It involves the use of formal processes to impart knowledge and help people to acquire the skills necessary for them to perform their jobs satisfactorily. It is described as one of several responses an organization can undertake to promote learning.

As Reynolds (2004) points out, training has a complementary role to play in accelerating learning: 'It should be reserved for situations that justify a more directed, expert-led approach rather than viewing it as a comprehensive and all-pervasive people development solution.' He also commented that the conventional training model has a tendency to 'emphasize subject-specific knowledge, rather than trying to build core learning abilities'.

The justification for training

Formal training is indeed only one of the ways of ensuring that learning takes place, but it can be justified when:

- the work requires skills that are best developed by formal instruction;
- different skills are required by a number of people, which have to be developed quickly to meet new demands and cannot be acquired by relying on experience;
- the tasks to be carried out are so specialized or complex that people are unlikely to master them on their own initiative at a reasonable speed;
- critical information must be imparted to employees to ensure they meet their responsibilities;
- a learning need common to a number of people has to be met, which can readily be dealt with in a training programme, for example induction, essential IT skills, communication skills.

Transferring training

It has been argued (Reynolds, 2004) that: 'The transfer of expertise by outside experts is risky since their design is often removed from the context in which work is created.' This is a fundamental problem and applies equally to internally run training courses where what has been taught can be difficult for people to apply in the entirely different circumstances in their workplace. Training can seem to be remote from reality and the skills and knowledge acquired can appear to be irrelevant. This particularly applies to management or supervisory training, but even the manual skills learnt in a training centre may be difficult to transfer.

This problem can be tackled by making the training as relevant and realistic as possible, anticipating and dealing with any potential transfer difficulties. Individuals are more likely to apply learning when they do not find it too difficult, believe what they learnt is relevant, useful and transferable, are supported by line managers, have job autonomy, believe in themselves and are committed and engaged. Transfer is also more likely if systematic training and 'just-in-time training' approaches are used, as described below.

Systematic training

Training should be systematic in that it is specifically designed, planned and implemented to meet defined needs. It is provided by people who know how to train and the impact of training is carefully evaluated. The concept was originally developed for the industrial training boards in the 1960s and consists of a simple four-stage model, as illustrated in Figure 38.3:

1. Identify training needs.
2. Decide what sort of training is required to satisfy these needs.
3. Use experienced and trained trainers to implement training.
4. Follow up and evaluate training to ensure that it is effective.

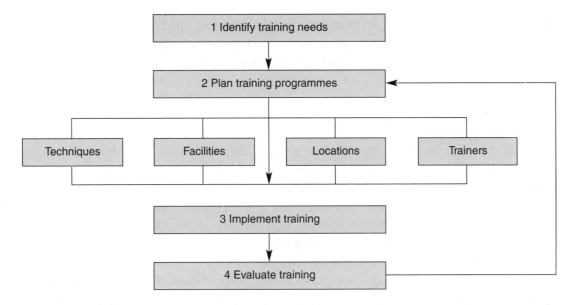

Figure 38.3 Systematic training model

Just-in-time training

Just-in-time training is training that is closely linked to the pressing and relevant needs of people by its association with immediate or imminent work activities. It is delivered as close as possible to the time when the activity is taking place. The training will be based on an identification of the latest requirements, priorities and plans of the participants, who will be briefed on the live situations in which their learning has to be applied. The training programme will take account of any transfer issues and aim to ensure that what is taught is seen to be applicable in the current work situation.

Types of training

Training programmes or events can be concerned with any of the following:

- manual skills;
- IT skills;
- team leader or supervisory training;
- management training;
- interpersonal skills, eg leadership, teambuilding, group dynamics, neurolinguistic programming;
- personal skills, eg assertiveness, coaching, communicating, time management;
- training in organizational procedures or practices, eg induction, health and safety, performance management, equal opportunity or managing diversity policy and practice.

Effective training practices

Effective training uses the systematic approach defined above with an emphasis on skills analysis. The purpose of the training should be clearly defined in terms of the 'criterion behaviour' required as a result of training, and the 'terminal behaviour' expected. The latter can be expressed as a statement along the lines of: 'On completing this training the participant will be able to...'. Defining criterion and terminal behaviours will provide the basis for evaluation, which is an essential element in the achievement of successful training.

The content of the training should be related to the work contexts of the participants. Ideally, their work should be made a central feature of the subject matter. Every opportunity should be taken to embed learning at work.

The training techniques used should be appropriate to the purpose of the course and to the characteristics of participants – their jobs, learning needs, previous experience, level of knowledge and skills, and how receptive they will be to being taught (motivated to learn). A blend of different techniques should be used where appropriate. It is particularly important in management, supervisory and interpersonal skills training to provide ample time for participation and active learning through discussion, case studies and simulations. Lectures should form a minor part of the course. Good instructional techniques as described below should be used in manual skills training.

Training techniques

Instruction

Job instruction techniques should be based on skills analysis and learning theory, as discussed in Chapters 13 and 37. The sequence of instruction should follow six stages:

1. Preparation for each instruction period means that the trainer must have a plan for presenting the subject matter and using appropriate teaching methods, visual aids and demonstration aids. It also means preparing trainees for the instruction that is to follow. They should want to learn. They must perceive that the learning will be relevant and useful to them personally. They should be encouraged to take pride in their job and to appreciate the satisfaction that comes from skilled performance.

2. Presentation should consist of a combination of telling and showing – explanation and demonstration.

3. Explanation should be as simple and direct as possible: the trainer explains briefly the ground to be covered and what to look for. He or she makes the maximum use of films, charts, diagrams and other visual aids. The aim should be to teach first things first and then proceed from the known to the unknown, the simple to the complex, the concrete to the abstract, the general to the particular, the observation to reasoning, and the whole to the parts and back to the whole again.

4. Demonstration is an essential stage in instruction, especially when the skill to be learnt is mainly a 'doing' skill. Demonstration takes place in three steps:
   - The complete operation is shown at normal speed to show the trainee how the task should be carried out eventually.
   - The operation is demonstrated slowly and in correct sequence, element by element, to indicate clearly what is done and the order in which each task is carried out.
   - The operation is demonstrated again slowly, at least two or three times, to stress the how, when and why of successive movements.

5. Practice consists of the learner imitating the instructor and then constantly repeating the operation under guidance. The aim is to reach the target level of performance for each element of the total task, but the instructor must constantly strive to develop coordinated and integrated performance, that is, the smooth combination of the separate elements of the task into a whole job pattern.

6. Follow-up continues during the training period for all the time required by the learner to reach a level of performance equal to that of the normal experienced

worker in terms of quality, speed and attention to safety. During the follow-up stage, the learner will continue to need help with particularly difficult tasks or to overcome temporary setbacks that result in a deterioration of performance. The instructor may have to repeat the presentation for the elements and supervise practice more closely until the trainee regains confidence or masters the task.

Lecture

A lecture is a talk with little or no participation except a question-and-answer session at the end. It is used to transfer information to an audience with controlled content and timing. When the audience is large, there may be no alternative to a 'straight lecture' if there is no scope to break it up into discussion groups.

The effectiveness of a lecture depends on the ability of the speaker to present material with the judicious use of visual aids. But there are several limits on the amount an inert audience can absorb. However effective the speaker, it is unlikely that more than 20 per cent of what was said will be remembered at the end of the day. And after a week, all will be forgotten unless the listeners have put some of their learning into practice. For maximum effectiveness, the lecture must never be longer than 30 or 40 minutes; it must not contain too much information (if the speaker can convey three new ideas that more than a half of the audience understands and remembers, the lecture will have been successful); it must reinforce learning with appropriate visual aids (but not too many); and it must clearly indicate the action that should be taken to make use of the material.

Discussion

The objectives of using discussion techniques are to:

- get the audience to participate actively in learning;
- give people an opportunity of learning from the experience of others;
- help people to gain understanding of other points of view;
- develop powers of self-expression.

The aim of the trainer should be to guide the group's thinking. He or she may, therefore, be more concerned with shaping attitudes than imparting new knowledge. The trainer has unobtrusively to stimulate people to talk, guide the discussion along predetermined lines (there must be a plan and an ultimate objective), and provide interim summaries and a final summary.

The following techniques can be used to get active participation:

- Ask for contributions by direct questions.
- Use open-ended questions that will stimulate thought.
- Check understanding; make sure that everyone is following the argument.
- Encourage participation by providing support rather than criticism.
- Prevent domination by individual members of the group by bringing in other people and asking cross-reference questions.
- Avoid dominating the group yourself. The leader's job is to guide the discussion, maintain control and summarize from time to time. If necessary, 'reflect' opinions expressed by individuals back to the group to make sure they find the answer for themselves. The leader's job is to help them reach a conclusion, not to do it for them.
- Maintain control – ensure that the discussion is progressing along the right lines towards a firm conclusion.

Case study

A case study is a history or description of an event or set of circumstances that is analysed by trainees in order to diagnose the causes of a problem and work out how to solve it. Case studies are mainly used in courses for managers and team leaders because they are based on the belief that managerial competence and understanding can best be achieved through the study and discussion of real events.

Case studies should aim to promote enquiry, the exchange of ideas, and the analysis of experience in order that the trainees can discover underlying principles that the case study is designed to illustrate. They are not light relief. Nor are they a means of reducing the load on the instructor. Trainers have to work hard to define the learning points that must come out of each case, and they must work even harder to ensure that these points do emerge.

The danger of case studies is that they are often perceived by trainees to be irrelevant to their needs, even if based on fact. Consequently, the analysis is superficial and the situation is unrealistic. It is the trainer's job to avoid these dangers by ensuring that the participants are not allowed to get away with half-baked comments. Trainers have to challenge assumptions and force people to justify their reasoning. Above all, they have to seize every chance to draw out the principles they want to illustrate from the discussion and to get the group to see how these are relevant to their own working situation.

Role-playing

In role-playing, the participants act out a situation by assuming the roles of the characters involved. The situation will be one in which there is interaction between two people or within a group. It should be specially prepared with briefs written for each participant explaining the situation and, broadly, their role in it. Alternatively, role-playing could emerge naturally from a case study when the trainees are asked to test their solution by playing the parts of those concerned.

Role-playing is used to give managers, team leaders or sales representatives practice in dealing with face-to-face situations such as interviewing, conducting a performance review meeting, counselling, coaching, dealing with a grievance, selling, leading a group or running a meeting. It develops interactive skills and gives people insight into the way in which people behave and feel.

The technique of 'role reversal', in which a pair playing, say, a manager and a team leader run through the case and then exchange roles and repeat it, gives extra insight into the feelings involved and the skills required.

Role-playing enables trainees to get expert advice and constructive criticism from the trainer and their colleagues in a protected training situation. It can help to increase confidence as well as developing skills in handling people. The main difficulties are either that trainees are embarrassed or that they do not take the exercise seriously and overplay their parts.

Simulation

Simulation is a training technique that combines case studies and role-playing to obtain the maximum amount of realism in classroom training. The aim is to facilitate the transfer of what has been learnt off the job to on-the-job behaviour by reproducing, in the training room, situations that are as close as possible to real life. Trainees are thus given the opportunity to practise behaviour in conditions identical to or at least very similar to those they will meet when they complete the course.

Group exercises

In a group exercise the trainees examine problems and develop solutions to them as a group. The problem may be a case study or it could be one entirely unrelated to everyday work. The aims of an exercise of this kind are to give members practice in working together and to obtain insight into the way in which groups behave in tackling problems and arriving at decisions.

Group exercises can be used as part of a team-building programme and to develop interactive skills. They can be combined with other techniques such as the discovery method, encouraging participants to find out things for themselves and work out the techniques and skills they need to use.

39

E-learning

WHAT IS E-LEARNING?

E-learning is defined by Pollard and Hillage (2001) as 'the delivery and administration of learning opportunities and support via computer, networked and web-based technology to help individual performance and development'. E-learning enhances learning by extending and supplementing face-to-face learning rather than replacing it.

The term 'e-learning' first appeared in the US in the mid-1990s but became prominent in the late 1990s. Like many HR practices, it was based on earlier developments such as computer-based training, supported online training, open or distance learning and informal e-learning derived from knowledge management approaches. The main difference is that e-learning is essentially web-based, although it can include the use of distributed technology products (mainly CD-ROMs), which do not require the user's computer to be networked.

E-learning is not so much about technology as about learning based on technology. However, it is the use of the intranet that has offered most scope for learning. In its fully developed form, e-learning is a more comprehensive approach to learning than the earlier developments, especially when blended with other learning methods.

The different types of e-learning are:

- self-paced e-learning when the learner is using technology but is not connected to instructors or other learners at the same time;
- live e-learning in which by the use of technology, the instructor and the learner are together at the same time but in different locations; and
- collaborative e-learning, which supports learning through the exchange and sharing of information and knowledge amongst learners by means of discussion forums, communities of practice, bulletin boards and chat rooms.

AIM OF E-LEARNING

In the words of Pollard and Hillage (2001) the objective is to provide for learning that is 'just in time, just enough and just for you'. It enables learning to take place when it is most needed ('just in time' as distinct from 'just in case') and when it is most convenient. Learning can be provided in short segments or bites that focus on specific learning objectives. It is 'learner-centric' in that it can be customized to suit an individual's learning needs – learners can choose different learning objects within an overall package.

THE TECHNOLOGY OF E-LEARNING

E-learning can offer up-to-date information to learners who are widely distributed geographically. Collaboration and the sharing of information between learners are possible, but learners tend to work much of the time in isolation.

The basic principle of e-learning is 'connectivity' – the process by which computers are networked, share information and connect people to people. This is provided for by what is often called 'the e-learning landscape or architecture', which refers to the hardware, software and connectivity components required to facilitate learning. In designing the system, consideration has to be given to 'functionality' – what each part is expected to do.

The main components of the e-learning 'landscape' are:

- *The learning management system (LMS)* – this provides users with access to various learning processes and enables self-paced e-learning to take place. It can also help with administration, including curriculum management, and course publishing.
- *The learning content management system (LCMS)* – this provides an authoring system for course or programme preparation, a collection of learning objects or

modules (sometimes called a repository), and a means of sending a completed course to a delivery system (sometimes called a delivery interface).

- *Learning portals* – these are access points to learning information and services that enable learners to locate content.

THE E-LEARNING PROCESS

The e-learning process comprises defining the system, encouraging access, advising and assisting individual learners, and encouraging and facilitating the creation of learning communities. E-learning focuses on the learner. It provides a means of satisfying individual learning needs. But individual learning may be supplemented by participation in learning groups or communities of interest in which members both gain and share knowledge.

The emphasis is on self-paced learning – learners control the rate at which they learn, although they may be given targets for completion and guidance from tutors on how they should learn. However, while self-directed learning is encouraged and provided for, the impact of e-learning is strongly influenced by how well support is provided to learners. It is the effectiveness of this support rather than the sophistication of the technology that counts. The quality of the content is important but it will be enhanced by support from tutors or 'e-moderators'. The latter as described by Salmon (2001) preside over the activities of a learning group in 'knowledge exchange forums', arranging contributions and information sharing and providing guidance and comments as appropriate.

E-learning programme content

E-learning programmes may cover common business applications and processes, induction programmes and, frequently, IT skills development. They are not so effective for developing soft skills such as team building, communication or presentation that rely on interpersonal contact. But programmes can still present basic principles that can prepare people for practical face-to-face sessions, provide reinforcement through post-event reading, help with self-assessment and lead to chatroom support.

Programmes may consist of generic content purchased from suppliers, but most organizations prefer customized web-based modules developed either in-house or outsourced to software firms that produce material to a specified design. The content should be constructed in accordance with the following pedagogic principles:

- learners must be stimulated by the learning process;
- the programme and content should be seen to be intrinsically relevant, the method of presentation should be interesting, use should be made of graphics, animations, audio, interactive simulations, scenarios, case studies, projects, question and answer sessions and problem-solving activities where appropriate – the programme should not simply involve 'page turning';
- learners must be encouraged to respond to stimuli and should be engaged in the learning process;
- learners should understand their learning goals, preferably working them out for themselves but with help where necessary;
- the programme should be constructed in incremental steps and presented in 'bite-sized chunks' or modules, each with clear objectives and outcomes;
- learners should be able to plan their learning (self-paced learning);
- learners must be able to measure their own progress but should be given feedback as well;
- learners should be encouraged to reflect on what they are learning by reference to their own experience.

The content can be prepared with the help of authoring tools such as Macromedia (Authorware and Flash).

Delivery of e-learning

E-learning is delivered through websites and the intranet; CD-ROMs are also used extensively. Provision can be made for online coaching and discussion forums. The content can be delivered through PowerPoint, video and audio clips, drag and drop questions, PDF files, links to websites, and web-enabled forums and learning communities.

Blended e-learning

In a sense blended e-learning is balanced learning in that a balance needs to be struck between electronic learning, face-to-face learning and informal group learning through teams and communities of interest. An example of a blended programme is shown in Figure 39.1

THE BUSINESS CASE FOR E-LEARNING

E-learning can enable flexibility of access and interrogation of high volumes of diverse learning resources in different locations. It can speed up the learning process

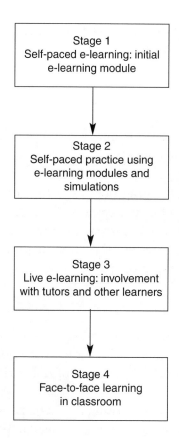

Figure 39.1 A blended learning programme

by as much as 50 per cent and focus on critical learning needs in the organization. The cost of training can be halved by decreasing the number of instructor hours. As stated by van Dam (2004):

> Self-paced e-learning can be taken *any time* and is therefore a just-in-time approach. E-learning can be taken *at any place* – in the office, at home or other locations, which eliminates the travel needs and costs. Skills acquisition and knowledge development will take place at *any pace* and *any path*, as the learning experience is solely driven by the participant, and therefore very personalized. *Anyone* in the organization can engage in e-learning and participate and share experience and knowledge in e-learning collaboration sessions.

DEVELOPING E-LEARNING PROCESSES

The main steps required to develop e-learning processes are described below.

Initial analysis

1. Define or re-define the human resource development strategy within the context of the organization's business strategy, external environment, culture and technologies.
2. Identify organizational learning needs – what should be invested in people in order to develop the intellectual capital of the organization, extend its stock of knowledge and skills and thus increase its organizational capability.
3. In the light of the above, assess the strengths and weaknesses of the present arrangements for developing people.

Scope for e-learning

4. Identify the overall scope for developing e-learning systems. The need to enhance present arrangements with a blended approach that uses complementary and mutually supportive methods of delivering learning also needs to be assessed.
5. Identify any areas in which e-learning might be particularly appropriate because there are well-established learning needs that can be met by electronic as well as more traditional means. Establish what specific opportunities technology offers to enhance knowledge. Establish the extent to which employees will have access to computers.

Development programmes

6. For each aspect of learning in which scope for e-learning has been established, produce a specification defining:

    – the learning need;
    – how e-learning will meet that need;
    – the learning system that should be used;
    – broadly, the content of the learning to be delivered;
    – how e-learning will blend with other forms of training;
    – the extent to which the programme is to cater for individual or group learning; and
    – who will be responsible within the organization for developing and delivering e-learning.

7. Decide on the extent to which learning systems, including the content of e-learning programmes, should be developed in-house, or purchased from outside suppliers. The factors to be taken into consideration will be:

- the availability of resources within the organization to develop content;
- the degree to which the material needs to be tailor-made to fit the organization;
- the likelihood of suitable material being available elsewhere; and
- the comparative costs of each option.

8. If it is decided that external suppliers should be used, identify possible organizations (on the basis of recommendations, as far as possible). The criteria for choice should be:

- understanding of the requirements;
- the learning methods employed (the pedagogic principles and theoretical perspectives from which the methods are derived);
- the outcomes associated with the methods and how they will be measured;
- suitability of learning material (fit with requirements); and
- cost.

9. Select and train tutors and e-moderators.
10. Ensure that facilities for e-learning (computers, learning resource centres) are available. Take into account the possible need to provide guidance to users of learning resource centres on the use of the equipment.

Implementation

11. Prepare briefing material.
12. Ensure that everyone is aware of the facilities for e-learning, the part they and their managers will play, and the support they will receive from tutors and moderators.
13. Ensure e-learning arrangements are linked to other HR initiatives, eg performance management, career planning and knowledge management.
14. Launch e-learning, possibly starting with a pilot scheme in a department or a specific area of learning, eg IT.

Evaluation

15. Monitor and evaluate the performance and impact of e-learning.

Examples

B&Q

All the content of the B&Q e-learning system was produced as customized learning modules focusing on the needs of store-based employees. For example, the 'show-room' module, which deals with selling kitchens and bathrooms, uses both audio and visual components with options for different customer types. All modules are delivered in bite-sized chunks and provide learners with information on their progress.

Black & Decker

The blended programme for sales representatives consists of 16 self-paced e-learning courses, on-the-job training, classroom training and mentoring.

Prudential Financial

New starters take part in the Life Centre new starters' programme for seven weeks. Sixty per cent of the programme time is self-paced e-learning using simulations extensively, and 40 per cent is instructor-led classroom learning.

Unilever

Unilever operates a leadership development blended programme that balances on-line work with classroom sessions and coaching. A web-enabled community tool is used, which begins with a virtual, experiential module in order to develop the thinking and dialogue prior to the face-to-face programme. It continues to support virtual teamwork and encourages participants to engage in learning beyond the programme itself. Assignments and projects are used throughout the programme. These include individual projects focused on personal development and business improvement, and a team business proposal project.

40

Management development

Management development is concerned with improving managers' performance in their present roles and preparing them for greater responsibilities in the future. It has been described by Mumford and Gold (2004) as 'an attempt to improve managerial effectiveness through a learning process'. In this chapter, the following aspects of management development are considered:

- its aims, needs and priorities;
- its requirements, nature as a business-led process and the elements involved in a management development processes;
- the main management development activities of analysis, assessment and strategy formulation;
- approaches to management development with an emphasis on integration, experiential and self-managed learning and personal development planning, and the use of competency-frameworks and development centres;
- the concept of emotional intelligence and its use in the development of leadership skills;
- the responsibility for management development.

AIMS OF MANAGEMENT DEVELOPMENT

Management development contributes to business success by helping the organization to grow the managers it requires to meet its present and future needs. It improves managers' performance, gives them development opportunities, and provides for management succession. Development processes may be *anticipatory* (so that managers can contribute to long-term objectives), *reactive* (intended to resolve or preempt performance difficulties) or *motivational* (geared to individual career aspirations). The particular aims are to:

- ensure that managers understand what is expected of them; agreeing with them objectives against which their performance will be measured and the level of competence required in their roles;
- improve the performance of managers in their present roles as a means of preparing them for greater responsibilities;
- identify managers with potential, encouraging them to prepare and implement personal development plans and ensuring that they receive the required development, training and experience to equip them for more demanding responsibilities within their own locations and elsewhere in the organization;
- provide for management succession, creating a system to keep this under review.

MANAGEMENT DEVELOPMENT: NEEDS AND PRIORITIES

Needs

A systematic approach to management development is necessary because the increasingly onerous demands made on line managers mean that they require a wider range of developed skills than ever before. Tamkin *et al* (2003) suggest that managers need the ability to:

- empower and develop people – understand and practise the process of delivering through the capability of others;
- manage people and performance – managers increasingly need to maintain morale whilst also maximizing performance;
- work across boundaries, engaging with others, working as a member of a team, thinking differently about problems and their solutions;

● develop relationships and a focus on the customer, building partnerships with both internal and external customers;
● balance technical and generic skills – the technical aspects of management and the management of human relationships.

Priorities

Hirsh *et al* (2000) suggest a number of priorities for management development. These are:

● combining a strong corporate architecture for management development with a capability for 'just in time' and local delivery to meet specific business needs;
● providing better information and advice for individual managers on how to think about their future direction in career terms and their learning needs;
● mainstreaming the skills required to manage self-development and to support the development of others; these skills include those of 'manager as coach' but also go wider and include informal career mentoring;
● finding ways of delivering more stretching and stimulating management development to the whole population of managers, not just those in very senior posts or identified as 'high potential'.

THE REQUIREMENTS, NATURE AND ELEMENTS OF MANAGEMENT DEVELOPMENT

Requirements

The CIPD (2002) sets out three key and mutually reinforcing requirements for connecting business challenges and management development:

1. Making the case for developing managers: convincing key stakeholders of the significance of management to business practice.
2. Making the connection between business strategies, organization and management development: clarifying the business purpose and outcomes for investing in management.
3. Managing the learning – getting the implementation right: designing, specifying, implementing and evaluating management development strategies that are 'fit for purpose'.

Nature

The most important thing to remember about the process of management development is that it must be business led even though it will be concerned with the development of individual performance and potential. The business has to decide what
sort of managers it needs to achieve its strategic goals and the business must decide
how it can best obtain and develop these managers. Even when the emphasis is on
self-development, as it should be, the business must still indicate the directions in
which self-development should go, possibly in the broadest of terms.

Elements

It has been suggested by Mumford (1993) that three elements have to be combined to
produce an effective management development system:

- *self-development* – a recognition that individuals can learn but are unlikely to be
  taught, and that the initiative for development often rests with the individual;
- *organization-derived development* – the development of the systems of formal development beloved of personnel and management development specialists;
- *boss-derived development* – those actions undertaken by a senior manager with
  others, most frequently around real problems at work.

Mumford also makes the point that managers think in terms of activities, not learning
opportunities, and therefore: 'Our main concern must be to facilitate learning
through our understanding of real work in the manager's world, rather than
attempting to impose separate management development processes.' He suggests
that formal management development processes do not always function as effectively as we would like because: 'We have put too much emphasis on planning ahead,
and not enough on enabling managers to use, understand and then build on their
past experiences.'

MANAGEMENT DEVELOPMENT ACTIVITIES

The three essential management development activities are the:

- analysis of present and future management needs;
- assessment of existing and potential skills and effectiveness of managers against
  those needs;
- production of strategies and plans to meet those needs.

Management development also involves management succession planning and career management activities as described in Chapter 26.

Analysis of needs

The analysis of the future needs for managers is carried out through human resource planning processes (see Chapter 25).

In today's changeable, if not chaotic, conditions it may not be feasible to make precise forecasts of the number of managers required. But what can and should be done is to assess the skills and competences managers will need to meet future demands and challenges arising from competitive pressures, new product-market strategies and the introduction of new technology.

Assessment of skills and competences

The assessment of skills and competences against these needs can be carried out by performance management processes as described in Part VII. It will be important, however, to include in these processes a means of identifying specific development needs and the agreement of development plans to meet not only current needs but anticipated future requirements.

These aspects of management development are discussed in the remaining sections of this chapter.

Management development strategy

The management development strategy will be concerned overall with what the organization intends to do about providing for its future management needs in the light of its business plans. The strategy will be concerned with the roles of the parties involved and with the approaches the organization proposes to use to develop its managers.

The prime aim of these benchmark statements is to identify the key facets that make up management development activities. They provide personnel and line managers with a means of conducting their own evaluation and analysis of the state of management development within their organization. Each facet or 'dimension' in the statements brings together such aspects as the links between the management development plan, the assessment of skills and identification of skill gaps, and the delivery of appropriate and effective training and development.

The facets are broken down into four aspects of performance:

- commitment to management development;
- reviewing the current position of management development;

- making progress in management development;
- excellence in management development.

The underpinning assumption in the framework is the importance of bringing together the elements of a management development strategy into a more integrated whole. The various components do not have separate existences of their own.

APPROACHES TO MANAGEMENT DEVELOPMENT

Management development should be regarded as a range of related activities rather than an all-embracing programme. The use of the word 'programme' to describe the process smacks too much of a mechanistic approach. It is important to start from an understanding of how managers learn, as considered below.

This does not imply that some systemization is not necessary; first, because many managers have to operate in more or less routine situations and have to be developed accordingly, and secondly, because organizations will not continue to thrive if they simply react to events. There must be an understanding of the approaches that can be used both to develop managers and also to assess existing managerial resources and how they meet the needs of the enterprise. And plans must be made for the development of those resources by selecting the best of the methods available. But this should not be seen as a 'programme' consisting of a comprehensive, highly integrated and rigidly applied range of management training and development techniques.

The management development activities required depend on the organization: its technology, its environment and its philosophy. A traditional bureaucratic/mechanistic type of organization may be inclined to adopt the programmed routine approach, complete with a wide range of courses, inventories, replacement charts, career plans and results-orientated review systems. An innovative and organic type of organization may rightly dispense with all these mechanisms. Its approach would be to provide its mangers with the opportunities, challenges and guidance they require, seizing the chance to give people extra responsibilities, and ensuring that they receive the coaching and encouragement they need. There may be no replacement charts, inventories or formal appraisal schemes, but people know how they stand, where they can go and how to get there.

As discussed later in this chapter, the role of formal training is much more limited than in the earlier approaches to management development, where it tended to predominate. As Hirsh and Carter (2002) emphasize:

Management training still needs to provide a coherent view of what managers need to learn, but delivery needs to be more flexible and fit into the busy working lives of managers... The development of interpersonal and leadership skills is a high priority and not easily achieved through conventional formal training.

How managers learn

It has often been said that managers learn to manage by managing – in other words, 'experience is the best teacher'. This is largely true, but some people learn much better than others. After all, a manager with 10 years' experience may have had no more than one year's experience repeated 10 times.

Differences in the ability to learn arise because some managers are naturally more capable or more highly motivated than others, while some will have had the benefit of the guidance and help of an effective boss who is fully aware of his or her responsibilities for developing managers. The saying quoted above could be expanded to read: 'Managers learn to manage by managing under the guidance of a good manager.' The operative word in this statement is 'good'. Some managers are better at developing people than others, and one of the aims of management development is to get all managers to recognize that developing their staff is an important part of their job. And for senior managers to say that people do not learn because they are not that way inclined, and to leave it at that, is to neglect one of their key responsibilities – to improve the performance of the organization by doing whatever is practical to improve the effectiveness and potentials of the managers.

To argue that managers learn best 'on the job' should not lead to the conclusion that managers are best left entirely to their own devices or that management development should be a haphazard process. The organization should try to evolve a philosophy of management development which ensures that consistent and deliberate interventions are made to improve managerial learning. Revans (1989) wants to take management development back into the reality of management and out of the classroom, but even he believes that deliberate attempts to foster the learning process through 'action learning' (see Chapter 38) are necessary.

The three basic approaches to management development are:

1. learning through work;
2. formal training; and
3. feedback, facilitation and support.

These can be achieved through both formal and informal means, as described below.

Formal approaches to management development

The formal approaches to management development include:

- development on the job through coaching, counselling, monitoring and feedback by managers on a continuous basis associated with the use of performance management processes to identify and satisfy development needs, and with mentoring;
- development through work experience, which includes job rotation, job enlargement, taking part in project teams or task groups, 'action learning', and secondment outside the organization;
- formal training by means of internal or external courses – although management training programmes are more likely to be delivered in a series of modules over a number of months rather than a single, long, residential course;
- structured self-development by following self-managed learning programmes agreed as a personal development plan or learning contract with the manager or a management development adviser – these may include guidance reading or the deliberate extension of knowledge or acquisition of new skills on the job;
- e-learning as part of a blended learning programme.

The formal approaches to management development are based on the identification of development needs through performance management or a development centre. The approach may be structured around a list of generic or core competences which have been defined as being appropriate for managers in the organization.

Informal approaches to management development

Informal approaches to management development make use of the learning experiences that managers meet during the course of their everyday work. Managers are learning every time they are confronted with an unusual problem, an unfamiliar task or a move to a different job. They then have to evolve new ways of dealing with the situation. They will learn if they analyse what they did to determine how and why it contributed to its success or failure. This retrospective or reflective learning will be effective if managers can apply it successfully in the future.

This is potentially the most powerful form of learning. The question is: can anything be done to help managers make the best use of their experience? This type of 'experiential' learning comes naturally to some managers. They seem to absorb, unconsciously and by some process of osmosis, the lessons from their experience, although in fact they they have probably developed a capacity for almost instantaneous analysis, which they store in their mental databank and which they can retrieve whenever necessary.

Ordinary mortals, however, either find it difficult to do this sort of analysis or do not recognize the need. This is where semi-formal approaches can be used to encourage and help managers to learn more effectively. These approaches include:

- emphasizing self-assessment and the identification of development needs by getting managers to assess their own performance against agreed objectives and analyse the factors that contributed to effective or less effective performance – this can be provided through performance management;
- getting managers to produce their own personal development plans or self-managed learning programmes;
- encouraging managers to discuss their own problems and opportunities with their bosses, colleagues or mentors in order to establish for themselves what they need to learn or be able to do.

An integrated approach to management development

An integrated approach to management development will make judicious use of both the formal and informal methods as described above. There are five governing principles:

- *The reality of management* – the approach to management development should avoid making simplistic assumptions on what managers need to know or do, based on the classical analysis of management as the processes of planning, organizing, directing and controlling. In reality managerial work is relatively disorganized and fragmented, and this is why many practising managers reject the facile solutions suggested by some formal management training programmes. As Kanter (1989) has said: 'Managerial work is undergoing such enormous and rapid change that many managers are reinventing their profession as they go.'
- *Relevance* – it is too easy to assume that all managers need to know about such nostrums as strategic planning, economic value added, balance sheet analysis, etc. These can be useful but they may not be what managers really need. Management development processes must be related to the needs of particular managers in specific jobs and these processes may or may not include techniques such as those listed above. Those needs should include not only what managers should know now but also what they should know and be able to do in the future, if they have the potential. Thus, management development may include 'broadening programmes' aimed at giving managers an understanding of the wider, strategic issues which will be relevant at higher levels in the organization.

- *Self-development* – managers need to be encouraged to develop themselves and helped to do so. Performance management will aim to provide this guidance.
- *Experiential learning* – if learning can be described as a modification of behaviour through experience then the principal method by which managers can be equipped is by providing them with the right variety of experience, in good time in the course of their careers, and by helping them to learn from that experience – coaching and action learning are methods of achieving this.
- *Formal training* – courses can supplement but can never replace experience and they must be carefully timed and selected or designed to meet particular needs. A 'sheep dip' approach which exposes all managers to the same training course may be desirable in some circumstances, but the focus should generally be on identifying and meeting individual learning needs.

Competency-based management development

Competency-based management development uses competency frameworks (see Chapter 11) as a means of identifying and expressing development needs and pointing the way to self-managed learning programmes or the provision of learning opportunities by the organization.

Competency-based management development may concentrate on a limited number of core or generic competences which the organization has decided will be an essential part of the equipment of their managers if they are going to take the organization forward in line with its strategic plans. For example:

- *strategic capability* to understand the changing business environment, opportunities for product-market development, competitive challenges and the strengths and weaknesses of their own organization in order to identify optimum strategic responses;
- *change management capability* to identify change needs, plan change programmes and persuade others to participate willingly in the implementation of change;
- *team management capability* to get diverse groups of people from different disciplines to work well together.
- *relationship management* to network effectively with others to share information and pool resources to achieve common objectives;
- *international management* to be capable of managing across international frontiers, working well with people of other nationalities.

Development centres

The aim of development centres is to help participants build up an awareness of the competences their job requires and to construct their own personal development plans to improve their performance in the present job and to enhance their careers.

Like assessment centres (see Chapter 27), development centres are built around definitions of competency requirements. Unlike assessment centres, however, development centres look ahead at the competencies needed in the future. The other significant difference between a development centre and an assessment centre is that in the latter case the organization 'owns' the results for selection or promotion purposes, while in the former case the results are owned by the individual as the basis for self-managed learning.

Development centres are not an event, nor a physical location. The activities of the centre offer participants the opportunity to examine and understand the competences they require now and in the future. Because 'behaviour predicts behaviour' the activities of the centre need to offer opportunities for competences to be observed in practice. Simulations of various kinds are therefore important features – these are a combination of case studies and role playing designed to obtain the maximum amount of realism. Participants are put into the position of practising behaviour in conditions very similar to those they will meet in the course of their everyday work.

An important part of the centre's activities will be feedback reviews, counselling and coaching sessions conducted by the directing staff, which will consist of full-time tutors and line managers who have been given special training in the techniques required.

The stages of a typical development centre as described by Hall and Norris (1992) are:

Prior to the centre delegates assess themselves against defined competencies.

Day 1

- Delegates test their pre-centre work with other delegates
- Individual task
- Structured self-insight
- Business simulation

Day 2

- Team roles questionnaire
- Personal profiles questionnaire
- Further counselling sessions and self-assessment procedures

Day 3

- Numerical reasoning tests
- Feedback on questionnaire
- Counselling on personal development plans
- Review of key points and findings

EMOTIONAL INTELLIGENCE AND LEADERSHIP QUALITIES

Management development should be concerned with enhancing leadership as well as extending and improving more general management skills. According to Goleman (1995), this process should take account of the concept of emotional intelligence as discussed in Chapter 10. Emotional intelligence has been defined by Goleman (1995) as being about:

- knowing what you are feeling and being able to handle those feelings without having them swamp you;
- being able to motivate yourself to get jobs done, be creative and perform at your peak;
- sensing what others are feeling and handling relationships effectively.

The possession of high levels of emotional intelligence is a necessary attribute for success as a leader.

Goleman has defined four components of emotional intelligence:

1. *Self-management* – the ability to control or redirect disruptive impulses and moods and regulate your own behaviour coupled with a propensity to pursue goals with energy and persistence. The six competencies associated with this component are self-control, trustworthiness and integrity, initiative and adaptability, comfort with ambiguity, openness to change and a strong desire to achieve.
2. *Self-awareness* – the ability to recognize and understand your moods, emotions and drives as well as their effect on others. This is linked to three competencies: self-confidence, realistic self-assessment and emotional self-awareness.
3. *Social awareness* – the ability to understand the emotional make-up of other people, and skill in treating people according to their emotional reactions. This is linked to six competencies: empathy, expertise in building and retaining talent, organizational awareness, cross-cultural sensitivity, valuing diversity, and service to clients and customers.

4. *Social skills* – proficiency in managing relationships and building networks to get the desired result from others and reach personal goals, and the ability to find common ground and build rapport. The five competencies associated with this component are leadership, effectiveness in leading change, conflict management, influence/communication, and expertise in building and leading teams.

The steps required to develop emotional intelligence suggested by Goleman (1999) are:

- assess the requirements of jobs in terms of emotional skills;
- assess individuals to identify their level of emotional intelligence – 360-degree feedback can be a powerful source of data;
- gauge readiness – ensure that people are prepared to improve their level of emotional intelligence;
- motivate people to believe that the learning experience will benefit them;
- make change self-directed – encourage people to prepare a learning plan which fits their interests, resources and goals;
- focus on clear manageable goals – the focus must be on immediate, manageable steps, bearing in mind that cultivating a new skill is gradual, with stops and starts; the old ways will reassert themselves from time to time;
- prevent relapse – show people how they can learn lessons from the inevitable relapses;
- give performance feedback;
- encourage practice, remembering that emotional competence cannot be improved overnight;
- provide models of desired behaviours;
- encourage and reinforce – create a climate that rewards self-improvement;
- evaluate – establish sound outcome measures and then assess performance against them.

RESPONSIBILITY FOR MANAGEMENT DEVELOPMENT

Management development is not a separate activity to be handed over to a specialist and forgotten or ignored. The success of a management development programme depends upon the degree to which all levels of management are committed to it. The development of subordinates must be recognized as a natural and essential part of any manager's job. But the lead must come from the top.

The traditional view is that the organization need not concern itself with management development. The natural process of selection and the pressure of competition will ensure the survival of the fittest. Managers, in fact, are born not made. Cream rises to the top (but then so does scum).

The reaction to this was summed up in Humble's (1963) phrase, 'programmitis and crown prince'. Management development was seen in its infancy as a mechanical process using management inventories, multicoloured replacement charts, 'Cook's tours' for newly recruited graduates, detailed job rotation programmes, elaborate points schemes to appraise personal characteristics, and endless series of formal courses.

The true role of the organization in management development lies somewhere between these two extremes. On the one hand, it is not enough, in conditions of rapid growth (when they exist) and change, to leave everything to chance – to trial and error. On the other hand, elaborate management development programmes cannot successfully be imposed on the organization. As Peter Drucker wisely said many years ago (1955): 'Development is always self-development. Nothing could be more absurd than for the enterprise to assume responsibility for the development of a man. [sic]. The responsibility rests with the individual, his abilities, his efforts'.

But he went on to say:

> Every manager in a business has the opportunity to encourage individual self-development or to stifle it, to direct it to or to misdirect it. He [sic] should be specifically assigned the responsibility for helping all men working with him to focus, direct and apply their self-development efforts productively. And every company can provide systematic development challenges to its managers.

Executive ability is eventually something that individuals must develop for themselves while carrying out their normal duties. But they will do this much better if they are given encouragement, guidance and opportunities by their company and managers. In McGregor's (1960) phrase: managers are grown – they are neither born nor made. The role of the company is to provide conditions favourable to faster growth. And these conditions are very much part of the environment and organizational climate of the company and the management style of the chief executive. The latter has the ultimate responsibility for management development. As McGregor wrote:

> The job environment of the individual is the most important variable affecting his [sic] development. Unless that environment is conducive to his growth, none of the other things we do to him or for him will be effective. This is why the 'agricultural' approach to management development is preferable to the 'manufacturing' approach. The latter leads, among other things, to the unrealistic expectation that we can create and develop managers in the classroom.

It is remarkable that today some people are still reciting these well-established principles as if they had just discovered them.

Personal development plans

Managers must therefore take the main responsibility for their own development. The organization can help and the manager's boss must accept some responsibility for encouraging self-development and providing guidance as necessary. But individuals should be expected to draw up their own personal development plans (see also Chapter 39), the content of which would be based on answers to the following questions:

- What knowledge and/or skills do you intend to gain? and/or
- What levels of competence are you planning to achieve?
- What are your learning objectives? These should be set out in the form of definitions of the areas in which your performance will improve and/or what new things you will be able to do after the learning programme.
- How are you doing to achieve your objectives? What tasks, projects, exercises or reading will you do? What educational or training courses would you like to attend? The development plan should be broken down into defined phases and specific learning events should be itemized. The duration of each phase and the total length of the programme should be set out together with the costs, if any.
- What resources will you need in the form of computer-based training material, books, videos, individual coaching, mentoring etc?
- What evidence will you show to demonstrate your learning? What criteria will be used to ensure that this evidence is satisfactory?

Role of the human resource development specialist

Management development is not a separate activity to be handed over to a specialist and forgotten or ignored. The success of management development depends upon the degree to which it is recognized as an important aspect of the business strategy – a key organizational process aimed at delivering results. All levels of management must therefore be committed to it. The development of their staff must be recognized as a natural and essential part of any manager's job and one of the key criteria upon which their performance as managers will be judged. But the lead must come from the top.

However, human resource development specialists still have a number of important roles as facilitators of the learning and development process. They:

- interpret the needs of the business and advise on how management development strategies can play their part in meeting these needs;
- act as advocates of the significance of management development as a business-led activity;
- make proposals on formal and informal approaches to management development;
- develop in conjunction with line management competency frameworks which can be used as the basis for management development;
- provide guidance to managers on how to carry out their developmental activities;
- provide help and encouragement to managers in preparing and pursuing their personal development plans – including advice on acquiring an NVQ, professional or academic qualifications;
- provide the learning material, including e-learning, managers need to achieve their learning objectives;
- act as tutors or mentors to individual managers or groups of managers as required;
- advise on the use and choice of external management education programmes;
- facilitate action learning projects;
- plan and conduct development centre;
- plan and conduct other formal learning events with the help of external providers as required.

41

Formulating and implementing learning and development strategies

This chapter deals with the formulation and implementation of learning and development strategies, the purpose of which is to provide a road map for the future and a basis upon which learning and development activities can be planned, The chapter deals with making the business case, creating a learning climate, identifying learning needs, planning and implementing learning and development activities, and evaluating the learning that has taken place.

MAKING THE BUSINESS CASE

The business case for learning and development should demonstrate how learning, training and development programmes will meet business needs. Kearns and Miller (1997) go as far as to claim that: 'If a business objective cannot be cited as a basis for designing training and development, then no training and development should be offered.'

The areas of the business strategy that depend on talented people should be analysed. The organization's strategic plans and their impact on knowledge and skill requirements should also be noted. For example, these might include the development of a high performance culture, productivity improvements, the innovation and launch of new products or services, achieving better levels of service delivery to customers, or the extended use of IT or other forms of technology. Any proposed learning and training interventions should specify how they would contribute to the achievement of these strategic goals.

A cost/benefit analysis is required that compares the benefits, expressed in quantified terms as far as possible, which will result from the learning activity. The business case has to convince management that there will be an acceptable return on the investment (ROI) in learning and training programmes. It can be difficult to produce realistic figures, although the attempt is worth making with the help of finance specialists. The case for investing in learning and development can refer to any of the following potential benefits:

- improve individual, team and corporate performance in terms of output, quality, speed and overall productivity;
- attract high-quality employees by offering them learning and development opportunities, increasing their levels of competence and enhancing their skills, thus enabling them to obtain more job satisfaction, to gain higher rewards and to progress within the organization;
- provide additional non-financial rewards (growth and career opportunities) as part of a total reward policy (see Chapter 42);
- improve operational flexibility by extending the range of skills possessed by employees (multiskilling);
- increase the commitment of employees by encouraging them to identify with the mission and objectives of the organization;
- help to manage change by increasing understanding of the reasons for change and providing people with the knowledge and skills they need to adjust to new situations;
- provide line managers with the skills required to manage and develop their people;
- help to develop a positive culture in the organization: one, for example, which is oriented towards performance improvement;
- provide higher levels of service to customers;
- minimize learning costs (reduce the length of learning curves).

DEVELOPING A LEARNING CULTURE

A learning culture is one that promotes learning because it is recognized by top management, line managers and employees generally as an essential organizational process to which they are committed and in which they engage continuously.

Reynolds (2004) describes a learning culture as a 'growth medium' that will 'encourage employees to commit to a range of positive discretionary behaviours, including learning' and which has the following characteristics: empowerment not supervision, self-managed learning not instruction, long-term capacity building not short-term fixes. It will encourage discretionary learning, which Sloman (2003a) believes takes place when individuals actively seek to acquire the knowledge and skills that promote the organization's objectives.

It is suggested by Reynolds (2004) that to create a learning culture it is necessary to develop organizational practices that raise commitment amongst employees and 'give employees a sense of purpose in the workplace, grant employees opportunities to act upon their commitment, and offer practical support to learning'. He proposes the following steps:

1. Develop and share the vision – belief in a desired and emerging future.
2. Empower employees – provide 'supported autonomy'; freedom for employees to manage their work within certain boundaries (policies and expected behaviours) but with support available as required.
3. Adopt a facilitative style of management in which responsibility for decision-making is ceded as far as possible to employees.
4. Provide employees with a supportive learning environment where learning capabilities can be discovered and applied, eg peer networks, supportive policies and systems, protected time for learning.
5. Use coaching techniques to draw out the talents of others by encouraging employees to identify options and seek their own solutions to problems.
6. Guide employees through their work challenges and provide them with time, resources and, crucially, feedback.
7. Recognize the importance of managers acting as role models: 'The new way of thinking and behaving may be so different that you must see what it looks like before you can imagine yourself doing it. You must see the new behaviour and attitudes in others with whom you can identify' (Schein, 1990).
8. Encourage networks – communities of practice.
9. Align systems to vision – get rid of bureaucratic systems that produce problems rather than facilitate work.

IDENTIFYING LEARNING NEEDS

All learning activities need to be based on an understanding of what needs to be done and why. The purpose of the activities must be defined and this is only possible if the learning needs of the organization and the groups and individuals within it have been identified and analysed.

The basis of learning needs analysis

Learning needs analysis is sometimes assumed to be concerned only with defining the gap between what is happening and what should happen, ie the difference between what people know and can do and what they *should* know and be able to do. This gap is what has to be filled by training.

But this 'deficiency' model of training – only putting things right that have gone wrong – is limited. Learning is much more positive than that. It is more concerned with identifying and satisfying development needs – fitting people to take on extra responsibilities, increasing all-round competence, equipping people to deal with new work demands, multiskilling, and preparing people to take on higher levels of responsibility in the future.

Areas for learning needs analysis

Learning needs should be analysed, first, for the organization as a whole – corporate needs; second, for departments, teams, functions or occupations within the organization – group needs; and third, for individual employees – individual needs. These three areas are interconnected, as shown in Figure 41.1. The analysis of corporate needs will lead to the identification of learning needs in different departments or occupations, while these in turn will indicate what individual employees need to learn. The process operates in reverse. As the needs of individual employees are analysed separately, common needs emerge that can be dealt with on a group basis. The sum of group and individual needs will help to define corporate needs, although there may be some superordinate learning requirements that can be related only to the company as a whole to meet its business development needs – the whole learning plan may be greater than the sum of its parts.

These areas of analysis are discussed below.

Analysis of business and human resource plans

Business and HR plans should indicate in general terms the types of skills and competencies that may be required in the future and the numbers of people with

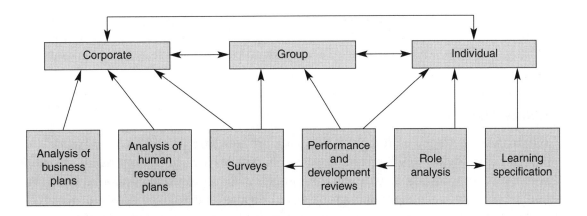

Figure 41.1 Learning needs analysis – areas and methods

those skills and competencies who will be needed. These broad indicators have to be translated into more specific plans that cover, for example, the outputs from training programmes of people with particular skills or a combination of skills (multiskilling).

Surveys

Special surveys may be carried out that analyse the information from a number of sources, eg performance reviews, to identify corporate and group learning and training needs. This information can be usefully supplemented by interviewing people to establish their views about what they need to learn. But they often find it difficult to articulate learning needs and it is best to lead with a discussion of the work they do and identify any areas where they believe that their performance and potential could be improved by a learning or training programme.

An analysis should also be made of any areas where future changes in work processes, methods or job responsibilities are planned, and of any common gaps in skills or knowledge or weaknesses in performance that indicate a learning need. Further information should be derived from the evaluation of training, as described at the end of this chapter.

Performance and development reviews

Performance management processes, as described in Part VII of this book, should be a prime source of information about individual learning and development needs. The performance management approach to learning concentrates on the preparation of performance improvement programmes, personal development plans and learning contracts that lead to jointly determined action plans. The emphasis is on identifying learning needs for continuous development or to produce specific improvements in performance.

Role analysis

Role analysis is the basis for preparing role profiles that provide a framework for analysing and identifying learning needs. Role profiles set out the key result areas of the role but, importantly, also define the competencies required to perform the role. A good performance management process will ensure that role profiles are updated regularly and the performance review will be built round an analysis of the results achieved by reference to the key result areas and agreed objectives. The competency framework for the role is used to assess the level of competency displayed in achieving, or as the case may be, not achieving those results. An assessment can then be made of any learning required to develop levels of competency. Ideally, this should be a self-assessment by individuals, who should be given every encouragement to identify learning needs themselves. But these can be discussed with the individuals' manager and agreement reached on how the learning needs should be met, by the individuals through self-managed learning, and/or with the help and support of their managers. The output of role analysis could be a learning specification, as illustrated in Figure 41.2.

PLANNING AND IMPLEMENTING LEARNING AND DEVELOPMENT PROGRAMMES

Every learning and development programme needs to be designed individually, and the design will continually evolve as new learning needs emerge, or when feedback indicates that changes are required. It is essential to consider carefully the objectives of the programme and to express these in the form of what behaviour is expected from those involved in the workplace (terminal behaviour). When planning a learning event, the process used should match the desired objectives for the event.

The basis of learning and development programmes

The planning and implementation of learning and development programmes is based on an understanding of learning needs. A training survey conducted in 2005

LEARNING SPECIFICATION	
Role title: Product Manager	**Department:** Marketing

What the role holder must understand	
Learning outcomes	*Learning methods*
• The product market	• Coaching: Marketing Manager and Advertising Manager
• The product specification	• Coaching: Operations Manager
• Market research availability	• Coaching: Market Research Manager
• Interpretation of marketing data	• Coaching: Market Research Manager
• Customer service requirements	• Customer Service Manager
• Techniques of product management	• Institute of Marketing courses

What the role holder must be able to do	
Learning outcomes	*Learning methods*
• Prepare product budget	• Coaching: Budget Accountant
• Prepare marketing plans	• Coaching: Mentor
• Conduct market reviews	• Coaching: Market Research Department
• Prepare marketing campaigns	• Read: Product Manager's Manual
• Specify requirements for advertisers and promotional material	• Read: Product Manager's Manual
• Liaise with advertising agents and creative suppliers	• Attachment to agency
• Analyse results of advertising campaigns	• Coaching: Mentor, read analyses
• Prepare marketing reports	• Read: previous reports, observe: marketing review meetings

Figure 41.2   A learning specification

(CIPD, 2005e) produced the data set out below in response to the question, 'Which skills does your organization need to develop in order to fulfil requirements in three years' time?' The respondents listed in order:

1. Management and leadership.
2. Communication.
3. Business skills.
4. Customer service.
5. Advanced technical skills.
6. Broader skill sets.
7. Coaching and mentoring.
8. Innovation.
9. IT skills.
10. Ability to adapt easily to change.

Account needs to be taken of the lessons that can be learnt from learning theory, especially those concerned with cognitive, experiential and social learning. These highlight the importance of providing people with the opportunity to learn for themselves, and emphasizes the importance of learning from experience and learning from other people. The concepts of self-directed learning and personal development planning are particularly important, but encouraging these processes needs to be reinforced by the provision of guidance and advice to learners, mainly from their line managers but also from learning specialists and through the provision by the organization of learning resource centres and e-learning programmes.

Responsibility for the implementation of learning

While individuals should be expected to take a considerable degree of responsibility for managing their own learning, they need the help and support of their line managers and the organization.

Line managers have a key role in planning and facilitating learning by conducting performance and development reviews, agreeing learning contracts and personal development plans with their staff, and helping staff to implement those plans through the provision of learning opportunities and coaching. But they have to be encouraged to do this. They should understand that the promotion of learning is regarded as an important aspect of their responsibilities and that their performance in carrying it out will be assessed. They also need guidance on how they should carry out their developmental role.

Responsibility for learning and development is being placed increasingly on managers and employees rather than training professionals. The latter are becoming learning facilitators rather than training providers or instructors. The direct role of training is becoming less important. As Stewart and Tansley (2002) point out, training specialists are focusing on learning processes, rather than the content of training courses. Carter *et al* (2003) argue that 'The shifting organizational forms of training, coupled with multiple delivery methods, are not leading to a single new role for the trainer, but rather an array of different role demands.' These roles include facilitator and change agent.

As facilitators, learning and development specialists analyse learning needs and make proposals on how these can best be satisfied. They provide facilities such as learning resource centres and e-learning programmes, and plan and implement training interventions, often outsourcing training to external providers. Importantly, they provide guidance to line managers and help them to develop their skills in assessing development needs, personal development planning and coaching. Additionally, they are there to give advice and help to individuals on their learning plans.

Learning and development activities

A balanced learning approach is required, making use of the various forms of learning and development referred to in Chapter 38. The aim should be to produce a coherent strategy that contains the plans for creating and maintaining a learning climate and developing and implementing complementary and mutually supportive learning activities such as coaching and mentoring. Details should be provided for each activity on its objectives, the methods to be used, its timing as part of a programme, how it is linked to other learning activities, who is responsible (emphasizing the role of individuals and their managers), and the business case for using it in terms of a cost/benefit assessment.

The extent to which organizations use different approaches as revealed by a survey conducted in 2004 (IRS, 2004g) is shown in Table 41.1.

Table 41.1   Use of learning activities (*Source:* IRS, 2004g)

Activity	No of organizations using 'regularly' or 'sometimes'
On-the-job induction	72
On-the-job skills updating	71
External conferences and workshops	70
Formal classroom training	67
Coaching	64
Mentoring	55
Off-the-job induction	49
Off-the-job skills updating	40
e-learning	35
Non-vocational training	22
Action learning sets	16

N = 79

EVALUATION OF LEARNING

It is important to evaluate learning in order to assess its effectiveness in producing the outcomes specified when the activity was planned and to indicate where improvements or changes are required to make the training even more effective. As Tamkin *et al* (2002) suggest:

> Learning can be modelled as a chain of impact from the planning of learning to meet organizational or individual learning needs to the learning that takes place in a learning event, from learning to changed behaviour, and from changed behaviour to impact on others and the organization as a whole.

It is at the planning stage that the basis upon which each category of learning event is to be evaluated should be determined. At the same time, it is necessary to consider how the information required for evaluation should be obtained and analysed.

Approaches to the evaluation of learning have traditionally concentrated on the evaluation of training events as described below. But the trend is to concentrate more on the validation of the total learning process.

Training evaluation defined

The process of evaluating training has been defined by Hamblin (1974) as: 'Any attempt to obtain information (feedback) on the effects of a training programme, and to assess the value of the training in the light of that information.' Evaluation leads to control, which means deciding whether or not the training was worthwhile (preferably in cost/benefit terms) and what improvements are required to make it even more cost-effective.

Evaluation is an integral feature of learning activities. In its crudest form, it is the comparison of objectives (criterion behaviour) with outcomes (terminal behaviour) to answer the question of how far the event has achieved its purpose. The setting of objectives and the establishment of methods of measuring results are, or should be, an essential part of the planning stage of any learning and development programme.

Levels of evaluation

Four levels of training evaluation have been suggested by Kirkpatrick (1994).

Level 1. Reaction

At this level, evaluation measures how those who participated in the training have reacted to it. In a sense, it is a measure of immediate customer satisfaction. Kirkpatrick suggests the following guidelines for evaluating reactions:

- determine what you want to find out;
- design a form that will quantify reactions;
- encourage written comments and suggestions;
- get 100 per cent immediate response;

- get honest responses;
- develop acceptable standards;
- measure reactions against standards, and take appropriate action;
- communicate reactions as appropriate.

Research by Warr *et al* (1999) has shown that there is relatively little correlation between learner reactions and measures of training, or subsequent measures of changed behaviour. But as Tamkin *et al* (2002) point out, despite this, organizations are still keen to get reactions to training, and used with caution this can produce useful information on the extent to which learning objectives were perceived to be met and why.

Level 2. Evaluating learning

This level obtains information on the extent to which learning objectives have been attained. It will aim to find how much knowledge was acquired, what skills were developed or improved, and the extent to which attitudes have changed in the desired direction. So far as possible, the evaluation of learning should involve the use of tests before and after the programme – paper and pencil, oral or performance tests.

Level 3. Evaluating behaviour

This level evaluates the extent to which behaviour has changed as required when people attending the programme have returned to their jobs. The question to be answered is the extent to which knowledge, skills and attitudes have been transferred from the classroom to the workplace. Ideally, the evaluation should take place both before and after the training. Time should be allowed for the change in behaviour to take place. The evaluation needs to assess the extent to which specific learning objectives relating to changes in behaviour and the application of knowledge and skills have been achieved.

Level 4. Evaluating results

This is the ultimate level of evaluation and provides the basis for assessing the benefits of the training against its costs. The objective is to determine the added value of learning and development programmes – how they contribute to raising organizational performance significantly above its previous level. The evaluation has to be based on 'before and after' measures and has to determine the extent to which the fundamental objectives of the training have been achieved in areas such as increasing sales, raising productivity, reducing accidents or increasing customer satisfaction.

Evaluating results is obviously easier when they can be quantified. However, it is not always easy to prove the contribution to improved results made by training as distinct from other factors and, as Kirkpatrick says: 'Be satisfied with evidence, because proof is usually impossible to get.' Perhaps the most powerful method of demonstrating that learning programmes pay is to measure the return on investment, as discussed below.

Return on investment as a method of evaluation

Return on investment (ROI) is advocated by some commentators as a means of assessing the overall impact of training on organizational performance. It is calculated as:

$$\frac{\text{Benefits from training (£)} - \text{costs of training (£)}}{\text{Costs of training (£)}} \times 100$$

Kearns and Miller (1997) believe that only this sort of measure is useful in evaluating the overall impact of training. They argue that particular hard measures should be used to evaluate specific training; for example, if development aims to bring about greater awareness of customers then it should still be measured by the eventual effect on customer spend, customer satisfaction and number of customers.

The pressure to produce financial justifications for any organizational activity, especially in areas such as learning and development, has increased the interest in ROI. The problem is that while it is easy to record the costs it is much harder to produce convincing financial assessments of the benefits. Kearns (2005a) provides a response to this concern:

> All business is about the art of speculation and the risk of the unknown. The trick here is not to try and work to a higher standard of credibility than anyone else in the organization. If accountants are prepared to guess about amortization costs or marketing directors to guess about market share why should a trainer not be prepared to have a guess at the potential benefits of training?

He recommends the use of 'a rule of thumb' when using ROI to the effect that any training should improve the performance of trainees by at least 1 per cent. Thus if the return on sales training is being measured, the benefits could be calculated as 1 per cent of profit on sales.

Use of evaluation tools

Research by The Industrial Society (2000) has shown that the Kirkpatrick model was used by 35 per cent of the 487 participants. Research by Twitchell *et al* (2000) found that many US organizations use levels 1 and 2 evaluations for at least some programmes, fewer than half even try level 3 and only a small percentage use level 4 evaluations.

The number of respondents to the IRS 2004 training survey using different types of evaluation is shown in Table 41.2.

Table 41.2 Use of evaluation tools (*Source:* IRS, 2004f)

Activity	No of organizations using 'regularly' or 'sometimes'
Immediate post-course questionnaire	74
Monitoring appraisal results	50
Observation of participants at work	49
Interviewing participants	48
Employee attitude surveys	44
Monitoring qualifications gained	42
Follow-up questionnaires	41
Monitoring test results	35
Survey line managers	34
Assessment of participant's action plans	31
Evaluation framework/model	28
Customer surveys	28
Analysis of output/quality data	25

N = 79

Application of evaluation

As Reid *et al* (2004) comment: 'The more care that has been taken in the assessment of needs and the more precise the objectives, the greater will be the possibility of effective evaluation.' This is the basis for conducting evaluation at various levels.

Like the similar levels of evaluation suggested by Hamblin in 1976 (reactions, learning, job behaviour, impact on unit and organizational performance) the levels defined by Kirkpatrick are links in the chain. Training produces reactions, which lead to learning, which leads to changes in job behaviour, which lead to results at unit and organizational level. Trainees can react favourably to a course – they can enjoy the experience – but learn little or nothing. They can learn something, but cannot, or will not, or are not allowed to apply it. They apply it but it does no good within their own areas. It does some good in their function, but does not improve organizational effectiveness.

Evaluation can take place at any level. In the Kirkpatrick scheme it is easier to start at level 1 and progress up with increasing difficulty to level 4. It could be argued that the only feedback from evaluation that matters is the result in terms of improved unit or organizational performance that training brings. But if this is hard to measure, training could still be justified in terms of any actual changes in behaviour that the programme was designed to produce. This is based on the assumption that the analysis of learning needs indicated that this behaviour is more than likely to deliver the desired results. Similarly, at the learning level, if a proper analysis of knowledge, skills and attitude requirements and their impact on behaviour has been conducted, it is reasonable to assume that if the knowledge, etc has been acquired, behaviour is likely to change appropriately. Finally, if all else fails, reactions are important in that they provide immediate feedback on the quality of training given (including the performance of the trainer), which can point the way to corrective action.

Part IX

Rewarding people

This part is concerned with the process of rewarding people in organizations. It starts in Chapter 42 with a general review of reward management, which includes descriptions of its application for directors and executives, sales staff and manual workers. This is followed in Chapter 43 with an examination of the concept of strategic reward. The rest of Part IX deals with the following aspects of reward management:

42

Reward management

This chapter provides an overview of reward management. The concept of reward management, its strategic and detailed aims and its philosophy are discussed initially. Reference is also made to the economic factors that affect levels of pay. This is followed by descriptions of the elements of a reward management system and the concept of total reward. The chapter ends with descriptions of particular applications of reward management for directors and executives, sales staff and manual workers.

REWARD MANAGEMENT DEFINED

Reward management is concerned with the formulation and implementation of strategies and policies, the purposes of which are to reward people fairly, equitably and consistently in accordance with their value to the organization and thus help the organization to achieve its strategic goals. It deals with the design, implementation and maintenance of reward systems (reward processes, practices and procedures) that aim to meet the needs of both the organization and its stakeholders.

THE AIMS OF REWARD MANAGEMENT

The aims of reward management are to:

- reward people according to what the organization values and wants to pay for;
- reward people for the value they create;
- reward the right things to convey the right message about what is important in terms of behaviours and outcomes;
- develop a performance culture;
- motivate people and obtain their commitment and engagement;
- help to attract and retain the high quality people the organization needs;
- create total reward processes that recognize the importance of both financial and non-financial rewards;
- develop a positive employment relationship and psychological contract;
- align reward practices with both business goals and employee values; as Brown (2001) emphasizes, the 'alignment of your reward practices with employee values and needs is every bit as important as alignment with business goals, and critical to the realization of the latter';
- operate fairly – people feel that they are treated justly in accordance with what is due to them because of their value to the organization: the 'felt-fair' principle of Jaques (1961);
- apply equitably – people are rewarded appropriately in relation to others within the organization, relativities between jobs are measured as objectively as possible and equal pay is provided for work of equal value;
- function consistently – decisions on pay do not vary arbitrarily and without due cause between different people or at different times;
- operate transparently – people understand how reward processes operate and how they are affected by them.

THE PHILOSOPHY OF REWARD MANAGEMENT

Reward management is based on a well-articulated philosophy – a set of beliefs and guiding principles that are consistent with the values of the organization and help to enact them. These include beliefs in the need to achieve fairness, equity, consistency and transparency in operating the reward system. The philosophy recognizes that if HRM is about investing in human capital from which a reasonable return is required, then it is proper to reward people differentially according to their contribution (ie the return on investment they generate).

The philosophy of reward management recognizes that it must be strategic in the sense that it addresses longer-term issues relating to how people should be valued for what they do and what they achieve. Reward strategies and the processes that are required to implement them have to flow from the business strategy.

Reward management adopts a 'total reward' approach, which emphasizes the importance of considering all aspects of reward as a coherent whole that is integrated with other HR initiatives designed to achieve the motivation, commitment, engagement and development of employees. This requires the integration of reward strategies with other HRM strategies, especially those concerning human resource development. Reward management is an integral part of an HRM approach to managing people.

The philosophy will be affected by the business and HR strategies of the organization, the significance attached to reward matters by top management, and the internal and external environment of the organization. The external environment includes the levels of pay in the labour market (market rates) and it is helpful to be aware of the economic theories that explain how these levels are determined, as summarized in Table 42.1.

THE ELEMENTS OF REWARD MANAGEMENT

The elements of reward management are described below.

Reward system

A reward system consists of:

- *Policies* that provide guidelines on approaches to managing rewards.
- *Practices* that provide financial and non-financial rewards.
- *Processes* concerned with evaluating the relative size of jobs (job evaluation) and assessing individual performance (performance management).
- *Procedures* operated in order to maintain the system and to ensure that it operates efficiently and flexibly and provides value for money.

Reward strategy

Reward strategy sets out what the organization intends to do in the longer term to develop and implement reward policies, practices and processes that will further the achievement of its business goals.

Table 42.1 Economic theories explaining pay levels

Name of theory	Summary of theory	Practical significance
The law of supply and demand	Other things being equal, if there is a surplus of labour and supply exceeds the demand, pay levels go down; if there is a scarcity of labour and demand exceeds the supply, pay goes up.	Emphasizes the importance of labour market factors in affecting market rates.
Efficiency wage theory	Firms will pay more than the market rate because they believe that high levels of pay will contribute to increases in productivity by motivating superior performance, attracting better candidates, reducing labour turnover and persuading workers that they are being treated fairly. This theory is also known as 'the economy of high wages'.	Organizations use efficiency wages theory (although they will not call it that) when they formulate pay policies which place them as market leaders or at least above the average.
Human capital theory	A worker has a set of skills developed by education and training which generates a stock of productive capital.	Employees and employers each derive benefits from investment in creating human capital. The level of pay should supply both parties with a reasonable return on that investment.
Agency theory	The owners of a firm (the principals) are separate from the employees (the agents). This difference can create 'agency costs' because the agents may not be so productive as the principals. The latter therefore have to devise ways of motivating and controlling the efforts of the former.	A system of incentives to motivate and reward acceptable behaviour. This process of 'incentive alignment' consists of paying for measurable results that are deemed to be in the best interests of the owners.
The effort bargain	Workers aim to strike a bargain about the relationship between what they regard as as reasonable contribution and what their employer is prepared to offer to elicit that contribution.	Management has to assess what level and type of inducements it has to offer in return for the contribution it requires from its workforce.

Reward policies

Reward policies address the following broad issues:

- the level of rewards, taking into account 'market stance', ie how internal rates of pay should compare with market rates, for example aligned to the median or the upper quartile rate;
- achieving equal pay;
- the relative importance attached to external competitiveness and internal equity;
- the approach to total reward;
- the scope for the use of contingent rewards related to performance, competence, contribution or skill;
- the role of line managers;
- transparency – the publication of information on reward structures and processes to employees.

Total reward

Total reward is the combination of financial and non-financial rewards available to employees.

Total remuneration

Total remuneration is the value of all cash payments (total earnings) and benefits received by employees.

Base or basic pay

The base rate is the amount of pay (the fixed salary or wage) that constitutes the rate for the job. It may be varied according to the grade of the job or, for manual workers, the level of skill required.

Base pay will be influenced by internal and external relativities. The internal relativities may be measured by some form of job evaluation. External relativities are assessed by tracking market rates. Alternatively, levels of pay may be agreed through collective bargaining with trade unions or by reaching individual agreements.

Base pay may be expressed as an annual, weekly or hourly rate. For manual workers this may be called a 'time rate' system of payment. Allowances for overtime, shift working, unsocial hours or increased cost of living in London or elsewhere may be added to base pay. The base rate may be adjusted to reflect increases in the cost of living or market rates by the organization, unilaterally or by agreement with a trade union.

Job evaluation

Job evaluation is a systematic process for defining the relative worth or size of jobs within an organization in order to establish internal relativities and provide the basis for designing an equitable grade structure, grading jobs in the structure and managing relativities. It does not determine the level of pay directly. Job evaluation can be analytical or non-analytical. It is based on the analysis of jobs or roles, which leads to the production of job descriptions or role profiles. Job evaluation is described in Chapter 44.

Market rate analysis

Market rate analysis is the process of identifying the rates of pay in the labour market for comparable jobs to inform decisions on levels of pay within the organization. A policy decision may be made on how internal rates of pay should compare with external rates – an organization's market stance. Market rate analysis is described in Chapter 45.

Grade and pay structures

Jobs may be placed in a graded structure according to their relative size. Pay levels in the structure are influenced by market rates. The pay structure may consist of pay ranges attached to grades, which provide scope for pay progression based on performance, competence, contribution or service. Alternatively, a 'spot rate' structure may be used for all or some jobs in which no provision is made for pay progression in a job. The various types of grade and pay structures are described in Chapter 46.

Contingent pay

Additional financial rewards may be provided that are related to performance, competence, contribution, skill or experience. These are referred to as 'contingent pay'. Contingent payments may be added to base pay, ie 'consolidated'. If such payments are not consolidated (ie paid as cash bonuses) they are described as 'variable pay'. Contingent pay schemes are described in Chapter 47.

Employee benefits

Employee benefits include pensions, sick pay, insurance cover, company cars and a number of other 'perks' as described in Chapter 48. They comprise elements of remuneration additional to the various forms of cash pay and also include provisions for employees that are not strictly remuneration, such as annual holidays.

Performance management

Performance management processes (see Part VII) define individual performance and contribution expectations, assess performance against those expectations, provide for regular constructive feedback and result in agreed plans for performance improvement, learning and personal development. They are a means of providing non-financial motivation and may also inform contingent pay decisions.

Non-financial rewards

These are rewards that do not involve any direct payments and often arise from the work itself, for example, achievement, autonomy, recognition, scope to use and develop skills, training, career development opportunities and high quality leadership.

The inter-relationships of these elements are shown in Figure 42.1.

TOTAL REWARD

The concept of total reward has emerged quite recently and is exerting considerable influence on reward management. This section of the chapter begins by defining what it means. The importance of the concept is then explained, and the section continues with an analysis of the components of total reward. It concludes with a description of how a total reward approach to reward management can be developed.

Total reward defined

As defined by Manus and Graham (2003), total reward 'includes all types of rewards – indirect as well as direct, and intrinsic as well as extrinsic'. Each aspect of reward, namely base pay, contingent pay, employee benefits and non-financial rewards, which include intrinsic rewards from the work itself, are linked together and treated as an integrated and coherent whole. Total reward combines the impact of the two major categories of reward as defined below and illustrated in Figure 42.2: 1) *transactional rewards* – tangible rewards arising from transactions between the employer and employees concerning pay and benefits; and 2) *relational rewards* – intangible rewards concerned with learning and development and the work experience.

A total reward approach is holistic: reliance is not placed on one or two reward mechanisms operating in isolation, and account is taken of every way in which people can be rewarded and obtain satisfaction through their work. The aim is to

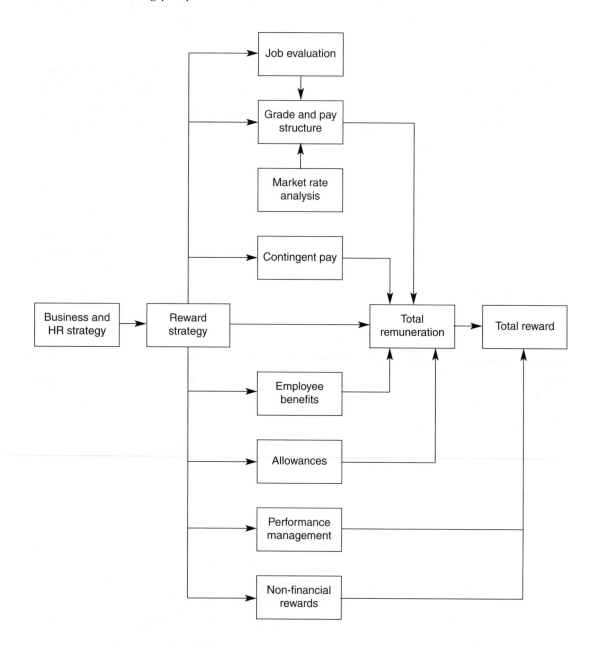

Figure 42.1 Reward management: elements and interrelationships

maximize the combined impact of a wide range of reward initiatives on motivation, commitment and job engagement. As O'Neal (1998) has explained: 'Total reward embraces everything that employees value in the employment relationship.'

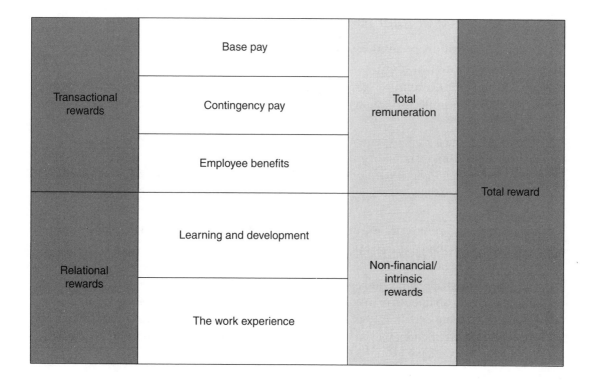

Figure 42.2 The components of total reward

An equally wide definition of total reward is offered by WorldatWork (2000) who state that total rewards are 'all of the employer's available tools that may be used to attract, retain, motivate and satisfy employees'. Thompson (2002) suggests that:

> Definitions of total reward typically encompass not only traditional, quantifiable elements like salary, variable pay and benefits, but also more intangible non-cash elements such as scope to achieve and exercise responsibility, career opportunities, learning and development, the intrinsic motivation provided by the work itself and the quality of working life provided by the organization.

The conceptual basis of total rewards is that of configuration or 'bundling', so that different reward processes are interrelated, complementary and mutually reinforcing. Total reward strategies are vertically integrated with business strategies, but they are also horizontally integrated with other HR strategies to achieve internal consistency.

The significance of total reward

Essentially, the notion of total reward says that there is more to rewarding people than throwing money at them.

For O'Neal (1998), a total reward strategy is critical to addressing the issues created by recruitment and retention as well as providing a means of influencing behaviour:

> It can help create a work experience that meets the needs of employees and encourages them to contribute extra effort, by developing a deal that addresses a broad range of issues and by spending reward dollars where they will be most effective in addressing workers' shifting values.

Perhaps the most powerful argument for a total rewards approach was made by Pfeffer (1998):

> Creating a fun, challenging, and empowered work environment in which individuals are able to use their abilities to do meaningful jobs for which they are shown appreciation is likely to be a more certain way to enhance motivation and performance – even though creating such an environment may be more difficult and take more time than simply turning the reward lever.

The benefits of a total reward approach are:

- *Greater impact* – the combined effect of the different types of rewards will make a deeper and longer-lasting impact on the motivation and commitment of people.
- *Enhancing the employment relationship* – the employment relationship created by a total reward approach makes the maximum use of relational as well as transactional rewards and will therefore appeal more to individuals.
- *Flexibility to meet individual needs* – as pointed out by Bloom and Milkovitch (1998): 'Relational rewards may bind individuals more strongly to the organization because they can answer those special individual needs.'
- *Talent management* – relational rewards help to deliver a positive psychological contract and this can serve as a differentiator in the recruitment market that is much more difficult to replicate than individual pay practices. The organization can become an 'employer of choice' and 'a great place to work', thus attracting and retaining the talented people it needs.

MODEL OF TOTAL REWARD

A model of total reward is shown in Figure 42.3.

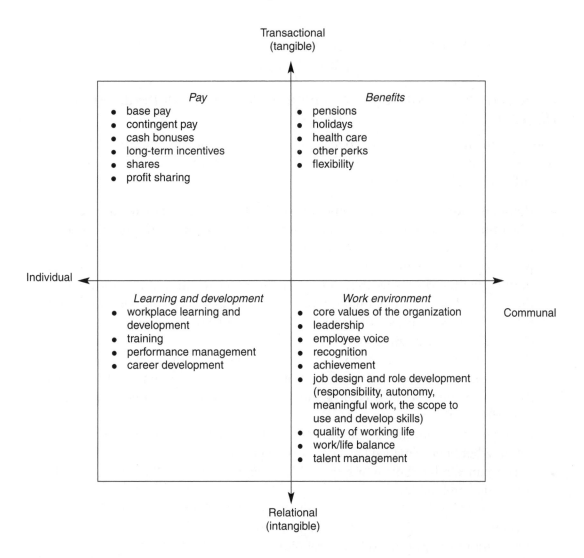

Figure 42.3 Model of total reward

The upper two quadrants – pay and benefits – represent transactional rewards. These are financial in nature and are essential to recruit and retain staff but can be easily copied by competitors. By contrast, the relational (non-financial) rewards produced by the lower two quadrants are essential to enhancing the value of the upper two quadrants. The real power, as Thompson (2002) states, comes when organizations combine relational and transactional rewards.

REWARD MANAGEMENT FOR DIRECTORS AND EXECUTIVES

Principles of corporate governance relating to remuneration of directors

The key principles of corporate governance as it affects the remuneration of directors, which emerged from various reviews, namely the Cadbury, Greenbury and Hampel Reports, are as follows:

- Remuneration committees should consist exclusively of non-executive directors. Their purpose is to provide an independent basis for setting the salary levels and the rules covering incentives, share options, benefit entitlements and contract provisions for executive directors. Such committees are accountable to shareholders for the decisions they take and the non-executive directors who sit on them should have no personal financial interests at stake. They should be constituted as sub-committees of company boards and boards should elect both the chairman and the members.
- Remuneration committees must provide a remuneration package sufficient to attract, retain and motivate directors but should avoid paying more than is necessary. They should be sensitive to wider issues, eg pay and employment conditions elsewhere in the company.
- Remuneration committees should take a robust line on the payment of compensation where performance has been unsatisfactory.
- Performance-related elements should be designed to align the interests of directors and shareholders.
- Any new longer-term incentive arrangement should, preferably, replace existing executive share option plans, or at least form part of an integrated approach, which should be approved by shareholders.
- The pension consequences and associated costs to the company of increases in base salary should be considered.
- Notice or service contract periods should be set at, or reduced to, a year or less. However, in some cases periods of up to two years may be acceptable.

Elements of directors' and senior executives' pay

The main elements of directors' and senior executives' pay are basic pay, bonus or incentive schemes, share option and share ownership schemes.

Basic pay

Decisions on the base salary of directors and senior executives are usually founded on largely subjective views about the market worth of the individuals concerned. Remuneration on joining the company is commonly settled by negotiation, often subject to the approval of a remuneration committee. Reviews of base salaries are then undertaken by reference to market movements and success as measured by company performance. Decisions on base salary are important not only in themselves but also because the level may influence decisions on the pay of both senior and middle managers. Bonuses are expressed as a percentage of base salary, share options may be allocated as a declared multiple of basic pay and, commonly, pension will be a proportion of final salary.

Bonus schemes

Virtually all major employers in the UK (90 per cent according to recent surveys by organizations such as Monks and Hay) provide annual incentive (bonus) schemes for senior executives. Bonus schemes provide directors and executives with cash sums based on the measures of company and, frequently, individual performance.

Typically, bonus payments are linked to achievement of profit and/or other financial targets and they are sometimes 'capped', ie a restriction is placed on the maximum amount payable. There may also be elements related to achieving specific goals and to individual performance.

Share option schemes

Many companies have share option schemes that give directors and executives the right to buy a block of shares on some future date at the share price ruling when the option was granted. They are a form of long-term incentive on the assumption that executives will be motivated to perform more effectively if they can anticipate a substantial capital gain when they sell their shares at a price above that prevailing when they took up the option.

Executive restricted share schemes

Under such schemes free shares are provisionally awarded to participants. These shares do not belong to the executive until they are released or vested; hence they are 'restricted'. The number of shares actually released to the executive at the end of a defined period (usually three or, less commonly, five years) will depend on performance over that period against specific targets. Thereafter there may be a further retention period when the shares must be held, although no further performance conditions apply.

REWARD MANAGEMENT FOR SALES STAFF

There are no hard-and-fast rules governing how sales representatives should be paid. It depends on the type of company, the products or services it offers its customers and the nature of the sales process – how sales are organized and made. The different methods are described in Table 42.2.

PAYING MANUAL WORKERS

The pay of manual workers takes the form of time rates, also known as day rates, day work, flat rates or hourly rates. Incentive payments by means of payment-by-results schemes may be made on top of a base rate.

Time rates

These provide workers with a predetermined rate for the actual hours they work. Time rates on their own are most commonly used when it is thought that it is impossible or undesirable to use a payment-by-results system, for example in maintenance work. From the viewpoint of employees, the advantage of time rates is that their earnings are predictable and steady and they do not have to engage in endless arguments with rate-fixers and supervisors about piece rate or time allowances. The argument against them is that they do not provide a direct incentive relating the reward to the effort or the results. Two ways of modifying the basic time rate approach are to adopt high day rates, as described below, or measured day work.

Time rates may take the form of what are often called high day rates. These are higher than the minimum time rate and may contain a consolidated bonus rate element. The underlying assumption is that higher base rates will encourage greater effort without the problems created when operating an incentive scheme. High day rates are usually above the local market rates, to attract and retain workers.

Table 42.2 Summary of payment and incentive arrangements for sales staff

Method	Features	Advantages	Disadvantages	When appropriate
Salary only	Straight salary, no commission or bonus	Encourage customer service rather than high pressure selling; deal with the problem of staff who are working in a new or unproductive sales territory; protects income when sales fluctuate for reasons beyond the individual's control	No direct motivation through money; may attract under-achieving people who are subsidized by high achievers; increases fixed costs of sales because pay costs are not flexed with sales results	When representing the company is more important than direct selling; staff have little influence on sales volume (they may simply be 'order takers'); customer service is all-important
Salary plus commission	Basic salary plus cash commission calculated as a percentage of sales volume or value	Direct financial motivation is provided related to what sales staff are there, to do ie generate sales; but they are not entirely dependent on commission – they are cushioned by their base salary	Relating pay to the volume or value of sales is too crude an approach and may result in staff going for volume by concentrating on the easier to sell products not those generating high margins; may encourage high-pressure selling as in some financial services firms in the 1980s and 1990s	When it is believed that the way to get more sales is to link extra money to results but a base salary is still needed to attract the many people who want to be assured of a reasonable basic salary which will not fluctuate but who still aspire to increase that salary by their own efforts
Salary plus bonus	Basic salary plus cash bonus based on	Provide financial motivation but targets or	Do not have a clear line of sight between	When: flexibility in providing rewards is

continued overleaf

Table 42.2 *continued*

Method	Features	Advantages	Disadvantages	When appropriate
	achieving and exceeding sales targets or quotas and meeting other selling objectives	objectives can be flexed to ensure that particular sales goals are achieved, eg high margin sales, customer service	effort and reward; may be complex to administer; sales representative may find them hard to understand and resent the use of subjective judgements on performance other than sales	important; it is felt that sales staff need to be motivated to focus on aspects of their work other than simply maximizing sales volume
Commission only	Only commission based on a percentage of sales volume or value is paid, there is no basic salary	Provide a direct financial incentive; attract high performing sales staff; ensure that selling costs vary directly with sales; little direct supervision required	Lead to high-pressure selling; may attract the wrong sort of people who are interested only in making sales and not customer service; focus attention on high volume rather than profitability	When: sales performance depends mainly on selling ability and can be measured by immediate sales results; staff are not involved in non-selling activities; continuing relationships with customers are relatively unimportant
Additional non-cash rewards	Incentives, prizes, cars, recognition, opportunities to grow	Utilize powerful non-financial motivators	May be difficult to administer; do not provide a direct incentive	When it is believed that other methods of payment need to be enhanced by providing additional motivators

Payment-by-result schemes

Payment-by-result (PBR) schemes provide incentives to workers by relating their pay or, more usually, part of their pay to the number of items they produce or the time taken to do a certain amount of work. The main types of PBR or incentive schemes for individuals are piece work, work measured schemes, measured day work and performance-related pay. Team bonus schemes are an alternative to individual PBR and plant-wide schemes can produce bonuses that are paid instead of individual or team bonuses, or in addition to them. Each of these methods is described in Table 42.3 together with an assessment of their advantages and disadvantages for employers and employees, and when they are appropriate.

Table 42.3   Comparison of shopfloor payment-by-result schemes

Select	Main features	For employers		For employees		When appropriate
		Advantages	**Disadvantages**	**Advantages**	**Disadvantages**	
Piece work	Bonus directly related to output.	Direct motivation; simple, easy and to operate.	Lose control over output; quality problems.	Predict and control earnings in the short-term; regulate pace of work themselves.	More difficult to predict and control earnings in the longer-term; work may be stressful and produce RSI.	Fairly limited application to work involving unit production controlled by the person eg agriculture, garment manufacture.
Work-measured schemes	Work measurement used to determine standard output levels over a period or standard times for job/tasks; bonus based by reference to performance ratings compared	Provides what appears to be a 'scientific' method of relating reward to performance; can produce significant increases in productivity, at least in the short-term.	Schemes are expensive, time-consuming and difficult to run and can too easily degenerate and cause wage drift because of loose rates.	Appear to provide a more objective method of relating pay to performance; employees can be involved in the rating process to ensure fairness.	Ratings are still prone to subjective judgement and earnings can fluctuate because of changes in work requirements outside the control of employees.	For short-cycle repetitive work where changes in the work mix or design changes are infrequent, down time is restricted, and manage-

continued

Table 42.3 *continued*

Select	Main features	For employers		For employees		When appropriate
		Advantages	Disadvantages	Advantages	Disadvantages	
	with actual performance or time saved.					ment and supervision are capable of managing and maintaining the scheme.
Measured day work	Pay fixed at a high rate on the understanding that a high level of performance against work-measured standards will be maintained.	Employees are under an obligation to work at the specified level of performance.	Performance targets can become easily attained norms and may be difficult to change.	High predictable earnings are provided.	No opportunities for individuals to be rewarded in line with their own efforts.	Everyone must be totally committed to making it work; high standards of work measure-ment are essential; good control systems to identify shortfalls on targets.
Perfor-mance related pay	Payments on top of base rates are made related to individual assessments of performance.	Reward individual contribution without resource to work measurement; relevant in high technology manufacturing.	Measuring performance can be difficult; no direct incentive provided.	Opportunity to be rewarded for own efforts without having to submit to a pressured PBR system.	Assessment informing performance pay decisions may be biased, inconsistent or unsupported by evidence.	As part of a reward harmoniza-tion (shop floor and staff) programme; as an alternative to work measured schemes or an en-hancement of a high day rate system.

continued

Table 42.3 *continued*

Select	Main features	For employers		For employees		When appropriate
		Advantages	**Disadvantages**	**Advantages**	**Disadvantages**	
Group or team basis	Groups or teams are paid bonuses on the basis of their performance as indicated by work measurement ratings or the achievement of targets.	Encourage team cooperation and effort; not too individualized.	Direct incentive may be limited; depends on good work measurement or the availability of clear group output or productivity targets.	Bonuses can be related clearly to the joint efforts of the group; fluctuations in earnings minimized.	Depend on effective work measurement, which is not always available; individual effort and contribution not recognized.	When team working is important and team efforts can be accurately measured and assessed; as an alternative to individual PBR if this is not effective.

43

Strategic reward

Strategic reward management is about the development and implementation of reward strategies and the philosophies and guiding principles that underpin them. It provides answers to two basic questions: 1) where do we want our reward practices to be in a few years' time? and 2) how do we intend to get there? It therefore deals with both ends and means. As an end it describes a vision of what reward processes will look like in a few years' time. As a means, it shows how it is expected that the vision will be realized.

The chapter starts with a definition of reward strategy and an explanation of why it is necessary. Consideration is then given to the structure and content of reward strategies. The guiding principles for inclusion in a reward strategy are discussed next and this is followed by a description of the development process and a note of the criteria for effectiveness. Examples of reward strategy are then given and implementation issues are assessed. The chapter ends with an examination of the important issue of line management capability.

REWARD STRATEGY DEFINED

Reward strategy is a declaration of intent that defines what the organization wants to do in the longer term to develop and implement reward policies, practices and processes that will further the achievement of its business goals and meet the needs of its stakeholders.

Reward strategy provides a sense of purpose and direction and a framework for developing reward policies, practices and process. It is based on an understanding of the needs of the organization *and* its employees and how they can best be satisfied. It is also concerned with developing the values of the organization on how people should be rewarded and formulating guiding principles that will ensure that these values are enacted.

Reward strategy is underpinned by a reward philosophy that expresses what the organization believes should be the basis upon which people are valued and rewarded. Reward philosophies are often articulated as guiding principles.

WHY HAVE A REWARD STRATEGY?

In the words of Brown (2001): 'Reward strategy is ultimately a way of thinking that you can apply to any reward issue arising in your organization, to see how you can create value from it.' There are four arguments for developing reward strategies:

1. You must have some idea where you are going, or how do you know how to get there, and how do you know that you have arrived (if you ever do)?
2. Pay costs in most organizations are by far the largest item of expense – they can be 60 per cent and often much more in labour-intensive organizations – so doesn't it make sense to think about how they should be managed and invested in the longer term?
3. There can be a positive relationship between rewards, in the broadest sense, and performance, so shouldn't we think about how we can strengthen that link?
4. As Cox and Purcell (1998) write: 'The real benefit in reward strategies lies in complex linkages with other human resource management policies and practices.' Isn't this a good reason for developing a reward strategic framework which indicates how reward processes will be associated with HR processes so that they are coherent and mutually supportive?

THE STRUCTURE OF REWARD STRATEGY

Reward strategy should be based on a detailed analysis of the present arrangements for reward, which would include a statement of their strengths and weaknesses. This, as suggested by the CIPD (2004e), could take the form of a 'gap analysis', which compares what is believed should be happening with what *is* happening and indicates which 'gaps' need to be filled. A format for the analysis is shown in Figure 43.1.

A diagnosis should be made of the reasons for any gaps or problems so that decisions can be made on what needs to be done to overcome them. It can then be structured under the headings set out below:

1. *A statement of intentions* – the reward initiatives that it is proposed should be taken.
2. *A rationale* – the reasons why the proposals are being made. The rationale should make out the business case for the proposals, indicate how they will meet business needs and set out the costs and the benefits. It should also refer to any people issues that need to be addressed and how the strategy will deal with them.
3. *A plan* – how, when and by whom the reward initiatives will be implemented. The plan should indicate what steps will need to be taken and should take account of resource constraints and the need for communications, involvement and training. The priorities attached to each element of the strategy should be indicated and a timetable for implementation should be drawn up. The plan should state who will be responsible for the development and implementation of the strategy.
4. *A definition of guiding principles* – the values that it is believed should be adopted in formulating and implementing the strategy.

THE CONTENT OF REWARD STRATEGY

Reward strategy may be a broad-brush affair simply indicating the general direction in which it is thought reward management should go. Additionally or alternatively, reward strategy may set out a list of specific intentions dealing with particular aspects of reward management.

Broad-brush reward strategy

A broad-brush reward strategy may commit the organization to the pursuit of a total rewards policy. The basic aim might be to achieve an appropriate balance between financial and non-financial rewards. A further aim could be to use other approaches to the development of the employment relationship and the work environment, which will enhance commitment and engagement and provide more opportunities for the contribution of people to be valued and recognized.

What should be happening	What is happening	What needs to be done
1. A total reward approach is adopted which emphasises the significance of both financial and non-financial rewards.		
2. Reward policies and practices are developed within the framework of a well-articulated strategy which is designed to support the achievement of business objectives and meet the needs of stakeholders.		
3. A job evaluation scheme is used which properly reflects the values of the organisation, is up-to-date with regard to the jobs it covers and is non-discriminatory.		
4. Equal pay issues are given serious attention. This includes the conduct of equal pay reviews which lead to action.		
5. Market rates are tracked carefully so that a competitive pay structure exists which contributes to the attraction and retention of high quality people.		
6. Grade and pay structures are based on job evaluation and market rate analysis, appropriate to the characteristics and needs of the organization and its employees, facilitate the management of relativities, provide scope for rewarding contribution, clarify reward and career opportunities, constructed logically, operate transparently and are easy to manage and maintain.		
7. Contingent pay schemes reward contribution fairly and consistently, support the motivation of staff and the development of a performance culture, deliver the right messages about the values of the organization, contain a clear 'line of sight' between contribution and reward and are cost-effective.		
8. Performance management processes contribute to performance improvement, people development and the management of expectations, operate effectively throughout the organization and are supported by line managers and staff.		

Figure 43.1   A reward gap analysis

continued

What should be happening	What is happening	What needs to be done
9. Employee benefits and pension schemes meet the needs of stakeholders and are cost-effective.		
10. A flexible benefits approach is adopted.		
11. Reward management procedures exist which ensure that reward processes are managed effectively and that costs are controlled.		
12. Appropriate use is made of computers (software and spreadsheets) to assist in the process of reward management.		
13. Reward management aims and arrangements are transparent and communicated well to staff.		
14. Surveys are used to assess the opinions of staff about reward and action is taken on the outcomes.		
15. An appropriate amount of responsibility for reward is devolved to line managers.		
16. Line managers are capable of carrying out their devolved responsibilities well.		
17. Steps are taken to train line managers and provide them with support and guidance as required.		
18. HR has the knowledge and skills to provide the required reward management advice and services and to guide and support line managers.		
19. Overall, reward management developments are conscious of the need to achieve affordability and to demonstrate that they are cost effective.		
20. Steps are taken to evaluate the effectiveness of reward management processes and to ensure that they reflect changing needs.		

Figure 43.1 *continued*

Examples of other broad strategic aims include:

- introducing a more integrated approach to reward management – encouraging continuous personal development and spelling out career opportunities;
- developing a more flexible approach to reward that includes the reduction of artificial barriers as a result of over-emphasis on grading and promotion;
- generally rewarding people according to their contribution;
- supporting the development of a performance culture and building levels of competence; and
- clarifying what behaviours will be rewarded and why.

Specific reward initiatives

The selection of reward initiatives and the priorities attached to them will be based on an analysis of the present circumstances of the organization and an assessment of the needs of the business and its employees. The following are examples of possible specific reward initiatives, one or more of which might feature in a reward strategy:

- the replacement of present methods of contingent pay with a pay for contribution scheme;
- the introduction of a new grade and pay structure, eg a broad-graded or career family structure;
- the replacement of an existing decayed job evaluation scheme with a computerized scheme that more clearly reflects organizational values;
- the improvement of performance management processes so that they provide better support for the development of a performance culture and more clearly identify development needs;
- the introduction of a formal recognition scheme;
- the development of a flexible benefits system;
- the conduct of equal pay reviews with the objective of ensuring that work of equal value is paid equally;
- communication programmes designed to inform everyone of the reward policies and practices of the organization;
- training, coaching and guidance programmes designed to increase line management capability (see also the last section of this chapter).

GUIDING PRINCIPLES

Guiding principles define the approach an organization takes to dealing with reward. They are the basis for reward policies and provide guidelines for the actions contained in the reward strategy. They express the reward philosophy of the organization – its values and beliefs about how people should be rewarded.

Members of the organization should be involved in the definition of guiding principles that can then be communicated to everyone to increase understanding of what underpins reward policies and practices. However, employees will suspend their judgement of the principles until they experience how they are applied. What matters to them are not the philosophies themselves but the pay practices emanating from them and the messages about the employment 'deal' that they get as a consequence. It is the reality that is important, not the rhetoric.

Reward guiding principles may refer to concerns such as:

- developing reward policies and practices that support the achievement of business goals;
- providing rewards that attract, retain and motivate staff and help to develop a high performance culture;
- maintaining competitive rates of pay;
- rewarding people according to their contribution;
- recognizing the value of all staff who are making an effective contribution, not just the exceptional performers;
- allowing a reasonable degree of flexibility in the operation of reward processes and in the choice of benefits by employees;
- devolving more responsibility for reward decisions to line managers.

An example of a statement of reward philosophy and guiding principles is given in Figure 43.2.

DEVELOPING REWARD STRATEGY

The formulation of reward strategy can be described as a process for developing and defining a sense of direction. The main phases are:

1. The *diagnosis* phase, when reward goals are agreed, current policies and practices assessed against them, options for improvement considered and any changes agreed.

Reward philosophy	Principles
• We will provide an innovative reward package that is valued by our staff and communicated brilliantly to reinforce the benefits of working for B&Q plc.	• Innovative and differentiated policies and benefits.
• Reward investment will be linked to company performance so that staff share in the success they create and, by going the extra mile, receive above average reward compared to local competitors.	• Basic salaries will be competitive. • Total compensation will be upper quartile. • We share the success of B&Q with all employees. • Increase variable pay as a percentage of overall to drive company performance. • Pay for performance. • Performance objectives must have line of sight for individuals/team.
• All parts of the total reward investment will add value to the business and reinforce our core purpose, goals and values.	• Non-cash recognition is a powerful driver of business performance. • Pay can grow without promotion. • Rewards are flexible around individual aspirations. • We will not discriminate on anything other than performance.

Figure 43.2   Reward philosophy and guiding principles at B&Q

2. The *detailed design* phase, when improvements and changes are detailed and any changes tested (pilot testing is important).
3. The *final testing and preparation* phase.
4. The *implementation* phase, followed by ongoing review and modification.

A logical step-by-step model for doing this is illustrated in Figure 43.3. This incorporates ample provision for consultation, involvement and communication with stakeholders, who include senior managers as the ultimate decision makers as well as employees and line managers.

In practice, however, the formulation of reward strategy is seldom as logical and linear a process as this. As explained in Chapter 7, strategies evolve. Reward strategists have to respond to changes in organizational requirements, which are happening all the time. They need to track emerging trends in reward management and may modify their views accordingly, as long as they do not leap too hastily on the latest bandwagon.

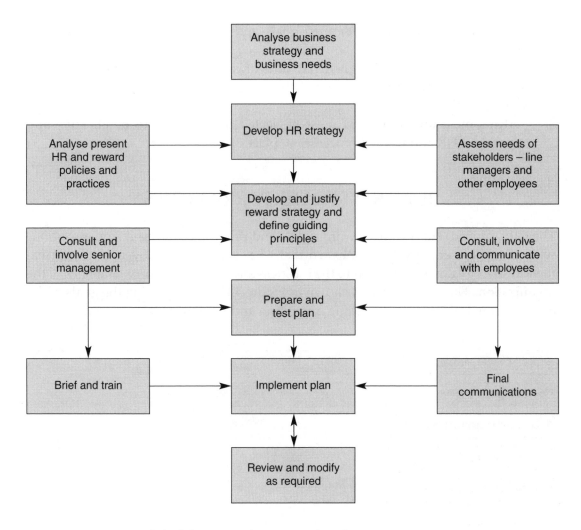

Figure 43.3 A model of the reward strategy development process

It may be helpful to set out reward strategies on paper for the record and as a basis for planning and communication. But this should be regarded as no more than a piece of paper that can be torn up when needs change – as they will – not a tablet of stone.

COMPONENTS OF AN EFFECTIVE REWARD STRATEGY

Brown (2001) has suggested that effective reward strategies have three components:

1. They have to have clearly defined goals and a well-defined link to business objectives.
2. There have to be well-designed pay and reward programmes, tailored to the needs of the organization and its people, and consistent and integrated with one another.
3. Perhaps most important and most neglected, there needs to be effective and supportive HR and reward processes in place.

REWARD STRATEGY PRIORITIES

The CIPD (2005d) survey into reward policy and practice covering 477 organizations with 1.5 million employees established that 45 per cent of employers had a formal reward strategy that was aligned to the business and human resource strategies of the organization. The top priority, as shown in Figure 43.4, is supporting the goals of the organization, followed by rewarding, recruiting and retaining high performers.

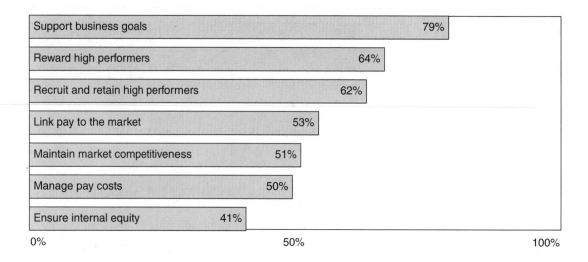

Figure 43.4 Reward strategy priorities (*Source*: CIPD 2005d)

EXAMPLES OF REWARD STRATEGIES

The source of the following examples of reward strategies is e-reward (2004a).

AEGON UK

A good example of the development of a reward strategy is provided by AEGON UK, the insurance group with 4,000 employees. Like many companies, AEGON UK's pay systems and supporting processes such as job evaluation and performance appraisal used to stand alone, apart from other HR processes. The company has adopted a more holistic approach to the development of its new reward system – which it calls the *Human Resources Integrated Approach* – so that from every angle staff can look at the elements of reward, pay management, performance management and career development and observe that they are consistent and linked. The stated objective of this programme is 'to develop a set of HR processes which are integrated with each other and with the business objectives'. In other words, AEGON UK aims to ensure that the processes of recruiting, retaining and motivating people, as well as measuring their performance, are in line with what the business is trying to achieve. *The Human Resources Integrated Approach* is underpinned by a competency framework. The established competencies form the basis of the revised HR processes:

- *Recruitment:* competency based with multi-assessment processes as the basic approach.
- *Reward:* market driven with overall performance dictating rate of progress of salaries within broad bands rather then existing grades.
- *Performance management:* not linked to pay, concentrated on personal development, objective setting and competency development.
- *Training and development:* targeted on key competencies and emphasizing self-development.

Norwich Union Insurance

Progression, Performance and Pay is the name given to Norwich Union Insurance's new total reward strategy. It comprises four main elements:

1. *Reward* – salary and benefits, variable pay, all-employee share option plan and incentive awards.
2. *Career framework* – meaningful job content and career opportunities.
3. *Performance* – challenging work; recognition and brand supporting behaviours.
4. *Development* – learning opportunities and personal development.

As stated in the Norwich Union Insurance's documentation and illustrated in Figure 43.5:

> These initiatives... support our commitment to the one team culture reflected in our balanced scorecard. The Progression, Performance & Pay framework is underpinned by the brand values: Progressive, Shared benefit and Integrity. These should be reflected in the way we agree objectives and use the skills, knowledge and behaviours model. Progression, Performance & Pay moves us towards 'total reward' where financial reward is just one element of the reward package. Other elements are benefits, recognition of performance, career opportunities and personal development. In our model these are expressed through reward, performance, career framework and development. This gives us the tools to help build NUI as a great place to work, which attracts and retains quality staff.

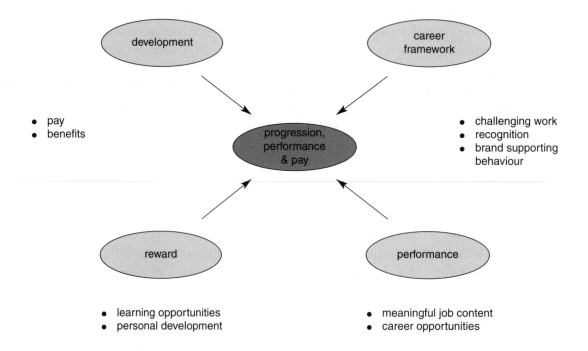

Figure 43.5 The Norwich Union Insurance Progression, Performance & Pay framework

The framework was accompanied by a commitment from senior management:

● to recognize our best people through career opportunities and reward packages;
● to develop all staff to their full potential;

- to widen career opportunities for all;
- to provide managers with the means to recognize and reward performance locally.

Integrated reward at Kwik-Fit

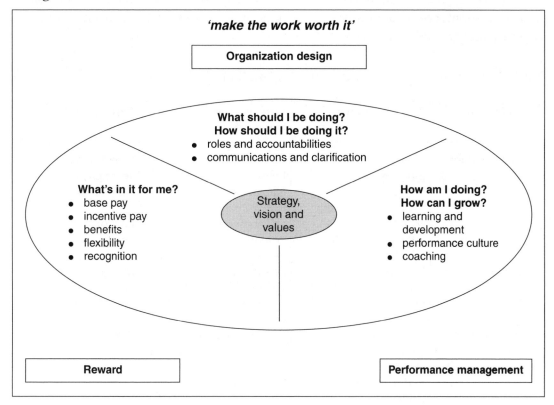

Figure 43.6   Integrated reward model – Kwik-fit

B&Q

Will Astill, Reward Manager of B&Q, a retail chain with 25,000 employees, which completed a strategic reward review in 2003, explained to e-reward that:

> An overriding theme running through our review was on the desirability of adopting a strategic approach. It wasn't a case of 'let's follow the best practice', nor were we lured into adopting the latest fads and fashions. Applying a bespoke system – taking what someone has done before and adapting it to your organization – will not push you ahead of rivals. Our emphasis throughout the two-year process was on what's right for the business.

Other examples

Other examples are given in Table 43.1 of the ways in which organizations have responded to the needs established by their business strategy and the business and reward issues they are facing. In each case the organizations started with broad-brush statements about their intentions and proceeded from there to prepare action plans and implementation programmes for specific innovations that had been fully justified by a cost/benefit analysis.

Table 43.1 Examples of reward strategies and their derivation

Organization	Business strategy	Business/reward issues	Reward strategy
Food distribution	Increase efficiency Innovate Cost reduction	Poor team work Inflexible Narrow focus	Broad-banding Team pay Gain-sharing
Engineering manufacturing	Maintain market share Increase competitive edge Develop more sophisticated planning processes	Skill-based pay not working PRP only for managers Performance appraisal ineffective	Link operating plan and performance management Replace skill-based pay Introduce PRP for all
International bank	International growth Enhance customer service Maintain market leadership	Transactional rather than relational approach Incremental scales Pay for jobs not people	Replace incremental scales Introduce contribution-related pay Revise performance management
Care provider, voluntary sector	Growth by improving service delivery Develop new projects Win more contracts	Flexibility Cost of people Competence of people	Competence-related pay Broad-banding

IMPLEMENTING REWARD STRATEGY

Formulation is easy, implementation is hard. In the UK more attention is now being given to how organizations can make things happen. It is recognized that a pragmatic approach is required – what's good is what works. It is also appreciated that implementation presents a massive change management challenge. The practical advice on managing changes in reward systems given by Paul Craven, Compensation Director, R&D, GlaxoSmithKline was: 'Don't expect people to change overnight and don't try to force change. It is better to reinforce desirable behaviour than to attempt to enforce a particular way of doing things.' The advice given by Nicki Denby, Performance and Reward Director, Diageo was to:

- keep it simple, but simple isn't easy;
- ensure that the HR department is not developing policies and practices on its own, which are then tagged as just another HR initiative rather than something which is owned by the organization as a whole;
- not only explain the planned changes, the rationale behind them, and how they affect the workforce, but also communicate details of who was involved in the development process so that unnecessary fears are allayed.

Will Astill of B&Q had three pieces of advice on implementation:

1. the value of in-depth employee consultation should never be undervalued;
2. no initiative should be implemented without looking at the return on investment; and
3. evaluate the effectiveness of programmes and take action as required.

REWARD STRATEGY AND LINE MANAGEMENT CAPABILITY

The trend is to devolve more responsibility for managing reward to line managers. Some will have the ability to respond to the challenge and opportunity; others will be incapable of carrying out this responsibility without close guidance from HR; some may never be able to cope. Managers may not always do what HR expects them to do and if compelled to, they may be half-hearted about it. This puts a tremendous onus on HR and reward specialists to develop line management capability, to initiate processes that can readily be implemented by line managers, to promote understanding by communicating what is happening, why it is happening and how it will affect everyone, to provide guidance and help where required and to provide formal training as necessary.

44

Job evaluation

Job evaluation is of fundamental importance in reward management. It provides the basis for achieving equitable pay and is essential as a means of dealing with equal pay for work of equal value issues. In the 1980s and 1990s job evaluation fell into disrepute because it was alleged to be bureaucratic, time-consuming and irrelevant in a market economy where market rates dictate internal rates of pay and relativities. However, as the e-reward 2003 survey of job evaluation showed, job evaluation is still practised widely and, indeed, its use is extending, not least because of the pressures to achieve equal pay.

In this chapter:

- job evaluation is defined;
- the different types of job evaluation schemes are described;
- information on the incidence of job evaluation is provided;
- the use of computers in job evaluation is discussed;
- the arguments for and against job evaluation are summarized;
- consideration is given to criteria for choice;
- the process of developing a point-factor scheme is described;
- conclusions are reached about using job evaluation effectively.

JOB EVALUATION DEFINED

Job evaluation is a systematic process for defining the relative worth or size of jobs within an organization in order to establish internal relativities. It provides the basis for designing an equitable grade and pay structure, grading jobs in the structure and managing job and pay relativities.

Aims

Job evaluation aims to:

- establish the relative value or size of jobs (internal relativities) based on fair, sound and consistent judgements;
- produce the information required to design and maintain equitable and defensible grade and pay structures;
- provide as objective as possible a basis for grading jobs within a grade structure, thus enabling consistent decisions to be made about job grading;
- enable sound market comparisons with jobs or roles of equivalent complexity and size;
- be transparent – the basis upon which grades are defined and jobs graded should be clear;
- ensure that the organization meets equal pay for work of equal value obligations.

The last aim is important. In its *Good Practice Guide on Job Evaluation Schemes Free of Sex Bias* the Equal Opportunities Commission (2003) states that: 'Non-discriminatory job evaluation should lead to a payment system which is transparent and within which work of equal value receives equal pay regardless of sex.'

Approaches

Job evaluation can be analytical or non-analytical. Jobs can also be valued by reference to their market rates – 'market pricing'. These approaches are described below.

ANALYTICAL JOB EVALUATION

Defined

Analytical job evaluation is the process of making decisions about the value or size of jobs, which are based on an analysis of the level at which various defined factors or elements are present in a job in order to establish relative job value. The set of factors used in a scheme is called the *factor plan*, which defines each of the factors used (which should be present in all the jobs to be evaluated) and the levels within each factor. Analytical job evaluation is the most common approach to job evaluation (it was used by 89 per cent of the organizations with job evaluation responding to the e-reward 2003 survey). The two main types of analytical job evaluation schemes are point-factor schemes and analytical matching, as described later.

Main features

The main features of analytical job evaluation as explained below are that it is systematic, judgemental, concerned with the person not the job and deals only with internal relativities.

Systematic

Analytical job evaluation is systematic in that the relative value or 'size' of jobs is determined on the basis of factual evidence on the characteristics of the jobs that have been analysed within a structured framework of criteria or factors.

Judgemental

Human judgement has to be exercised at a number of points in the job evaluation process. Although job evaluations are based on factual evidence, this has to be interpreted. The information provided about jobs through job analysis can sometimes fail to provide a clear indication of the levels at which demands are present in a job. The definitions in the factor plan may not precisely indicate the level of demand that should be recorded. Judgement is required in making decisions on the level and therefore, in a point-factor or factor comparison scheme, the score. The aim is to maximize objectivity but it is difficult to eliminate a degree of subjectivity. As the Equal Opportunities Commission (EOC) states in its *Good Practice Guide on Job Evaluation Schemes Free of Sex Bias* 2003: 'It is recognized that to a certain extent any assessment of a job's total demands relative to another will always be subjective.'

A fundamental aim of any process of job evaluation is to provide frameworks or approaches that ensure, as far as possible, that consistent judgements are made based on objectively assessed information. To refer to an evaluation as 'judgemental' does not necessarily mean that it is inaccurate or unsound. Correct judgements are achieved when they are made within a defined framework and are based on clear evidence and sound reasoning. This is what a job evaluation scheme can do if the scheme is properly designed and properly applied.

Concerned with the job not the person

This is the iron law of job evaluation. It means that when evaluating a job the only concern is the content of that job in terms of the demands made on the job holder. The performance of the individual in the job must not be taken into account. But it should be noted that while *performance* is excluded, in today's more flexible organizations the tendency is for some people, especially knowledge workers, to have flexible roles. Individuals may have the scope to enlarge or enrich their roles and this needs to be taken into account when evaluating what they do. Roles cannot necessarily be separated from the people who carry them out. It is people who create value, not jobs.

Concerned with internal relativities

When used within an organization, job evaluation in the true sense as defined above (ie not market pricing as described later) can only assess the relative size of jobs in that organization. It is not concerned with external relativities, that is, the relationship between the rates of pay of jobs in the organization and the rates of pay of comparable jobs elsewhere (market rates).

Types of analytical schemes

Point-factor evaluation

Point-factor schemes are the most commonly used type of analytical job evaluation. The methodology is to break down jobs into factors or key elements representing the demands made by the job on job holders, the competencies required and, in some cases, the impact the job makes. It is assumed that each of the factors will contribute to job size (ie the value of the job) and is an aspect of all the jobs to be evaluated but to different degrees. Using numerical scales, points are allocated to a job under each factor heading according to the extent to which it is present in the job. The separate factor scores are then added together to give a total score, which represents job size.

Analytical matching

Like point-factor job evaluation, analytical matching is based on the analysis of a number of defined factors. Grade or level profiles are produced which define the characteristics of jobs in each grade in a grade structure in terms of those factors. Role profiles are produced for the jobs to be evaluated set out on the basis of analysis under the same factor headings as the grade profiles. The role profiles are then 'matched' with the range of grade or level profiles to establish the best fit and thus grade the job.

Alternatively or additionally, role profiles for jobs to be evaluated can be matched analytically with generic role profiles for jobs that have already been graded.

Analytical matching may be used to grade jobs following the initial evaluation of a sufficiently large and representative sample of 'benchmark' jobs, ie jobs that can be used as a basis for comparison with other jobs. This can happen in large organizations when it is believed that it is not necessary to go through the whole process of point-factor evaluation for every job. This especially applies where 'generic' roles are concerned, ie roles that are performed by a number of job holders, which are essentially similar although there may be minor differences. When this follows a large job evaluation exercise as in the NHS Agenda for Change programme, the factors used in the grade and role profiles will be the same as those used in the point-factor job evaluation scheme.

Factor comparison

The original and now little used factor comparison method compared jobs factor by factor using a scale of money values to provide a direct indication of the rate for the job. The main form of factor comparison now in use is graduated factor comparison, which involves comparing jobs factor by factor with a graduated scale. The scale may have only three value levels – for example lower, equal, higher – and factor scores are not necessarily used.

It is a method often used by the independent experts engaged by Employment Tribunals to advise on an equal pay claim. Their job is simply to compare one job with one or two others, not to review internal relativities over the whole spectrum of jobs in order to produce a rank order. Independent experts may score their judgements of comparative levels, in which case graduated factor comparison resembles the point-factor method, except that the number of levels and range of scores are limited, and the factors may not be weighted.

Proprietary brands

There are a number of job evaluation schemes offered by management consultants. By far the most popular is the Hay Guide Chart Profile Method, which is a factor comparison scheme. It uses three broad factors (know-how, problem solving and accountability) each of which is further divided into sub-factors, although these cannot be scored individually. Definitions of each level have been produced for each sub-factor to guide evaluators and ensure consistency of application.

NON-ANALYTICAL JOB EVALUATION

Non-analytical job evaluation compares whole jobs to place them in a grade or a rank order – they are not analysed by reference to their elements or factors. Non-analytical schemes do not meet the requirements of equal value law. The main non-analytical schemes are described below.

Job classification

This is the most common non-analytical approach. Jobs as defined in job descriptions are slotted into grades in a hierarchy by comparing the whole job with a grade definition and selecting the grade that provides the best fit. It is based on an initial definition of the number and characteristics of the grades into which jobs will be placed. The grade definitions may therefore refer to such job characteristics as skill, decision making and responsibility. Job descriptions may be used that include information on the presence of those characteristics but the characteristics are not assessed separately when comparing the description with the grade definition.

Job ranking

Whole-job ranking is the most primitive form of job evaluation. The process involves comparing jobs with one another and arranging them in order of their perceived size or value to the organization. In a sense, all evaluation schemes are ranking exercises because they place jobs in a hierarchy. The difference between simple ranking and analytical methods such as point-factor rating is that job ranking does not attempt to quantify judgements. Instead, whole jobs are compared – they are not broken down into factors or elements although, explicitly or implicitly, the comparison may be based on some generalized concept such as the level of responsibility.

Paired comparison ranking

Paired comparison ranking is a statistical technique that is used to provide a more sophisticated method of whole-job ranking. It is based on the assumption that it is always easier to compare one job with another than to consider a number of jobs and attempt to build up a rank order by multiple comparisons.

The technique requires the comparison of each job as a whole separately with every other job. If a job is considered to be of a higher value than the one with which it is being compared it receives two points; if it is thought to be equally important, it receives one point; if it is regarded as less important, no points are awarded. The scores are added for each job and a rank order is obtained.

A simplified example of a paired comparison ranking is shown in Figure 44.1.

Job reference	a	b	c	d	e	f	Total score	Ranking
A	–	0	1	0	1	0	2	5=
B	2	–	2	2	2	0	8	2
C	1	0	–	1	1	0	3	4
D	2	0	1	–	2	0	5	3
E	1	0	1	0	–	0	2	5=
F	2	2	2	2	2	–	10	1

Figure 44.1 A paired comparison

The advantage of paired comparison ranking over normal ranking is that it is easier to compare one job with another rather than having to make multi-comparisons. But it cannot overcome the fundamental objections to any form of whole-job ranking – that no defined standards for judging relative worth are provided and it is not an acceptable method of assessing equal value. There is also a limit to the number of jobs that can be compared using this method – to evaluate 50 jobs requires 1,225 comparisons.

Paired comparisons can also be used analytically to compare jobs on a factor by factor basis.

Internal benchmarking

Internal benchmarking is what people often do intuitively when they are deciding on the value of jobs, although it has never been dignified in the job evaluation texts as a formal method of job evaluation. It simply means comparing the job under review with any internal job that is believed to be properly graded and paid, and placing the job under consideration into the same grade as that job. The comparison is often made on a whole-job basis without analysing the jobs factor by factor.

Market pricing

Market pricing is the process of assessing rates of pay by reference to the market rates for comparable jobs and is essentially external benchmarking. Strictly speaking, market pricing is not a process of job evaluation in the sense that those described above are – they only deal with internal relativities and are not directly concerned with market values, although in conjunction with a formal job evaluation scheme, establishing market rates is a necessary part of a programme for developing a pay structure.

However, the term 'market pricing' in its extreme form is used to denote a process of directly pricing jobs on the basis of external relativities with no regard to internal relativities. This approach was widely publicized in the US in the mid-1990s as a reaction to what was regarded as too much emphasis on internal relativities ('a job is worth what the market says it is worth') accompanied by over-bureaucratic job evaluation. It sat alongside attempts at developing broad-banded pay structures (ie structures with a limited number of grades or bands). The approach has board level appeal because of the focus on competitiveness in relation to the marketplace for talent.

The acceptability of market pricing is heavily dependent on the quality and detail of market matching as well as the availability of robust market data. It can therefore vary from analysis of data by job titles to detailed matched analysis collected through bespoke surveys focused on real market equivalence. Market pricing can produce an indication of internal relativities even if these are market driven. But it can lead to pay discrimination against women where the market has traditionally been discriminatory. It does not satisfy UK equal pay legislation.

Market pricing can be done formally by the analysis of published pay surveys, participating in 'pay clubs', conducting special surveys, obtaining the advice of recruitment consultants and agencies and, more doubtfully, by studying advertisements. In its crudest form, market pricing simply means fixing the rate for a job at the level necessary to recruit or retain someone. To avoid a successful equal pay claim, any difference in pay between men and women carrying out work of equal value based on market rate considerations has to be 'objectively justified'.

THE INCIDENCE OF JOB EVALUATION

Despite considerable criticism in the 1990s, job evaluation has not diminished in use in the UK or in many other countries. A survey of job evaluation practice in the UK (e-reward, 2003) found that 44 per cent of the 236 organizations contributing to the research had a formal job evaluation scheme, and 45 per cent of those who did not have such a scheme intended to introduce one. Analytical schemes were used by 89 per cent of the respondents, of which 70 per cent used point-factor rating. The most popular non-analytical approach was job classification. Schemes developed in-house ('home grown' schemes) were used by 37 per cent of the respondents.

A 'proprietary brand', ie one provided by consultants, was used by 37 per cent of respondents and 26 per cent used a hybrid or tailored version of a proprietary brand. The Hay Guide Chart Profile method dominated the market (83 per cent of the proprietary brand schemes). Organizations opting for a proprietary brand did so because of its credibility and, especially with Hay, its link to a market rate database. Organizations opting for a home grown approach did so because they believed this would ensure that it could be shaped to meet the strategic needs of the organization and fit its technology, structure, work processes and business objectives. A minority of respondents mentioned the scope for aligning the scheme with their competency framework.

COMPUTER-ASSISTED JOB EVALUATION

Computers can be used to help directly with the job evaluation process.

Types of schemes

There are two types of computer-assisted systems.

First, there are *job analysis-based schemes* such as that offered by Link Consultants in which the job analysis data is either entered direct into the computer or transferred to it from a paper questionnaire. The computer software applies predetermined rules based on an algorithm that reflects the organization's evaluation standards to convert the data into scores for each factor and produce a total score. The algorithm replicates panel judgements both on job factor levels and overall job score.

Secondly, there are *interactive schemes* using software such as that supplied by Pilat UK (Gauge) in which the job holder and his or her manager sit in front of a PC and are presented with a series of logically interrelated questions forming a question tree; the answers to these questions lead to a score for each of the built-in factors in turn and a total score.

Advantages of computer-assisted job evaluation

Computer-assisted job evaluation systems can:

- provide for greater consistency – the same input information will always give the same output result because the judgemental framework on which the scheme is based (the algorithm) can be applied consistently to the input data;
- offer extensive database capabilities for sorting, analysing and reporting on the input information and system outputs;
- speed up the job evaluation process once the initial design is complete.

Disadvantages of computer-assisted job evaluation

Computer-assisted job evaluation systems can lack transparency – the evaluation in conventional computer-assisted schemes is made in a 'black box' and it can be difficult to trace the connection between the analysis and the evaluation and therefore to justify the score. This is not such a problem with interactive schemes in which job holders participate in evaluations and the link between the answer to a question and the score can be traced in the 'question trees'.

Computer-assisted job evaluation systems can also appear to by-pass the evaluation process through joint management/employee panels, which is typical in conventional schemes; however, this problem can be reduced if panels are used to validate the computer-generated scores.

CRITERIA FOR CHOICE

The main criteria for selecting a job evaluation scheme are that it should be:

- *Analytical* – it should be based on the analysis and evaluation of the degree to which various defined elements or factors are present in a job.
- *Thorough in analysis and capable of impartial application* – the scheme should have been carefully constructed to ensure that its analytical framework is sound and appropriate in terms of all the jobs it has to cater for. It should also have been tested and trialled to check that it can be applied impartially to those jobs.
- *Appropriate* – it should cater for the particular demands made on all the jobs to be covered by the scheme.
- *Comprehensive* – the scheme should be applicable to all the jobs in the organization covering all categories of staff, and the factors should be common to all those jobs. There should therefore be a single scheme that can be used to assess relativities across different occupations or job families and to enable benchmarking to take place as required.
- *Transparent* – the processes used in the scheme from the initial role analysis through to the grading decision should be clear to all concerned.
- *Non-discriminatory* – the scheme must meet equal pay for work of equal value requirements.

A summary of the various approaches to job evaluation and their advantages and disadvantages is given in Table 44.1.

Table 44.1 Comparison of approaches to job evaluation

Scheme	Characteristics	Advantages	Disadvantages
Point-factor rating	An analytical approach in which separate factors are scored and added together to produce a total score for the job which can be used for comparison and grading purposes.	As long as it is based on proper job analysis, point-factor schemes provide evaluators with defined yardsticks that help to increase the objectivity and consistency of judgements and reduce the over-simplified judgement made in non-analytical job evaluation. They provide a defence against equal value claims as long as they are not in themselves discriminatory.	Can be complex and give a spurious impression of scientific accuracy – judgement is still needed in scoring jobs. Not easy to amend the scheme as circumstances, priorities or values change.
Analytical matching	Grade profiles are produced which define the characteristics of jobs in each grade in a grade structure in terms of a selection of defined factors. Role profiles are produced for the jobs to be evaluated set out on the basis of analysis under the same factor headings as the grade profiles. Role profiles are 'matched' with the range of grade profiles to establish the best fit and thus grade the job.	If the matching process is truly analytical and carried out with great care, this approach saves time by enabling the evaluation of a large number of jobs, especially generic ones, to be conducted quickly and in a way which should satisfy equal value requirements.	The matching process could be more superficial and therefore suspect than evaluation through a point-factor scheme. In the latter approach there are factor level definitions to guide judgements and the resulting scores provide a basis for ranking and grade design which is not the case with analytical matching. Although matching on this basis may be claimed to be analytical, it might be difficult to prove this in an equal value case.
Job classification	Non-analytical – grades are defined in a structure in terms of the level of responsibilities involved in a hierarchy. Jobs are allocated to grades by	Simple to operate; standards of judgement when making comparisons are provided in the shape of the grade definitions.	Can be difficult to fit complex jobs into a grade without using over-elaborate grade definitions; the definitions tend to be so

continued

Table 44.1 *continued*

Scheme	Characteristics	Advantages	Disadvantages
	matching the job description with the grade description (job slotting).		generalized that they are not much help in evaluating borderline cases or making comparisons between individual jobs; does not provide a defence in an equal value case.
Ranking	Non-analytical – whole job comparisons are made to place them in rank order.	Easy to apply and understand.	No defined standards of judgement; differences between jobs not measured; does not provide a defence in an equal value case.
Internal benchmarking	Jobs or roles are compared with benchmark jobs that have been allocated into grades on the basis of ranking or job classification and placed in whatever grade provides the closest match of jobs. The job descriptions may be analytical in the sense that they cover a number of standard and defined elements.	Simple to operate; facilitates direct comparisons, especially when the jobs have been analysed in terms of a set of common criteria.	Relies on a considerable amount of judgement and may simply perpetuate existing relativities; dependent on accurate job/role analysis; may not provide a defence in an equal value case.
Market pricing	Rates of pay are aligned to market rates – internal relativities are therefore determined by relativities in the market place. Not strictly a job evaluation scheme.	In line with the belief that 'a job is worth what the market says it is worth'. Ensures that pay is competitive.	Relies on accurate market rate information which is not always available; relativities in the market may not properly reflect internal relativities; pay discrimination may be perpetuated.

Making the choice

The choice has to be made by reference to the criteria referred to earlier and to the advantages and disadvantages of the alternative approaches listed above. But the overwhelming preference for analytical schemes shown by the e-reward survey suggests that the choice is fairly obvious. The advantages of using a recognized analytical approach that satisfies equal value requirements appear to be overwhelming. Point-factor schemes were used by 70 per cent of those respondents and others used analytical matching, often in conjunction with the points scheme.

There is much to be said for adopting point-factor methodology as the main scheme, but using analytical matching in a supporting role to deal with large numbers of generic roles not covered in the original benchmarking exercise. Analytical matching can be used to allocate generic roles to grades as part of the normal job evaluation operating procedure to avoid having to resort to job evaluation in every case. The tendency in many organizations is to assign to job evaluation a supporting role of this nature rather than allowing it to dominate all grading decisions and thus involve the expenditure of much time and energy.

THE CASE FOR AND AGAINST JOB EVALUATION

The case for

The case for properly devised and applied job evaluation, especially analytical job evaluation, is that:

- it can make the criteria against which jobs are valued explicit and provide a basis for structuring the judgement process;
- an equitable and defensible pay structure cannot be achieved unless a structured and systematic process is used to assess job values and relativities;
- a logical framework is required within which consistent decisions can be made on job grades and rates of pay;
- the factor plan and the process of job evaluation can be aligned to the organization's value system and competency framework and therefore reinforce them as part of an integrated approach to people management;
- analytical schemes provide the best basis for achieving equal pay for work of equal value and are the only acceptable defence in an equal pay case;
- a formal process of job evaluation is more likely to be accepted as fair and equitable than informal or *ad hoc* approaches – and the degree of acceptability will be considerably enhanced if the whole process is transparent.

The case against

The case against job evaluation has been presented vociferously. Critics emphasize that it can be bureaucratic, inflexible, time-consuming and inappropriate in today's organizations. Opponents such as Nielsen (2002) take exception to the fact that job evaluation is not concerned with external relativities, which, they claim, are what really matter. Schemes can decay over time through use or misuse. People learn how to manipulate them to achieve a higher grade and this leads to the phenomenon known as grade drift – upgradings that are not justified by a sufficiently significant increase in responsibility. Job evaluators can fall into the trap of making *a priori* judgements. They may judge the validity of a job evaluation exercise according to the extent to which it corresponds with their preconceptions about relative worth. The so-called 'felt-fair' test is used to assess the acceptability of job evaluations, but a rank order is felt to be fair if it reproduces their notion of what it ought to be.

These criticisms mainly focus on the way in which job evaluation is operated rather than the concept of job evaluation itself. Like any other management technique, job evaluation schemes can be misconceived and misused. And the grade and pay structures developed through job evaluation seldom last for more than a few years and need to be replaced or adjusted to remedy decay or reflect new ways of working.

Those who criticize job evaluation because it is only concerned with internal relativities fail to understand that job evaluation exists to grade jobs, not to price them. Of course, when developing the pay structures superimposed on grade structures it is necessary to take account of external relativities and this will mean reconciling the different messages provided by job evaluation and market rate surveys. If the latter indicate that attracting and retaining good quality staff is only feasible if rates of pay are higher than those indicated by the grading of the job, then it may be necessary to pay market supplements, but to avoid claims that equal pay is not being provided, these must be objectively justified on the basis of evidence on competitive rates.

DESIGNING A POINT-FACTOR JOB EVALUATION SCHEME

The process of designing a job evaluation scheme is demanding and time-consuming, as is stressed by Armstrong *et al* (2003). This section considers the design and process criteria and the design and implementation programme.

Design and process criteria

It is necessary to distinguish between the design of a scheme and the process of operating it. Equal pay considerations have to be taken into account in both design and process.

Design principles

The design principles are that:

- the scheme should be based on a thorough analysis of the jobs to be covered and the types of demands made on those jobs to determine what factors are appropriate;
- the scheme should facilitate impartial judgements of relative job size;
- the factors used in the scheme should cover the whole range of jobs to be evaluated at all levels without favouring any particular type of job or occupation and without discriminating on the grounds of sex, race, disability or for any other reason – the scheme should fairly measure features of female-dominated jobs as well as male-dominated jobs;
- through the use of common factors and methods of analysis and evaluation, the scheme should enable benchmarking to take place of the relativities between jobs in different functions or job families;
- the factors should be clearly defined and differentiated – there should be no double counting;
- the levels should be defined and graduated carefully;
- sex bias must be avoided in the choice of factors, the wording of factor and level definitions and the factor weightings – checks should be carried out to identify any bias.

Process principles

The process principles are that:

- the scheme should be transparent, everyone concerned should know how it works – the basis upon which the evaluations are produced;
- appropriate proportions of women, those from ethnic minorities and people with disabilities should be involved in the process of developing and applying job evaluation;
- the quality of role analysis should be monitored to ensure that analyses produce accurate and relevant information that will inform the job evaluation process and will not be biased;

- consistency checks should be built into operating procedures;
- the outcomes of evaluations should be examined to ensure that sex or any other form of bias has not occurred;
- particular care is necessary to ensure that the outcomes of job evaluation do not simply replicate the existing hierarchy – it is to be expected that a job evaluation exercise will challenge present relativities;
- all those involved in role analysis and job evaluation should be thoroughly trained in the operation of the scheme and in how to avoid bias;
- special care should be taken in developing a grade structure following a job evaluation exercise to ensure that grade boundaries are placed appropriately and that the allocation of jobs to grades is not in itself discriminatory;
- there should be scope for the review of evaluations and for appeals against gradings;
- the scheme should be monitored to ensure that it is being operated properly and that it is still fit for its purpose.

The design and implementation programme

The design and implementation of a point-factor job evaluation scheme can be a demanding and time-consuming affair. In a large organization it can take two years or more to complete a project. Even in a small organization it can take several months. Many organizations seek outside help from management consultants or ACAS in conducting the programme. An example of a programme is given in Figure 44.2.

Activities 1 to 6 form the initial design phase and activities 7 to 12 form the application of the design and implementation phases. Full descriptions of these phases follow.

The scheme design programme

Figure 44.3 shows the steps required to design a point-factor job evaluation scheme.

Step 1. Decide to develop scheme

The decision to develop a new point-factor job evaluation scheme follows an analysis of the existing arrangements, if any, for job evaluation, and a diagnosis of any problems.

Step 2. Prepare detailed project programme

The detailed project programme could be set out in a bar chart, as illustrated in Figure 44.2.

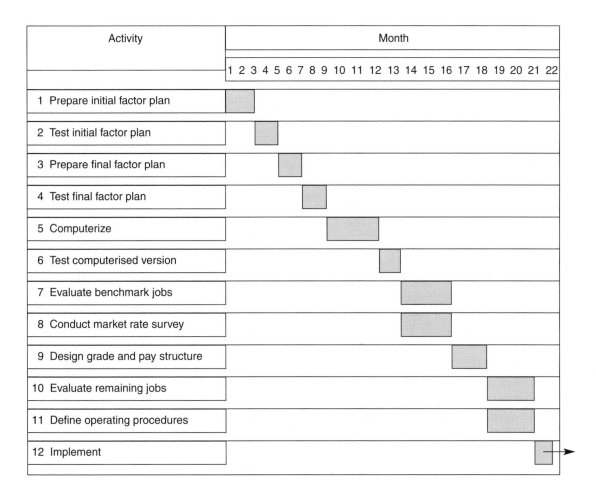

Figure 44.2   A typical job evaluation programme

Step 3. Select, brief and train design team

The composition of the design team should have been determined broadly at Step 1. Members are usually nominated by management and the staff or union(s) (if they exist). It is very desirable to have a representative number of women and men and the major ethnic groups employed in the organization. It is also necessary to appoint a facilitator.

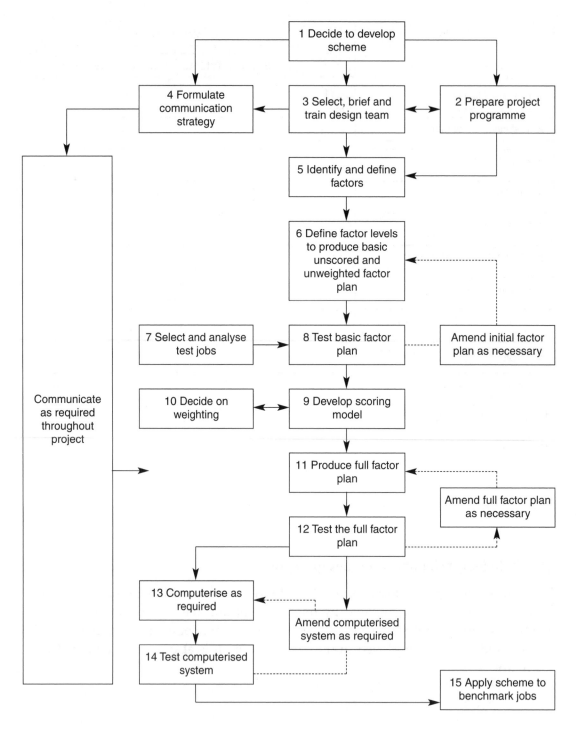

Figure 44.3 Design sequence

Step 4. Formulate communication strategy

It is essential to have a communication strategy. The introduction of a new job evaluation will always create expectations. Some people think that they will inevitably benefit from pay increases, others believe that they are sure to lose money. It has to be explained carefully, and repeatedly, that no one should expect to get more and that no one will lose. The strategy should include a preliminary communication setting out what is proposed and why, and how people will be affected. Progress reports should be made at milestones throughout the programme, for example when the factor plan has been devised. A final communication should describe the new grade and pay structure and spell out exactly what is to happen to people when the structure is introduced.

Step 5. Identify and define factors

Job evaluation factors are the characteristics or key elements of jobs that are used to analyse and evaluate jobs in an analytical job evaluation scheme. The factors must be capable of identifying relevant and important differences between jobs that will support the creation of a rank order of jobs to be covered by the scheme. They should apply equally well to different types of work, including specialists and generalists, lower-level and higher-level jobs, and not be biased in favour of one sex or group. Although many of the job evaluation factors used across organizations capture similar job elements (this is an area where there are some enduring truths), the task of identifying and agreeing factors can be challenging.

The e-reward survey (2003) established that the eight most frequently used factors by the respondents with analytical schemes were:

1. Knowledge and skill.
2. Communications and contacts.
3. Judgement and decision-making.
4. Impact.
5. People management.
6. Freedom to act.
7. Working environment.
8. Responsibility for financial resources.

Step 6. Define factor levels to produce the basic factor plan

The factor plan is the key job evaluation document. It guides evaluators on making decisions about the levels of demand. The basic factor plan defines the levels within each of the selected factors. A decision has to be made on the number of levels (often five, six or seven), which has to reflect the range of responsibilities and demands in the jobs covered by the scheme.

Step 7. Select and analyse test jobs

A small representative sample of jobs should be identified to test the scheme. A typical proportion would be about 10 per cent of the jobs to be covered. These are then analysed in terms of the factors.

Step 8. Test basic factor plan

The factors forming the basic factor plan are tested by the design team on a representative sample of jobs. The aim of this initial test is to check on the extent to which the factors are appropriate, cover all aspects of the jobs to be evaluated, are non-discriminatory, avoid double counting and are not compressed unduly. A check is also made on level definitions to ensure that they are worded clearly, graduated properly and cover the whole range of demands applicable to the jobs to be evaluated so that they enable consistent evaluations to be made.

Step 9. Develop scoring model

The aim is to design a point-factor scheme that will operate fairly and consistently to produce a rank order of jobs, based on the total points score for each job. Each level in the factor plan has to be allocated a points value so that there is a scoring progression from the lowest to the highest level.

Step 10. Decide on the factor weighting

Weighting is the process of attaching more importance to some factors than others through the scoring system (explicit weighting) or as a result of variations in the number of levels or the choice of factors (implicit weighting).

Step 11. Prepare full factor plan

The outcome of stages 9 and 10 is the full scored and weighted factor plan, which is tested in Step 12.

Step 12. Test the full factor plan

The full factor plan incorporating a scoring scheme and either explicit or implicit weighting is tested on the same jobs used in the initial test of the draft factors. Further jobs may be added to extend the range of the test.

Step 13. Computerize

The steps set out above will produce a paper-based scheme and this is still the most popular approach. The e-reward survey (2003) found that only 28 per cent of respondents with job evaluation schemes used computers to aid evaluation. But full computerization can offer many advantages, including greater consistency, speed and the elimination of much of the paperwork. There is also the possibility of using computers to help manage and support the process without using computers as a substitute for grading design teams.

Computer-assisted schemes use the software provided by suppliers, but the system itself is derived from the paper-based scheme devised by the methods set out above. No job evaluation design team is required to conduct evaluations, but it is necessary to set up a review panel that can validate and agree the outcomes of the computerized process. No one likes to feel that a decision about their grade has been made by a computer on its own, and hard lessons have been learnt by organizations that have ended up with fully automated but discriminatory systems.

Step 14. Test the computerized scheme

The computerized scheme is tested to ensure that it delivers an acceptable rank order.

Step 15. Apply and implement

When the final design of the paper or computerized scheme has been tested as satisfactory the application and implementation programme can begin.

CONCLUSIONS

It could be claimed that every time a decision is made on what a job should be paid requires a form of job evaluation. Job evaluation is therefore unavoidable, but it should not be an intuitive, subjective and potentially biased process. The issue is how best to carry it out analytically, fairly, systematically, consistently, transparently and, so far as possible, objectively, without being bureaucratic, inflexible or resource-intensive. There are five ways of dealing with this issue:

1. Use a tested and relevant analytical job evaluation scheme to inform and support the processes of designing grade structures, grading jobs, managing relativities and ensuring that work of equal value is paid equally.
2. Ensure that job evaluation is introduced and managed properly.
3. Consider using computers to speed up processing and decision-making while at the same time generating more consistent evaluations and reducing bureaucracy.
4. Recognize that thorough training and continuing guidance for evaluators is essential, as is communication about the scheme, its operation and objectives to all concerned.
5. Review the operation of the scheme regularly to ensure that it is not decaying and continues to be appropriate and trusted.

45

Market rate analysis

PURPOSE

To ensure that pay levels are competitive, it is necessary to track market rates for the jobs within the organization, especially those that are particularly vulnerable to market pressures because of scarcity factors. This is sometimes called benchmarking.

Job evaluation schemes can be used to determine internal relativities, but, in themselves, they cannot price jobs. To a large extent, pay levels are subject to market forces which have to be taken into account in fixing the rates for particular jobs. Some specialized jobs may not be subject to the same external pressures as others, but it is still necessary to know what effect market rates are likely to have on the pay structure as a whole before deciding on internal pay differentials which properly reflect levels of skill and responsibility. It has also to be accepted that market pressures and negotiations affect differentials within the firm.

THE CONCEPT OF THE MARKET RATE

The concept of the market rate, even in the local labour market, is an imprecise one. There is no such thing as *the* market rate, unless this is represented by a universally applied national pay scale, and such cases are now rare. There is always a range of rates paid by different employers, even for identical jobs, because of different pay policies on how they want their rates to compare with the market rates. This is particularly so in managerial jobs and other occupations where duties can vary considerably, even if the job title is the same, and where actual pay is likely to be strongly influenced by the quality and value to the business of individuals. It is therefore possible to use pay surveys only to provide a broad indication of market rates. Judgement has to be used in interpreting the results of special enquiries or the data from published surveys. And there is often plenty of scope for selecting evidence which supports whatever case is being advanced.

THE INFORMATION REQUIRED

When making market comparisons, the aim should be to:

- obtain accurate and representative data covering base pay, bonuses and benefits;
- compare like with like in terms of the type and size of the job and the type of organization – this is the process of 'job matching';
- obtain up-to-date information;
- interpret data in the light of the organization's circumstances and needs;
- present data in a way that indicates the action required.

JOB MATCHING

The aim in conducting a pay survey is to compare like with like – the process of job matching. The various methods of job matching in ascending order of accuracy are:

- *job title* – often very misleading;
- *brief (two or three lines) description of job and level of responsibility* – this provides better guidance for matching jobs but still leaves much scope for inaccuracy;
- *capsule job descriptions* which define the job and its duties in two or three hundred words, some indication being given of the size of the job in such terms as resources controlled – these can provide a better basis for job matching but may still not produce the ideal degree of accuracy;
- *full job descriptions* which provide more details about the job but demand a considerable amount of effort in making the comparisons;

● *job evaluation* can be used in support of a job description to obtain reasonably accurate information on comparative job sizes, but it is very time consuming unless it is done through the UK surveys run on this basis by firms such as Hay and Wyatt.

PRESENTATION OF DATA

Data can be presented in two ways:

1. *Measures of central tendency*:
   – arithmetic mean (average);
   – median – the middle item in a distribution of individual items, this is the most commonly used measure because it avoids the distortions to which arithmetic averages are prone.
2. *Measures of dispersion*:
   – upper quartile – the value above which 25 per cent of the individual values fall;
   – lower quartile – the value below which 25 per cent of the individual values fall;
   – interquartile range – the difference between the upper and lower quartiles.

SOURCES OF INFORMATION

The following are the sources of information available on market rates:

● published surveys;
● special surveys;
● club surveys;
● advertisements.

These are described below and a comparison between them and other sources is made in Table 45.1.

Published surveys

There is a wide range of published surveys which either collect general information about managerial salaries or cover the pay for specialist professional, technical or office jobs. The general surveys which are available 'over the counter' include those published by Reward, Monks Publications and Remuneration Economics. Incomes Data Services publishes a *Directory of Salary Surveys* which is a consumer's guide to all the major surveys.

When using a published survey it is necessary to check on:

- the information provided;
- the size and composition of the participants;
- the quality of the job matching information;
- the extent to which it covers the jobs for which information is required;
- the degree to which it is up to date;
- how well data are presented.

Published surveys are a quick and not too expensive way of getting information. But there may be problems in job matching and the information may be somewhat out of date.

Special surveys

Special surveys can be 'do it yourself' affairs or they can be conducted for you by management consultants. The latter method costs more but it saves a lot of time and trouble and some organizations may be more willing to respond to an enquiry from a reputable consultant.

Special surveys can be conducted as follows:

1. Decide what information is wanted.
2. Identify the 'benchmark' jobs for which comparative pay data are required. This could have been done as part of a job evaluation exercise.
3. Produce capsule job descriptions for those jobs.
4. Identify the organizations that are likely to have similar jobs.
5. Contact those organizations and invite them to participate. It is usual to say that the survey findings will be distributed to participants (this is the quid pro quo) and that individual organizations will not be identified.
6. Provide participants with a form to complete together with notes for guidance and capsule job descriptions.
7. Analyse the returned forms and distribute a summary of the results to participants.

Special surveys can justify the time and trouble, or expense, by producing usefully comparable data. It may, however, be difficult to get a suitable number of participants to take part, either because organizations cannot be bothered or because they are already members of a survey club or take part in a published survey.

Club surveys

Club surveys are conducted by a number of organizations who agree to exchange information on pay in accordance with a standard format and on a regular basis. They have all the advantages of special surveys plus the additional benefits of saving a considerable amount of time and providing regular information. It is well worth joining one if you can. If a suitable club does not exist, you could always try to start one, but this takes considerable effort.

Advertisements

Many organizations rely on the salary levels published in recruitment advertisements. But these can be very misleading as you will not necessarily achieve a good match and the quoted salary may not be the same as what is finally paid. However, although it is highly suspect, data from advertisements can be used to supplement other more reliable sources.

Other market intelligence

Other market intelligence can be obtained from the publications of Incomes Data Services and Industrial Relations Services. This may include useful information on trends in the 'going rate' for general, across-the-board pay increases which can be used when deciding on what sort of uplift, if any, is required to pay scales.

Using survey data

The use of market survey data as a guide on pay levels is a process based on judgement and compromise. Different sources may produce different indications of market rate levels. As a result you may have to produce what might be described as a 'derived' market rate based on an assessment of the relative reliability of the data. This would strike a reasonable balance between the competing merits of the different sources used. This is something of an intuitive process.

Once all the data available have been collected and presented in the most accessible manner possible (ie job by job for all the areas the structure is to cover), reference points can be determined for each pay range in a graded structure as described in Chapter 46. This process will take account of the place in the market the business wishes to occupy, ie its market 'stance' or 'posture'.

Table 45.1 Summary of sources of market data

Source	Brief description	Advantages	Disadvantages
General national published surveys	Available for purchase – provide an overall picture of pay levels for different occupations in national and regional labour markets.	Wide coverage, readily available, continuity allows trend analyses over time, expert providers.	Risk of imprecise job matching, insufficiently specific, quickly out of date.
Local published surveys	Available for purchase – provide an overall picture of pay levels for different occupations in the local labour market.	Focus on local labour market especially for administrative staff and manual workers.	Risk of imprecise job matching, insufficiently specific, quickly out of date, providers may not have expertise in pay surveys.
Sector surveys	Available for purchase – provide data on a sector such as charities.	Focus on a sector where pay levels may differ from national rates, deal with particular categories in depth.	Risk of imprecise job matching, insufficiently specific, quickly out of date.
Industrial surveys	Surveys, often conducted by employer and trade associations on jobs specific to an industry.	Focus on an industry, deal with particular categories in depth, quality of job matching may be better than general or sector surveys.	Job matching may still not be entirely precise, quickly out of date.
Special surveys	Surveys specially conducted by an organization.	Focused, reasonably good job matching, control of participants, control of analysis methodology.	Takes time and trouble, may be difficult to get participation, sample size may therefore be inadequate.
Pay clubs	Groups of employers who regularly exchange data on pay levels.	Focused, precise job matching, control of participants, control of analysis methodology, regular data, trends data, more information may be available on benefits and pay policies.	Sample size may be too small, involve a considerable amount of administration, may be difficult to maintain enthusiasm of participants.

continued

Table 45.1 *continued*

Source	Brief description	Advantages	Disadvantages
Published data in journals	Data on settlements and pay levels available from IDS or IRS, and on national trends in earnings from the New Earnings Survey.	Readily accessible.	Mainly about settlements and trends little specific well matched information on pay levels for individual jobs.
Job advertisements	Pay data obtained from job advertisements.	Readily accessible, highly visible (to employees as well as employers), up to date.	Job matching very imprecise, pay information may be misleading.
Management consultants' databases	Pay data obtained from the databases maintained by management consultants.	Based on well-researched and matched data.	Only obtainable from specific consultants.
Analysis of recruitment data	Pay data derived from analysis of pay levels required to recruit staff.	Immediate data.	Data random and can be misleading because of small sample.
Other market intelligence	Pay data obtained from informal contacts or networks.	Provide good background.	Imprecise, not regularly available.

46

Grade and pay structures

Grade and pay structures are an important part of reward systems. If properly designed and maintained they provide a logically designed framework within which an organization's pay policies can be implemented. They enable the organization to determine where jobs should be placed in a hierarchy, define pay levels and the scope for pay progression, and provide the basis upon which relativities can be managed, equal pay achieved and the processes of monitoring and controlling the implementation of pay practices can take place. A grade structure can also serve as a medium through which the organization communicates the career and pay opportunities available to employees.

GRADE STRUCTURE DEFINED

A grade structure consists of a sequence or hierarchy of grades, bands or levels into which groups of jobs that are broadly comparable in size are placed. There may be a single structure that contains grades or bands and which is defined by their number and width (width is the scope the grade or band provides for pay progression). Alternatively the structure may be divided into a number of job or career families consisting of groups of jobs where the essential nature and purpose of the work are similar but the work is carried out at different levels.

PAY STRUCTURE DEFINED

A pay structure defines the different levels of pay for jobs or groups of jobs by reference to their relative internal value as determined by job evaluation, to external relativities as established by market rate surveys and, sometimes, to negotiated rates for jobs. It provides scope for pay progression in accordance with performance, competence, contribution or service.

There may be a single pay structure covering the whole organization or there may be one structure for staff and another for manual workers, but this is becoming less common. There has in recent years been a trend towards 'harmonizing' terms and conditions between different groups of staff as part of a move towards single status. This has been particularly evident in many public sector organizations in the UK, supported by national agreements on 'single status'. Executive directors are sometimes treated separately where reward policy for them is decided by a remuneration committee of non-executive directors.

A grade structure becomes a pay structure when pay ranges, brackets or scales are attached to each grade, band or level. In some broad-banded structures, as described below, reference points and pay zones may be placed within the bands and these define the range of pay for jobs allocated to each band.

GUIDING PRINCIPLES FOR GRADE AND PAY STRUCTURES

Grade and pay structures should:

- be appropriate to the culture, characteristics and needs of the organization and its employees;
- facilitate the management of relativities and the achievement of equity, fairness, consistency and transparency in managing gradings and pay;
- be capable of adapting to pressures arising from market rate changes and skill shortages;
- facilitate operational flexibility and continuous development;
- provide scope as required for rewarding performance, contribution and increases in skill and competence;
- clarify reward, lateral development and career opportunities;
- be constructed logically and clearly so that the basis upon which they operate can readily be communicated to employees;
- enable the organization to exercise control over the implementation of pay policies and budgets.

TYPES OF GRADE AND PAY STRUCTURE

The types of pay structures as described below are narrow-graded, broad-graded, broad-banded, job family, career family and pay spine. Some organizations use spot rates for all or some of their employees and although this approach does not constitute a pay structure, it is described below as a feature of some pay systems. Spot rate systems can be expanded by developing individual job grades.

Narrow-graded structure

A narrow-graded structure, as illustrated in Figure 46.1, consists of a sequence of job grades into which jobs of broadly equivalent value are placed. There may be 10 or more grades and long-established structures, especially in the public sector, may have as many as 18 grades. Grades may be defined by a bracket of job evaluation points so that any job for which the job evaluation score falls within the points bracket for a grade would be allocated to that grade. Alternatively, grades may be defined by grade definitions or profiles, which provide the information required to match jobs set out under job demand factor headings (analytical matching). This information can be supplemented by reference to benchmark jobs that have been already graded as part of the structure design exercise.

'Mid-point management' techniques are often used to analyse and control pay policies by comparing actual pay with the reference point that is regarded as the policy pay level. 'Compa-ratios' can be used to measure the relationship between actual and policy rates of pay as a percentage. If the two coincide, the compa-ratio is 100 per cent. Compa-ratio analysis can be used to establish how pay practice (actual pay) compares with pay policy (the rate for a person who is fully qualified and competent in his or her job).

The problem with narrow-graded structures is that they encourage 'grade drift', ie unjustified upgradings. This takes place because it is difficult to differentiate between successive grades even with the help of job evaluation.

Broad-graded structures

Broad-graded structures, as illustrated in Figure 46.2, have six to nine grades rather than the 10 or more grades contained in narrow-graded structures. They may include 'reference points' or 'market anchors', which indicate the rate of pay for a fully competent performer in the grade and are aligned to market rates in accordance with 'market stance' policy. The grades and pay ranges are defined and managed in the same way as narrow-graded structures except that the increased width of the grades

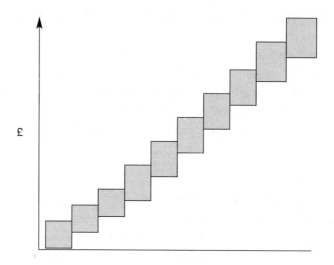

Figure 46.1 A narrow, multi-graded structure

means that organizations sometimes introduce mechanisms to control progression in the grade so that staff do not inevitably reach its upper pay limit. The mechanisms available consist of:

- *Reference point control* – scope is provided for progression according to competence by increments to the reference point. Thereafter, individuals may earn cash bonuses for high achievement that may be consolidated up to the maximum pay for the grade if high achievement levels are sustained.
- *Threshold control* – a point is defined in the pay range beyond which pay cannot increase unless individuals achieve a defined level of competence and achievement.
- *Segment or zone control* – an extension of threshold control, which involves dividing the grade into a number (often three) of segments or zones.

Broad-graded structures are used to overcome or at least alleviate the grade drift problem endemic in multi-graded structures. If the grades are defined, it is easier to differentiate them, and matching (comparing role profiles with grade definitions or profiles to find the best fit) becomes more accurate. But it may be difficult to control progression and this would increase the costs of operating them, although these costs could be offset by better control of grade drift.

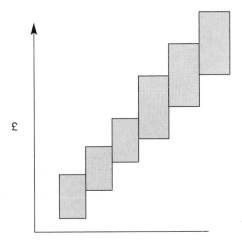

Figure 46.2 A broad-graded structure

Broad-banded structures

Broad-banded structures compress multi-graded structures into four or five 'bands', as illustrated in Figure 46.3. The process of developing broad-banded structures is called 'broad-banding'. In its original version, a broad-banded structure contained no more than five bands, each with, typically, a span of 70 to 100 per cent. Bands were unstructured and pay was managed much more flexibly than in a conventional graded structure (no limits may be defined for progression, which depended on competence and the assumption of wider role responsibilities) and much more attention was paid to market rates that governed what were in effect the spot rates for jobs within bands. Analytical job evaluation was often felt to be unnecessary because of the ease with which jobs could be allocated to one of a small number of bands. The difference between broad bands and broad grades is that the latter still generally adopt a fairly conventional approach to pay management by the use of analytical job evaluation, mid-point management, compa-ratio analysis and pay matrix techniques.

However, structure often crept in. It started with reference points aligned to market rates around which similar roles could be clustered. These were then extended into zones for individual jobs or groups of jobs, which placed limits on pay progression, as illustrated in Figure 46.4. Job evaluation was increasingly used to define the boundaries of the band and to size jobs as a basis for deciding where reference points should be placed in conjunction with market pricing. The original concept of broad-banding was therefore eroded as more structure was introduced and job evaluation became more prominent to define the structure and meet equal pay requirements. Zones within broad bands began to look rather like conventional grades.

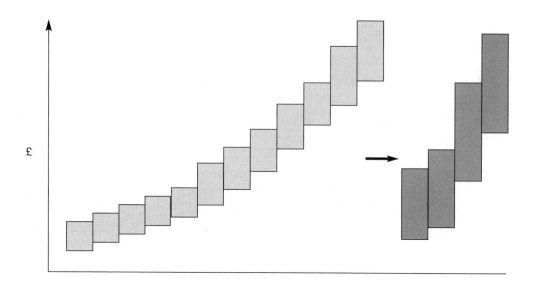

Figure 46.3 Narrow and broad-banded structures

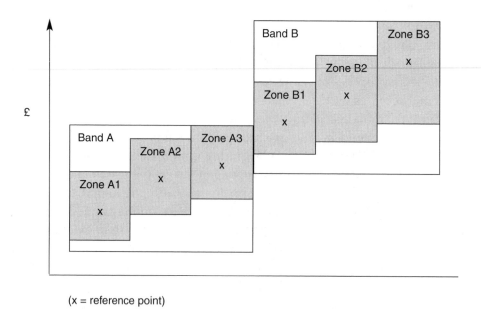

(x = reference point)

Figure 46.4 A broad-banded structure with zones

Job family structures

Job families consist of jobs in a function or occupation such as marketing, operations, finance, IT, HR, administration or support services, which are related through the activities carried out and the basic knowledge and skills required, but in which the levels of responsibility, knowledge, skill or competence levels required differ. In a job family structure, as shown in Figure 46.5, different job families are identified and the successive levels in each family are defined by reference to the key activities carried out and the knowledge and skills or competences required to perform them effectively. They therefore define career paths – what people have to know and be able to do to advance their career within a family and to develop career opportunities in other families. Typically, job families have between six and eight levels as in broad-graded structures. Some families may have more levels than others.

In contrast to career family structures (see below) each family in a job family structure may in effect have its own pay structure that takes account of different levels of market rates between families (this is sometimes called 'market grouping'). The level or grade structures may also differ between families to reflect any special family role characteristics. Because the size of jobs and rates of pay can vary between the same levels in different job families, there may be no read-across between them unless use is made of analytical job evaluation.

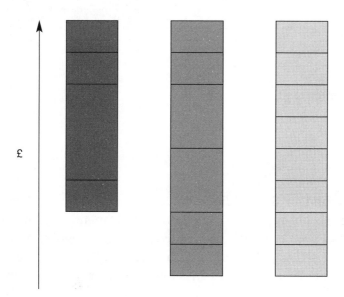

Figure 46.5   A job family structure

Career family structures

Career family structures, as shown in Figure 46.6, resemble job family structures in that there are a number of different 'families'. The difference is that in a career family, jobs in the corresponding levels across each of the career families are within the same size range and, if an analytical job evaluation scheme is used, this is defined by the same range of scores. Similarly, the pay ranges in corresponding levels across the career families are the same. In effect, a career structure is a single graded structure in which each grade has been divided into families.

Career family structures focus on career mapping and career development as part of an integrated approach to human resource management. This is as important a feature of career families as the pay structure element, possibly even more so.

Career families			
Operations	Administration	Finance	IT
Level 1	Level 1	Level 1	Level 1
Level 2	Level 2	Level 2	Level 2
Level 3	Level 3	Level 3	Level 3
Level 4	Level 4	Level 4	Level 4
Level 5	Level 5	Level 5	Level 5
Level 6	Level 6	Level 6	Level 6

evaluation points £   job

Figure 46.6   A career family structure

Pay spines

Pay spines are found in the public sector or in agencies and charities that have adopted a public sector approach to reward management. As illustrated in Figure 46.7, they consist of a series of incremental 'pay points' extending from the lowest to the highest paid jobs covered by the structure. Typically, pay spine increments are between 2.5 and 3 per cent. They may be standardized from the top to the bottom of the spine, or the increments may vary at different levels, sometimes widening towards the top. Job grades are aligned to the pay spine and the pay ranges for the grades are defined by the relevant scale of pay points. The width of grades can vary and job families may have different pay spines. Progression through a grade is based on service, although an increasing number of organizations provide scope for accelerating increments or providing additional increments above the top of the scale for the grade to reward merit.

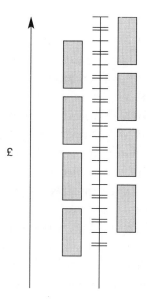

Figure 46.7   A pay spine

Spot rates

Some organizations do not have a graded structure at all for any jobs or for certain jobs such as directors. Instead they use 'spot rates'. They may also be called the 'rate for the job', more typically for manual jobs where there is a defined skilled or semi-skilled market rate that may be negotiated with a trade union. Spot rates are quite often used in retail firms for customer service staff.

Spot rates are sometimes attached to a person rather than a job. Unless they are negotiated, rates of pay and therefore relativities are governed by market rates and managerial judgement. Spot rates are not located within grades and there is no defined scope for progression while on the spot rate. There may, however, be scope for moving on to higher spot rates as skill, competence or contribution increases. Job holders may be eligible for incentive bonuses on top of the spot rate.

Spot rates may be used where there is a very simple hierarchy of jobs, as in some manufacturing and retailing companies. They may be adopted by organizations that want the maximum amount of scope to pay what they like. They often exist in small or start-up organizations that do not want to be constrained by a formal grade structure and prefer to retain the maximum amount of flexibility. But they can result in serious inequities that may be difficult to justify.

Individual job grades

Individual job grades are, in effect, spot rates to which a defined pay range of, say, 20 per cent on either side of the rate has been attached to provide scope for pay progression based on performance, competence or contribution. Again, the mid-point of the range is fixed by reference to job evaluation and market rate comparisons.

Individual grades are attached to jobs not people, but there may be more flexibility for movement between grades than in a conventional grade structure. This can arise when people have expanded their role and it is considered that this growth in the level of responsibility needs to be recognized without having to upgrade the job. Individual job grades may be restricted to certain jobs, for example more senior managers where flexibility in fixing and increasing rates of pay is felt to be desirable. They provide for greater flexibility than more conventional structures but can be difficult to manage and justify and can result in pay inequities. The 'zones' that are often established in broad-banded structures have some of the characteristics of individual job grades.

Summary

A summary of the features of the different pay structures, their advantages and disadvantages and when they may be appropriate is given in Table 46.1.

Incidence of different types of structure

Figure 46.8 shows the incidence of different types of structure as established by the e-reward survey (2004c). Broad-graded structures are now the most popular. They are replacing narrow-graded structures rather than broad-banding, which is relatively little used. There are a fair number of job family structures but few career family structures.

DESIGNING GRADE AND PAY STRUCTURES

Design options

There is a choice of structure, as shown in Table 46.1, and whichever structure is selected, there will be a number of design options. The first decision to make is where

Table 46.1 Summary analysis of different grade and pay structures

Type of structure	Features	Advantages	Disadvantages	When appropriate
Narrow-graded	A sequence of job grades –10 or more Narrow pay ranges eg 20 per cent – 40 per cent Progression usually linked to performance	Clearly indicate pay relativities Facilitate control Easy to understand	Create hierarchical rigidity Prone to grade drift Inappropriate in a de-layered organization	In a large bureau-cratic organization with well defined hierarchies When close and rigid control is required When some but not too much scope for pay progression related to performance or contribution is wanted
Broad-graded	A sequence of between 6 and 9 grades Fairly broad pay ranges eg 40 to 50% Progression linked to contribution and may be controlled by thresholds or zones	As for narrow graded structures but in addition: the broader grades can be defined more clearly better control can be exercised over grade drift	Too much scope for pay progression Control mechanisms can be provided but they can be difficult to manage May be costly	Desirable to define and differentiate grades more accurately as an aid to better precision when grading jobs Grade drift problems exist More scope wanted to reward contribution
Broad-banded	A series of, often 5 or 6 'broad' bands Wide pay bands – typically between 50 and 80% Progression linked to contribution and competence	More flexible Reward lateral development and growth in competence Fit new style organizations	Create unrealistic expectations of scope for pay rises Seem to restrict scope for promotion Difficult to understand Equal pay problems	In de-layered, process-based, flexible organizations Where more flexibility in pay determination is wanted Where the focus is on continuous improvement and lateral development

continued

Table 46.1   *continued*

Type of structure	Features	Advantages	Disadvantages	When appropriate
Job family	Separate grade and pay structures for job families containing similar jobs Progression linked to competence and/or contribution	Can appear to be divisive May inhibit lateral career development May be difficult to maintain internal equity between job families unless underpinned by job evaluation	Facilitate pay differentiation between market groups. Define career paths against clear criteria	When there are distinct market groups which need to be rewarded differentially Where there are distinct groups of jobs in families
Pay spine	A series of incremental pay points covering all jobs Grades may be superimposed Progression linked to service	Easy to manage Pay progression not based on managerial judgement	No scope for differentiating rewards according to performance May be costly as staff drift up the spine	In a public sector or voluntary organization where this is the traditional approach and it therefore fits the culture Where it is believed to be impossible to measure differential levels of performance fairly and consistently

to place grade boundaries which, as described below, is usually informed by a job evaluation exercise. Decisions on grade boundaries will be influenced by considerations affecting the number and width of grades. Further options exist on the pay structure concerning the differentials between grades, the degree to which there should be overlap between grades, if any, and the method of pay progression within grades. In broad-banded structures there is also choice on the infrastructure (the use of reference points or zones), and in career or job family structures there are options concerning the number of families, the composition of families and the basis upon which levels should be defined.

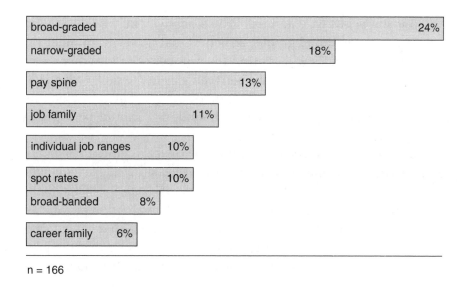

n = 166

Figure 46.8   Type of grade and pay structure

Deciding on grade boundaries

An analytical job evaluation exercise will produce a rank order of jobs according to their job evaluation scores. A decision then has to be made on where the boundaries that will define grades should be placed in the rank order. So far as possible, boundaries should divide groups or clusters of jobs which are significantly different in size so that all the jobs placed in a grade are clearly smaller than the jobs in the next higher grade and larger than the jobs placed in the next lower grade.

Fixing grade boundaries is one of the most critical aspects of grade structure design following an analytical job evaluation exercise. It requires judgement – the process is not scientific and it is rare to find a situation when there is one right and obvious answer. In theory, grade boundaries could be determined by deciding on the number of grades in advance and then dividing the rank order into equal parts. But this would mean drawing grade boundary lines arbitrarily and the result could be the separation of groups of jobs that should properly be placed in the same grade.

The best approach is to analyse the rank order to identify any significant gaps in the points scores between adjacent jobs. These natural breaks in points scores will then constitute the boundaries between clusters of jobs that can be allocated to adjacent grades. A distinct gap between the highest rated job in one grade and the lowest rated job in the grade above will help to justify the allocation of jobs between grades. It will therefore reduce boundary problems leading to dissatisfaction with gradings when the distinction is less well defined. Provisionally, it may be decided in advance when designing a conventional graded structure that a certain number of grades is required, but the gap analysis will confirm the number of grades that is appropriate, taking into account the natural divisions between jobs in the rank order. However, the existence of a number of natural breaks cannot be guaranteed, which means that judgement has to be exercised as to where boundaries should be drawn when the scores between adjacent jobs are close.

In cases where there are no obvious natural breaks, the guidelines that should be considered when deciding on boundaries are as follows:

- Jobs with common features as indicated by the job evaluation factors are grouped together so that a distinction can be made between the characteristics of the jobs in different grades – it should be possible to demonstrate that the jobs grouped into one grade resemble each other more than they resemble jobs placed in adjacent grades.
- The grade hierarchy should take account of the organizational hierarchy, ie jobs in which the job holder reports to a higher level job holder should be placed in a lower grade, although this principle should not be followed slavishly when an organization is over-hierarchical with, perhaps, a series of one-over-one reporting relationships.
- The boundaries should not be placed between jobs mainly carried out by men and jobs mainly carried out by women.
- The boundaries should ideally not be placed immediately above jobs in which large numbers of people are employed.
- The grade width in terms of job evaluation points should represent a significant step in demand as indicated by the job evaluation scheme.

Number of grades, levels or bands

The considerations to be taken into account when deciding on the number of grades levels or bands are:

- The range and types of roles to be covered by the structure.
- The range of pay and job evaluation points scores to be accommodated.
- The number of levels in the organizational hierarchy (this will be an important factor in a broad-banded structure).
- Decisions on where grade boundaries should be placed following a job evaluation exercise, which has produced a ranked order of jobs – this might identify the existence of clearly defined clusters of jobs at the various levels in the hierarchy between which there are significant differences in job size.

- The fact that within a given range of pay and responsibility, the greater the number of grades the smaller their width and vice versa – this is associated with views on what is regarded as the desirable width of a range, taking into account the scope for progression, the size of increments in a pay spine and equal pay issues.
- The problem of 'grade drift' (unjustified upgradings in response to pressure, lack of promotion opportunities or because job evaluation has been applied laxly), which can be increased if there are too many narrow grades.

Width of grades

The factors affecting decisions on the width of grades or bands are:

- Views on the scope that should be allowed for performance, contribution or career progression within grade.
- Equal pay considerations – wide grades, especially extended incremental scales, are a major cause of pay gaps between men and women simply because women, who are more likely to have career breaks than men, may not have the same opportunity as men to progress to the upper regions of the range; male jobs may therefore cluster towards the top of the range while women's may cluster towards the bottom.
- V on the number of grades – the greater the number the smaller the width.
- Decisions on the value of increments in a pay spine – if it is believed, as in local government and as a result of an ACAS equal pay case that the number of increments should be restricted, for equal pay or other reasons, but that the number of grades should also be limited, then it is necessary to increase the value of the increments.
- In a broad-banded structure, the range of market rates and job evaluation scores covering the jobs allocated to the band.

Differentials between pay ranges

Differentials between pay ranges should provide scope to recognize increases in job size between successive grades. If differentials are too close – less than 10 per cent – many jobs become borderline cases, which can result in a proliferation of appeals and arguments about grading. Large differentials below senior management level of more than 25 per cent can create problems for marginal or borderline cases because of the amount at stake. Experience has shown that in most organizations with conventional grade structures, a differential of between 16 and 20 per cent is appropriate except, perhaps, at the highest levels.

Pay range overlap

There is a choice on whether or not pay ranges should overlap and if so, by how much. The amount of overlap, if any, is a function of range width and differentials. Large overlaps of more than 10 per cent can create equal pay problems where, as is quite common, men are clustered at the top of their grades and women are more likely to be found at the lower end.

Pay progression

There is a choice of methods of pay progression between the fixed service-related increments common in the public sector, and the other forms of contingent pay, namely performance, competence or contribution-related, as described in Chapter 47.

The grade and pay structure design process

An analytical job evaluation scheme is usually the basis for designing a graded structure and it can be used in the initial stages of designing a broad-banded or career/job family structure. In the case of graded structures, decisions on the number and width of grades are generally based on an analysis of the rank order of scores produced by job evaluation.

This approach is used less often in the design of broad-banded or career/job family structures, where the most common method is to make a provisional advance decision on the number of bands or career family levels, and then position roles in bands (often by reference to market rates) or allocate roles into levels by an 'analytical matching' process, as described in Chapter 44. Job evaluation may only be used at a later stage to validate the positioning of roles in bands or the allocation of jobs to family levels, check on relativities and, sometimes, define the bands or levels in job evaluation score terms. The initial decision on the number of bands or levels and their definition may, however, be changed in the light of the outcome of the allocation, matching and evaluation processes.

More rarely, the grade and pay structure design is conducted by means of a non-analytical job classification exercise (see Chapter 44), which defines a number of single grades. Jobs are then slotted into the grades by reference to the grade definitions. The basic sequence of steps for designing a grade and pay structure is illustrated in Figure 46.9. Note the emphasis on communication and involvement at all stages.

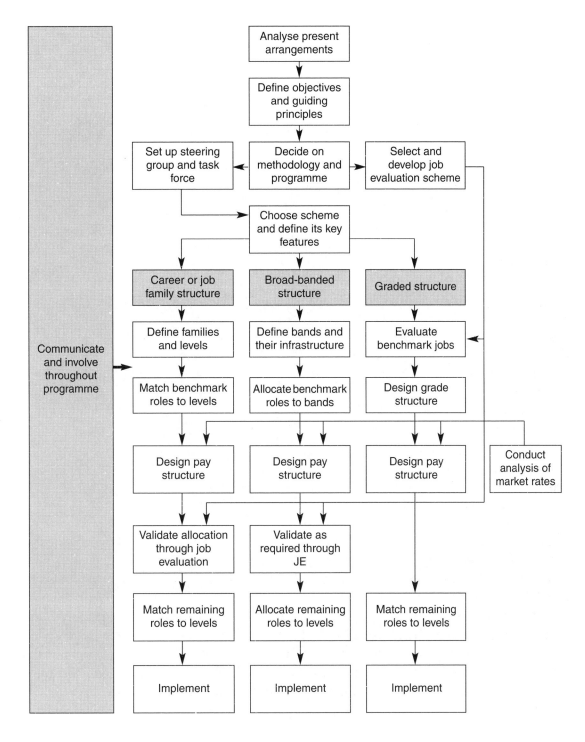

Figure 46.9 Flow chart: design of a new grade and pay structure

47

Contingent pay

This chapter starts with a definition of contingent pay and details of its incidence. It then deals with individual contingent pay under the following headings:

- contingent pay as a motivator;
- arguments for and against contingent pay;
- alternatives to contingent pay;
- criteria for success;
- performance-related pay;
- competence-related pay;
- contribution-related pay;
- skill-based pay;
- service-related pay;
- choice of scheme;
- readiness for contribution pay;
- developing and implementing contingent pay.

The chapter concludes with a description of team pay schemes and schemes that pay for organizational performance. Incentives for sales staff and manual workers are covered in Chapter 42.

CONTINGENT PAY DEFINED

Contingent pay provides an answer to the two fundamental reward management questions: what do we value, and what are we prepared to pay for? Individual contingent pay relates financial rewards to the performance, competence, contribution or skill of individual employees. However, pay related to service is also in a sense contingent pay and is therefore considered separately towards the end of the chapter. Contingent pay may also be provided for teams and for organizational performance.

THE INCIDENCE OF CONTINGENT PAY

The e-reward survey of contingent pay (2004b) established that 189 schemes were used by the 100 respondents in the proportions shown in Figure 47.1.

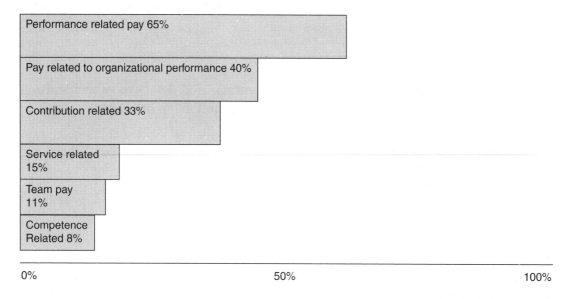

Figure 47.1 Incidence of contingent pay schemes

Performance-related pay remains the most common approach and a large proportion of organizations relate pay to organizational performance. Contribution-related pay (a combination of performance and competence pay) is used to a surprisingly high extent considering that as a defined concept it did not really exist until the end of the 1990s, when it was introduced by Brown and Armstrong (1999). Service-related pay persists in the public and voluntary sectors, but neither team pay nor competence-related pay is much used.

THE NATURE OF INDIVIDUAL CONTINGENT PAY

Contingent pay may be consolidated in base pay or provided in the form of cash lump sum bonuses. The latter arrangement is called 'variable pay'. This is sometimes referred to as 'pay at risk', which has to be re-earned, as distinct from consolidated pay, which is usually regarded as continuing as long as the person remains in the job and performs it satisfactorily.

Contingent pay schemes are based on processes for measuring or assessing performance, competence, contribution or skill. These may be expressed as ratings, which are converted by means of a formula to a payment. Alternatively, there may be no formal ratings and pay decisions are based on broad assessments rather than a formula.

INDIVIDUAL CONTINGENT PAY AS A MOTIVATOR

Many people see contingent pay as the best way to motivate people. But it is simplistic to assume that it is only the extrinsic motivators in the form of pay that create long-term motivation. The total reward concept, as explained in Chapter 42, emphasizes the importance of non-financial rewards as an integral part of a complete package. The intrinsic motivators, which can arise from the work itself and the working environment, may have a deeper and longer-lasting effect.

Incentives and rewards

When considering contingent pay as a motivator a distinction should be made between financial incentives and rewards.

Financial incentives are designed to provide direct motivation. They tell people how much money they will get in the future if they perform well – 'Do this and you will get that'. A shop floor payment-by-result scheme and a sales representative's commission system are examples of financial incentives.

Financial rewards act as indirect motivators because they provide a tangible means of recognizing achievements, as long as people expect that what they do in the future will produce something worthwhile, as expectancy theory suggests. Rewards can be retrospective – 'You have achieved this, therefore we will pay you that.' But rewards can also be prospective: 'We will pay you more now because we believe you have reached a level of competence that will produce high levels of performance in the future.'

ARGUMENTS FOR AND AGAINST INDIVIDUAL CONTINGENT PAY

Arguments for

The most powerful argument for individual contingent pay is that those who contribute more should be paid more. It is right and proper to recognize achievement with a financial and therefore tangible reward. This is preferable to paying people just for 'being there', as happens in a service-related system.

The e-reward survey of contingent pay (2004b) found that, in order of importance, the following were the main reasons given by the respondents for using contingent pay:

1. To recognize and reward better performance.
2. To attract and retain high quality people.
3. To improve organizational performance.
4. To focus attention on key results and values.
5. To deliver a message about the importance of performance.
6. To motivate people.
7. To influence behaviour.
8. To support cultural change.

Arguments against

The main arguments against individual contingent pay are that:

- the extent to which contingent pay schemes motivate is questionable – the amounts available for distribution are usually so small that they cannot act as an incentive;
- the requirements for success as set out below are exacting and difficult to achieve;
- money by itself will not result in sustained motivation – as Kohn (1993) points out, money rarely acts in a crude, behaviourist, Pavlov's dog manner;
- people react in widely different ways to any form of motivation – it cannot be assumed that money will motivate all people equally, yet that is the premise on which contribution pay schemes are based;

- financial rewards may possibly motivate those who receive them, but they can demotivate those who don't, and the numbers who are demotivated could be much higher than those who are motivated;
- contingent pay schemes can create more dissatisfaction than satisfaction if they are perceived to be unfair, inadequate or badly managed, and, as explained below, they can be difficult to manage well;
- contingent pay schemes depend on the existence of accurate and reliable methods of measuring performance, competence, contribution or skill, which might not exist;
- contingent pay decisions depend on the judgement of managers which, in the absence of reliable criteria, could be partial, prejudiced, inconsistent or ill-informed;
- the concept of contingent pay is based on the assumption that performance is completely under the control of individuals when in fact, it is affected by the system in which they work;
- contingent pay, especially performance-related pay schemes, can militate against quality and teamwork.

Another powerful argument against contingent pay is that it has proved difficult to manage. Organizations, including the Civil Service, rushed into performance-related pay in the 1980s without really understanding how to make it work. Inevitably problems of implementation arose. Studies such as those conducted by Bowey (1982), Kessler and Purcell (1992), Marsden and Richardson (1994) and Thompson (1992) have all revealed these difficulties. Failures are usually rooted in implementation and operating processes, especially those concerned with performance management, the need for effective communication and involvement, and line management capability.

The last factor is crucial. The success of contingent pay rests largely in the hands of line managers. They have to believe in it as something that will help them as well as the organization. They must also be good at practising the crucial skills of agreeing targets, measuring performance fairly and consistently, and providing feedback to their staff on the outcome of performance management and its impact on pay. Line managers can make or break contingent pay schemes.

Wright (1991) summed it all up: 'Even the most ardent supporters of per-formance-related pay recognize that it is difficult to manage well', and Oliver (1996) made the point that 'performance pay is beautiful in theory but difficult in practice'.

Conclusions

A comprehensive study by Brown and Armstrong (1999) into the effectiveness of contingent pay as revealed by a number of research projects produced two overall conclusions: 1) contingent pay cannot be endorsed or rejected universally as a principle; and 2) no type of contingent pay is universally successful or unsuccessful. They concluded their analysis of the research findings by stating that 'the research does show that the effectiveness of pay-for-performance schemes is highly context and situation-specific; and it has highlighted the practical problems which many companies have experienced with these schemes'.

ALTERNATIVES TO INDIVIDUAL CONTINGENT PAY

The arguments against contribution pay set out above convince many people that it is unsatisfactory, but what is the alternative? One answer is to rely more on non-financial motivators. But it is still necessary to consider what should be done about pay. The reaction in the 1990s to the adverse criticisms of PRP was to develop the concept of competence-related pay that fitted in well with the emphasis on competencies (the competency industry). This approach, as described later, in theory overcame some of the cruder features of PRP but still created a number of practical difficulties and has never really taken off. In the late 1990s the idea of contribution-related pay emerged, as advocated by Brown and Armstrong (1999). This combines the output-driven focus of PRP with the input (competence) oriented focus of competence-related pay and has proved to be much more appealing than either performance or competence-related pay.

However, many people still have reservations about this approach from the viewpoint of achieving the fair and consistent measurement of contribution. So what are the alternatives for them? Team pay is often advocated because it removes the individualistic aspect of PRP and accords with the belief in the importance of teamwork, but although team pay is attractive, it is often difficult to apply and it still relies on performance measurement.

The traditional alternative is service-related pay, as described later in this chapter. This certainly treats everyone equally (and therefore appeals to trade unions) but pays people simply for being there, and this could be regarded as inequitable in that rewards take no account of relative levels of contribution.

The other common alternative is a spot rate system as described in Chapter 46. Most people, however, want and expect a range of base pay progression, however that is determined, and spot rates are not much used in larger organizations except for senior managers, shop floor and sales staff.

CRITERIA FOR SUCCESS

The following are the success criteria for individual contingent pay:

- Individuals should have a clear line of sight between what they do and what they will get for doing it. A line of sight model adapted from Lawler (1988) is shown in Figure 47.2. The concept expresses the essence of expectancy theory: that motivation only takes place when people expect that their effort and contribution will be rewarded. The reward should be clearly and closely linked to accomplishment or effort – people know what they will get if they achieve defined and agreed targets or standards and can track their performance against them.
- The rewards are worth having.
- Fair and consistent means are available for measuring or assessing performance, competence, contribution or skill.
- People must be able to influence their performance by changing their behaviour and developing their competences and skills.
- The reward should follow as closely as possible the accomplishment that generated it.

Figure 47.2   Line of sight model

These are ideal requirements and few schemes meet them in full. That is why individual contingent pay arrangements as described below can often promise more than they deliver.

PERFORMANCE-RELATED PAY

Methods of operating PRP vary considerably but its typical main features are summarized in Figure 47.3 and described below.

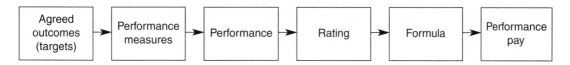

Figure 47.3   Performance-related pay

Basis of scheme

Pay increases are related to the achievement of agreed results defined as targets or outcomes. Scope is provided for consolidated pay progression within pay brackets attached to grades or levels in a graded or career family structure, or zones in a broad-banded structure. Such increases are permanent – they are seldom if ever withdrawn. Alternatively or additionally, high levels of performance or special achievements may be rewarded by cash bonuses, which are not consolidated and have to be re-earned. Individuals may be eligible for such bonuses when they have reached the top of the pay bracket for their grade, or when they are assessed as being fully competent, having completely progressed along their learning curve. The rate of pay for someone who reaches the required level of competence can be aligned to market rates according to the organization's pay policy.

Pay progression

The rate and limits of progression through the pay brackets are typically but not inevitably determined by performance ratings, which are often made at the time of the performance management review but may be made separately in a special pay review. Some organizations do not base PRP increases on formal ratings and instead rely on a general assessment of how much the pay of individuals should increase by reference to performance, potential, the pay levels of their peers and their 'market worth' (the rate of pay it is believed they could earn elsewhere).

Conclusions on PRP

PRP has all the advantages and disadvantages listed for contingent pay. Many people feel the latter outweigh the former. It has attracted a lot of adverse comment, primarily because of the difficulties organizations have met in managing it. Contribution-related pay schemes are becoming much more popular.

COMPETENCE-RELATED PAY

The main features of competence-related pay schemes are illustrated in Figure 47.4 and described below.

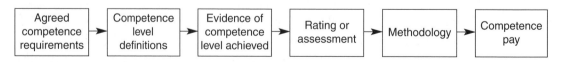

Figure 47.4   Competence-related pay

Basis of scheme

People receive financial rewards in the shape of increases to their base pay by reference to the level of competence they demonstrate in carrying out their roles. It is a method of paying people for the ability to perform now and in the future.

As in the case of PRP, scope is provided for consolidated pay progression within pay brackets attached to grades or levels in a narrow-graded or career family structure, or zones in a broad-banded structure (competence pay is often regarded as a feature of such structures).

Pay progression

The rate and limits of progression through the pay brackets can be based on ratings of competence using a PRP-type matrix, but they may be governed by more general assessments of competence development.

Conclusions on competence-related pay

Competence-related pay is attractive in theory because it can be part of an integrated competency-based approach to HRM. However, the idea of competence-related pay raises two questions. The fundamental question is, 'What are we paying for?' Are we paying for competencies, ie how people behave, or competences, ie what people have to know and be able to do to perform well? If we are rewarding good behaviour (competencies) then a number of difficulties arise. It has been suggested by Sparrow (1996) that these include the performance criteria on which competencies are based, the complex nature of what is being measured, the relevance of the results to the organization, and the problem of measurement. He concluded that 'we should avoid over-egging our ability to test, measure and reward competencies'.

Other fundamental objections to the behavioural approach have been raised by Lawler (1993). He expresses concern about schemes that pay for an individual's personality traits and emphasizes that such plans work best 'when they are tied to the ability of an individual to perform a particular task and when there are valid measures available of how well an individual can perform a task'. He also points out that, 'generic competencies are not only hard to measure, they are not necessarily related to successful task performance in a particular work assignment or work role'.

This raises the second question: 'Are we paying for the possession of competence or the use of competence?' Clearly it must be the latter. But we can only assess the effective use of competence by reference to performance. The focus is therefore on results and if that is the case, competence-related pay begins to look suspiciously like performance-related pay. It can be said that the difference between the two in these circumstances is all 'smoke and mirrors'. Competence-related pay could be regarded as no more than a more acceptable name for PRP.

Competence-related pay sounds like a good idea but it has not been taken up to a great extent because of the problems mentioned above.

CONTRIBUTION-RELATED PAY

Contribution-related pay, as modelled in Figures 47.5 and 47.6, is a process for making pay decisions that are based on assessments of both the outcomes of the work carried out by individuals and the inputs in terms of levels of competence and competency that have influenced these outcomes. In other words, it pays not only for what they do but how they do it. Contribution-related pay focuses on what people in organizations are there to do, that is, to contribute by their skill and efforts to the achievement of the purpose of their organization or team.

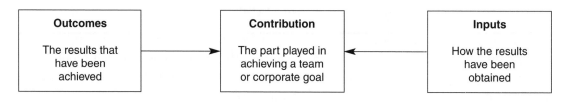

Figure 47.5 Contribution pay model (1)

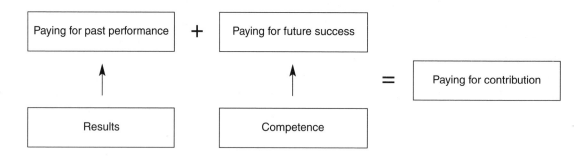

Figure 47.6 Contribution pay model (2)

The case for contribution-related pay was made by Brown and Armstrong (1999) as follows:

> Contribution captures the full scope of what people do, the level of skill and competence they apply and the results they achieve, which all contribute to the organization achieving its long-term goals. Contribution pay works by applying the mixed model of performance management: assessing inputs and outputs and coming to a conclusion on the level of pay for people in their roles and their work; both to the organization and in the market; considering both past performance and their future potential.

Main features

Contribution-related pay rewards people for both their performance (outcomes) and their competence (inputs). Pay awards can be made as consolidated pay increases, but in some schemes there is also scope for cash bonuses. The features of contribution-related pay are illustrated in Figure 47.7.

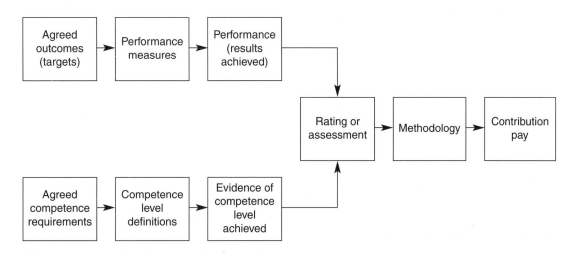

Figure 47.7 Contribution-related pay

A pay for contribution scheme incorporating competence and contribution pay in the form of consolidated increases and cash bonuses developed for the Shaw Trust is modelled in Figure 47.8.

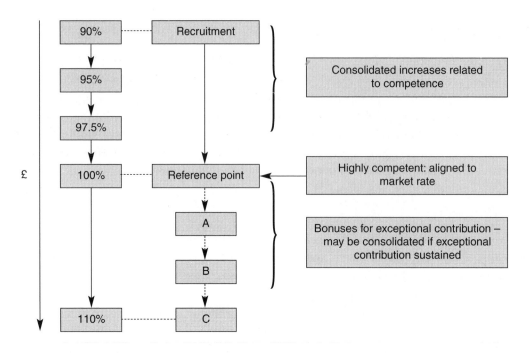

Figure 47.8   Contribution-related pay model (Shaw Trust)

SKILL-BASED PAY

Defined

Skill-based pay provides employees with a direct link between their pay progression and the skills they have acquired and can use effectively. It focuses on what skills the business wants to pay for and what employees must do to demonstrate them. It is therefore a people-based rather than a job-based approach to pay. Rewards are related to the employee's ability to apply a wider range or a higher level of skills to different jobs or tasks. It is not linked simply to the scope of a defined job or a prescribed set of tasks.

A skill may be defined broadly as a learnt ability that improves with practice over time. For skill-based pay purposes the skills must be relevant to the work. Skill-based pay is also known as 'knowledge-based pay', but the terms are used interchangeably, knowledge being regarded loosely as the understanding of how to do a job or certain tasks.

Application

Skill-based pay was originally applied mainly to operatives in manufacturing firms, but it has been extended to technicians and workers in retailing, distribution, catering and other service industries. The broad equivalent of skill-based pay for managerial, professional and administrative staff and knowledge workers is competence-related pay, which refers to expected behaviour as well as, often, to knowledge and skill requirements. There is clearly a strong family resemblance between skill- and competence-related pay – each is concerned with rewarding the person as well as the job. But they can be distinguished both by the way in which they are applied, as described below, and by the criteria used.

Main features

Skill-based pay works as follows:

- Skill blocks or modules are defined. These incorporate individual skills or clusters of skills that workers need to use and which will be rewarded by extra pay when they have been acquired and the employee has demonstrated the ability to use them effectively.
- The skill blocks are arranged in a hierarchy, with natural break points between clearly definable different levels of skills.
- The successful completion of a skill module or skill block will result in an increment in pay. This will define how the pay of individuals can progress as they gain extra skills.
- Methods of verifying that employees have acquired and can use the skills at defined levels are established.
- Arrangements for 'cross-training' are made. These will include learning modules and training programmes for each skill block.

Conclusions

Skill-based pay systems are expensive to introduce and maintain. They require a considerable investment in skill analysis, training and testing. Although in theory a skill-based scheme will pay only for necessary skills, in practice individuals will not be using them all at the same time and some may be used infrequently, if at all. Inevitably, therefore, payroll costs will rise. If this increase is added to the cost of training and certification, the total of additional costs may be considerable. The advocates of skill-based pay claim that their schemes are self-financing because of the resulting increases in productivity and operational efficiency. But there is little evidence that such is the case. For this reason, skill-based schemes have never been very popular in the UK and some companies have discontinued them.

SERVICE-RELATED PAY

Defined

Service-related pay provides fixed increments that are usually paid annually to people on the basis of continued service either in a job or a grade in a pay spine structure. Increments may be withheld for unacceptable performance (although this is rare) and some structures have a 'merit bar', which limits increments unless a defined level of 'merit' has been achieved. This is the traditional form of contingent pay and is still common in the public and voluntary sectors and in education and the health service, although it has largely been abandoned in the private sector.

Arguments for

Service-related pay is supported by many unions because they perceive it as being fair – everyone is treated equally. It is felt that linking pay to time in the job rather than performance or competence avoids the partial and ill-informed judgements about people that managers are prone to make. Some people believe that the principle of rewarding people for loyalty through continued service is a good one.

Arguments against

The arguments against service-related pay are that:

- it is inequitable in the sense that an equal allocation of pay increases according to service does not recognize the fact that some people will be contributing more than others and should be rewarded accordingly;
- it does not encourage good performance; indeed, it rewards poor performance equally;
- it is based on the assumption that performance improves with experience, but this is not automatically the case – it has been said that a person with five years' experience may in practice only have had one year's experience repeated five times;
- it can be expensive – everyone may drift to the top of the scale, especially in times of low staff turnover, but the cost of their pay is not justified by the added value they provide.

The arguments against service-related pay have convinced most managements, although some are concerned about managing any other form of contingent-pay schemes (incremental pay scales do not need to be managed at all). They may also have to face strong resistance from their unions and can be unsure of what exit strategy they should adopt if they want to change. They may therefore stick with the *status quo*.

CHOICE OF APPROACH

The first choice is whether or not to have contingent pay related to performance, competence, contribution or skill. Public or voluntary sector organizations with fixed incremental systems (pay spines), where progression is solely based on service, may want to retain them because they do not depend on possibly biased judgements by managers and they are perceived as being fair – everyone gets the same – and easily managed. However, the fairness of such systems can be questioned. Is it fair for a poor performer to be paid more than a good performer simply for being there?

The alternatives to fixed increments are either spot rates or some form of contingent pay. Spot rate systems in their purest form are generally only used for senior managers, shop floor or retail workers, and in smaller organizations and new businesses where the need for formal practices has not yet been recognized.

If it is decided that a more formal type of contingent pay for individuals should be adopted, the choice is between the various types of performance pay, competence-related or contribution-related pay and skill-based pay, as summarized in Table 47.1. The alternative to individual contingent pay is team pay, as described later. Pay related to organizational performance is another alternative, although some organizations have such schemes in addition to individual contingent pay.

READINESS FOR INDIVIDUAL CONTINGENT PAY

The 10 questions to be answered when assessing readiness for individual contingent pay are:

1. Is it believed that contingent pay will benefit the organization in the sense of enhancing its ability to achieve its strategic goals?
2. Are there valid and reliable means of measuring performance?
3. Is there a competency framework and are there methods of assessing levels of competency objectively (or could such a framework be readily developed)?

Table 47.1 Comparison of individual contingent pay schemes

Type of scheme	Main features	Advantages	Disadvantages	When appropriate
Performance-related pay	Increases to basic pay or bonuses are related to assessment of performance	May motivate (but this is uncertain) Links reards to objectives Meets the need to be rewarded for achievement Delivers message that good performance is important and will be rewarded	May *not* motivate Relies on judgements of performance which may be subjective Prejudicial to teamwork Focuses on outputs, not quality Relies on good performance management processes Difficult to manage well	For people who are likely to be motivated by money In organizations with a performance-orientated culture When performance can be measured objectively
Competence-related pay	Pay increases are related to the level of competence	Focus attention on need to achieve higher levels of competence Encourages competence development Can be integrated with other applications of competency-based HR management	Assessment of competence levels may be difficult Ignores outputs – danger of paying for competences that will not be used Relies on well-trained and committed line managers	As part of an integrated approach to HRM where competencies are used across a number of activities Where competence is a key factor where it may be inappropriate or hard to measure outputs Where well-established competency frameworks exist

continued

Table 47.1 *continued*

Type of scheme	Main features	Advantages	Disadvantages	When appropriate
Contribution-related pay	Increases in pay or bonuses are related both to inputs (competence) and outputs (performance)	Rewards people not only for what they do but how they do it	As for both PRP and competence-related pay – it may be hard to measure contribution and it is difficult to manage well	When it is believed that a well-rounded approach covering both inputs and outputs is appropriate
Skill-based pay	Increments related to the acquisition of skills	Encourages and rewards the acquisition of skills	Can be expensive when people are paid for skills they don't use	On the shop floor or in retail organizations
Service-related pay	Increments related to service in grade	No scope for bias, easy to manage	Fails to reward those who contribute more	Where this is the traditional approach and trade unions oppose alternatives

4. Are there effective performance management processes that line managers believe in and carry out conscientiously?
5. Are line managers willing to assess performance or contribution and capable of doing so?
6. Are line managers capable of making and communicating contingent pay decisions?
7. Is the HR function capable of providing advice and guidance to line managers on managing contingent pay?
8. Can procedures be developed to ensure fairness and consistency in assessments and pay decisions?
9. Are employees and trade unions willing to accept the scheme?
10. Do employees trust management to deliver the deal?

DEVELOPING AND IMPLEMENTING INDIVIDUAL CONTINGENT PAY

The 10 steps required to develop and implement individual contingent pay are:

1. Analyse culture, strategy and existing processes, including the grade and pay structure, performance management and methods of progressing pay or awarding cash bonuses.
2. Decide which form of contingent pay is most appropriate.
3. Set out aims that demonstrate how contribution pay will help to achieve the organization's strategic goals.
4. Communicate aims to line managers' staff and involve them in the development of the scheme.
5. Determine how the scheme will operate.
6. Develop or improve performance management processes covering the selection of performance measures, decisions on competence requirements, methods of agreeing objectives and the procedure for conducting joint reviews.
7. Communicate intentions to line managers and staff.
8. Pilot test the scheme and amend as necessary.
9. Provide training to all concerned.
10. Launch the scheme and evaluate its effectiveness after the first review.

TEAM-BASED PAY

Team-based pay provides rewards to teams or groups of employees carrying out similar and related work that is linked to the performance of the team. Performance may be measured in terms of outputs and/or the achievement of service delivery standards. The quality of the output and the opinion of customers about service levels are also often taken into account.

As described by Armstrong and Ryden (1996), team pay is usually paid in the form of a bonus that is shared amongst team members in proportion to their base rate of pay (much less frequently, it is shared equally). Individual team members may be eligible for competence-related or skill-based pay but not for performance-related pay.

Advantages of team pay

Team pay can:

- encourage effective teamworking and co-operative behaviour;

- clarify team goals and priorities;
- enhance flexible working within teams;
- encourage multiskilling;
- provide an incentive for the team collectively to improve performance;
- encourage less effective team members to improve to meet team standards.

Disadvantages of team pay

The disadvantages of team pay are that:

- it only works in cohesive and mature teams;
- individuals may resent the fact that their own efforts are not rewarded specifically;
- peer pressure, which compels individuals to conform to group norms, could be undesirable.

Conditions suitable for team pay

Team pay is more likely to be appropriate when:

- teams can be readily identified and defined;
- teams are well established;
- the work carried out by team members is interrelated – team performance depends on the collective efforts of team members;
- targets and standards of performance can be determined and agreed readily with team members;
- acceptable measurements of team performance compared with targets and standards are available;
- generally, the formula for team pay meets the criteria for performance pay.

ORGANIZATION-WIDE SCHEMES

Organization-wide bonus schemes pay sums of money to employees that are related to company or plant-wide performance. They are designed to share the company's prosperity with its employees and thus to increase their commitment to its objectives and values. Because they do not relate reward directly to individual effort, they are not effective as direct motivators, although gain-sharing schemes can focus directly on what needs to be done to improve performance and so get employees involved in productivity improvement or cost-reduction plans. The two main types of schemes are gain sharing and profit sharing.

Gain sharing

Gain sharing is a formula-based company or factory-wide bonus plan that provides for employees to share in the financial gains resulting from increases in added value or another measure of productivity. The link between their efforts and the payout can usefully be made explicit by involving them in analysing results and identifying areas for improvement.

Profit sharing

Profit sharing is the payment to eligible employees of sums in the form of cash or shares related to the profits of the business. The amount shared may be determined by a published or unpublished formula or entirely at the discretion of management. Profit sharing differs from gain sharing in that the former is based on more than improved productivity. A number of factors outside the individual employee's control contribute to profit. Gain sharing aims to relate its payouts much more specifically to productivity and performance improvements within the control of employees. It is not possible to use profit-sharing schemes as direct incentives as for most employees the link between individual effort and the reward is so remote. But they can increase identification with the company and many managements operate profit-sharing schemes because they believe that they should share the company's success with its employees.

Share ownership schemes

There are two main forms of share ownership plans: Share Incentive Plans (SIPS) and Save-As-You-Earn (SAYE) schemes. These can be Inland Revenue-approved and if so, produce tax advantages as well as linking financial rewards in the longer term to the prosperity of the company.

Share incentive plans

Share incentive plans must be Inland Revenue-approved. They provide employees with a tax-efficient way of purchasing shares in their organization to which the employer can add 'free', 'partnership' or 'matching' shares and which can also be issued as shares. There is a limit to the amount of free shares that can be provided to employees (£3,000 a year in 2004). Employees can use up to £1,500 a year (in 2004) out of pre-tax and pre-National Insurance Contributions pay to buy partnership shares, and employers can give matching shares at a ratio of up to two matching shares for each partnership share.

Save-As-You-Earn schemes

SAYE schemes must be Inland Revenue-approved. They provide employees with the option to buy shares in the company in three, five or seven years' time at today's price, or a discount of up to 20 per cent of that price. Purchases are made from a savings account to which the employee pays an agreed sum each month. The monthly savings must be between £5 and £250. Income tax is not chargeable when the option is granted.

48

Employee benefits, pensions and allowances

EMPLOYEE BENEFITS

Definition

Employee benefits are elements of remuneration given in addition to the various forms of cash pay. They also include items that are not strictly remuneration, such as annual holidays.

Objectives

The objectives of the employee benefits policies and practices of an organization are to:

- provide an attractive and competitive total remuneration package which both attracts and retains high-quality employees;
- provide for the personal needs of employees;
- increase the commitment of employees to the organization;
- provide for some people a tax-efficient method of remuneration.

Note that these objectives do not include 'to motivate employees'. This is because the normal benefits provided by a business seldom make a direct and immediate impact on performance. They can, however, create more favourable attitudes towards the business which can improve commitment and organizational performance in the longer term.

Main types of employee benefits

Benefits can be divided into the following categories:

- *Pension schemes*: these are generally regarded as the most important employee benefit.
- *Personal security*: these are benefits which enhance the individual's personal and family security with regard to illness, health, accident or life insurance.
- *Financial assistance*: loans, house purchase schemes, relocation assistance and discounts on company goods or services.
- *Personal needs*: entitlements which recognize the interface between work and domestic needs or responsibilities, eg holidays and other forms of leave, child care, career breaks, retirement counselling, financial counselling and personal counselling in times of crisis, fitness and recreational facilities.
- *Company cars and petrol*: still a much appreciated benefit in spite of the fact that cars are now more heavily taxed.
- *Other benefits:* which improve the standard of living of employees such as subsidized meals, clothing allowances, refund of telephone costs, mobile phones (as a 'perk' rather than a necessity) and credit card facilities.
- *Intangible benefits*: characteristics of the organization which contribute to the quality of working life and make it an attractive and worthwhile place in which to be employed.

Taxation

It should be remembered that most benefits are taxable as 'benefits in kind', the notable exceptions being approved pension schemes, meals where these are generally available to employees, car parking spaces, professional subscriptions and accommodation where this is used solely for performing the duties of the job.

Flexible benefits

Flexible benefit schemes (sometimes called cafeteria schemes) allow employees to decide, within certain limits, on the make-up of their benefits package. Schemes can allow for a choice within benefits or a choice between benefits. Employees are allocated an individual allowance to spend on benefits. This allowance can be used to switch between benefits, to choose new ones or to alter the rate of cover within existing benefits. Some core benefits such as sick pay may lie outside the scheme and cannot be 'flexed'. Employees can shift the balance of their total reward package between pay and benefits, either adding to their benefits allowance by sacrificing salary or taking any unspent benefit allowance as cash.

Flexible benefit schemes provide employees with a degree of choice on what benefits they want, according to their needs. A flexible benefit policy can save employers money on benefits that are neither wanted nor needed.

Total remuneration

The concept of total remuneration is based on the principle of treating all aspects of pay and benefits provision as a whole. The cost to the business and the value to the individual of each element can be assessed with the object of adjusting the package according to organizational and individual needs. Consideration can also be given to the overall competitiveness of the total package in the market place.

OCCUPATIONAL PENSION SCHEMES

The reasons for having a worthwhile pension scheme are that it:

- demonstrates that the organization is a good employer;
- attracts and retains high-quality people by helping to maintain competitive levels of total remuneration;
- indicates that the organization is concerned about the long-term interests of its employees.

Definition

An occupational pension scheme is an arrangement under which an employer provides pensions for employees when they retire, income for the families of members who die, and deferred benefits to members who leave. A 'group scheme' is the typical scheme which provides for a number of employees.

Operation

Occupational pension schemes are administered by trusts which are supposed to be outside the employer's control. The trustees are responsible for the pension fund from which pension benefits are paid.

The pension fund is fed by contributions from employers and usually (but not always) employees. The size of the fund and its capacity to meet future commitments depend both on the size of contributions and on the income the trustees can generate. They do this by investing fund money with the help of advisers in stocks, shares and other securities, or through an insurance company. In the latter case, insurance companies offer either a *managed fund* – a pool of money managed by the insurance company for a number of clients – or a *segregated fund* which is managed for a single client.

Contributions

In a *contributory scheme* employees as well as employers make contributions to the pension fund. Pensionable earnings are total earnings from which may be excluded such payments as overtime or special bonuses. A sum equal to the State flat rate pension may also be excluded.

The level of contributions varies considerably, although in a typical contributory scheme, employees would be likely to contribute about 5 per cent of their earnings and employers would contribute approximately twice that amount.

Approved scheme

Members of an occupational scheme that has been approved by the Inland Revenue (an *approved scheme*) obtain full tax relief on their contributions. The company also recovers tax on its contributions and the income tax deductible from gains realized on UK investments. This makes a pension fund the most tax-efficient form of saving available in the UK.

Employers can establish unapproved pension schemes which provide benefits in excess of approved schemes but at the expense of the generous tax allowances for the latter type of scheme.

Retiring age and sex discrimination

Traditionally, the retiring age was 65 for men and 60 for women. However, under the Sex Discrimination Act (1986), it is unlawful for employers to require female employees to retire at an earlier age than male employees. In its judgement on the *Barber v Guardian Royal Exchange* case on 17 May 1990 the European Court ruled that pension was 'pay' under Article 119 of the Treaty of Rome (which provided for equal pay) and that it was unlawful to discriminate between men and women with regard to pension rights. It has since been agreed that pensions would not be considered as pay prior to 17 May 1990.

Benefits statements

Every member of an occupational scheme is entitled to an annual statement setting out his or her prospective benefits.

Types of occupational pension schemes

A defined benefit or *final salary* group pension scheme offers a guaranteed pension, part of which may be surrendered for a tax-free cash sum. In its final pay or salary form, the pension is a fraction of final pensionable earnings for each year of service (typically 1/60th). To achieve the maximum two-thirds pension in a 1/60th scheme would therefore take 40 years' service. Defined benefit schemes provide employers with a predictable level of pension. But for employers, they can be costly and unpredictable because they have to contribute whatever is necessary to buy the promised benefits.

In a defined contribution or *money purchase* scheme employers fix the contributions they want to pay for employees by undertaking to pay a defined percentage of earnings irrespective of the benefits available on retirement. The retirement pension is therefore whatever annual payment can be purchased with the money accumulated in the fund for a member.

A defined contribution scheme offers the employee unpredictable benefits because these depend on the total value of the contributions invested, the investment returns achieved and the rate at which the accumulated fund can be converted into pension on retirement. For the employer, however, it offers certainty of costs.

Stakeholder pensions

All employers with five or more people on their payroll are obliged to provide access to a stakeholder pension for employees who have no access to a company pension. Stakeholder pensions will be money-purchase schemes and, initially, employers do not have to make a contribution and employees are not required to take them out (although these conditions may be changed). Employers can designate a stakeholder scheme from a provider but in choosing one are required to consult with the employees concerned.

Developments in pension provision

As the CIPD (2003b) comments:

> The last decade has seen a significant change in the nature of occupational schemes offered to new employees. There has been a shift away from defined benefit schemes for new employees in favour of defined contribution schemes. There has also been a significant growth in mixed and hybrid types of pension plan, and a reduction in the proportion of the total workforce who are members of occupational schemes of any type.

The move away from defined benefit (final salary) schemes has largely been because of the increasing and unpredictable costs of such schemes. But as the CIPD states, 'An important driver of these changes has been demographic, with a declining birth rate and fall in the average retirement age, combining with the significant increase in life expectancy to push up scheme costs. Greater labour market flexibility may also be a contributory factor.' Some organizations such as the civil service are introducing money purchase schemes to help to recruit and retain younger employees in specialist fields.

The contribution of HR

As suggested by the CIPD, HR can contribute to the development of pensions policy by:

- defining and communicating clear pension goals aligned to the needs of the organization and its staff;
- advising on the design and implementation of appropriate schemes to achieve these goals – flexibility and choice on provision are important components of these designs to meet the needs of a more diverse workforce;
- educating managers and employees so that they can take on personal responsibility and make informed choices on the way they want to work and move into retirement, with the appropriate pension provision to achieve this.

ALLOWANCES AND OTHER PAYMENTS TO EMPLOYEES

The main areas in which allowances and other special payments may be made to employees are:

- *Location allowances* – London and large town allowances may be paid because of housing and other cost-of-living differentials. Allowances are paid as an addition to basic pay although many employers in effect consolidate them by paying the local market rate which takes into account explicit or implicit location allowances and costs.
- *Subsistence allowances* – the value of subsistence allowances for accommodation and meals varies greatly between organizations. Some have set rates depending on location or the grade of employee. Others allow 'reasonable' rates without any set scale but usually, and desirably, with guidelines on acceptable hotel and meal costs.
- *Overtime payments* – most manual workers are eligible for paid overtime as well as many staff employees up to management level. Higher-paid staff may receive time off in lieu if they work longer hours. Typically organizations that make overtime payments give time and a half as an overtime premium from Monday to Saturday, with double time paid on Sundays and statutory holidays. Some firms also pay double time from around noon on Saturday. Work on major statutory holidays such as Christmas Day and Good Friday often attracts higher overtime premiums.
- *Shift payments* are made at rates which usually vary according to the shift arrangement. A premium of, say, one-third of basic pay may be given to people working nights while those on an early or late day shift may receive less, a premium, say, of one-fifth of basic pay.
- *Stand-by and call-out allowances* may be made to those who have to be available to come in to work when required. The allowance may be made as a standard payment added to basic pay. Alternatively, special payments may be made for unforeseen call-outs.

49

Managing reward systems

Managing reward systems is a complex and demanding business. This chapter deals with the subject in seven parts:

1. Preparation and use of forecasts and budgets.
2. Evaluating the reward system.
3. Pay reviews.
4. Control.
5. Reward procedures.
6. Responsibility for reward management.
7. Communicating to employees.

REWARD BUDGETS AND FORECASTS

Reward budgets and forecasts are concerned with overall payroll costs and the costs of general and individual pay increases.

Payroll budgets

A payroll budget is a statement of the planned allocation and use of human resources required to meet the objectives of the organization. It is usually a major part of the master budget. The budget is based on forecast levels of activity which determine the number of people required. The annual payroll budget is a product of the number of people to be employed and the rates at which they will be paid during the budget year. It will incorporate the cost of benefits (eg pensions contributions) and the employer's National Insurance contributions. The budget will be adjusted to take account of forecasts covering increases or decreases to employee numbers, the likely costs of general and individual pay reviews, changes to the pay structure and increases to the cost of employee benefits.

Managers in charge of budget centres will have their own payroll budget which they have to account for. This budget will incorporate forecasts of pay increases as well as the manager's assessment of the numbers of employees needed in different categories. Managers will be required to ensure that individual pay increases are made within that budget, which may, however, be flexed upwards or downwards if activity levels or the assumptions on which forecast pay increases were based change.

Review budgets

A general review budget simply incorporates the forecast costs of any across-the-board pay increases that may be granted or negotiated during the budget year. Individual performance review budgets may be expressed as the percentage increase to the payroll that can be allowed for performance, skill-based or competence-related increases. The size of the budget will be affected by the following considerations:

- the amount the organization believes it can afford to pay on the basis of budgeted revenue, profit, and payroll costs;
- the organization's policies on pay progression – the size and range of increases;
- any allowances that may need to be made for increasing individual rates of pay to remove anomalies, for example after a job evaluation exercise.

The basic budget would be set for the organization as a whole but, within that figure, departmental budgets could be flexed to reflect different needs and circumstances. Pay modelling techniques which cost alternative pay review proposals on distributions of awards can be used to prepare individual review budgets. Increasingly, organizations are replacing individual review budgets with a total payroll budgeting approach. This means that departmental heads have to fund individual increases from their payroll budget. In effect, they are expected to add value from performance pay or at least ensure that it is self-financing.

EVALUATING THE REWARD SYSTEM

The reward system should be audited regularly to assess its effectiveness, the extent to which it is adding value and its relevance to the present and future needs of the organization. This audit should include an assessment of opinions about the reward system by its key users and those who are affected by it. This leads to a diagnosis of strengths and weaknesses and an assessment of what needs to be done and why.

The operation of the reward system should be monitored continually by the HR department through such audits and by the use of compa-ratios and attrition analysis as discussed below. In particular it is necessary to analyse data on upgradings, the effectiveness with which performance management processes are functioning and the amount paid out on pay-for-performance schemes and the impact they are making on results.

Internal relativities should also be monitored by carrying out periodic studies of the differentials that exist vertically within departments or between categories of employees. The studies should examine the differentials built into the pay structure and also analyse the differences between the average rates of pay at different levels. If it is revealed that because of changes in roles or the impact of pay reviews differentials no longer properly reflect increases in job values and/or are no longer 'felt fair', then further investigations to establish the reasons for this situation can be conducted and, if necessary, corrective action taken.

External relativities should be monitored by tracking movements in market rates by studying published data and conducting pay surveys as described in Chapter 42.

No reward innovations should take place unless a cost–benefit analysis has forecast that they will add value. The audit and monitoring processes should establish the extent to which the predicted benefits have been obtained and check on the costs against the forecast.

Compa-ratio analysis

A compa-ratio (short for comparative ratio) measures the relationship in a graded pay structure between actual and policy rates of pay as a percentage. The policy value used is the midpoint or reference point in a pay range which represents the 'target rate' for a fully competent individual in any job in the grade. This point is aligned to market rates in accordance with the organization's market stance policy.

Compa-ratios are used to define where an individual is placed in a pay range. The analysis of compa-ratios indicates what action might have to be taken to slow down or accelerate increases if compa-ratios are too high or too low compared with the policy level. This process is sometimes called 'midpoint management'.

Compa-ratios are calculated as follows:

$$\frac{\text{actual rate of pay}}{\text{mid or reference point of range}} \times 100$$

A compa-ratio of 100 per cent means that actual and policy pay are the same. Compa-ratios which are higher or lower than 100 per cent mean that, respectively, pay is above or below the policy target rate. For example, if the target (policy) rate in a range were £20,000 and the average pay of all the individuals in the grade were £18,000, the compa-ratio would be 90 per cent.

Compa-ratios establish differences between policy and practice and the reasons for such differences need to be established.

Analysing attrition

Attrition or slippage takes place when employees enter jobs at lower rates of pay than the previous incumbents. If this happens payroll costs will go down given an even flow of starters and leavers and a consistent approach to the determination of rates of pay. In theory attrition can help to finance pay increases within a range. It has been claimed that fixed incremental systems can be entirely self-financing because of attrition, but the conditions under which this can be attained are so exceptional that it probably never happens.

Attrition can be calculated by the formula: total percentage increase to payroll arising from general or individual pay increases minus total percentage increase in average rates of pay. If it can be proved that attrition is going to take place, the amount involved can be taken into account as a means of at least partly financing individual pay increases. Attrition in a pay system with regular progression through ranges and a fairly even flow of starters and leavers is typically between 2 and 3 per cent but this should not be regarded as a norm.

CONDUCTING PAY REVIEWS

Pay reviews are general or 'across-the-board' reviews in response to movements in the cost of living or market rates or following pay negotiations with trade unions, or individual reviews that determine the pay progression of individuals in relation to their performance or contribution, or individual reviews. They are one of the most visible aspects of reward management (the other is job grading) and are an important means of implementing the organization's reward policies and demonstrating to employees how these policies operate.

Employees expect that general reviews will maintain the purchasing power of their pay by compensating for increases in the cost of living. They will want their levels of pay to be competitive with what they could earn outside. And they will want to be rewarded fairly and equitably for the contribution they make.

General reviews

General reviews take place when employees are given an increase in response to general market rate movements, increases in the cost of living, or union negotiations. General reviews are often combined with individual reviews, but employees are usually informed of the general and individual components of any increase they receive. Alternatively the general review may be conducted separately to enable better control to be achieved over costs and to focus employees' attention on the performance-related aspect of their remuneration.

Some organizations have completely abandoned the use of across-the-board reviews. They argue that the decision on what people should be paid should be an individual matter, taking into account the personal contribution people are making and their 'market worth' – how they as individuals are valued in the marketplace. This enables the organization to adopt a more flexible approach to allocating pay increases in accordance with the perceived value of individuals to the organization.

The steps required to conduct a general review are:

1. Decide on the budget.
2. Analyse data on pay settlements made by comparable organizations and rates of inflation.
3. Conduct negotiations with trade unions as required.
4. Calculate costs.
5. Adjust the pay structure – by either increasing the pay brackets of each grade by the percentage general increase or by increasing pay reference points by the overall percentage and applying different increases to the upper or lower limits of the bracket, thus altering the shape of the structure.
6. Inform employees.

Individual reviews

Individual pay reviews determine contingent pay increases or bonuses. The e-reward 2004 survey of contribution pay found that the average size of the contingent pay awards made by respondents to the CIPD 2003 performance management survey (Armstrong and Baron, 2004) was 3.3 per cent. Individual awards may be based on ratings, an overall assessment that does not depend on ratings, or ranking, as discussed below.

Individual pay reviews based on ratings

Managers propose increases on the basis of their performance management ratings within a given pay review budget and in accordance with pay review guidelines. Forty-two per cent of the respondents to the CIPD 2003/4 performance management survey used ratings to inform contingent pay decisions. Approaches to rating were discussed in Chapter 33.

There may be a direct link between the rating and the pay increase, for example:

Rating	% Increase
A	6
B	4
C	3
D	2
E	0

Alternatively, a pay matrix may be used which relates pay increases to both the rating and position in the pay range. Many people argue that linking performance management too explicitly to pay prejudices the essential developmental nature of performance management. However, realistically it is accepted that decisions on performance-related or contribution-related increases have to be based on some form of assessment. One solution is to 'decouple' performance management and the pay review by holding them several months apart, and 45 per cent of the respondents to the CIPD 2003/4 survey (Armstrong and Baron, 2004) separated performance management reviews from pay reviews (43 per cent of the respondents to the e-reward 2004 survey separated the review). There is still a read-across but it is not so immediate. Some try to do without formulaic approaches (ratings and pay matrices) altogether, although it is impossible to dissociate contingent pay completely from some form of assessment.

Doing without ratings

Twenty-seven per cent of the respondents to the 2004 e-reward survey of contingent pay did without ratings. The percentage of respondents to the 2003/4 CIPD performance management survey who did not use ratings was 52 per cent (this figure is too high to be fully reliable and may have been inflated by those who treat service-related increments, which do not depend on ratings, as contingent pay). One respondent to the e-reward survey explained that in the absence of ratings, the approach they used was 'informed subjectivity', which meant considering ongoing performance in the form of overall contribution.

Some companies adopt what might be called an holistic approach. Managers propose where people should be placed in the pay range for their grade, taking into account their contribution and pay relative to others in similar jobs, their potential, and the relationship of their current pay to market rates. The decision may be expressed in the form of a statement that an individual is now worth £21,000 rather than £20,000. The increase is 5 per cent, but what counts is the overall view about the value of a person to the organization, not the percentage increase to that person's pay.

Ranking

Ranking is carried out by managers who place staff in a rank order according to an overall assessment of relative contribution or merit and then distribute performance ratings through the rank order. The top 10 per cent could get an A rating, the next 15 per cent a B rating, and so on. The ratings determine the size of the reward. But ranking depends on what could be invidious comparisons and only works when there are a number of people in similar jobs to be ranked.

Guidelines to managers on conducting individual pay reviews

Whichever approach is adopted, guidelines have to be issued to managers on how they should conduct reviews. These guidelines will stipulate that they must keep within their budgets and may indicate the maximum and minimum increases that can be awarded, with an indication of how awards could be distributed. For example, when the budget is 4 per cent overall, it might be suggested that a 3 per cent increase should be given to the majority of their staff and the others given higher or lower increases as long as the total percentage increase does not exceed the budget. Managers in some companies are instructed that they must follow a forced pattern of distribution but, only 8 per cent of the respondents to the 2003/4 CIPD survey used this method.

To help them to explore alternatives, managers may be provided with a spreadsheet facility in which the spreadsheets contain details of the existing rates of staff and which can be used to model alternative distributions on a 'what if' basis. Managers may also be encouraged to 'fine tune' their pay recommendations to ensure that individuals are on the right track within their grade according to their level of performance, competence and time in the job compared with their peers. To do this, they need guidelines on typical rates of progression in relation to performance, skill or competence, and specific guidance on what they can and should do. They also need information on the positions of their staff in the pay structure relative to the policy guidelines.

Conducting individual pay reviews

The steps required to conduct an individual pay review are:

1. Agree budget.
2. Prepare and issue guidelines on the size, range and distribution of awards and on methods of conducting the review.
3. Provide advice and support.
4. Review proposals against budget and guidelines and agree modifications to them if necessary.
5. Summarize and cost proposals and obtain approval.
6. Update payroll.
7. Inform employees.

It is essential to provide advice, guidance and training to line managers as required. Some managers will be confident and capable from the start; others will have a lot to learn.

CONTROL

Control over the implementation of pay policies generally and payroll costs in particular will be easier if it is based on:

- a clearly defined and understood pay structure;
- specific pay review guidelines and budgets;
- defined procedures for grading jobs and fixing rates of pay;
- clear statements of the degree of authority managers have at each level to decide on rates of pay and increases;
- an HR function which is capable of monitoring the implementation of pay policies and providing the information and guidance managers require and has the authority and resources (including computer software) to do so;
- a systematic process for monitoring the implementation of pay policies and costs against budgets.

REWARD PROCEDURES

Reward management procedures are required to achieve and monitor the implementation of reward management policies. They deal with methods of fixing pay on appointment or promotion and dealing with anomalies. They will also refer to methods of appealing against grading or pay decisions, usually through the organization's normal appeals procedure.

Procedures for grading jobs

The procedures for grading new jobs or re-grading existing ones should lay down that grading or re-grading can only take place after a proper job evaluation study. It is necessary to take action to control grade drift (unjustified upgradings) by insisting that this procedure is followed. Pressures to upgrade because of market forces or difficulties in recruitment or retention should be resisted. These problems should be addressed by such methods as market premiums or creating special market groups of jobs.

Fixing rates of pay on appointment

Line managers should have a major say in pay offers and some freedom to negotiate when necessary, but they should be required to take account of relevant pay policy guidelines which should set out the circumstances in which pay offers above the minimum of the range can be made. It is customary to allow a reasonable degree of freedom to make offers up to a certain point, eg the 90 per cent level in an 80 to 120 per cent pay range. Pay policies frequently allow offers to be made up to the midpoint or reference point depending on the extent to which the recruit has the necessary experience, skills and competences. Offers above the midpoint should be exceptional because they would leave relatively little room for expansion. Such offers will sometimes be made because of market pressures, but they need to be very carefully considered because of the inevitably of grade drift unless the individual is promoted fairly soon. If the current rates are too low to attract good candidates, it may be necessary to reconsider the scales or to agree on special market rate premiums. To keep the latter under control, it is advisable to require that they should only be awarded if they are authorized by the personnel department or a more senior manager. Many organizations require that all offers should be vetted and approved by a member of the personnel function and/or a higher authority.

Promotion increases

Promotion increases should be meaningful, say 10 per cent or more. They should not normally take the promoted employee above the midpoint or reference point in the pay range for his or her new job so that there is adequate scope for performance-related increases. One good reason for having reasonably wide differentials is to provide space for promotions.

Dealing with anomalies

Within any pay structure, however carefully monitored and maintained, anomalies will occur and they need to be addressed during a pay review. Correction of anomalies will require higher level increases for those who are under-paid relative to their performance and time in the job, and lower levels of increase for those who are correspondingly over-paid. It is worth noting that over-payment anomalies cannot be corrected in fixed incremental structures, and this is a major disadvantage of such systems. The cost of anomaly correction should not be huge in normal circumstances if at every review managers are encouraged to 'fine tune' their pay recommendations as suggested earlier.

In a severely anomalous situation, which may be found at the implementation stage of a new structure or at a major review, a longer-term correction programme may be necessary either to mitigate the demotivating effects of reducing relative rates of pay or to spread costs over a number of years.

As well as individual anomaly correction there may be a need to correct a historical tendency to over-pay or under-pay whole departments, divisions or functions by applying higher or lower levels of increases over a period of time. This would involve adjustments to pay review budgets and guidelines and, obviously, it would have to be handled with great care.

RESPONSIBILITY FOR REWARD

The trend is to devolve more responsibility for pay decisions to line managers, especially those concerned with individual pay reviews. But there are obvious dangers. These include inconsistency between managers' decisions, favouritism, prejudice (gender or racial) and illogical distributions of rewards. Research has shown that many managers tend not to differentiate between the performance of individual members of their staff. Ratings can be compressed, with most people clustered around the midpoint and very few staff rated as good or poor performers.

Devolving more authority to line managers may in principle be highly desirable but managers must be briefed thoroughly on their responsibilities, the organization's pay policies (including methods of progressing pay), the principles to be followed in conducting review and how they should interpret and apply pay review guidelines. The need to achieve equity and a reasonable degree of consistency across the organization should be emphasized. Managers should be given whatever training, guidance and help they need to ensure that they are capable of exercising their discretionary powers wisely. This training should cover:

- how information on market rates supplied by the personnel department should be interpreted and used;
- how data provided by the personnel department on the levels of pay and pay progression histories of individual members of staff and the distribution of pay by occupation throughout the department should be used as the basis for planning pay;
- methods of assessing performance and contribution levels;
- how to interpret any generic competence profiles to assess individual development needs and agree career pathways;
- how to assess competence requirements for specific roles (as they exist now or as they may develop), and how to counsel employees on the preparation of personal development plans;
- methods of reviewing progress in achieving these plans and in career development, and how to interpret information from these reviews when making pay decisions;
- generally, how to distribute rewards within budgets, fairly, equitably and consistently by reference to assessments of contribution, competence, progress or growth.
- the guidance available from the personnel function on how to manage pay – it should be emphasized that guidance must always be sought if line managers have any doubts as to how they should exercise their discretion.

Full devolution implies that the decisions of managers on pay increases are not reviewed and questioned as long as they keep within their budgets. However, it is usual for senior managers, personnel or pay specialists to monitor pay proposals to spot inconsistencies or what appear to be illogical recommendations, especially when the scheme is initiated or with newly appointed managers. The use of computerized personnel information systems makes it easier for managers to communicate their proposals and for the personnel department to monitor them. If the personnel department is involved, it should aim to provide support and guidance, not to act as a police force. Monitoring can be relaxed as managers prove that they are capable of making good pay decisions.

COMMUNICATING TO EMPLOYEES

Employee reward systems communicate messages to employees about the beliefs of the organization on what is felt to be important when valuing people in their roles. They deliver two messages: this is how we value your contribution; this is what we are paying for. It is therefore important to communicate to employees collectively about the reward policies and practices of the organization and individually about how those policies affect them – now and in the future. Transparency is essential.

What to communicate to employees generally

Employees generally should understand:

- the *reward policies* of the organization in setting pay levels, providing benefits and progressing pay;
- the *pay structure* – grades and pay ranges and how the structure is managed;
- the *benefits structure* – the range of benefits provided, with details of the pension scheme and other major benefits;
- *methods of grading and regrading jobs* – the job evaluation scheme and how it operates;
- *pay progression* – how pay progresses within the pay structure and how pay decisions affecting employees collectively and individually are made;
- *pay-for-performance schemes* – how individual, team and organization-wide schemes work and how employees can benefit from them;
- *pay for skill or competence* – how any skill-based or competence-based schemes work, the aims of the organization in using such schemes, and how employees can benefit from them;
- *performance management* – how performance management processes operate and the parts played by managers and employees;
- *reward developments and initiatives* – details of any changes to the reward system, the reasons for such changes, and how employees will be affected by them – the importance of doing this thoroughly cannot be over-emphasized.

What to communicate to individual employees

Individual employees should know and understand:

- their *job grade* and how it has been determined;
- the basis upon which their *present rate* of pay has been determined;
- the *pay opportunities* available to them – the scope in their grade for pay progression, the basis upon which their pay will be linked to their performance and the acquisition and effective use of skills and competences as their career develops, and what actions and behaviour are expected of them if their pay is to progress;
- *performance management* – how their performance will be reviewed and the part they play in agreeing objectives and formulating personal development and performance improvement plans;
- *the value of the employee benefits they receive* – the level of total remuneration provided for individuals by the organization, including the values of such benefits as pension and sick pay schemes;
- *appeals and grievances* – how they can appeal against grading and pay decisions or take up a grievance on any aspect of their remuneration.

Part X

Employee relations

EMPLOYEE RELATIONS DEFINED

Employee relations consist of all those areas of human resource management that involve relationships with employees – directly and/or through collective agreements where trade unions are recognized. Employee relations are concerned with generally managing the employment relationship as considered in Chapter 15.

These relationships deal with the agreement of terms and conditions of employment and with issues arising from employment. They will not necessarily be subject to collective agreements or joint regulation. Employee relations, therefore, cover a broader spectrum of the employment relationship than industrial relations, which are usually regarded as being essentially about dealings between managements and trade unions. This wider definition recognizes the move away from collectivism towards individualism in the ways in which employers relate to their employees. The move in this direction has been prompted by a growing insistence on management's prerogative supported by the philosophy of HRM, the requirement to meet competition with slimmer and more efficient organizations, a massive restructuring of industry in the 1980s, the 1980s concept of the market economy and free enterprise and by trade union legislation.

Employee relations practices include formal processes, procedures and channels of communication. It is important to remember, however, that employee relations are mainly conducted on a day-to-day informal basis by line managers and team leaders; without the framework of employment and employee relations policies but acting mainly on their own initiative.

PLAN

This part covers the broad subject of employee relations under the following headings:

- *the framework of employee relations – the conceptual framework to industrial relations. The HRM approach to employee relations developments in industrial relations and the parties involved (Chapter 50);*
- *employee relations processes, including collective bargaining (Chapter 51);*
- *negotiating and bargaining skills (Chapter 52);*
- *processes for employee involvement and participation (employee voice) and communications (Chapters 53 and 54).*

50

The framework of employee relations

The purpose of this chapter is to provide a review of the complex subject of employee relations. It starts with a summary of the elements of employee relations and then deals with the following industrial and employee relations concepts:

- the systems theory of industrial relations, which sees the subject as a system of regulations and rules;
- the types of regulations and rules contained in the system;
- the nature of collective bargaining and bargaining power;
- the unitarist and pluralist views about the basis of the relationship between management and trade unions in particular or employees in general;
- the reconciliation of interests;
- individualism and collectivism as approaches to employee relations;
- the voluntarist approach to industrial relations and its decline;
- human resource management (HRM) as a new paradigm for employee relations;
- the role of the employee relations function.

The chapter continues with a summary of developments in industrial relations and a review of the current industrial relations scene. The chapter concludes with a description of the various parties to industrial relations and the institutions, agencies and officers involved.

THE ELEMENTS OF EMPLOYEE RELATIONS

The elements of employee relations consist of:

- The formal and informal employment policies and practices of the organization.
- The development, negotiation and application of formal systems, rules and procedures for collective bargaining, handling disputes and regulating employment. These serve to determine the reward for effort and other conditions of employment, to protect the interests of both employees and their employers, and to regulate the ways in which employers treat their employees and how the latter are expected to behave at work.
- Policies and practices for employee voice and communications.
- The informal as well as the formal processes that take place in the shape of continuous interactions between managers and team leaders or supervisors on the one hand and employee representatives and individuals on the other. These may happen within the framework of formal agreements but are often governed by custom and practice and the climate of relationships that has been built up over the years.
- The philosophies and policies of the major players in the industrial relations scene: the government of the day, management and the trade unions.
- A number of parties each with different roles. These consist of the state, management, employers' organizations, the trade unions, individual managers and supervisors, HR managers, employee representatives or shop stewards and employees.
- The legal framework.
- A number of institutions such as the Advisory, Conciliation and Arbitration Service (ACAS) and the employment tribunals.
- The bargaining structures, recognition and procedural agreements and practices which have evolved to enable the formal system to operate.

INDUSTRIAL RELATIONS AS A SYSTEM OF RULES

Industrial relations can be regarded as a system or web of rules regulating employment and the ways in which people behave at work. The systems theory of industrial relations, as propounded by Dunlop (1958), states that the role of the system is to produce the regulations and procedural rules that govern how much is distributed in the bargaining process and how the parties involved, or the 'actors' in the industrial relations scene, relate to one another. According to Dunlop, the output of the system takes the form of:

> The regulations and policies of the management hierarchy; the laws of any worker hierarchy; the regulations, degrees, decisions, awards or orders of governmental agencies; the rules and decisions of specialized agencies created by the management and worker hierarchies; collective bargaining arrangements and the customs and traditions of the work place.

The system is expressed in many more or less formal or informal guises: in legislation and statutory orders, in trade union regulations, in collective agreements and arbitration awards, in social conventions, in managerial decisions, and in accepted 'custom and practice'. The 'rules' may be defined and coherent, or ill-defined and incoherent. Within a plant the rules may mainly be concerned with doing no more than defining the *status quo* which both parties recognize as the norm from which deviations may be made only by agreement. In this sense, therefore, an industrial relations system is a normative system where a norm can be seen as a rule, a standard, or a pattern for action which is generally accepted or agreed as the basis upon which the parties concerned should operate.

Systems theory, however, does not sufficiently take into account the distribution of power between management and trade unions, nor the impact of the state. Neither does it adequately explain the role of the individual in industrial relations.

TYPES OF REGULATIONS AND RULES

Job regulation aims to provide a framework of minimum rights and rules. Internal regulation is concerned with procedures for dealing with grievances, redundancies or disciplinary problems and rules concerning the operation of the pay system and the rights of shop stewards. External regulation is carried out by means of employment legislation, the rules of trade unions and employers' associations, and the regulative content of procedural or substantive rules and agreements.

Procedural rules are intended to regulate conflict between the parties to collective bargaining, and when their importance is emphasized, a premium is being placed on industrial peace. *Substantive rules* settle the rights and obligations attached to jobs. It is interesting to note that in the UK, the parties to collective agreements have tended to concentrate more on procedural than on substantive rules. In the USA, where there is greater emphasis on fixed-term agreements, the tendency has been to rely more on substantive rules.

COLLECTIVE BARGAINING

The industrial relations system is regulated by the process of collective bargaining, defined by Flanders (1970) as a social process that 'continually turns disagreements into agreements in an orderly fashion'. Collective bargaining aims to establish by negotiation and discussion agreed rules and decisions on matters of mutual concern to employers and unions as well as methods of regulating the conditions governing employment.

It therefore provides a framework, often in the form of a collective agreement, within which the views of management and unions about disputed matters that could lead to industrial disorder can be considered with the aim of eliminating the causes of the disorder. Collective bargaining is a joint regulating process, dealing with the regulation of management in its relationships with work people as well as the regulation of conditions of employment. It has a political as well as an economic basis – both sides are interested in the distribution of power between them as well as the distribution of income.

Collective bargaining can be regarded as an exchange relationship in which wage–work bargains take place between employers and employees through the agency of a trade union. Traditionally, the role of trade unions as bargaining agents has been perceived as being to offset the inequalities of individual bargaining power between employers and employees in the labour market.

Collective bargaining can also be seen as a political relationship in which trade unions, as Chamberlain and Kuhn (1965) noted, share industrial sovereignty or power over those who are governed, the employees. The sovereignty is held jointly by management and union in the collective bargaining process.

Above all, collective bargaining is a power relationship that takes the form of a measure of power sharing between management and trade unions (although recently the balance of power has shifted markedly in the direction of management).

Bargaining power

The extent to which industrial sovereignty is shared by management with its trade unions (if at all) depends upon the relative bargaining powers of the two parties. Bargaining power can be defined as the ability to induce the other side to make a decision that it would otherwise not make. As Fox and Flanders (1969) commented:

'Power is the crucial variable which determines the outcome of collective bargaining.' It has been suggested by Hawkins (1979) that a crucial test of bargaining power is 'whether the cost to one side in accepting a proposal from the other is higher than the cost of not accepting it'. Singh (1989) has pointed out that bargaining power is not static but varies over time. He also notes that:

> Bargaining power is inherent in any situation where differences have to be reconciled. It is, however, not an end in itself and negotiations must not rely solely on bargaining power. One side may have enormous bargaining power, but to use it to the point where the other side feels that it is impossible to deal with such a party is to defeat the purpose of negotiations.

Atkinson (1989) asserts that:

- what creates bargaining power can be appraised in terms of subjective assessments by individuals involved in the bargaining process;
- each side can guess the bargaining preferences and bargaining power of the other side;
- there are normally a number of elements creating bargaining power.

Forms of collective bargaining

Collective bargaining takes two basic forms, as identified by Chamberlain and Kuhn (1965):

- *conjunctive bargaining*, which 'arises from the absolute requirement that some agreement – any agreement – may be reached so that the operations on which both are dependent may continue', and results in a 'working relationship in which each party agrees, explicitly or implicitly, to provide certain requisite services, to recognize certain seats of authority, and to accept certain responsibilities in respect of each other';
- *cooperative bargaining*, in which it is recognized that each party is dependent on the other and can achieve its objectives more effectively if it wins the support of the other.

A similar distinction was made by Walton and McKersie (1965), who referred to *distributive bargaining* as the 'complex system of activities instrumental to the attainment of one party's goals when they are in basic conflict with those of the other party' and to *integrative bargaining* as the 'system of activities which are not in fundamental conflict with those of the other party and which therefore can be integrated to some degree'. Such objectives are said to define 'an area of common concern, a purpose'.

THE UNITARY AND PLURALIST VIEWS

There are two basic views expressed about the basis of the relationship between management and trade unions in particular or employees in general: the unitary and the pluralist perspectives.

The unitary view is typically held by managements who see their function as that of directing and controlling the workforce to achieve economic and growth objectives. To this end, management believes that it is the rule-making authority. Management tends to view the enterprise as a unitary system with one source of authority – itself – and one focus of loyalty – the organization. It extols the virtue of teamwork, where everyone strives jointly to a common objective, everyone pulls their weight to the best of their ability, and everyone accepts their place and function gladly, following the leadership of the appointed manager or supervisor. These are admirable sentiments, but they sometimes lead to what McClelland (1963) referred to as an orgy of 'avuncular pontification' on the part of the leaders of industry. This unitary view, which is essentially autocratic and authoritarian, has sometimes been expressed in agreements as 'management's right to manage'. The philosophy of HRM with its emphasis on commitment and mutuality is based on the unitary perspective.

In contrast, the *pluralist view*, as described by Fox (1966), is that an industrial organization is a plural society, containing many related but separate interests and objectives which must be maintained in some kind of equilibrium. In place of a corporate unity reflected in a single focus of authority and loyalty, management has to accept the existence of rival sources of leadership and attachment. It has to face the fact that in Drucker's (1951) phrase, a business enterprise has a triple personality: it is at once an economic, a political and a social institution. In the first, it produces and distributes incomes. In the second, it embodies a system of government in which managers collectively exercise authority over the managed, but are also themselves involved in an intricate pattern of political relationships. Its third personality is revealed in the plant community, which evolves from below out of face-to-face relations based on shared interests, sentiments, beliefs and values among various groups of employees.

Pluralism conventionally regards the workforce as being represented by 'an opposition that does not seek to govern' (Clegg, 1976). Pluralism, as described by Cave (1994), involves 'a balance of power between two organized interests and a sufficient degree of trust within the relationship (usually) for each side to respect the other's legitimate and, on occasions, separate interests, and for both sides to refrain from pushing their interest separately to the point where it became impossible to keep the show on the road'. It has been noted by Guest (1995) that: 'The tradition of bargaining at plant or even organization level has reinforced a pluralistic concept.'

THE RECONCILIATION OF INTERESTS

The implication of the pluralistic approach to employee relations is that there has to be some process for reconciling different interests. This can be achieved through formal agreements where there are recognized trade unions or staff associations. The absence of these may indicate that management adopts a unitarist philosophy. But it is to be hoped that in these circumstances management's efforts to increase mutuality and gain commitment adopt a stakeholder or partnership approach which at least involves consultation with employees on how the joint interests of the organization and its members can best be satisfied.

The process of reconciling interests has been modelled by Gennard and Judge (1997), as shown in Figure 50.1.

INDIVIDUALISM AND COLLECTIVISM

Purcell (1987) argues that the distinction between pluralist and unitary frames of management has 'provided a powerful impetus to the debate about management style, but the mutually exclusive nature of these categories has limited further development'. Moreover, wide variations can be found within both the unitary and the pluralist approach. He therefore suggests an alternative distinction between 'individualism' – policies focusing on individual employees – and 'collectivism' – the extent to which groups of workers have an independent voice and participate in decision making with managers. He believes that companies can and do operate on both these dimensions of management style.

VOLUNTARISM AND ITS DECLINE

The essence of the systems theory of industrial relations is that the rules are jointly agreed by the representatives of the parties to employment relations; an arrangement

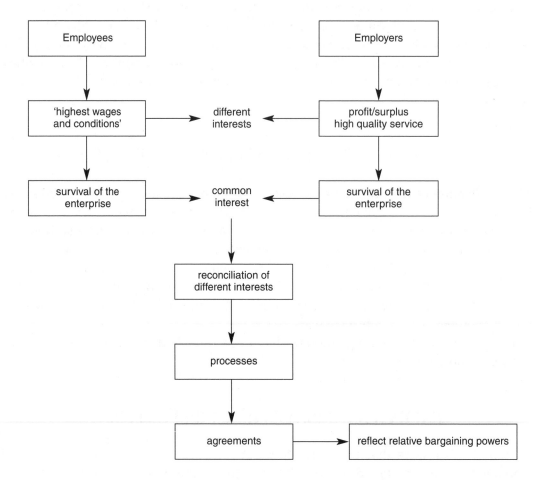

Figure 50.1 Employee relations: reconciliation of interests

which, it is believed, makes for readier acceptance than if they were imposed by a third party such as the State. This concept of voluntarism was defined by Kahn-Freund (1972) as 'the policy of the law to allow the two sides by agreement and practice to develop their own norms and their own sanctions and to abstain from legal compulsion in their collective relationship'. It was, in essence, voluntarism that came under attack by government legislation from 1974 onwards, including the principle of 'immunities' for industrial action and the closed shop.

THE HRM APPROACH TO EMPLOYEE RELATIONS

The HRM model

The philosophy of HRM has been translated into the following prescriptions, which constitute the HRM model for employee relations:

- a drive for commitment – winning the 'hearts and minds' of employees to get them to identify with the organization, to exert themselves more on its behalf and to remain in it, thus ensuring a return on their training and development;
- an emphasis on mutuality – getting the message across that 'we are all in this together' and that the interests of management and employees coincide;
- the organization of complementary forms of communication, such as team briefing, alongside traditional collective bargaining – ie approaching employees directly as individuals or in groups rather than through their representatives;
- a shift from collective bargaining to individual contracts;
- the use of employee involvement techniques such as quality circles or improvement groups;
- continuous pressure on quality – total quality management;
- increased flexibility in working arrangements, including multi-skilling, to provide for the more effective use of human resources, sometimes accompanied by an agreement to provide secure employment for the 'core' workers;
- emphasis on teamwork;
- harmonization of terms and conditions for all employees.

The key contrasting dimensions of traditional industrial relations and HRM have been presented by Guest (1995) as follows:

Table 50.1 Contrasting dimensions of industrial relations and HRM

Dimension	Industrial Relations	HRM
Psychological contract Behaviour references	Compliance Norms, custom and practice	Commitment Values/mission
Relationships	Low trust, pluralist, collective	High trust, unitarist, individual
Organization design	Formal roles, hierarchy, division of labour, managerial control	Flexible roles, flat structure, teamwork/autonomy, self control

Guest notes that this model aims to support the achievement of the three main sources of competitive advantage identified by Porter (1980), namely, innovation, quality and cost leadership. Innovation and quality strategies require employee commitment while cost leadership strategies are believed by many managements to be achievable only without a union. 'The logic of a market-driven HRM strategy is that where high organisational commitment is sought, unions are irrelevant. Where cost advantage is the goal, unions and industrial relations systems appear to carry higher costs.'

An HRM approach is still possible if trade unions are recognized by the organization. In this case, the strategy might be to marginalize or at least side-step them by dealing direct with employees through involvement and communications processes.

THE CONTEXT OF INDUSTRIAL RELATIONS

Industrial relations are conducted within the external context of the national political environment, the international context and the internal context of the organization.

The political context

The political context is formed by the government of the day. Conservative administrations from 1979 to 1997 set out to curb the power of the trade unions through legislation and succeeded to a degree. Labour administrations have not made any major changes to existing legislation except in the area of trade union recognition.

The European context

Employee relations in the UK are affected by European Union regulations and initiatives. A number of Articles in the original treaty of Rome referred to the promotion of improvements in working conditions and the need to develop dialogue between the two sides of industry. It seems likely that the conduct of employee relations in Britain will be increasingly affected by EU directives, such as those concerning works councils and working hours.

The organizational context

The need to 'take cost out of the business' has meant that employers have focused on the cost of labour – usually the highest and most easily reduced cost. Hence 'the lean organization' movement and large-scale redundancies, especially in manufacturing.

There has been pressure for greater flexibility and increased management control of operations, which has had a direct impact on employee relations policies and union agreements.

The widespread introduction of new technology and information technology has aimed to increase productivity by achieving higher levels of efficiency and reducing labour costs. Organizations are relying more on a core of key full-time employees, leaving the peripheral work to be undertaken by subcontractors and the increasing numbers of part-timers – women *and* men. This has reduced the number of employees who wish to join unions or remain trade union members.

DEVELOPMENTS IN INDUSTRIAL RELATIONS

Developments in the practice of industrial relations since the 1950s can be divided into the following phases:

1. The traditional system existing prior to the 1970s.
2. The Donovan analysis of 1968.
3. The interventionist and employment protection measures of the 1970s.
4. The 1980s programme for curbing what were perceived by the Conservative Government to be the excesses of rampant trade unionism.

The traditional system – to 1971

Relations prior to 1971 and indeed for most of the 1970s could be described as a system of collective representation designed to contain conflict. Voluntary collective bargaining between employees and employers' associations was the central feature of the system, and this process of joint regulation was largely concerned with pay and basic conditions of employment, especially hours of work in industry, and legal abstention on the part of the state and the judiciary. During this period and, in fact, for most of the twentieth century, the British system of industrial relations was characterized by a tradition of voluntarism.

The Donovan analysis

The high incidence of disputes and strikes, the perceived power of the trade unions and some well-publicized examples of shop steward militancy (although the majority were quite amenable) contributed to the pressure for the reform of industrial relations which led to the setting up of the Donovan Commission. This concluded in 1968 that the formal system of industry-wide bargaining was breaking down. Its key findings were that at plant level, bargaining was highly fragmented and ill-organized, based on informality and custom and practice. The Commission's prescription was for a continuation of voluntarism, reinforced by organized collective bargaining arrangements locally, thus relieving trade unions and employers' associations of the 'policing role', which they so often failed to carry out. This solution involved the creation of new, orderly and systematic frameworks for collective bargaining at plant level by means of formal negotiation and procedural agreements.

Since Donovan, comprehensive policies, structures and procedures to deal with pay and conditions, shop steward facilities, discipline, health and safety, etc have been developed at plant level to a substantial extent. The support provided by Donovan to the voluntary system of industrial relations was, however, underpinned by a powerful minority note of reservation penned by Andrew Shonfield in the 1968 report of the Royal Commission. He advocated a more interventionist approach, which began to feature in government policies in the 1970s.

Interventionism in the 1970s

The received wisdom in the 1960s, as reflected in the majority Donovan report, was that industrial relations could not be controlled by legislation. But the Industrial Relations Act introduced by the Conservative Government in 1971 ignored this belief and drew heavily on Shonfield's minority report. It introduced a strongly interventionist legal framework to replace the voluntary regulation of industrial relations systems. Trade unions lost their general immunity from legal action and had to register under the Act if they wanted any rights at all. Collective agreements were to become legally binding contracts and a number of 'unfair industrial practices' were proscribed. Individual workers were given the right to belong or not belong to a trade union but no attempt was made to outlaw the closed shop. But the Act failed to make any impact, being ignored or side-stepped by both trade unions and employers, although it did introduce the important general right of employees 'not to be unfairly dismissed'.

The Labour Government of 1974 promptly repealed the 1971 Industrial Relations Act and entered into a 'social contract' with the trade unions which incorporated an agreement that the Trades Union Congress (TUC) would support the introduction of a number of positive union rights. These included a statutory recognition procedure and in effect meant that the unions expressed their commitment to legal enforcement as a means of restricting management's prerogatives.

Statutory rights were also provided for minimum notice periods, statements of terms and conditions, redundancy payments and unfair dismissal.

The 1980s – curbing the trade unions

The strike-ridden 'winter of discontent' in 1978 and the return of a Conservative Government in 1979 paved the way for the ensuing step-by-step legislation which continued throughout the 1980s and into the early 1990s.

The ethos of the Conservative Governments in the 1980s was summed up by Phelps Brown (1990) as follows:

> People are no longer seen as dependent on society and bound by reciprocal relationship to it; indeed the very notion of society is rejected. Individuals are expected to shift for themselves and those who get into difficulties are thought to have only themselves to blame. Self-reliance, acquisitive individualism, the curtailment of public expenditure, the play of market forces instead of the restraints and directives of public policy, the prerogatives of management instead of the power of the unions, centralisation of power instead of pluralism.

The legislation on trade unions followed this ethos and was guided by an ideological analysis expressed in the 1981 Green Paper on *Trade Union Immunities* as follows: 'Industrial relations cannot operate fairly and efficiently or to the benefit of the nation as a whole if either employers or employees collectively are given predominant power – that is, the capacity effectively to dictate the behaviour of others.'

The government described industrial relations as 'the fundamental cause of weakness in the British economy', with strikes and restrictive practices inhibiting the country's ability to compete in international markets. The balance of bargaining power was perceived to have moved decisively in favour of trade unions which were described as 'irresponsible, undemocratic and intimidatory', while the closed shop was described as being destructive of the rights of the individual worker.

Developments since 1990

Kessler and Bayliss (1992) commented that 'the needs of employers have increasingly been towards enterprise orientated rather than occupationally orientated trade unions'. They also noted that: 'It is clear that the significance of industrial relations in many firms has diminished. It is part of a management controlled operation – a branch of human resource management. It is no longer a high profile problem-ridden part of personnel management as it so often was in the 1970s.'

Guest (1995) noted that the industrial relations system may continue as a largely symbolic 'empty shell', insufficiently important for management to confront and eliminate, but retaining the outward appearance of health to the casual observer:

'Management sets the agenda, which is market-driven, while industrial relations issues are relatively low on the list of concerns.'

Conclusions of the Workplace Employee Relations Survey (WERS) 2004

The results showed some significant changes (from the 1988 survey). Most striking of all, perhaps, was the continuing decline of collective labour organization. Employees were less likely to be union members than they were in 1998; workplaces were less likely to recognize unions for bargaining over pay and conditions; collective bargaining was less prevalent. Even so, the rate of decline seemed to have slowed down from that seen in earlier periods and the joint regulation of terms and conditions remains a reality for many employees in Britain: one-half of employees were employed in workplaces with a recognized trade union; one-third were union members; and 40 per cent had their pay set through collective bargaining.

THE PARTIES TO INDUSTRIAL RELATIONS

The parties to industrial relations are:

- the trade unions;
- shop stewards or employee representatives;
- the Trades Union Congress (the TUC);
- management;
- employer's organizations;
- the Confederation of British Industry;
- various institutions, agencies and officers.

The role of each of these parties is summarized below

The trade unions

Traditionally the fundamental purpose of trade unions is to promote and protect the interests of their members. They are there to redress the balance of power between employers and employees. The basis of the employment relationship is the contract of employment. But this is not a contract between equals. Employers are almost always in a stronger position to dictate the terms of the contract than individual employees. Trade unions, as indicated by Freeman and Medoff (1984), provide workers with a 'collective voice' to make their wishes known to management and thus bring actual and desired conditions closer together. This applies not only to terms of employment such as pay, working hours and holidays, but also to the way in which individuals are treated in such aspects of employment as the redress of grievances, discipline and redundancy. Trade unions also exist to let management know that there will be, from time to time, an alternative view on key issues affecting employees. More broadly, unions may see their role as that of participating with management on decision making on matters affecting their members' interests.

Within this overall role, trade unions have had two specific roles, namely to secure, through collective bargaining, improved terms and conditions for their members, and to provide protection, support and advice to their members as individual employees.

An additional role, that of providing legal, financial and other services to their members, has come into prominence more recently.

Trade union structure

Trade unions are run by full-time central and, usually, district officials. There may be local committees of members. National officials may conduct industry-wide or major employer pay negotiations while local officials may not be involved in plant negotiations unless there is a 'failure to agree' and the second stage of a negotiating procedure is invoked. Major employers who want to introduce significant changes in agreements or working arrangements may deal direct with national officials.

The trade union movement is now dominated by the large general unions and the merged craft and public service unions.

Shop stewards

Shop stewards or employee representatives may initially be responsible for plant negotiations, probably with the advice of full-time officials. They will certainly be involved in settling disputes and resolving collective grievances and in representing individual employees with grievances or over disciplinary matters. They may be members of joint consultative committees, which could be wholly or partly composed of trade union representatives.

At one time, shop stewards were the ogres of the industrial relations scene. Undoubtedly there were cases of militant shop stewards, but where there are recognized trade unions, managements have generally recognized the value of shop stewards as points of contact and channels of communication.

The Trades Union Congress (TUC)

The TUC acts as the collective voice of the unions. Its roles are to:

- represent the British trade union movement in the UK and internationally;
- conduct research and develop policies on trade union, industrial, economic and social matters and to campaign actively for them;
- regulate relationships between unions;
- help unions in dispute;
- provide various services (eg research) to affiliated unions.

But the TUC has effectively been marginalized by successive Conservative governments and is but a shadow of its former self, especially since its interventionary role concerning union disputes over membership (the Bridlington rules) has now effectively been abolished by legislation.

International union organizations

The two main international union organizations are the European Trade Union Confederation and the International Trade Union Confederation. At present neither of these makes much impact on the UK, but this could change.

Staff associations

Staff associations may sometimes have negotiating and/or representational rights but they seldom have anything like the real power possessed by a well-organized and supported trade union. They are often suspected by employees as being no more than management's poodle. Managements have sometimes encouraged the development of staff associations as an alternative to trade unions but this strategy has not always worked. In fact, in some organizations the existence of an unsatisfactory staff association has provided an opportunity for a trade union to gain membership and recognition. Staff associations have their uses as channels of communication, and representatives can play a role in consultative processes and in representing colleagues who want to take up grievances or who are being subjected to disciplinary proceedings.

The role of management

The balance of power has undoubtedly shifted to managements who now have more choice over how they conduct relationships with their employees. But the evidence is that there has been no concerted drive by managements to de-recognize unions. As Kessler and Bayliss (1992) point out: 'If managers in large establishments and companies wanted to make changes they looked at ways of doing so within the existing arrangements and if they could produce the goods they used them. Because managers found that the unions did not stand in their way they saw no reason for getting rid of them.' They argued that management's industrial relations objectives are now generally to:

- control the work process;
- secure cost-effectiveness;
- reassert managerial authority;
- move towards a more unitary and individualistic approach.

As Storey (1992a) found in most of the cases he studied, there was a tendency for managements to adopt HRM approaches to employee relations while still coexisting with the unions. But they gave increasing weight to systems of employee involvement, in particular communication, which bypass trade unions.

Employers' organizations

Traditionally, employers' organizations have bargained collectively for their members with trade unions and have in general aimed to protect the interests of those members in their dealings with unions. Multi-employers or industry-wide bargaining, it was believed, allowed companies to compete in product markets without undercutting their competitors' employment costs and prevented the trade unions 'picking off' individual employers in a dispute.

The trend towards decentralizing bargaining to plant level has reduced the extent to which employers' organizations fulfil this traditional role, although some industries such as building and electrical contracting with large numbers of small companies in competitive markets have retained their central bargaining function, setting a floor of terms and conditions for the industry.

The Confederation of British Industry (CBI)

The CBI is a management organization which is only indirectly concerned with industrial relations. It provides a means for its members to influence economic policy and it provides advice and services to them, supported by research.

Institutions, agencies and officers

There are a number of bodies and people with a role in employee relations, as described below.

The Advisory Conciliation and Arbitration Service (ACAS)

ACAS was created by the government but functions independently. It has three main statutory duties:

- to resolve disputes;
- to provide conciliatory services for individuals in, for example, unfair dismissal cases;
- to give advice, help and information on industrial relations and employment issues.

ACAS helps to resolve disputes in three ways: collective conciliation, arbitration and mediation.

During the 1980s and early 1990s the use of ACAS's collective conciliation and arbitration services declined considerably. But the individual conciliation case load has been very heavy and the ACAS advisory work has flourished. These are aimed at encouraging non-adversarial approaches to preventing and resolving problems at work by facilitating joint working groups of employers, employees and their representatives.

The Central Arbitration Committee (CAC)

The CAC is an independent arbitration body that deals with disputes. It arbitrates at the request of one party but with the agreement of the other. It does not handle many arbitrations but it deals more frequently with claims by trade unions for disclosure of information for collective bargaining purposes.

Employment tribunals

Employment tribunals are independent judicial bodies that deal with disputes on employment matters such as unfair dismissal, equal pay, sex and race discrimination and employment protection provisions. They have a legally qualified chair and two other members, one an employer, the other a trade unionist.

The Employment Appeal Tribunal (EAT)

The EAT hears appeals from the decisions of industrial tribunals on questions of law only.

ROLE OF THE HR FUNCTION IN EMPLOYEE RELATIONS

The HR function provides guidance and training and will develop and help to introduce and maintain formal processes; but it does not do line managers' jobs for them. However, in their role as industrial relations specialists, HR practitioners may deal directly with trade unions and their representatives. They are also likely to have a measure of responsibility for maintaining participation and involvement processes and for managing employee communications. They can and should play a major part in developing employee relations strategies and policies that aim to:

- achieve satisfactory employment relationships, taking particular account of the importance of psychological contracts;
- build stable and cooperative relationships with employees which recognize that they are stakeholders in the organization and minimize conflict;
- achieve commitment through employee involvement and communications processes;
- develop mutuality – a common interest in achieving the organization's goals through the development of organizational cultures based on shared values between management and employees;
- clarify industrial relations processes with trade unions and build harmonious relationships with them on a partnership basis.

In these capacities HR practitioners can make a major contribution to the creation and maintenance of a good employee relations climate.

51

Employee relations processes

Employee relations processes consist of the approaches and methods adopted by employers to deal with employees either collectively through their trade unions or individually. They will be based on the organization's articulated or implied employee relations policies and strategies as examined in the first two sections of this chapter. The way in which they are developed and how they function will be influenced by, and will influence, the employee relations climate, the concept of which is examined in the third section of the chapter.

Industrial relations processes, ie those aspects of employee relations that are concerned with the dealings between employers and trade unions, consist of:

- approaches to recognizing or de-recognizing trade unions;
- formal methods of collective bargaining;
- partnership as an approach to employee relations;
- the informal day-to-day contacts on employment issues that take place in the workplace between management and trade union representatives or officials;
- features of the industrial relations scene such as union membership in the workplace, the check-off and strikes.

These processes are considered later in this chapter. Negotiating techniques and skills as an aspect of collective bargaining are dealt with separately in the next chapter. In addition there are the employee relations processes of involvement, participation and communication which are discussed in Chapter 53.

The outcomes of these processes are various forms of procedural and substantive agreements and employment procedures, including harmonization of terms and conditions, and the approaches used by organizations to manage with and without trade unions. These are described in the last three sections of this chapter.

EMPLOYEE RELATIONS POLICIES

Approaches to employee relations

Four approaches to employee relations policies have been identified by Industrial Relations Services (1994):

- *Adversarial:* the organization decides what it wants to do, and employees are expected to fit in. Employees only exercise power by refusing to cooperate.
- *Traditional:* a good day-to-day working relationship but management proposes and the workforce reacts through its elected representatives.
- *Partnership:* the organization involves employees in the drawing up and execution of organization policies, but retains the right to manage.
- *Power sharing:* employees are involved in both day-to-day and strategic decision making.

Adversarial approaches are much less common than in the 1960s and 1970s. The traditional approach is still the most typical but more interest is being expressed in partnership, as discussed later in this chapter. Power sharing is rare.

Nature and purpose of employee relations policies

Against the background of a preference for one of the four approaches listed above, employee relations policies express the philosophy of the organization on what sort of relationships between management and employees and their unions are wanted, and how they should be handled. A partnership policy will aim to develop and maintain a positive, productive, cooperative and trusting climate of employee relations.

When they are articulated, policies provide guidelines for action on employee relations issues and can help to ensure that these issues are dealt with consistently. They provide the basis for defining management's intentions (its employee relations strategy) on key matters such as union recognition and collective bargaining.

Policy areas

The areas covered by employee relations policies are:

- *trade union recognition* – whether trade unions should be recognized or de-recognized, which union or unions the organization would prefer to deal with, and whether or not it is desirable to recognize only one union for collective bargaining and/or employee representational purposes;
- *collective bargaining* – the extent to which it should be centralized or decentralized and the scope of areas to be covered by collective bargaining;
- *employee relations procedures* – the nature and scope of procedures for redundancy, grievance handling and discipline;
- *participation and involvement* – the extent to which the organization is prepared to give employees a voice on matters that concern them;
- *partnership* – the extent to which a partnership approach is thought to be desirable;
- *the employment relationship* – the extent to which terms and conditions of employment should be governed by collective agreements or based on individual contracts of employment (ie collectivism versus individualism);
- *harmonization* of terms and conditions of employment for staff and manual workers;
- *working arrangements* – the degree to which management has the prerogative to determine working arrangements without reference to trade unions or employees (this includes job-based or functional flexibility).

When formulating policies in these areas, organizations may be consciously or unconsciously deciding on the extent to which they want to adopt the HRM approach to employee relations. This emphasizes commitment, mutuality and forms of involvement and participation that mean that management approaches and communicates with employees directly rather than through their representatives.

Policy choices

There is, of course, no such thing as a model employee relations policy. Every organization develops its own policies. In a mature business these will be in accordance with established custom and practice, its core values and management style and the actual or perceived balance of power between management and unions. In younger organizations, or those being established on a green field site, the policies will depend on the assumptions and beliefs of management and, where relevant, the existing philosophy and policies of the parent organization. In both these cases policies will be affected by the type of people employed by the organization, its business strategies, technology, the industry or sector in which it operates, and its structure (for example, the extent to which it is centralized or decentralized).

The following four policy options for organizations on industrial relations and HRM have been described by Guest (1995):

- *The new realism – a high emphasis on HRM and industrial relations.* The aim is to integrate HRM and industrial relations. This is the policy of such organizations as Rover, Nissan and Toshiba. A review of new collaborative arrangements in the shape of single-table bargaining (IRS, 1993) found that they were almost always the result of employer initiatives, but that both employers and unions seem satisfied with them. They have facilitated greater flexibility, more multi-skilling, the removal of demarcations and improvements in quality. They can also extend consultation processes and accelerate moves towards single status.
- *Traditional collectivism – priority to industrial relations without HRM.* This involves retaining the traditional pluralist industrial relations arrangements within an eventually unchanged industrial relations system. Management may take the view in these circumstances that it is easier to continue to operate with a union, since it provides a useful, well-established channel for communication and for the handling of grievance, discipline and safety issues.
- *Individualized HRM – high priority to HRM with no industrial relations.* According to Guest, this approach is not very common, excepting North American-owned firms. It is, he believes, 'essentially piecemeal and opportunistic'.
- *The black hole – no industrial relations.* This option is becoming more prevalent in organizations in which HRM is not a policy priority for managements but where they do not see that there is a compelling reason to operate within a traditional industrial relations system. When such organizations are facing a decision on whether or not to recognize a union, they are increasingly deciding not to do so. And, as shown by Millward (1994), non-union firms are not replacing the unions with an HRM strategy. Marginson *et al* (1993) similarly found no support for a non-union HRM strategy.

Policy formulation

Employee relations policies usually evolve in the light of the circumstances of the firm, traditional practices, management's values and style and the power of trade unions to exert influence. They will change as new situations emerge and these may include competitive pressure, new management, a takeover, different views amongst employees about the value of trade unions, or new trade union policies. Sometimes these changes will be deliberate. Management may decide that it no longer has any use for trade unions and will therefore de-recognize them. On other occasions the changes will simply emerge from the situation in which management finds itself.

The evolutionary and emergent nature of employee relations policies is the most typical case. But there is much to be said for managements occasionally to sit back and think through their policies in order to establish the extent to which they are still appropriate. This review should be based on an analysis of current policies and their relevance to the changing environment of the organization. The analysis could be extended to discussions with union representatives within the firm and local or even national officials to obtain their views. Employees could also be consulted so that their views could be obtained and acted upon, thus making it more likely that they will accept and be committed to policy changes. If there is a staff association, its role as a representative body should be reconsidered. Alternatively, the case for setting up a staff association should be reviewed. The outcome of attitude surveys designed to elicit the opinions of employees on matters of general concern to them can provide additional information on which to base policy decisions.

The result of such a review might, for example, be a decision not to make a frontal assault on the union, but simply to diminish its power by restricting the scope of collective bargaining and bypassing it and its shop stewards through more direct approaches to individual employees. As recent surveys have shown, this, rather than outright de-recognition, has been the typical policy of unionized firms. And it is probable in most of these cases that the policy evolved over time, rather than being formulated after a systematic review.

Alternatively, processes of consultation with trade unions and employees may lead to the development of a more positive policy of partnership with the trade union which recognizes the mutual advantages of working together.

Expressing policy

Most organizations seem reluctant to commit their employee relations policies to writing. And this is understandable in the light of their fluid nature and, in some cases, the reluctance of managements to admit publicly that they are anti-union.

Policies that are deeply embedded as part of the managerial philosophy and values of the organization do not need to be formalized. They will be fully understood by management and will therefore be acted upon consistently, especially when they are in effect broad expressions of the views of management rather than specific action guidelines.

The argument for having written policies is that everyone – line managers, team leaders and employees generally – will be clear about where they stand and how they are expected to act. Firms may also want to publish their employee relations policies to support a 'mutual commitment' strategy. But this presupposes the involvement of employees in formulating the policies.

EMPLOYEE RELATIONS STRATEGIES

Nature and purpose

Employee relations strategies set out how objectives such as those mentioned above are to be achieved. They define the intentions of the organization about what needs to be done and what needs to be changed in the ways in which the organization manages its relationships with employees and their trade unions. Like all other aspects of personnel or HR strategy, employee relations strategies will flow from the business strategy but will also aim to support it. For example, if the business strategy is to concentrate on achieving competitive edge through innovation and the delivery of quality to its customers, the employee relations strategy may emphasize processes of involvement and participation, including the implementation of programmes for continuous improvement and total quality management. If, however, the strategy for competitive advantage, or even survival, is cost reduction, the employee relations strategy may concentrate on how this can be achieved by maximizing cooperation with the unions and employees and by minimizing detrimental effects on those employees and disruption to the organization.

Employee relations strategies should be distinguished from employee relations policies. Strategies are dynamic. They provide a sense of direction, and give an answer to the question 'how are we going to get from here to there?' Employee relations policies are more about the here and now. They express 'the way things are done around here' as far as dealing with unions and employees is concerned. Of course they will evolve but this may not be a result of a strategic choice. It is when a deliberate decision is made to change policies that a strategy for achieving this change has to be formulated. Thus if the policy is to increase commitment, the strategy could consider how this might be achieved by involvement and participation processes.

Strategic directions

The intentions expressed by employee relations strategies may direct the organization towards any of the following:

- changing forms of recognition, including single union recognition, or de-recognition;
- changes in the form and content of procedural agreements;

- new bargaining structures, including decentralization or single-table bargaining;
- the achievement of increased levels of commitment through involvement or participation;
- deliberately bypassing trade union representatives to communicate directly with employees;
- increasing the extent to which management controls operations in such areas as flexibility;
- generally improving the employee relations climate in order to produce more harmonious and cooperative relationships;
- developing a 'partnership' with trade unions, recognizing that employees are stakeholders and that it is to the advantage of both parties to work together (this could be described as a unitarist strategy aiming at increasing mutual commitment).

Formulating strategies

Like other business and HR strategies, those concerned with employee relations can, in Mintzberg's (1987) words, 'emerge in response to an evolving situation'. But it is still useful to spend time deliberately formulating strategies and the aim should be to create a shared agenda which will communicate a common perspective on what needs to be done. This can be expressed in writing but it can also be clarified through involvement and communication processes.

EMPLOYEE RELATIONS CLIMATE

The employee relations climate of an organization represents the perceptions of management, employees and their representatives about the ways in which employee relations are conducted and how the various parties (managers, employees and trade unions) behave when dealing with one another. An employee relations climate can be good, bad or indifferent according to perceptions about the extent to which:

- management and employees trust one another;
- management treats employees fairly and with consideration;
- management is open about its actions and intentions – employee relations policies and procedures are transparent;
- harmonious relationships are generally maintained on a day-to-day basis, which results in willing cooperation rather than grudging submission;

- conflict, when it does arise, is resolved without resort to industrial action and resolution is achieved by integrative processes which result in a 'win–win' solution;
- employees are generally committed to the interests of the organization and, equally, management treats them as stakeholders whose interests should be protected as far as possible.

Improving the climate

Improvements to the climate can be attained by developing fair employee relations policies and procedures and implementing them consistently. Line managers and team leaders who are largely responsible for the day-to-day conduct of employee relations need to be educated and trained on the approaches they should adopt. Transparency should be achieved by communicating policies to employees, and commitment increased by involvement and participation processes. Problems that need to be resolved can be identified by simply talking to employees, their representatives and their trade union officials. Importantly, as discussed below, the organization can address its obligations to the employees as stakeholders and take steps to build trust.

An ethical approach

Businesses aim to achieve prosperity, growth and survival. Ideally, success should benefit all the stakeholders in the organization – owners, management, employees, customers and suppliers. But the single-minded pursuit of business objectives can act to the detriment of employees' well-being and security. There may be a tension between accomplishing business purposes and the social and ethical obligations of an organization to its employees. But the chances of attaining a good climate of employee relations are slight if no attempt is made to recognize and act on an organization's duties to its members.

An ethical approach will be based on high-commitment and high-involvement policies. The commitment will be mutual and the arrangements for involvement will be genuine, ie management will be prepared not only to listen but to act on the views expressed by employees or at least, if it cannot take action, the reasons why will be explained. It will also be transparent and, although the concept of a 'job for life' may no longer be valid in many organizations, at least an attempt will be made to maintain 'full employment' policies.

Building trust

The Institute of Personnel and Development's (IPD) statement *People Make the Difference* (1994) makes the point that much has been done in recent years to introduce a sense of reality into employee relations. But, according to the IPD, 'Managers should not kid themselves that acquiescence is the same thing as enthusiastic involvement. The pace of life and changing work patterns in the future will put a strain on the best of relationships between employees and managers.'

The IPD suggests that employee relations policies aimed at building trust should be based on the principles that employees cannot just be treated as a factor of production and that organizations must translate their values concerning employee relations into specific and practical action. In too many organizations, inconsistency between what is said and what is done undermines trust, generates employee cynicism and provides evidence of contradictions in management thinking.

UNION RECOGNITION AND DE-RECOGNITION

Recognition

An employer fully recognizes a union for the purposes of collective bargaining when pay and conditions of employment are jointly agreed between management and trade unions. Partial recognition takes place when employers restrict trade unions to representing their members on issues arising from employment. An independent trade union can apply to the CAC for recognition, which will agree where either a majority of the workers already belong to the union, or when the union wins majority support for recognition by at least 40 per cent of those entitled to vote in a secret ballot.

Single union recognition

The existence of a number of unions within one organization was frequently criticized in the 1980s because of the supposed increase in the complexity of bargaining arrangements and the danger of inter-union demarcation disputes (who does what). The answer to this problem was thought to be single union representation through single union deals. These had a number of characteristics that were considered to be advantageous to management.

Single-union deals have the following typical features:

- a single union representing all employees, with constraints put on the role of union full-time officials;

- flexible working practices – agreement to the flexible use of labour across traditional demarcation lines;
- single status for all employees – the harmonization of terms and conditions between manual and non-manual employees;
- an expressed commitment by the organization to involvement and the disclosure of information in the form of an open communications system and, often, a works council;
- the resolution of disputes by means of devices such as pendulum arbitration, a commitment to continuity of production and a 'no-strike' provision.

Single-union deals have generally been concluded on green field sites, often by Japanese firms such as Nissan, Sanyo, Matshushsita and Toyota. A 'beauty contest' may be held by the employer to select a union from a number of contenders. Thus, the initiative is taken by the employer, who can lay down radical terms for the agreement.

Factors influencing recognition or de-recognition

Employers are in a strong position now to choose whether they recognize a union or not, which union they want to recognize and the terms on which they would grant recognition, for example a single union and a no-strike agreement.

When setting up on green field sites employers may refuse to recognize unions. Alternatively they hold 'beauty contests', as mentioned above, to select the union they prefer to work with, which will be prepared to reach an agreement in line with what management wants.

An organization deciding whether or not to recognize a union will take some or all of the following factors into account:

- the perceived value or lack of value of having a process for regulating collective bargaining;
- if there is an existing union, the extent to which management has freedom to manage; for example, to change working arrangements and introduce flexible working or multi-skilling;
- the history of relationships with the union;
- the proportion of employees who are union members and the degree to which they believe they need the protection their union provides; a decision on de-recognition has to weigh the extent to which its perceived advantages outweigh the disadvantages of upsetting the *status quo*;
- any preferences as to a particular union, because of its reputation or the extent to which it is believed a satisfactory relationship can be maintained.

In considering recognition arrangements employers may also consider entering into a 'single union deal' as described above.

COLLECTIVE BARGAINING ARRANGEMENTS

Collective bargaining arrangements are those set up by agreements between managements, employers' associations, or joint employer negotiating bodies and trade unions to determine specified terms and conditions of employment for groups of employees. Collective bargaining processes are usually governed by procedural agreements and result in substantive agreements and agreed employee relations procedures.

The considerations to be taken into account in developing and managing collective bargaining arrangements are:

- collective agreements;
- the level at which bargaining should take place;
- single-table bargaining where a number of unions are recognized in one workplace;
- dispute resolution.

Collective agreements

Collective agreements can be classified as procedural agreements or substantive agreements. The former provide the framework for collective bargaining, and the latter are the outcome of collective bargaining. Two forms of collective procedural agreements have become prominent: partnership agreements and new-style agreements.

Procedural agreements

Procedural agreements set out the respective responsibilities and duties of managers and unions, the steps through which the parties make joint decisions, and the procedure to be followed if the parties fail to agree. Their purpose is to regulate the behaviour of the parties to the agreement, but they are not legally enforceable, and the degree to which they are followed depends on the goodwill of both parties or the balance of power between them. Procedural agreements are seldom broken and, if so, never lightly. The basic presumption of collective bargaining is that both parties will honour agreements that have been made freely between them. An attempt to make collective agreements legally enforceable in the 1971 Industrial Relations Act failed because employers generally did not seek to enforce its provisions.

A typical procedural or procedure agreement contains the following sections:

- a preamble defining the objectives of the agreement;
- a statement that the union is recognized as a representative body with negotiating rights;
- a statement of general principles, which may include a commitment to use the procedure (a no-strike clause) and/or a status quo clause which restricts the ability of management to introduce changes outside negotiated or customary practice;
- a statement of the facilities granted to unions, including the rights of shop stewards and the right to hold meetings;
- provision for joint negotiating committees (in some agreements);
- the negotiating or disputes procedure;
- provision for terminating the agreement.

The scope and content of such agreements can, however, vary widely. Some organizations have limited recognition to the provision of representational rights only, others have taken an entirely different line in concluding single-union deals which, when they first emerged in the 1980s, were sometimes dubbed 'new style agreements', or referred to as the 'new realism'.

An agreement may incorporate or have attached to it employee relations procedures such as those concerned with grievances, discipline and redundancy. In addition, agreements are sometimes reached on health and safety procedures.

Substantive agreements

Substantive agreements set out agreed terms and conditions of employment, covering pay and working hours and other aspects such as holidays, overtime regulations, flexibility arrangements and allowances. Again, they are not legally enforceable. A substantive agreement may detail the operational rules for a payment-by-results scheme which could include arrangements for timing or re-timing and for payments during waiting time or on new, untimed, work.

Partnership agreements

A partnership agreement is one in which both parties (management and the trade union) agree to work together to their mutual advantage and to achieve a climate of more cooperative and therefore less adversarial industrial relations.

The rationale for partnership is that it is a way of getting away from confrontational industrial relations to the mutual benefit of both management and employees.

Partnership deals can at least attempt to balance the needs of employees for job security with the aims of management to maximize flexibility.

Common features

The common features of partnership as defined by Reilly (2001) are:

- *Mutuality* – both sides recognize that there are areas of commonality, of shared interest.
- *Plurality* – it is recognized that there are areas of difference as well as areas of common interest.
- *Trust and respect* – for the intentions of the other side and for legitimate differences in interests.
- *Agreement without coercion* – there is an intention to solve problems through consensus, recognizing business and employee needs.
- *Involvement and voice* – opportunities are provided for employees to shape their work environment and have their opinions heard.
- *Individualist and collectivist dimension* – this is achieved through direct and indirect (ie representative) forms of employee involvement.

Problems

The concept of partnership captured attention when it first emerged, but it has not become a major feature of the industrial relations scene. The TUC estimates that there are only about 60 genuine partnership deals in existence. Reilly (2001) notes that the concept can come under pressure for a number of reasons. Three of the key factors are:

1. misunderstanding of what partnership is all about;
2. lack of trust, lack of support and increased evocation over the benefits of partnership; and
3. disagreements that are not resolved and infect relationships.

Senior management may not really believe in partnership and make unilateral decisions without consultation; support may come from full-time trade union officials but is not backed by shop stewards; and employees may reject the partnership notion, seeing their representatives as management 'poodles' unable to look after their interests properly. Partnership may mean that employees and their representatives can be well informed, consulted and have a voice, but in the end management decides.

New-style agreements

The so-called 'new style agreements' emerged in the 1990s to achieve improvements in the conclusion and operation of negotiating and bargaining arrangements. As described by Farnham (2000), a major feature of these agreements was that their negotiating and disputes procedures were based on the mutually accepted 'rights' of the parties expressed in the recognition agreement. The intention was to resolve any differences of interests on substantive issues between the parties by regulations, with pendulum arbitration providing a resolution of those issues where differences exist. As originally conceived, new style agreements typically included provision for single-union recognition, single status, labour flexibility, a works council, and a no-strike clause to the effect that issues should be resolved without recourse to industrial action. Some or all of these provisions may still be made in agreements, but are not usually packaged as 'new style' agreements.

Bargaining levels

There has been a pronounced trend away from multi-employer bargaining, especially in the private sector. This has arisen because of decentralization and a reluctance on the part of central management to get involved.

Single-table bargaining

Single-table bargaining brings together all the unions in an organization as a single bargaining unit. The reasons organizations advance for wanting a 'single-table deal' are:

- a concern that existing multi-unit bargaining arrangements not only are inefficient in terms of time and management resources but are also a potential source of conflict;
- the desire to achieve major changes in working practices, which it is believed can be achieved only through single-table bargaining;
- a belief in the necessity of introducing harmonized or single-status conditions.

Marginson and Sisson (1990), however, identified a number of critical issues which need to be resolved if single-table bargaining is to be introduced successfully. These comprise:

- the commitment of management to the concept;
- the need to maintain levels of negotiation which are specific to particular groups below the single-bargaining table;

- the need to allay the fears of managers that they will not be able to react flexibly to changes in the demand for specific groups of workers;
- the willingness of management to discuss a wider range of issues with union representatives – this is because single-table bargaining adds to existing arrangements a top tier in which matters affecting all employees, such as training, development, working time and fringe benefits can be discussed;
- the need to persuade representatives from the various unions to forget their previous rivalries, sink their differences and work together (not always easy);
- the need to allay the fears of trade unions that they may lose representation rights and members, and of shop stewards that they will lose the ability to represent members effectively.

These are formidable requirements to satisfy, and however desirable single-table bargaining may be, it will never be easy to introduce or to operate.

Third-party dispute resolution

The aim of collective bargaining is, of course, to reach agreement, preferably to the satisfaction of both parties. Negotiating procedures, as described in the next section of this chapter, provide for various stages of 'failure to agree' and often include a clause providing for some form of third-party dispute resolution in the event of the procedure being exhausted. The processes of dispute resolution as identified by IRS (2004d) are conciliation, arbitration and mediation.

Conciliation

An attempt through informal discussions to help parties in a dispute to reach their own agreement. The third party does not recommend or decide on a settlement. One advantage of this process is that it helps the parties to retain ownership of the resolution of the problem, which can, in turn, engender greater commitment to its implementation. Conciliation is the most frequently used form of third-party involvement.

Arbitration

The parties put the issue to an independent third party for determination. The parties agree in advance to accept the arbitrator's decision as a means of finally resolving the matter. There is sometimes a reluctance to use this method as it removes control over the final outcome from employers, employees or trade unions.

Mediation

Formal but non-binding recommendations or proposals are put forward for further consideration by the parties. The use of dispute mediation is rare, partly because it is seen as a halfway house. There is sometimes a feeling that if conciliation cannot succeed, it may be best simply to go all the way to arbitration.

INFORMAL EMPLOYEE RELATIONS PROCESSES

The formal processes of union recognition, collective bargaining and dispute resolution described earlier in this chapter provide the framework for industrial relations in so far as this is concerned with agreeing terms and conditions of employment and working arrangements and settling disputes. But within or outside that framework, informal employee relations processes are taking place continuously.

Informal employee relationships take place whenever a line manager or team leader is handling an issue in contact with a shop steward, an employee representative, an individual employee or a group of employees. The issue may concern methods of work, allocation of work and overtime, working conditions, health and safety, achieving output and quality targets and standards, discipline or pay (especially if a payment-by-results scheme is in operation, which can generate continuous arguments about times, standards, re-timings, payments for waiting time or when carrying out new tasks, and fluctuations or reductions in earnings because of alleged managerial inefficiency).

Line managers and supervisors handle day-to-day grievances arising from any of these issues and are expected to resolve them to the satisfaction of all parties without involving a formal grievance procedure. The thrust for devolving responsibility to line managers for personnel matters has increased the onus on them to handle employee relations effectively. A good team leader will establish a working relationship with the shop steward representing his or her staff which will enable issues arising on the shop-floor or with individual employees to be settled amicably before they become a problem.

Creating and maintaining a good employee relations climate in an organization may be the ultimate responsibility of top management, advised by personnel specialists. But the climate will be strongly influenced by the behaviour of line managers and team leaders. The HR function can help to improve the effectiveness of this behaviour by identifying and defining the competences required, advising on the selection of supervisors, ensuring that they are properly trained, encouraging the development of performance management processes that provide for the assessment of the level of competence achieved by line managers and team leaders in handling employee relations, or by providing unobtrusive help and guidance as required.

OTHER FEATURES OF THE INDUSTRIAL RELATIONS SCENE

There are four features of the industrial relations scene which are important, besides the formal and informal processes discussed above. These features are harmonization, union membership arrangements within the organization, the 'check-off' system, and strikes and other forms of industrial action (which should more realistically be called industrial inaction if it involves a 'go slow' or 'work to rule').

Harmonization

Harmonization is the process of introducing the same conditions of employment for all employees. It is distinguished by Roberts (1990) from single status and staff status as follows:

- Single status is the removal of differences in basic conditions of employment to give all employees equal status. Some organizations take this further by putting all employees into the same pay and grading structure.
- Staff status is a process whereby manual and craft employees gradually receive staff terms and conditions of employment, usually upon reaching some qualifying standard, for example length of service.
- Harmonization means the reduction of differences in the pay structure and other employment conditions between categories of employee, usually manual and staff employees. The essence of harmonization is the adoption of a common approach and criteria to pay and conditions for all employees. It differs from staff status in that, in the process of harmonization, some staff employees may have to accept some of the conditions of employment of manual workers.

According to Duncan (1989), the pressure towards harmonization has arisen for the following reasons:

- *New technology* – status differentials can obstruct efficient labour utilization, and concessions on harmonization are invariably given in exchange for an agreement on flexibility. Moreover, technology, by de-skilling many white-collar jobs and enhancing the skills of former blue-collar workers, has made differential treatment harder to defend.

- *Legislation* – equal pay, the banning of sex and racial discrimination, and employment protection legislation have extended to manual workers rights that were previously the preserve of staff. The concept of equal value has been a major challenge to differentiation between staff and manual workers.
- *Improving productivity* by the more flexible use of labour.
- *Simplifying personnel administration* and thereby reducing costs.
- *Changing employee attitudes* and so improving commitment, motivation and morale.

In Roberts' view, questions of morality are probably of least importance.

Union membership within organizations

The closed shop, which enforced union membership within organizations, has been made illegal. But many managers prefer that all their employees should be in the union because on the whole it makes their life easier to have one channel of representation to deal with industrial relations issues and also because it prevents conflict between members and non-members of the union.

The 'check-off' system

The 'check-off' is a system that involves management in deducting the subscriptions of trade union members on behalf of the union. It is popular with unions because it helps to maintain membership and provides a reasonably well guaranteed source of income. Managements have generally been willing to cooperate as a gesture of good faith to their trade union. They may support a check-off system because it enables them to find out how many employees are union members. Employers also know that they can exert pressure in the face of industrial action by threatening to end the check-off. However, the Trade Union and Employment Rights Act 1993 provides that if an employer is lawfully to make check-off deductions from a worker's pay, there must be prior written consent from the worker and renewed consent at least every three years. This three-year renewal provision can inhibit the maintenance of the system.

Strikes

Strikes are the most politically charged of all the features of industrial relations. The Conservative Government in the 1980s believed that 'strikes are too often a weapon of first rather than last resort'. However, those involved in negotiation – as well as trade unions – have recognized that a strike is a legitimate last resort if all else fails. It is a factor in the balance of power between the parties in a negotiation and has to be taken into account by both parties.

Unlike other Western European countries, there is no legal right in Britain for workers or their unions to take strike action. What has been built up through common law is a system of legal liability that suspends union liability for civil wrongs or 'torts' as long as industrial action falls within the legal definition of a trade dispute and takes place 'in contemplation of furtherance of a trade dispute'.

The Conservative Government's 1980s and 1990s legislation has limited this legal immunity to situations where a properly conducted ballot has been conducted by the union authorizing or endorsing the action and where the action is between an employer and their direct employees, with all secondary or sympathy action being unlawful. Immunity is also removed if industrial action is taken to impose or enforce a closed shop or where the action is unofficial and is not repudiated in writing by the union. The impact of this law is to deter the calling of strikes without careful consideration of where the line of legal immunity is now drawn and of the likely result of a secret ballot. But the secret ballot can in effect legitimize strike action.

The number of strikes and the proportion of days lost through strike action have diminished significantly in the UK since the 1970s. This reduction has been caused more by economic pressures than by the legislation. Unions have had to choose between taking strike action, which could lead to closure, or survival on the terms dictated by employers with fewer jobs. In addition, unions in manufacturing found that their members who remained in jobs did well out of local productivity bargaining and threatened strike action.

MANAGING WITH TRADE UNIONS

Ideally, managements and trade unions learn to live together, often on a give and take basis, the presumption being that neither would benefit from a climate of hostility or by generating constant confrontation. It would be assumed in this ideal situation that mutual advantage would come from acting in accordance with the spirit as well as the letter of agreed joint regulatory procedures. However, both parties would probably adopt a realistic pluralist viewpoint, recognizing the inevitability of differences of opinion, even disputes, but believing that with goodwill on both sides they could be settled without recourse to industrial action.

Of course, the reality in the 1960s and 1970s was often different. In certain businesses, for example in the motor and shipbuilding industries, hostility and confrontation were rife. And newspaper proprietors tended to let their unions walk all over them in the interests of peace and profit.

Times have changed. As noted earlier, trade union power has diminished and managements have tended to seize the initiative. They may be content to live with trade unions but they give industrial relations lower priority. They may feel that it is easier to continue to operate with a union because it provides a useful, well-established channel for communication and for the handling of grievance, discipline and safety issues. In the absence of a union, management would need to develop its own alternatives, which would be costly and difficult to operate effectively. The trade union and the shop stewards remain a useful lubricant. Alternatively, as Smith and Morton (1993) suggest, the management perspective may be that it is safer to marginalize the unions than formally to de-recognize them and risk provoking a confrontation: 'Better to let them wither on the vine than receive a reviving fertilizer'. However, the alternative view was advanced by Purcell (1979) who argued that management will have greater success in achieving its objectives by working with trade unions, in particular by encouraging union membership and participation in union affairs.

Four types of industrial relations management have been identified by Purcell and Sisson (1983):

- *Traditionalists* have unitary beliefs and are anti-union with forceful management.
- *Sophisticated paternalists* are essentially unitary but they do not take it for granted that their employees accept the organization's objectives or automatically legitimize management decision making. They spend considerable time and resources in ensuring that their employees adopt the right approach.
- *Sophisticated moderns* are either constitutionalists, where the limits of collective bargaining are codified in an agreement but management is free to take decisions on matters that are not the subject of such an agreement, or consultors, who accept collective bargaining but do not want to codify everything in a collective agreement, and instead aim to minimize the amount of joint regulation and emphasize joint consultation with 'problems' having to be solved rather than 'disputes' settled.
- *Standard moderns* are pragmatic or opportunist. Trade unions are recognized, but industrial relations are seen as primarily fire-fighting and are assumed to be non-problematic unless events prove otherwise. This is by far the most typical approach.

MANAGING WITHOUT TRADE UNIONS

Most organizations do, in fact, manage without trade unions; they constitute what Guest (2001) refers to as the 'black hole'. Millward *et al* (1992) established from the third *Workplace Industrial Relations Survey* (2004) that the characteristics of union-free employee relations were as follows:

- Employee relations were generally seen by managers as better in the non-union sector than in the union sector.
- Strikes were almost unheard of.
- Labour turnover was high but absenteeism was no worse.
- Pay levels were generally set unilaterally by management.
- The dispersion of pay was higher, it was more market related and there was more performance-related pay. There was also a greater incidence of low pay.
- In general, no alternative methods of employee representation existed as a substitute for trade union representation.
- Employee relations were generally conducted with a much higher degree of informality than in the union sector. In a quarter of non-union workplaces there were no grievance procedures and about a fifth had no formal disciplinary procedures.
- Managers generally felt unconstrained in the way in which they organized work.
- There was more flexibility in the use of labour than in the union sector, which included the greater use of freelance and temporary workers.
- Employees in the non-union sector are two and a half times as likely to be dismissed as those in unionized firms and the incidence of compulsory redundancies is higher.

The survey concluded that many of the differences between unionized and non-unionized workplaces could be explained by the generally smaller size of the non-union firms and the fact that many such workplaces were independent, rather than being part of a larger enterprise.

Another characteristic not mentioned by the survey is the use by non-unionized firms of personal contracts as an alternative to collective bargaining. In theory, employees are free to negotiate such contracts, but as an Anglia Polytechnic University (1995) study found, little bargaining activity takes place in the 500 workplaces they surveyed. The conclusion was that the personal contract 'reflects inherent inequality of bargaining power' and this suggests that there is a continuing role for trade unions.

This does not paint a very satisfactory picture of employee relations from the workers' point of view, but it is probably typical of smaller, independent firms. Some of the latter may be what Marchington (1995b) describes as the traditional sweatshop employer. The pressure on the firm could be to control costs and increase flexibility and responsiveness to customer demands. These are objectives which management may feel could only be achieved without union interference.

Some larger organizations, for example IBM and Marks & Spencer, manage without unions by, in effect, adopting a 'union substitution' policy. This offers a complete employment package, which can be seen by employees as an attractive alternative to trade union membership. The package is likely to include highly competitive pay with harmonized employment conditions, recruitment tests designed to select people who match organizational norms, a focus on employee communications and information sharing, induction programmes that aim to get employees to accept the organization's ethos, an emphasis on training and career development and a commitment to providing secure and satisfying work. Such businesses may broadly adhere to the HRM model (although they would not describe it as such, and this is the approach they used before HRM was invented).

HRM techniques for increasing commitment through involvement and communication processes provide a route that some organizations without unions follow in order to maintain a satisfactory employee relations climate. But it is not easy. Unless HRM fits the core values of the organization and is in accord with its management style, and unless a coherent and integrated approach is adopted to introducing HRM processes, it is unlikely to succeed.

52

Negotiating and bargaining

Collective bargaining requires the exercise of negotiating skills. Bargaining skills are also necessary during the process of negotiating collective substantive agreements on terms and conditions of employment. Negotiating skills are required in many other aspects of HRM, including, for example, agreeing individual contracts of employment and outsourcing contracts, but this chapter concentrates on those used in collective bargaining. This chapter covers the nature and process of negotiation and bargaining, bargaining conventions, the stages of negotiation and, in summary, the skills required.

THE NATURE OF NEGOTIATING AND BARGAINING

To negotiate is to converse with a view to finding terms of agreement. To bargain is to go through the steps required to come to terms on a transaction. Collective bargaining is essentially a process of negotiation – of conferring and, it is hoped, reaching agreement without resorting to force (although hard words may be exchanged on the way).

Within this negotiating process bargaining takes place. This means coming to terms on a settlement, which in a pay negotiation may be somewhere between the union's opening demand of, say, 4 per cent increase and the employer's first response of, say, 2 per cent. The point at which a settlement is achieved between these figures will depend on the relative bargaining power of the two parties, the realism of the offer or response, the level of bargaining skills the parties can deploy and the sheer determination of either party to press its point or not to concede (this may be a function of bargaining power).

NEGOTIATING

Negotiating take place when two parties meet to reach an agreement. This can be a convergent process (in commercial terms this is sometimes referred to as a 'willing buyer – willing seller' situation) where both parties are equally keen to reach a win–win agreement. Clearly, if this can be achieved rather than a win–lose outcome, the future relationships between the parties are more likely to be harmonious. Certainly, the primary aim of any negotiator should be to proceed on this basis.

But some negotiations can be described as 'divergent' in which one or both of the parties aim to win as much as they can from the other while giving away as little as possible. In these circumstances, negotiating can be a war game. It is a battle in the sense that the bargainers are pitting their wits against each other while also bringing in the heavy artillery in the shape of sanctions or threatened sanctions. As with other battles, the negotiation process can produce a pyrrhic victory in which both sides, including the apparent winner, retire to mourn their losses and lick their wounds. It is a game in the sense that both sides are trying to win, but there are various conventions or rules that the parties tacitly adopt or recognize, although they may break them in the heat of the battle.

Negotiations can normally be broken down into four stages:

1. preparing for negotiation: setting objectives, defining strategy and assembling data;
2. opening;
3. bargaining;
4. closing.

Before analysing these stages in detail it may be helpful to consider the process of bargaining and list the typical conventions that operate when bargaining takes place.

The process of bargaining

The process of bargaining consists of three distinct, though related, functions. First, bargainers state their bargaining position to their opposite numbers. Second, they probe weaknesses in the bargaining position of their opposite numbers and try to convince them that they must move, by stages if this is inevitable, from their present position to a position closer to what the bargainer wants. Third, they adjust or confirm their original estimate of their own bargaining position in the light of information gleaned and reactions from their opposite numbers, in order that, if the time comes to put an estimate of bargaining position to the test, the ground chosen will be as favourable as possible.

The essence of the bargaining process was described by Peters (1968):

> In skilful hands the bargaining position performs a double function. It conceals and it reveals. The bargaining position is used to indicate – to unfold gradually, step by step – the maximum expectation of the negotiator, while at the same time concealing, for as long as necessary, his minimum expectation. By indirect means, such as the manner and timing of the changes in your bargaining position, you, as a negotiator, try to convince the other side that your maximum expectation is really your minimum breaking-off point. Since you have taken an appropriate bargaining position at the start of negotiations, each change in your position should give ever-clearer indications of your maximum expectation. Also, each change should be designed to encourage or pressure the other side to reciprocate with as much information as you give them.

Bargaining conventions

There are certain conventions in collective bargaining which most experienced and responsible negotiators understand and accept, although they are never stated and, indeed, may be broken in the heat of the moment, or by a tyro in the bargaining game. These conventions help to create an atmosphere of trust and understanding which is essential to the maintenance of the type of stable bargaining relationship that benefits both sides. Some of the most generally accepted conventions are listed below:

- Whatever happens during the bargaining, both parties are using the bargaining process in the hope of coming to a settlement.
- While it is preferable to conduct negotiations in a civilized and friendly manner, attacks, hard words, threats, and (controlled) losses of temper are sometimes used by negotiators to underline determination to get their way and to shake their opponent's confidence and self-possession – but these should be treated by both sides as legitimate tactics and should not be allowed to shake the basic belief in each other's integrity or desire to settle without taking drastic action.
- Off-the-record discussions are mutually beneficial as a means of probing attitudes and intentions and smoothing the way to a settlement, but they should not be referred to specifically in formal bargaining sessions unless both sides agree in advance.

- Each side should normally be prepared to move from its original position.
- It is normal, although not inevitable, for the negotiation to proceed by alternate offers and counter-offers from each side which lead steadily towards a settlement.
- Concessions, once made, cannot be withdrawn.
- Firm offers must not be withdrawn, although it is legitimate to make and withdraw conditional offers.
- Third parties should not be brought in until both parties are agreed that no further progress would be made without them.
- The final agreement should mean exactly what it says – there should be no trickery, and the terms agreed should be implemented without amendment.
- So far as possible, the final settlement should be framed in such a way as to reduce the extent to which the other party obviously loses face or credibility.

Preparing for negotiation

Negotiations take place in an atmosphere of uncertainty. Neither side knows how strong the other side's bargaining position is or what it really wants and will be prepared to accept. They do not know how much the other party will be prepared to concede or the strength of its convictions.

In a typical pay negotiation unions or representative bodies making the claim will define three things:

- the target they would like to achieve;
- the minimum they will accept;
- the opening claim which they believe will be most likely to help achieve the target.

Employers define three related things:

- the target settlement they would like to achieve;
- the maximum they would be prepared to concede;
- the opening offer they will make which would provide them with sufficient room to manoeuvre in reaching their target.

The difference between the union's claim and the employer's offer is the negotiating range. If your maximum exceeds their minimum, this will indicate the settlement range. This is illustrated in Figure 52.1. In this example the chance of settlement without too much trouble is fairly high. It is when your maximum is less than their minimum, as in Figure 52.2, that the trouble starts. Over a period of time a negotiation where a settlement range exists proceeds in the way demonstrated in Figure 52.3.

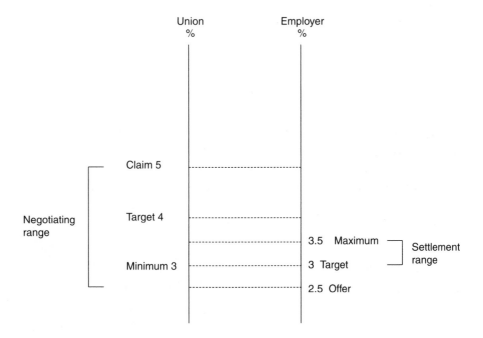

Figure 52.1   Negotiating range within a settlement range

Objectives

The objectives in the form of a target settlement and initial and minimum/maximum offers and agreements will be conditioned by:

- the perceptions of both parties about the relative strengths of their cases;
- the relative power of the two parties;
- the amount of room for negotiation the parties want to allow;
- the employer's ability to pay;
- the going rate elsewhere;
- the rate of inflation – although employers are reluctant to concede that it is their job to protect their employees from inflation, the cost of living is often one of the chief arguments advanced by a union for an increase.

Strategy

Negotiating strategy should clearly be designed to achieve the target settlement, with the maximum the negotiator is prepared to concede being the fall-back position. Two decisions are required:

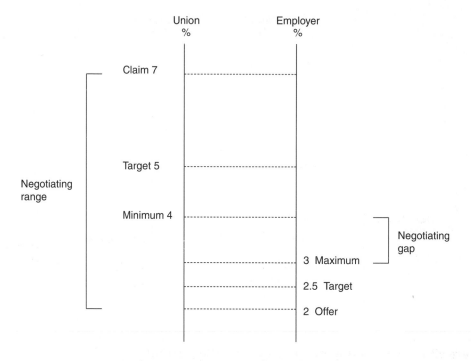

Figure 52.2   Negotiating range with a negotiating gap

1.   The stages to follow in moving from, in the union's case, the opening claim to the final agreement, and in the employer's case from the initial to the closing offer. This is dependent on the amount of room for negotiating that has been allowed.
2.   The negotiating package the employer wants to use in reply to whatever package the union has put forward. The employer's aim should be to provide scope for trading concessions during the course of negotiations. From their viewpoint, there is also much to be said for having in reserve various conditions which they can ask the unions to accept in return for any concessions they may be prepared to make. Employers might, for example, ask for an extended period before the next settlement in return for an increase in their offer.

Preparation steps

Negotiators must prepare carefully for negotiations so that they do not, in Aneurin Bevan's phrase, 'go naked to the conference table'. The following steps should be taken:

●   List the arguments to be used in supporting your case.

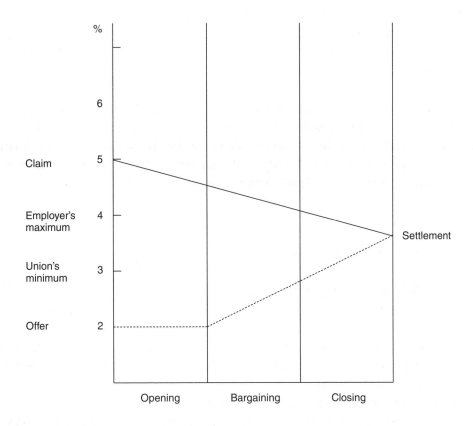

Figure 52.3 Stages of a negotiation

- List the likely arguments or counter-arguments that the other party is likely to use.
- List the counter-arguments to the arguments of the other side.
- Obtain the data you need to support your case.
- Select the negotiating team – this should never have fewer than two members, and for major negotiations should have three or more: one to take the lead and do most of the talking, one to take notes and feed the negotiator with any supporting information required, and the others to observe opposite numbers and play a specific part in negotiations in accordance with their brief.
- Brief the members of the negotiating team on their roles and the negotiating strategy and tactics that are to be adopted – if appropriate, prepared statements or arguments should be issued at this stage to be used as required by the strategic plan.

- Rehearse the members of the team in their roles; they can be asked to repeat their points to other members and deal with responses from them; or someone can act as devil's advocate and force the leader or other members of the team to handle awkward points or negotiating ploys.

At this stage it may be possible to meet one or more members of the other side informally to sound out their position, while they sound out yours. This 'early warning' system can be used to condition either side to modify their likely initial demands or responses by convincing them either of the strength of your own position or their determination to persist with the claim or to resist.

Opening

Opening tactics can be as follows:

- Open realistically and move moderately.
- Challenge the other side's position as it stands; do not destroy their ability to move.
- Explore attitudes, ask questions, observe behaviour and, above all, listen in order to assess the other side's strengths and weaknesses, their tactics and the extent to which they may be bluffing.
- Make no concessions of any kind at this stage.
- Be non-committal about proposals and explanations (do not talk too much).

Bargaining

After the opening moves, the main bargaining phase takes place in which the gap is narrowed between the initial positions and the parties attempt to persuade each other that their case is strong enough to force the other side to close at a less advantageous point than they had planned. The following tactics can be employed:

- Always make conditional proposals: 'If you will do this, then I will consider doing that' – the words to remember are: if… then…
- Never make one-sided concessions: always trade off against a concession from the other party: 'If I concede x, then I expect you to concede y'.
- Negotiate on the whole package: negotiations should not allow the other side to pick off item by item.
- Keep the issues open to extract the maximum benefit from potential trade-offs.

Closing

When and how negotiators should close is a matter of judgement, and depends on an assessment of the strength of the other side's case and their determination to see it through. There are various closing techniques:

- making a concession from the package, preferably a minor one which is traded off against an agreement to settle – the concession can be offered more positively than in the bargaining stage: 'If you will agree to settle at x, then I will concede y';
- doing a deal: splitting the difference, or bringing in something new, such as extending the settlement time scale, agreeing to back-payments, phasing increases, or making a joint declaration of intent to do something in the future (eg introducing a productivity plan);
- summarizing what has happened to date, emphasizing the concessions that have been made and the extent to which movement has been made and stating that the final position has been reached;
- applying pressure through a threat of the dire consequences which will follow if a 'final' claim is not agreed or a 'final' offer is not accepted;
- giving the other side a choice between two courses of action.

Employers should not make a final offer unless they mean it. If it is not really their final offer and the union calls their bluff they may have to make further concessions and their credibility will be undermined. Each party will, of course, attempt to force the other side into revealing the extent to which they have reached their final position. But negotiators should not allow themselves to be pressurized. If negotiators want to avoid committing themselves and thus devaluing the word 'final', they should state as positively as they can that this is as far as they are prepared to go. But bargaining conventions accept that further moves may still be made on a *quid pro quo* basis from this 'final position'.

NEGOTIATING AND BARGAINING SKILLS

Negotiating skills

The main negotiating skills are:

- *analytical ability* – the capacity to assess the key factors which will affect the negotiating stance and tactics of both sides, and to use this assessment to ensure that all the facts and argument that can be used to support the negotiator's case or prejudice the other party's case are marshalled;

- *empathy* – the ability to put oneself in the other party's shoes to understand not only what they are hoping to achieve but also why they have these expectations and the extent to which they are determined to fulfil them;
- *planning ability* – to develop and implement negotiating strategies and tactics but to be prepared to be flexible about the tactics in the light of developments during negotiations;
- *interactive skills* – the capacity to relate well with other people, to be persuasive without being domineering, to make a point without using it as an opportunity to make the other side lose face, to show respect to the other side's arguments and points if they are valid while questioning them if they are dubious, to respond quickly to changing moods and reactions so that the opportunity can be seized to make progress towards consensus (and the achievement of consensus is the ultimate aim);
- *communicating skills* – the ability to convey information and arguments clearly, positively and logically while also being prepared to listen to the other side and to respond appropriately.

Bargaining skills

The basic bargaining skills are:

- the ability to sense the extent to which the other side wants or indeed expects to achieve its claims or sustain its offer;
- the reciprocal ability not to give real wants away (bargaining, as was mentioned earlier, is about concealing as well as revealing) – in the market place it is always easier for sellers to drive a hard bargain with buyers who have revealed somehow that they covet the article;
- flexible realism – the capacity to make realistic moves during the bargaining process to reduce the claim or increase the offer which will demonstrate that the bargainer is seeking a reasonable settlement and is prepared to respond appropriately to movements made by the other side;
- respect – the ability to demonstrate to the other party that the negotiator respects their views and takes them seriously even if he or she disagrees with them;
- sensitivity – the ability to sense changes in moods and directions or weaknesses in arguments and respond quickly to press home a point.

Acquiring the skills

Negotiating and bargaining skills are developed through experience. To a certain extent they can be taught in the classroom through role plays and simulations but these can never replace the reality of sitting down with the other side and discussing claims and counter-offers, making points, handling confrontation and working out and applying the tactics required to reach a satisfactory settlement. It is useful to be aware of the need to apply the skills listed above but they only become meaningful during actual negotiation.

The best way to learn is by being a subsidiary member of a team with the scope to observe and comment on the tactics, approaches and skills used by both sides and, increasingly, to make planned contributions. A good team leader will nurse the tyro negotiator and will review the nature of each negotiating session to assess what went right or wrong, and why. This is how the writer learnt his negotiating skills and it served him in good stead when faced with the task of leading negotiating teams at plant, local and national level in the stimulating, exciting but sometimes frustrating process of negotiation.

53

Employee voice

The phrase 'employee voice' refers to the say employees have in matters of concern to them in their organization. Employee voice processes answer the question posed by Beardwell (1998): 'What is the most important expression of employee perspectives within any organization?' In this chapter the notion of employee voice is first defined, and reference is made to the more traditional but closely associated concepts of participation and involvement. The rest of the chapter is devoted to describing the various employee voice processes that can be developed in organizations.

THE CONCEPT OF EMPLOYEE VOICE

As defined by Boxall and Purcell (2003), 'Employee voice is the term increasingly used to cover a whole variety of processes and structures which enable, and sometimes empower employees, directly and indirectly, to contribute to decision-making in the firm.' Employee voice can be seen as 'the ability of employees to influence the actions of the employer' (Millward *et al* 2000). The concept covers the provision of opportunities for employees to register discontent and modify the power of management. It embraces involvement, and more significantly, participation.

INVOLVEMENT AND PARTICIPATION

Involvement means that management allows employees to discuss with it issues that affect them but that management retains the right to manage. It is primarily a management-driven concept. Participation is about employees playing a greater part in the decision making process. It is therefore much closer to the concept of employee voice systems, that is, arrangements for ensuring that employees are given the opportunity to influence management decisions and to contribute to the improvement of organizational performance.

PURPOSES OF EMPLOYEE VOICE

The purposes of employee voice have been defined by Marchington *et al* (2001) as follows:

- *Articulation of individual dissatisfaction* – to rectify a problem with management or prevent deterioration of relations.
- *Expression of collective organization* – to provide a countervailing source of power to management.
- *Contribution to management decision making* – to seek improvements in work organization, quality and productivity.
- *Demonstration of mutuality and cooperative relations* – to achieve long term viability for the organization and its employees.

THE FRAMEWORK FOR EMPLOYEE VOICE

The framework for employee voice has been modelled by Marchington *et al* (2001) as shown in Figure 53.1. This framework identifies two dimensions of voice: first, individual employees, and second, collective; that is, union and other representation. The shared agenda of involvement and partnership is a form of upward problem solving. This is on the same axis as the contested agenda of grievances and collective bargaining. These are not absolutes. Organizations will have tendencies toward shared or contested agendas, just as there will be varying degrees of direct and indirect involvement, although they are unlikely to have partnership and traditional collective bargaining at the same time. As Kochan *et al* (1986) point out, one of the strongest factors affecting the choice of approach to employee voice is the attitude of management towards unions.

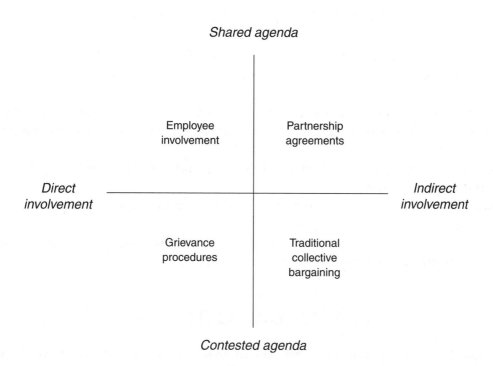

Figure 53.1 A framework for employee voice

(Source: M. Marchington, A. Wilkinson, P Ackers and A. Dandon, *Management Choice and Employee Voice*, CIPD, 2001)

EXPRESSION OF EMPLOYEE VOICE

The degree to which employees have a voice will vary considerably. At one end of the scale there is unilateral management, where employees have no voice at all. At the other end, employees might have complete self-management and control as in a cooperative, although this is rare. In between, the steps in the degree to which employees have voice, as defined by Boxall and Purcell (2003), are:

- little voice – information provided;
- downward – right to be told;
- some – opportunity to make suggestions;
- two way – consulted during decision making;
- two way plus – consulted at all stages of decision making and implementation;
- a lot – the right to delay a decision;
- power to affect outcome – the right to veto a decision;
- substantial – equality or co-determination in decision making.

FACTORS AFFECTING CHOICE

Research carried out by Marchington *et al* (1992) identified a number of factors that influenced employers to implement employee involvement or voice initiatives:

● *information and education* – a desire to 'educate' employees more fully about aspects of the business and to convince them of the 'logic' of management's actions;
● *secure enhanced employee contributions* – seeking employee ideas and using them to improve performance;
● *handling conflict at work and promoting stability* – providing a safety valve for the expression of employees' views;
● *a mechanism for channelling employee anxieties and misgivings* without their resorting to the disputes procedure and industrial action.

FORMS OF EMPLOYEE VOICE

As defined by Marchington *et al* (2001), the main methods of employee voice fall into two categories: representative participation and upward problem solving.

Representative participation

● *Joint consultation* – a formal mechanism which provides the means for management to consult employee representatives on matters of mutual interest (discussed in more detail below).
● *Partnership schemes* – these emphasize mutual gains and tackling issues in a spirit of cooperation rather than through traditional adversarial relationships.
● *European Works Councils* – these may be set up across European sites as required by EU legislation.
● *Collective representation* – the role of trade unions or other forms of staff association in collective bargaining and representing the interests of individual employees and groups of employees. This includes the operation of grievance procedures.

Upward problem solving

● *Electronic media* – the intranet.
● *Two way communication* – meetings between managers and their staff, or briefing groups.

- *Attitude surveys* – seeking the opinions of staff through questionnaires (discussed in more detail below).
- *Suggestion schemes* – the encouragement of employees to make suggestions, often accompanied by rewards for accepted ideas (discussed in more detail below).
- *Project teams* – getting groups of employees together with line managers to develop new ideas, processes, services or products or to solve problems (quality circles and improvement groups come into this category, although the former have generally failed to survive as a specific method of involvement).

JOINT CONSULTATION

Joint consultation enables managers and employee representatives to meet on a regular basis in order to exchange views, to make good use of members' knowledge and expertise, and to deal with matters of common interest that are not the subject of collective bargaining.

For joint consultation to work well it is first necessary to define, discuss and agree its objectives. These should be related to tangible and significant aspects of the job, the process of management, or the formulation of policies that affect the interests of employees. They should not deal only with peripheral matters such as welfare, social amenities or the quality of the sausages in the staff restaurant. Consultation should take place before decisions are made. Management must believe in and must be seen to believe in involving employees. Actions speak better than words, and management should demonstrate that it will put into effect the joint decisions made during discussions. The unions must also believe in participation as a genuine means of giving them voice and advancing the interests of their members, and not simply as a way of getting more power. They should show by their actions that they are prepared to support unpopular decisions to which they have been a party.

Joint consultation machinery should be in line with any existing systems of negotiation and representation. It should not be supported by management as a possible way of reducing the powers of the union. If this naive approach is taken, it will fail – it always does. Joint consultation should be regarded as a process of integrative bargaining complementary to the distributive bargaining that takes place in joint negotiating committees.

Consultative committees should always relate to a defined working unit, should never meet unless there is something specific to discuss, and should always conclude their meetings with agreed points which are implemented quickly.

Employee and management representatives should be properly briefed and trained, and have all the information they require. Managers and team leaders should be kept in the picture, and as appropriate, involved in the consultation process. It is clearly highly undesirable for them to feel that they have been left out.

ATTITUDE SURVEYS

Attitude surveys are a valuable way of involving employees by seeking their views on matters that concern them. Attitude surveys can provide information on the preferences of employees, give warning on potential problem areas, diagnose the cause of particular problems, and compare levels of job satisfaction, commitment and morale in different parts of the organization.

Methods of conducting attitude surveys

There are three methods of conducting attitude surveys:

- *By the use of structured questionnaires*. These can be issued to all or a sample of employees. The questionnaires may be standardized ones, such as the Brayfield and Rothe Index of Job Satisfaction, or they may be developed specially for the organization. The advantage of using standardized questionnaires is that they have been thoroughly tested, and in many cases norms are available against which results can be compared. Additional questions specially relevant to the company can be added to the standard list. A tailor-made questionnaire can be used to highlight particular issues, but it may be advisable to obtain professional help from an experienced psychologist, who can carry out the skilled work of drafting and pilot testing the questionnaire and interpreting the results. Questionnaires have the advantage of being relatively cheap to administer and analyse, especially when there are large numbers involved. Many organizations use electronic means (the intranet) to seek the views of employees generally or on particular issues. An example of an attitude survey dealing with views on pay is given in the Appendix.
- *By the use of interviews*. These may be 'open ended' or depth interviews in which the discussion is allowed to range quite freely. Alternatively they may be semi-structured in that there is a checklist of points to be covered, although the aim of the interviewer should be to allow discussion to flow around the points so that the frank and open views of the individual are obtained. Alternatively, and more rarely, interviews can be highly structured so that they become no more than the spoken application of a questionnaire. Individual interviews are to be preferred

because they are more likely to be revealing, but they are expensive and time-consuming and not so easy to analyse. Discussions through 'focus groups' (groups of employees convened to focus their attention on particular issues) are a quicker way of reaching a large number of people, but the results are not so easy to quantify, and some people may have difficulty in expressing their views in public.

- *By a combination of questionnaire and interview.* This is the ideal approach because it combines the quantitative data from the questionnaire with the qualitative data from the interviews. It is always advisable to accompany questionnaires with some depth interviews, even if time permits only a limited sample. An alternative approach is to administer the questionnaire to a group of people and then discuss the reactions to each question with the group. This ensures that a quantified analysis is possible but enables the group, or at least some members of it, to express their feelings more fully.
- *By the use of focus groups.* A focus group is a representative sample of employees whose attitudes and opinions are sought on issues concerning the organization and their work. The essential features of a focus group are that it is structured, informed, constructive and confidential.

Assessing results

It is an interesting fact that when people are asked directly if they are satisfied with their job, most of them (70 to 90 per cent) will say they are. This is regardless of the work being done, and often in spite of strongly held grievances. The probable reason for this phenomenon is that while most people are willing to admit to having griev-ances – in fact, if invited to complain, they will complain – they may be reluctant to admit, even to themselves, to being dissatisfied with a job that they have no imme-diate intention of leaving. Many employees have become reconciled to their work, even if they do not like some aspects of it, and have no real desire to do anything else. So they are, in a sense, satisfied enough to continue, even if they have complaints. Finally, many people are satisfied with their job overall, although they grumbled about many aspects of it.

Overall measures of satisfaction do not, therefore, always reveal anything inter-esting. It is more important to look at particular aspects of satisfaction or dissatisfac-tion, to decide whether or not anything needs to be done. In these circumstances, the questionnaire will indicate only a line to be followed up. It will not provide the answers. Hence the advantage of individual meetings or focus group discussions to explore in depth any issue raised.

SUGGESTION SCHEMES

Suggestion schemes can provide a valuable means for employees to participate in improving the efficiency of the company. Properly organized, they can help to reduce the feelings of frustration endemic in all concerns where people think they have good ideas but cannot get them considered because there are no recognized channels of communication. Normally only those ideas outside the usual scope of employees' duties are considered, and this should be made clear, as well as the categories of those eligible for the scheme – senior managers are often excluded.

The basis of a successful suggestion scheme should be an established procedure for submitting and evaluating ideas, with tangible recognition for those that have merit, and an effective system for explaining to employees without discouraging them that their ideas cannot be accepted.

The most common arrangement is to use suggestion boxes, with possibly a special form for entering a suggestion. Alternatively, or additionally, employees can be given the name of an individual or a committee to whom suggestions should be submitted. Managers and team leaders must be stimulated to encourage their staff to submit suggestions, and publicity in the shape of posters, leaflets and articles in the company magazine should be used to promote the scheme. The publicity should give prominence to the successful suggestions and how they are being implemented.

One person should be made responsible for administering the scheme. He or she should have the authority to reject facetious suggestions, but should be given clear guidance on the routing of suggestions by subject matter to departments or individuals for their comments. The administrator deals with all communications, and if necessary may go back to the individual who submitted the suggestion to get more details of, for example, the savings in cost or improvements in output that should result from the idea.

It is desirable to have a suggestion committee consisting of management and employee representatives, to review suggestions in the light of the comments of any specialist functions or executives who have evaluated them. This committee should be given the final power to accept or reject suggestions, and be able if necessary to call for additional information or opinion before making its decision. The committee could also decide on the size of any award within established guidelines, such as a proportion of savings during the first year. There should be a standard procedure for recording the decisions of the committee and informing those who made suggestions of the outcome – with reasons for rejection if appropriate.

PLANNING FOR VOICE

The forms of voice appropriate for an organization depend upon the values and attitudes of management, and if they exist trade unions, and the current climate of employee relations. Planning should be based on a review of the existing forms of voice, which includes discussions with stakeholders (line managers, employees and trade union representatives) on the effectiveness of existing arrangements and any improvements required. In the light of these discussions, new or revised approaches can be developed, but it is necessary to brief and train those involved in the part they should play.

54

Communications

Organizations function by means of the collective action of people, yet each individual is capable of taking independent action which may not be in line with policy or instructions, or may not be reported properly to other people who ought to know about it. Good communications are required to achieve coordinated results.

Organizations are subject to the influence of continuous change which affects the work employees do, their well-being and their security. Change can be managed only by ensuring that the reasons for and the implications of change are communicated to those affected in terms which they can understand and accept.

Individuals are motivated by the extrinsic reward system and the intrinsic rewards coming from the work itself. But the degree to which they are motivated depends upon the amount of responsibility and scope for achievement provided by their job, and upon their expectations that the rewards they will get will be the ones they want, and will follow from the efforts they make. Feelings about work and the associated rewards depend very much on the effectiveness of communications from their managers or team leaders and within the company.

Above all, good two-way communications are required so that management can keep employees informed of the policies and plans affecting them, and employees can react promptly with their views about management's proposals and actions. Change cannot be managed properly without an understanding of the feelings of those affected by it, and an efficient system of communications is needed to understand and influence these feelings.

But the extent to which good communications create satisfactory relationships rather than simply reducing unsatisfactory ones, can be exaggerated. A feature of management practices is the way in which different management theories become fashionable or influential for a while and then decline in favour. Among these has been the 'good communications' theory of management. This approach to dealing with management problems is based upon the following assumptions:

● The needs and aims of both employees and management are, in the long run, the same in any organization. Managers' and employees' ideas and objectives can all be fitted together to form a single conceptual framework.
● Any differences in opinion between management and employees are due to misunderstandings which have arisen because communications are not good enough.
● The solution to industrial strife is to improve communications.

This theory is attractive and has some validity. Its weakness is that the assumptions are too sweeping, particularly the belief that the ultimate objectives of management and workers are necessarily identical. The good communications theory, like paternalism, seems to imply that a company can develop loyalty by keeping people informed and treating them well. But people working in organizations have other and, to them, more important loyalties elsewhere – and why not?

The existence of different loyalties and points of view in an organization does not mean that communication is unimportant. If anything the need for a good communications system becomes even greater when differences and conflict exist. But it can only alleviate those differences and pave the way to better cooperation. It cannot solve them.

It is therefore necessary to bear in mind that the group with which we identify – the reference group – influences our attitudes and feelings. 'Management' and the 'the union' as well as our family, our ethnic background, our political party and our religious beliefs (if any) constitute a reference group and colour our reactions to information. What each group 'hears' depends on its own interests. Shared experiences and common frames of reference have much more influence than exhortations from management. Employees may feel they have nothing to do with them because it conflicts with what they already believe.

However, although there may be limitations on the extent to which communication strategies can enhance mutuality and commitment, there is no doubt that it is essential for managements to keep people informed on matters that affect them and to provide channels for them to express their views. This is particularly necessary when new employment initiatives are taking place and effective change management is very much about communicating management's intentions to people and making sure that they understand how they will be affected.

COMMUNICATION AREAS AND OBJECTIVES

The main communication areas and their associated objectives are set out in Table 54.1.

Employee relations are mainly affected by managerial and internal communications, although external communications are an additional channel of information. The strategy for managerial communications is concerned with planning and control procedures, management information systems and techniques of delegating and giving instructions. These matters are outside the scope of this book, except in so far as the procedures and skills can be developed by training programmes.

COMMUNICATIONS STRATEGY

The strategy for internal communications should be based on analyses of:

- what management wants to say;
- what employees want to hear;
- the problems being met in conveying or receiving information.

These analyses can be used to indicate the systems of communication that need to be developed and the education and training programmes required to make them work. They should also provide guidance on how communications should be managed and timed. Bad management and poor timing are frequently the fundamental causes of ineffective communication.

What management wants to say

What management wants to say depends upon an assessment of what employees need to know, which, in turn, is affected by what they want to hear.

Management usually aims to achieve three things: first, to get employees to understand and accept what management proposes to do in areas that affect them; second, to obtain the commitment of employees to the objectives, plans and values of the organization; and, third, to help employees to appreciate more clearly the contribution they can make to organizational success and how it will benefit them.

Table 54.1 Communication areas and objectives

	Communication Area	Objectives
I. MANAGERIAL	1. the communication downwards and sideways of corporate or functional objectives, policies plans and budgets to those who have to implement them	to ensure that managers and supervisors receive clear, accurate and prompt information on what they are expected to achieve to further the company's objectives
	2. the communication downwards of direct instructions from a manager to a subordinate on what the latter has to do	to ensure that the instructions are clear and precise and provide the necessary motivation to get people into action
	3. the communication upwards and sideways of proposals, suggestions and comments on corporate or functional objectives, policies and budgets from those who have to implement them	to ensure that managers and supervisors have adequate scope to influence corporate and functional decisions on matters about which they have specific expertise and knowledge
	4. the communication upwards and sideways of management information on performance and results	to enable management to monitor and control performance in order that, as necessary, opportunities can be exploited or swift corrective action taken
II. INTERNAL RELATIONS	5. the communication downwards of information on company plans, policies or performance	to ensure that (i) employees are kept informed of matters that affect them, especially changes to working conditions, and factors influencing their prosperity and security; (ii) employees are encouraged to identify themselves more completely with the company
	6. the communication upwards of the comments and reactions of employees to what is proposed will happen or what is actually happening in matters that affect them	to ensure that employees are given an opportunity to voice their suggestions and fears and that the company is in a position to amend its plans in the light of these comments
III. EXTERNAL RELATIONS	7. the receipt and analysis of information from outside which affects the company's interests	to ensure that the company is fully aware of all the information on legislation and on marketing, commercial, financial and technological matters that affect its interests
	8. the presentation of information about the company and its products to the government, customers and the public at large	to exert influence in the interests of the company, to present a good image of the company, and to persuade customers to buy its products or services

Communications from management should be about values, plans, intentions and proposals (with the opportunity for discussion with and feedback from employees) as well as about achievements and results. Exhortations should not be used: no one listens to them. It is better to concentrate on specific requirements rather than resorting to general appeals for abstract things such as improved quality or productivity. The requirements should be phrased in a way which emphasizes how all concerned will actually work together and the mutual benefits that should result.

What employees want to hear

Clearly, employees want to hear about and to comment upon the matters that affect their interests. These will include changes in working methods and conditions, changes in the arrangements for overtime and shift working, company plans which may affect pay or security, and changes in terms and conditions of employment. It is management's job to understand what employees want to hear and plan its communications strategy accordingly. Understanding can be obtained by conducting 'focus groups' discussions which bring together groups of employees to focus on particular issues that concern them, by means of attitude surveys, by asking employee representatives, by informally listening to what employees say, and by analysing grievances to see if improved communications could modify them.

Analysing communication problems

Specific examples of employee relations problems where communication failures have been the cause or a contributory factor should be analysed to determine exactly what went wrong and what needs to be done to put it right. The problems may be any of those listed earlier in this chapter, including lack of appropriate channels of communication, lack of appreciation of the need to communicate, and lack of skill in overcoming the many formidable barriers to communication. Problems with channels of communication can be dealt with by introducing new or improved communications systems. Lack of skill is a matter for education and training.

COMMUNICATION SYSTEMS

Communication systems can be divided into those using an intranet, those using the written word such as magazines, newsletters, bulletins and notice-boards, and those using oral methods such as meetings, briefing groups and public address systems. The aim should be to make judicious use of a number of channels to make sure that the message gets across.

Communications through an intranet system

Organizations are increasingly relying on an internal e-mail system (the intranet) to communicate information, especially in workplaces where all or most of the employees have direct or indirect access to a computer. The advantage of intranet communications is that they can be transmitted swiftly to a wide audience. They can also be used for two-way communications – employees can be invited to respond to questions or surveys.

Magazines

Glossy magazines or house journals are an obvious way to keep employees informed about the company and are often used for public relations purposes as well. They can extol and explain the achievements of the company and may thus help to increase identification and even loyalty. If employees are encouraged to contribute (although this is difficult), the magazine can become more human. The biggest danger of this sort of magazine is that it becomes a public relations exercise which is seen by employees as having little relevance to their everyday affairs.

Newsletters

Newsletters aim to appear more frequently and to angle their contents more to the immediate concerns of employees than the glossier form of house magazine. To be effective, they should include articles specifically aimed at explaining what management is planning to do and how this affects everyone. They can also include more chatty 'human interest' material about the doings of employees to capture the attention of readers. Correspondence columns can provide an avenue for the expression of employees' views and replies from management, but no attempt should be made to censor letters (except those that are purely abusive) or to pull punches in reply. Anonymous letters should be published if the writer gives his name to the editor.

The key factor in the success of a newsletter or any form of house magazine is the editor, who should be someone who knows the company and its employees and can be trusted by everyone to be frank and fair. Professional expertise is obviously desirable but it is not the first consideration, as long as the editor can write reasonably well and has access to expert help in putting the paper together. It is often a good idea to have an editorial board consisting of management and employee representatives to advise and assist the editor.

Organizations often publish a newsletter in addition to a house magazine, treating the latter mainly as a public relations exercise and relying on the newsletter as the prime means of communicating with employees.

Bulletins

Bulletins can be used to give immediate information to employees which cannot wait for the next issue of a newsletter; or they can be a substitute for a formal publication if the company does not feel that the expense is justified. Bulletins are useful only if they are distributed quickly and are seen by all interested employees. They can simply be posted on notice-boards or, more effectively, given to individual employees and used as a starting point for a briefing session if they contain information of sufficient interest to merit a face-to-face discussion.

Notice-boards

Notice-boards are an obvious but frequently misused medium for communications. The biggest danger is allowing boards to be cluttered up with uninteresting or out-of-date material. It is essential to control what goes on to the boards and to appoint responsible people to service them by removing out-of-date or unauthorized notices.

A more impressive show can be made of notices and other material if an information centre is set up in the restaurant or some other suitable place where the information can be displayed in a more attractive and compelling manner than on a typical notice-board.

Employee involvement

Employee involvement through such means as consultative committees provides a channel for two-way communication. Sometimes, however, they are not particularly effective, either because their thunder has been stolen by union negotiation committees, or because their proceedings are over-formalized and restricted and fail to address the real issues. It is essential to disseminate the information revealed at committees around the offices and works, but it is impossible to rely on committee members to do this. Minutes can be posted on notice-boards, but they are seldom read, usually because they contain too much redundant material.

DVDs

Specially made DVDs can be a cost-effective method of getting across personal messages (eg from the chief executive) or information about how the company is doing. They can, however, be regarded by employees as too impersonal and/or too slick to have any real meaning.

Team briefing

The concept of team briefing (previously called briefing groups), as originally developed by the Industrial Society, is a device to overcome the restricted nature of joint consultative committees by involving everyone in an organization, level by level, in face-to-face meetings to present, receive and discuss information. Team briefing aims to overcome the gaps and inadequacies of casual briefings by injecting some order into the system.

Team briefing should operate as follows:

1. *Organization*
   - cover all levels in an organization;
   - fewest possible steps between the top and bottom;
   - between 4 and 18 in each group;
   - run by the immediate leader of each group at each level (who must be properly trained and briefed).
2. *Subjects*
   - policies – explanations of new or changed policies;
   - plans – as they affect the organization as a whole and the immediate group;
   - progress – how the organization and the group are getting on;
   - people – new appointments, points about personnel matters (pay, security, procedures).
3. *Sequence* – the briefing groups should work to a brief prepared by the board on key issues. This briefing is written up and cascaded down the organization. The briefing group meetings should, however, allow for discussion of the brief, and the system should cater for any reactions or comments to be fed back to the top. This provides for two-way communication.
4. *Timing and duration:*
   - a minimum of once a month for those in charge of others and once every two months for every individual in the organization – but meet only if there is something to say;
   - duration not longer than 20–30 minutes.

The merit of team briefing is that it enables face-to-face communications to be planned and, to a reasonable degree, formalized. It is easy, however, for it to start on a wave of enthusiasm and then to wither away because of lack of sufficient drive and enthusiasm from the top downward, inadequately trained and motivated managers and team leaders, reluctance of management to allow subjects of real importance to be discussed throughout the system, and insufficient feedback upwards through each level.

A team briefing system must be led and controlled effectively from the top, but it does require a senior manager with specific responsibility to advise on the subject matter and the preparation of briefs (it is important to have well-prepared material to ensure that briefing is carried out consistently and thoroughly at each level), to train managers and team leaders, and to monitor the system by checking on the effectiveness and frequency of meetings.

Part XI

Health, safety and welfare

This part deals with the services provided by the HR department in order to help the organization meet its legal and social responsibilities to ensure a healthy and safe place of work, to help employees cope with their personal problems, to help elderly and retired employees and, in some cases, to make recreational facilities available.

55

Health and safety

Health and safety policies and programmes are concerned with protecting employees – and other people affected by what the company produces and does – against the hazards arising from their employment or their links with the company.

Occupational health programmes deal with the prevention of ill-health arising from working conditions. They consist of two elements:

- *occupational medicine*, which is a specialized branch of preventive medicine concerned with the diagnosis and prevention of health hazards at work and dealing with any ill-health or stress that has occurred in spite of preventive actions;
- *occupational hygiene*, which is the province of the chemist and the engineer or ergonomist engaged in the measurement and control of environmental hazards.

Safety programmes deal with the prevention of accidents and with minimizing the resulting loss and damage to persons and property. They relate more to systems of work than the working environment, but both health and safety programmes are concerned with protection against hazards, and their aims and methods are clearly inter-linked.

The Royal Society for the Prevention of Accidents (Bibbings, 2003) has made the following observation on accident prevention:

We fail to prevent accidents not just because of incomplete control of the circumstances which give rise to them, but because of our partial knowledge of how things really are and, of course, our inevitably incomplete knowledge of what will happen in the future. Human beings in this sense fail to bring order to an essentially chaotic and dangerous world – not just because it defies their efforts to control it but because they do not fully understand its complexity and randomness. The result is a potentially dangerous tendency to deny that error and disorder are permanent features of the natural world and all human undertakings in particular. We become complacent and fail to take preventative action. Good investigation of accidents, where it takes place, tends almost invariably to show that failures to prevent them are rooted either in weaknesses in risk assessment or in the implementation of control measures.

MANAGING HEALTH AND SAFETY AT WORK

It is estimated by the Health and Safety Executive (HSE) that in the UK about 500 people are killed at work every year and several hundred thousand more are injured or suffer ill-health. It is also estimated that, apart from the pain and misery caused to those directly or indirectly concerned, the total cost to British employers of work-related injury and illness exceeds £4 billion a year.

The achievement of a healthy and safe place of work and the elimination to the maximum extent possible of hazards to health and safety are the responsibility of everyone employed in an organization, as well as those working there under contract. But the onus is on management to achieve and indeed go beyond the high standard in health and safety matters required by the legislation – the Health and Safety at Work etc. Act in 1974 and the various regulations laid down in the Codes of Practice.

The importance of healthy and safe policies and practices is, sadly, often underestimated by those concerned with managing businesses and by individual managers within those businesses. But it cannot be emphasized too strongly that the prevention of accidents and elimination of health and safety hazards are a prime responsibility of management and managers in order to minimize suffering and loss.

THE IMPORTANCE OF HEALTH AND SAFETY IN THE WORKPLACE

The achievement of the highest standards of health and safety in the workplace is important because the elimination, or at least minimization, of health and safety hazards and risks is the moral as well as the legal responsibility of employers – this is the over-riding reason. Close and continuous attention to health and safety is important because ill-health and injuries inflicted by the system of work or working conditions cause suffering and loss to individuals and their dependants. In addition, accidents and absences through ill-health or injuries result in losses and damage for the organization. This 'business' reason is very much less significant than the 'human' reasons given above but it is still a consideration, albeit a tangential one.

As described in this chapter, managing health and safety at work is a matter of:

- developing health and safety policies;
- conducting risk assessments which identify hazards and assess the risks attached to them;
- carrying out health and safety audits and inspections;
- implementing occupational health programmes;
- managing stress;
- preventing accidents;
- measuring health and safety performance;
- communicating the need for good health and safety practices;
- training in good health and safety practices;
- organizing health and safety.

BENEFITS OF WORKPLACE HEALTH AND SAFETY

Research by the Health and Safety Executive (2004a) in 19 case-study organizations such as AstraZeneca, Severn Trent Water and Transco, established that the tangible benefits from better health and safety management include higher productivity, lower absence, avoiding the cost of accidents and litigation, meeting client demands, and improved staff morale and employee relations. These organizations have managed to overcome the common perception that health and safety is a compliance or staff welfare issue, and use initiatives in this area to add value to the business. Employers in the study made a number of headline savings from investing in occupational health and safety:

- Rolls Royce saved £11 million through improved absence management;
- in one month, St Bartholomew's Hospital and the London NHS Trust recouped the cost of flu injections for staff;
- manual-handling injuries were eliminated and the resultant lost hours reduced to zero at furniture retailer MFI;

- British Polythene Industries saved £12 for every £1 spent on manual handling improvements;
- The Port of London Authority cut absence by 70 per cent.

HEALTH AND SAFETY POLICIES

Written health and safety policies are required to demonstrate that top management is concerned about the protection of the organization's employees from hazards at work and to indicate how this protection will be provided. They are, therefore, first, a declaration of intent, second, a definition of the means by which that intent will be realized, and third, a statement of the guidelines that should be followed by everyone concerned – which means all employees – in implementing the policy.

The policy statement should consist of three parts:

- the general policy statement;
- the description of the organization for health and safety;
- details of arrangements for implementing the policy.

The general policy statement

The general policy statement should be a declaration of the intention of the employer to safeguard the health and safety of employees. It should emphasize four fundamental points:

- that the safety of employees and the public is of paramount importance;
- that safety takes precedence over expediency;
- that every effort will be made to involve all managers, team leaders and employees in the development and implementation of health and safety procedures;
- that health and safety legislation will be complied with in the spirit as well as the letter of the law.

Organization

This section of the policy statement should describe the health and safety organization of the company through which high standards are set and achieved by people at all levels in the organization.

This statement should underline the ultimate responsibility of top management for the health and safety performance of the organization. It should then indicate how key management personnel are held accountable for performance in their areas. The role of safety representatives and safety committees should be defined, and the duties of specialists such as the safety adviser and the medical officer should be summarized.

CONDUCTING RISK ASSESSMENTS

What is a risk assessment?

Risk assessments are concerned with the identification of hazards and the analysis of the risks attached to them.

A *hazard* is anything that can cause harm (eg working on roofs, lifting heavy objects, chemicals, electricity etc). A *risk* is the chance, large or small, of harm actually being done by the hazard. Risk assessments are concerned with looking for hazards and estimating the level of risk associated with them. As suggested by Holt and Andrews (1993), risk can be calculated by multiplying a severity estimate by a probability estimate. That is, risk = severity × probability.

The purpose of risk assessments is, of course, to initiate preventive action. They enable control measures to be devised on the basis of an understanding of the relative importance of risks. Risk assessments must be recorded if there are five or more employees.

There are two types of risk assessment. The first is *quantitative risk assessment*, which produces an objective probability estimate based upon risk information that is immediately applicable to the circumstances in which the risk occurs. The second is *qualitative risk assessment*, which is more subjective and is based on judgement backed by generalized data. Quantitative risk assessment is preferable if the specific data are available. Qualitative risk assessment may be acceptable if there are little or no specific data as long as it is made systematically on the basis of an analysis of working conditions and hazards and informed judgement of the likelihood of harm actually being done.

Looking for hazards

The following, as suggested by the HSE and others, are typical activities where accidents happen or there are high risks:

- receipt of raw materials, eg lifting, carrying;
- stacking and storage, eg falling materials;

- movement of people and materials, eg falls, collisions;
- processing of raw materials, eg exposure to toxic substances;
- maintenance of buildings, eg roof work, gutter cleaning;
- maintenance of plant and machinery, eg lifting tackle, installation of equipment;
- using electricity, eg using hand tools, extension leads;
- operating machines, eg operating without sufficient clearance, or at an unsafe speed; not using safety devices;
- failure to wear protective equipment, eg hats, boots, clothing;
- distribution of finished jobs, eg movement of vehicles;
- dealing with emergencies, eg spillages, fires, explosions;
- health hazards arising from the use of equipment or methods of working, eg VDUs, repetitive strain injuries from badly designed work stations or working practices.

The HSE suggests that most accidents are caused by a few key activities. It advises that assessors should concentrate initially on those that could cause serious harm. Operations such as roof work, maintenance and transport movement cause far more deaths and injuries each year than many mainstream activities.

When carrying out a risk assessment it is also necessary to consider who might be harmed, eg employees, visitors (including cleaners and contractors and the public when calling in to buy products or enlist services).

Hazards should be ranked according to their potential severity as a basis for producing one side of the risk equation. A simple three-point scale can be used such as 'low', 'moderate' and 'high'. A more complex severity rating scale has been proposed by Holt and Andrews (1993), as follows:

1. *Catastrophic* – imminent danger exists, hazard capable of causing death and illness on a wide scale.
2. *Critical* – hazard can result in serious illness, severe injury, property and equipment damage.
3. *Marginal* – hazard can cause illness, injury, or equipment damage, but the results would not be expected to be serious.
4. *Negligible* – hazard will not result in serious injury or illness; remote possibility of damage beyond minor first-aid case.

Assessing the risk

When the hazards have been identified it is necessary to assess how high the risks are. The HSE suggests that this involves answering three questions:

- What is the worst result?
- How likely is it to happen?
- How many people could be hurt if things go wrong?

A probability rating system can be used such as the one recommended by Holt and Andrews:

1. *Probable* – likely to occur immediately or shortly.
2. *Reasonably probable* – probably will occur in time.
3. *Remote* – may occur in time.
4. *Extremely remote* – unlikely to occur.

Taking action

Risk assessment should lead to action. The type of action can be ranked in order of potential effectiveness in the form of a 'safety precedence sequence' as proposed by Holt and Andrews:

- *Hazard elimination* – use of alternatives, design improvements, change of process.
- *Substitution* – for example, replacement of a chemical with one which is less risky.
- *Use of barriers* – removing the hazard from the worker or removing the worker from the hazard.
- *Use of procedures* – limitation of exposure, dilution of exposure, safe systems of work (these depend on human response).
- *Use of warning systems* – signs, instructions, labels (these also depend on human response).
- *Use of personal protective clothing* – this depends on human response and is used as a side measure only when all other options have been exhausted.

Monitoring and evaluation

Risk assessment is not completed when action has been initiated. It is essential to monitor the hazard and evaluate the effectiveness of the action in eliminating it or at least reducing it to an acceptable level.

HEALTH AND SAFETY AUDITS

What is a health and safety audit?

Risk assessments identify specific hazards and quantify the risks attached to them. Health and safety audits provide for a much more comprehensive review of all aspects of health and safety policies, and procedures and practices programmes. As defined by Saunders (1992):

> A safety audit will examine the whole organisation in order to test whether it is meeting its safety aims and objectives. It will examine hierarchies, safety planning processes, decision-making, delegation, policy-making and implementation as well as all areas of safety programme planning.

Who carries out a health and safety audit?

Safety audits can be conducted by safety advisers and/or personnel specialists but the more managers, employees and trade union representatives are involved, the better. Audits are often carried out under the auspices of a health and safety committee with its members taking an active part in conducting them.

Managers can also be held responsible for conducting audits within their departments and, even better, individual members of these departments can be trained to carry out audits in particular areas. The conduct of an audit will be facilitated if check lists are prepared and a simple form used to record results.

Some organizations also use outside agencies such as the British Safety Institute to conduct independent audits.

What is covered by a health and safety audit?

A health and safety audit should cover:

Policies

- Do health and safety policies meet legal requirements?
- Are senior managers committed to health and safety?
- How committed are other managers, team leaders and supervisors to health and safety?
- Is there a health and safety committee? If not, why not?
- How effective is the committee in getting things done?

Procedures:

How effectively do the procedures:

- support the implementation of health and safety policies?
- communicate the need for good health and safety practices?
- provide for systematic risk assessments?
- ensure that accidents are investigated thoroughly?
- record data on health and safety which are used to evaluate performance and initiate action?
- ensure that health and safety considerations are given proper weight when designing systems of work or manufacturing and operational processes (including the design of equipment and work stations, the specification for the product or service, and the use of materials)?
- provide safety training, especially induction training and training when jobs or working methods are changed?

Safety practices

- To what extent do health and safety practices in all areas of the organization conform to the general requirements of the Health and Safety at Work Act and the specific requirements of the various regulations and codes of practice?
- What risk assessments have been carried out? What were the findings? What actions were taken?
- What is the health and safety performance of the organization as shown by the performance indicators? Is the trend positive or negative? If the latter, what is being done about it?
- How thoroughly are accidents investigated? What steps have been taken to prevent their recurrence?
- What is the evidence that managers and supervisors are really concerned about health and safety?

What should be done with the audit?

The audit should cover the questions above but its purpose is to generate action. Those conducting the audit will have to assess priorities and costs and draw up action programmes for approval by the Board.

SAFETY INSPECTIONS

Safety inspections are designed to examine a specific area of the organization – operational department or manufacturing process – in order to locate and define any faults in the system, equipment, plant or machines, or any operational errors that might be the source of accidents. Safety inspections should be carried out on a regular and systematic basis by line managers and supervisors with the advice and help of health and safety advisers. The steps to be taken in carrying out safety inspections are as follows:

- Allocate the responsibility for conducting the inspection.
- Define the points to be covered in the form of a checklist.
- Divide the department or plant into areas and list the points to which attention needs to be given in each area.
- Define the frequency with which inspections should be carried out – daily in critical areas.
- Use the check lists as the basis for the inspection.
- Carry out sample or spot checks on a random basis.
- Carry out special investigations as necessary to deal with special problems such as operating machinery without guards to increase throughput.
- Set up a reporting system (a form should be used for recording the results of inspections).
- Set up a system for monitoring that safety inspections are being conducted properly and on schedule and that corrective action has been taken where necessary.

OCCUPATIONAL HEALTH PROGRAMMES

Almost 20 million working days a year are lost because of work-related illness. Two million people say they suffer from an illness they believe was caused by their work. Muscular disorders, including repetitive strain injury and back pain, are by far the most commonly reported illnesses with 1.2 million affected, and the numbers are rising. The next biggest problem is stress, which 500,000 people say is so bad that it is making them ill. These are large and disturbing figures and they show that high priority must be given to creating and maintaining programmes for the improvement of occupational health.

The control of occupational health and hygiene problems can be achieved by:

- eliminating the hazard at source through design and process engineering;
- isolating hazardous processes and substances so that workers do not come into contact with them;
- changing the processes or substances used, to promote better protection or eliminate the risk;
- providing protective equipment, but only if changes to the design, process or specification cannot completely remove the hazard;
- training workers to avoid risk;
- maintaining plant and equipment to eliminate the possibility of harmful emissions, controlling the use of toxic substances and eliminating radiation hazards;
- good housekeeping to keep premises and machinery clean and free from toxic substances;
- regular inspections to ensure that potential health risks are identified in good time;
- pre-employment medical examinations and regular checks on those exposed to risk;
- ensuring that ergonomic considerations (ie, those concerning the design and use of equipment, machines, processes and workstations) are taken into account in design specifications, establishing work routines and training – this is particularly important as a means of minimizing the incidence of repetitive strain injury (RSI);
- maintaining preventive medicine programmes which develop health standards for each job and involve regular audits of potential health hazards and regular examinations for anyone at risk.

Particular attention needs to be exercised on the control of noise, fatigue and stress. Control of stress should be regarded as a major part of any occupational health programme.

MANAGING STRESS

There are four main reasons why organizations should take account of stress and do something about it:

1. They have the social responsibility to provide a good quality of working life.
2. Excessive stress causes illness.
3. Stress can result in inability to cope with the demands of the job, which, of course, creates more stress.

4. Excessive stress can reduce employee effectiveness and therefore organizational performance.

The ways in which stress can be managed by an organization include:

- *job design* – clarifying roles, reducing the danger of role ambiguity and conflict and giving people more autonomy within a defined structure to manage their responsibilities;
- *targets and performance standards* – setting reasonable and achievable targets which may stretch people but do not place impossible burdens on them;
- *placement* – taking care to place people in jobs that are within their capabilities;
- *career development* – planning careers and promoting staff in accordance with their capabilities, taking care not to over- or under-promote;
- *performance management processes*, which allow a dialogue to take place between managers and individuals about the latter's work, problems and ambitions;
- *counselling* – giving individuals the opportunity to talk about their problems with a member of the personnel department or the company medical officer, or through an employee assistance programme;
- *management training* in performance review and counselling techniques and in what managers can do to alleviate their own stress and reduce it in others;
- *work–life balance policies* which take account of the pressures on employees who have responsibilities as parents, partners or carers, and which can include such provisions as special leave and flexible working hours.

The Health and Safety Executive (2003) has named the following 'beacons of excellence' for stress prevention:

- *Senior management commitment* – stress interventions are unlikely to be implemented successfully without the long-term commitment of management.
- *Participative approach* – involving employees from all levels of the organization at every stage in a stress management programme increases the likelihood of a successful outcome.
- *Stress prevention strategy* – this should cover the aims of interventions, tasks, responsibilities and resources available.
- *Risk assessment and task analysis* – an appraisal of work activities should enable an employer to recognize stress hazards before interventions are designed.
- *Work-related and worker-related prevention and management* – interventions should be designed to tackle the causes of stress emanating from the work environment and support individuals who are not protected by the first set of interventions, or who are subject to special stressors.

ACCIDENT PREVENTION

The prevention of accidents is achieved by:

- identifying the causes of accidents and the conditions under which they are most likely to occur;
- taking account of safety factors at the design stage – building safety into the system;
- designing safety equipment and protective devices and providing protective clothing;
- carrying out regular risk assessments audits, inspections and checks and taking action to eliminate risks;
- investigating all accidents resulting in damage to establish the cause and to initiate corrective action;
- maintaining good records and statistics in order to identify problem areas and unsatisfactory trends;
- conducting a continuous programme of education and training on safe working habits and methods of avoiding accidents;
- leadership and motivation – encouraging methods of leadership and motivation that do not place excessive demands on people.

MEASURING HEALTH AND SAFETY PERFORMANCE

The saying that 'if you can't measure it you can't manage it' is totally applicable to health and safety. It is essential to know what is happening, and it is even more essential to measure trends as a means of identifying in good time where actions are necessary.

The most common measures are:

- *The frequency rate:*

$$\frac{\text{Number of injuries} \times 100,000}{\text{Number of hours worked}}$$

- *The incidence rate:*

$$\frac{\text{Number of injuries} \times 1,000}{\text{Average number employed during the period}}$$

- *The severity rate* – the days lost through accidents or occupation health problems per 1,000,000 hours worked.

  Some organizations adopt a 'total loss control' approach which covers the cost of accidents to the business under such headings as pay to people off work, damage to plant or equipment and loss of production. A cost severity rate can then be calculated, which is the total cost of accidents per 1,000,000 hours worked.

COMMUNICATING THE NEED FOR BETTER HEALTH AND SAFETY PRACTICES

As Holt and Andrews (1993) observe, various forms of propaganda selling the health and safety message have been used for many years, although: 'They are now widely felt to be of little value in measurable terms in changing behaviour and influencing attitudes to health and safety issues.' But they believe that it is still necessary to deliver the message that health and safety is important as long as this supplements rather than replaces other initiatives. They suggest that the following steps can be taken to increase the effectiveness of safety messages:

- *Avoid negatives* – successful safety propaganda should contain positive messages, not warnings of the unpleasant consequences of actions.
- *Expose correctly* – address the message to the right people at the point of danger.
- *Use attention-getting techniques carefully* – lurid images may only be remembered for what they are, not for the message they are trying to convey.
- *Maximize comprehension* – messages should be simple and specific.
- *Messages must be believable* – they should address real issues and be perceived as being delivered by people (ie. managers) who believe in what they say and are doing something about it.
- *Messages must point the way to action* – the most effective messages call for positive actions that can be achieved by the receivers and will offer them a tangible benefit.

Approaches to briefing staff on the importance of health and safety

Advice to a group of staff on the importance of health and safety in the workplace must be based on a thorough understanding of the organization's health and safety policies and procedures and an appreciation of the particular factors affecting the health and safety of the group of people concerned. The latter can be based on information provided by risk assessments, safety audits and accident reports. But the advice must be positive – why health and safety is important and how accidents can be prevented. The advice should not be over-weighted by awful warnings.

The points to be made include:

- a review of the health and safety policies of the organization with explanations of the reasoning behind them and a positive statement of management's belief that health and safety is a major consideration because (1) it directly affects the well-being of all concerned; and (2) it can, and does, minimize suffering and loss;
- a review of the procedures used by the organization for the business as a whole and in the particular area to assess risks and audit safety position;
- an explanation of the roles of the members of the group in carrying out their work safely and giving full consideration to the safety of others;
- a reiteration of the statement that one of the core values of the organization is the maintenance of safe systems of work and the promotion of safe working practices.

HEALTH AND SAFETY TRAINING

Health and safety training is a key part of the preventative programme. It should start as part of the induction course. It should also take place following a transfer to a new job or a change in working methods. Safety training spells out the rules and provides information on potential hazards and how to avoid them. Further refresher training should be provided and special courses laid on to deal with new aspects of health and safety or areas in which safety problems have emerged.

ORGANIZING HEALTH AND SAFETY

Health and safety concerns everyone in an establishment although the main responsibility lies with management in general and individual managers in particular. The specific roles are summarized below:

- *Management* develops and implements health and safety policies and ensures that procedures for carrying out risk assessments, safety audits and inspections are implemented. Importantly, management has the duty of monitoring and evaluating health and safety performance and taking corrective action as necessary.

- *Managers* can exert the greater influence on health and safety. They are in immediate control and it is up to them to keep a constant watch for unsafe conditions or practices and to take immediate action. They are also directly responsible for ensuring that employees are conscious of health and safety hazards and do not take risks.

- *Employees* should be aware of what constitutes safe working practices as they affect them and their fellow workers. While management and managers have the duty to communicate and train, individuals also have the duty to take account of what they have heard and learned in the ways they carry out their work.

- *Health and safety advisers* advise on policies and procedures and on healthy and safe methods of working. They conduct risk assessments and safety audits and investigations into accidents in conjunction with managers and health and safety representatives, maintain statistics and report on trends and necessary actions.

- *Medical advisers* have two functions: preventive and clinical. The preventive function is most important, especially on occupational health matters. The clinical function is to deal with industrial accidents and diseases and to advise on the steps necessary to recover from injury or illness arising from work. They do not usurp the role of the family doctor in non-work-related illnesses.

- *Safety committees* consisting of health and safety representatives advise on health and safety policies and procedures, help in conducting risk assessments and safety audits, and make suggestions on improving health and safety performance.

56

Welfare services

Welfare services may be provided for matters concerning employees which are not immediately connected with their jobs although they may be connected generally with their place of work. These matters will include individual services relating to employees' welfare such as private help with counselling on personal problems, assistance with problems of health or sickness and special services for retired employees. Group services may include the provision of social and sporting activities and restaurants. Child-care facilities may be provided for individual employees but on a collective basis.

WHY PROVIDE WELFARE SERVICES?

There are arguments against the provision of welfare services. They imply do-gooding and the HR fraternity has spent many years trying to shake off its association with what it, and others, like to think of as at best peripheral and at worst redundant welfare activities. Welfare is provided by the state services – why should industrial, commercial or public sector organizations duplicate what is already there? The private affairs of employees and their out-of-work interests should not be the concern of their employers. It is selfish to maintain large playing fields and sports pavilions if they are going to be used by a minute proportion of staff for a very limited period of time – the space and facilities could be better used by the community. The argument that the provision of employee welfare services increases the loyalty and motivation of employees has long been exploded. If such services are used at all, they are taken for granted. Gratitude, even if it exists, is not a motivating factor.

The case against employee welfare services is formidable; the last point is particularly telling and there is some truth in each of the others – although there are limitations to their validity. State welfare services are, in theory, available to all, but the ability of social workers to give individual advice, especially on problems arising from work, is limited in terms of both time and knowledge. It is all too easy for people to fall into the cracks existing in the decaying edifice of the welfare state.

The case for providing employee welfare services rests mainly on the abstract grounds of the social responsibility of organizations for those who work in them. This is not paternalism in the Victorian sense – turkeys at Christmas – nor in the traditional Japanese sense, where the worker's whole life centres on the employer. Rather, it is simply the realization that in exchange for offering their services, employees are entitled to rather more than their pay, benefits and healthy and safe systems of work. They are also entitled to consideration as human beings, especially when it is remembered that many of their personal problems arise in the context of work and are best dealt with there. People's worries and the resulting stress may well arise from work and their concerns about security, money, health, and relationships with others. But they also bring their personal problems to work; and many of these cannot be solved without reference to the situation there – they may require time off to deal with sick children or partners, or care for relatives, or advice on how to solve their problems and so minimize interference with their work.

The argument for employee welfare services at work was well put by Martin (1967):

> Staff spend at least half their waking time at work or in getting to it or leaving it. They know they contribute to the organization when they are reasonably free from worry, and they feel, perhaps inarticulately, that when they are in trouble they are due to get something back from the organization. People are entitled to be treated as full human beings with personal needs, hopes and anxieties; they are employed as people; they bring themselves to work, not just their hands, and they cannot readily leave their troubles at home.

The social argument for employee welfare services is the most compelling one, but there is also an economic argument. Increases in morale or loyalty may not result in commensurate or, indeed, in any increases in productivity, but undue anxiety can result in reduced effectiveness. Even if welfare services cannot increase individual productivity, they can help to minimize decreases. Herzberg's two-factor model, in effect, placed welfare among the hygiene factors, but he did not underestimate the importance of 'hygiene' as a means of eliminating or at least reducing causes of anxiety or dissatisfaction.

A further practical argument in favour of employee welfare services is that a reputation for showing concern helps to improve the image of the firm as a good employer and thus assists in recruitment. Welfare may not directly increase productivity, but it may increase commitment and help in the retention of key employees.

A strong case for employee welfare services therefore exists, and the real question is not 'Why welfare?' but 'What sort of welfare?' This question needs to be answered in general terms before discussing the type of welfare services that can be provided and how they should be organized.

WHAT SORT OF WELFARE SERVICES?

Welfare services fall into two categories:

- individual or personal services in connection with sickness, bereavement, domestic problems, employment problems, and elderly and retired employees;
- group services, which consist of sports and social activities, clubs for retired staff and benevolent organizations.

Principles of personal casework

Individual services require personal casework, and the most important principle to adopt is that this work should aim to help individuals to help themselves. The employer, manager or HR specialist should not try to stand between individuals and their problems by taking them out of their hands. Emergency action may sometimes have to be taken on behalf of individuals, but, if so, it should be taken in such a way that they can later cope with their own difficulties. Welfare action must start on the basis that disengagement will take place at the earliest possible moment when individuals can, figuratively, stand on their own two feet. This does not mean that follow-up action is unnecessary, but it is only to check that things are going according to plan, not to provide additional help unless something is seriously wrong.

Personal services should be provided when a need is established, and a welfare need exists where it is clear that help is required, that it cannot be given more effectively from another source, and that the individual is likely to benefit from the services that can be offered.

In an organizational setting, an essential element in personal casework services is confidentiality. There is no point in offering help or advice to people if they think that their personal problems are going to be revealed to others, possibly to the detriment of their future careers. This is the argument for having specialized welfare officers in organizations large enough to be able to afford them. They can be detached in a way that line managers and even personnel managers cannot be.

Principles for providing group services

Group services, such as sports or social clubs, should not be laid on because they are 'good for morale'. There is no evidence that they are. They are costly and should be provided only if there is a real need and demand for them, arising from a very strong community spirit in a company or lack of local facilities. In the latter case, the facilities should be shared in an agreed and controlled way with the local community.

INDIVIDUAL SERVICES

Sickness

These services aim to provide help and advice to employees absent from work for long periods because of illness. The practical reason for providing them is that they should help to speed the return of the employee to work, although it is not part of the employee services function to check up on possible malingerers. The social reason is to provide employees with support and counsel where a need exists. In this context, a need exists where employees cannot help themselves without support and where such aid is not forthcoming from the state medical or welfare services or the employees' own families.

Needs can be established by keeping in touch with an absent employee. This should be not done by rushing round as soon as anyone has been absent for more than, say, 10 days or has exhausted sickness benefit from work. It is generally better to write to sick absentees, expressing general concern and good wishes for a speedy recovery and reminding them that the firm can provide help if they wish, or simply asking them if they would like someone to visit them – with a stamped, addressed envelope for their reply. Such letters should preferably be sent by the employee's line manager.

There will be some cases where the employee is reluctant to request help or a visit, and the company may have to decide whether a visit should be made to establish if help is required. This will be a matter of judgement based on the known facts about employees and their circumstances.

Visits can be made by the line manager, a personnel officer, or a specialized full- or part-time sick visitor. Some organizations use retired employees for this purpose. Alternatively, arrangements can be made for a colleague to pay the visit. The aims of the visit should be, first, to show employees that their firm and colleagues are concerned about their welfare; second, to alleviate any loneliness they may feel; and, third, to provide practical advice or help. The latter may consist of putting them in touch with suitable organizations or ensuring that such organizations are informed and take action. Or more immediate help may be provided to deal with pressing domestic problems.

Bereavement

Bereavement is a time when many people need all the help and advice they can get. The state welfare services may not be able to assist and families are often non-existent or unhelpful. Established welfare organizations in industry, commerce or the public sector attach a lot of importance to this service. The advice may often be no more than putting the bereaved employee or the widow or widower of an employee in touch with the right organizations, but it is often extended to help with funeral arrangements and dealing with will and probate matters.

Domestic problems

Domestic problems seem the least likely area for employee welfare services. Why should the organization intervene, even when asked, in purely private matters? If, for example, employees get into debt, that is surely their own affair. What business is it of the organization?

These are fair questions. But employers who have any real interest in the well-being of staff cannot ignore appeals for help. The assistance should not consist of bailing people out of debt whenever they get into trouble, or acting as an amateur marriage guidance or family casework officer. But, in accordance with the basic principle of personal casework already mentioned, employees can be counselled on how to help themselves or where to go for expert advice. A counselling service could be provided by company staff or through an employee assistance programme (see page 852). It can do an immense amount of good simply by providing an opportunity for employees to talk through their problems with a disinterested person. The help can be provided either through internal counselling services or by means of employee assistance programmes as described later in this chapter.

There is indeed a limit to how much can or should be done in the way of allowing employees to pour out their troubles but, used with discretion, it is a valuable service.

Employment problems

Employment problems should normally be solved by discussion between the individual and his or her manager or team leader, or through the company's grievance procedure. There may be times, however, when employees have problems over interpersonal relations, bullying, or feelings of inadequacy, about which they want to talk to a third party. Such counselling talks, as a means of relieving feelings and helping people to work through their problems for themselves, can do a lot of good, but extreme caution must be displayed by any HR people who are involved. They must not cut across line management authority, but, at the same time, they must preserve the confidentiality of the discussion. It is a delicate business, and where it affects relationships between individuals and their managers, it is one in which the giving of advice can be dangerous. The most that can be done is to provide a counselling service which gives employees an opportunity to talk about their problems and allows the counsellor to suggest actions the employee can take to put things right. Counsellors must not comment on the actions of anyone else who is involved. They can comment only on what the employee who seeks their help is doing or might do.

Elderly and retired employees

Employee services for elderly employees are primarily a matter of preparing them for retirement and dealing with any problems they have in coping with their work. Preparation for retirement is a valuable service that many firms offer. This may be limited to advising on the classes and facilities local authorities provide for people prior to retirement, or when they have retired, or it may be extended to running special pre-retirement courses held during working hours.

Some companies have made special provision for elderly employees by setting aside jobs or work areas for them. This has its dangers. Treating employees as special cases ahead of their time may make them over-aware of their condition or too dependent on the services provided for them. There is much to be said for treating elderly employees as normal workers, even though the health and safety services may take particular care to ensure that the age of the worker does not increase the danger of accident or industrial disease.

Retired employees, particularly those with long service, deserve the continuing interest of their former employer. The interest need not be oppressive, but continuing sick visiting can be carried out, and social occasions can be provided for them.

GROUP WELFARE SERVICES

Group employee services mainly consist of restaurants, sports and social clubs, and nursery facilities, although some companies still support various benevolent societies which provide additional help and finance in times of need.

Company restaurant facilities are obviously desirable in any reasonably sized establishment where there is relatively little choice of facilities in the vicinity. Alternatively, luncheon vouchers can be provided.

A massive investment in sports facilities is usually of doubtful value unless there is nothing else in the neighbourhood and, in accordance with the principles mentioned earlier, the company is prepared to share its facilities with the local community. In a large company in a large town, it is very difficult to develop feelings of loyalty towards the company teams or to encourage people to use the sports club. Why should they support an obscure side when their loyalties have always been directed to the local club? Why should they travel miles when they have perfectly adequate facilities near at hand? Such clubs are usually supported by small cliques who have little or no influence over the feelings of other employees, who leave the enthusiasts to get on with whatever they are doing.

The same argument applies to social clubs, especially those run by paternalistic companies. It is different when they arise spontaneously from the needs of employees. If they want to club together, then the company should say good luck to them and provide them with a reasonable amount of support. The subsidy, however, should not be complete. The clubs should generate their own funds as well as their own enthusiasm. Facilities can be provided within the firm's premises if they are needed and readily available. An investment in special facilities should be made only if there is a real likelihood of their being used regularly by a large proportion of employees. This is an area where prior consultation, before setting up the facility, and self-government, when it has been established, are essential.

Child care or nursery facilities (crèches) have obvious value as a means of attracting and retaining parents who would not otherwise be able to work on a full or part-time basis.

PROVISION OF EMPLOYEE WELFARE SERVICES

It seems obvious that the HR department should provide employee welfare services. Inevitably, HR staff will be dealing with cases and providing advice because they are in constant contact with employees and may be seen to be disinterested. It is to be hoped that they will also have some expertise in counselling.

Increasingly, however, it is being recognized that employee welfare is the responsibility of line management and supervision. If the latter take on their proper role as team leaders rather than their traditional autocratic and directive role, they should be close enough to each member of their team to be aware of any personal problems affecting their work. They should be trained in identifying symptoms and at least be able to refer people for counselling if it is clear that they need more help than the team leader can provide.

Employee welfare services can be provided for either internally by means of a counselling service or externally through an agency which runs employee assistance programmes (EAPs).

INTERNAL COUNSELLING SERVICES

Internal counselling services can be provided by full-time staff or volunteers who may work on a part-time basis. No specific academic qualifications are required for this work, but those carrying it out should be carefully assessed for suitable and relevant experience and they should have undergone extended training in counselling methods.

EMPLOYEE ASSISTANCE PROGRAMMES

Employee assistance programmes (EAPs) originated in the US in the 1960s. The idea was slow to catch on in the UK, but it is now becoming more accepted.

There are a number of external agencies which provide EAP services. They offer, on a contractual basis, a 24-hour phone service giving employees and their families access to counselling on a range of problems including stress, alcohol and drug abuse, marital breakdown and financial and legal problems. Most services identify the problem and arrange for a relevant specialist to phone back, although face-to-face counselling may also be offered, either at local offices or at surgeries on company premises. In addition, employers may refer employees direct to the service. Where long-term treatment relating to alcohol and drug problems or psychological problems is needed, employees are referred to state services.

Confidentiality is guaranteed by all EAPs to users, although employers are usually provided with a periodic statistical report on take-up of the service, which may be broken down by sex, seniority, department or type of problem. Advocates of the programmes argue that the anonymity they offer makes them particularly suitable for use in this country since it helps overcome the traditional British reluctance to discuss personal matters. Larger EAP providers offer clients the option of reports on average statistics based on work for comparable companies. Additional services include workplace seminars on problems identified as particularly prevalent, training of managers and personnel staff and related literature. The service may be charged for at a per capita rate or according to take-up, which can be as much as 25 per cent of the workforce.

Part XII

Employment and HRM services

This handbook emphasizes the importance of strategic considerations in formulating HR policies and planning HR programmes to achieve defined objectives. The fact remains, however, that much of human resource management is about managing the employment relationship, service delivery and dealing with the problems that will always arise when people work together, as considered in Chapter 57.

This also includes the various employment policies and procedures and approaches needed to ensure that both employees and the organization feel that their needs are being satisfied, as discussed in Chapter 58.

Organizations also need to maintain a comprehensive HR information system, not only to maintain employee records but also, and importantly, to build a computerized database which will assist in strategic decision taking. This is covered in Chapter 59.

57

Employment practices

Employment practices should be concerned with fundamental aspects of the employment relationship as expressed in the organization's HR policies (see Chapter 10) and procedures. They should take account of the requirements of relevant UK and European legislation and case law, which it is beyond the scope of the handbook to cover in detail. Recent Acts and Regulations which are important include those concerning the minimum wage, working time and part-time workers. The last of these is especially significant because it requires that part-time workers should be entitled to the same terms and conditions as full-time workers, including pro rata pay.

Note should also be taken of the UK Human Rights Act (1998) which gave further effect to rights and freedoms guaranteed under the European Convention on Human Rights. However, the rights are essentially civil and political rather than economic or social rights, and they only apply to a narrow range of employment. Moreover, they are not directly enforceable against an employer unless it is an 'obvious' public authority. It has, however, been held by the European Court of Human Rights that statutory rights should not be unlawfully dismissed or discriminated against as they can be regarded as 'civil rights'. Provisions inserted into the Employment Rights Act must be interpreted by employment tribunals in a way that is compatible with the European Convention right to freedom of expression. This could apply to whistle-blowing.

Employment practices need to be established in the following areas as described in this chapter:

- terms and conditions and contracts of employment;
- mobility clauses;
- transfer practices (including transfer between undertakings);
- promotion practices;
- flexible working;
- attendance management;
- equal opportunity and ethnic monitoring;
- managing diversity;
- data protection;
- sexual harassment;
- smoking;
- bullying;
- substance abuse at work;
- AIDS;
- use of e-mails;
- work-life balance.

Administrative procedures for dealing with the legal requirements for maternity leave and pay and sick pay will also have to be developed.

TERMS AND CONDITIONS AND CONTRACTS OF EMPLOYMENT

Terms and conditions of employment which apply generally or to groups of employees need to be defined in the areas included in the contract of employment as described below.

Individual contracts of employment must satisfy the provisions of contracts of employment legislation. They include a statement of the capacity in which the person is employed and the name or job title of the individual to whom he or she is responsible. They also include details of pay, allowances, hours, holidays, leave and pension arrangements and refer to relevant company policies, procedures and rules. Increasing use is being made of fixed-term contracts.

The basic information that should be included in a written contract of employment varies according to the level of job, but the following check list sets out the typical headings:

- job title;
- duties, preferably including a flexibility clause such as: 'The employee will perform such duties and will be responsible to such person, as the company may from time to time require', and, in certain cases: 'The employee will work at different locations as required by the company.'
- the date when continuous employment starts and basis for calculating service;
- the rate of pay, allowances, overtime and shift rates, method and timing of payment;
- hours of work including lunch break and overtime and shift arrangements;
- holiday arrangements:
  - days paid holiday per year;
  - calculation of holiday pay;
  - qualifying period;
  - accrual of holidays and holiday pay;
  - details of holiday year;
  - dates when holidays can be taken;
  - maximum holiday that can be taken at any one time;
  - carry-over of holiday entitlement;
  - public holidays.
- sickness:
  - pay for time lost;
  - duration of sickness payments;
  - deductions of National Insurance benefits;
  - termination due to continued illness;
  - notification of illness (medical certificate);
- length of notice due to and from employee;
- grievance procedure (or reference to it);
- disciplinary procedure (or reference to it);
- works rules (or reference to them);
- arrangements for terminating employment;
- arrangements for union membership (if applicable);
- special terms relating to rights to patents and designs, confidential information and restraints on trade after termination of employment;
- employer's right to vary terms of the contract subject to proper notification being given.

MOBILITY CLAUSES

Case law has established that employers can invoke mobility clauses which specify that the employee must work in any location as required by the employer as long as that discretion is exercised reasonably and not in such a way as to prevent the employee being able to carry out his or her part of the contract. A mobility clause could, however, be held to discriminate against women, who may not be in a position to move (*Meade-Hill and another vs British Council*, 1995). The acid test is whether or not the employer acts reasonably.

TRANSFER PRACTICES

Flexibility and redeployment in response to changing or seasonal demands for labour is a necessary feature of any large enterprise. The clumsy handling of transfers by management, however, can do as much long-lasting harm to the climate of employee relations as ill-considered managerial actions in any other sphere of personnel practice.

Management may be compelled to move people in the interests of production. But in making the move, managers should be aware of the fears of those affected in order that they can be alleviated as much as possible.

The basic fear will be of change itself – a fear of the unknown and of the disruption of a well-established situation: work, pay, environment, colleagues and workmates, and travelling arrangements. There will be immediate fears that the new work will make additional and unpalatable demands for extra skill or effort. There will be concern about loss of earnings because new jobs have to be tackled or because of different pay scales or bonus systems. Loss of overtime opportunities or the danger of shift or night work may also arouse concern.

Transfer policies should establish the circumstances when employees can be transferred and the arrangements for pay, resettlement and retraining. If the transfer is at the company's request and to suit the convenience of the company, it is normal to pay the employee's present rate or the rate for the new job, whichever is higher. This policy is easiest to apply in temporary transfers. It may have to be modified in the case of long-term or permanent transfers to eliminate the possibility of a multi-tiered pay structure emerging in the new location, which must cause serious dissatisfaction among those already employed there.

When transfers are made to avoid redundancy in the present location, the rate for the job in the new department should be paid. Employees affected in this way would, of course, be given the choice between being made redundant or accepting a lower-paid job.

The policies should also provide guidelines on how requests from employees for transfer should be treated. The normal approach should be to give a sympathetic hearing to such requests from long-serving employees, especially if the transfer is wanted for health or family reasons. But the transferred employees would have to accept the rate for the job in their new department.

The procedures for handling transfers may have to include joint consultation or discussions with workers' representatives on any major transfer programme. If regular transfers take place because of seasonal changes, it is best to establish a standard procedure for making transfers which would be managed by department supervisors, but they should be made aware of company policies and procedures and the need to treat the human problems involved with care and consideration.

The Transfer of Undertakings (Protection of Employment) Regulations 1981 (TUPE) provided that, following a business transfer arising from a merger or acquisition, all employees working in the business to be transferred automatically transfer into the employment of the merged business or the business making the acquisition. Following the transfer, they retain their existing terms and conditions of employment except for pensions. Employers have to give information about the business transfer to a recognized trade union.

PROMOTION PRACTICES

The aims of the promotion procedures of a company should be, first, to enable management to obtain the best talent available within the company to fill more senior posts and, second, to provide employees with the opportunity to advance their careers within the company, in accordance with the opportunities available (taking into account equal opportunity policies) and their own abilities.

In any organization where there are frequent promotional moves and where promotion arrangements cause problems, it is advisable to have a promotion policy and procedure which is known to both management and employees and this procedure should take full account of equal opportunity policies (it is often incorporated in equal opportunity policy statements). The basic points that should be included in such a procedure are:

- Promotion vacancies should be notified to the HR department.
- Vacancies should be advertised internally.
- Departmental managers should not be allowed to refuse promotions within a reasonable time unless the individual has been in the department for less than, say, one year, or the department has recently suffered heavy losses through promotions or transfers.

- Promotion opportunities should be open to all, irrespective of race, creed, sex or marital status.

FLEXIBLE WORKING

The range of possible working patterns as listed by IRS (2004d) is:

- *Part-time working* – an employee's contractual hours are less than the standard full-time hours, which can involve working any number of hours over any number of days.
- *Job-sharing* – the contractual hours are split between two employees, although not necessarily on a 50/50 basis.
- *Time-off-in lieu (TOIL)* – any additional hours worked can be taken as time off at a later date.
- *Flexitime* – start and finish times are flexible, provided they are outside core hours, and any excess or deficit in the time worked is carried over to the next period.
- *Homeworking or teleworking* – ranging from occasional days spent working at home or an arrangement where an employee works entirely from home.
- *Career breaks* – unpaid leave with an understanding that an employee can return to employment at the end of the agreed period.
- *Shift working* – set periods of working, often designed to provide 24-hour cover as a three-shift system or sometimes operating as a two-shift system or a 'twilight shift' which lasts from, say, 5 pm to 9 pm.
- *Shift swapping* – employees are able to exchange their allocated shifts amongst themselves on the understanding that full cover will be provided.
- *Self-rostering* – employees have responsibility for negotiating which shifts they will work but the employer determines the shift pattern.
- *Annualized hours* – where contractual hours are calculated over a 12-month period to potentially suit both an employee's needs and business demand.
- *Compressed hours* – an employee works their standard number of hours but within a shorter time scale, such as fewer days.
- *Staggered hours* – this allows for alternative start, break and finish times.
- *Additional leave entitlement* – either paid or unpaid, with the necessary adjustment of salary payments.
- *V-time working* – a reduction in hours for a set period.
- *Unique working pattern* – an individualized arrangement that can combine more than one flexible working option.

The Workshop Employee Relations Survey (2005) found that the following flexible arrangements were used:

- Reduced hours – 70 per cent.
- Change in working pattern – 45 per cent.
- Flexitime – 35 per cent.
- Job-sharing – 31 per cent.
- Homeworking – 26 per cent.
- Term-time only – 20 per cent.
- Compressed hours – 16 per cent.
- Annualized hours – 6 per cent.

As reported by IRS (2004d), the Yorkshire Building Society has a flexible working policy that makes clear the availability of flexible working to all employees. A business case has to be made for working flexibly and the criteria used to make a decision are:

- an analysis of the role's tasks, their frequency and duration;
- the workflow of the role, including an analysis of the telephone log;
- the complexity of tasks undertaken;
- the workload of the role, using work measurement data where available;
- the structure of the department and staff resourcing;
- the level of supervision needed for the role and back-up available;
- the effect on other staff of the flexible working arrangement;
- the cost impact of the new arrangement;
- other issues particular to the working of the department or branch.

ATTENDANCE MANAGEMENT

Attendance management is the process of controlling absenteeism and time-keeping.

Absenteeism

Absenteeism is a serious problem. A CIPD survey (IPD 1993a) established that the average absence rate per employee was equivalent to nine working days a year.

Causes of absence

The causes of absence have been analysed by Huczynski and Fitzpatrick (1989) under three headings: job situation factors, personal factors and attendance factors.

Job situation factors include:

- Job scope – a high degree of task repetitiveness is associated with absenteeism although job dissatisfaction itself is a contributory rather than a primary cause of absence.
- Stress – it is estimated that 40 million working days are lost each year in the UK through stress. This can be attributed to workload, poor working conditions, shift work, role ambiguity or conflict, relationships and organizational climate.
- Frequent job transfers increase absenteeism.
- Management style — the quality of management, especially immediate supervisors, affects the level of absenteeism.
- Physical working conditions.
- Work group size — the larger the organization, the higher the absence rate.

Personal factors include:

- Employee values – for some workers, doing less work for the same reward improves the deal made with the employer (the effort-reward bargain). The following positive outcomes of absence have been shown by research to be particularly important to employees: break from routine, leisure time, dealing with personal business and a break from co-workers.
- Age – younger employees are more frequently absent than older ones.
- Sex – women are more prone to sickness absence than men.
- Personality – some people are absence-prone (studies have noted that between 5 and 10 per cent of workers account for about half of the total absence, while a few are never absent at all).

Attendance factors include:

- Reward systems — as pay increases, attendance improves.
- Sick pay schemes may increase absenteeism.
- Work group norms can exert pressure for or against attendance.

Control of absenteeism

Absenteeism can be disruptive and costly. It needs to be controlled. The steps required to achieve effective absence control are:

- *commitment* on the part of management to reduce the cost of absenteeism;
- *trust* – the control of absenteeism is more likely to be achieved if employees are trusted – companies that are operating on this basis provide sickness benefit for all workers and rely upon the commitment and motivation of their employees (which they work hard at achieving) to minimize abuse, but they reserve the right to review sickness benefit if the level of sickness absence is unacceptable;
- *information* – sadly, a trusting approach will not necessarily work and hard, accurate information on absence is required – this can be provided by computerized systems;
- *a documented attendance policy* which spells out the organization's views on absenteeism and the rules for sick pay;
- *regular training for managers and team leaders* which ensures that they are aware of their responsibilities for controlling absenteeism and indicates the actions they can take;
- *getting managers to conduct return-to-work interviews* to welcome employees back and, if appropriate, enquire about the cause of absence and what can be done by the employee or the manager to reduce future occurrences;
- *communications* which inform employees why absence control is important;
- *counselling* for employees at return-to-work interviews which provides advice on any attendance problems they may have and creates trust;
- *disciplinary procedure* – this must be operated fairly and consistently.

In addition, as reported by IRS (2004d): 'It is now increasingly recognized that offering employees flexible working options can play a significant role in developing a more positive and longer-lasting solution to non-attendance.' In a survey by the Work Foundation on maximizing attendance (2003a), 36 per cent of respondents cited flexible working patterns as one of the five most effective ways of managing attendance and reducing absence.

The importance of keeping contact with employees absent through sickness has been emphasized by the Health and Safety Executive (HSE) and IRS. The HSE (2004b) guidelines to employees confirm that keeping in contact represents a key factor in helping employees return to work after a long-term absence. However, they note that contact can be a sensitive topic because some employees may feel pressed to come back to work too early. The HSE suggests that discussions with absent staff must be clearly focused on the employee's well-being and their return to work. Managers need to address issues where the employee might need help and also what the employer can do to aid their return to work. IRS (2005) reported that their survey on long-term absence had shown that 'easy and regular contact with employees on sick leave leads to a quicker return to work'. The most frequently used method of contact is by letter (65 per cent) followed by telephone calls to the employee's house by their line manager (57 per cent) or by the HR department (55 per cent). Visits to the employee's home are used less frequently. Many organizations have policies or guidance notes that stipulate the method, timing and frequency of contacts.

EQUAL OPPORTUNITY

Equal opportunity policies were considered in Chapter 10. To get them into action the following are the key steps as set out in the Chartered Institute of Personnel and Development's 2002 code of conduct:

1. *The recruitment process*:
    -   have accurate, up-to-date job descriptions which are not sex biased;
    -   avoid over-inflated job criteria in person specifications;
    -   check that job requirements are really necessary to the job and are not a reflection of traditional biased practices;
    -   guard against sex/race stereotyping in advertisements and recruitment literature.
2. *The interview – to reduce interview bias*:
    -   provide training to all who conduct selection interviews;
    -   ensure that only trained interviewers conduct preliminary interviews;
    -   avoid discriminatory questions, although interviews can discuss with applicants any domestic or personal circumstances which might have an adverse effect on job performance as long as this is done without making assumptions based on the sex of the applicant.
3. *Training*:
    -   check that women and men have equal opportunities to participate in training and development programmes;
    -   take late entrants into training schemes;
    -   ensure that selection criteria for training do not discriminate against women;
    -   consider using positive training provisions for women and ethnic minorities.
4. *Promotion*:
    -   improve performance review procedures to minimize bias;
    -   avoid perpetuating the effects of past discriminatory practices in selection for promotion;
    -   do not presume that women or minorities do not want promotion.

ETHNIC MONITORING

The Commission for Racial Equality's (CRE) guide on ethnic monitoring recommends that analyses of the workforce should be conducted in sufficient detail to show whether there is an under-representation in more skilled jobs and grades, as well as whether there are general concentrations of ethnic minority employees in certain jobs, levels or departments in the organization. The Chartered Institute of Personnel and Development Equal Opportunities Code states that the most important processes to monitor are recruitment and selection since these are easily influenced by prejudice or indirect discrimination. But the proportion of ethnic minorities at different levels in the organization should also be checked regularly.

The CRE has suggested that ethnic monitoring should collect employment information under the following ethnic classifications:

- white;
- black-Caribbean;
- black-African;
- black-other;
- Indian;
- Pakistani;
- Bangladeshi;
- Chinese;
- other (those describing themselves in this category should be invited to provide further information).

The results of ethnic monitoring should be used to establish whether:

- in comparison with the workforce as a whole, or in comparison with the local labour market, ethnic minority workers are significantly under- or over-represented in any area;
- representative numbers of ethnic minorities apply for and are accepted for jobs;
- higher or lower proportions of employees from ethnic minorities leave the organization;
- there are any disparities in the proportion of members of ethnic minorities.

If necessary, positive affirmative action, as recommended by the CRE, can be taken along the following lines:

- job advertisements designed to reach members of under-represented groups;
- the use of employment agencies and careers offices in areas where these groups are concentrated;
- recruitment and training for school leavers designed to reach members of these groups;
- encouragement of employees from these groups to apply for promotion or transfer opportunities;
- training for promotion or skill training for employees of these groups who lack particular expertise but show potential.

MANAGING DIVERSITY

The CIPD (2005b) states that:

> Diversity is an inclusive term based on recognizing all kinds of difference. It is about 'valuing everyone as an individual'. It recognizes that people from different backgrounds can bring fresh ideas and perceptions... which can make the work done more efficient and products and services better... Diversity is an inclusive concept that covers all kinds of difference that go beyond the traditional understanding of what equal opportunity is about.

As described by Kandola and Fullerton (1998):

> The basic concept of managing diversity accepts that the workforce consists of a diverse population of people. The diversity consists of visible and non-visible differences which will include factors such as sex, age, background, race, disability, personality and work-style. It is founded on the premise that harnessing these differences will create a productive environment in which everybody feels valued, where their talents are being fully utilized and in which organizational goals are met.

Managing diversity is about ensuring that all people maximize their potential and their contribution to the organization. It means valuing diversity, that is, valuing the differences between people and the different qualities they bring to their jobs which can lead to the development of a more rewarding and productive environment.

Kandola and Fullerton quote the following 10 most successful initiatives adopted by organizations who are pursuing diversity policies:

1. introducing equal rights and benefits for part-time workers (compared with full-time workers);

2. allowing flexibility in uniform/dress requirements;
3. allowing time off for caring for dependants beyond that required by law, eg extended maternity/paternity leave;
4. benefits provided for employees' partners are equally available to same-sex and different-sex partners;
5. buying specialized equipment, eg braille keyboards;
6. employing helpers/signers for those who need them;
7. training trainers in equal opportunities;
8. eliminating age criteria from selection decisions;
9. providing assistance with child care;
10. allowing staff to take career breaks.

They use the acronym MOSAIC to describe the characteristics of a diversity oriented organization:

Mission and values that are strong and positive and where effective successful diversity management is a necessary long-term goal.

Objective and fair processes exist within the organization and these are audited regularly to ensure that power does not sit within informal networks, and no one group of employees dominates at any level.

Skilled workforces aware of the effects of biases and prejudices on their decision-making, and managers who manage the diversity effectively while stressing excellence in individual and team performance.

Active flexibility means that the diversity-oriented organization will display increasing flexibility, not only in its working patterns but also in its practices, policies and procedures.

Individual focus – organizations must guard against averaging out group differences or similarities by creating segregated groups.

Culture that empowers achieved through openness, engendering trust between all individuals through an absence of prejudice and discrimination.

THE DATA PROTECTION ACT

The Data Protection Act (1998) is built round the eight data protection principles included in the 1984 Data Protection Act. The most important of these is that data should be accessible to the individuals concerned, who may, where appropriate, correct or erase them. The 1998 Act covers manually maintained records (eg filing systems) as well as records held on a computer database. It also places restrictions on the processing of sensitive data, which includes data on racial or ethnic origin, political opinions, religious beliefs, trade union membership, physical or mental health, sex life, and the commission or alleged commission of any offence. Under the Act, employees must give explicit consent to the processing of personal data, especially sensitive data.

SEXUAL HARASSMENT

Sadly, sexual harassment has always been a feature of life at work. Perhaps it is not always quite so blatant today as it has been in the past, but it is still there, in more or less subtle forms, and it is just as unpleasant.

Persons subject to harassment can take legal action but, of course, it must be the policy of the company to make it clear that it will not be tolerated.

Problems of dealing with harassment

The first problem always met in stamping out sexual harassment is that it can be difficult to make a clear-cut case. An accusation of harassment can be hard to prove unless there are witnesses. And those who indulge in this practice usually take care to carry it out on a one-to-one basis. In this situation, it may be a case of one person's word against another's. The harasser, almost inevitably a man, resorts to two defences: one, that it did not take place ('it was all in her mind'); and two, that if anything did take place, it was provoked by the behaviour of the female. In these situations, whoever deals with the case has to exercise judgement and attempt, difficult though it may be, to remove any prejudice in favour of the word of the man, the woman, the boss or the subordinate.

The second problem is that victims of sexual harassment are often unwilling to take action and in practice seldom do so. This is because of the actual or perceived difficulty of proving their case. But they may also feel that they will not get a fair hearing and are worried about the effect making such accusations will have on how they are treated by their boss or their colleagues in future – whether or not they will have substantiated their accusation.

The third and possibly the most deep-rooted and difficult problem of all is that sexual harassment can be part of the culture of the organization – a way of life, a 'norm', practised at all levels.

Solutions

There are no easy solutions to these problems. It may be very hard to eradicate sexual harassment completely. But an effort must be made to deal with it and the following approaches should be considered:

1. Issue a clear statement by the chief executive that sexual harassment will not be tolerated. The absolute requirement to treat all people equally, irrespective of sex, role, creed, sexual orientation or disability, should be one of the fundamental values of the organization. This should be reinforced by the explicit condemnation of harassment as a direct and unacceptable contravention of that value.

2. Back up the value statement with a policy directive on sexual harassment (see Chapter 8) which spells out in more detail how the company deplores it, why it is not acceptable and what people who believe they are being subjected to harassment can do about it.

3. Reinforce the value and policy statements by behaviour at senior level which demonstrates that they are not simply words but that these exhortations have meaning.

4. Ensure that the company's policy on harassment is stated clearly in induction courses and is conveyed to everyone in the form of a strong reminder on promotion.

5. Make arrangements for employees subjected to sexual harassment to be able to seek advice, support and counselling in total confidence without any obligation to take a complaint further. A counsellor can be designated to provide advice and assistance covering such functions as:
   - offering guidance on handling sexual harassment problems;
   - assisting in resolving problems informally by seeking, with the consent of the complainant, a confidential and voluntary interview with the person complained against in order to pursue a solution without resource to the formal disciplinary or grievance procedure;
   - assisting in submitting a grievance if the employee wishes to complain formally;
   - securing an undertaking, where appropriate, by the person who is the subject of the complaint to stop the behaviour which has caused offence;
   - counselling the parties as to their future conduct where a problem has been resolved without recourse to formal procedures.

6. Create a special procedure for hearing complaints about sexual harassment – the normal grievance procedure may not be suitable because the sexual harasser

could be the employee's line manager. The procedure should provide for employees to bring their complaint to someone of their own sex, should they so choose.

7. Handle investigations of complaints with sensitivity and due respect for the rights of both the complainant and the accused. Ensure that hearings are conducted fairly, both parties being given an equal opportunity to put their case. The principles of natural justice mentioned earlier in this chapter should prevail. Care should be taken to ensure that the careers and reputations of neither party are unjustly affected.

8. Where sexual harassment has taken place, crack down on it. It should be stated in the policy that it is regarded as gross industrial misconduct and, if it is proved, makes the individual liable to instant dismissal. Less severe penalties may be reserved for minor cases but there should always be a warning that repetition will result in dismissal.

9. Ensure that everyone is aware that the organization does take action when required to punish those who indulge in sexual harassment.

10. Provide training to managers and team leaders to ensure that the policy is properly implemented and to make them aware of their direct responsibility to prevent harassment taking place and to take action if it does.

SMOKING

Smoking policies at work are designed to provide employees with a healthy and efficient workplace and to avoid conflict. A smoking policy should be developed in consultation with employees and may involve the use of an opinion survey. Most smokers agree to the right of non-smokers to work in air free from tobacco smoke. Smoking policies can involve a total ban on all smoking except, usually, in a smoking-permitted area away from the workplace. Remember that smokers do have some rights and that a ban in all areas may be oppressive. Sometimes, by agreement, there is a partial ban with separate working areas for those who wish to smoke. Kitchens and lifts are always non-smoking areas and rest rooms generally are.

It is sometimes appropriate to introduce smoking bans in stages, starting by restricting smoking in meeting rooms, corridors and canteens before extending the restriction to other communal and work areas.

SUBSTANCE ABUSE AT WORK

Substance abuse is the use of alcohol, drugs or other substances which cause difficulties at work such as absenteeism, low performance standards and interpersonal problems, for example, unpredictable reactions to criticism, paranoia, irritability, avoiding colleagues, borrowing money or physical or verbal abuse of colleagues. A policy on how to deal with incidents of substance abuse (see Chapter 8) is necessary because:

- many employers have some employees with a drink problem and possibly a drug problem;
- substance abuse may be a result of work pressures, for which employers must take some responsibility;
- employers are required to maintain a safe and healthy work environment.

BULLYING

Bullying is a form of harassment and can be very unpleasant. It is perhaps one of the most difficult aspects of employee relationship to control – it can be hard to prove that bullying has taken place and employees may be very reluctant to complain about a bullying boss, simply because he or she is a bully. But this does not mean that the organization should ignore the problem. A policy should be published which states that bullying constitutes unacceptable behaviour and indicating that those who indulge in the practice can face severe disciplinary action. It should be announced that anyone who is being bullied has the right to discuss the problem with someone in the HR department or lodge a complaint, and in such discussions employees should also have the right to be accompanied by a representative.

But as the CIPD (2005a) states: 'Tackling a difficult and complex subject like bullying at work is about much more than having a policy in the staff handbook. It is not just about an absence of negatives, but about actively defining and promoting positive working relationships.' The emphasis, according to the CIPD, must be on building a culture of respect with the following features:

- Positive behaviours that everyone can expect from one another are defined and communicated.
- Everyone is supported in accepting responsibility for his or her behaviour and actions. Bullies are not punished and isolated but helped to acknowledge the impact of their behaviours, and to change.

- Everyone accepts responsibility for finding solutions.
- Top team behaviour is regarded as vital in reinforcing positive behaviours and creating a culture that goes beyond lip-service.
- Internal buddies/listeners and trained mediators can also help to deal with bullying at an early stage before conflict becomes entrenched, relationships break down and more formal routes are taken.

AIDS

There are no logical reasons why AIDS should be treated differently from any other disease that employees may be carrying, many of which are contagious and some of which are fatal. However, AIDS is a frightening and threatening disease which has received enormous publicity, not all of which has been accurate. Because of this fact it is necessary to develop a company policy (see Chapter 8).

E-MAILS

Increasingly, companies are cracking down on staff using e-mails at work for private purposes (eg online shopping), surfing the internet, or sending pornographic e-mails through the company's intranet. Employers are concerned about the waste of time and money and the undesirability of pornographic or defamatory material being distributed round the office. They are often, therefore, introducing policies which state that the sending of offensive e-mails is prohibited and that the senders of such messages are subject to normal disciplinary procedures. They may also prohibit any browsing or downloading of material not related to the business, although this can be difficult to enforce. Some companies have always believed that reasonable use of the telephone is acceptable, and that policy may be extended to e-mails.

If it is decided that employees' e-mails should be monitored to check on excessive or unacceptable use, then this should be included in an e-mail policy as set out in Chapter 8.

The legal position needs to be considered. The Lawful Business Practice Regulations (2000) permit access to e-mails by employers as long as they have taken reasonable steps to inform the parties concerned. However, the Code of Practice issued by the Data Protection Commission suggests that employers should not check sites accessed by employees, but should clarify what can or cannot be downloaded. The Code also suggests that the term 'pornography' is not sufficiently precise, and the Commissioner does not believe that there needs to be a ban on downloading unsuitable material even if other employees find it offensive, and that employers should simply deal with cases as they arise. Many employers may find it difficult to accept this suggestion, but 'proportionality' is required in dealing with any problems, ie there may be situations when a dismissal for 'gross misconduct' is inappropriate, and employers should be aware that downloading unsuitable material can be done innocently.

WORK-LIFE BALANCE

Work-life balance employment practices are concerned with providing scope for employees to balance what they do at work with the responsibilities and interests they have outside work and so reconcile the competing claims of work and home by meeting their own needs as well as those of their employers. The term work-life balance has largely replaced 'family friendly policy'. As Kodz *et al* (2002) explain, the principle of work-life balance is that: 'There should be a balance between an individual's work and their life outside work, and that this balance should be healthy.'

As defined by the Work Foundation (2003b), the concept of work-life balance is 'about employees achieving a satisfactory equilibrium between work and non-work activities (ie parental responsibilities and wider caring duties, as well as other activities and interests). The Work Foundation recommends that practical day-to-day business and related needs should be considered when organizations set about selecting the range of work-life options that should be made available to staff, whether on a collective basis (as for example flexitime arrangements) or on an individual level (say, allowing an individual to move to term-time working provisions). Individual requests for particular working arrangements generally need to be considered on a case-by-case basis, but it is important for a culture to exist that does not discourage employees from making such requests. In addition to fearing the reaction of line managers, the risk of career-damage is a common reason for poor take-up of work-life balance arrangements. Line management will need to be convinced that work-life balance measures are important and pay off in terms of increased engagement.

The IRS (2002) considers that, 'Flexible working is considered the most practical solution to establishing an effective work-life balance.' The term 'flexible working' covers flexitime, home working, part-time working, compressed working weeks, annualized hours, job sharing and term-time only working. It also refers to special leave schemes, which provide employees with the freedom to respond to a domestic crisis or to take a career break without jeopardizing their employment status. For example, ASDA operates a range of schemes designed to give carers and others the flexibility to maintain a healthy work-life balance. Work-life options available for

ASDA 'colleagues' include childcare leave, shift-swapping and study leave.

However, as IRS points out, there is more to work-life balance than flexible working: 'Creating an environment in which staff who opt to work flexibly and those who raise work-life issues will require a cultural shift in many organizations, backed by senior level support.'

Kodz *et al* (2002) quote figures from an IES survey that showed the following proportion of employees offering some form of flexibility:

- Part-time working – 76 per cent.
- Care leave – 55 per cent.
- Varying hours – 38 per cent.
- Compassionate leave – 38 per cent.
- Career breaks – 27 per cent.
- Workplace counselling or stress management – 26 per cent.
- Working from home – 22 per cent.
- Flexitime – 11 per cent.
- Term-time working – 6 per cent.
- Help with child care in school holidays – 6 per cent.
- Job sharing – 5 per cent.
- Reduced hours – 4 per cent.
- Crèche – 1 per cent.

The respondents to the survey indicated that the successful implementation of work-life balance practices required a change in culture and attitudes within the organization. Also, line managers have a key role.

The Work Foundation (2003b) survey of work-life balance established that the most common work-life balance measures taken by employers were the provision of part-time working (90 per cent), family/emergency leave (85 per cent) and general unpaid leave (78 per cent). Formal policies are most likely to be found in public and voluntary sector organizations (35 per cent) and least likely to be found in manufacturing (14 per cent). Management resistance is the most common difficulty met in introducing work-life balance policies.

But the work-life balance survey conducted by the DTI in 2003 found that there was a high level of support amongst employers (65 per cent). But 65 per cent also said that it was not easy. A large proportion of employers (74 per cent) believed that people who work flexibly are just as likely to be promoted as those that do not.

The DTI survey established that the benefits claimed for introducing work-life balance policies were:

- improved productivity and quality of work;
- improved commitment and morale;
- reduced staff turnover;
- reduced casual absence;
- improved utilization of new recruits.

Work-life balance policies can lower absence and help to tackle the low morale and high degrees of stress that can lead to retention problems as employees tire of juggling work and life responsibilities. The research conducted by the Institute of Employment Studies (Kodz *et al*, 2002) identified employees who were staying longer with their firms because of access to flexible working arrangements.

58

HRM procedures

Human resource management procedures set out the ways in which certain actions concerning people should be carried out by the management or individual managers. In effect they constitute a formalized approach to dealing with specific matters of policy and practice. They should be distinguished from HR policies as described in Chapter 10. These describe the approach the organization adopts to various aspects of people management and define key aspects of the employment relationship. They serve as guidelines on people management practices but do not necessarily lay down precisely the steps that should be taken in particular situations. Procedures are more exacting. They state what *must* be done as well as spelling out how to do it. It is desirable to have the key HRM procedures written down to ensure that HR policies are applied consistently and in accordance with both legal requirements and ethical considerations. The existence of a written and well-publicized procedure ensures that everyone knows precisely what steps need to be taken when dealing with certain significant and possibly recurring employment issues.

The introduction or development of HR procedures should be carried out in consultation with employees and, where appropriate, their representatives. It is essential to brief everyone on how the procedures operate and they should be published either in an employee handbook or as a separate document. Line managers may need special training on how they should apply the procedures and the HR department should provide guidance wherever necessary. HR will normally have the responsibility of ensuring that procedures are followed consistently.

The main areas where procedures are required are those concerned with handling grievances and disciplinary, capability and redundancy issues.

GRIEVANCE PROCEDURE

Grievance procedures spell out the policy on handling grievances and the approach to dealing with them. An example of a grievance procedure is given below.

Grievance procedure

POLICY

It is the policy of the company that employees should:

- be given a fair hearing by their immediate supervisor or manager concerning any grievances they may wish to raise;
- have the right to appeal to a more senior manager against a decision made by their immediate supervisor or manager;
- have the right to be accompanied by a fellow employee of their own choice, when raising a grievance or appealing against a decision.

The aim of the procedure is to settle the grievance as nearly as possible to its point of origin.

PROCEDURE

The main stages through which a grievance may be raised are as follows:

1. The employee raises the matter with his or her immediate team leader or manager and may be accompanied by a fellow employee of his or her own choice.
2. If the employee is not satisfied with the decision, the employee requests a meeting with a member of management who is more senior than the team leader or manager who initially heard the grievance. This meeting takes place within five working days of the request and is attended by the manager, the manager responsible for personnel, the employee appealing against the deci-

---

sion, and, if desired, his or her representative. The manager responsible for personnel records the result of the meeting in writing and issues copies to all concerned.

3. If the employee is still not satisfied with the decision, he or she may appeal to the appropriate director. The meeting to hear this appeal is held within five working days of the request and is attended by the director, the manager responsible for personnel, the employee making the appeal, and, if desired, his or her representative. The manager responsible for personnel records the result of this meeting in writing and issues copies to all concerned.

DISCIPLINARY PROCEDURE

Disciplinary procedures set out the stages through which any disciplinary action should proceed. An example is given below.

Disciplinary procedure (part 1)

POLICY

It is the policy of the company that if disciplinary action has to be taken against employees it should:

- be undertaken only in cases where good reason and clear evidence exist;
- be appropriate to the nature of the offence that has been committed;
- be demonstrably fair and consistent with previous action in similar circumstances;
- take place only when employees are aware of the standards that are expected of them or the rules with which they are required to conform;
- allow employees the right to be represented by a representative or colleague during any formal proceedings;
- allow employees the right to know exactly what charges are being made against them and to respond to those charges;
- allow employees the right of appeal against any disciplinary action.

RULES

The company is responsible for ensuring that up-to-date rules are published and available to all employees.

PROCEDURE

The procedure is carried out in the following stages:

1. *Informal warning.* A verbal or informal warning is given to the employee in the first instance or instances of minor offences. The warning is administered by the employee's immediate team leader or manager.

2. *Formal warning.* A written formal warning is given to the employee in the first instance of more serious offences or after repeated instances of minor offences. The warning is administered by the employee's immediate team leader or manager – it states the exact nature of the offence and indicates any future disciplinary action which will be taken against the employee if the offence is repeated within a specified time limit. A copy of the written warning is placed in the employee's personnel record file but is destroyed 12 months after the date on which it was given, if the intervening service has been satisfactory. The employee is required to read and sign the formal warning and has the right to appeal to higher management if he or she thinks the warning is unjustified. The HR manager should be asked to advise on the text of the written warning.

3. *Further disciplinary action.* If, despite previous warnings, an employee still fails to reach the required standards in a reasonable period of time, it may become necessary to consider further disciplinary action. The action taken may be up to three days' suspension without pay, or dismissal. In either case the departmental manager should discuss the matter with the personnel manager before taking action. Staff below the rank of departmental manager may only recommend disciplinary action to higher management, except when their manager is not present (for example, on night-shift), when they may suspend the employee for up to one day pending an inquiry on the following day. Disciplinary action should not be confirmed until the appeal procedure has been carried out.

Disciplinary procedure (part 2)
SUMMARY DISMISSAL

An employee may be summarily dismissed (ie given instant dismissal without notice) only in the event of gross misconduct, as defined in company rules. Only departmental managers and above can recommend summary dismissal, and the action should not be finalized until the case has been discussed with the HR manager and the appeal procedure has been carried out. To enable this review to take place, employees should be suspended pending further investigation, which must take place within 24 hours.

APPEALS

In all circumstances, an employee may appeal against suspension, dismissal with notice, or summary dismissal. The appeal is conducted by a member of management who is more senior than the manager who initially administered the disciplinary action. The HR manager should also be present at the hearing. If he or she wishes, the employee may be represented at the appeal by a fellow employee of his or her own choice. Appeal against summary dismissal or suspension should be heard immediately. Appeals against dismissal with notice should be held within two days. No disciplinary action that is subject to appeal is confirmed until the outcome of the appeal.

If an appeal against dismissal (but not suspension) is rejected at this level, the employee has the right to appeal to the chief executive. The head of HR and, if required, the employee's representative should be present at this appeal.

CAPABILITY PROCEDURE

Some organizations deal with matters of capability under a disciplinary procedure, but there is a good case to be made for dealing with poor performance issues separately, leaving the disciplinary procedure to be invoked for situations such as poor timekeeping. An example of a capability procedure follows.

Capability procedure

POLICY

The company aims to ensure that performance expectations and standards are defined, performance is monitored and employees are given appropriate feedback, training and support to meet these standards.

Procedure

1. If a manager/team leader believes that an employee's performance is not up to standard an informal discussion will be held with the employee to try to establish the reason and to agree the actions required to improve performance by the employee and/or the manager/team leader. If, however:

    (a) it is agreed that the established standards are not reasonably attainable, they will be reviewed;

    (b) it is established that the performance problems are related to the employee's personal life, the necessary counselling/support will be provided;

    (c) it is decided that the poor performance emanates from a change in the organizations' standards, those standards will be explained to the employee and help will be offered to obtain conformity with the standards;

    (d) it is apparent that the poor performance constitutes misconduct, the disciplinary procedure will be invoked.

2. Should the employee show no (or insufficient) improvement over a defined period (weeks/months), a formal interview will be arranged with the employee (together with a representative if so desired). The aims of this interview will be to:

    (a) explain clearly the shortfall between the employee's performance and the required standard;

    (b) identify the cause(s) of the unsatisfactory performance and to determine what – if any – remedial treatment (eg training, retraining, support, etc) can be given;

    (c) obtain the employee's commitment to reaching that standard;

    (d) set a reasonable period for the employee to reach the standard and agree on a monitoring system during that period; and

    (e) tell the employee what will happen if that standard is not met.

    The outcome of this interview will be recorded in writing and a copy will be given to the employee.

3. At the end of the review period a further formal interview will be held, at which time:
    (a) if the required improvement has been made, the employee will be told of this and encouraged to maintain the improvement;
    (b) if some improvement has been made but the standard has not yet been met, the review period will be extended;
    (c) if there has been no discernible improvement this will be indicated to the employee and consideration will be given to whether there are alternative vacancies that the employee would be competent to fill; if there are, the employee will be given the option of accepting such a vacancy or being dismissed;
    (d) if such vacancies are available, the employee will be given full details of them in writing before being required to make a decision;
    (e) in the absence of suitable alternative work, the employee will be informed and invited to give his or her views on this before the final decision is taken, to take disciplinary action, including dismissal.
4. Employees may appeal against their dismissal. The appeal must be made within three working days.

REDUNDANCY PROCEDURE

Redundancy procedures aim to meet statutory, ethical and practical considerations when dealing with this painful process. An example of a procedure is given below.

Redundancy procedure (part 1)
DEFINITION

Redundancy is defined as the situation in which management decides that an employee or employees are surplus to requirements in a particular occupation and cannot be offered suitable alternative work.

Employees may be surplus to requirements because changes in the economic circumstances of the company mean that fewer employees are required, or because changes in methods of working mean that a job no longer exists in its previous form. An employee who is given notice because he or she is unsuitable or inefficient is not regarded as redundant and would be dealt with in accordance with the usual disciplinary or capability procedure.

OBJECTIVES

The objectives of the procedure are to ensure that:

- employees who may be affected by the discontinuance of their work are given fair and equitable treatment;
- the minimum disruption is caused to employees and the company;
- as far as possible, changes are effected with the understanding and agreement of the unions and employees concerned.

PRINCIPLES

The principles governing the procedure are as follows:

- The trade unions concerned will be informed as soon as possible of the possibility of redundancy.
- Every attempt will be made to:
  - absorb redundancy by the natural wastage of employees;
  - find suitable alternative employment within the company for employees who might be affected, and provide training if this is necessary;
  - give individuals reasonable warning of pending redundancy in addition to the statutory period of notice.
- If alternative employment in the company is not available and more than one individual is affected, the factors to be taken into consideration in deciding who should be made redundant will include:
  - length of service with the company;
  - age (especially those who could be retired early);
  - value to the company;
  - opportunities for alternative employment elsewhere.
- The first three of these factors should normally be regarded as the most important; other things being equal, however, length of service should be the determining factor.
- The company will make every endeavour to help employees find alternative work if that is necessary.

Redundancy procedure (part 2)

PROCEDURE

The procedure for dealing with employees who are surplus to requirements is set out below.

Review of employee requirements

Management will continuously keep under review possible future developments which might affect the number of employees required, and will prepare overall plans for dealing with possible redundancies.

Measures to avoid redundancies

If the likelihood of redundancy is foreseen, the company will inform the union(s), explaining the reasons, and in consultation with the union(s) will give consideration to taking appropriate measures to prevent redundancy.

Departmental managers will be warned by the management of future developments that might affect them in order that detailed plans can be made for running down staff, retraining, or transfers.

Departmental managers will be expected to keep under review the work situation in their departments in order that contingency plans can be prepared and the manager responsible for personnel warned of any likely surpluses.

Consultation on redundancies

If all measures to avoid redundancy fail, the company will consult the union(s) at the earliest opportunity in order to reach agreement.

Selection of redundant employees

In the event of impending redundancy, the individuals who might be surplus to requirements should be selected by the departmental manager with the advice of the manager responsible for personnel on the principles that should be adopted.

The manager responsible for personnel should explore the possibilities of transferring affected staff to alternative work.

The manager responsible for personnel should inform management of proposed action (either redundancy or transfer) to obtain approval.

The union(s) will be informed of the numbers affected but not of individual names.

The departmental manager and the HR manager responsible for personnel will jointly interview the employees affected either to offer a transfer or, if a suitable alternative is not available, to inform them they will be redundant. At this interview, full information should be available to give to the employee on, as appropriate:

- the reasons for being surplus;
- the alternative jobs that are available;
- the date when the employee will become surplus (that is, the period of notice);
- the entitlement to redundancy pay;
- the employee's right to appeal to an appropriate director;
- the help the company will provide.

Redundancy procedure (part 3)

An appropriate director will hear any appeals with the manager responsible for personnel.

The manager responsible for personnel will ensure that all the required administrative arrangements are made.

If the union(s) have any points to raise about the selection of employees or the actions taken by the company, these should be discussed in the first place with the manager responsible for personnel. If the results of these discussions are unsatisfactory, a meeting will be arranged with an appropriate director.

Alternative work within the company

If an employee is offered and accepts suitable alternative work within the company, it will take effect without a break from the previous employment and will be confirmed in writing. If the offer is refused, the employee may forfeit his or her redundancy payment. Employees will receive appropriate training and will be entitled to a four-week trial period to see if the work is suitable. This trial period may be extended by mutual agreement to provide additional training. During this period, employees are free to terminate their employment and if they do, would be treated as if they had been made redundant on the day the old job ended. They would then receive any redundancy pay to which they are entitled.

Alternative employment

Employees for whom no suitable work is available in the company will be given reasonable opportunities to look for alternative employment.

59

Computerized human resource information systems

As defined by Kettley and Reilly (2003), a computerized human resource information system consists of 'a fully integrated, organization-wide network of HR-related data, information, services, databases, tools and transactions'. Such a system can be described as 'e-HR', meaning 'the application of conventional, web and voice technologies to improve HR administration, transactions and process performance'. They suggest that the reasons for adopting e-HR are:

- HR service improvement;
- cost-cutting and operational efficiency;
- the desire of the HR function to change the nature of its relationship with employees and line managers;
- the transformation of HR into a customer-focused and responsive function;
- the offer of services that fit the new world of work and are attractive to current and future staff.

BENEFITS OF A COMPUTERIZED HUMAN RESOURCE INFORMATION SYSTEM

According to IDS (2002), the benefits of a computerized human resource management system are:

- increased access to HR data;
- streamlined and standardized processes;
- more consistent and accurate data;
- a higher internal profile for HR.

HR INFORMATION STRATEGY

The HR strategy of an organization in relation to HR information is concerned first with the use of computerized information for strategic decision making, second with the range of applications which should be included in the system and finally with the provision to line managers of the facility to have direct access to any personnel data they need to manage their own teams in a devolved organization.

Strategic decision taking

The strategic areas involving computerized information and the knowledge gained from analysing that information include macro concerns about organization, human resource requirements, the utilization of human resources, employee development and organizational health.

Specifically the information may focus on areas such as:

- organization development – how the structure may need to adapt to future needs and how IT can enable structural change, for example, high performance team structures;
- human resource plans, especially those concerned with 'mapping' future competence requirements and enlarging the skills base;
- determination of future development and training needs;
- determination of the performance and personality characteristics of the people who will be successful in the organization;
- assessment of the 'health' of the organization measured by attitude surveys and turnover and absence statistics, leading to the development of motivation, retention and absence control strategies;

- analysis of productivity levels as the basis for productivity improvement programmes;
- analysis of the scope for cutting down the number of employees – taking unnecessary costs out of the business.

Range of applications

There is an immense range of applications to choose from, starting from basic employee records and extending to highly sophisticated 'expert' systems which focus on fundamental HR decision areas.

THE FUNCTIONS OF A COMPUTERIZED HR SYSTEM

The basic functions of a computerized HR system are to:

- hold personal details about individual employees including career history, skills and qualifications, leave and absence records;
- hold details about employees' jobs, including grade, pay and benefits, hours, locations, job description or role definition;
- produce reports summarizing different aspects of this information.

The additional 'functionality' that a system can incorporate comprises:

- the recording and analysis of absence, attendance and labour turnover, which includes making comparisons between different occupations and locations and producing data on trends;
- recruitment and training administration;
- job evaluation;
- sophisticated modelling tools for such activities as human resource planning and reward management, which enable the system to be used to support strategic decision-making;
- linkages to the internet (for example as part of an internet recruitment system) or to the internal intranet.

It is useful to distinguish between transactional (HR processes such as records, recruitment and e-learning) application and relational systems (communication, knowledge management and enhancing the employer brand).

Systems may be completely integrated with payroll, or more commonly they maintain a direct link. Some systems are entirely stand-alone. There may be one comprehensive software package to cover all applications, or specialized software for such functions as attendance management or job evaluation may be used.

THE TECHNICAL INFRASTRUCTURE

Human resource information system

This provides the information required to manage HR processes. These may be core employee database and payroll systems but can be extended to include such systems as recruitment, e-learning, performance management and reward. The system may be web-based, enabling access to be remote or online and at any time.

HR/corporate intranet

An intranet is an electronic network that enables information to be communicated across organizations. It posts static data such as information on HR policies and communications about employee facilities such as learning opportunities and flexible benefits. It can include links that enable managers and other employees to interface directly with HR applications and make changes or enquiries.

B2E portal

A B2E portal provides a single intranet screen that enables the organization to gather and present information and gives people ready access to it.

Application service provider

An application service provider (ASP) carries out on behalf of the organization all or much of the administration of the human resource information system. Organizations, often smaller or medium-sized, can use an ASP to outsource the burden of running the system.

RATING OF SYSTEM FEATURES

Research conducted by the IPD and the Institute for Employment Studies (IPD, 1999b) established that the systems features rated highly by organizations were:

- employee records;
- payroll;
- sick pay and maternity pay calculations;
- equal opportunity monitoring;
- production of standard letters and contracts;
- absence recording and monitoring;
- annual leave records;
- enquiries;
- attendance recording;
- disciplinary recording.

The features that were not so highly rated were:

- psychometric testing;
- IiP evaluation;
- shift or roster planning;
- organization charting;
- succession planning;
- 'what-if' modelling;
- jobs/skills matching;
- workforce planning;
- training needs analysis;
- appraisal records;
- salary modelling.

AN EFFECTIVE SYSTEM

The IPD guide on using computerized personnel systems (1999b) states that an effective system will have the following features:

- meets business needs;
- user-friendliness;
- good reporting facilities;
- flexibility;
- value for money;
- good supplier support;
- reliability.

PROBLEMS AND HOW TO DEAL WITH THEM

The 1999 IPD guide lists a number of typical problems and suggests how they can be dealt with. The problems and their solutions are set out in Table 59.1.

Table 59.1 Computer system problems and solutions

Problem	Solution
Poor data quality	Pay particular attention to getting accurate data into the system by training and monitoring
Lack of understanding of the system by users	Provide 'contextual training' covering: ● data sources (who provides the data and in what form) ● why different pieces of data are collected ● links to other systems
Inadequate coding of data producing unhelpful reports	Take care in setting up coding structures and train users in how to use codes
Lack of clarity about responsibilities for generating information on how the system can be used to generate useful information	Ensure that care is taken in specifying responsibilities and spelling out how information can be used supported by training and continuing guidance (a 'help line' to a systems or networks manager is a good idea)
Inadequate reporting capability – this is an aspect of systems that causes most dissatisfaction	● Define report specifications carefully in advance ● Take care in designing report layouts and contents on the basis of surveys of user needs ● Check views about the quality of reports and amend them as necessary
Line managers resent having to contribute or maintain information	● Minimize form filling ● Ensure that managers can access the system easily, possibly via the intranet ● Advise managers on how they can use the system to their benefit

Involving line managers

With the universal availability of personal computers (PCs) and the development of distributed data processing in local area networks (LANS) and the wide area networks (WANS), it is possible for data for use by line managers to be downloaded from the centre (a mainframe, minicomputer or UNIX system). Managers can also maintain their own data and manipulate the figures by the use of spreadsheets, for example, considering alternative ways of distributing their budget for a payroll increase among their staff. All this will, of course, be subjected to intensive security so that information goes only to authorized people and some data may be on a 'read only' basis.

The strategy for extending the system to line managers will clearly be entirely dependent on the organization's policies for devolving personnel decisions to them. But if this is the policy, its implementation will be much more likely to take place if the information required by line managers is made available.

DEVELOPING A COMPUTERIZED HR INFORMATION SYSTEM

The design decisions that have to be made when developing an e-HR system are concerned with the type and proportion of services to be delivered, the best means of delivery and the use of the system shared by HR service centres. The challenges, as described by Kettley and Reilly (2003) are:

- aligning e-HR investment with the strategy of the business;
- taking into account the needs of a varied workforce, including their access to and familiarity with technology;
- customizing e-HR;
- avoiding information overload;
- making an impact on HR and organizational performance.

They emphasize that it is important to avoid simply computerizing an existing process. It is necessary to take a 'process thinking' approach, ie to redesign the process and then computerize. This might involve significant streamlining of existing processes.

Overall approach

The following are the typical stages in the development of an HR information system.

- Establish the current and future needs of the business and how these impinge on HR, and the implications for information systems.

- Define what outputs are required from the system in the form of information and reports.
- Prepare a high-level statement of requirement.
- Identify the options available to meet the HR business requirements.
- Prepare a recommendation on how to proceed for executive approval and buy-in. This must be supported both by a financial evaluation and by an analysis of the benefits to the business and any associated changes in business practices. A transition plan will be required which sets out the sequence of activities that would allow the organization to move swiftly and efficiently to any new system with the minimum of disruption.

Preferred characteristics of an information system

The preferred characteristics of an information system are:

- direct input of data at source;
- systems that can be used by the 'occasional user', not just a dedicated expert;
- systems able to deal with administrative processes, not simply a management information system;
- systems that provide the information needed by line managers in an easily understood format.

The range of applications will be defined by the information strategy. It will be vital to ensure that the hardware is appropriate to the organizational requirements in that PCs and terminals are provided where needed and are linked together in a network as required.

It is equally essential to ensure that the system is designed in such a way as to hold all the base data needed to provide management information. The system should be user-friendly, bearing in mind that the task which demands most time in using a system is data entry and that the enquiry system for obtaining information must be as easy to learn and use as possible.

The detailed points to be considered when developing a system are:

- the choice of hardware;
- database management;
- the degree to which the system is integrated with the payroll;
- the choice of software;
- the development programme.

Choice of hardware

There may be no choice of hardware – some systems are still linked to a mainframe computer. But networked PC systems using either mini or microcomputers are common, especially in larger organizations.

Database management

The system should be founded on a database – a self-describing collection of integrated personnel records. Particular attention has to be paid to the database management system (DBMS), the program or set of programs that develops and uses the database and database applications. Careful attention has also to be given to the design of database forms: data entry forms which are custom developed, video displays used to enter and change data, queries using standard query language (SQL) and report forms which are the hard copy output of database data. The base data is likely to be of much better quality if it is used in such day-to-day processes as recruitment, training administration and job evaluation.

Integration

Although many organizations have separated the payroll and purely personnel applications (the former usually being controlled by the accounts department), there is a lot to be said for having an integrated system. This makes economic use of one comprehensive database and facilitates such processes as flexible payment (cafeteria) systems.

Software

There is a massive and almost bewildering choice of software packages for application programs to provide information and generate reports. The software houses are constantly innovating and developing their products and between them provide something for everyone. However, if the organization has its own systems analysis and programming resources there are advantages in developing tailor-made software. But great care will need to be taken to debug the system, especially if a distributed system involving line managers is being created.

However, most organizations use an external supplier although the HR application market is highly fragmented, as an IRSI (2004i) survey into the use of human resource management information systems found. The two basic approaches are the 'integrated best-of-breed model', which links applications from separate specialist providers to produce what is in effect a bespoke system, or the 'application suite' model, with one vendor supplying a linked group of modules. If an external supplier is used the choice should be made as follows:

- research the HR software market through trade exhibitions and publications;
- review HR processes and existing systems;
- produce a specification of system requirements;
- send an invitation to tender to several suppliers;
- invite suppliers to demonstrate their products;
- obtain references from existing customers, including site visits;
- analyse and score the product against the specification.

The development programme

The 10 steps required to develop and implement an information system are:

1. Determine objectives – are they to save administrative costs, speed up processing, provide advanced decision support, or a combination of any of these?
2. Prepare a business case for the system, setting out the benefits and the costs.
3. Carry out a feasibility study to consider applications and their likely costs and benefits. This study could be carried out in-house or with the help of outside consultants or software houses who provide a consultancy service. The feasibility study will broadly analyse and define user requirements and ensure that all concerned are aware of what is being planned, how they will benefit from it and the contribution they will be expected to make to the development and application of the system. The information the system will be required to store and process and the uses to which the information will be put should be specified. Account should be taken of the provisions of the Data Protection Act (1998) as described in Chapter 55.
4. Prepare a requirements specification which will set out in detail what the system is expected to do and how the company would like to use it. This specification can be used to brief hardware and software suppliers before selecting the system.
5. Select the system in the form of the hardware and the software required. This may involve decisions on the extent to which existing hardware or systems (eg payroll systems) will be used. The need and scope for networking, that is, linking users by means of terminals, will also need to be considered.
6. Plan the implementation programme to ensure that the objectives will be achieved within a given time scale and in line with the cost budget.
7. Involve users to ensure that everyone who will benefit from the system (line

managers as well as members of the personnel department) can contribute their ideas and thus feel that it is their system rather than one imposed upon them.

8. Control the project against the implementation programme to ensure that it delivers what is required, on time and within the budget. As *The IPD Guide on Implementing Computerized Personnel Systems* (1997b) emphasizes, it is essential to ensure that the selection and implementation of a system is a managed process. This means selecting an individual to act as project manager with the responsibility for dealing with all the steps listed above.

9. Provide training to all users to ensure that they can operate and get the most out of the system.

10. Monitor performance to ensure that the system lives up to expectations.

APPLICATIONS

As established by the IRSI (2004i) survey, in many respects the core functionality in use is concerned with administrative processes, particularly absence management (very popular), training and development, reward, payroll and recruitment and selection. Most HR functions use their HRM information system to change pay rates, alter employee records, monitor absence figures and download forms for manual completion. Not many organizations use their IT systems strategically for workforce planning, tracking the skills of individuals and making the data available for analysis and action. Some but by no means all organizations were developing self-service applications such as employees changing their personal details, and booking on training courses directly. The main potential applications are summarized below.

Personal records

These can include personal details, job details, employment contracts, pay details, performance appraisal, contacts and addresses and employee transactional data. The latter includes all the special items of information a company may need for its employees including qualifications, special skills and competences, training, absence, medical history and discipline.

Business to employees (B2E)

As defined by Watson Wyatt Worldwide (2002), business to employee (B2E) processes involve the application of any computer technology enabling managers and employees to have direct access to HR and other workplace services for communication, performance reporting, team management and learning, in addition to administrative applications. A self-service approach can be adopted, which allows managers or staff to access personal records and update them or add new information, subject to rigorous security arrangements.

Human resource planning

An information system can be used to model the effects on groups of people within the organization of change over time in the numbers and structure of each group and movements into, through and out of each group. Such a model looks at the organization, using a staffing system consisting of grades and flows. The user has considerable freedom in defining the number and type of flows required whether into, through, or out of each level of the system, ie:

- flows in – recruitment, transfers in;
- flows out – transfers out, retirement, resignation (uncontrolled losses), early retirement (controlled losses).

Employee turnover monitoring and control

Computer models can monitor and help in the control of employee turnover. They can therefore provide a critical input to other areas of human resource decision making such as policies on recruitment, promotion, redeployment, training and career planning.

Employee scheduling

An information system can be used to provide an integral system for matching the numbers of employees to business needs. The process of scheduling human resources to meet output in processing targets is becoming increasingly complex with the availability of more flexible ways of deploying people. They include multi-skilling (employees who are capable of carrying out different tasks and are not subject to trade-union-imposed constraints in doing so), the use of contract workers, the use of outworkers (people working at home or in another centre, a process which is facilitated by computer networking and electronic mailing), twilight shifts, more part-timers, job sharing etc.

Human resource planning is an interactive process which is always using output from one part of the process to influence another part of the process. Thus, assessments of the demand and supply of people, scheduling policies and possibilities, and the scope for flexing workloads and the use of people all influence the human resource supply policies adopted by the organization.

Employee profiling

Profiling is a particular aspect of employee scheduling concerned with the matching of staff to workloads and ensuring that the right number of people are available to meet fluctuations in activity levels over time. Profiling techniques are used where there are measurable volumes of work that can be costed and forecast with reasonable accuracy. Profiling can be linked with employee budgeting control in the sense that the use of people is both constrained and influenced by the cash budget and performance and employee establishment targets.

Profiling models can be used to:

- monitor and analyse employee utilization;
- test the effects of moving some activities to different times of the year and analyse their predicted impact on the employment profile;
- monitor movements in expenditure on pay and other employee benefits and carry out sensitivity tests on the impact of different pay assumptions;
- forecast future employee requirements;
- synchronize the recruitment of permanent and temporary employees with forecast workloads;
- flex employee budgets on the basis of revised activity level forecasts;
- control employee budgets.

Skills inventories and audits

Many organizations need to store detailed information about the skills, competences and experience of the individuals they employ. A separate skills inventory can be linked to a personnel database in order that any individual changes in experience or additional training can be fed through automatically to it.

Periodical audits can be carried out by the information system of the skills and competences available in the organization. These can be compared with estimates of current and future requirements to identify areas where recruitment or training action is required.

Competency modelling

Competency modelling brings together organization planning and performance management data to establish the skills or competencies required to do particular jobs. This assists in appointment, promotion and training decisions. Competency analysis looks both at what tasks have to be carried out and the competencies required. Profiles can then be developed by the computer and matched to assessments of current job holders or job applicants.

Recruitment

A recruitment system can carry out the following tasks:

- storage of applicants' details;
- retrieval and amendment of those details;
- matching CVs to person specifications for short-listing purposes;
- link with Internet recruiting processes;
- letter writing (linking the system to word-processing facilities) – acknowledgements, invitations to interview, offers and rejections;
- management reports, analysis of response by media and monitoring recruitment costs.

Computerized recruitment control packages not only automate recruitment correspondence (coupling the system with word processors) but also enable users to determine instantly who has applied for which post, track progress in recruiting for a specific post and match and process internal candidates (applicant tracking systems).

The database can be used in more advanced applications to assist in establishing selection profiles with the standards against which potential job holders can be assessed in order that the right people can be appointed to or promoted into jobs.

As reported by Kettley and Reilly (2003), the United Biscuits graduate recruitment portal is a competency-based pre-screening tool. It allows people to review online details of the company, its jobs and career development opportunities. Interested applicants are invited to go through pre-screening by entering their personal details, filing academic information, and completing a questionnaire focused on United Biscuits' high performance behaviours derived from the company's top 100 managers.

If successful at this level, applicants are given a unique password enabling access to the website's next level, where applications to specific functions can be made.

Reward management

The system can be used for pay modelling and to carry out a number of reward administration activities. It can also be used in job evaluation.

Pay models provide the answers to 'what if?' questions such as, 'How much would it cost if we gave x per cent to this part of the company, y per cent to another part of the company, and implemented the following special package across these job functions?'

A system can also:

- analyse and report on average pay or pay distributions by job, grade, age or length of service;
- calculate compa-ratios to show how average pay in a range differs from the target pay;
- calculate the effects of attrition;
- assist in job evaluation;
- forecast future payroll costs on the basis of assumptions about numbers, promotions and pay levels;
- administer pay reviews, producing review forms, analysing proposals against the budgets and calculating the cost of performance-related pay awards in accordance with different assumptions about amounts and the distribution of awards within a budget;
- provide information to line managers which will guide them to their pay decisions;
- generate instructions to adjust pay as well as letters to individuals informing them of their increases.

Performance management

An information system can help to operate performance management, generating forms, analysing and reporting on the result of performance reviews showing the distribution of people with different degrees of potential or performing at different levels, and highlighting individuals with particular skills or special promise. This system can be linked to others to provide an integrated basis for creating and implementing human resource management policies.

Computer-managed learning

A system can be used for computer-managed learning by:

- storing e-learning modules on the database, which enables trainers to select an appropriate module or mix of modules to meet a specified learning need;
- analysing the training recommendations contained in performance review reports to identify collective and individual training needs;
- identifying suitable training courses to meet training needs;

- making arrangements for off-the-job courses;
- informing employees about the arrangements for courses;
- handling correspondence about training courses;
- storing data on standard or individually tailored induction, continuation or development training programmes, including syllabi, routings, responsibilities for giving training, test procedures and progress reporting;
- generating instructions and notes for guidance for all concerned with providing or undergoing on-the-job training programmes;
- storing progress reports and monitoring achievements against training objectives;
- producing reports summarizing current and projected training activities and calculating the output of training programmes – this can be linked to human resource planning models including those designed to determine the input of trainees required for training schemes;
- recording and monitoring training expenditure against budget.

Computers can also be used as training aids.

Career management

A system can help in the implementation of career management policies and procedures which embrace both career planning and management development. The system does this by analysing the progression of individuals and comparing the results of that analysis, first, with assessments of organizational requirements as generated by the human resource planning models and, second, with the outputs of the performance management system.

Absence control

Absence control can be carried out with the help of computerized time recording and attendance systems which:

- record clocking-on or -out time and the hours actually worked;
- enable employees to record the time spent on particular jobs;
- get employees to explain the reason for late arrival, early departure, or any other absence;
- can be linked to the payroll system for pay and bonus calculation purposes and to a flexible working hours system;
- provide team leaders with a statement showing the length and reasons for absence.

Advanced systems link information obtained from clocking-on or -out direct to a screen in team leaders' offices so that they can have instant information on how many people are at work and on the incidence of lateness.

Equal opportunity monitoring

The system can store records of the ethnic composition of the workforce. This information can be analysed to produce data on the distribution of ethnic minorities by occupation, job grade, age, service and location. The analysis could show the overall proportion of ethnic minority employees compared with the proportion in each job grade. Similar statistics can be produced for men and women. The analysis can be extended to cover career progression, splitting the results of the overall analysis into comparisons of the rate at which women and men of different ethnic groups progress.

Expert systems

Knowledge-based software or expert systems are computer programs which contain knowledge about particular fields of human activity and experience, which, through linkages and rules built into the system design, can help solve human resource management problems. Unlike a database system which stores, sorts, manipulates, and presents bits of information – ie data – expert systems store, sort, manipulate and present managers with ready-to-use knowledge of management practice, written in a language that management understands, as opposed to computerese.

Expert systems are developed through a process of knowledge engineering which starts from a knowledge base containing facts and a body of expertise ('heuristics', or rules of thumb) about the use of those facts. These 'rules' enable decisions to be made on the basis of factual information presented to the computer. Thus, a fact may be information on employee turnover during the last three years, and the rule of thumb may be the method by which turnover could be predicted over the next three years. These facts and rules are processed by what is termed the 'inference engine', which solves problems or makes predictions, and the results of this process are presented to the user in the 'user interface'.

An expert system can produce a list of suitable candidates for promotion by using information from the database. If more information were required, it would ask the user to answer questions. It would also respond to users' questions about why particular candidates had been identified, by giving details of qualifications, performance appraisal results and so on.

What can loosely be described as expert systems are also used in job evaluation applications where they make use of a database of job analyses and evaluations in order to make consistent judgements about evaluation scores. This is done by:

- defining the evaluation rules;
- programming the computer to ask appropriate questions concerning each factor in a job to enable it to apply the evaluation rules – this involves the analysis of structured questionnaires which have been specially designed to facilitate the systematic collection and analysis of data;
- applying the rules consistently and determining the factor score for the job;
- grading and ranking jobs;
- storing the information in the computer's memory so that it can be called to the screen or printed at any time.

AUDITING THE SYSTEM

As suggested by Robinson (1999), regular audit of the system should be carried out to obtain answers to these questions:

- Is the system being used efficiently and effectively?
- Are there any barriers to the effective use of the system?
- Does the technology enable managers or merely dictate to them?
- Are there any aspects of the system which are causing dissatisfaction in the HR department, with senior management or line managers?
- Are there any problems with data inaccuracy?
- Are reports accurate, helpful and used for decision-making?
- What is the functionality of the system? That is, what does the system do, and how well does it do it? What additional functions might be useful?
- How effective are the systems links, the use of data in different applications?

Appendix

Example of an attitude survey

Purpose

The purpose of this survey is to obtain your opinion on the existing pay arrangements and the performance appraisal process in XYZ Ltd. Your views and those of all the other staff of the company who are being asked to complete this questionnaire will provide a valuable input to the work currently being carried out to devise new approaches to pay and performance appraisal. Feedback on the overall results of the survey will be provided to all staff.

Confidentiality

Your answers to the questionnaire will be completely confidential. No individual will be identified and no one in the company will see the forms, which will be analysed by an independent research firm. You are being asked to identify your function but that is simply to make comparisons; the forms will not be analysed on an individual basis.

Completing and forwarding the survey form

Please complete the form and send it by 1st July in the attached envelope which is addressed to the firm which will be carrying out the analysis.

How to complete the questionnaire

The questionnaire will take about 15 minutes to complete. Please indicate your views about the statements overleaf by placing a ring around the number which most closely matches your opinion. For example:

	Strongly agree	*Inclined to agree*	*Neither agree nor disagree*	*Inclined to disagree*	*Strongly disagree*
I like my job	(1)	2	3	4	5

Function/department

Please circle one of the following:

1. corporate office;

2. marketing;

3. manufacturing;

4. finance;

5. IT;

6. HR;

7. customer service;

8. marketing, development, fundraising, PR, HR.

	QUESTIONNAIRE					
	I believe that:	*Strongly agree*	*Inclined to agree*	*Neither agree nor disagree*	*Inclined to disagree*	*Strongly disagree*
1	My pay adequately rewards me for my contribution	1	2	3	4	5
2	The pay system is clear and easy to understand	1	2	3	4	5
3	It is right for staff to be rewarded according to their contribution	1	2	3	4	5
4	The basis upon which my pay is determined is fair	1	2	3	4	5
5	Highly competent staff should be paid more than less competent staff	1	2	3	4	5
6	Rates of pay in the Company are not consistent with levels of responsibility	1	2	3	4	5
7	My rate of pay compares favourably with rates paid outside the Company	1	2	3	4	5
8	My pay does not reflect my performance	1	2	3	4	5
9	The current pay system encourages better performance	1	2	3	4	5
10	The pay system badly needs to be reviewed	1	2	3	4	5
11	I am clear about the standards of performance I am expected to achieve	1	2	3	4	5
12	I do not understand the competence levels I am expected to reach	1	2	3	4	5
13	The performance appraisal scheme is helpful	1	2	3	4	5
14	I receive good feedback from my manager on my performance	1	2	3	4	5
15	My manager is not really interested in carrying out my appraisal	1	2	3	4	5
16	I am motivated by my performance review meeting	1	2	3	4	5
17	The process of setting objectives and reviewing achievements is fair	1	2	3	4	5
18	The assessment of my performance by my manager is objective and fair	1	2	3	4	5
19	Performance appraisal does not help me to improve my performance	1	2	3	4	5
20	Performance appraisal clearly indicates any further training I might need	1	2	3	4	5

References

ACAS (1982) *Developments in Harmonization: Discussion Paper No 1*, London

ACAS (1991) *Effective Organizations: The people factor, ACAS Advisory Booklet No 6*, ACAS, London

Accounting for People Task Force (2003) *Accounting for People*, DTI, London

Adair, J (1973) *The Action-Centred Leader*, McGraw-Hill, London

Adams, J S (1965) Injustice in social exchange, in *Advances in Experimental Psychology*, Vol. 2, ed L Berkowitz, Academic Press, New York

Adams, K (1991) Externalisation vs specialisation: what is happening to personnel?, *Human Resource Management Journal*, **14**, pp 40–54

Adler N J and Ghader, F (1990) Strategic human resource management: a global perspective, in *International Human Resource Management*, ed R Pieper, De Gruter, Berlin/New York

Akinnusi, D K (1991) Personnel management in Africa: a comparative analysis of Ghana, Kenya and Nigeria, in *International Human Resource Management*, ed C Brewster and S Tyson, Pitman, London

Alderfer, C (1972) *Existence, Relatedness and Growth*, New York, The Free Press

Aldous, H (2000) Education and business: partners in building human capital, in *Human Capital and Corporate Regulation*, ed A Carey and N Sleigh-Johnson, Institute of Chartered Accountants, London

Allport, G (1954) The historical background of modern social psychology, in *Theoretical Models and Personality*, ed G Lindzey, Addison-Wesley, Cambridge, MA

Allport, G (1960) The open system in personality theory, *Journal of Abnormal and Social Psychology*, **61**, pp 301–311

Anglia Polytechnic University (1995) *Collectivism or Individualism in Employee Contracts*, Employment Relations, Research and Development Centre, Chelmsford

Argyle, M (1989) *The Social Psychology of Work*, Penguin, Harmondsworth

Argyris, C (1957) *Personality and Organization*, Harper & Row, New York

Argyris, C (1970) *Intervention Theory and Method*, Addison-Wesley, Reading, MA

Argyris, C (1991) Teaching smart people how to learn, *Harvard Business Review*, May-June, pp 54–62

Argyris, C (1992) *On Organizational Learning*, Blackwell, Cambridge, MA

Argyris, C (1993) *Knowledge for Action: A guide to overcoming barriers to organizational change*, Jossey Bass, San Fransisco, CA

Argyris, C and Schon, D A (1996) *Organizational Learning: A theory of action perspective*, Addison Wesley, Reading, MA

Armstrong, M (1977) *A Handbook of Personnel Practice*, 6th edn, Kogan Page, London

Armstrong, M (1987) Human resource management: a case of the emperor's new clothes, *Personnel Management*, August, pp 30–35

Armstrong, M (1989) *Personnel and the Bottom Line*, Institute of Personnel Management, London

Armstrong M (1996) *A Handbook of Personnel Management Practice*, 6th edn, Kogan Page, London

Armstrong, M (1999) *Employee Reward*, 2nd edn, Institute of Personnel and Development, London

Armstrong, M (2000a) The name has changed but has the game remained the same?, *Employee Relations*, **22**(6), pp 576–89

Armstrong, M (2000b) *Team Rewards*, CIPD, London

Armstrong, M and Baron, A (1995) *The Job Evaluation Handbook*, IPD, London

Armstrong, M and Baron, A (1998) *Performance Management: The new realities*, IPD, London

Armstrong, M and Baron, A (2002) *Strategic HRM: The key to improved business performance*, CIPD, London

Armstrong, M and Baron, A (2004) *Managing Performance: Performance management in action*, CIPD, London

Armstrong, M and Brown, D (1998) Relating competencies to pay: the UK experience, *Compensation & Benefits Review*, May/June, pp 28–39

Armstrong, M and Brown, D (2001) *Pay: The new dimensions*, CIPD, London

Armstrong M and Long, P (1994) *The Reality of Strategic HRM*, IPD, London

Armstrong, M and Murlis, H (1998) *Reward Management*, 4th edn, Kogan Page, London

Armstrong, M and Ryden, O (1996) *The IPD Guide on Team Reward*, IPD, London

Armstrong, M, Cummins, A, Hastings, S and Wood, W (2003) *Guide to Job Evaluation*, Kogan Page, London

Arnold, J, Robertson, I T and Cooper, C L (1991) *Work Psychology*, Pitman, London

Arthur, J (1990) *Industrial Relations and Business Strategies in American Steel Minimills*, Unpublished PhD dissertation, Cornell University

Arthur, J B (1992) The link between business strategy and industrial relations systems in American steel mills, *Industrial and Labor Relations Review*, **45**(3), pp 488–506

Arthur, J (1994) Effects of human resource systems on manufacturing performance and turnover, *Academy of Management Review*, **37**(4), pp 670–87

Atkinson, G (1989) *The Effective Negotiator*, Negotiating Systems Publications, Newbury

Atkinson, J (1984) Manpower strategies for flexible organizations, *Personnel Management*, August, pp 28–31

Atkinson, J and Meager, N (1986) *Changing Patterns of Work*, IMS/OECD, London

Bailey, T (1993) *Discretionary Authority and the Organization of Work: Employee participation and work reform since Hawthorne*, Working Paper, Columbia University, New York

Baillie, J (1995) *The Changing Nature of Work and the Psychological Contract*, IPD (unpublished)

Bales, R F (1950) *Interaction Process Analysis*, Addison-Wesley, Reading, MA

Bandura, A (1977) *Social Learning Theory*, Prentice-Hall, Englewood Cliffs, NJ

Bandura, A (1982) Self-efficacy mechanism in human agency, *American Psychologist*, **37**, pp 122–47

Bandura, A (1986) *Social Boundaries of Thought and Action*, Prentice-Hall, Englewood Cliffs, NJ

Barnard, C (1938) *The Functions of an Executive*, Harvard University Press, Boston, MA

Barney, J (1991) Firm resources and sustained competitive advantage, *Journal of Management*, **17**, pp 99–120

Bartlett, C A and Ghoshal, S (1991) *Managing Across Borders: The transnational solution*, London Business School, London

Bartlett, C A and Ghoshal, S (1993) Beyond the M-form: toward a management theory of the firm, *Strategic Management Journal*, 14, pp 23–46

Bartlett, C A and Ghoshal, S (2000) *Transnational Management Text: Cases and readings on cross-boarder Management*, Harvard Business School Press, Boston, MA

Bass, B M and Vaughan, J A (1966) *Training in Industry: The management of learning*, Tavistock, London

Bates, R A and Holton, E F (1995) Computerised performance monitoring: a review of human resource issue, *Human Resource Management Review*, Winter, pp 267–88

Beardwell, I (1998) Voices on, *People Management*, 28 May, pp 32–36

Beatty, R W, Huselid, M A and Schneier, C E (2003) Scoring on the business scorecard, *Organizational Dynamics*, **32**(2), pp 107–21

Becker, B E and Gerhart, S (1996) The impact of human resource management on organizational performance: progress and prospects, Academy of Management Journal, **39**(4), pp 779–801

Becker, B E, Huselid, M A, Pickus, P S and Spratt, M F (1997) HR as a source of shareholder value: research and recommendations, *Human Resource Management*, Spring, **36**(1), pp 39–47

Becker, B E, Huselid, M A and Ulrich, D (2001) *The HR Scorecard: Linking people, strategy, and performance*, Harvard Business School Press, Boston, MA

Beckhard, R (1969) *Organization Development: Strategy and models*, Addison-Wesley, Reading, MA

Beckhard, R (1989) A model for the executive management of transformational change in G Salaman, (ed) *Human Resource Strategies*, Sage, London

Beer, M (1981) Performance appraisal – dilemmas and possibilities, *Organization Dynamics*, Winter, pp 24–36

Beer, M (1984) Reward systems, in M Beer, B Spector, P R Lawrence and D Quinn Mills, *Managing Human Assets*, New York, The Free Press

Beer, M and Ruh, R A (1976) Employee growth through performance management, *Harvard Business Review*, July/August, pp 59–66

Beer, M and Spector, B (1985) Corporate transformations in human resource management, in R Walton and P Lawrence (eds) *HRM Trends and Challenges*, Harvard University Press, Boston, MA

Beer, M, Eisenstat, R and Spector, B (1990) Why change programs don't produce change, *Harvard Business Review*, November/December, pp 158–66

Beer, M, Spector, B, Lawrence, P, Quinn Mills, D and Walton, R (1984) *Managing Human Assets*, The Free Press, New York

Belbin, M (1981) *Management Teams: Why they succeed or fail*, Heinemann, Oxford

Bell, W and Hanson, C (1987) *Profit Sharing and Profitability*, Kogan Page, London

Bennis, W (1960) *Organizational Development*, Addison-Wesley, Reading, MA

Bennis, W and Nanus, B (1985) *Leaders*, Harper & Row, New York

Bento, R and Ferreira, L (1992) Incentive pay and organisational culture, in W Bruns (ed) *Performance Measurement, Evaluation and Incentives*, Harvard Business School Press, Boston, MA

Berlet, K and Cravens, D (1991) *Performance Pay as a Competitive Weapon*, Wiley, New York

Berridge, J (1992) Human resource management in Britain, *Employee Relations*, **14**(5) pp 62–85

Bessant, J, Caffyn, S, Gilbert, J and Harding, R (1994) Rediscovering continuous improvement, *Technovation*, **14**(3), pp 17–29

Bevan, S, Barber, L and Robinson, D (1997) *Keeping the Best: A practical guide to retaining key employees*, Institute for Employment Studies, Brighton

Bevan, S and Thompson, M (1991) Performance management at the cross roads, *Personnel Management*, November, pp 36–39

Bibbings, R (2003) Hearsay and heresy, *The RoSPA Occupational Health and Safety Journal*, July, pp 51–52

Billson, I (1998) How just-in-time training can support business-led competency development, *Competency*, Spring, pp 21–24

Birchall, D and Lyons, L (1995) *Creating Tomorrow's Organisation*, Pitman, London

Blackburn, R M and Mann, R (1979) *The Working Class in the Labour Market*, Macmillan, London

Blackler, F (1995) Knowledge, knowledge work and experience *Organization Studies*, **16**(6), pp 16–36

Blake, P (1988) The knowledge management explosion, *Information Today*, **15**(1), pp 12–13

Blake, R and Mouton, J (1964) *The Managerial Grid*, Gulf Publishing, Houston

Blake, R, Shepart, H and Mouton, J (1964) Breakthrough in Organizational Development, *Harvard Business Review*, **42**, pp 237–58

Blinkorn, S and Johnson C (1990) The insignificance of personality testing, *Nature*, **348**, pp 20–27

Bloom, M and Milkovich, G T (1998) Rethinking international compensation, *Compensation and Benefits Review*, April, pp 17–27

Blyton, P and Turnbull, P (eds) (1992) *Reassessing Human Resource Management*, Sage Publications, London

Bontis, N (1996) There's a price on your head: managing intellectual capital strategically, *Business Quarterly*, Summer, pp 4–47

Bontis, N (1998) Intellectual capital: an exploratory study that develops measures and models, *Management Decision*, **36**(2), pp 63–76

Bontis, N, Dragonetti, N C, Jacobsen, K and Roos, G (1999) The knowledge toolbox: a review of the tools available to measure and manage intangible resources, *European Management Journal*, **17**(4), pp 391–402

Boudreau, J W (1988) Utility analysis, in *Human Resource Management: Evolving roles and responsibilities*, ed. L Dyer, Bureau of National Affairs, Washington, DC

Bower, J L (1982) 'Business policy in the 1980s, *Academy of Management Review*, **7**(4), pp 630–38

Bowey, A (1982) *The Effects of Incentive Pay Systems*, Department of Employment, Research Paper 36, DOE, London

Bowles, M L and Coates, G (1993) Image and substance: the management of performance as rhetoric or reality?, *Personnel Review*, **22**(2), pp 3–21

Boxall, P F (1992) Strategic HRM: a beginning, a new theoretical direction, *Human Resource Management Journal*, **2**(3), pp 61–79

Boxall, P F (1993) The significance of human resource management: a reconsideration of the evidence, *The International Journal of Human Resource Management*, **4**(3), pp 645–65

Boxall, P (1994) Placing HR strategy at the heart of the business, *Personnel Management*, July, pp 32–35

Boxall, P (1996) The strategic HRM debate and the resource-based view of the firm, *Human Resource Management Journal*, **6**(3), pp 59–75

Boxall, P (1999) Human resource strategy and competitive advantage: a longitudinal study of engineering consultancies, *Journal of Management Studies*, **36**(4), pp 443–63

Boxall, P and Purcell, J (2003) *Strategic Human Resource Management*, Palgrave Macmillan, Basingstoke

Boyatzis, R (1982) *The Competent Manager,* Wiley, New York

Boyett, J H and Conn, H P (1995) *Maximum Performance Management*, Glenbridge Publishing, Oxford

Bradley, P, Hendry, C and Perkins, P (1999) Global or multi-local? The significance of international values in reward strategy, in *International HRM: Contemporary issues in Europe*, ed C Brewster and H Harris, Routledge, London

Braverman, H (1974) *Labour and Monopoly Capital*, Monthly Review Press, New York

Brayfield, A H and Crockett, W H (1955) Employee attitudes and employee performance, *Psychological Bulletin*, **52**, pp 346–424

Brewster, C (1993) Developing a 'European' model of human resource management, *The International Journal of Human Resource Management*, **4**(4), pp 765–84

Brewster, C (1999) Strategic Human Resource Management: the value of different paradigms, in *Strategic Human Resource Management*, ed R S Schuler and S E Jackson, Blackwell, Oxford

Brewster, C (2004) European perspectives of human resource management, *Human Resource Management Review*, **14**(4), pp 365–82

Brewster, C and Holt Larsen, H (1992) Human resource management in Europe: evidence from ten countries, *International Journal of Human Resource Management*, **3**(3), pp 409–34

Brewster, C and Lloyd, J (1994) The changing face of union negotiations, *Human Resources*, Summer, pp 148–52

Brockbank, W, Ulrich, D and Beatty, D (1999) HR professional development: creating the future creators at the University of Michigan Business School, *Human Resource Management*, **38**, Summer, pp 111–17

Brown, D (1998) Presentation to the Compensation Forum meeting, February

Brown, D (2001) *Reward Strategies, From Intent to Impact*, CIPD, London

Brown, J A C (1954) *The Social Psychology of Industry*, Penguin Books, Harmondsworth

Brown, D and Armstrong, M (1997) Terms of endearment, *People Management*, 11 September, pp 36–38

Brown, D and Armstrong, M (1999) *Paying for Contribution*, Kogan Page, London

Brumbach, G B (1988) Some ideas, issues and predictions about performance management, *Public Personnel Management*, Winter, pp 387–402

Buchanan, D (1987) Job enrichment is dead: long live high performance work design!, *Personnel Management*, May, pp 40–43

Buchanan, D and Huczynski, A (1985) *Organizational Behaviour*, Prentice-Hall, Englewood Cliffs, NJ

Bulla, D N and Scott, P M (1994) Manpower requirements forecasting: a case example, in *Human Resource Forecasting and Modelling*, ed D Ward, T P Bechet and R Tripp, The Human Resource Planning Society, New York

Burdett, J O (1991) What is empowerment anyway?, *Journal of European Industrial Training*, **15**(6), pp 23–30

Burgess, S and Rees, H (1996) Job tenure in Britain, *Economic Journal*, March, pp 334–44

Burgoyne, J (1988a) *Competency Approaches to Management Development*, Centre for the Study of Management Learning, University of Lancaster

Burgoyne, J (1988b) Management development for the individual *and* the organization, *Personnel Management*, June, pp 40–44

Burgoyne, J (1994) As reported in *Personnel Management Plus*, May, p 7

Burgoyne, J (1999) Design of the times, *People Management*, 3 June, pp 39–44

Burner, D (1996) *Managing Change: A Strategic Approach to Organizational Dynamics*, 2nd edn, Pitman, London

Burns, J M (1978) *Leadership*, Harper & Row, New York

Burns, T and Stalker, G (1961) *The Management of Innovation*, Tavistock, London

Burt, C (1954) The differentiation of intellectual ability, *British Journal of Educational Psychology*, **24**, pp 45–67

Caldwell, R (2001) Champions, adapters, consultants and synergists: the new change agents in HRM, *Human Resource Management Journal*, **11**(3), pp 39–52

Caldwell, R (2004) Rhetoric, facts and self-fulfilling prophesies: exploring practitioners' perceptions of progress in implementing HRM, *Industrial Relations Journal*, **35**(3), pp 196–215

Campbell, J P (1990) Modelling the performance prediction problem in industrial and organizational psychology, in *Handbook of Industrial and Organizational Psychology*, ed M P Dunnette and L M Hugh, Blackwell, Cambridge, MA

Cannon, T (2000) Knowledge entrepreneurs and the responsible corporation, in *Human Capital and Corporate Regulation*, ed Anthony Carey and Nigel Sleigh-Johnson, Institute of Chartered Accountants, London

Cappelli, P (1999) *Employment Practices and Business Strategy*, Oxford University Press, New York

Cappelli, P (2000) A market-driven approach to retaining talent, *Harvard Business Review*, January/February, pp 103–11

Cappelli, P (2001) Making the most of on-line recruiting, *Harvard Business Review*, **70**(3), pp 134–48

Cappelli, P and Crocker-Hefter, A (1996) Distinctive human resources are firms' core competencies, *Organizational Dynamics*, Winter, pp 7–22

Cappelli, P and Singh, H (1992) Integrating strategic human resources and strategic management, in *Research Frontiers in Industrial Relations and Human Resources*, ed D Lewin, O Mitchell and P Scheller, Industrial Relations Research Association, Madison, Win

Carter, A, Hirsh, W and Aston, J (2002) *Resourcing the Training and Development Function*, Report No 390, Institute of Employment Studies, Brighton

Casson, J (1978) *Re-evaluating Company Manpower Planning in the Light of Some Practical Experiences*, Institute of Manpower Studies, Brighton

Cattell, R B (1963) *The Sixteen Personality Factor Questionnaire*, Institute for Personality and Ability Training, Illinois

Cave, A (1994) *Organizational Change in the Workplace*, Kogan Page, London

Centre for Workforce Development (1998) *The Teaching Firm: Where productive work and learning converge*, Newton, MA

CFO Research Services (2003) *Human Capital Management: The CFO's perspective*, CFO Publishing, Boston, MA

Chadwick, C and Cappelli, P (1998) Alternatives to generic strategy typologies in human resource management, in P Wright, L Dyer, J Boudreau and G Milkovich (eds) *Research in Personnel and Human Resource Management*, JAI Press, Greenwich, CT

Chamberlain, N W and Kuhn, J (1965) *Collective Bargaining*, McGraw-Hill, New York

Chartered Institute of Personnel and Development (2000) *Labour Turnover Report*, CIPD, London

Chartered Institute of Personnel and Development (2002) *Developing Managers for Business Performance*, CIPD, London

Chartered Institute of Personnel and Development (2002) *Code of Conduct for Equal Opportunities*, CIPD, London

Chartered Institute of Personnel and Development (2003a) *Employee Absence*, CIPD, London

Chartered Institute of Personnel and Development (2003b) *Human Capital: External reporting framework*, CIPD, London

Chartered Institute of Personnel and Development (2003c) *Reward Management 2003: A Survey of Policy and Practice*, CIPD, London

Chartered Institute of Personnel and Development (2004a) *How to Develop a Reward Strategy*, CIPD, London

Chartered Institute of Personnel and Development (2004b) *Human Capital Reporting: An internal perspective*, CIPD, London

Chartered Institute of Personnel and Development (2004c) *Professional Standards*, CIPD, London

Chartered Institute of Personnel and Development (2004d) *Survey of Recruitment, Retention and Turnover*, CIPD, London

Chartered Institute of Personnel and Development (2004e) *How to Develop a Reward Strategy*, CIPD, London

Chartered Institute of Personnel and Development (2005a) *Bullying at Work: Beyond policies to a culture of respect*, CIPD, London

Chartered Institute of Personnel and Development (2005b) *Managing Diversity*, CIPD, London

Chartered Institute of Personnel and Development (2005c) *Recruitment, Retention and Turnover Survey*, CIPD, London

Chartered Institute of Personnel and Development (2005d) *Reward Survey*, CIPD, London

Chartered Institute of Personnel and Development (2005e) *Training and Development Survey*, CIPD, London

Chell, E (1985) *Participation and Organisation*, Macmillan, London

Chell, E (1987) *The Psychology of Behaviour in Organisations*, Macmillan, London

Child, J (1977) *Organization: A guide to problems and practice*, Harper & Row, London

Chiumento (2004) *Get Engaged*, Chiumento, London

Clegg, H (1976) *The System of Industrial Relations in Great Britain*, Blackwell, Oxford

Clutterbuck, D (2004) *Everyone Needs a Mentor*, CIPD, London

Coleman, J S (1990) *Foundations of Social Theory*, University of Harvard Press, Cambridge, MA

Competency and Emotional Intelligence (2003/4) Raising performance through competencies: the tenth benchmarking survey

Cook, M (1993) *Personnel Selection and Productivity*, Wiley, Chichester

Cooke, R and Lafferty, J (1989) *Organizational Culture Inventory*, Human Synergistic, Plymouth, MI

Cooper, C (2000) In for the count, *People Management*, 12 October, pp 28–33

Cooper, R (1973) Task characteristics and intrinsic motivation, *Human Relations*, August, pp 387–408

Coopey, J and Hartley, J (1991) Reconsidering the case for organizational commitment, *Human Resource Management Journal*, **3**, Spring, pp 18–31

Council for Excellence in Management and Leadership (2002), *Report on Human Capital Reporting*, CEML, London

Cox, A and Purcell, J (1998), Searching for leverage: pay systems, trust, motivation and commitment in SMEs, in *Trust, Motivation and Commitment*, ed S J Perkins and St John Sandringham, Strategic Remuneration Centre, Faringdon

Cyert, R M and March, J G (1963) *A Behavioural Theory of the Firm*, Prentice-Hall, Englewood Cliffs, NJ

Daft, R L and Weick, K E (1984) Towards a model of organisations as interpretation systems, *Academy of Management Review*, **9**, pp 284–95

Dale, M (1994) Learning organizations, in C Mabey and P Iles (eds), *Managing Learning*, Routledge, London

Daniels, A C (1987) What is PM? *Performance Management*, July, pp 8–12

Davenport, T H (1996) Why re-engineering failed: the fad that forgot people, *Fast Company*, Premier Issue, pp 70–74

Davenport, T O (1999) *Human Capital*, Jossey Bass, San Francisco, CA

Davenport, T H and Prusak, L (1998) *Working Knowledge: How organizations manage what they know*, Harvard Business School Press, Boston, MA

Davis, L E (1966) The design of jobs, *Industrial Relations*, **6**

Deal, T and Kennedy, A (1982) *Corporate Cultures*, Addison-Wesley, Reading, MA

Deary, I J and Matthews, G (1993) Personality traits are alive and well. *The Psychologist*, **6**, pp 299–311

Delaney, J T and Huselid, M A (1996) The impact of human resource management practices on perceptions of organizational performance, *Academy of Management Journal*, **39**(4), pp 949–69

Delery, J E and Doty, H D (1996) Modes of theorizing in strategic human resource management: tests of universality, contingency and configurational performance predictions, *International Journal of Human Resource Management*, **6**, pp 656–70

Deloitte & Touche and Personnel Today (2002) *Measuring Human Capital Value, 2002 Survey*, Deloitte & Touche/*Personnel Today*, London

deLong, T and Vijayaraghavan, V (2003) Let's hear it for B players, *Harvard Business Review*, June, pp 96–102

Deming, W E (1982) *Quality, Productivity and Competitive Position*, MIT Centre for Advanced Engineering Study, Cambridge, MA

Deming, W E (1986) *Out of the Crisis*, MIT Centre for Advanced Engineering Study, Cambridge, MA

Denison, D R (1996) What *is* the difference between organizational culture and organizational climate? A native's point of view on a decade of paradigm wars, *Academy of Management Review*, July, pp 619–54

Digman, L A (1990) *Strategic Management – Concepts, Decisions, Cases*, Irwin, Georgetown, Ontario

Dowling, P J, Weech, D E and Schuler, R S (1999) *International Human Resource Management: Managing people in a multinational context*, South Western College Publishing, Cincinnati, OH

Drucker, P (1951) *The New Society*, Heinemann, London

Drucker, P (1955) *The Practice of Management*, Heinemann, London

Drucker, P (1967) *The Effective Executive*, Heinemann, London

Drucker, P (1988) The coming of the new organization, *Harvard Business Review*, January/February, pp 45–53

Drucker, P (1993) *Post-Capitalist Society*, Butterworth-Heinmann, Oxford

Drucker, P (1995) The information executives truly need, *Harvard Business Review*, Jan–Feb, pp 54–62

Dulewicz, V (1989) Assessment centres as the route to competence, *Personnel Management*, November, pp 56–59

Dulewicz, V and Higgs, M (1999) The seven dimensions of emotional intelligence, *People Management*, 28 October, p 53

Duncan, C (1989) Pay and payment systems, in B Towers (ed) *A Handbook of Industrial Relations Practice*, Kogan Page, London

Dunlop, J T (1958) *Industrial Relations Systems*, Holt, New York

Dyer, L and Holder, G W (1998) Strategic human resource management and planning, in L Dyer (ed) *Human Resource management: Evolving roles and responsibilities*, Bureau of National Affairs, Washington, DC

Dyer, L and Reeves, T (1995) Human resource strategies and firm performance: what do we know and where do we need to go? *The International Journal of Human Resource Management*, **6**(3), September, pp 656–70

Eagleton, T (1983) *Literary Theory*, Blackwell, Oxford

Easterby-Smith, M (1997) Disciplines of organizational learning: contributions and critiques, *Human Relations*, **50**(9), pp 1085–1113

Easterby-Smith, M and Araujo, J (1999) *Organizational learning: current opportunities, in Organisational Learning and the Learning Organization*, ed M Easterby-Smith, Sage, London

The Economic and Social Research Council and the Tomorrow Project (2005) *Workers on the Move*, ECRS, London

Edenborough, R (1994) *Using Psychometrics*, Kogan Page, London

Edvinson, L and Malone, M S (1997) *Intellectual Capital: Realizing your company's true value by finding its hidden brainpower*, Harper Business, New York

Edwards, M R and Ewen, A T (1996) *360-degree Feedback*, American Management Association, New York

Edwards, M R, Ewen, A T and O'Neal, S (1994) Using multi-source assessment to pay people not jobs, *ACA Journal*, Summer, pp 6–17

Egan, G (1990) *The Skilled Helper: A systematic approach to effective helping*, Brooks Cole, London

Egan, G (1995) A clear path to peak performance, *People Management*, 18 May, pp 34–37

Eggert, M (1991) *Outplacement: A guide to management and delivery*, Institute of Personnel Management, London

Ehrenberg, R G and Smith, R S (1994) *Modern Labor Economics*, Harper Collins, New York

Eldridge, J and Crombie, A (1974) *The Sociology of Organizations*, Allen & Unwin, London

Elliot, L (1996) Dealing with the dirty end of jobs for life, *The Guardian*, 23 April, p 14

Elliott, R F (1991) *Labor Economics*, McGraw-Hill, Maidenhead

Emery, F F (1980) Designing socio-technical systems for greenfield sites, *Journal of Occupational Behaviour*, **1**(1), pp 19–27

Engelmann, C H and Roesch, C H (1996) *Managing Individual Performance*, American Compensation Association, Scottsdale, Arizona

Equal Opportunities Commission (2003) *Good Practice Guide – Job Evaluation Free of Sex Bias*, EOC, Manchester

Equal Opportunities Commission (2004) *Illustrated Advertisements*, EOC, Manchester

Eraut, M J, Alderton,G, Cole, G and Senker, P (1998) Development of knowledge and skills in employment, *Economic and Social Research Council*, London

e-reward (2003) *Survey of Job Evaluation*, e-reward.co.uk, Stockport

e-reward (2004a) *Reward Case Studies*, e-reward.co.uk, Stockport

e-reward (2004b) *Survey of Contingent Pay*, e-reward.co.uk, Stockport

e-reward (2004c) *Survey of Pay Structures*, e-reward.co.uk, Stockport

e-reward (2005) *Survey of Performance Management*, e-reward.co.uk, Stockport

Erez, M (1977) Feedback: a necessary condition for the goal-setting performance relationship, *Journal of Occupational Psychology*, **62**(5), pp 624–27

Erez, M and Zidon, I (1984) Effect of good acceptance on the relationship of goal difficulty on performance, *Journal of Applied Psychology*, **69**(1), pp 69–78

Eysenck, H J (1953) *The Structure of Human Personality*, Methuen, London

Fadel, J J and Petti, M (2001) International HR policy basics, in *International HRM*, ed M H Albrecht, Blackwell, Oxford

Farnham, D (2000) *Employee Relations in Context*, 2nd edn, Institute of Personnel and Development, London

Fayol, H (1916) *Administration Industrielle et General*, Translated by C Storrs as *General and Industrial Management*, Pitman, London, 1949

Fein, M (1970) *Approaches to Motivation*, Hillsdale, NJ

Financial Times (2005) *Best Workplaces Report*, Financial Times, London

Fine, S A (1988), Functional job analysis, in *The Job Analysis Handbook for Business, Industry and Government*, ed S Gael, Wiley, New York

Fitz-enj, J (2000) *The ROI of Human Capital*, American Management Association, New York

Flanders, A (1970) *Management and Unions: The theory and reform of industrial relations*, Faber and Faber, London

Fletcher, C (1984) What's new in performance appraisal, *Personnel Management*, February, pp 20–22

Fletcher, C (1991) Study shows personality tests are 'useless' for predicting performance, *Personnel Management Plus*, p 3

Fletcher, C (1993) *Appraisal: Routes to improved performance*, Institute of Personnel Management, London

Follett, M P (1924) *Creative Experience*, Longmans Green, New York

Fombrun, C J, Tichy, N M, and Devanna, M A (1984) *Strategic Human Resource Management*, Wiley, New York

Fowler, A (1987) When chief executives discover HRM, *Personnel Management*, January, p 3

Fowler, A (1991a) An even-handed approach to graphology, *Personnel Management*, March, pp 40–43

Fowler, A (1996) *Induction* 3rd edn, Institute of Personnel and Development, London

Fox, A (1966) 'Industrial sociology and industrial relations, *Royal Commission on Trade Unions and Employers' Associations Research Paper No. 3*, HMSO, London

Fox, A (1973) *Beyond Contract*, Faber and Faber, London

Fox, A and Flanders, A (1969) Collective bargaining: from Donovan to Durkheim, in A Flanders (ed) *Management and Unions*, Faber and Faber, London

Freeman, R and Medoff, J (1984) *What do Unions do?* Basic Books, New York

French, J R and Raven, B (1959) The basis of social power, in D Cartwright, (ed) *Studies in Social Power*, Institute for Social Research, Ann Arbor, Mich

French, W L and Bell, C H (1990/1994) *Organization Development*, Prentice-Hall, Englewood Cliffs, NJ

French, W L, Kast, F E and Rosenzweig, J E (1985) *Understanding Human Behaviour in Organizations*, Harper & Row, New York

Friedman, A (1977) *Industry and Labour: Class structure and monopoly capitalism*, London, Macmillan

Furnham, A and Gunter, B (1993) *Corporate Assessment*, Routledge, London

Gagne, R M (1977) *The Conditions of Learning*, 3rd edn, Rinehart and Wionston, New York

Galbraith, J R (1973) *Organizational Design*, Addison-Wesley, Reading, MA

Gallie, D, White, M, Cheng, Y and Tomlinson, M (1998) *Restructuring the Employment Relationship*, The Clarendon Press, Oxford

Garratt, R (1990) *Creating a Learning Organization*, Institute of Directors, London

Garvin, D A (1993) Building a learning organization, *Harvard Business Review*, July–August, pp 78–91

Gennard, J and Judge, G (1997) *Employee Relations*, Institute of Personnel and Development, London

Gennard, J and Kelly, J (1994) Human resource management: the views of personnel directors, *Human Resource Management Journal*, **5**(1), pp 15–32

Geppert, M (1996) Paths of managerial learning in the East German context, *Organization Studies*, **17**(2), pp 249–68

Ghoshal, S and Bartlett, C A (1993) Changing the role of top management: beyond structure to process, *Harvard Business Review*, January–February, pp 86–96

Giles, L, Kodz, J and Evans, C (1997) *Productive Skills for Process Operatives*, Institute of Employment Studies, IES Report 336

Gilmer, B (1961) *Industrial Psychology*, McGraw-Hill, New York

Gluckman, M (1964) *Closed Systems and Open Minds*, Oliver and Boyd, London

Goldthorpe, J H, Lockwood, D C, Bechofer, F and Platt, J (1968) *The Affluent Worker: Industrial attitudes and behaviour*, Cambridge University Press, Cambridge

Goleman, D (1995) *Emotional Intelligence*, Bantam, New York

Goleman, D (1998), *Working With Emotional Intelligence*, Bloomsbury, London

Goleman, D (1999) *Emotional Intelligence*, presentation made at CIPD annual conference, October

Gomez-Mejia, L R and Balkin, D B. (1992) *Compensation, Organizational Strategy, and Firm Performance*, Southwestern Publishing, Cincinnati

Goold, M and Campbell, A (1986) *Strategies and Styles: The role of the centre in managing diversified corporations*, Oxford, Blackwell

Gospel, H (1992) *Markets, Firms and the Management of Labour*, Cambridge University Press, Cambridge

Grant, R M (1991) The resource-based theory of competitive advantage: implications for strategy formulation, *California Management Review*, **33**(3), pp 114–35

Gratton, L (1999) People processes as a source of competitive advantage, in *Strategic Human Resource Management*, eds L Gratton, V H Hailey, P Stiles and C Truss, Oxford University Press, Oxford

Gratton, L A (2000) Real step change, *People Management*, 16 March, pp 27–30

Gratton, L and Hailey, V H (1999) The rhetoric and reality of new careers, in *Strategic Human Resource Management*, eds L Gratton, V H Hailey, P Stiles and C Truss, Oxford University Press, Oxford

Gratton, L, Hailey, V H, Stiles, P and Truss, C (1999) *Strategic Human Resource Management*, Oxford University Press, Oxford

Guest, D E (1984) What's new in motivation, *Personnel Management*, May, pp 30–33

Guest, D E (1987) Human resource management and industrial relations, *Journal of Management Studies*, **14**(5), pp 503–21

Guest, D E (1989a) Human resource management: its implications for industrial relations, in J Storey (ed), *New Perspectives in Human Resource Management*, Routledge, London

Guest, D E (1989b) Personnel and HRM: can you tell the difference? *Personnel Management*, January, pp 48–51

Guest, D E (1990) Human resource management and the American dream, *Journal of Management Studies*, **27**(4), pp 378–97

Guest, D E (1991) Personnel management: the end of orthodoxy, *British Journal of Industrial Relations*, **29**(2), pp 149–76

Guest, D E (1992a) *Motivation After Herzberg*, Unpublished paper delivered at the Compensation Forum, London

Guest, D E (1992b) Human resource management in the UK, in B Towers (ed) *The Handbook of Human Resource Management*, Blackwell, Oxford

Guest, D E (1993) Current perspectives on human resource management in the United Kingdom, in C Brewster (ed) *Current Trends in Human Resource Management in Europe*, Kogan Page, London

Guest, D E (1995) Human resource management: trade unions and industrial relations, in J Storey (ed) *Human Resource Management; A critical text*, Routledge, London

Guest, D E (1997) Human resource management and performance; a review of the research agenda, *The International Journal of Human Resource Management*, **8**(3), pp 263–76

Guest, D E (1999a) Human resource management: the workers' verdict, *Human Resource Management Journal*, **9**(2), pp 5–25

Guest, D E (1999b) *Do People Strategies Really Enhance Business Success and if so, Why Don't More People Use Them?* Presentation at the Annual Conference of the Institute of Personnel and Development, October

Guest D E (2001) Industrial relations and human resource management, in *Human Resource Management: A critical text*, ed J Storey, Thomson Learning, London

Guest, D E and Conway, N (1997) *Employee Motivation and the Psychological Contract*, Institute of Personnel and Development, London

Guest, D E and Conway, N (1998) *Fairness at Work and the Psychological Contract*, Institute of Personnel and Development, London

Guest, D E and Conway, N (2002) Communicating the psychological contract: an employee perspective, *Human Resource Management Journal*, **12**(2), pp 22–39

Guest, D E and Conway, N (2005) *Well-being and the Psychological Contract*, CIPD, London

Guest D E and Fatchett, D (1974) *Worker Participation: Industrial Control and Performance*, Institute of Personnel Management, London

Guest, D E and Hoque, K (1994) Yes, personnel management does make the difference, *Personnel Management*, November, pp 40–44

Guest, D E and Hoque, K (1995) An assessment and further analysis of the 1990 Workshop Industrial Relations Survey in Guest, D E, Tyson, S, Doherty, N, Hoque, K and Viney K (eds) *The Contribution of Personnel Management to Organizational Performance*, IPD, London

Guest, D E and Horwood, R (1981) Characteristics of the successful personnel manager, *Personnel Management*, May, pp 18–23

Guest, D E and Peccei, R (1994) The nature and causes of effective human resource management, *British Journal of Industrial Relations*, June, pp 219–42

Guest, D E, Conway, N, Briner, R and Dickman, M (1996) *The State of the Psychological Contract in Employment: Issues in people management*, Institute of Personnel and Development, London

Guest, D E, Michie, J, Sheehan, M and Conway, N (2000a) *Employment Relations, HRM and Business Performance*, Chartered Institute of Personnel and Development, London

Guest, D E, Michie, J, Sheehan, M and Metochi, M (2000b) *Effective People Management: Initial Findings of the Future of Work Survey*, Chartered Institute of Personnel and Development, London

Guilford, J P (1967) *The Nature of Human Intelligence*, McGraw-Hill, New York

Guion, R M (1958) Industrial morale (a symposium) – the problems of terminology, *personne; Psychology*, **11**, pp 59–64

Guzzo, R A and Noonan, K A (1994) Human resource practices as communication and the psychological contract, *Human Resource Management*, Fall

Hackman, J R and Oldham, G R (1974) Motivation through the design of work: test of a theory, *Organizational Behaviour and Human performance*, **16**(2), pp 250–79

Haley, J (1999) Localisation as an ethical response to internationalisation, in *International HRM: Contemporary issues in Europe*, ed C Brewster and H Harris, Routledge, London

Hall, D T (1984) Human resource development and organizational effectiveness, in *Strategic Human Resource Managemnt*, ed D Fombrun, N Tichy and M A Devenna, Wiley, New York

Hall, R (1992) The strategic analysis of intangible resources, *Strategic Management Journal*, **13**, pp 135–44

Hall, R (1996) Supply Change Management – the challenge for the 21st century, Paper presented to the CIPS Conference at Durham University Business School, 9 May

Hall, L and Torrington, D (1998) *The Human Resource Function*, FT/Pitman, London

Hall, P and Norris, P (1992) Development centres: making the learning organization happen, *Human Resources*, Autumn, pp 126–28

Halpin, A and Winer, B A (1957) *Factorial Study of the Leader Behaviour Description*, Ohio State University

Hamblin, A C (1974) *Evaluation and Control of Training*, McGraw-Hill, Maidenhead

Hamel, G and Prahalad C K (1989) Strategic intent, *Harvard Business Review*, May–June, pp 63–76

Handy, C (1981) *Understanding Organizations*, Penguin Books, Harmondsworth

Handy, C (1984) *The Future of Work*, Blackwell, Oxford

Handy, C (1989) *The Age of Unreason*, Business Books, London

Handy, C (1994) *The Empty Raincoat*, Hutchinson, London

Handy, L, Devine, M and Health, L (1996) *360-Degree Feedback: Unguided missile or powerful weapon?* Ashridge Management Group, Berkhamstead

Hansen, M T, Nohria, N and Tierney, T (1999) What's your strategy for managing knowledge? *Harvard Business Review*, March–April, pp 106–16

Harre, R (1979) *Social Being*, Blackwell, Oxford

Harris, H and Brewster, C (1999) International human resource management: the European contribution, in *International HRM: Contemporary issues in Europe*, ed C Brewster and H Harris, Routledge, London

Harris, H, Brewster, C and Sparrow, P (2003) *International Human Resource Management*, CIPD, London

Harrison, R (1972) Understanding your organization's character, *Harvard Business Review*, **5**, pp 119–28

Harrison, R (1997) *Employee Development*, 2nd edn, Institute of Personnel and Development, London

Harrison, R (2000) *Employee Development*, 2nd edn, IPM, London

Harrison, R (2002) *Learning and Development*, 1st edn CIPD, London

Harrison, R (2005) *Learning and Development*, 2nd edn, CIPD, London

Hartley, V (2005) *Open for Business: HR and human capital reporting*, IIES, Brighton

Hawkins, K A (1979) *A Handbook of Industrial Relations Practice*, Kogan Page, London

Hayes Committee on Personnel Management (1972) *Training for the Management of Human Resources*, Department of Employment, HMSO, London

Health and Safety Executive (2003) *Beacons of Excellence in Stress Prevention*, HSE, London

Health and Safety Executive (2004a) *The Development of Case Studies that Demonstrate the Business Benefit of Effective Management of Health and Safety*, HSE, London

Health and Safety Executive (2004b) *Managing Sickness Absence and the Return to Work*, HSE, London

Heider, F (1958) *The Psychology of Interpersonal Relationships*, Wiley, New York

Heller, R (1972) *The Naked Manager*, Barrie & Jenkins, London

Hendry, C (1995) *Human Resource Management: A strategic approach to employment*, Butterworth-Heinemann, Oxford

Hendry, C and Pettigrew, A (1986) The practice of strategic human resource management, *Personnel Review*, **15**, pp 2–8

Hendry, C and Pettigrew, A (1990) Human resource management: an agenda for the 1990s, *International Journal of Human Resource Management*, **1**(3), pp 17–43

Hermanson, R (1964) *Accounting for Human Assets*, Bureau of Business and Economic Research, Michigan State University, Occasional Paper, November

Herriot, P, Hirsh, W and Riley, P (1988) *Trust and Transition: Managing the employment relationship*, Wiley, Chichester

Herzberg, F (1968) One more time: how do you motivate employees? *Harvard Business Review*, January–February, pp 109–20

Herzberg, F W, Mausner, B and Snyderman, B (1957) *The Motivation to Work*, Wiley, New York

Heskett, J (1986) *Managing in the Service Economy*, Harvard Business School Press, Boston, MA

Hiltrop, J M (1995) The changing psychological contract: the human resource challenge of the 1990s, *European Management Journal*, **13**(3), pp 286–94

Hirsh, W (2000) *Succession Planning Demystified*, Report No 372, Institute of Employment Studies

Hirsh, W and Carter, A (2002) *New Directions in Management Development*, Paper 387, Institute of Employment Studies

Hirsh, W, Pollard, E and Tamkin, P (2000) Management development *IRS Employee Development Bulletin*, November, pp 8–12

Hofstede, G (1980) *Cultural Consequences: International differences in work-related values*, Sage, Beverley Hills, CA

Holbeche, L (1998) *Motivating People in Lean Organizations*, Butterworth-Heinemann, Oxford

Holt, A and Andrews, H (1993) *Principles of Health and Safety at Work*, IOSH Publishing, London

Honey, P (1998) The debate starts here, *People Management*, 1 October, pp 28–29

Honey, P and Mumford, A (1996) *The Manual of Learning Styles*, 3rd edn, Honey Publications, Maidenhead

Hope-Hailey, V, Gratton, L, McGovern, P, Stiles, P and Truss, C (1998) A chameleon function? HRM in the '90s, *Human Resource Management Journal*, **7**(3), pp 5–18

Hoque, K and Moon, M (2001) Counting angels: a comparison of personnel and HR specialists, *Human Resource Management Journal*, **11**(3), pp 5–22

Hoyle, E (1995) 'The school as a learning organisation, *AERA Conference*, San Francisco, CA, April

Huczynski, A and Fitzpatrick, M J (1989) M*anaging Employee Absence for a Competitive Edge*, Pitman, London

Hull, C (1951) *Essentials of Behaviour*, Yale University Press, New Haven, CT

Humble, J (1963) Programmitis and crown princes, *The Manager*, December

Huselid, M A (1995) The impact of human resource management; an agenda for the 1990s, *The International Journal of Human Resource Management*, **1**(1), pp 17–43

Huselid, M A and Becker, B E (1996) Methodological issues in cross-sectional and panel estimates of the human resource-firm performance link, *Industrial Relations*, **35**(3), pp 400–22

Huselid, M A, Jackson, S E, Schuler, R S (1997) Technical and strategic human resource management effectiveness as determinants of firm performance, *Academy of Management Journal*, **40**(1) pp 171–88

Hutchinson, S and Purcell, J (2003) *Bringing Policies to Life: The vital role of front line managers in people management*, CIPD, London

Hutchinson, S and Wood, S (1995) *Personnel and the Line: Developing the Employment Relationship*, IPD, London.

Ichniowski, C, Shaw, K and Prennushi, G (1997) The effects of human resource management practices on productivity: a study of steel finishing lines, *The American Economic Review*, June

IDS (2002) *Human Resource Management Systems*, IDS, London

IDS (2004) Searching for the magic bullet, *HR Study 783*, October pp 2–6

Industrial Participation Association (1995) *Towards Industrial Partnership*, IPA, London

The Industrial Society (1974) *Practical Policies for Participation*, The Industrial Society, London

The Industrial Society (1999) *Managing Best Practice: Coaching*, IDS, London

The Industrial Society (2000) *Managing Best Practice, Training evaluation*, IDS, London

Institute of Personnel and Development (1993a) *Code of Professional Conduct*, IPD, London

Institute of Personnel and Development (1993b) *Quality: People management matters*, London

Institute of Personnel and Development (1993c) *Code on Employee Involvement and Participation*, IPD, London

Institute of Personnel and Development (1994) *People Make the Difference*, IPD, London

Institute of Personnel and Development (1995) *The Development of the New Psychological Contract*, (unpublished)

Institute of Personnel and Development (1997a) *Key Facts on Psychological Testing*, IPD, London

Institute of Personnel and Development (1997b) *The IPD Guide on Implementing Computerised Personnel Systems*, IPD, London

Institute of Personnel and Development (1998a) *IPD 1998 Performance Pay Survey: Executive Summary*, London

Institute of Personnel and Development (1998b) *The IPD Guide to Outsourcing*, IPD, London.

Institute of Personnel and Development (1999a) *Organisational Development – Whose Responsibility?* IPD, London

Institute of Personnel and Development (1999b) *The IPD Guide on Using Your Computerised Personnel Effectively*, IPD, London

Institute of Personnel Management (1992a) *Performance Management in the UK: an analysis of the issues*, IPM, London

Institute of Personnel Management (1992b) *Statement on Counselling in the Workplace*, IPM, London

Institute of Personnel and Development (1997) *Key Facts on Psychological Testing IPD*, London

Institute of Personnel and Development (1999) *Key Facts on References* IPD, London

IRS (2003) Trends in performance management, *Employment Review*, 1 August 2003, pp 12–19

IRS (2004a) Recruiters march in step with online recruitment, *Employment Review* no 792, 23 January, pp 44–48

IRS (2004b) Survey of HR roles and responsibilities, *Employment Review* no 795, March, pp 9–15

IRS (2004c) Managing to make the best hiring choice, *Employment Review* no 796, 19 March, pp 43–48

IRS (2004d) Managing attendance the flexible way, *Employment Review* no 798, 16 April, pp 19–24

IRS (2004e) From the outside looking in: third-party dispute resolution, *Employment Review*, 23 July, pp 8–15

IRS (2004f) A graphic illustration: getting the best from recruitment ads, *Employment Review* no 805, 6 August, pp 42–48

IRS (2004g) Training survey, *Employment Review* no 807, September, pp 10–17

IRS (2004h) It pays to talk: gauging the employment relationship, November, pp 9–16

IRS (2004i) Systems error? How HR chooses and uses information systems, *Employment Review* no 812, November, pp 9–15

IRS (2005) Absence essentials: maintaining contact, *Employment Review* no 818, February, pp 23–24

IRS Employee Development Bulletin no 54 (1994) Management development, pp 10–12

IRS Employee Development Bulletin (2000), November, pp 8–12

IRS Employment Trends no 500 (1991) 20 years of industrial relations, p 2

IRS Employment Trends no 544 (1993) Multi-employer bargaining, pp 6–8

IRS Employment Trends no 556 (1994) Where are the unions going, pp 14–16

IRS Employment Trends no 807 (2004) Training Survey, pp 10–17

IRS Management Review (1996) *Using Human Resources to Achieve Strategic Objectives*, IRS, London

IRS Management Review (2002) *Work/life Balance*, IRS, London

Ishikawa, Kaoru, (1976) *Guide to Quality Control*, Asian Productivity Organization, Tokyo

James, R and Sells, S B (1981) Psychological climate: theoretical perspectives and empirical research, in D Magnusson (ed) *Towards a Psychology of Situations: An interactional perspective*, Erlbaum, Hillsdale, NJ

Janis, I (1972) *Victims of Groupthink*, Houghton Mifflin, Boston, MA

Jaques, E (1961) *Equitable Payment*, Heinemann, London

Johnson, G and Scholes, K (1993) *Exploring Corporate Strategy*, Prentice Hall, Hemel Hempstead

Johnson, G and Scholes, K (1997) *Exploring Corporate Strategy*, Prentice Hall, Hemel Hempstead

Johnston, J (1991) An empirical study of repatriation of managers in UK multinationals, *Human Resource Management Journal*, **1**(4), pp 102–108.

Jones, P, Palmer, J, Whitehead, D and Needham, P (1995) Prisms of performance, *The Ashridge Journal*, April, pp 10–14

Jones, T W (1995) Performance management in a changing context, *Human Resource Management*, Fall, pp 425–42

Jung, C (1923) *Psychological Types*, Routledge Kegan Paul, London

Juran, J N (1979) *Quality Control Handbook*, McGraw-Hill, New York

Kahn, R (1974) *Organizational Stress*, Wiley, New York

Kahn-Freund, O (1972) *Labour and the Law*, Stevens, London

Kakabadse, A (1983) *The Politics of Management*, Gower, Aldershot

Kalleberg, A L and Loscocco, K A (1983) Aging, values and rewards: explaining age differences in job satisfaction, *American Sociological Review*, **48**, pp 323–36

Kamoche, K (1996) Strategic human resource management within a resource capability view of the firm, *Journal of Management Studies*, **33**(2), pp 213–33

Kandola, R and Fullerton, J (1994) *Managing the Mosaic*: *Diversity in action*, Institute of Personnel and Development, London

Kane, J S (1996) The conceptualisation and representation of total performance effectiveness, *Human Resource Management Review*, Summer, pp 123–45

Kanter, R M (1984) *The Change Masters*, Allen & Unwin, London

Kanter, R M (1989) *When Giants Learn to Dance*, Simon & Schuster, London

Kaplan, R S and Norton, D P (1992) The balanced scorecard – measures that drive performance, *Harvard Business Review.* January/February, pp 71–79

Kaplan, R S and Norton, D P (1996) *The Balanced Scorecard,* Harvard Business School Press, Boston, MA

Katz, D and Kahn, R (1966) *The Social Psychology of Organizations,* John Wiley, New York

Katzenbach, J and Smith, D (1993) *The Magic of Teams,* Harvard Business School Press, Boston, MA

Kay, J (1993) *Functions of Corporate Success,* Oxford University Press, Oxford

Kearns, P (2005a) *Evaluating the ROI From Learning,* CIPD, London

Kearns, P (2005b) *Human Capital Management,* Reed Business Information, Sutton, Surrey

Kearns, P and Miller, T (1997) Measuring the impact of training and development on the bottom line, *FT Management Briefings,* Pitman, London

Keenoy, T (1990a) HRM: a case of the wolf in sheep's clothing, *Personnel Review,* **19**(2), pp 3–9

Keenoy, T (1990b) HRM: rhetoric, reality and contradiction, *International Journal of Human Resource Management,* **1**(3), pp 363–84

Keenoy, T (1997) HRMism and the images of re-presentation, *Journal of Management Studies,* **4**(5), pp 825–41

Keenoy, T and Anthony, P (1992) HRM: metaphor, meaning and morality, in P Blyton and P Turnbull (eds) *Reassessing Human Resource Management,* Sage Publications, London

Keep, E (1989) Corporate training strategies, in J Storey (ed) *New Perspectives on Human Resource Management,* Blackwell, Oxford

Kelley, H H (1967) Attribution theory in social psychology, in D Levine (ed), *Nebraska Symposium on Motivation,* University of Nebraska Press, Lincoln, NB

Kelly, G (1955) *The Psychology of Personal Constructs,* Norton, New York

Kenney, J and Reid, M (1994) *Training Interventions,* 4th ed, Institute of Personnel and Development, London

Kerrin, M and Kealey M (2003) *e-Recruitment: Is it delivering?* Report No 402, Institute of Employment Studies, Brighton

Kessels, J (1996) Knowledge productivity and the corporate curriculum, in *Knowledge Management: Organisation, Competence and Methodology: Proceedings of the Fourth International ISMICK Symposium,* ed J F Scjhreinmakers, October

Kessler, J and Purcell, J (1992) Performance-related pay: objectives and application, *Human Resource Management Journal,* **2**(3), pp 16–33

Kessler, S and Bayliss, F (1992) *Contemporary British Industrial Relations,* Macmillan, London

Kessler, S and Undy, R (1996) *The New Employment Relationship: Examining the psychological contract*, Institute of Personnel and Development, London

Kettley, P and Reilly, P (2003) *e HR: An introduction*, Report No 398, Institute of Employment Studies, Brighton

Kim, D H (1993) The link between individual and organizational learning, *Sloane Management Review*, Fall, pp 37–50

Kirkpatrick, D L (1994) *Evaluating Training Programs*, Berret-Koehler, San Francisco

Kissler, G D (1994) The new employment contract, *Human Resource Management*, **33**(3), pp 335–52

Kochan, T A, Katz, H and McKenzie, R (1986) *The Transformation of American Industrial Relations*, Basic Books, New York

Kochan, T A and Dyer, L (1993) Managing transformational change: the role of human resource professionals, *International Journal of Human Resource Management*, **4**(3), pp 569–90

Kodz, J, Harper, H and Dench, S (2002) *Work-Life Balance: Beyond the rhetoric*, Report No 384, Institute of Employment Studies, Brighton

Kohn, A (1993) Why incentive plans cannot work, *Harvard Business Review*, September–October, pp 54–63

Kolb, D A, Rubin, I M and McIntyre, J M (1974) *Organizational Psychology: An experimental qpproach*, Prentice-Hall, Englewood Cliffs, NJ

Kotter, J (1990) What leaders really do, *Harvard Business Review*, May/June, pp 103–11

Kotter, J J (1995) *A 20% Solution: Using rapid re-design to build tomorrow's organization today*, Wiley, New York

Koys, D and De Cotiis, T (1991) Inductive measures of organizational climate, *Human Relations*, **44**, pp 265–85

Latham, G and Locke, R (1979) Goal setting – a motivational technique that works, *Organizational Dynamics*, Autumn, pp 68–80

Latham, G P, Saari, L M, Pursell, E D and Campion, M A (1980) The situational interview, *The Journal of Applied Psychology*, **65**, pp 442–47

Laurent, A (1986) The cross-cultural puzzle in international human resource management, *Human Resource Management*, **21**, pp 91–102

Lawler, E E (1969) Job design and employee motivation, *Personnel Psychology*, **22**, pp 426–35

Lawler, E E (1986) What's wrong with point-factor job evaluation, *Compensation and Benefits Review*, March–April, pp 20–28

Lawler, E E (1988) Pay for performance: making it work, *Personnel*, October, pp 68–71

Lawler, E E (1990) *Strategic Pay*, Jossey-Bass, San Francisco, CA

Lawler, E E (1993) Who uses skill-based pay, and why, *Compensation & Benefits Review*, March-April, pp 22–26

Lawrence, P R and Lorsch, J W (1969) *Developing Organizations*, Addison-Wiley, Reading, MA

Lawrence, P R and Lorsch, J W (1976) *Organization and Environment*, Harvard University Press, Cambridge, MA

Lawson, P (1995) Performance management: an overview, in *The Performance Management Handbook*, ed M Walters, Institute of Personnel and Development, London

Leadbeater, C (2000) *New Measures for the New Economy*, Centre for Business Performance, London

Leary-Joyce, J (2004) *Becoming an Employer of Choice*, CIPD, London

Leavitt, H J (1951) Some effects of certain communication patterns on group performance, *Journal of Abnormal Psychology*, **14**(3), pp 457–81

Leblanc B (2001) European competitiveness – some guidelines for companies, in *International HRM*, ed M H Albrecht, Blackwell, Oxford

Legge, K (1978) *Power, Innovation and Problem Solving in Personnel Management*, McGraw-Hill, Maidenhead

Legge, K (1987) Women in personnel management: uphill climb or downhill slide? In Spencer, A and Podmore, D (eds) *Women in a Man's World*, Tavistock Publications, London

Legge, K (1989) Human resource management: a critical analysis, in J Storey (ed) *New Perspectives in Human Resource Management*, Routledge, London

Legge, K (1995) *Human Resource Management; Rhetorics and Realities*, Macmillan, London

Legge, K (1998) The morality of HRM, in C Mabey, D Skinner and T Clark (eds) *Experiencing Human Resource Management*, Sage, London

Lengnick-Hall, C A and Lengnick-Hall, M L (1990) *Interactive Human Resource Management and Strategic Planning*, Quorum Books, Westport, CT

Leventhal, G S (1980) What should be done with equity theory?, in G K Gergen, M S Greenberg and R H Willis (eds) *Social Exchange: Advances in theory and research*, Plenum, New York

Levinson, D (1978) *The Seasons of Man's Life*, Knopf, New York

Lewin, K (1947) Frontiers in group dynamics, *Human Relations*, **1**(1), pp 5–42

Lewin, K (1951) *Field Theory in Social Science*, Harper & Row, New York

Liff, S (2000) Manpower or HR planning: what's in a name?, in S Bach and K Sisson (eds), *Personnel Management*, 3rd edn, Blackwell, Oxford

Likert, R (1961) *New Patterns of Management*, Harper & Row, New York

Likert, R (1967) *The Human Organization*, McGraw-Hill, New York

Likierman, A (2005) How to measure the performance of HRM, *People Management*, 11 August, pp 44–45

Littler, C and Salaman, G (1982) Bravermania and beyond: recent theories of the labour process, *Sociology*, **16**(2), pp 215–69

Litwin, G H and Stringer, R A (1968) *Motivation and Organizational Climate*, Harvard University Press, Boston, MA

Locke, E A (1984) Effect of self-efficacy, goals and task strategies on task performance, *Journal of Applied Psychology*, **69**(2), pp 241–51

London M and Beatty, R W (1993) 360-degree feedback as competitive advantage, *Human Resource Management*, Summer/Fall, pp 353–72

Low, J and Siesfield, T (1998) *Measures that Matter*, Ernst & Young, Boston, MA

Luthans, F and Kreitner, R (1975) *Organizational Behaviour Modification*, Scott-Foresman, Glenview, IL

Mabey, C and Salaman, G (1995) *Strategic Human Resource Management*, Blackwell Business, Oxford

Mabey, C, Skinner, D and Clark, T (1998) *Experiencing Human Resource Management*, Sage, London

McClelland, D C (1973) Testing for competence rather than intelligence, *American Psychologist*, **28**(1), pp 1–14

McClelland, G (1963) *British Journal of Industrial Relations*, June, p 278

McCrae, R and Costa, P (1989) More reasons to adopt the five factor model, *American Psychologist*, **44**, pp 451–52

MacDuffie, J P (1995) Human resource bundles and manufacturing performance, *Industrial Relations Review*, **48**(2), pp 199–221

McGregor, D (1957) An uneasy look at performance appraisal, *Harvard Business Review*, May–June, pp 89–94

McGregor, D (1960) *The Human Side of Enterprise*, McGraw-Hill, New York

Mackay, L and Torrington, D (1986) *The Changing Nature of Personnel Management*, Institute of Personnel Management, London

McLean, A (1981) Organization Development: A case of the Emperor's new clothes? *Personnel Review*, **4**(1), pp 38–46

Macneil, R (1985) Relational contract: what we do and do not know, *Wisconsin Law Review*, pp 483–525

Makin, P, Cooper, C and Cox, C (1996) *Organizations and the Psychological Contract*, BPS Books, Leicester

Mangham, L L (1979) *The Politics of Organizational Change*, Associated Business Press, London

Mansfield, B (1999) What is 'competence' all about? *Competency*, **6**(3), pp 24–28

Mansfield, B and Mitchell, L (1986), *Towards a Competent Workforce*, Gower, Aldershot

Mant, A (1970) *The Experienced Manager*, British Institute of Management, London

Mant, A (1996) The psychological contract, Presentation at IPD National Conference, October

Manus, T M and Graham, M D (2003) *Creating a Total Rewards Strategy*, American Management Association, New York

Marchington, M (1985) *Joint Consultation Revisited*, Glasgow University, Glasgow

Marchington, M (1995a) Fairy tales and magic wands: new employment practices in perspective, *Employee Relations*, Spring, pp 51–66

Marchington, M (1995b) Employee relations, in *Strategic Prospects for HRM*, ed S Tyson, Institute of Personnel and Development, London

Marchingon M and Goodman, J (1992) *New Developments in Employee Involvement*, Employment Department, Sheffield

Marchington, M and Wilkinson, A (1996) *Core Personnel and Development*, Institute of Personnel and Development, London

Marchington, M, Wilkinson, A, Ackers, P and Dundon, A (2001) *Management Choice and Employee Voice*, CIPD, London

Margerison, C (1976) A constructive approach to appraisal, *Personnel Management*, July, pp 30–33

Margerison, C and McCann, R (1986) The Margerison/McCann team management resource: theory and application, *International Journal of Manpower*, 7(2), pp 1–32

Marginson, P, Armstrong, P, Edwards, P and Purcell, J (1993) The control of industrial relations in large companies: an initial analysis of the Second Company Level Industrial Relations Survey, *Warwick Papers in Industrial Relations No. 45*, University of Warwick, Coventry

Marginson, P and Sisson, K (1990) Single table talk, *Personnel Management*, May, pp 46–49

Markham, C (1987) *Practical Consulting*, Institute of Chartered Accountants, London

Marsden, D and French, S (1998) *What a Performance: Performance-related pay in the public services*, Centre for Economic Performance, London

Marsden D and Richardson R (1994) Performing for pay?, *British Journal of Industrial Relations*, 32(2), pp 243–61

Marsh, A (1981) *Employee Relations Policy and Decision Making*, Gower, Aldershot

Marsick, V J (1994) Trends in managerial invention: creating a learning map, *Management Learning*, 21(1) pp 11–33

Martin, A O (1967) *Welfare at Work*, Batsford, London

Marx, K (translated in 1976) *Capital, Penguin*, Harmondsworth

Maslow, A (1954) *Motivation and Personality*, Harper & Row, New York

Mayo, A (1992) A framework for career management, *Personnel Management*, February, pp 36–39

Mayo, A (1999) Making human capital meaningful, *Knowledge Management Review*, January/February, pp 26–29

Mayo, A (2001) *The Human Value of the Enterprise: Valuing people as assets*, Nicholas Brealey, London

Mayo, A and Lank, E (1994) *The Power of Learning: A guide to gaining competitive advantage*, Institute of Personnel and Development, London

Mayo, E (1933) *Human Problems of an Industrial Civilisation*, Macmillan, London

Mecklenberg, S, Deering, A and Sharp, D (1999) Knowledge management: a secret engine of corporate growth, *Executive Agenda*, **2**, pp 5–15

Meyerson, D and Martin, J (1987) Cultural studies and integration of three different views, *Journal of Management Studies*, **24**(6), pp 623–47

Mezirow, J A (1985) A critical theory of self-directed learning, in *Self-directed Learning: From theory to practice*, ed S Brookfield, Jossey-Bass, San Fransisco, CA

Miles, R E and Snow C C (1978) *Organizational Strategy, Structure and Process*, McGraw-Hill, New York

Milkovitch, M and Wigdor (1991) *Pay for Performance: Evaluating performance appraisal and merit pay*, National Academy Press, Washington, DC

Miller, E and Rice, A (1967) *Systems of Organization*, Tavistock, London

Miller, L, Rankin, N and Neathey, F (2001) *Competency Frameworks in UK Organizations*, CIPD, London

Miller, P (1987) Strategic industrial relations and human resource management: distinction, definition and recognition, *Journal of Management Studies*, **24**, pp 101–09.

Miller, P (1989) Strategic human resource management: what it is and what it is'nt, *Personnel Management*, February, pp 46–51

Miller, P (1991) Strategic human resource management: an assessment of progress, *Human Resource Management Journal*, **1**(4), pp 23–39

Miller, R and Stewart, J (1999) Opened university, *People Management*, **5**(12), pp 42–46

Millward, N (1994) *The New Industrial Relations?* Policy Studies Institute, Poole

Millward, N, Bryn, A and Forth, J (2000) *All Change At Work?* Routledge, London

Millward, N, Stevens, M, Smart, D and Hawes, W R (1992) *Workplace Industrial Relations in Transition*, Dartmouth Publishing, Hampshire

Mintzberg, H (1973) *The Nature of Managerial Work*, Harper & Row, New York

Mintzberg, H (1978) Patterns in strategy formation, *Management Science*, May, pp 934–48

Mintzberg, H (1981) Organization design: fashion or fit, *Harvard Business Review*, January/February, pp 103–16

Mintzberg, H (1983a) *Power in and Around Organizations*, Prentice-Hall, Englewood Cliffs, NJ

Mintzberg, H (1983b) *Structure in Fives*, Prentice-Hall, Englewood Cliffs, NJ

Mintzberg, H (1987) Crafting strategy, *Harvard Business Review*, July/August, pp 66–74

Mintzberg, H, Quinn, J B and James, R M (1988) *The Strategy Process: Concepts, contexts and cases*, Prentice-Hall, Englewood Cliffs, NJ

Mirabile, R J (1998), Leadership competency development, competitive advantage for the future, *Management Development Forum*, **1**(2), pp 1–15

Mirvis, P and Hall, D (1994) Psychological success and the boundary-less career, *Journal of Organisational Behaviour*, **15**, pp 361–80

Mischel, W (1968) *Personality and Assessment*, Wiley, New York

Mischel, W (1981) *Introduction to Personality*, Holt, Rinehart and Winston, New York

Mohrman, S A and Lawler, E E (1998) The new human resources management: creating the strategic business partnership, in *Tomorrow's Organization: Crafting winning capabilities in a dynamic world*, S A Mohrman, J R Galbraith and E E Lawler, Jossey-Bass, San Francisco, CA

Monks, K (1992) Models of personnel management: a means of understanding the diversity of personnel practices, *Human Resource Management Journal*, **3**(2), pp 29–41

Mueller, F (1996) Human resources as strategic assets: an evolutionary resource-based theory, *Journal of Management Studies*, **33**(6), pp 757–85

Mullen, B and Cooper, C (1994) The relation between group cohesiveness and performance: an integration, *Psychological Bulletin*, **115**, pp 210–27

Mumford, A (1993) How managers can become developers, *Personnel Management*, June, pp 42–45

Mumford, A and Gold, J (2004) *Management Development: Strategies for action*, CIPD, 2004

Munro Fraser, J (1954) *A Handbook of Employment Interviewing*, Macdonald and Evans, London

Murlis, H and Fitt, D (1991) Job evaluation in a changing world, *Personnel Management*, May, pp 39–43

Nadler, D A and Tushman, M L (1980) A congruence model for diagnosing organizational behaviour, *Resource Book in Macro-Organizational Behaviour*, R H Miles (ed), Goodyear Publishing, Santa Monica, CA

Nahpiet, J and Ghoshal, S (1998), Social capital, intellectual capital and the organizational advantage, *Academy of Management Review*, **23**(2), pp 24–266

Nalbantian, R, Guzzo, R A, Kieffer, D and Doherty, J (2004) *Play to your Strengths*, McGraw-Hill, New York

The National Online Recruitment Survey (2003) *Enhance Media*, Winter, London

New Learning for New Work Consortium (1999) *Managing Learning for Added Value*, Institute of Personnel and Development, London

Newcomb, T M (1966) On the definition of attitudes, in M Jahoda and N Warren (eds), *Attitudes*, Penguin, Harmondsworth

Newton, T and Findlay, P (1996) Playing god?: the performance of appraisal, *Human Resource Management Journal*, **6**(3), pp 42–56

Nielsen, N H (2002) Job content evaluation techniques based on Marxian economics, *WorldatWork Journal*, **11**(2), pp 52–62

Nonaka, I (1991) The knowledge creating company, *Harvard Business Review*, Nov–Dec, pp 96–104

Nonaka, I (1994) A dynamic theory of organisational knowledge creation, *Organisation Science*, **5**, pp 14–37

Nonaka, I and Takeuchi, H (1995), *The Knowledge Creating Company*, Oxford University Press, New York

Noon, M (1992) HRM: a map, model or theory? in P Blyton and P Turnbull (eds) *Reassessing Human Resource Management*, Sage Publications, London

OECD (1998) *Human Capital Investment: An international comparison*, Organization for Economic Cooperation and Development, Paris

Oliver, J (1996) Cash on delivery, *Management Today*, August, pp 6–9

O'Neal, S (1998) The phenomenon of total rewards, *ACA Journal*, **7**(3), pp 8–12

Opsahl, R and Dunnette, M (1966) The role of financial compensation in industrial motivation, *Psychological Bulletin*, **66**, pp 94–118

Oracle (2005) *Human Capital Management*, People Management, London

O'Reilly, C A and Pfeffer, J (2000) *Hidden Value: How great companies achieve extraordinary results*, Harvard Business School press, Boston, MA

Ouchi, W G (1981) *Theory Z*, Addison-Wesley, Reading, MA

Pascale, R (1990) *Managing on the Edge*, Viking, London

Pascale, R and Athos, A (1981) *The Art of Japanese Management*, Simon & Schuster, New York

Patterson, M G, West, M A, Lawthom, R and Nickell, S (1997) *Impact of People Management Practices on Performance*, Institute of Personnel and Development, London

Pearce, J A and Robinson, R B (1988) *Strategic Management: Strategy formulation and implementation*, Irwin, Georgetown, Ontario

Pearn, K and Kandola, R (1993) *Job Analysis*, Institute of Personnel Management, London

Pedler, M and Burgoyne J (1994) *A Manager's Guide to Self Development*, McGraw Hill, Maidenhead

Pedler, M, Boydell, T and Burgoyne, J (1989) Towards the learning company, *Management Education and Development*, **20**(1), pp 1–8

Pedler, M, Burgoyne, J and Boydell, T (1991) *The Learning Company: A strategy for sustainable development*, McGraw-Hill, London

Penrose, E (1959) *The Theory of the Growth of the Firm*, Blackwell, Oxford

Perkins, S J (1997) *Internationalization: The people dimension*, Kogan Page, London

Perkins, S and Hendry, C (1999) *The IPD Guide on International Reward and Recognition*, Institute of Personnel and Development, London

Perrow, C (1980) The Short and Glorious History of Organizational Theory, in R H Miles (ed) *Resource Book in Macro-Organizational Behaviour*, Goodyear Publishing, Santa Monica, CA

Peters, J (1968) *Strategies and Tactics in Labour Negotiations*, McGraw-Hill, New York

Peters, T (1988) *Thriving on Chaos*, Macmillan, London

Peters, T and Austin, N (1985) *A Passion for Excellence*, Collins, Glasgow

Peters, T and Waterman, R (1982) *In Search of Excellence*, Harper & Row, New York

Pettigrew, A and Whipp, R (1991) *Managing Change for Competitive Success*, Blackwell, Oxford

Pfeffer, G (1998) *The Human Equation*, Harvard Business School Press, Boston

Pfeffer, J (1994) *Competitive Advantage Through People*, Harvard Business School Press, Boston

Pfeffer, J (2001) *Fighting the War for Talent is Hazardous for your Organization*, Stanford University Graduate School of Business, Stanford, CA

Pfeffer, J and Cohen, Y (1984) Determinants of internal labour markets in organizations, *Administrative Science Quarterly*, **29**, pp 550–72

Pfeffer, J and Salancik, G R (1978) *The External Control of Organizations: A resource dependence perspective*, Harper & Row, New York

Phelps Brown, H (1990) The counter revolution of our time, *Industrial Relations*, **29**(1), pp 306–20

Pickard, J (1995) Prepare to make a moral judgement, *People Management*, 4 May, pp 22–25, 27

Pickard, J (1997) A yearning for learning, *People Management*, **3**(5), pp 34–35

Pil, F K and MacDuffie, J P (1996) The adoption of high-involvement work practices, *Industrial Relations*, **35**(3), pp 423–55

Pil, F K and MacDuffie, J P (1999) Organizational and environmental factors influencing the use and diffusion of high-involvement work practices, in *Employment Practices and Business Strategy*, ed P Capelli, Oxford University Press, New York

Pioro, I and Baum, N (2005) How to design better job application forms, *People Management*, 16 June, pp 42–43

Pollard, E and Hillage, J (2001) *Explaining e-Learning*, Report No 376, Institute of Employment Studies

Porter, L W (1961) A study of perceived need satisfaction in bottom and middle management jobs, *Journal of Applied Psychology*, **45**, pp 1–10

Porter, L W and Lawler, E E (1968) *Managerial Attitudes and Performance*, Irwin-Dorsey, Homewood, Illinois

Porter, L W, Steers, R, Mowday, R and Boulian, P (1974) Organizational commitment, job satisfaction and turnover amongst psychiatric technicians, *Journal of Applied Psychology*, **59**, pp 603–09

Porter, M (1980) *Competitive Strategy,* The Free Press, New York

Porter, M (1985) *Competitive Advantage: Creating and sustaining superior performance,* The Free Press, New York

Prahalad, C K and Hamel, G (1990) The core competences of the corporation, *Harvard Business Review,* May–June, pp 79–91

Pritchard, D and Murlis, H (1992) *Jobs, Roles and People,* Nicholas Brearley, London

Purcell, J (1979) A strategy for management control in industrial relations, in J Purcell and R Smith (eds) *The Control of Work,* Macmillan, London

Purcell, J (1987) Mapping management styles in employee relations, *Journal of Management Studies,* September, pp 78–91

Purcell, J (1989) The impact of corporate strategy on human resource management, in J Storey (ed) *New Perspectives on Human Resource Management,* Routledge, London

Purcell, J (1993) The challenge of human resource management for industrial relations research and practice, *The International Journal of Human Resource Management,* **4**(3), pp 511–27

Purcell, J (1994) Personnel earns a place on the board, *Personnel Management,* February, pp 26–29

Purcell, J (1999) Best practice or best fit: chimera or cul-de-sac, *Human Resource Management Journal,* **9**(3), pp 26–41

Purcell, J (2001) The meaning of strategy in human resource management, in *Human Resource Management: A critical text,* second edn, ed J Storey, Thompson Learning, London

Purcell, J and Sisson, K (1983) Strategies and practice in the management of industrial relations, in G Bain (ed) *Industrial Relations in Britain,* Blackwell, Oxford

Purcell, J, Hutchinson, S and Kinnie, N (1998) *The Lean Organisation,* Institute of Personnel and Development, London

Purcell, J, Kinnie, K, Hutchinson, Rayton, B and Swart, J (2003) *People and Performance: How people management impacts on organisational performance,* CIPD, London

Purcell, J, Kinnie, K, Hutchinson, Swart, J and Rayton, B (2005) *Vision and Values: Organizational culture and values as a source of competitive advantage,* CIPD, London

Putnam, R (1996) Who killed civic America?, *Prospect,* March, pp 66–72

Quinn, J B (1980) Managing strategic change, *Sloane Management Review,* **11**(4/5), pp 3–30

Quinn Mills, D (1983) Planning with people in mind, *Harvard Business Review,* November–December, pp 97–105

Rankin, N (2002) Raising performance through people: the ninth competency survey, *Competency & Emotional Intelligence,* January, pp 2–21

Reay, D G (1994) *Understanding How People Learn,* Kogan Page, London

Recruitment Development Report (1991) New ways of managing your human resources: a survey of top employers, *Industrial Relations Review*, March

Reed, A (2001) *Innovation in Human Resource Management*, CIPD, London

Reich, R (1991) *The Work of Nations: Preparing ourselves for 21st century capitalism*, Simon & Schuster, London

Reid, M A and Barrington, H (1999) *Training Interventions*, 6th edn, CIPD, London

Reid, M A, Barrington, H and Brown B (2004) *Human Resource Development: Beyond training interventions*, CIPD, London

Reilly, P (1999) *The Human Resource Planning Audit*, Cambridge Strategy Publications, Cambridge

Reilly, P (2000) *HR Shared Services and the Re-alignment of HR*, Institute for Employment Studies, Brighton

Reilly, P (2001) *Partnership Under Pressure: How does it survive?*, Report No 383, Institute for Employment Studies, Brighton

Report of the Royal Commission on Trades Unions and Employer's Associations (1968) HMSO, London

Revans, R W (1971) *Developing Effective Managers*, Longman, Harlow

Revans, R W (1989) *Action Learning*, Blond and Briggs, London

Reynolds, J (2002) Method and modems: the real value of e-learning, *People Management*, April, pp 42–43

Reynolds, J (2004) *Helping People Learn*, CIPD, London

Reynolds, J, Caley, L and Mason, R (2002) *How Do People Learn?* CIPD, London

Richardson, R and Thompson, M (1999) *The Impact of People Management Practices on Business Performance: A literature review*, Institute of Personnel and Development, London

Risher, H (2003) Re-focusing performance management for high performance, *Compensation & Benefits Review*, October, pp 20–30

Roberts, C (1990) *Harmonization: Whys and Wherefores*, Institute of Personnel Management, London

Roberts, G (1997) *Recruitment and Selection: A competency approach*, Institute of Personnel and Development, London

Robertson, I T and Cooper, C L (1983) *Human Behaviour in Organizations*, Macdonald & Evans, Plymouth

Robertson, I T and Smith, M (1985) *Motivation and Job Design*, Institute of Personnel Management, London

Robertson, I T, Smith, M and Cooper, D (1992) *Motivation*, Institute of Personnel Management, London

Robinson, D (1999) *The Human Resource Information System Audit*, Cambridge Strategy Publications, Cambridge

Rodger, A (1952) *The Seven-Point Plan*, National Institute of Industrial Psychology, London

Roethlisberger, F and Dickson, W (1939) *Management and the Worker*, Harvard University Press, Cambridge, MA

Rogers, A (1996) *Teaching Adults*, Open University Press, London

Rogers, C R (1983) *Freedom to Learn*, Merrill, Columbus, Ohio

Rosow, J and Casner-Lotto, J (1998) *People, Partnership and Profits: the new labor-management agenda*, Work in America Institute, New York

Rothwell, S (1995) Human resource planning in J Storey (ed) *Human Resource Management: A critical text*, Routledge, London

Rousseau, D M (1988) The construction of climate in organizational research, in L C Cooper and I Robertson (eds) *International Review of Industrial and Organizational Psychology*, Wiley, Chichester

Rousseau, D M and Greller, M M (1994) Human resource practices: administrative contract makers, *Human Resource Management*, **33**(3), pp 385–401

Rousseau, D M and Wade-Benzoni, K A (1994) Linking strategy and human resource practices: how employee and customer contracts are created, *Human Resource Management*, **33**(3), pp 463–89

Royal Bank of Scotland (2005) *Policy Statement*, unpublished

Rugles, R (1998) The state of the notion, *Californian Management Review*, **40**(3), pp 80–89

Rumelt, R P (1984) Toward a strategic theory of the firm, in *Competitive Strategic Management*, ed R Lamb, Prentice-Hall, Englewood Cliffs, NJ

Ryle, G (1949) *The Concept of Mind*, Oxford University Press, Oxford

Sako, M (1994) The informational requirement of trust in supplier relations: evidence from Japan, the UK and the USA, unpublished

Salancik, G R (1977) Commitment and the control of organizational behaviour and belief, in *New Directions in Organizational Behaviour*, ed B M Staw and G R Salancik, St Clair Press, Chicago

Salmon, G (2001) Far from remote, *People Management*, 27 September, pp 34–36

Saunders, R (1992) *The Safety Audit*, Pitman, London

Saville, P and Sik, G (1992) Personality questionnaires: current issues and controversies, *Human Resources Management Yearbook*, A P Services, London, pp 28–32

Scarborough, H and Carter, C (2000) *Investigating Knowledge Management*, Chartered Institute of Personnel and Development, London

Scarborough, H and Elias, J (2002) *Evaluating Human Capital*, CIPD, London

Scarborough, H, Swan, J and Preston, J (1999) *Knowledge Management: A Literature Review*, Institute of Personnel and Development, London

Schaffer, R (1991) Demand better results – and get them, *Harvard Business Review*, March–April, pp 142–49

Schein, E H (1969) *Process Consultation; Its role in organisational development*, Addison-Wesley, Reading, MA

Schein, E H (1965) *Organizational Psychology*, Prentice-Hall, Englewood Cliffs, NJ

Schein, E H (1969) *Process Consultation: Its role in organizational development*, Addison-Wesley, Reading, MA

Schein, E H (1977) *Career Dynamics*, Addison-Wesley, Reading, MA

Schein, E H (1984) Coming to a new awareness of culture, *Sloan Management Review*, Winter, pp 1–15

Schein, E H (1985) *Organization Culture and Leadership*, Jossey Bass, New York

Schein, E H (1990) Organizational culture, *American Psychologist*, **45**, pp 109–19

Schiffman, A and Kanuk, J (1994) Corporate Culture, *American Psychologist*, **49**, pp 251–75

Schmitt, N, Gooding, R Z, Noe, R A and Kirsch, M (1984) Meta-analysis of validity studies published between 1964 and 1982 and the investigation of study characteristics, *Personnel Psychology*, **37**(3), pp 407–22

Schramm, J (2001) *The Change Agenda*, CIPD, London

Schuler, R S (1992) Strategic human resource management: linking people with the strategic needs of the business, *Organizational Dynamics*, **21**(1), pp 18–32

Schuler, R S, Dowling, P J and De Cieri, H (1993) An integrative framework of strategic international human resource management, *International Journal of Human Resource Management*, December, pp 717–64

Schuler, R S and Jackson, S E (1987) Linking competitive strategies with human resource management practices, *Academy of Management Executive*, **9**(3), pp 207–19

Schuller, T (2000) Social and human capital; the search for appropriate technomethodology, *Policy Studies*, **21**(1), pp 25–35

Schultz, T W (1961) Investment in human capital, *American Economic Review*, **51**, March, pp 1–17

Schultz, T W (1981) *Investing in People: The economics of population quality*, University of California

Scott, A (1994) *Willing Slaves?: British workers under human resource management*, Cambridge University Press, Cambridge

Sears, D (2003) *Successful Talent Strategies*, American Management Association, New York

Selznick, P (1957) *Leadership and Administration*, Row, Evanston, IL

Senge, P (1990) *The Fifth Discipline: The art and practice of the learning organization*, Doubleday, London

Shaw, R B (1997) *Trust in the Balance*, Jossey Bass, San Francisco, CA

Sheard, A (1992) Learning to improve performance, *Personnel Management*, November, pp 40–45

Sims, R R (1994) Human resource management's role in clarifying the new psychological contract, *Human Resource Management*, **33**(3), Fall, pp 373–82

Singh, R (1989) Negotiations, in B Towers (ed) *A Handbook of Industrial Relations Practice*, Kogan Page, London

Sisson, K (1990) Introducing the Human Resource Management Journal, *Human Resource Management Journal*, **1**(1), pp 1–11

Sisson, K (1995) Human resource management and the personnel function, in J Storey (ed) *Human Resource Management: A critical text*, Routledge, London

Skinner, B F (1974) *About Behaviourism*, Cape, London

Sloan, A P (1963) *My Years With General Motors*, Doubleday, New York

Sloman, M (1999) Seize the day, *People Management*, 20 May, p 31

Sloman, M (2001) *The E-Learning Revolution*, CIPD, London

Sloman, M (2003a) E-learning: stepping up the learning curve, *Impact*, CIPD, January, pp 16–17

Sloman, M (2003b) *Training in the Age of the Learner*, CIPD, London

Smart, D (1983) *Selection Interviewing*, Wiley, New York

Smilansky, J (2005) *The Systematic Management of Executive Talent*, Hydrogen, London

Smith, J M and Robertson, I T (1986) *The Theory and Practice of Systematic Staff Selection*, Macmillan, London

Smith, M (1984) *Survey Item Blank*, MCB Publications, Bradford

Smith, M (1988) Calculating the sterling values of selection, *Guidance and Assessment Review*, **4**(1), pp 6–8

Smith, M and Robertson, I T (1986) *The Theory and Practice of Systematic Staff Selection*, Macmillan, London

Smith, P and Morton, G (1993) Union exclusion and decollectivisation of industrial relations in contemporary Britain, *British Journal of Industrial Relations*, **31**(1), pp 97–114

Sparrow, P R (1996) Too true to be good, *People Management*, 5 December, pp 22–27

Sparrow, P R (1999b) International reward system: to converge or not to converge, in C Brewster and H Harris (eds) *International HRM: Contemporary issues in Europe*, Routledge, London

Sparrow, P R (1999a) *The IPD Guide on International Recruitment, Selection and Assessment*, Institute of Personnel and Development, London

Sparrow, P R and Hiltrop J-M (1997) Redefining the field of human resource management: a battle between national mindsets and forces of business transition?, *Human Resource Management*, **36**(2), pp 201–19

Spearman, C (1927) *The Abilities of Man*, Macmillan, New York

Spindler, G S (1994) Psychological contracts in the workplace: a lawyer's view, *Human Resource Management*, **33**(3), pp 325–33

Stacey, R D (1993) Strategy as order emerging from chaos, *Long Range Planning*,

Stephenson, J (2001) Learner managed learning – an emerging pedagogy for learning on-line, in *Teaching and Learning On-line*, ed J.Stephenson, Kogan Page, London

Stern, E and Sommerlad, E (1999) *Workplace Learning, Culture and Performance*, Institute of Personnel and Development, London

Stevens, J (1998) *High-performance Working is for Everone*, IPD, London

Stewart, J and Tansley, C (2002) *Training in the Knowledge Economy*, CIPD, London

Storey, J (1985) The means of management control, *Sociology*, **19**(2), pp 193–212

Storey, J (1987) Developments in the management of human resources: an interim report, *Warwick Papers on Industrial Relations*, No 17, University of Warwick

Storey, J (1989) From personnel management to human resource management, in Storey, J (ed) *New Perspectives on Human Resource Management*, Routledge, London

Storey, J (1992a) *New Developments in the Management of Human Resources*, Blackwell, Oxford

Storey, J (1992b) HRM in action: the truth is out at last, *Personnel Management*, April, pp 28–31

Storey, J (1993) The take-up of human resource management by mainstream, companies: key lessons from research, *The International Journal of Human Resource Management*, **4**(3), pp 529–57

Storey, J (1995) Human resource management: still marching on or marching out? in J Storey (ed) *Human Resource Management: A critical text*, Routledge, London

Storey, J and Sisson, K (1990) Limits to transformation: human resource management in the British context, *Industrial Relations Journal*, **21**(1), pp 60–65

Strauss, G and Sayles, L R (1972) *Personnel: The human problems of management*, Prentice-Hall, Eaglewood Cliffs, NJ

Swart, J and Kinnie, N (2004) *Managing the Careers of Professional Knowledge Workers*, CIPD, London

Swart, J, Kinnie, N and Purcell, J (2003) *People and Performance in Knowledge Intensive Firms*, CIPD, London

Tamkin, P, Barber, L and Hirsh, W (1995) *Personal Development Plans: Case studies of practice*, The Institute for Employment Studies, Brighton

Tamkin, P, Hirsh, W and Tyers, ? (2003) *Clone (?) to Champion: The making of better people managers*, Report No 389 Institute of Employment Studies, Brighton

Tamkin, P, Yarnall, J and Kerrin, M (2002) *Kirkpatrick and Beyond: A review of training evaluation*, Report 392, Institute of Employment Studies, Brighton

Tampoe, M (1993) Motivating knowledge workers: the challenge for the 1990s, *Long-range Planning*, **26**(2) pp 37–44

Tan, J (2000) Knowledge management – just more buzzwords? *British Journal of Administrative Management*, March/April, pp 10–11

Tannenbaum S I, Beard R L and Sales, E (1992) Team building and its influence on team effectiveness: an examination of conceptual and empirical developments, in *Issues, Theory and Research in Industrial/Organizational Psychology*, ed K Kelley, North Holland, London

Tarique, I and Caligiri, P (1995) Training and development of international staff, in *International Human Resource Management*, ed A-W Herzorg and J V Ruyssevelde, Sage Publications, London

Taylor, F W (1911) *Principles of Scientific Management*, Harper, New York

Taylor, S (1998) *Employee Resourcing*, Institute of Personnel and Development, London

Taylor, S (2002) *People Resourcing*, CIPD, London

Thompson, M (1998) Trust and reward, in *Trust, Motivation and Commitment: A reader*, ed Stephen Perkins and St John Sandringham, Strategic Remuneration Research Centre, Faringdon

Thompson, P (2002) *Total Reward*, CIPD, London

Thurley, K (1979) *Supervision: A reappraisal*, Heinemann, London

Thurley, K (1981) Personnel management: a case for urgent treatment, *Personnel Management*, August, pp 24–29

Thurstone, L L (1940) Current issues in factor analysis, *Psychological Bulletin*, **30**, pp 26–38

Toplis, J, Dulewicz, V, and Fletcher, C (1991) *Psychological Testing*, Institute of Personnel Management, London

Torrington, D P (1989) Human resource management and the personnel function, in J Storey, (ed) *New Perspectives on Human Resource Management*, Routledge, London

Townley, B (1989) Selection and appraisal: reconstructing social relations? in *New Perspectives in Human Resource Management*, ed J Storey, Routledge, London

Trist, E L, Higgin, G W, Murray, H and Pollack, A B (1963) *Organizational Choice*, Tavistock, London

Truss, C (1999) Soft and hard models of HRM, in *Strategic Human Resource Management*, ed L Gratton, V H Hailey, P Stiles, and C Truss, Oxford University Press, Oxford

Truss, C (2001) Complexities and controversies in linking HRM with organizational outcomes, *Journal of Management Studies,* 38(8), December, pp 1121–49

Trussler, S (1998) The rules of the game, *Journal of Business Strategy*, **19**(1), pp 16–19

Tsui, A S and Gomez-Mejia, L R (1988) Evaluating human resource effectiveness, in *Human Resource Management: Evolving roles and responsibilities*, ed L Dyer, Bureau of National Affairs, Washington, DC

Tuckman, B (1965) Development sequences in small groups, *Psychological Bulletin*, **63**, pp 123–56

Turner, A N and Lawrence, P R (1965) *Industrial Jobs and the Worker: An investigation of response to task attributes*, Harvard University Graduate School of Business Administration, Boston, MA

Turnow, W W (1993) Introduction to special issue on 360-degree feedback, *Human Resource Management*, Spring, pp 311–16

Twitchell, S, Holton, E F and Trott, J W (2000) Technical training evaluation processes in the United States, *Performance Improvement Quarterly*, **13** (3), pp 84–109

Tyler, T R and Bies, R J (1990) Beyond formal procedures: the interpersonal context of procedural justice, in *Applied Social Psychology and Organizational Settings,* ed J S Carrol, Lawrence Earlbaum, Hillsdale, NJ

Tyson, S (1985) Is this the very model of a modern personnel manager, *Personnel Management*, **26**, pp 35–39

Tyson, S (1987) The management of the personnel function, *Journal of Management Studies*, September, pp 523–32

Tyson, S (1997) Human resource strategy: a process for managing the contribution of HRM to organizational performance, *The International Journal of Human Resource Management*, **8** (3), pp 277–90

Tyson, S and Fell, A (1986) *Evaluating the Personnel Function*, Hutchinson, London

Tyson, S and Witcher, M (1994) Getting in gear: post-recession HR management, *Personnel Management*, August, pp 20–23

Ulrich, D (1995) Shared services: from vogue to value, *Human Resource Planning*, **18** (3) pp 12–23

Ulrich, D (1997) *Human Resource Champions*, Harvard Business School Press, Boston, MA

Ulrich, D (1998) A new mandate for human resources, *Harvard Business Review*, January–February, pp 124–34

Ulrich, D and Black, J S (1999) Worldly wise, *People Management*, 28 October, pp 42–46

Ulrich, D and Brockbank, W (2005a) *The HR Value Proposition*, Harvard Press, Cambridge, MA

Ulrich, D and Brockbank, W (2005b) Role call, *People Management*, 16 June, pp 24–28

Ulrich, D and Lake, D (1990) *Organizational Capability: Competing from the inside out,* Wiley, New York

Urwick, L F (1947) *Dynamic Administration*, Pitman, London

US Department of Labor (1993) *High Performance Work Practices and Work Performance,* US Government Printing Office, Washington, DC

van Dam, N (2004) *The E-learning Field Book*, McGraw-Hill, New York

Vernon, P E (1961) *The Structure of Human Abilities*, Methuen, London

Vroom, V (1964) *Work and Motivation*, Wiley, New York

Walker, J W (1992) *Human Resource Strategy*, McGraw-Hill, New York

Walker, N (2004) Creating a talent mindset: a five-step roadmap, *Strategic HR Review*, **3** (6), pp 20–23

Walton, R E (1969) *Interpersonal Peacemaking: Confrontations and third party peace-making*, Addison-Wesley, Reading, MA

Walton, R E (1985a) From control to commitment in the workplace, *Harvard Business Review*, **63**, pp 76–84

Walton, R E (1985b) Towards a strategy of eliciting employee commitment based on principles of mutuality, in *HRM Trends and Challenges*, ed R E Walton and P R Lawrence, Harvard Business School Press, Boston, MA

Walton, J (1999) *Strategic Human Resource Development*, Financial Times/Prentice Hall, Harlow

Walton, R E and McKersie, R B (1965) *Behavioural Theory of Labour Negotiations*, McGraw-Hill, New York

Ward, P (1995) A 360-degree turn for the better, *People Management*, February, pp 20–22

Warr, P B, Bird, M W and Rackham, N (1970) *Evaluation of Management Training*, Gower, Aldershot

Watkins, K and Marsick, V (1993) *Sculpting the Learning Organization*, Falmer Press, London

Watson, A (1977) *The Personnel Managers*, Routledge and Kegan Paul, London

Watson Wyatt Human Capital Index (2001) Watson Wyatt, London

Watson Wyatt Worldwide (2002) *B2E Survey Results*, People Management Resources, New York

Weber, M (1946) *From Max Weber*, ed H H Gerth and C W Mills, Oxford University Press, Oxford

Wedderburn, Lord (1989) Freedom of association and philosophies of labour law, *Industrial Law Journal*, **18**, p 28

Weiner, B (1974) *Achievement Motivation and Attribution Theory*, General Learning Press, New Jersey

Welch, J (1991) Quoted in *Managing People and Organizations*, J Gabarro (ed), Harvard Business School Publications, Boston, MA

Wenger, E (1998) *Communities of Practice: Learning, meaning and identity*, Cambridge University Press, Cambridge

Wenger, E and Snyder, W M (2000) Communities of practice: the organizational frontier, *Harvard Business Review*, January–February, pp 33–41

West, M A and Slater J A (1995) Teamwork: myths, reality and research, *Occupational Psychologist*, April, pp 24–29

West, P (1996) The learning organization: losing the luggage in transit? *Journal of European Industrial Training*, **18**(11), pp 30–38

Whipp, R (1992) HRM: competition and strategy, in P Blyton and P Turnbull (eds) *Reassessing Human Resource Management*, Sage Publications, London

Whitehead, M (1998) Employee happiness levels impact on the bottom line, *People Management*, 10 December, p 14

Whittington, R (1993) *What Is Strategy – and does it matter?* Routledge, London

Wick, C W and Leon, L S (1995) Creating a learning organisation: from ideas to action, *Human Resource Management*, Summer, pp 299–311

Wickens, P (1987) *The Road to Nissan*, Macmillan, London

Williams, A (1998) Organizational learning and the role of attitude surveys, *Human Resource Management Journal*, **8**(4), pp 51–65

Williams, A, Dobson, P and Walters, M (1989) *Changing Culture: New organizational approaches*, IPA, London

Willmott. H (1993) Strength is ignorance, slavery is freedom: managing culture in modern organizations, *Journal of Management Studies*, **29**(6), pp 515–52

Wilson, N A B (1973) *On the Quality of Working Life*, HMSO, London

Womack, J and Jones, D (1970) *The Machine That Changed the World*, Rawson, New York

Wood, S (1996) High commitment management and organization in the UK, *The International Journal of Human Resource Management*, February, pp 41–58

Wood, S and Albanese, M (1995) Can we speak of a high commitment management on the shop floor? *Journal of Management Studies*, March, pp 215–47

Wood, R and Payne, T (1998) *Competency-based Recruitment and Selection*, Wiley, Chichester

Woodruffe, C (1990) *Assessment Centres*, Institute of Personnel Management, London

Woodruffe, C (1991) Competent by any other name, *Personnel Management*, September, pp 30–33

Woodward, J (1965) *Industrial Organization*, Oxford University Press, Oxford

Woodward, J (1968) Resistance to change, *Management International Review*, **8**

Wooldridge, B and Floyd, S W (1990) The strategy process, middle management involvement and organizational performance', *Strategic Management Journal*, **11**, pp 231–41

Wooldridge, E (1989) The Donovan analysis: does it still stand? *Personnel Management*, June, pp 38–42

Work Foundation (2003a) *Maximising Attendance*, Work Foundation, London

Work Foundation (2003b) *Work-life Balance*, Work Foundation, London

Workplace Employee Relations Survey: Summary (2005) HMSO, Norwich

World Bank (2000) *Intellectual Capital*, Word Bank website

WorldatWork (2000) *Total Rewards: From strategy to implementation*, WorldatWork, Scottsdale, AZ

Wright, D S and Taylor, A (1970) *Introducing Psychology*, Penguin, Harmondsworth

Wright, P M and Snell, S A (1998) Towards a unifying framework for exploring fit and flexibility in strategic human resource management, *Academy of Management Review*, **23**(4), pp 756–72

Wright, V (1991) Performance-related pay, in F Neale (ed) *The Handbook of Performance Management*, Institute of Personnel Management, London

Youndt, M A (2000) 'Human resource considerations and value creation: the mediating role of intellectual capital', Paper delivered at National Conference of US Academy of Management, Toronto, August

Zuboff, S (1988) *In the Age of the Smart Machine*, Basic Books, New York

Subject index

Author index